This book examines the gradual decline of slavery forty years of colonial rule. At the time of the British one of the largest slave societies in modern history. the colonial state instituted policies of abolishing the legal status of slavery, encouraging them to buy their own freedom. A great financial burden was, therefore, placed on slaves. Since freedom was far too expensive to purchase quickly, many were not able to do so. Even when they were able to earn a wage, the region was still very poor and emancipation usually took years to achieve. In fact, it was not until 1936 that slavery was finally abolished.

It was even more difficult for female slaves to gain their freedom. In the view of colonial officials, women had no identity other than their status as dependants upon men, whether as wives, concubines, daughters, or sisters. As a consequence, many went free only after their masters died, particularly if they were concubines.

The authors have written a thoughtful and provocative book which raises doubts over the moral legitimacy of both the Sokoto Caliphate and the colonial state. They chart the development of British colonial policy towards resolving the dilemma of slavery and how to end it.

U A W

SLOW DEATH FOR SLAVERY

AFRICAN STUDIES SERIES 76

GENERAL EDITOR
J. M. Lonsdale, *Lecturer in History and Fellow of Trinity College, Cambridge*

ADVISORY EDITORS
J. D. Y. Peel, *Professor of Anthropology and Sociology, with special reference to Africa, School of Oriental and African Studies, University of London*

Published in collaboration with
THE AFRICAN STUDIES CENTRE, CAMBRIDGE

A list of books in this series will be found at the end of this volume

SLOW DEATH FOR SLAVERY

The course of abolition in
Northern Nigeria, 1897–1936

PAUL E. LOVEJOY
York University, Ontario

JAN S. HOGENDORN
Colby College, Maine

CAMBRIDGE
UNIVERSITY PRESS

Published by the Press Syndicate of the University of Cambridge
The Pitt Building, Trumpington Street, Cambridge CB2 1RP
40 West 20th Street, New York, NY 10011–4211, USA
10 Stamford Road, Oakleigh, Victoria 3166, Australia

First published 1993

Printed in Great Britain at the University Press, Cambridge

A catalogue record for this book is available from the British Library

Library of Congress cataloguing in publication data
Lovejoy, Paul E.
Slow death for slavery: the course of abolition in Northern
Nigeria, 1897–1936 / Paul E. Lovejoy and Jan S. Hogendorn.
        p.   cm. – (African studies series:76)
Includes bibliographical references (p.   ).
ISBN 0 521 37469 3 (hardback)
1. Slavery – Nigeria, Northern – History – 20th century.   2. Slaves –
Nigeria, Northern – Emancipation – History – 20th century.
I. Hogendorn, Jan S.   II. Title.   III. Series.
HT1334.N6L68   1993
326′.09669′5–dc20   92-18406   CIP

ISBN 0 521 37469 3 hardback
ISBN 0 521 44702 X paperback

CE

Dedicated to Malam Bawa of Hanwa,
descendant of slaves and local historian, who first
introduced us to a slave's life on a *rinji* in Northern Nigeria

Contents

Maps

x

Tables

Preface

Writing a volume on Northern Nigeria's slave system, one of the largest slave societies in modern history, poses more than ordinary difficulty, because no books on the subject have come before. Prior to this study, only about twenty articles have been published on our topic. Thus this first book-length study of slavery in the region of Northern Nigeria bears little similarity to the work on American slavery of Ulrich Phillips, Kenneth Stamp, Stanley Elkins, Eugene Genovese, or Stanley Engerman. These scholars could draw on an already existing wealth of information, whereas we could not.

Our direct interest in the slave system of the Sokoto Caliphate, and the painfully slow end of that system extending over many years of British colonial rule, dates from the year 1975. In that year, we were visiting academics at Ahmadu Bello University in Zaria. Jan Hogendorn had just published an article on the economics of the Atlantic slave trade that included a section on slave supply conditions within West Africa. He commented that he wished he had some of this knowledge when writing his Ph.D. thesis on Northern Nigerian groundnut production, since slaves surely played a part in the development of this crop. Paul Lovejoy noted that slaves had figured in his own Ph.D. thesis on the kola trade between the Sokoto Caliphate and Asante. Many wealthy kola merchants of slave origin had subsequently invested heavily in slave-based agriculture. The realization that slavery was important in these two famous and overlapping lines of commerce led to many fruitful conversations that involved other, wider questions. What role had slavery played in the economy of the Sokoto Caliphate? What must life have been like for the slaves on a *rinji* (plantation) before the British conquest? How did slavery come to an end? We have been studying slavery in Northern Nigeria ever since.

Collaboration has been invaluable because the dimensions of the task were large, and because it was helpful to have an economist and an historian working together. Initially, our joint venture involved collecting oral data, first by ourselves working with translators, and later as organizers of students sent into the field. Hogendorn did much of the early interviewing on which later research was based, while Lovejoy supervised over a dozen students who recorded interviews arising from the preliminary work. The material was ultimately transcribed, much of it translated into English, and tapes and transcripts were deposited in the Northern History Research Scheme at Ahmadu Bello University. These interviews also formed the basis of several BA dissertations. Though some said the effort would be unproductive, that neither slaves nor masters would be willing to speak of the old days, the data proved to be rich and easily collectable. Many of these interviews are now being prepared for publication.

Later our attention turned to the archives; there was more in the British colonial records at the Public Record Office, in the reminiscences of colonial officials collected at Rhodes House, Oxford, and in the missionary and commercial records, than we had expected. Our initial impression that the colonial records in the Nigerian archives would mostly be duplicates of messages sent home proved to be quite wrong. Large numbers of reports on slavery and emancipation are not available outside of these archives, and as we later discovered, there are major gaps in the Nigerian archives that are recoverable at Rhodes House and elsewhere.

The first book on a subject so large will inevitably have major omissions and distortions, and it is incumbent on us to identify what we would have done had our documentation been better, had we spent even more time digesting the materials we have, or had we pursued the collection of oral data with additional interviews. First, we do not examine all of what became Northern Nigeria, only those parts of it that had been emirates in the Sokoto Caliphate. The largest area excluded in this study is Borno; similarly a number of smaller states and numerous non-Muslim communities that remained independent of the Caliphate are not considered. Furthermore, we do not examine the portion of the Caliphate that lay outside what became the borders of Northern Nigeria – the eight western emirates incorporated into French territory, and the large sub-emirates of Adamawa that became part of German Kamerun – although we pick up a little of their story once Northern Cameroons was mandated to Britain after the First World War. The additional research needed to cover Borno and the non-British territories would have seriously compromised our timetable, which was already stretched.

Another area of omission concerns the masters. We do not do full justice to the analysis of slave ownership. We seldom grapple with questions such as the differences of opinion and action among slave owners, or how these masters acted on an individual level to abet or oppose the dictates of the colonial government and the desires of their own slaves. Did merchants, aristocrats, and clerics behave as masters in similar fashion or differently? What were their class loyalties in determining whether there was a community of interest or stark division in the reception accorded the British efforts to reform and in the long run abolish slavery? When and under what conditions did slaves and masters reach a mutually acceptable accord? Were there important regional differences among the emirates? Only on occasion do we examine these questions.

We realize fully how difficult it is to establish what individual slaves thought and did. Though our analysis sometimes borders on the socio-logical, based on our knowledge of individual cases obtained from oral data or court records, and on the (usually biased) view of the colonial officials and other Europeans, we are all too aware that actual testimony by slaves is rare and difficult to put into proper perspective. It is even more difficult to speculate on the motivations and actions of slave women, because the history of Hausa women in general is so poorly understood. Nonetheless, our efforts to uncover the reactions of slaves to British rule has been a driving force in our research.

We have rather boldly identified the ideological and sometimes even the psychological forces working on the various colonial officials. It is difficult, perhaps impossible, to understand and interpret the many reports of these officials as they expound on the slavery issue without taking into account their class, their Victorian/Edwardian upbringing and training, and the whole collection of their resulting preconceived judgments and prejudices. Merely identifying the sexual preferences, political commitments, and class loyalties of the British officials on the spot opens a Pandora's Box that is well worthy of study in and of itself.

Economics has a major place in our study, perhaps even more so than it did in the denouement of slavery elsewhere in the world. Unfortunately, however, the implicit and explicit calculus of the masters, the slaves, the colonial government, the Caliphate aristocracy, and the merchants com-bined and interacted in complex ways, and the local data on production, income, and income distribution are usually so imperfect as to leave many unanswered questions. Even so, it is clear that a great financial burden was placed on the slaves, and that Northern Nigeria is the world's outstanding example of a slave system where emancipation was achieved in part by the self-purchase of the slaves themselves. Yet freedom was far too expensive to purchase quickly, and many slaves were never able to buy it. Long after transport improvements made it possible for slaves to earn much higher cash incomes through the sale of crops (especially groundnuts and cotton) for export, the region was still very poor, and emancipation for those able to achieve it usually took many years.

The study of female slaves presents a special problem, because they have been largely ignored in the documents. References to "slaves" usually mean male slaves. The attitude of the British, discussed in Chapter 4, was that women had no identity other than that connected with males. This British stance together with Islamic chauvinism has been largely responsible for adumbrating the experience of female slaves, who have been largely (and understandably, given their neglect in the source material) ignored by his-torians. Much more could be attempted in examining the status of female slaves from the western and Islamic points of view; we have limited ourselves to demonstrating that female slaves were always treated as if they should be dependants of men, whether as wives, concubines, sisters, daughters, or wards.

We do not deal specifically with children, who increasingly were the major targets of slavers during the illegal period of the slave trade under colonial rule. Children were relatively easy to hide, and they could be more readily bullied into submission than adults. The evidence in the colonial records is abundant that a slave trade consisting mostly of children continued well into the 1930s, and there are scattered references to enslavement of children even after that. Tragic as this late and illegal trade was, we have chosen not to devote much attention to it because of the demands of space and time.

Nor do we follow in detail the experience of royal slaves, who had a range of special privileges under the Caliphate, some of which continued long after the imposition of colonial rule. The slaves of high officials served as tax collectors, policed the emirates, made up the elite musketeer corps of the emirate armies, were the messengers in the Caliphate's postal system, and otherwise served in a number of ways as functionaries of the Muslim state bureaucracy. Despite occasional efforts to purge these slaves under colonialism, they continued to be the backbone of aristocratic rule in the British period. Royal slaves were proud of their status, and as late as the 1950s and 1960s their descendants, still obviously esteeming their social rank of "royal slave," could be found serving in a variety of official positions. Even today, examples of this remnant of the slave system can be found in the entourages of the emirs, doggedly and from all appearances voluntarily persisting in their servility. If only by virtue of their large numbers, the royal slaves of the Islamic state will in the future surely be a major topic for research and analysis, but that study is one we have chosen not to undertake.

Finally, we must call attention to the difficulties we faced in obtaining information on the decisions and actions taken by slaves who fled their masters in the aftermath of the colonial conquest. Wherever possible, we have attempted to identify motivations and patterns of flight, but concerning those who fled there is a noticeable vacuum in the documents – a not surprising consequence of the absconding slaves' unwillingness to be found. For reconstructing their collective experience, it has often been necessary to rely on supposition rather than documentation. Consequently, our analysis is merely circumstantial, suggestive of a range of possibilities, albeit limited ones for which there were few substitutes.

Portions of the book have appeared in modified form elsewhere. Our approach to the subject was first outlined in "The Reform of Slavery in Early Colonial Northern Nigeria."[1] Some of Chapter 3 was published as "The Development and Execution of Frederick Lugard's Policies Toward Slavery in Northern Nigeria,"[2] and an update was subsequently published as "Keeping Slaves in Place: The Secret Debate on the Slavery Question in

Northern Nigeria, 1900–1904."[3] The part of Chapter 2 on revolutionary Mahdism and portions of Chapter 4 on concubinage are revised here from earlier discussion as well.[4]

We would like to acknowledge the assistance and support of many people who provided documents, collected materials, read various versions of the typescript, and otherwise offered criticism and advice. We would like to mention the following: A. H. M. Kirk-Greene, Kenneth Swindell, Colin Newbury, M. G. Smith, R. J. Gavin, A. S. Mohammed, Kimba Idrissa, Ralph Austen, Martin Klein, Ann O'Hear, M. B. Duffill, Suzanne Miers, and Richard Roberts, all of whom provided advice and encouragement at various times during our research. Ibrahim Jumare, Stephen Giles, Philip Afeadie, Abdullahi Sule-Kano, and Philip Murphy assisted with the collection of archival and other materials. Ahmadu Maccido, Yusufu Yunusa, Yau Haruna, M. Y. Ahmed, Muhammed Lawal, and Aliyu Bala Umar conducted interviews, either with one or other of the authors or under our supervision. Toyin Falola, Ann O'Hear, Stefano Fenoaltea, and Ibrahim Jumare commented extensively on the typescript, for which we are particularly grateful. We also wish to thank Katherine Rogers, Kwabena Opare-Akurang, and Pauline Marsh for their assistance.

We wish to thank the Social Sciences and Humanities Research Council of Canada for financial assistance to Lovejoy and to the Guggenheim Foundation for assistance to Hogendorn. In addition, York University and Colby College have provided extensive support, and Ahmadu Bello University provided financial assistance in support of data collection in 1975–76. Institutional support also came from Linacre College, Oxford, the Centre of West African Studies, the University of Birmingham, Rhodes House Library, Oxford, the Nigerian National Archives at Kaduna and Ibadan, and Arewa House in Kaduna.

1

Slavery and the British conquest of Northern Nigeria

At the time of the colonial conquest (1897–1903), the Sokoto Caliphate had a huge slave population, certainly in excess of 1 million and perhaps more than 2.5 million people.[1] This slave population had arisen in the course of the nineteenth century, during which the area stretching from modern Burkina Faso in the west, through Niger and northern Nigeria as far east as Cameroun was consolidated into the thirty emirates and numerous sub-emirates that comprised this large, Muslim state. The Caliphate itself was responsible for the enslavement of the servile population through war, slave raiding, and the demand for tribute from subjugated communities. As the colonial conquest began, slavery was very much a functioning institution. People were still being enslaved, and the trade in slaves was of considerable proportions. It is no wonder, then, that slavery figured prominently in the conquest itself.[2]

It is now widely recognized that slavery was common in many parts of the world well into the modern era, not only in the Americas but also throughout the Islamic world and in China, India, and southeast Asia.[3] The Ottoman Empire certainly had a large slave population, and many of its slaves came from sub-Saharan Africa, including the Sokoto Caliphate.[4] Recent scholarship has tended to treat slavery as a world-wide phenomenon, with significant sub-divisions that can be identified with classical antiquity, medieval Europe, Islam, the non-Muslim areas of Asia, and Africa. Much more research has been done on slavery in the Americas than elsewhere, but there were many more slaves in other places and at other times than in the Americas.

Of modern slave societies, the United States probably had more slaves than the Caliphate, about 4 million in 1860. Brazil's slave population of 1.5 million in 1888, the date of abolition there, was at the lower end of the estimate for the Sokoto Caliphate. The numbers of slaves in the British Caribbean in 1834, approximately 450,000, and in Cuba at the start of gradual emancipation in 1870, about 290,000, were quite small by comparison.[5] Hence when the British abolished the legal status of slavery for those parts of the Caliphate that were to become Northern Nigeria, they were dealing with a slave population the scale of which was huge even by the standards of the slave economies of the Americas.

From these large figures immediately arise a host of questions and quali-fications. Surely slavery was very different in the Sokoto Caliphate than it was in the United States or Brazil (or even China), and surely the process of emancipation must have followed a different course. The Caliphate bridged many frontiers which must have influenced slavery there. It was a Muslim state and hence had similarities with slavery in other Islamic societies, including the Ottoman Empire. It was located in Africa, where slavery was very common in the nineteenth century. Indeed parts of the Caliphate had ethnic associations, such as Yoruba, that were similar to those of areas that were beyond its frontiers and were not Muslim. Furthermore, the Caliphate contributed to the transatlantic slave trade early in the nineteenth century and therefore had remote connections to the supply mechanism for the slavery of the Americas. Since very little is known about the internal operations of slavery in the Caliphate, and since even less is known about the destruction of slavery in that region, it is difficult to complete the com-parisons. This study, which examines the impact of the European occupation (1897–1903) on slavery and traces British colonial policies that resulted in the reform and ultimate demise of slavery, partly remedies this deficiency.[6]

The colonial conquest undermined the old and well-established institution of slavery in the Sokoto Caliphate. The invading armies of the French, Germans, and British partitioned the Caliphate, the French taking the western extremities, the Germans absorbing the eastern fringe, and the British occupying the central, heavily populated emirates. The French portions became part of Afrique Occidentale Française; the German domains were incorporated into Kamerun; while the British fashioned their territory into the Protectorate of Northern Nigeria. The Caliphate was exceptional in that three European powers participated in its partition.

The abolition of slavery varied considerably in the three colonial terri-tories, both with respect to the timing and nature of reforms and with respect to the extent of the commitment to their implementation. Gradually, each of the colonial empires suppressed slave raiding and then the trade in slaves, although both enslavement, especially kidnaping, and slave trading lasted well into the twentieth century in parts of the former Caliphate, no matter which European power was in control. The French instituted reforms that ended the legitimacy of slavery in all courts and tribunals in 1903, with the result that there was a massive exodus of slaves, especially in 1906.[7] For several years after the German occupation of Adamawa in 1902, nothing was done to eliminate domestic slavery in the Muslim emirates. The policy adopted in southern Kamerun, whereby the government regulated con-ditions of slavery and legislated a program of self-purchase, was extended to Caliphate territory.[8] The British were concerned to minimize the potential disruptions of full emancipation and therefore used the power of the colonial state to keep slaves in place. As we argue in this book, the British abolished

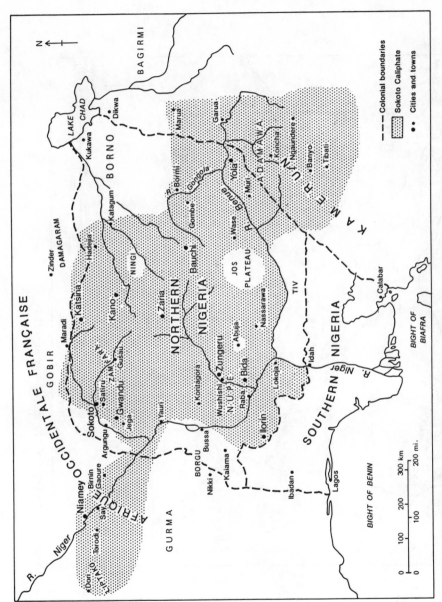

Map 1 Sokoto Caliphate: French, British, and German spheres

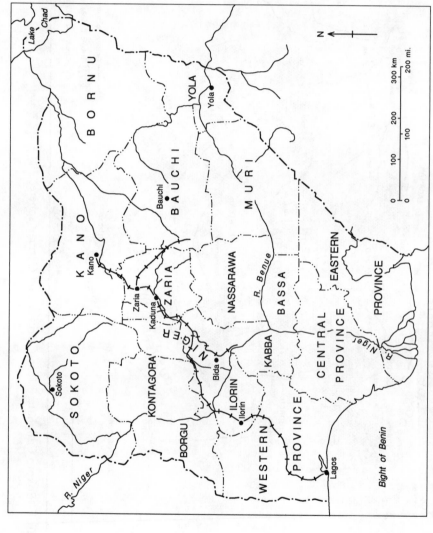

Map 2 Provinces of Northern Nigeria, 1916

the legal status of slavery in colonial courts, but not in the Islamic courts.

Regardless of these differences, many slaves escaped during and shortly after the conquest and other slaves resisted in more subtle ways. In any event, slavery eventually declined into insignificance in all the colonial areas, but only after several decades. Because the overwhelming portion of the slaves were in the British sphere, this study concentrates on that part of the Caliphate which became Northern Nigeria. German participation in this process ended in the First World War, when most of those parts of Kamerun that had been part of the Sokoto Caliphate were brought under the rule of Northern Nigeria and hence back into line with developments common to most of the former Caliphate. The French parts of the Caliphate are best understood in the context of slavery policy in l'Afrique Occidentale Française. Sometimes developments in l'AOF influenced events across the long border with Northern Nigeria, as in the Mahdist uprising of 1905–1906, but generally the eight French emirates remained separated from the central regions of the former Caliphate.

Slavery and emancipation

The struggle to end slavery has been a major theme of world history since the end of the eighteenth century. Most scholars have concentrated on the abolition of the transatlantic slave trade and the process of emancipation in the Americas. The great expansion of slavery in Africa, particularly in the nineteenth century, and the subsequent emancipation of slaves there have received much less attention. Ironically, it is only recently that scholars have begun to examine slavery and emancipation in the homeland of the slaves who populated the Americas.[9] An understanding of the process of emancipation in Africa adds perspective to the similar struggle in the Americas, just as neglect of the African experience distorts that perspective.

Historically, the emancipation of slaves occurred in a number of different contexts.[10] Slaves achieved freedom through revolution, as in St. Domingue in the 1790s. They were granted freedom because of the pressures abolitionists applied in the political arena, as in the British West Indies in 1834 and in the United States in the 1850s and 1860s (although the British and US cases were remarkably different). The slave revolt in Jamaica in 1831–32 was a major factor in the decision of the British Parliament to enact the emancipation decree of 1834, and the United States had to fight a civil war to resolve its slavery issues. In Brazil, general emancipation only occurred in 1888, after slavery had virtually disappeared from the rest of the Americas. Brazilians came to realize that abolition was unavoidable; at the time of emancipation, the number of free blacks exceeded the slave population three to one, which was a major factor in ending slavery there.[11] Emancipation in Cuba was a prolonged and complicated process that occurred over an eighteen-year period that began in 1870 with the freeing of newborn children and old people and was not complete until 1888 with the ending of apprenticeship.[12]

The avenues to emancipation become more varied, if not more muddy, once the rest of the world is taken into consideration. In some places, slaves suffered under modified forms of servitude that were intended to disguise the continuation of a system of oppression – slavery remained in all but name. Slavery continued in most Islamic countries, even into the twentieth century, because it was thought that religion somehow made a difference. In Portuguese Africa slaves became *libertos*, a change in name but not in status and conditions. These cases, and others too, thinly disguised the continuation of slavery in a remarkably successful attempt to satisfy abolitionists, who appear to have become increasingly worn out by their struggle against slavery.

The British implemented quite different policies in Asia, Africa, and the Americas. A consideration of these differences should serve as a corrective to the usual picture of Britain as the champion of the anti-slavery movement. At one extreme of relative moderation, British policy in the West Indies allowed a transition period of so-called apprenticeship, during which time slaves continued to work for their masters in almost the same way as under slavery. The number of hours of work required of slaves was set at forty-five per week. Such a regime lasted from 1834 to 1838. In addition Parliament compensated slave owners with cash payments. In sharp contrast, the Native House Rule Ordinance of Southern Nigeria recognized slaves as members of the master's household and hence under the master's virtually absolute authority. There was very little difference from slavery. Masters continued to benefit from the labor of their slaves, even receiving legal support if "house members" refused to work. The Native House Rule Ordinance allowed for the continuation of slavery under another name.

Yet another strategy was the British policy, first developed in Asia and later applied in parts of Africa, including Northern Nigeria, that abolished the "legal status" of slavery. Under this approach, slavery was no longer recognized as a legal institution in the courts, although slavery itself was not abolished and slaves were not emancipated, unless they or some third party compensated their owners. Because the legal distinction between slave and free was removed, the courts could not be used to recover slaves, and slaves could leave their masters without any formal emancipation. This policy, first introduced in India in 1843, in Malaya later in the same year, and in Ceylon and Hong Kong in 1844, was subsequently adopted in Africa as well, first in the Gold Coast in 1874 and later in Zanzibar and the Royal Niger Company territories in 1897. The policy was continued when the Royal Niger Company ceded its claims to the British government upon the creation of the Protectorate of Northern Nigeria in 1900, and the Zanzibar decree was extended to the Kenya coast in 1907.[13]

The range of possibilities in the decline of slavery fell on a continuum running from freedom obtained in open revolt through various mechanisms that continued to justify some form of servility. At the one extreme, masters received no compensation for the loss of their slaves. Far more often, however, masters continued to benefit from slavery, but on a decreasing scale. In the British West Indies masters received paid compensation and a period of forced labor. In Southern Nigeria, masters continued to benefit from the full labor of their slaves but were denied the legal replenishment of slave supply. In Northern Nigeria and elsewhere, slaves or interested third parties compensated the owners, who usually continued to benefit directly from the labor of the slaves as well. There was no government compensation for masters.

The process of emancipation of slaves in the Sokoto Caliphate, often described as "gradual" but in fact "jerky," did not resemble any of the situations that obtained in the Americas and more closely falls on that end of the continuum whereby slavery was allowed to survive under some modified form. We follow the decline of slavery during the course of four decades from 1897 to 1936. As we will demonstrate, British policy aimed at reforming slavery and thereby protected an otherwise doomed institution for some years. This policy was largely crafted by Sir Frederick (Later Lord) Lugard, High Commissioner of Northern Nigeria (1900–1906), Governor of Northern and Southern Nigeria (1912–14) and Governor of (united) Nigeria (1914–18). A consideration of Lugard's role in the abolition of slavery figures prominently in this study.

The world-wide variations in the patterns of emancipation highlight the struggle associated with the end of slavery. Masters and slaves had different interests, and the issue of how slavery would end revolved around political power. Slaves usually had little of that. Masters, by contrast, could participate in the process of emancipation, as they did in Northern Nigeria, if they recognized its inevitability and still retained a political position. A fundamental proposition of early colonial rule in this British Protectorate was the need to convince slave owners that they could benefit from the modifications in the slave system that were introduced. To understand the implications of British reforms, it is necessary to consider the possibilities facing both masters and slaves.

Because slaves were property, masters everywhere had a strong financial interest in securing compensation during the process of emancipation. Masters could be compensated for the loss of their slaves through cash payments, continued labor under conditions which resembled slavery, a share of crops, or a combination of money, goods, and labor. All these methods obtained in Northern Nigeria. While the British government granted monetary compensation and otherwise made provision for continued labor in the West Indies, in Northern Nigeria slaves were encouraged or expected to buy their own freedom through self-purchase (*fansar kai*) or otherwise to acquire their freedom through ransom (*fansa*) by third parties. Both government compensation and payments from slaves clearly reduced the losses inflicted on masters, the difference being whether or not the slaves or the government paid. Compensation of some sort was almost always obtained by the masters, except where the slaves revolted (St. Domingue), or where there was civil war (United States), or where slaves ran away.

7

Policies that intended to control emancipation and thereby promote the payment of compensation were often designed to prevent slaves from gaining access to land. Masters were allowed to maintain their proprietary rights in land, thereby forcing former slaves to become sharecroppers and tenant farmers. The research of Kenneth Swindell and M. G. Smith suggests this strategy was widespread in Northern Nigeria,[14] and of course, it was certainly the case in the United States and elsewhere. Slaves could also be forced into contracts which were tantamount to slavery. Strictly speaking there were no such contracts in Northern Nigeria, but many slaves did enter into contractual arrangements (*murgu*) that allowed them to seek employment on their own account and thereby obtain the time necessary to earn money for self-purchase (see Chapter 7).

The economic impact of emancipation on masters and slaves varied considerably, therefore. Masters could receive compensation from governments or from slaves, or from both, or they might be deprived of any compensation whatever. Slaves could avoid paying compensation through immediate emancipation; revolt, escape from slavery, and government action could all produce this result. Theoretically, slaves could even receive some economic support – in effect, compensation to them – but it will not seem surprising that no such program was ever instituted. The United States came closest to compensating slaves, but the proposal of the Radical Republicans to allocate forty acres and a mule to each former slave was never legislated. Such a possibility did not even come close to implementation anywhere else.

Slaves also ran away in very large numbers, true of every slave society that has been studied in detail, including the present case. The Underground Railway of US history was a particularly well-organized form of escape, but the flight of slaves by sea from Cape Town or the smaller islands of the Caribbean was no less important for the individuals seeking freedom.[15] Escape probably involved many more slaves than those who rose in rebellion. The effect on masters was similar, whether or not escape was well organized or haphazard. It deprived masters of what they considered to be their property without compensation. Furthermore, escape was usually more frequent at the time of emancipation in those places where slaves were expected to continue working for their masters. In such situations, escape must be interpreted as a direct attempt by slaves to free themselves without accepting some gradual plan for freedom.

Analysis of slavery and emancipation has focused very largely on the slave economies of the Americas. As we have seen, however, the Sokoto Caliphate was one of the largest slave societies in modern times, and it must have its due. Slavery in the Sokoto Caliphate was indeed distinct from the slave systems in the Americas, as M. G. Smith demonstrated almost forty years ago in his provocative comparison of Zaria and Jamaica.[16] Even though we have much more to learn about slavery in the Sokoto Caliphate before a full comparison can be undertaken, Smith's analysis serves as a useful starting point in highlighting the sharp contrast between the slave societies of the Americas and slavery in the Muslim emirates of the Sokoto Caliphate.

Zaria Emirate, a constituent part of the Sokoto Caliphate, can be taken as representative of the larger Muslim state. Located in the interior of Africa, Zaria was virtually isolated from the capitalist world market, so that the impact of the world economy on slavery was minimal. Slavery was interpreted within an Islamic religious and legal tradition that was many centuries old. The Emirate was actively involved in enslavement as well as the exploitation of slave labor. Indeed the continued acquisition of new captives was essential in sustaining the number of slaves in Zaria. There was no racial difference between masters and slaves, although ethnic distinctions were clearly articulated as a result of the enslavement of non-Muslim populations. While most slaves were assigned agricultural work, some performed essential functions of government, and many had the possibility of achieving emancipation for themselves or their children. The children of slave concubines were particularly likely to inherit a free status. We concur with Smith on these points.

Jamaica, by contrast, was also part of a large empire, but the British Empire was far more dispersed and varied than the Sokoto Caliphate. Slavery in Jamaica was more similar to slavery elsewhere in tropical America than to slavery in the British Empire as a whole. Its economy was closely integrated with the capitalist world market, which had a strong impact on the development of slavery. Jamaica was superficially Christian with a relatively recent legal tradition involving slavery. There was no mechanism for enslavement, other than through the birth of children, so that it was necessary to import slaves from Africa; biological regeneration was not sufficient to maintain the slave population, and once slave imports were prohibited, the number of slaves declined considerably. As is clearly recognized as a significant dimension of slavery in the Americas, there was a sharp racial division between slaves and masters. Slaves were essentially confined to economic activities, especially the production of sugar cane for export. While a few slaves were emancipated, even the children of masters and slave women had unpredictable futures. Smith has clearly identified many of the striking differences between slavery in Jamaica and Zaria.

The differences aside, each of these slave regimes had to cope with the problem of how to bring the institution of slavery to an end. The dissimilarities in their methods for doing so were as wide as the differences in the slave systems themselves. In the chapters that follow we explore the course of abolition in the Protectorate of Northern Nigeria and the process of historical change that modified slavery under conditions of colonialism over a period of forty years. The slow death of slavery in Northern Nigeria contrasts with the sudden emancipation of slaves through revolution and civil war. In order to understand the long transition that occurred in Northern Nigeria, it is first necessary to examine the early interaction between Britain and the Sokoto Caliphate.

Slavery and the British penetration of the Sokoto Caliphate

British justification of the conquest of the Sokoto Caliphate was intertwined with attitudes towards slavery. The anti-slavery legacy stretched back over a century before 1900. As the foremost slaver of the late eighteenth century and the abolitionist force of the nineteenth century, Britain had an ideological heritage that was torn by conflicting views of the infamous institution. The masters of empire had come to understand the complexities of slavery. Britain had declared moral outrage over the transatlantic trade it once dominated, had emancipated slaves in the West Indies even while profits from slave production were high, had pressured other slave powers to acquiesce in post-Napoleonic "British" Europe without slavery, and had trivialized slavery in the Asian Empire that had been won during the period of British ascendancy. In nineteenth-century Africa, slavery was an embarrassment, a hangover from an earlier intoxication. The ideology of anti-slavery engaged Britons in a dialogue that recognized the reality of the Caliphate political economy and pretended a willingness to accept the inevitable consequences of conquest. But the "men-on-the-spot" were determined not to let slavery stand in their way, so that at times they used anti-slavery rhetoric for their own purposes but without having any intention of freeing very many slaves. How they interpreted the British heritage in the context of military conquest differed considerably.

There was an anti-slavery component to Britain's relations with the Sokoto Caliphate from the first official encounters in the 1820s, as Adu Boahen has argued. The missions of Hugh Clapperton and the Lander brothers promoted alternatives to the slave trade by establishing treaties of commerce and friendship with the important countries of the African interior, most especially with the Sokoto Caliphate.[17] The result of these early expeditions had little direct impact on slavery questions, other than collecting information on the relative advantages of the trans-Saharan routes versus the Niger River as a means of tapping the commerce of the interior. The importance of slavery was duly reported.

The interconnections between commerce, diplomatic links and abolition were most noticeable in the great anti-slave-trade crusade of T. F. Buxton in 1841.[18] Buxton's commitment to the abolition of slavery, as the acknowledged leader of Britain's anti-slavery movement, is unquestioned; perhaps it is less well known that his plans for the Niger River stumbled into the heart of one of the largest slave societies of its day. In retrospect, the efforts of the Niger expedition appear naive. The ideology of anti-slavery and the technology of newly industrial Britain were pitted against a powerful slavocracy whose control of the largest state in Africa could not be immediately threatened by the voyage of a few steamboats up the Niger.

Buxton's intention was to persuade African states along the Niger and Benue Rivers to substitute "innocent trade," as the phrase was, for the slave trade.[19] The expedition failed to learn much about the Sokoto Caliphate, other than the fact that "the countries bordering on the middle and lower parts of the river [Niger] supply the western coast of Africa with slaves, and a large proportion of them are sent overland from Kabba to the different parts in the Bight of Benin," that is, following routes south from Nupe and Ilorin to the coast.[20] Buxton's vision of agricultural development as a weapon against the slave trade proved illusory, although the "model farm" established just below the Niger–Benue confluence near present-day Lokoja did acquire lasting notoriety as the inspiration for Charles Dickens' satire in *Bleak House*.[21] During its brief existence, moreover, the farm offered sanctuary to fugitive slaves, which was the first sign that the British presence might have more disturbing influences on slavery in the Caliphate than even the abolitionists imagined.[22]

With the failure of the Niger expedition, the attentions of the British government and the Anti-Slavery Society, still interested in the pursuit of "legitimate" trade as the way to end the slave trade, turned once more to an approach across the Sahara. In 1849, James Richardson, under the sponsorship of the Foreign Office, undertook an expedition which, among other aims, had as its first object to further the elimination of the slave trade by promoting commerce in "legitimate articles of trade and barter." A draft treaty was supplied to Richardson, the first three clauses of which spoke of the abolition of slavery, the slave trade, and human sacrifice. Understandably given the political climate and the economic reality of the Caliphate, the clauses on slavery were not included in the treaties eventually negotiated.[23]

In 1854, Macgregor Laird obtained a government subsidy for a new expedition up the Niger that included the by-now usual directive to ascertain if the slave trade could be replaced by legitimate commerce. The Church Missionary Society had a representative aboard, looking towards future missions – the Reverend Samuel Crowther, the famous Yoruba priest who had been a slave, and who for many years headed the mission eventually established at Lokoja. Despite British intentions, however, the Caliphate remained largely unaffected by the movement to abolish the slave trade. Another expedition was undertaken in 1857 with instructions to develop British trade "practically to show the advantage of legitimate trade over the debasing and demoralising traffic in slaves."[24] In November, 1859, its leader, W. B. Baikie, started a settlement, named Lokoja, which was in the Emirate of Bida.[25]

With a post on the margins of the Caliphate, British policy towards the slave trade in that region first encountered the problem of fugitive slaves. That runaways might be useful was rapidly apparent. John Glover, who arranged relief supplies for the fledgling settlement, recruited a number of Hausa freed slaves in Sierra Leone who wanted to return to their homeland, but had not for fear of being taken by slavers while on the journey. Glover took them back to Lagos with him. Somehow the fact that he had recruited former Hausa slaves became known, and some Hausa slaves in the vicinity of Lagos ran away to join his expedition. Glover welcomed these recruits, despite several confrontations with their masters. On its march north from Lagos, the column was refused passage through Abeokuta because of the fugitive slaves. There was a brief struggle in which the fugitives proved helpful.[26] Other escaped slaves were employed as carriers, some of whom had initially been captured in the civil wars leading to the foundation of the Emirate of Bida.[27]

The possibility of turning slaves into soldiers struck Glover, and when he was later appointed Governor of Lagos, "those very men were the nucleus of the Haussa Constabulary." Glover recruited the first hundred men himself, and the name "Glover's Hausas" had considerable currency.[28] As we shall see, later British military forces continued the tradition of enroling runaway slaves.

It is not surprising, therefore, that former slaves figured ever more importantly in the population of Lokoja, with the inevitable consequence of friction with the Caliphate and especially the Emirate of Bida. In an effort to consolidate a precarious position on the edge of the Sokoto Caliphate, Baikie saw a way of implementing his anti-slavery ideals with the need for recruits. As Howard Pedraza relates,

> At the end of four years of perseverance there were some 200 natives who had either been redeemed from slavery by Baikie or who had put themselves directly under his protection. He bought slaves at the rate of three to ten bags of cowries per head, each bag costing 12s 6d, but it is obvious that he had not the means to redeem on a wholesale scale and it must have been the fugitives seeking sanctuary who formed a major part of his community. During his first year or two he fed daily at least fifty people free of charge and had some twenty natives on daily pay.[29]

When Baikie departed from Lokoja in 1864, he left behind redeemed slaves who had taken his name, a tradition that has carried on to this day in Lokoja.[30]

In a letter from Queen Victoria to Etsu Masaba, "King of Nufi," that was delivered on July 20, 1865, the anti-slavery intentions of the British government were made clear, although how Caliphate officials received the message is not. According to the communication, Britain made it known that

> Our chief wish is to put a stop to traffic in slaves, and to prevent their being carried away in ships by wicked men from Africa to Foreign countries and we ask your Highness to use your great influence to put a stop to this traffic and to prevent the ways that are undertaken in many cases for the sole purpose of procuring slaves to be sold for shipment beyond the seas.[31]

Official British policy was not opposed to slavery, however. As the Queen's despatch made clear, "We would also ask your Highness to encourage your subjects and the slaves within your territories to bring the produce of their country to trade with the merchants who will go from this country to trade with your people."[32] The promotion of "legitimate" trade was fully compatible with the production of goods for export by slaves.

The initiative for a British settlement withered, nonetheless, and once again the Caliphate was isolated from abolitionist sentiments.[33] Even though a British consulate had been decided upon in 1866, and a consul actually arrived on September 1, 1867, the subsidies that supported Lokoja were ended in 1866. The consulate lasted only a short time, being abandoned in 1869. When a British diplomatic agent, W. H. Simpson, arrived at Lokoja in 1871, he found trade much diminished and a population of only about 500. Simpson negotiated a treaty with the *etsu* (emir) in which Bida guaranteed the protection of British merchants and allowed for improved opportunities for trade.[34] Slavery was not an important issue.

By this time, five trading companies were operating on the Niger, mostly south of the Caliphate. Despite earlier rhetoric connecting "legitimate" trade with the fight against the slave trade, these trading interests had little concern with slavery. Private companies, operating without subsidies and generally small, were in business for profit, and profit did not obviously lie in offending the slave societies on whose margins the companies operated. The next few years brought repeated attempts to combine and extract monopoly profits, without more than nominal regard for the commitment to fight the slave trade. By the end of the 1860s, furthermore, the transatlantic slave trade had declined into insignificance and abolitionists were turning their attention elsewhere, but not to the Sokoto Caliphate. The American Civil War had ended slavery there, leaving slavery in the Americas a viable but doomed institution only in Cuba and Brazil. It is unlikely that any of the abolitionists noticed that the Sokoto Caliphate now had more slaves than anywhere in the Americas.

Slavery and the Royal Niger Company

Slavery continued to be a marginal feature of British interests along the Niger in the 1870s, but abolitionist sentiments were always just below the surface, if for no other reason than political considerations. As John Flint has demonstrated, the consolidation of the various commercial companies on the Niger into the United African Company in 1879 attempted to impose a monopoly on the commerce of the Niger River. Further mergers were in order, resulting in the National African Company in 1886. George Goldie was instrumental in the various reorganizations and mergers which attempted to profit from the rapid expansion on the Niger and Benue.[35] Concern over the prevalence of slavery in the Sokoto Caliphate was not a factor in these rivalries.

The Berlin Conference of 1884, arranged among European powers to limit the commercial war waging throughout the continent, strongly influenced subsequent developments. For Britain, the conference established British paramountcy in the Niger–Benue region, which undermined German and French activities for the time being. The Berlin accord also condemned the slave trade, but no common action was agreed on. Each European power

13

was left free to take the steps it desired. The conservative British position that slavery would be abolished in territories to be annexed in the future, but in protectorates it need not be challenged, was not disputed at the conference.[36] This distinction between protectorates and other colonial territory had important implications for the future Protectorate of Northern Nigeria. On the one hand, anti-slavery interests accepted the distinction and hence were far less critical of British policy in protectorates than in colonies. On the other hand, this legalism would be extended to the policy on slavery in 1897 through the ruse of abolishing only the legal status of slavery, leaving slavery otherwise largely alone (see below).

As a result of international competition, commercial treaties were an important feature of the relations with the various polities along the Niger and Benue, the most important of which was always the Caliphate.[37] The treaties signed with Caliphate officials included ones with the Emirate of Bida in 1884 (reconfirmed March 19, 1885), the sub-emirate of Nassarawa (October 24, 1884), the Emirate of Muri (January 31, 1885), Sokoto (June 1, 1885), Gwandu (June 13, 1885), and the sub-emirate of Keffi (July 22, 1885).[38] The Company later claimed that these documents conferred elements of sovereignty, but in fact, the treaties only secured extra-territorial commercial rights, comparable to similar treaties with the Ottoman Empire and elsewhere.

The demarcation of British interests in what was to become Northern Nigeria meant that the government looked with favor on the lobbying effort by Goldie and the National African Company to obtain a royal charter, which took effect on July 10, 1886. Thus, on July 13 of that year the NAC became the Royal Niger Company Chartered and Limited. As the agency for British penetration of the Caliphate, Goldie's Niger Company adopted the rhetoric of anti-slavery to justify its political ambitions and its commercial intentions. The charter of the Royal Niger Company endorsed the pronouncements of the Berlin Conference that declared war on the slave trade. Article 6 of the charter read as follows:

> the Company shall, to the best use of its power, discourage and, as far as may be practicable, abolish by degrees any system of domestic servitude existing among the native inhabitants; and no foreigner, whether European or not, shall be allowed to own Slaves of any kind in the Company's territories.[39]

Like its unchartered predecessors, however, the RNC was a trading company designed to earn profits for its shareholders – and so it was obviously not going to antagonize the Sokoto Caliphate, its major trading partner in the interior of West Africa, unless it believed in the existence of great gains to compensate for the costs.[40] As Flint rightly states, "even slavery would not be suppressed by force, the Company had not the power and already had enough on its hands."[41]

In 1890, the Company had ten stations and some treaty relations along the Benue above Lokoja, and seven mostly less busy stations above Lokoja on the Niger, stretching to Rabba. All this territory was in the Sokoto Caliphate. By contrast, there were twenty-three posts below Lokoja, many bustling.[42] The Company had little physical presence outside the posts and beyond the reach of its armed steamers, but in the vicinity of the latter it had complete control of the waterways. The reality was closely in accord with Caliphate perceptions of the Company, which wanted to encourage foreign trade and keep foreigners confined to enclaves governed by formal treaties of commercial extra-territoriality, as in other Muslim countries of the time. There was no desire to sell slaves to Christians, and hence the lack of British interest in purchasing slaves was not a problem. Nor does it appear that RNC anti-slave treaties were of any serious concern.

This all changed in 1890, when the Company responded to diplomatic manoeuvers in Europe arising out of the Brussels Anti-Slave Trade Conference of 1889–90. As Suzanne Miers has demonstrated, the Brussels conference was the "culmination" of Britain's campaign against the slave trade.[43] Its General Act for the Repression of the Slave Trade was enacted by the European powers as the Scramble for Africa was being launched. While the focus of the conference was on eastern and central Africa, Goldie was quick to respond to the opportunity. He could use the anti-slavery language of the conference to justify a more aggressive stance along the Niger and Benue.

Lokoja became a focus for bad relations between the Company and the Caliphate. The Company tried to increase its rights of extra-territoriality, but slavery led to confrontations that the RNC would have preferred to avoid. In 1890, Caliphate authorities at Bida, the largest of the Nupe emirates, attempted to bring the Company to account for harboring fugitive slaves. The Emirate of Bida still claimed sovereignty over the territory south of the Niger, including Lokoja, and maintained troops in the region. As a result of friction between Bida and the Company, Bida sent troops into Lokoja itself which led in turn to reprisals by the RNC Constabulary. The Company then formally annexed Lokoja, ignoring Bida's protests. Annual payments due under the treaty signed in 1885 were discontinued, and the RNC and Bida were set for further collisions.[44]

Over the next several years, the Company defended its annexation, while Bida attempted to consolidate its position on the south side of the Niger, in the area of Koton Karfi, immediately north of Lokoja, and in the Benue Valley further east. As Flint has noted, friction resulted in escaped slaves finding "sanctuary either in the company's stations, or in the mission centres of the Church Missionary Society."[45] The crisis was eased temporarily after a visit by Goldie himself in 1891.

> When he arrived at Lokoja Goldie felt that war with Nupe [Bida] was a distinct possibility, and he blamed his own officials for interfering with the institution of slavery, in his opinion not justified by the terms of the company's treaty with Nupe, which made no mention of slaves.[46]

When Goldie met the *etsu* and his chief minister at Bida on January 24, 1892, he gave every assurance that the Company would respect its treaty, and he guaranteed that he would halt any Company interference with slavery in Nupe territory. But the RNC obtained sovereignty over Lokoja.[47]

Goldie was less than honest in his assurances to Bida on the slavery issue. The RNC increasingly relied on an ideological stance of pursuing the anti-slavery crusade to justify its legitimacy in Europe. The Company had received its royal charter with difficulty, and it was no easy matter to keep it. Fortuitously for the RNC, the Brussels Anti-Slave Trade Conference gave the Company the ideological cover for commercial aggression. The RNC steadily continued its campaign of signing treaties that emphasized peaceful commerce while prohibiting the slave trade, with 306 in existence by 1894.[48] Such a course inevitably brought new problems for the Company. A dispute following the invasion of Jibu in 1891 led to the expulsion of the Company's agents from the Emirate of Muri, up the Benue, and scandal ensued in 1891 when the French Mizon expedition helped Emir Muhammadu Abubakar Nya of Muri to settle scores with rebellious subjects, which included raiding for slaves.[49] In July 1893, the Company instituted a river blockade of Muri to counter this French activity along the Benue. Anti-slavery pronouncements were clearly to the fore.

In the next year, imperial activities against the Caliphate accelerated. On the one hand, the British government at Lagos engaged in a series of skirmishes with the Emirate of Ilorin that led to the annexation of territory that Ilorin claimed.[50] On the other hand, the Company attempted to check the French advance after Dahomey fell under French rule on June 22, 1894. The race to Nikki was on, with Captain Frederick Lugard, fresh from East Africa, the British contestant against the French. As a result on January 1, 1895, the RNC proclaimed a protectorate over Bussa and Nikki, which were not part of the Caliphate but adjacent to its territory to the southwest.

With tension rising, slavery remained in the picture. As Flint relates, in the summer of 1896

> The old policy of "diplomacy" was breaking down in Nupe. The constabulary officers, many of them seconded from the British army, were finding it difficult to obey their orders not to interfere with Nupe [Bida] slave raiding. Early in 1896 Goldie had personally gone out to the Niger to try to re-establish discipline.[51]

As will be demonstrated below, we can add to Flint's interpretation that Bida was raiding for slaves, which was indeed the case, but Bida was also recapturing fugitive slaves, which had become a serious concern of Caliphate officials. Even so, at the level of Company policy, slavery could certainly serve a purpose. As Flint explains the events leading up to the RNC invasion of Bida and Ilorin in 1897,

> The motive of the war would be announced as the suppression of slavery and slave-raiding. With victory, the company would no longer be an obscure trading company which Englishmen only heard of by reading rather disturbing reports of allegations in Parliament. It would then not be so easy for Chamberlain to revoke the charter ... public opinion would want to know why a

16

company which had recently ventured so much should now be bought up ignominiously[52]

Slavery was the issue that justified Company intervention.

The hypocrisy that underlay this position is easy to recognize. The Company had often used the suppression of slave raiding and the slave trade as an excuse when a convenient one was wanted for punishing small states, while "in other cases a blind eye was turned on slavery in exchange for commercial favors."[53] Now, however, there was to be no blind eye, only a jaundiced one. Ironically, in view of the later policy of maintaining slavery in modified form, the suppression of slave raiding would be the battle cry of the conquest, first by the RNC and then by the Protectorate of Northern Nigeria after January 1, 1900.

Through the agency of the RNC, the British conquest of the Sokoto Caliphate began in 1897 with the invasion of Bida in January and Ilorin a month later. The invasion also initiated a dramatic acceleration in the evolution of British policy towards slavery and allowed the massive flight of slaves during and immediately after military campaigns (see Chapter 2). While British and Caliphate intentions towards slaves mattered, it should be observed at this point that many slaves acted on their own initiative regardless of these intentions. Nonetheless, relations between the RNC and the Caliphate set the boundaries with which slaves had to contend. Slavery was a central issue, both because the RNC interfered with slave raiding and because slaves deserted their masters in large numbers when they had the opportunity to do so.

Goldie's decision to launch an expedition against Bida was intended to demonstrate that the RNC should continue to be the agent of British imperialism. He was engaged in a political struggle against Joseph Chamberlain to prove that an outmoded royal company could persevere in the Age of Imperialism. Anti-slavery ideology could be useful. So, when he attacked Bida and Ilorin in early 1897, he used the slavery issue to keep the Colonial Office off his back. He made his views clear in 1898, in the introduction to Vandeleur's account of the conquest: "If Europe had no material interest to protect and develop in Africa, it would still have the same right, the same duty to extirpate slave-raiding that a man has to knock down a ruffian whom he sees maltreating a woman or child in the street."[54] He justified the invasion of the Caliphate in terms of suppressing slave raiding.

The Company utilized a little over half the total force of the recently enlarged Constabulary, plus a number of seconded officers from the British army, for the campaigns against Bida and Ilorin.[55] Goldie himself accompanied the expedition. The Company's troops moved against a large segment of the Bida army located south of the Niger, estimated to number 6,000 men and commanded by Makun Muhammad. The RNC's flotilla of steamers patrolled the Niger to prevent a junction of this army with the main body of Bida forces to the north of the river. In early January 1897, Makun Muhammad's army was unable to cross the Niger. Poorly led, it disintegrated under the pressure and presented no further threat to the Constabulary.[56]

The RNC Constabulary was now free to cross the Niger itself.[57] It fought a battle near Bida on January 26; and the city was shelled and occupied on January 28. The attacks of Bida's estimated 30,000 infantry and 1,000 cavalry were futile against the massed Maxims and artillery, and the effective volley firing by the Company's troops. Etsu Abubakar fled, and Makun Muhammad signed a treaty at Kusogi on February 5 that recognized him as *etsu* and ceded the south bank of the Niger to the RNC. It was symptomatic of the Company's military operations that it was unable to occupy all that it had conquered, however. The troops soon departed, and eventually Abuba-kar returned to Bida, where Makun Muhammad readily surrendered authority to him.[58]

Next, the RNC moved on Ilorin, which had already engaged in a number of encounters with British Lagos. An RNC expedition left Jebba on February 10. An Ilorin army of 8,000–10,000 (about 800 cavalry) assaulted the expedition on February 15, with no better results than those obtained by the Nupe army.[59] The city of Ilorin fell immediately. As at Bida, when the Constabulary departed on February 19 it left behind no company administration whatsoever, with the exception of a single clerk who remained on the scene. A garrison was established during the next year.

The Company proceeded to consolidate its position along the Niger and Benue Rivers. In April, the small emirate of Lafiagi and the town of Pategi were annexed, and Shonga, another emirate, was annexed the following month. Wurio, in Muri Emirate, was sacked later that year as well.[60] The Royal Niger Company now controlled the Niger Valley and maintained a strong military presence along the Benue.

This was the situation on July 19, 1897, when the Royal Niger Company declared that "the legal status of slavery shall stand abolished ... in the Niger Territories."[61] This decree, almost a ruse, followed the Indian model of legal-status abolition. The simplicity of the announcement is deceptive, considering that its adoption set the course for slavery policy for the next forty years. Issued as it was after the withdrawal of forces from Bida and Ilorin, moreover, the decree had little immediate effect on slavery elsewhere in the Sokoto Caliphate. RNC officials were confused over whether or not the intention was to emancipate slaves or leave domestic slavery alone, as we shall see in the next chapter. Furthermore, Goldie appears not to have thought too much about what it meant to abolish the legal status of slavery. As noted, his real intention was to employ anti-slavery rhetoric in the interests of the Company, and for him that meant an attack on slave raiding, not slavery itself.

Subsequent RNC military manoeuvers were undertaken as measures designed to stop slave raiding, whether or not such raiding was going on. The decree of June 19, 1897 was used as a cover for the aggressive activities of the Company. In June 1898, the small Nupe Emirates of Lapai and Agaye, to the east of Bida, were occupied; Lapai town was destroyed, and Agaye became a military outpost. In August 1898, a Company force briefly established a base at Illo, far up the Niger River in Gwandu territory, but it was abandoned after a skirmish with Caliphate forces. Wase, a sub-emirate of Bauchi, was sacked in September 1898, and various towns in Muri were raided in 1899.[62] If the Company believed that its successful campaign against Bida and Ilorin and forays into Muri, Bauchi, and Gwandu would save its charter, its hopes were in vain.

The British government was far too concerned with French expansion to allow the RNC to manage the imperial response, and consequently on July 23, 1897, Chamberlain issued instructions for the raising of the West African Frontier Force (WAFF), to be paid for by the government. Colonel Frederick Lugard, promoted to Brigadier for the occasion, was put in charge.[63] He left England in March 1898 to take command of the new imperial unit, which consisted of two battalions of infantry (1,200 men each at full strength), one stationed at Lokoja and the other at Jebba, two batteries of artillery, and a company of engineers. Headquarters were established at Jebba.[64] Recruiting and training went on during the first half of 1898, and the earliest operations were conducted in cooperation with the RNC Constabulary.

The decision to end the Company's chartered rule was subsequently taken. A debate on revocation took place in Parliament from July 26 to August 4, 1899.[65] The southern part of the RNC's territory was attached to the Oil Rivers protectorate, transferred from the Foreign Office to the Colonial Office and named thereafter the Protectorate of Southern Nigeria. The Charter was actually revoked on December 28, 1899, and by an Order in Council of December 27, 1899, a new protectorate named Northern Nigeria was established, its High Commissioner empowered to legislate by proclamation.[66] Goldie refused to be considered for the position, which went instead to Lugard, commander of the WAFF, and the logical candidate anyway. The RNC became merely a commercial company renamed the Niger Company. Goldie's strategy to prove the worth of a chartered company in the imperial cause had failed. What the Royal Niger Company had started, the Protectorate of Northern Nigeria would have to finish, and that included dealing with the issue of slavery.

The RNC had employed the rhetoric of anti-slavery to justify its actions in the southern emirates of the Caliphate. Slave raiding south of the Niger ended, and a policy of abolishing the legal status of slavery was instituted. In addition, as we will see (Chapter 2), military actions and ideological pronouncements against slavery had an immediate impact on the Caliphate. On the one hand, political instability arising from the invasion of the various emirates enabled thousands of slaves to desert their masters. On the other hand, Caliphate officials were made aware that British occupation not only undermined the sovereignty of the Caliphate but also was a frontal attack on the institution of slavery.

The British protectorate and the suppression of slave raiding

On January 1, 1900, his first day as High Commissioner of the new Protectorate of Northern Nigeria, Lugard issued a proclamation that warned the Caliphate of his intention to fight slavery. In a poor translation, this proclamation was sent to Caliph Abdurrahaman at Sokoto, and to selected emirs as well. The very first word was intended to be "Declaration" but was rendered with the Arabic characters for "Shouting," undoubtedly a bad beginning. In the second paragraph appeared the exaggerated claim that the Royal Niger Company by its laws had "prevented the perpetration of venomous crimes as well as great sins such as homicide, slavery, raiding of the poor people and similar things."[67] Paragraph 5 stated that the great Queen of England had chosen new people to "discourage trade in alcoholic drinks and in slaves." In fact, alcohol was not an issue, since its consumption was already illegal in the Caliphate, but it appeared that both slavery and the slave trade would be brought under attack. This was actually not the immediate intent, and it was unlike Lugard to make a slip of this sort. That was not the only mistake in this strange document, however, which must have inflamed Caliphate officials because it implied a breach of existing treaties concerning the Caliphate's independence, and because in addition it implied British suzerainty. It is hardly a surprise that the Caliph did not deign to reply, and after that, little diplomacy took place before the conquest of Sokoto itself.

Lugard's first military moves were justified to the Colonial Office as actions against slave raiding, and consequently, a WAFF detachment moved north into the Emirate of Kontagora, where it saw frequent action with "slave raiders" in the latter months of 1900. The WAFF unit established its base at the sub-emirate of Wushishi on the Kaduna River. Subsequently, Lugard would locate his capital only a few kilometers away at a site to be named Zungeru. Lugard thought that the Kaduna River would be an important route northward, although it turned out that the river itself was too shallow for most of the year. Nonetheless, Wushishi/Zungeru was a strategic point on the Kaduna, and the railway would be built along the river.

The Emirate of Kontagora, under Sarkin Sudan Ibrahim, was portrayed as the most notorious slave-raiding entity of the day. In August, 1900, Lugard reported to the Colonial Office that in a recent raid the Kontagora emir "took 4,000 slaves and killed all whom he caught who were useless as slaves."[68] Major O'Neill, who was in command of the Wushishi detachment, had

> a series of small engagements with slave-raiding parties, chiefly belonging to Bida and Kontagora. Parties from these two chiefs had closed the Kaduna waterway and fired on our canoes, had laid waste a vast tract of country, pillaging and burning the villages, and carrying off slaves, their efforts being more especially directed against those villages which had shown hospitality to,

or friendship with, Europeans ... It is probable that in consequence of his continued hostility I shall very soon be compelled to break the power of Kontagora, who is a slave raider of the worst type, and has harried and desolated a great area of country, and is said to have captured 8,000 slaves this season. Whatever the number of slaves captured may be, there is little doubt at least an equal number will have been killed.[69]

The language of conquest required that the WAFF stop Caliphate officials from conducting "slave raids."[70]

Both Kontagora and Bida, as well as the other Nupe emirates, faced a serious crisis because of British military occupation – slaves were running away in considerable numbers, and non-Muslim communities that had previously paid tribute were in open revolt (see Chapter 2). Kontagora and Bida were actively policing the countryside in an effort to control slaves, recapture fugitives, and force subjugated communities to honor tributary arrangements that included the forwarding of slaves. These emirates were also enslaving people, but labeling all military actions as "slave raiding" was a serious and conscious oversimplification. And in the case of some charges against Bida, as Mason has demonstrated, there was deliberate "falsification."[71]

The skirmishes around Wushishi would no doubt have given way to a full-scale operation much sooner than was the case, but inconveniently for Lugard, 1,200 troops (over half the strength of the WAFF) were in Asante. They did not return until December 1900, whereupon an attack on Kontagora was soon underway.[72] A force commanded by Lt.-Col. G. V. Kemball saw action against Sarkin Sudan Ibrahim's army, numbering about 5,000, on January 31 and February 1, 1901. The Kontagora army was reported to have suffered only about fifty casualties in their lost cause; the Emir fled to regroup further north.

Bida and Ilorin, both weakened by the campaigns of 1897, were next on Lugard's agenda, and their defeat this time led to permanent occupation. Ilorin was the easier case, with Emir Sulayman accepting a Resident without fighting. The city was troubled in the latter part of 1900, and unrest continued until well after the fall of the northern emirates in 1903. But the small force stationed in Ilorin was able to keep the peace.[73] Bida, accused of complicity in the "slave raiding" around Wushishi, required an expedition, and on February 19, 1901, the WAFF marched on Bida. Resistance was limited and ineffectual. Etsu Abubakar fled, the city was entered, and Makun Muhammad was made *etsu* once again, his second appointment by the British and this time for good.[74] Bida forces suffered many casualties, and "the W.A.F.F. proceeded to plunder the Nupes."[75] As Mason has noted, "Lugard's injunction against slave-raiding" made it amply clear that

even before Muhammedu [*sic*] sat on the throne [in 1901] he must have accepted that the southern provinces were irrecoverable. Slave raiding was at an end, too. Thus was the motor of the state both stripped and deprived of replacement parts.[76]

The small Nupe emirates east of Bida offered little resistance.

With the south reasonably secure, attention turned far up the Niger to the west, and that move too was connected with the slavery issue. From the vicinity of the WAFF garrison established in 1900 at Illo near the border with Dahomey, a column sacked Raha and burned Kalgo in Gwandu Emirate "as a punishment for slave-raiding."[77] Further in that direction, a WAFF force marched to Argungu. The British presence at Argungu, located on the Sokoto River in a commanding position close to both Gwandu and Sokoto, was a provocative move, especially since Argungu headed a confederation (together with the Zarma stronghold of Dosso and the Arewa capital at Birnin Konni) that had maintained its independence from the Caliphate since the middle of the nineteenth century.[78] The fact that the French had found a trusted ally in Dosso in its subjugation of the western emirates only reinforced Caliphate fears that the threat from the West was real.

Lugard now departed on one of his long leaves, leaving William Wallace in charge. Wallace had been an active administrator in the Company's days, and he was active with the government as well. Yola, the capital of Adamawa Emirate in the east, was the next target. A movement against that distant territory was delayed until success attended the moves against Kontagora and Bida, and until all troops had returned from the Asante War. Wallace had already characterized Adamawa's Lamido Zubairu as a principal slaver, advising the Colonial Office

> that nearly the whole of the raw slaves recently released and placed at Lokoja have passed through Adamawa, and that the Emir of Yola is now the worst offender in the matter of slave raiding in this Protectorate. He openly defies the Government, and recently sent a message, through the Niger Company's agents, asking "when he was to receive a visit from these new white men who would not show so much patience as the Company had shown towards him"; this had reference to a message I sent to him shortly before the transfer, warning him that the Government would not exercise the same leniency towards him as the Company had.[79]

The excuse that slave raiding required British intervention was once again used to effect. Lugard too wrote that Yola was now the center of the Caliphate's slave trade, with "huge numbers" involved. This explanation justified the strong expedition despatched in his absence.[80]

By 1901, the British had made plans to occupy Zaria as well. Sarkin Sudan Ibrahim had retreated into Zaria territory, where he was not well received and therefore began attacking villages. As a result, Emir Kwassau of Zaria was willing to accept British assistance in protecting his territory. Conflict between the two emirs appears to have related to differences within the Caliphate aristocracy over how best to respond to British aggression, either by full resistance, which Ibrahim favored, or accommodation, which Kwassau advocated. R. A. Adeleye suggests that Ibrahim's internecine raids were motivated by a need for land on which to settle and for provisions as well, but it is more likely that internal Caliphal political differences account for the conflict.[81] As we have seen, Ibrahim and the deposed *etsu* of Bida, Abubakar, took a hard line in their opposition to the British. Kwassau seems to have sided with those Caliphate officials who were more accommodating. In this case, Kwassau was closer to Makun Muhammad, who was once again *etsu* of Bida, than to the ousted Abubakar.[82] In any event, Emir Kwassau allowed the WAFF to move into Zaria territory in January 1902. This time Sarkin Sudan Ibrahim submitted to British troops without bloodshed, along with "thousands of slaves recently captured."[83] Lugard reiterated the theme of the conquest – the successful campaign to curtail slave raiding. Meanwhile, the British moved north from the Benue into Zaria's sub-emirates, with Nassarawa also occupied in early 1902.[84]

Now that Zaria had ostensibly put itself under British protection, a Resident (Captain Abadie) and a garrison were placed there, only eighty miles from Kano, in mid April 1902. By then, Emir Kwassau regretted British support. According to Assistant Resident Reginald Popham Lobb, mounting resistance in Zaria was related to anti-slavery measures:

> All that has been done and only that by a threat of force is to have the sale of slaves in the market stopped ... There were 300 in irons there a few days before and they were being hawked about the streets. Of course the sale goes on in the slave houses, it's inevitable, and if we stopped it by force the disaffected people would simply bolt to Kano. So we must settle Kano at once.[85]

As Popham Lobb's comments reveal, the corollary to stopping the Caliphate from enslaving people was to close the slave markets of the major towns.

Furthermore, a new theme was added to the litany of conquest – the interception of tribute payments in slaves. Zaria managed to send its annual tribute of one hundred slaves to Sokoto after the British garrison had established itself in the town, even though pickets were in place to stop this transfer.[86] In August, Popham Lobb wrote that

> The king [of Zaria] has been told, some weeks ago, that if he took a single slave as tribute again, there would be trouble. We have news of a batch of 30, who are to be smuggled into the town tomorrow night, so we have sent out spies along the road, and 10 soldiers disguised in ordinary native kit, with their rifles underneath their gowns. If we bag the slaves we shall get hold of the king at once, and send him down country, then the fun will begin.[87]

When further tribute was collected, Emir Kwassau was arrested and brought to Zungeru in September.[88] Not only was slave raiding prohibited, but the forwarding of slaves as tribute was also taboo.

By the autumn of 1902, The British had conquered Bida, Ilorin, Agaye, Lapai, Kontagora, Muri, Bauchi, Gombe, Zaria, and Yola, and all had administrations in place, even though some of these continued to send tribute to Sokoto secretly. Most of the emirs were ousted on charges of slave raiding in one form or another; whatever the ostensible reason, they were removed because they opposed the British. In every case their replacements undertook to obey the new laws against "slave raiding." In addition, Borno was conquered, and the British had an ally in Argungu. The central provinces of Kano, Sokoto, Katsina, and Gwandu were surrounded, with the French in control of Caliphate territory in the west and occupying the country to the north. Some of the minor emirates were still independent as well, including Hadejia, Kazaure, Katagum, Azare, and Daura.[89]

At this crucial point Sultan Abdurrahaman died (October 10, 1902), thereby throwing the central Caliphate into a state of confusion. Attahiru I became the new caliph on October 13, and plans for the defense of the central Caliphate resumed.[90] Lugard chose this time to plan the invasion of Kano and Sokoto, although he expected criticism from the Colonial Office for proceeding without authorization, which was certainly required, because Britain was recovering from the Boer War. Since it would be unwise to admit that the reason for prompt action was a result of the opportunity presented by the abrupt succession, Lugard had to find a more acceptable explanation.

In anticipation of the inevitable objections that he would face at the Colonial Office, Lugard returned frequently to the subject of slavery in justifying his decision to invade Kano and the other central emirates. The cessation of tribute payments in slaves now became the principal reason for the invasion. On November 21, 1902, he wrote:

> Apart from the great impetus to trade which will be given by the inclusion of Sokoto, Kano, and Katsena under the Administration, I anticipate that the settlement of this question will have a great effect in quieting the Emirates of Zaria, Bautshi, and Yola, which will never settle down until these States have given their allegiance to British rule. The annual tribute in slaves can then be effectively stopped. Although I am using every effort to prevent it, I believe that strenuous counter-efforts are being made by these Emirs to collect and send the slaves surreptitiously.[91]

Of course tribute payments and enslavement were linked, since only new slaves were forwarded to Sokoto as tribute.

The immediate *casus belli* was the death of Resident Maloney in Keffi on October 3, 1902. Maloney had been posted to the new province of Nassarawa, which had been fashioned out of the southern districts of Zaria Emirate, only a few months earlier. This province included the sub-emirate of Keffi, under the rule of Magajin Keffi Dan Yamusa. Soon after the British occupation in July 1902, Maloney forbade Keffi's annual forays against non-Muslims, which he called slave raids, but he was killed trying to enforce his orders. Soon after the confrontation, the Magajin Keffi fled to Kano, where he was welcomed and treated with honor. This incident provided the excuse for Lugard to move on Kano, but the fact that Lugard had already sketched the provinces that he would carve out of the central emirates indicates that another excuse would soon have been found if this one had not arisen.[92] Nonetheless, once again Lugard could claim that he was moving against slave raiders.

To abolitionists in Britain, Kano was the cynosure of the Caliphate's slave trade, and it did indeed import large numbers of slaves, although by this time it was not particularly active in capturing new slaves. By the end of 1902, anticipation of an attack was running high in Kano. During the year, the Kano walls and gates had been reinforced, and many towns in the emirate had repaired their smaller walls and redug their trenches.[93] In particular the ground from Bebeji north was defended by a series of fortified positions that were intended to lend support to one another in case of attack.

Slavery was never the only reason for the conquest. To justify a yet more extended operation, Lugard now called to the attention of the Colonial Office a letter from the late Caliph Abdurrahaman, which Lugard interpreted to be a declaration of war.[94] The invasion of Sokoto was preemptive, Lugard now claimed. He also brought up the need to protect the Anglo-French boundary commission which had arrived at Lokoja on November 1, 1902, and was just then in the process of demarcating the frontier from the Niger River to Lake Chad, which of course cut through Caliphate territory; therefore its presence could hardly be justified unless the Caliphate was occupied.[95]

The latter stages of the Boer War had, however, much diluted the imperial resolve at the Colonial Office, and military expeditions in Africa were not the fashion they once had been, even in as good a cause as Lugard claimed this one was. Because Joseph Chamberlain was stitching together peace in South Africa, the Earl of Onslow was left to counsel caution. His letter dated January 28, 1903 chided Lugard for preparing an advance on Kano, suggesting that the High Commissioner was exceeding his instructions.

> You are aware that the policy of His Majesty's Government has always been to avoid, if possible, any rupture with Sokoto, although they have not concealed from themselves that the measures which they authorised you to take to suppress slave-raiding would probably bring us into conflict sooner or later with the Sultan. It is necessary, in the interests both of humanity and of trade, that slave-raiding by organized bands, causing widespread misery and bloodshed and depopulating the country, should be met by force and suppressed so far as this can be done with the troops at your disposal; but there is no desire on the part of His Majesty's Government to destroy the existing forms of administration or to govern the country otherwise than through its own rulers.[96]

Even so, the Colonial Office in the end acquiesced, as was so often the case in its relations with Lugard. The conquest of Kano, Sokoto, Gwandu, and Katsina quickly followed.

Indecision among the senior Caliphate officials made the situation particularly precarious for the central emirates. As noted above, preoccupation with the accession of Caliph Attahiru I gave Lugard his opportunity. On January 2, 1903 Emir Aliyu left Kano for Sokoto to pay homage to the new caliph, taking with him many high Kano officials and 2,000 horsemen, probably because Caliph Attahiru I planned a coordinated defense against the invasion. Kano city was left in the hands of two slave officials and other troops, who were assigned the task of resisting the British advance while Aliyu consulted with Attahiru I. Perhaps Aliyu did not expect the attack to come so soon; perhaps Attahiru ordered Emir Aliyu to Sokoto. Whatever his reasons, the Emir's absence was catastrophic when the attack came a month later.[97]

Colonel T. N. Morland commanded the move on Kano. Bebeji, the first fortress in Kano Emirate, fell rather easily; other fortified towns en route were deserted by their garrisons; the Challawa River was crossed on February 2, and Kano was reached the next morning. Attempts to effect a breach at the Zaria gate having failed, an attack was made further west at the Kabuga gate. After the gate was penetrated, various groups attempted to flee, but they encountered mounted infantry patrols which killed many. Of the Kano army estimated by Moreland to consist of 800 cavalry and 5,000 infantry, an estimated 300 were killed.[98]

Emir Aliyu, returning from his untimely visit to Sokoto, heard this unwelcome news near Kaura Namoda and refused to believe it. Finally convinced, he fled. The Magajin Keffi, who had been the ostensible cause of the move on Kano, returned to Sokoto with the Emir's entourage. Both defections undermined this portion of the Kano army even before its final battle. At Kwatarkwashi on February 25 a first skirmish occurred, while on the morning of February 26 a battle took place at Rawiyya just north of Kwatarkwashi. The result was yet another defeat for a Caliphate army. After these actions, Abbas, the Wombai of Kano, led the defeated battalions back to Kano, where they surrendered and were disarmed on March 6.[99] Abbas became the British emir.

WAFF forces concentrated at Kaura Namoda on February 27 for the march on Sokoto, towards which they embarked on March 3. Kemball, now Brigadier-General, was in command. They were joined at Shagari on March 11 by Captain Merrick's force from Argungu. Merrick first moved to Shagari, where he ordered the Emir of Gwandu to submit. The Emir responded that there would be no resistance, and on March 12 Gwandu was occupied.[100] The stage was set for the final assault of Sokoto.

The opposition at Sokoto consisted of about 2,000 cavalry and 4,000 infantry.[101] On March 15 in a short action of less than 20 minutes outside the walls, the main body of the Sokoto army was defeated, while other units were dispersed in actions lasting for about 1½ hours. Caliph Attahiru I fled to the east. A new caliph, Attahiru II, was installed (he had been a candidate for the position a few months earlier), and Major Alder Burdon became the Resident. On March 23, the main WAFF force returned to Kano, leaving a garrison of 200 with Burdon.[102]

The conquest was now almost complete. After Sokoto's fall, Lugard moved on to Katsina and confirmed Emir Abubakar in his position. The small Emirate of Jama'are was occupied in the same month, while Hadejia, Kazaure and Daura were taken soon after.[103] Meanwhile, ex-Caliph Attahiru I moved steadily eastward with his large entourage, joined en route by many thousands of loyalists. Finally this mass of people reached Bormi, the former headquarters of Jibril's Mahdist community in Gombe Emirate. In an unsuccessful action of May 13, 1903 (the 1st Battle of Bormi) Captain Sword's WAFF detachment failed to take the former caliph, but on July 27 at the 2nd Battle of Bormi the defenders faced a concentration of WAFF units and suffered very heavy casualties. At least 600 were believed to have died in this action, including Attahiru I and probably (but not with complete certainty) the Magajin Keffi as well. British casualties were higher than in any action of the conquest, 84, including 12 dead.[104] Resistance of this intensity could have made a difference if it had occurred at any time in the preceding six years, but these were the last military resources available, and now they were gone.

Suppression of slave raiding and slave trading

As is clear from this summary of the conquest, the attack on slavery in the Sokoto Caliphate was intimately associated with the British advance. By the 1890s, the century-long abolitionist crusade had found its way into imperialist rhetoric, but in making the transition from evangelical conviction to imperial ideology, abolitionism became less concerned with freeing slaves from an inhumane system of labor and more with justifying the conquest itself.[105] Afterwards, colonial policies attempted to protect local economies, and hence the slave masters, from the inevitable dislocation associated with abolition.[106] Now the anti-slavery movement was radical neither in effect nor in intent: it first served to rationalize imperial ambitions, and then it became a conservative force in protecting the very people who exploited slaves.

By early 1903, Lugard claimed that he had ended all large-scale slave raiding and that the public slave markets in the major cities were closed. He felt morally justified in the conquest on the basis of these anti-slavery measures, as he made clear just after Kano fell:

> The advocates of conciliation at any price who protest against military operations in Northern Nigeria appear to forget that their nation has assumed before God and the civilised world the responsibility of maintaining peace and good order in the area declared as a British Protectorate, and that the towns of Kano and Sokoto are ruled by an alien race who buy and sell the people of the country in large public slave markets daily, these being now – thanks to the British rule – the last remaining centres of this traffic; that methods of cruelty involving a total disregard for human suffering are daily practised ... The military operations so much deprecated have, in the great cities of Bida, of Kontagora, of Yola, of Bautshi, of Illorin, of Zaria, and elsewhere, led to the suppression of these things ... The task upon which I am employed is one of prevention of the daily bloodshed which has already denuded this country of probably half its population and even the suppression of the forces of tyranny and unrest has been achieved with almost no bloodshed at all.[107]

As Resident Abadie explained the policy from Zaria, "The best way to stop slavery in this country is to first ensure the supply of men slaves being absolutely done away with, i.e. by stopping all slave raiding, and then at the same time stop all buying and selling of slaves."[108] By 1903, overt slave dealing had been confined to frontier markets that would be systematically closed as well.

The more difficult task of preventing occasional slave trading would plague the colonial regime for much longer, although tribute payments in slaves were easily terminated. The efforts to stop enslavement and the sale of slaves would embrace the whole Protectorate, including the former enemies of the Caliphate, because trade slaves moved in all directions. As we shall see (Chapter 9), Lugard was premature in asserting that organized raiding was over. Raiding was not fully suppressed until 1920, and enslavement on a smaller scale continued for even longer, particularly in non-Muslim areas. The many non-Muslim communities in the hills and plains of the Benue basin were particularly difficult to police. There would be considerable trouble in suppressing the pawning of children in times of famine and other duress, and pawned children often fell into the hands of slave traders. Nonetheless, British intentions were clear to Muslims and non-Muslims alike. Assistant Resident Stanley was especially blunt when he warned the Tiv of Muri Emirate in June 1903 "not to catch slaves to eat or sell."[109]

The rhetoric of anti-slavery had served Lugard well in justifying the conquest of the Sokoto Caliphate. Despite occasional criticism in Britain, he had managed to acquire an empire in the midst of the difficult period of the Boer War. He had many supporters in Britain, including his journalist wife, Flora Shaw, who were fully convinced of the need to stop slave raiding. As the *African Review* editorialized on January 16, 1904:

> Sir Frederick Lugard shows very clearly, as we have repeatedly pointed out in the columns in reply to ill-informed criticisms in some of our contemporaries, that the Fulani were merely rapacious foreign conquerors whose *regime* had degenerated at the present day into one of unlimited massacre, pillage, and slave-raiding, and that the Hausa inhabitants of the country, far from opposing our advance, have welcomed the breaking of the powers of their oppressors with the greatest joy ... Lugard ... [has] put an end by armed force (there being no other alternative) to the awful miseries and depopulation which the Fulani slave-raiders were causing throughout Northern Nigeria.[110]

Even his critics in Northern Nigeria shared the general view that the conquest was desirable. The Rev. Walter R. Miller, who often complained of government complacency, extended the charges against the Fulbe aristocracy from slave raiding to other "atrocities, as narrated by trustworthy Hausas and some royal Fillanis," in a special report to Lugard on "cruel punishments for unstated crimes."[111]

Thus it came as one of the most startling reversals of the colonial era, given these charges and the language of the conquest, when Lugard proceeded to rely on the very "slave raiders" that he had just been condemning. Lugard's regime would depend on the entire apparatus of the Caliphate, including its army in the crushing of the Satiru revolt of 1906 (see Chapter 2).

The aristocracy in particular would be kept in power. Even the notorious Ibrahim, "the Destroyer" of Kontagora, was reinstated.[112]

The hypocrisy of the slavery issue should have been apparent to anyone interested in looking at the occupation of the Sokoto Caliphate between 1897 and 1903, but apparently no one in the anti-slavery circles in Britain seemed to have noticed. The suppression of slave raiding and the likely death of the slave trade were enough to command the respect of the tired abolitionists of the British movement. Lugard understood well the issues surrounding slavery at the time. He also knew that British rule could not be consolidated with the aid of slaves, unless they continued to work for their masters. It is easy to be cynical about Lugard's commitment to abolition, and no doubt there is ample evidence to leave the matter at that.

Nothing concerning Lugard's use of slave raiding as a cover for imperialistic action should detract from the undoubted abhorrence of such activity among many colonial officials and the military, even including Lugard himself. Slave raiding was a good excuse for action that involved other motives as well. Raiding did exist, it was highly disruptive to society, and colonial officials believed in the virtue of its elimination. In later years, they were proud of extirpating the traffic in human beings.

Whether or not a cynical interpretation is applied to Lugard's motives, it is important to recognize that his vision of Indirect Rule required the careful management of the slavery issue. Colonialism was not just "evil" in its consequences; it undermined the aristocracy of the Caliphate in the short run but succeeded in reinforcing the same class in the long run. The process by which this transformation of a ruling class dependent upon slave labor and the enslavement of people through raiding and war into a ruling class assured of a tax base and income derived from land is the story of the twentieth century. The slaves of the Caliphate joined the peasantry of Northern Nigeria, not as a result of a quick reaction to capitalist penetration but after a prolonged series of adjustments in the terms of servility that resulted from the interaction between Muslim aristocrats and British administrators. Lugard tried to anticipate the changes in a manner that consolidated British rule, while advancing his own career.

As we will demonstrate, Lugard succeeded in most of his aims, despite the immediate problems. It was not possible to conquer a large Islamic state such as the Sokoto Caliphate on the basis of an anti-slavery crusade without slaves concluding that their time had come. But slaves were merely pawns in Lugard's ambitious game. He was preoccupied with details relating to his official relations at home in Britain, public opinion in the English-speaking world, and the implementation of military power in the context of British expansion. Lugard accepted the likelihood that many slaves would try to escape, but he was not especially interested in their humanity. Slaves were largely irrelevant to Lugard's grand vision; they were mere objects that had to be managed carefully so that they would not cause too much trouble.

But reform certainly did not mean the end of slavery, which survived as an institution. Not until 1936 did Ordinance No. 16 declare all people born in or brought into Nigeria to be free.[113] Even then, slavery persisted in modified form for royal slaves, and concubinage continued. Nonetheless, there were no subsequent decrees affecting the status of these slaves.[114] Today people can still be found who are considered slaves, although the actual number of people still technically so has declined to relative insignificance. The death of slavery, pronounced by so many observers, has been a protracted one and is still not over.

2

Fugitive slaves and the crisis in slavery policy

The conquest of the Sokoto Caliphate was undertaken as an anti-slavery campaign against a Muslim state in which slavery was essential to its economy and the bedrock of its society. Yet neither the Royal Niger Company nor the Protectorate government wanted to end slavery or encourage any dislocation that might impede the consolidation of colonial rule. During the RNC period of the conquest from 1897 to 1900, there was considerable confusion over the slavery issue, particularly with respect to escaped slaves. Goldie and his senior officers said they would not harbor fugitives, but they often did. The actions of the Protectorate government were more consistent, but even then it took a year or more to make it clear to subordinates that fugitives were not to be protected, unless there were signs of severe ill treatment. Official policy appeared to allow slaves to leave their masters if they so chose, but in practice they were to be discouraged, even obstructed. Despite the use of abolitionist rhetoric to justify the conquest, British imperialism was committed to the continuation of slavery, abolishing only its legal status.

The ideological overtones of the conquest were bound to filter through to the slaves nonetheless, especially since the pronouncements on slavery seemed to mean that slavery was over and the actions of the RNC and the Protectorate government often indicated as much. As Lugard himself admitted, many slaves thought the conquest meant the end of slavery, and as a result "the slaves deserted because they had heard that domestic slavery would be abolished."[1] British actions seemed unclear. On the one hand, slave raiding was outlawed, the slave trade curtailed, and the payment of tribute in slaves was no longer allowed. Yet, on the other hand, the Protectorate officials repeatedly stated that domestic slavery continued. It is understandable that there was confusion over British intentions and that many people, slaves and masters alike, thought that slavery itself was finished.

Given the situation, it was inevitable that a certain number of slaves would escape during the military campaigns of the conquest. We estimate that the scale of the exodus was of the order of a few hundred thousand slaves, perhaps 10 percent of the total slave population (see below). Considering the size of the slave population, it could hardly have been otherwise. For a while desertions had the useful effect of undermining the Caliphate. Many of the soldiers in the RNC Constabulary and the WAFF were ex-slaves who were hardly sympathetic to the Caliphate slave system. Some military officers, too, thought that the intention of legal-status abolition was to free slaves, which was convenient to do anyway, but once they were told otherwise, they followed orders. By 1901 or so, colonial staff and military officials understood that slaves were not to leave their masters. The British conquest was not for the purpose of ending slavery, despite the ideological overtones of abolition.

Neither the Royal Niger Company nor the Protectorate government wanted slaves to escape. Goldie, Lugard, and all of their subordinates, except the military officers who were temporarily confused by the anti-slavery ideology of the conquest, were in agreement that slaves should be kept in place. The question was how. The major difference between the RNC and the Protectorate on this issue was that the RNC was too disorganized and understaffed for the task of conquest to attempt consistency on policy and action. The Protectorate, under Lugard's direction, had a clearer vision. The consolidation of British rule would necessitate political stability and social order, and slaves on the run were an unsettling influence. The few missionaries who might have influenced public opinion back home in Britain were kept out of the way as much as possible, and they proved to be relatively quiet on the slavery issue anyway. Neither the "abolitionist" military officers nor the missionaries had any significant influence on developments.

The size of the slave population was such that even if a small proportion of slaves ran away, the scale of the exodus would have been enormous. Igor Kopytoff is probably correct in saying that if only 10 percent of a slave population expressed its discontent in an overt manner, as through flight, then the extent of opposition was not of particularly serious consequence to the slave regime.[2] But if the regime had perhaps two million slaves, as in the case of the Sokoto Caliphate, the number of people involved would be a major historical phenomenon nonetheless. As indicated, our best guess is that perhaps two hundred thousand slaves did desert their masters during the British invasion of the Sokoto Caliphate and the period of colonial consolidation. Because the exodus was stretched out over a decade or so, the social and economic impact was probably less than such large numbers might suggest. Nonetheless, the demographic implications were considerable.

Furthermore, the colonial state had to anticipate the possibility of even more serious displacement. If approximately two hundred thousand slaves could leave, then it was conceivable that slaves might band together and stage a coordinated uprising. Masters might even fear this possibility and overreact to the demands of slaves, or they might give in too quickly in the context of a situation which might appear uncontrollable. As Burdon noted in 1906, "the preconceived ideas of the people regarding British action on the question [of slavery]" was the cause of much dissatisfaction among slave owners, who held the British responsible for "the loss of their slaves."[3] The conquest *did* entail considerable reflection. And to the extent that slaves ran away, colonial officials and local aristocrats had good reason to ponder their new, even if unwanted, partnership. The test of the colonial conquest was how well the British regime would be able to convince the aristocracy and the merchant class that their interests could be accommodated under British rule.

The slave exodus from Nupe and Ilorin, 1897–1900

The military occupation of Bida and Ilorin in January and February 1897 set in motion a massive exodus of slaves that continued for the duration of Royal Niger Company rule along the Niger.[4] Several reasons contributed to the flight of slaves. First, the Company did not have tight discipline over its officers and employees. As we have noted, there was genuine confusion over the Company's policy, and even the actions of Goldie himself did not help to clear up the confusion. Sometimes he stated succinctly that fugitives were to be sent back, while other times he acquiesced in their flight. The senior administration realized the potential troubles slave desertions might cause, but some officers and officials welcomed the flight of slaves because such desertions weakened the enemy and seemed to be consistent with the anti-slavery ideology expressed by the campaign.[5] Second, missionaries at Lokoja tended to be abolitionists, and while there were never many missionaries and they had little influence on Company policy, their presence did not make it any easier to maintain a conservative position on slavery.[6]

Third, many soldiers in the RNC Constabulary and the newly formed West African Frontier Force were of slave origin, and most were thus hostile to the Caliphate.[7] Though there is nothing to indicate that these soldiers were in favor of abolishing slavery or that they explicitly encouraged slaves to desert, their very presence demonstrated that the British were willing to employ fugitives and ex-slaves, and indirectly, therefore, the Constabulary and the WAFF must have been a visible expression of anti-slavery sentiment to many slaves and slave owners alike. The soldiers themselves, however, typically wanted females and servants, and their wives also wanted servants, especially children. Consequently, soldiers acquired slaves, despite haphazard efforts on the part of white officers to prevent such acquisitions.

Official RNC policy during the conquest was at best muddled. Seymour Vandeleur later wrote that the RNC had "formally proclaimed ... the cessation of slavery," and that "slavery would be at the end from this time."[8] Certainly Goldie had no such intention in mind. As we have noted. Goldie was committed to a policy of abolishing the legal status of slavery, not slavery itself, but he only got around to instituting this policy several months after the occupation of Bida and Ilorin, on June 19, 1897. He suggested that the CMS missionaries interpret the abolition of the legal status of slavery carefully: "it would be a misfortune if the entire social system of the Territories were too rapidly revolutionized. Immense numbers of slaves would be unable to support themselves and families if they rashly sever themselves from the present social system. Harm would be done if slaves were encouraged to leave their masters."[9] Goldie asked the CMS "not to encourage, far less initiate," any action by slaves to leave their masters.

Alder Burdon, who was in charge of the RNC Constabulary after the initial invasion of Bida and Ilorin, insisted that the executive officers of the Company "were not affecting any wholesale freeing of slaves, [but] were in fact in many cases inducing fugitive slaves to return to their masters, and were openly expressing their disapproval of certain missionaries who were telling the natives that the meaning of the new law was that no one was to be a slave any more."[10] By the time he became Resident at Bida in 1901, Burdon had a pro-slavery reputation. Captain Abadie summarized Burdon's position succinctly: he "takes the side of the master and wants to back him up as much as possible."[11]

Despite official opposition, the invasion of Bida in 1897 established the pattern of the exodus; slaves fled in the wake of military action or whenever they thought they could get away.[12] According to later reports, "thousands of slaves and farm labourers deserted and established themselves on the south of the [Niger] river" at the time of the occupation.[13] As Mason has noted,

> From early 1897, the slave plantations, the army and the economic life in the capital [Bida] began to deteriorate for want of men. Slaves at work on the *tungazi* [plantations] began to slip away more regularly. There had always been a trickle of slaves returning to their homes. Now there was a flood. The Yorubas and Afemais returning southwards across the Niger were joined in their flight by Nupes crossing the Kaduna on the road to the west.[14]

Makun Muhammad, whom the Company had tried to install as *etsu*, complained that "all our slaves are running away to the other side of the river."[15] Because Makun Muhammad headed the faction in Bida that was most willing to collaborate with the RNC, his report was taken as a serious warning that a major exodus was underway. Musa, a government translator who was a slave in Bida during this period, later told G. D. Hazzledine that he received "less food and more blows" following the Company invasion. Masters were trying to keep slaves in place.[16]

Similar reports of mass desertions came from Ilorin. According to Vandeleur, as RNC forces withdrew from the city on February 19, 1897,

> the road was at first blocked by crowds of Hausa people – traders, refugees, and slaves, carrying their goods in baskets on their heads, and on donkeys – who intended to accompany the column. Numbers of slaves had come into the camp at Ilorin to have their chains knocked off their legs ... Thousands of people must have accompanied us, and several recruits were obtained on the way – men who had been brought as slaves to Ilorin from the interior of

Hausaland, and who now found relations and friends amongst the successful soldiery.[17]

An estimated 3,000 runaway slaves accompanied the column as it marched towards the Niger.[18]

The exodus was so extensive that Emir Sulayman complained bitterly to Company officials that "all the slaves in the town belonging to me and my people ran away with your men, and I am afraid they will not come back again to their masters."[19] Although Goldie wondered who would plant crops during the coming rains, he ignored the Emir's pleas "to send back these people to me." Instead, the Emir was reminded that the Royal Niger Company was opposed to slavery.[20]

Continued Company activities along the Niger in 1898, including the occupation of Lapai and Agaye, the two small Nupe emirates to the east of Bida, contributed to the fragile situation.[21] The Company's presence at Jebba, Bajibo, and other places was a sign to slaves that they could flee. According to William Wallace,

> in every place where the Company were in effective occupation all slaves who desired to do so deserted their masters "en bloc" and this wholesale desertion took place not only along the whole of the right bank of the Niger from Illorin to Jebba and Iddah but embraced also the district of Igarra and the Nupe [Kakanda] Canoe Slaves who were the backbone of the river canoe traffic.[22]

The Company may not have been fully aware of the crisis it was causing. Bajibo and Jebba were in the western part of Bida Emirate, where there had long been considerable opposition to central authority. The flight of slaves westward across the Kaduna River, as well as south across the Niger, challenged the very existence of the Emirate.

Formal annexation of the territory south of the Niger, which was one of the provisions of the Treaty of Kusogi (February 5, 1897) with Bida, meant that fugitive slaves could find sanctuary there. RNC pretensions over the "province" of Kabba were now fully recognized, and as a result "thousands of slaves – many of them no doubt originally raided from the Province – deserted their Nupe masters and established settlements, at first round Lokoja, and later further south."[23] Between the first occupation of Bida in January 1897 and the formal annexation in early 1901, "Yagbas [were] dribbling back to their homes ... [across the Niger]; if escape from Bida had not been so very easy Nupe would have sucked the Yagba district dry in an incredibly short time."[24] The Yagba, a sub-section of the Yoruba, had been a prime target for Bida slave raiders, but they were not the only slaves to run away. Slaves of Igbomina and other origins also seized the opportunity to flee.

Vandeleur noted that "some of the Hausa people [i.e., fugitives] who had come with us were ferried over in canoes to the northern bank to return to their homes, others were offered a free passage down to Lokoja, where a new settlement was to be formed about 6 miles further down the river, and close to the spot selected by the ill-fated government expedition of 1841."[25] With Goldie's blessing, one hundred of these fugitives were allowed to settle in a new community called Victoria, where missionaries converted them to Christianity.[26] James Willcocks, second in command of the WAFF, also harbored fugitive slaves in 1898, sending them out of reach of their masters.[27]

In his address to the annual meeting of the RNC on the invasion of Bida and Ilorin, Goldie admitted that there was an "enormous exodus of slaves from regions under Fulah [Fulani] rulers," and that the Company was dealing with the exodus by granting fugitive slaves "allotments of unoccupied land in regions devastated and depopulated by these Fulahs."[28] Despite the size of the exodus, Goldie still believed that there was "no reason to fear any violent dislocation of social relations in the Niger Territories." It should be noted that Goldie's admission that the RNC was in fact providing sanctuary for fugitive slaves, despite his stated opposition to doing so, may well have caused Lugard problems after 1900. Lugard inherited the mantle of liberality towards fugitives, which created difficulties with his most senior subordinates, especially among former RNC officials who favored a tough stance against fugitives (see Chapter 3).

Escaped slaves were a large proportion of the WAFF, as Sam Ukpabi has shown, although the size of the WAFF was never so great as to have had a noticeable impact on the scale of desertions. Even if the carrier corps, which also attracted fugitive slaves, is taken into account, the number of fugitives so employed was not very large.[29] Nonetheless, as Gann and Duignan have noted in discussing the WAFF, "the British relied at first on ex-slaves, aliens in the land where they served, men who owed everything to the colonial forces that clothed them, fed them, paid them, protected them against their former masters, and often placed them in positions of power."[30] Vandeleur referred to his soldiers as "former slaves of the Fulahs" who now had "defeated their dreaded masters."[31] There are even reports of WAFF fears that a few of the fugitives being enlisted were not after all disgruntled slaves, but had been instructed to join, spy out training methods, and then desert.[32] Later in the colonial period, Governor Girouard, Lugard's successor, also admitted that fugitive slaves had furnished "a certain number of the soldiers [and] a great proportion of Government carriers."[33] According to Sir Charles Orr, Lugard preferred to recruit Hausa-speaking pagans, many of whom would have been escaped slaves.[34]

Recruiting missions deliberately encouraged runaway slaves to join the force. When Lt. H. Bryan undertook a recruiting mission through Bauchi in late September to early October 1898, Emir Umar accused him of enlisting fugitive slaves. Bryan's caravan was searched, but no fugitives were identified, probably because 28 of 105 recruits had fled. According to Bryan, the Emir's instructions were "to kill any slaves who refused to turn back."

> This news frightened the recruits considerably and during the next few days, out of a total of 28 [new recruits], 9 deserted. Lieut MacNaughten reports that desertions followed immediately on the arrival of a messenger from Bauchi

during his visits to Pali and Guora. Messengers from Bauchi followed me to Ako and Gaturi ... [where] the messenger stated that I had taken some of the Emir's slaves, both men and women.[35]

Bryan did his best to hold the recruits. He even had deserters shot. His report makes it clear that the accusations of enlisting fugitive slaves were substantially correct, but as Ukpabi has observed, the CO did not appreciate the execution of recruits.[36]

Similarly, Captain N. M. Lynch, on another recruiting expedition to Gombe in December 1898, reported that of 105 recruits,

> a large proportion ... were slaves. Of course, there is a limit to the number of slaves that may be taken without producing a universally hostile feeling. However, I was always kept well informed as to the current of public opinion, and, by meting out speedy punishment to anyone who interfered with my recruits or any of my caravan, I inspired a wholesome respect, and the owners of slaves thought it best to submit to the inevitable, especially as I pointed out to them that the freemen who enlisted, principally Fulani, subsequently deserted, and that slaves did not do so.[37]

Most of Lynch's recruits "were not natives of either Bauchi or Gombe" but originally came from Borno, enslaved at the time of Rabih's invasion in 1893.

Emir Umar of Gombe claimed that Lynch's corporal was his former slave and that he was due "the price of him." Lynch would "not entertain any idea of compensation" because "the Corporal in question was a 'Dimajo' (fulfulde), i.e. was born in the house of his master, and as such, even according to their own native law, was not, under ordinary circumstances liable to be sold." Lynch's interpretation of Caliphate law was flawed, of course. A second-generation slave could be sold, and in any case such a slave was not free unless his master granted him his freedom. Under Caliphate law, Emir Umar was right in seeking compensation. Lynch would not have been convinced, because "in any case he was now a Queen's soldier, and had been so for a year."[38]

Many fugitive slaves were women and children. When Willcocks intercepted a small caravan from Ilorin, bound northwards for Illo, the slave women and children

> beheld the Union Jack, according to custom, raised; immediately the unfortunate creatures made a rush for it and held on to the staff, asking for protection from their owners. The non-commissioned officer sent them over to my camp, and during the enquiry they informed me that they had heard of and seen this same flag near Jebba, where everyone had been saying that under its folds no slavery could exist. I had them released and given clothing and food, and eventually sent them down the Niger with one of our escorts. The only explanation the owner of the caravan had to offer was that he had been misinformed as to this village being in our possession, and had he known it he would not have come that way.[39]

On another occasion at Jebba, Willcocks released more women and children, and when he pronounced their freedom, "They fell on their faces and lay prostrate, weeping with joy."[40] Subsequently, many women became attached to WAFF soldiers, and children were often kept on as "servants." Under these circumstances, it would have been heartless not to have been an abolitionist. Otherwise the fate of most fugitive women and children is simply not known.

By 1900, therefore, the Royal Niger Company, and the WAFF following on its heels, had set in motion a demographic and social movement of major proportions for the emirates along the Niger River. Even during the period of inaction in anticipation of the establishment of the Protectorate of Northern Nigeria slaves continued to run, and Bida in particular could do very little to recover fugitives who fled south of the Niger into territory that it no longer controlled. The uncertain fate of the RNC when compounded with its lack of effective direction on the slavery issue set in motion a fugitive slave exodus that was difficult to reverse.

Slave unrest in the southern emirates, 1900–1902

In January 1900, High Commissioner Lugard faced a fugitive slave crisis the size of which presented serious problems for the new regime. Since his immediate concern was to continue the British advance into the Caliphate, he did not want the slave exodus to interfere. Lugard had already demonstrated his antipathy to escaped slaves in East Africa, and within a matter of weeks of assuming control of the Protectorate of Northern Nigeria he issued secret instructions that slaves were to be discouraged from absconding (see Chapter 3). His decidedly hostile view to fugitive slaves can be discerned in his comments on the slaves who fled Nupe after 1897; in his opinion they simply wanted "to lead a life of vagrancy in Lokoja, or of comparative idleness in the surrounding country."[41]

Lugard was prepared to take "executive" action if necessary, should fugitive slaves cause a crisis. His views are clearly recorded for posterity in his 1906 *Instructions to Political and Other Officers*, which incorporated *verbatim* his earlier concern that the slave exodus might lead to a slave uprising or other disorder so extensive as to warrant severe action. If such unrest had occurred any time during the conquest of the emirates, he explained what would have been done:

> But suppose that the case [of slave desertion] took place near a very large native town; that the Resident was aware that both masters and slaves were watching it as a test case; that his decision to free the man might herald a break-up of the whole organisation of the town, and even a rising which he had not the Force to control, and the master and Chiefs were obdurate. In such an extreme case, it might be necessary to resort to expediency: to connive, that is to say, at the escape of the slave, and to avoid the necessity of giving a public decision. Finally, if recourse to the assertion of their freedom was made by such large numbers of slaves as to involve the dangers described, the Resident would report with the utmost despatch to the High Commissioner, who might find it necessary to temporarily place the district under special rules for the public safety.[42]

As far as we know, Lugard never instituted this executive action, but the fact that his subordinates understood that they had the full support of the High Commissioner must have had an important impact on how military and political officers handled escaped slaves.

In 1900, relations with Bida were particularly strained because of slave desertions, and the move inland from the Niger River only increased the fears of slave owners that they would lose their slaves. According to British intelligence, the *etsu* of Bida had been "driven to desperation by the loss of the farm slaves and of his revenue," which was largely dependent upon the product of slave labor.[43] The establishment of the advanced military post at Wushishi only heightened these fears, and Kontagora now faced a similar exodus.[44] By mid 1900 both Bida and Kontagora were doing everything they could to restrain the slave population. As already noted, efforts to recapture slaves were labeled "slave raiding," and as a result there were clashes between WAFF detachments and the armies of Bida and Kontagora.

Of course Bida and Kontagora, as part of the Caliphate, would have resisted the British conquest anyway; the slavery issue was an aggravation that resulted from the British advance and should not be misconstrued as the only factor in resistance. Because of the slavery issue, however, it was not clear how best to resist and what the consequences would be of that resistance. Islamic integrity, political independence and attitudes towards slavery all warranted consideration in determining the response to the British advance. What is perhaps most revealing, however, is that local Caliphate officials were often as concerned to intimidate their slaves as to confront the British advance.

The political upheaval in Kontagora and Bida in 1900–1901 was serious. The rural areas north of Bida and around Wushishi in Kontagora, where there were large concentrations of slaves, were in open rebellion. Furthermore, the two emirates faced the renunciation of political subordination in non-Muslim districts. In addition there were the rumblings of revolutionary Mahdism, which drew its support from the "lower orders," in Bida town itself. This resistance appears to have been interrelated and constituted one of the most serious challenges to the Caliphate during the period of the British conquest. As Mason has noted, Bida faced "slave desertions and rural revolts on an unprecedented scale."[45] With the occupation of Wushishi, Kontagora had a similar problem.

As early as March 1900, WAFF forces were involved in skirmishes north of Bida and Lugard sent survey parties to explore the region as far as Lemu and Gwarjiko, including parts of Agaye. Lugard referred to this action as providing "a powerful fighting force in case of difficulties with the Emirs of Bida, Kontagora and Zaria." According to Mason,

> Extending its operations from its riverain enclave, the British detachment soon occupied an area as far as twenty miles to the south of Wushishi. The effect of the British patrols on this northern perimeter of the [Bida] kingdom was two-fold. Neither was calculated to provide much relief for the Bida *ticizi*

[office holders]. The flight of slaves continued. Some sought to get away from the Bida area while others, presumably those who feared the British more than they objected to the Bida government, fled from farms and villages to seek refuge in the capital. Pleas made by the *Makun* to Lugard to restrain his men fell on deaf ears. So did protests from *Etsu* Abubakar that the [Caliphate] army nearest Wushishi was from Kontagora, not Bida. As there was no visibly peaceful means to restrain the invaders, an army was again raised in Bida. This was not done without difficulty. A force was sent northwards to meet the British, who had probably attacked the *Etsu*'s slave plantation at this time and, despite both the *Makun*'s and the *Etsu*'s protests, had refused to withdraw.[46]

The Bida forces were routed, and Lugard decided to move his headquarters from Jebba to Wushishi.

By March 1900, the WAFF was allowing fugitives to cross its lines, and "thousands of refugees crowded into the protected villages for safety."[47] According to Abadie, when the Emir of Wushishi fled to Bida, "the Gwaris, always very difficult for the Fulani to control, became absolutely independent as did in fact the other tribes, only to a lesser degree, being nearer and more in touch with the white man."[48] Pagans who had paid tribute to Kontagora and Bida and slaves alike were told, "No more slaves – you are all free men," so that "they all consider themselves under the white man, who never interferes with them, nor demands tribute, but uses his soldiers and people to their protection." In consequence, "Wushishi has been a haven of refuge."[49] In April, Lugard admitted to CMS missionary Walter Miller that he had "a large number of slaves on his hands."[50] The number increased further when Colonel Kemball despatched two strong parties in pursuit of Ibrahim Nagwamatse, which "compelled him to abandon all his slaves and retinue."[51] Despite this set-back, Nagwamatse was able to regroup and retreat north-east towards Zaria. He still controlled "a great mass of slaves," whom he took with him.[52]

By August 1901, almost all slaves around Wushishi had deserted. According to Molesworth, the only slaves left were "cripples and old people who were unable to run away."[53] By the end of the year, Wushishi was almost deserted except for the WAFF's own laborers and carriers, most of whom were fugitive slaves themselves. According to Abadie,

> All this is owing to the fact that George (a short time Asst. Resident here) went round the country telling them all they were free and no more slaves would be made etc. with the result they refused to obey their headmen and say they are free. All very well in theory but not in practice. When these people are first freed they become lazy and good for nothing and do no good to the country and only plant sufficient food to keep themselves. Here everything is in a muddle.[54]

Abadie's hostility to the fugitives should not disguise the extent of the exodus or the fact that the WAFF employed some of the fugitives.

The situation was equally serious around Bida. In August 1901 Burdon reported that "the majority of the farm slaves have run away, the farms are left untilled, this cultivated Province is reverting to 'bush' and there is famine in Bida."[55] Some slave owners tried to retard the exodus by "gathering their slaves from the farms before they could desert to the whiteman" in order to prevent "the wholesale liberation of slaves."[56] Nonetheless, in November 1901, Wallace estimated that some 30,000 slaves had crossed the Niger since Bida was first occupied in 1897, and that "the population in Bida Province and at Wushishi and Jebba have been in a state of semi-starvation for months."[57] In Agaye and Lapai,

> Things were ... bad: farms were being deserted by the slaves and such was the state of unrest that cultivation had almost ceased. The Fulani ruling classes were rapidly becoming desperate at the state of the country.[58]

It is no wonder that *West Africa* reported on October 19, 1901 that the "evil effects" of interfering with "domestic slavery" were "being felt in the provinces of Nupe and Ilorin. It upset the internal economy of the whole country, and the male slaves instead of working on their masters' farms became rogues and vagabonds and the females – something worse."[59]

Unrest among the slave population reached such proportions that there was a virtual slave rebellion underway. In September, "slave bandits" were operating unchecked around Bida.[60] Popham Lobb reported in November that there had been "several cases in the last week or two of runaway slaves (runaways 'because the whiteman told them all slaves were free' is the invariable formula) who have led looting parties into villages, saying they were sent by the whiteman, & have commandeered right & left."[61] Slaves were roaming "through the country looting and raiding in the white man's name, a practice which has already given more trouble than almost anything else that we have had to deal with."[62]

Slaves seized land at Paieko in Kontagora Emirate, according to Burdon's report of November 7:

> The natural results of the wholesale freeing of slaves has made itself apparent in a state of Anarchy round Paieko. The farm slaves of the Sarikin Paieko were apparently told by Major O'Neill that they were free. They immediately considered they were also free to appropriate their master's property, seized the farms on which they were employed, stole their master's produce and sold it to the whiteman and up till now have prevented their master from sending other men to work his farms or from collecting his property.[63]

Despite the many efforts of Burdon and other officials, therefore, slave unrest had reached new proportions. Not only were slaves fleeing, but a revolt was underway.

Efforts to reestablish order

In December 1901, Abadie attempted to reintroduce some measure of control around Wushishi, both among slaves and among the tributary

41

communities that, alongside the servile population, were engaged in serious unrest. As he reported, he had considerable difficulty in doing so:

> The Gwari people and Bauchi and Kanuku people all round here having been freed for 2 years naturally resent being put under their old oppressor and enemy the Fulani, and are quite ready even to fight against us to avoid such a calamity. They want talking to very gently just now and I have had a busy time and work from 8 a.m. to 6 p.m. without more than $\frac{1}{2}$ an hour off.[64]

It is perhaps not surprising that these communities harbored many fugitives, since they had long been a major source of slaves for the Caliphate. Hence the cessation of slave raiding, the termination of tribute payments, and the provision of sanctuary for fugitive slaves were all interrelated. Abadie tried to tell the Gwari that British policy did not sanction the flight of slaves.

> Naturally it is incomprehensible to them and now the white man has brought back the hated Fulani as King to again worry us and raid us, as they think, all as before. One tribe, the Gwaris, told Hall last month that they would sooner die fighting the white man, than obey the Fulani again and absolutely refused to come even to see the King.[65]

According to Mason, the British reoccupation of Bida in 1901 restored some order to an otherwise volatile situation, with the result that "many of the slaves who had fled the *tungazi* [plantations] were returned to bondage."[66]

The armies of Kontagora and Wushishi were defeated near Maska on February 21, 1902. Ibrahim's "enormous following, estimated at 20,000 people," included many "recently captured slaves [who] fled into the bush and found their way back to their villages."[67] Abadie estimated the number of slaves who ran away at "about 12,000":

> as I anticipated a very large number of people ran away, these being the slaves who had been caught during the last few years. I found 4 men and women bound with ropes on the way. These I released and heard that they had been caught 3 days before at the Gates of Zaria with 32 others by [Sarkin Sudan Ibrahim of] Kontagora.[68]

Many of the defeated officials and their families were escorted back to Wushishi and other places. They were allowed to keep "domestic slaves,"[69] who were estimated to number 5,000. Some 600 slaves were repatriated to Wushishi, while 4,200 were sent back to Kontagora. The remainder, 188 people, were sent to Bida.[70] Lugard's own estimate of "recently captured" slaves who were in the Kontagora contingent defeated by Abadie and Porter in March 1902 was 6,000: "it is probable that they at once seized the opportunity of escaping into the bush to find their way back to their homes."[71] At Birnin Gwari on April 6 1902, Abadie also reported that he "met every day in the road people returning to Bida, Kontagora and Wushishi."[72]

A tough line against fugitives was drawn as the WAFF moved north, first in the quest to capture Kontagora's Emir Ibrahim and then to occupy Zaria.

At Birnin Gwari, Abadie sought to erase the image that the British would allow slaves to flee. After negotiating with the defeated Kontagora forces, he reported that the

> bulk of the Kontagora people are now preparing to come down ... [T]he more I see the more I realise what howling mistakes have been committed in dealing with these people. Not that I am an advocate of peaceful negotiation with people like these from commencement, far from it. I consider they all want one good lesson to really shew them the power of the white man, and make them feel it but that after the first lesson they could be very quickly brought with a little tact to see the advantage of many of our customs and freedom of trade and the only sore point to come being the abolishing of slavery.[73]

The problem with Abadie's reflections was that he did not make it clear who would benefit the most from the "lesson" – slaves or masters. By preventing further desertions and by returning fugitives to their masters, the Caliphate aristocracy could be relieved of one of its worst fears of British colonialism, nevertheless.

The occupation of Zaria was a time to impress on Caliphate officials and slave owners that the British would not encourage the flight of slaves. Abadie, now Resident of Zaria, would "allow domestic slavery i.e. household slaves born in slavery by all means for the present, and I will go even further uphill, by allowing masters to retain all the slaves in their possession, the day the slave market is stopped."[74] He wanted "to keep things quiet, and prevent people from running away." Zaria was the first emirate to have a Resident "without being broken and it will be a splendid thing if it can be done without using force."[75] Abadie's instructions were to do everything possible to keep slaves in place so that the problem of slaves deserting would not spread to Kano and Sokoto when WAFF troops moved north. Nonetheless, the task could only be accomplished with difficulty. He admitted that he was

> so afraid that all slaves will run away. They have been so often misled by whitemen (who ought to know better) saying "No more slavery, everyone is free, etc. etc." and what is the result? Slaves run away and the whole country whose constitution is built up on slavery becomes a desert.[76]

His Assistant Resident, Popham Lobb, confirmed his fears. He reported that there were "a lot of slavery cases":

> the men in the barracks are always a centre of generally very willing attraction; their wives collect small runaway slaves and they themselves collect fresh wives, and everyday the various masters and mistresses come to complain and identify them.[77]

There was trouble on the Karo plantation of Baba's family throughout this unsettled period; first at the time that Sarkin Sudan Ibrahim invaded Zaria and then with the British occupation.[78] Many slaves left. Furthermore, there was a mass escape from Biye, a plantation near Zaria that had 100 or more slaves:

> Some months after the British had established themselves in Zaria [1902], about half the slaves at Biye gathered near the foot of the town's great cottonsilk tree. They had secretly armed themelves with bows and arrows and had prepared foodstuffs for a long march. Shouting "Who can claim us as slaves now," they volleyed arrows into the air, and with loud singing began a march south with their wives and children. They were not heard from again.[79]

There were many such escapes,[80] and slaves continued to desert for several years, particularly during the famine of early 1905. At that time, there was "some sullen discontent which was augmented by the desertion of slaves, and the inadequate amount of land under food crops."[81]

There were equally severe difficulties as WAFF troops moved into Nassarawa and Bauchi. In Nassarawa, "a large number of slaves ran away" in September 1901, which was only the beginning of trouble there.[82] Near the sub-emirate of Wase, slaves congregated at Yelwa, according to a report by Wilkin, who casually wrote home, October 28, 1901, that "Yellua is a big town [near Wase] more than half a mile across ... It is peopled by runaway slaves from Wase and Bauchi. The king is a Hausa from Bauchi."[83] More slaves fled when Bauchi was occupied. Ngas slaves, in particular, escaped *en masse*. According to colonial reports, there had been a severe famine among the Ngas in the mid 1890s, "when the entire Angass tribe sold themselves into slavery, but with the advent of British rule they deserted their masters and returned, and the Angass Hills are now thickly populated."[84]

In Bauchi, C. L. Temple imposed tough measures to prevent slaves from deserting. As far as he was concerned, "for many years the existence of domestic slaves or serfs will have to be countenanced in order to avoid the greater evil of entirely upsetting the social system."[85] Hence in 1902, he was capturing fugitive slaves and maintaining "a register of all such handed back to their owners."

> They will be brought before me on the first day of each month; I shall question each as to the treatment he receives and as to the treatment his fellow serfs [*sic*] receive and shall act accordingly.

Temple freed slaves who "bore the marks of ill usage," and he attempted to impress upon masters that beating slaves would no longer be allowed. Such masters were "severely reprimanded ... and forbidden ... to repeat the offence under penalty of all his serfs being taken from him."[86]

The exodus continued in Yola as well, although Wallace would later claim that he had contained it there (see Chapter 3). In 1902, slaves were deserting the farms around Yola in such numbers that a mob of local slave owners attacked the British fort. A severe famine did not help the situation, and indeed the famine may have been exacerbated by the flight of slaves.[87] A common complaint in Yola, and elsewhere as well, was that fugitive slaves were involved in criminal activities: "In fact they comprise the sole source of the criminal classes in this Province."[88] Fugitive slaves were also accused of abducting people and selling them in turn into slavery.[89] Indeed, one report of 1904 bemoaned the fact that "runaway slaves are a great thorn in the side of the Administration."[90]

Slave desertions after the conquest of Kano and Sokoto

The British conquest of Kano, Sokoto, and the other northern emirates resulted in severe dislocation in the rural areas, which included the flight of slaves, peasant resistance against emirate authorities, and anti-British agitation.[91] As S. U. Grier recalled much later, many slave owners suffered "real hardship" because of "the desertion of large numbers of slaves when we captured such places as Kontagora, Kano and Sokoto."[92] Lugard attempted to prevent this dislocation, of course, but slaves fled anyway.

A Vernacular Proclamation was posted in each of the major cities that made the British position clear. The translation of the Kano Proclamation read as follows (although to the best of our knowledge the Hausa original has not survived, and hence it is not possible to determine Lugard's exact phrasing):

> And be it known to all masters and slaves that any slave who is ill treated and has just cause of complaint may come to the Resident, who will enquire into the matter and set him free if his story is true and he is willing to work for wages and support himself, but others who have no cause of complaint and are working in the house or in the fields shall continue in their occupations and not leave them.[93]

In Sokoto Lugard posted a similar proclamation, also in Hausa, and he addressed the Waziri and other officials who had not joined Attahiru I on March 21, 1903, when he retreated from Sokoto towards the east on his *hijra* in search of the Mahdi. He told them

> If slaves are ill-treated they will be set free as your Koran orders, otherwise Government does not desire to interfere with existing domestic relations. But slaves set free must be willing to work and not remain idle.[94]

He continued to Katsina, where he repeated his containment policy. Later tradition remembers the British decree as *hana bauta*, that is, "preventing slavery." But this meant that the British were outlawing enslavement and trade, not slavery itself.

Lugard's own description of the handling of fugitive slaves is an excellent indication of how he put into practice the difference between the "executive" enforcement of slavery and the "legal" abolition of its status:

> On leaving Sokoto I had a very disagreeable task to perform. Hundreds of slaves had secretly crowded into our camp, hundreds more clambered over the walls to follow us, and no prohibition would stop them. Turned out of the line of march, they ran parallel to us through the fields, or ran on ahead. I had promised not to interfere with existing domestic slaves; I had no food for these crowds, and in front of us was a desert untraversed and unmapped, in which the infrequent wells were far apart, and could only supply a very limited

amount of water. Moreover, this exodus of slaves would leave Sokoto ruined, and its social fabric a chaos. There was nothing to be done but to send these poor wretches back, and instruct the Resident to enquire into all deserving cases. We did so, and presently found that the King of Gober [Gobir], who was following me with an army of 300 or 400 wild horsemen of the desert, had appropriated all he could catch. We made him disgorge them, and set them at liberty to return. Doubtless very many bolted to neighbouring towns, but I considered my obligations of honour and of necessity were satisfied when I turned them out of my own following, and I did not enquire too curiously what became of them.[95]

Burdon, putting into effect Lugard's sentiments, reported to Lugard on March 1, 1903: "I have carefully explained to the Sarikin Muslimin the steps taken by Y.Ex. and the other columns to prevent slaves accompanying them, & also the difficulties encountered owing to the failure on the part of him & his people to adequately second our efforts. He quite understood the position and is very grateful for what has been done. The failure on his side is partly due to a very natural fear & partly to the absence from Sokoto of the majority of the Masters."[96]

Despite these efforts, Resident Cargill reported that there was "considerable lawlessness" in rural Kano, as Fulani officials were "driven out."[97] According to his reports "the slaves of the Fulani deserted them in large numbers"[98] after the conquest. Cargill thought that much of the unrest was the result of two factors: "hatred of the Hausa peasantry towards the Fulani and that of the Fulani peasantry to ourselves."[99]

Furthermore, the appeal of Caliph Attahiru I to join the pilgrimage and await the Mahdi attracted some disaffected people – "all the body of the lawless elements of the lower classes." Even peasantry "of the better classes" flocked to Attahiru I.[100] Unfortunately, it is difficult to disentangle the various strands of Kano unrest, because Cargill was careful in what he reported and because he later destroyed most of his files. Peasant protest against the Fulbe aristocracy, slave desertions, anti-British agitation, and the flight of Attahiru I all took place at the same time. While it is not possible to discern how much of this trouble arose from the exodus of slaves, it is nonetheless clear that "many of the slave class ran away."[101]

Fugitive slaves were accused of joining "the idle or criminal classes ... personating soldiers and looting and robbing." Lugard believed that the leaders of these fugitives were "former Government employee[s] or deserter[s]," who may well have been originally slaves themselves, given the fact that the British recruited many of their soldiers, carriers, and laborers from among escaped slaves. While there is little information on these fugitive slave bands, they are reported to have been "armed with a pistol or a white man's coat" that were obtained from those "enlisted in the military or police." The bands roamed the countryside "and blackmailed their former masters or robbed traders and villagers passing near the barracks." As Cargill observed, "They did not desire our rule or Fulani rule, but no rule at all."

According to Lugard, "It cost much time and effort to get rid of these scoundrels, and to put a stop to such practices."[102]

Despite these reports, Cargill insisted that "complaints of assertion of freedom by slaves are extremely rare," the reason being that "a discontented slave simply runs away" and the British were never told.[103] Cargill's information is far from consistent. In 1904, he claimed that "many [of the slaves] who ran away at the time of the annexation of Kano have returned," and "the slavery question ... has caused scarcely any difficulty in this province." What could this mean, considering his own admissions and the testimonies of others?[104] In 1907, Cargill, once more contradicting what he sometimes wrote, reported that slave desertions were still a problem in Kano, but now slaves did not necessarily flee from the Emirate, or if they did, they were as likely to move into adjacent emirates as to return to non-Muslim districts to the south.

> The slaves are becoming more self-assertive and less willing to work for their masters. There is now practically nothing to prevent slaves asserting their freedom by the simple process of walking away from their masters and earning wages on the railway or elsewhere.[105]

As the Resident noted, "during the past year 20,000 people have crossed from the western part of Kano into Southern Katsena – due partly to the cessation of Maradi raids from the north – and land which is very fertile is being rapidly cleared and put into cultivation." Cargill also observed "the tendency of the Kano people to push into and cultivate the Ningi bush to the south-east of Kano," and there were new settlements in Katagum as well.[106] Cargill's reports are silent on the extent to which fugitive slaves were involved in much of this resettlement, but it seems likely that many were.

According to oral sources, the Kano exodus appears to have been considerable.[107] Merchants suffered in particular. Tsakuwa, the wealthy Kano leather manufacturer who owned many slaves at the end of the nineteenth century, experienced a serious reversal because "as soon as the white men came they [the slaves] all ran away."[108] The family of Yeye, like other merchant households, lost most of their slaves when the British arrived.[109] Hill records a tradition in Dorayi, near Kano, of slaves escaping after their master received a prison sentence for slave trading. Hill does not date this episode, but it likely occurred within the first few years of the British occupation.[110] The "ruined mansions" of mechants in Kano, noticed in 1932, attested to the earlier prosperity based on slave plantations which came to an end in the early years of colonial rule.[111] Sarkin Bagarmi, the overseer of the Gogel plantation of the Emir of Kano, attests to the fact that many slaves ran back to their home towns after the arrival of the British: "In both the city and the villages, slaves were given papers [of freedom] but some slaves left without them." The fugitives included Bagirmi, Sari, Gulai, and Farlomi slaves.[112] Da'u Bello's father owned a plantation at Amarawa, but as was the case with many wealthy families, "his slaves ran away."[113] S. U.

Grier, who began his career in Northern Nigeria in 1906, confirmed the impact on Kano. He learned that some Kano slave owners experienced "real hardship" during the conquest and for a period thereafter because of the "desertion of large numbers of slaves."[114]

Sokoto was also hard hit by slave escapes, in part because virtually the whole laboring population was slave and in part because the Sokoto aristocracy, preoccupied with defending the Caliphate, resisted the British advance more stoutly than their counterparts in most emirates, as already noted. Grier believed that Sokoto was as affected by slave desertions as Kano, Kontagora, and other parts of the Caliphate.[115] As noted above, slaves flocked to the WAFF regiment as it departed from Sokoto, and while many of those slaves were returned to their masters, others, especially women, sought protection with the WAFF in Sokoto. As Burdon noted in a report of April 30, 1903, soldiers tried to prevent slave women from being returned to their masters.[116] C. W. Orr, Acting Resident in Sokoto, reported a year later that "slaves of course continue to run to 'barracks' but thanks to the loyal & willing cooperation of the Officer Commanding in the endeavour to prevent this, the masters do not suffer the losses which they would do otherwise."[117] Orr also referred to the case of a woman from Gwandu who complained of being sold by the Sarkin Gwandu, "but she cannot be traced, disappeared with a party of soldiers."

Information from the districts surrounding Sokoto is scanty, although the Zarma slave owners at Bonkanu and Gawase in Korre and Binji Districts lost almost all of their slaves in the first year or two of colonial rule, and as a result "their large farms went out of cultivation at the British occupation." According to Arnett, the Zarma owned large numbers of slaves because

> formerly Sokoto owners of idle or refractory slaves were accustomed to transfer them either by sale or temporarily to the Zabermawa settlers at Bonkanu and Gawase in Kworre and Binji Districts. These Zabermawa who settled there about 50 or 60 years ago were notoriously hard and merciless to their slaves, making them work their large farms in chains allowing them no family life and giving them a bare subsistence as prisoners with heavy and brutal punishments.[118]

Consequently, Arnett noted that "it is not surprising to learn that these Zabermawa now own very few slaves."

Court records from Sokoto reveal that slaves were still running away from their masters in 1908. There were fifty-nine judicial cases involving "fugitive slaves" in that year, which is a particularly large number by comparison with the number of other slavery cases. In addition there were three cases of "illegal transfer," twenty-eight cases of "manumission," and forty-seven instances of "general" problems involving slaves.[119] While the statistics for manumissions and slave trading are fairly standard for this period, rarely are fugitive slaves mentioned as a subject for the Islamic courts, and in no other year for which data have been found were there as many slavery cases, in total or for fugitives, as there were in Sokoto in 1908. As Resident Temple observed, "desertions in general" continued to be a problem. Fugitives were still trying to gain access to military posts, even though they were often returned to their masters. Some of the other cases were more difficult to resolve.[120] In 1913, Argungu was accused of offering sanctuary to escaped slaves; indeed one report charged that "the Argungu people are inclined to encourage slaves to run away from Sokoto or Gando [Gwandu] and settle here," a practice that was "severely checked when discovered."[121] In Sokoto, at least, the fugitive problem continued quite late.

Colonial reports from the southern parts of the Caliphate confirm the fact that many slaves fled from the central, Hausa emirates after the conquest. In 1904, for example, G. W. Webster complained of the "difficulty with regard to runaway slaves ... from Hausa [areas to the north], who have gained their freedom, in consequence of our occupation of Kano and Sokoto." The slaves were returning to their old homes in Nassarawa Province.[122] By 1904 so "many runaway slaves from the north are settling in the province" that there was a noticeable increase in population.[123] Indeed a

> regular city of refuge ... has been formed in the Mada country South of Jemaa Darroro and a large number are also returning to the Bassa country North of Umaisha along the Toto road ...; some 200 are said to have returned to Katakwa, a Bassa town on the Modu River some 30 miles North-East of Umaisha, alone, saying they had returned by the power of the whitemen.[124]

That the fugitives credited their success in escaping to "the power of the whitemen" reveals that slaves were conscious of the revolutionary possibilities of the European conquest. They had to take their chances quickly before the new regime could consolidate its hold.

As Webster observed, there were many "absconding slaves" in Nassarawa Province.

> The repudiation of their obligations by both household and farm slaves is causing much trouble in the Keffi district. The masters complain that they have no power over them at all, if a slave is told to do any work that is at all distasteful he refuses and threatens to go away and leave his master.[125]

Because of "the constant stream of complaints in Keffi of slaves running away," Webster summoned the largest owners to reassure them, but he was informed by the masters that "unless we can beat and tie them up if they run, there is no medicine, since we cannot sell them." It may be that Webster encouraged the owners to punish their slaves, given his statement that "all my sympathies are with the master[s]."[126]

> The extent to which this absconding had been going on only came to my notice last month [February 1904], in consequence of enquiries into the cause of the difficulty in obtaining labour in this district, on which I reported to Your Excellency in February. I am now doing my best to discourage any further cases, as apart from the hardship to the owners, it has the effect of rendering labour scarce and dear, and thereby threatens to hamper the development of the country. There is another objection to the wholesale absconding of these

49

slaves, i.e. that they are mostly confirmed loafers and seem more likely to become the nucleus of a future professional criminal class than useful citizens.

But I cannot see that we have any means of really dealing with such absconders. In the case of the household slaves, they are at least very useless members of the community, and I do not think their desertion calls for so much attention.

But in the case of the farm servants it is very different, as their desertion threatens to check the development of agriculture.[127]

Webster feared that the success of those slaves who ran away would "do much harm by encouraging others by their example to desert their masters."[128]

The hinterland of Nassarawa rapidly became a sanctuary for slaves, whole villages being populated by fugitives, according to Webster's reports. The Emir of Keffi sent delegations to the villages of refuge, and sometimes these messengers were able to bring fugitives back, although whether or not they used force is not known. Webster succeeded in convincing some slaves – often concubines – to stay with their masters, while in other cases he arranged for a price to be paid in lieu of liberty. Such tactics did not always work; indeed the impression in Webster's reports is that a peaceful resolution was the exception. Several villages, for example, "refused point blank to send any [fugitives] in and have driven out the Emir's messengers with insults or even blows." At least three villages were involved in these episodes. Webster was determined that "these pagan towns should not be allowed to give the runaways asylum, especially in a Province like this where many of the slaves have been caught within the last 20 years from villages one or two days distant."[129] Lugard was not pleased with the situation in Nassarawa and told Webster that "these runaway slave villages are to be discouraged. No village can be started without Resident's sanction ... As long as your province affords an asylum, all the present serf population will run away. If they are denied a place, they will not run away."[130]

In Abuja, as well as at Keffi, "the greater number of slaves have been seized from the surrounding country and most of them too recently to have forgotten their old ties so that they are naturally inclined to take advantage of our advent to run to their old homes."[131] Many others became "traders on their own account."[132] Controlling the whole area of southern Zaria was a major problem.

Slaves continued to move south, sometimes in large numbers. In certain parts of Zaria Province, there were "whole towns peopled by ex-slaves freed [sic] by the Fulani";[133] ex-slaves to be sure, but unlikely "freed" by their masters. Other evidence suggests that the inhabitants of these villagers were fugitive slaves, not slaves who had been granted their freedom. When he first arrived in Zaria in 1906, Assistant Resident Grier thought that only "occasionally" did slaves run away from Zaria and "some other big Mahomedan towns & go back to their tribe,"[134] but by the end of the year he found out differently. When he was attempting to ascertain why Kafi, a village near

Fuka, refused to pay its taxes, he discovered that it was a haven for fugitive slaves.

> I got a number of the natives together & with the king of Fuka squatting on a mat near me, asked for an explanation. All my remarks were translated into their own language, but I suddenly discovered that was quite unnecessary – every man knew Hausa, every man was a fugitive slave! Finally one man came forward & said we will do everything you wish, we have no intention of disobeying, but we will not obey the king of Fuka. He is the man who hunted us down, who caught & sold us, we will not obey him.

The Fuka official, who was Gwari by origin, owed allegiance to Kontagora. Grier realized the difficulty of the situation and transferred the village to Paieko, the same town which had earlier experienced land seizures by slaves.[135]

Grier guessed that fully two-thirds of the Gwari population had been carried off into slavery, and while he found many returned slaves and at least one village of escaped slaves, he could not account for "the thousands of pagans who were caught." As far as he could tell in 1908, "only a very small percentage have ever found their way back."[136] Even though fugitive slaves probably did not want to be identified, Grier continued to find evidence that slaves had returned. In 1911, in a revealing confession of his own prejudices, he wrote to his mother that the "few really human people one meets down here have been slaves & have returned to their homes." He observed that "in practically no tribe are there not some runaway slaves who have learnt Hausa from their masters."[137]

The Resident in Bida drew attention to "the return of fugitive tribes from across the borders of Ilorin, Zaria and Keffi to their old homes in Nupe [which is] balanced by enslaved Yagbas and Kukuruku families returning to Kabba and Ilorin."[138] That the Resident referred to "fugitive *tribes*" is instructive, for the term "tribe" suggests that either fugitives were traveling in large groups or individuals and small numbers of fugitives were coming together once they reached safe country. As Lugard noted in 1905,

> The Yagba slaves have left for their old homes south of the Niger, while natives have immigrated from Illorin, and the Gwari villages in the northeast, and the Bassas in the east are filling up. This movement is taking place in greater or lesser degree throughout the whole Protectorate, the scattered members of tribes and clans driven from their homes by decades of slave-raiding and war are gradually returning, while an equally pronounced migration from the walled cities to the agricultural lands is noticeable. In spite of the fact that the slave farms are now deserted, new land is everywhere taken up.[139]

According to Lugard, many of these fugitives were "migrating to distant places to make new villages."[140] There was a "constant return of people from Nassarawa, Ilorin, and Zaria Provinces," including "fugitives from the Ganaga War in 1881."[141]

One such concentration was the town of Pategi on the south bank of the Niger. In 1898 Pategi was a small town, but by 1905 it had an estimated population of 10,000, many of whom were fugitives.[142] Missionary Judd, of the Sudan Interior Mission, reported in 1903 that "all slaves are free when they reach Patagi," which suggests that Pategi had been a sanctuary during the unrest of 1901.[143] In August 1903, Judd took in a woman who had fled from Bida. "The man she belonged to sent for her and she would have been taken back into slavery but the woman she was staying with brought her to us for protection so we took her in." She was held "for the Government until we can find out what they want us to do with her." It is not clear what happened to this woman, but Judd would only continue to shelter her "if we can arrange it with the government."[144] As this case demonstrates, Lugard's concerns about missionary sympathies for fugitive slaves appear to have been justified, but the SIM, at least, was willing to abide by government policy not to encourage the desertion of slaves.

Despite these havens in areas within or adjacent to Caliphate territory, many slaves moved further south still. As Mason and Obayemi have demonstrated, Yaba, Kiri, Bunu, Ebira, and others who had resisted the raids from Nupe, and to a lesser extent from Ilorin, had retreated to defensible hills and caves. The best land was left vacant. The fugitives moved back into this country, thereby reversing a half-century or more of depopulation.[145] Old shrines, long abandoned, were reactivated, and whenever possible people reestablished kinship and community connections that had been temporarily severed through enslavement. The resettlement could not recreate society as it had once been, although the fugitives probably tried to do so; population densities continued to be much lower than in the past, while some people went to Lagos and other towns in the south. And as a few reports indicate, there were social tensions as a result of the return of fugitives. This is understandable since some people had been sold into slavery or pawned, and there were many old scores to settle as well as old relationships to reestablish. The emigration to Kabba Province was still visible in 1907, when there was "a steady return of slaves from other provinces during the year. Their return has caused some social complications and litigations." The movement was considered "unsettling."[146]

Kontagora, which had suffered the extreme upheaval of 1900–1901, gradually recovered some of its people by 1905. "The meagre population of this devastated province is reported to have increased by about 10,000 during the year, owing to the return of people to their former districts and the influx of ex-slaves."[147] As a result of the resettlement, the population of Kontagora had recovered to an estimated 80,000 people.[148]

> As regards slavery, this Province is peculiar. The one constant complaint of the ruling class is that they have no slaves. The power of the Fulani was so utterly broken when Kontagora was taken by Government troops, that thousands of slaves took the opportunity to make their escape. They have since been gradually returning to the villages from which they were originally raided, and are settling down to farming, thus slowly increasing the population.[149]

In Dakarkari country, one of the non-Muslim areas that Kontagora had raided, "there has been a considerable influx of freed slaves to their former homes."[150]

Further east in Muri, the southward movement of fugitive slaves continued for several years after the conquest. As reported in 1904,

> There is a large influx of settlers from the north, due partly to the famine, partly to dislike of Fulani rule, partly to local dissensions, in which the immigrants had been worsted, and partly to the fertility of the Benue Valley ... A separate class of immigrants are pagans who have been enslaved during recent years, and have escaped, principally from Bauchi.[151]

As is the case with many reports, it is difficult to assess the relative importance of the fugitive factor, since many of those fleeing famine and "Fulani rule" may well not have been slaves. Nonetheless, the identification of a specific "class" of fugitives indicates that the size of the slave exodus was large. In 1907, "immigration from the north into the three settled divisions of the province [Jalingo Division, containing the Emirate of Muri; Amar Division, containing Wase; Ibi Division, containing Awe] continues, and the general trend of the population is from the towns back to the land."[152]

G. N. Barclay, in his Annual Report for Yola Province in 1905, observed:

> The number of slaves who come [to British officials] and demand their freedom is no indication of the number of runaways. Slaves know that their masters cannot recapture them and do not bother about coming to the Government for their freedom. This is especially the case with male slaves who simply leave their masters and follow their own devices.[153]

Barclay anticipated "that the near future will bring a large immigration of fugitive slaves and of Pagans to Yola, which will more than counterbalance the emigration of Fulani slave-dealers."[154] Only fifty-three slaves had been freed in 1905, "but the number who have left their masters without reference to the Government is vastly in excess of this. In this province the slaves are reported to be idle and threaten their masters with desertion, so that the latter are compelled to pamper and conciliate them."[155]

The slave exodus was captured in contemporary verse. When the British arrived in Kano, slaves assembled at the palace of the Shettima, near the central mosque, where the British had hoisted the Union Jack. They are remembered to have danced, and they sang the following refrain:

> A flag-touching dance,
> Is performed by freeborns alone.
> Anybody who touches the flag,
> Becomes free.
> He and his father [master],
> Become equals.[156]

Melvyn Hiskett, who has collected other poetry from the period, has noted the extent of dissatisfaction among slave owners. The poems that he obtained had an "implicit ... complaint against the freeing of slaves, for many of the younger male slaves had seen this [the conquest] as an opportunity to rush off and make their fortunes as itinerant traders, and when they failed, had ended up as head-carriers for the British."[157] According to Hiskett, the escape of slaves upset marital relations, because slaves who had once performed much of the work were no longer there. As one poet expressed the desperation of slave owners who now could not maintain their wives in purdah,

> I have no slave, I am not able to practice purdah,
> I have no slave girl who shall fetch water,
> Who will go to the bush and fetch me a little wood.[158]

The poem of the Kano poet Umaru Salga, denouncing the conquest of the "Christians," complains about the ending of slavery: "For slaves with joy have become free men. They say, 'We are not [slaves].' And it has come about that each one goes off on his own."[159] According to the learned Imam Imoru, many slaves "became free with joy":

> They were saying "We refuse to be slaves because the Christians are here." They all regained their freedom; they were boasting because of the Christians.[160]

In contrast to the conclusion of some scholars, many slaves and slave owners considered that the conquest introduced a major period of adjustment in matters relating to slavery. The transition was far from being "painless" or "gradual," as Watts has surmised.[161]

Revolutionary Mahdism and the exodus of slaves

A major concern of the British administration and the Caliphate aristocracy alike was that slaves would stage an insurrection. The early troubles of 1901 in Kontagora and Nupe had virtually amounted to a slave revolt, though directed against Caliphate officials rather than the British. Lugard even warned his Residents of the possibility of revolt, but by late in 1905, no one any longer believed that such a danger persisted.

Consequently, the colonial administration was completely taken by surprise in early 1906, when an uprising involving fugitive slaves occurred at the sprawling village of Satiru, only twenty kilometers south of Sokoto. The Satiru revolt was organized and led by revolutionary Mahdist clerics opposed to the Caliphate government, who encouraged slaves to leave their masters.[162] The revolt resulted in an unprecedented defeat for the West African Frontier Force and rekindled widespread alarm that a general slave uprising would occur. At first it was not clear whether the Caliphate aristocracy would remain faithful to the colonial cause or seize the opportunity to force a British retreat. But the aristocracy feared revolutionary Mahdism more than British colonialism, and despite some reluctance to support the British and some sympathy for the rebels, in the end the aristocrats threw their full support behind the British. Eventually the rebellion was suppressed with such brutality by the allied armed forces of the British and the Caliphate that slaves never again resorted to revolt. That option was permanently foreclosed. Instead, the suppression of the insurrection exposed the necessity of an alliance between the aristocrats and colonialists.

The British misjudged the Mahdist threat, which is remarkable since Mahdism had been a major concern of British imperial policy in Islamic regions since the death of General "Chinese" Gordon at Khartoum in 1884.[163] Furthermore, the extent of Mahdist influence in Northern Nigeria was well understood: Borno had become a Mahdist state after Rabih's conquest in the 1890s, the successors of Hayatu, the grandson of Usman dan Fodio, were rounded up during the British conquest, and the *hijra* of Caliph Attahiru I to Bormi, a Mahdist stronghold, in 1903, appealed to Mahdist sympathies. Finally, and most remarkably, the British seemed to have been unaware that the Mahdist uprising had actually begun in December 1905, in adjacent parts of the Caliphate that were now under French rule.

After the event, it is possible to see that the British had concerned themselves only with the type of Mahdism supported by the aristocracy. They failed to recognize the existence of another strand of Mahdism, one that appealed to slaves. There had been warnings. During the slave unrest in Nupe in 1901, a Mahdist agent had been arrested in Bida for stirring up trouble. He was considered a rabble-rouser who was attempting to inflame the "lower orders." British officials did not apparently notice that this Mahdist agent was very different from Rabih, Attahiru I, and other Mahdists close to the center of political power. The Bida agent was not associated with the aristocracy, and he was directing his campaign against the Caliphate government. Even if the British had known about the Mahdist uprising in French territory, therefore, it would have been surprising if they had recognized its potential to attract slaves.

The Mahdist uprising began at Kobkitanda in French Niger on December 8, 1905, after a decade or more of revolutionary Mahdist agitation in the Sokoto Caliphate and adjacent territory in the central and western Sudan.[164] The initial action involved radical Zarma clerics and their supporters, who directed their uprising against Zarmakoy Auta of Dosso, who was a principal supporter of French rule in the area immediately to the west of British territory. The revolutionary leader at Kobkitanda was the blind Zarma cleric Saybu dan Makafo, who commanded considerable support in the western emirates of the Caliphate, including the Emir of the sub-emirate of Karma. After the defeat of the Mahdist forces at Kobkitanda by the French, Saybu made his way to the Mahdist stronghold at Satiru in British Northern Nigeria.

Satiru was an autonomous Mahdist community that had been established in about 1894.[165] Located on the borders of four great fiefs, Danchadi, Dange, Shuni, and Bodinga, Satiru became a refuge for escaped slaves and other discontented elements.[166] Its original inhabitants were poor clerics and their followers, who came from the capital districts of Sokoto and Gwandu. They were hostile to the Caliphate aristocracy, and, after the conquest, to the British as well. Escaped slaves flocked to this community and eventually made up a strong element in its population, probably a majority.

The Satiru leaders, in alliance with Mahdists in French territory, planned an uprising for the Id-al-Kabir, which that year was on February 5, 1906. The Kobkitanda uprising was actually premature, because of an incident involving tax collectors, and the revolt at Satiru was late, because other Mahdists in the area refused to join the revolt as scheduled. The Satiru uprising, therefore, did not begin until February 14 because of this dissention within the ranks of the Mahdists.

Despite this confusion among the Mahdists, the uprising was a coordinated revolt against colonialism, both British and French, and it was also directed against those who collaborated with the colonialists, whether they were officials of the Caliphate or not.[167] The Muslim clerics, with Saybu Dan Makafo as the principal, provided the leadership; the Mahdist movement provided an ideology that was anti-aristocratic and anti-colonialist; the appeal was great enough that many discontented people flocked to Satiru. Along with fugitive slaves, the other main participants were the radical clerics and some disgruntled peasants who attached themselves to the clerics.

Revolutionary Mahdism can be distinguished from other forms of Mahdism in three important respects: first, it advocated the overthrow of the Caliphate government even before the imposition of colonial rule; second, it exhibited a dimension of class struggle in that it had few, if any, Fulbe supporters and tended towards hostility to the aristocracy; third, most of its supporters were poor peasants and fugitive slaves, and indeed the revolutionary Mahdists opposed slavery and welcomed runaway slaves to their cause.[168] Revolutionary Mahdism did not encourage emigration, unlike other forms of Mahdism, and it was associated with the expected appearance of Isa (Jesus) as well as the Mahdi Himself. With the colonial conquest, revolutionary Mahdism assumed a new dimension: it sought the expulsion of the colonial authorities and the overthrow of those officials who were collaborating with colonialism.

It would be an exaggeration to characterize the revolutionary Mahdism of 1905–1906 as entirely anti-Fulbe and therefore based only on ethnic cleavage, or primarily a revolt of the slaves. Both overtones were strong, however. It is striking that after the rebels were finally defeated, no Fulbe bodies were reported among the dead at Satiru.[169] Furthermore, the first reflections by colonial officials in March 1906 laid considerable stress on the role of runaway slaves in the rebellion.

After routing a British expedition on February 14, the Satiru Mahdists made punishing attacks on neighbouring towns and villages. Danchadi was burned on March 6 and Dange on March 8. Resident Burdon reported that "all the thickly populated country between these two was devastated."[170] The Satiru rebels specifically attacked slave plantations, apparently to liberate slaves. Among the places burned between February 16 and early March were Runjin Kwarai and Runjin Gawo, both of which were plantations. Similarly treated were Rudu Makera, Jaredi, Dandin Mahe, Zangalawa, Bunazawa, Hausawan Maiwa, and Kindiru, and a number of these settlements appear to have been slave estates, too. The towns of Shuni, Bodinga, and Sifawa, which were the centers for these plantations, were evacuated.[171]

Particularly worrisome to the British were the wider expressions of support for the uprising. Officials reported signs of disaffection in Katsina and Zamfara, the loyalty of the Emir of Gwandu was in doubt, and there were rumblings even in Sokoto town itself.[172] The longer the Satirawa went unchastised, the greater the risk that broader disaffection would surface.

Despite the gravity of the situation, the Sokoto aristocracy proved pacific towards the British and hostile to the rebels. These slave-holding aristocrats in this case had interests parallel to those of the colonial authorities: revolts involving fugitive slaves must be suppressed. The aristocracy, too, was deeply concerned and chose to remain allied with British interests. One major consequence of the Satiru revolt was that the aristocracy came to realize it was possible to reach an accommodation with British rule. The slavery issue was central to that realization.

Fugitive slaves and the Satiru revolt

Although it has not been possible to identify the actual proportion of fugitive slaves among the disaffected poor who made up most of the rebel force at Satiru, it *is* clear that fugitive slaves were a major factor in the revolt. According to A. S. Mohammed, who has studied the question with care, "the only people who joined the rebellion were poor peasants and slaves who escaped from their masters."[173] Mohammed's work has established that the Satiru Mahdists "encouraged the emigration of slaves."[174] In fact the radical clerics of the village believed that slavery was a prime example of the injustice of Caliphate society. According to Maidamma Mai Zari, Dutsen Assada ward, Sokoto, "the leaders of Satiru abolished slavery and as a consequence ... slaves flocked to them." Moreover, "the freedom of these fugitives was effectively and strenuously guarded."[175]

The first British reports concerning Satiru confirmed the importance of the slavery issue. In his despatch of February 21, 1906, Burdon stated: "As far as I can learn the adherents who at one time flocked to it [the Satiru cause] were nearly all run away slaves."[176] This interpretation made sense to Lugard at the time, and he therefore informed the Colonial Office that the Satiru Mahdists were "mostly fugitive slaves, and I suppose some outlaws from French territory," a reference to Saybu Dan Makafo and his followers.[177] In his official report of March 7, Lugard still subscribed to this theory:

> it appears that the rising was instigated by an outlaw from French territory named Dan Makafo, who gathered together a band of malcontents and

runaway slaves, and forced Malam Isa, the son of a man who had previously [in 1904] declared himelf Mahdi to head the rising.[178]

Burdon, whose interpretation Lugard depended upon, was on the spot and had time to make inquiries, and his language indicates that he had done so. This assessment should be given considerable weight, unaffected as it was by the later official reluctance to admit that slaves were part of the revolt. Temple, who became Resident of Sokoto in 1907, lent his support to this theory. After noting that "desertions of domestic slaves are a serious menace to the peace and prosperity of Mohammedan States," he observed, "I heartily concur with Major Burdon who writes that this was probably one of the causes of the Satiru rising."[179]

When the dead were examined on the battlefield, the apparent ethnic composition of the rebels was striking. Not a single Fulbe body was reported among the two thousand or so dead rebels. How would people know who was Fulbe and who was not? The Fulbe officials who were involved in the inspection certainly did not recognize anyone. Burdon grasped the significance of this ethnic dimension in his report to Lugard:

> Satiru was a Hausa village and only Hausas or their kindred races have joined them. All the faces on the battlefield had Gobir, Kebbi, Zanfara, Katsena and other such tribal marks. Not a single Fulani *talaka* [commoner] joined them.[180]

Mohammed, on the basis of oral sources, presents a similar picture, although he allows for the fact that there may have been "some non-Habe and non-Muslims among the Satirawa since quite a number of the slaves owned by the *Sarakuna* [i.e., title holders] and *Attajirai* [wealthy merchants] were from other societies."[181] He states that the ethnic groups included Zamfarawa, Gobirawa, Gimbanawa, Kabawa (Kebbi), Azbinawa (Azben), Arawa (Arewa), and Katsinawa. It is significant that other non-Hausa identities are not remembered, despite the presence of large numbers of fugitive slaves. By staying to fight, the fugitive slaves in effect had renounced their other loyalties and were fighting as Hausa.

The uprising of 1905–1906 deserves comparison with the unrest in Kontagora and Bida in 1901. In both cases, the disaffected population hated the Fulbe. The subjugated Gwari of Kontagora and northern Bida were bitter as a result of years of slave raiding and taxation, while the slaves, many of whom were Gwari, were tired of the oppression of agricultural slavery. The fugitive slaves, disgruntled peasants, and clerics at Satiru had similar kinds of grievances arising from slavery and aristocratic exactions. Nonetheless, the two situations were different in one important respect. In 1901, many British officers were sympathetic to the Gwari and the discontented slave population, and there was some willingness to let slaves escape and to allow the Gwari to assert their independence from Fulbe hegemony. By 1905, there was no British support for the Satiru uprising. Indeed, revolutionary Mahdists preached that the imposition of colonialism marked the advent of the millennium, which would result in the end of slavery and oppression. With this ideology, the clerics provided the leadership for a movement that appealed to a variety of discontented elements, including fugitive slaves. No such ideology had prevailed in Kontagora and Bida in 1901.

Colonial policy and the revolt at Satiru

After the Satiru uprising was crushed in early March, the British and the Sokoto authorities permitted the Sokoto levies to run riot at Satiru in order to set a bloody example for would-be revolutionaries, be they fugitive slaves or anyone else. Thousands of people were killed or forced back into slavery. The surviving leaders, including blind Dan Makafo, were tried and publicly executed in Sokoto. Not a single house was left standing at Satiru, and a curse was pronounced on its site, so that not even today is the location inhabited. It was thought that the Satiru community had to be thoroughly destroyed, even to the point of extermination, to prevent the uprising from becoming a dangerous precedent. Bellicose settlements of fugitive slaves, offering haven for like-minded slaves, might find encouragement. Satiru itself demonstrated that such settlements might spring up not only in some mountain fastness, but only a few kilometers from the capital. If this were condoned, it was unlikely that the slave masters of Northern Nigeria would be cooperative. As the British saw it, to protect indirect rule they had to allow severe treatment at Satiru, and if that amounted to brutality, then so be it. Slaves everywhere in Northern Nigeria, when they heard of this massacre, would think again about rising in arms against their masters and the British colonial government. That the action was effective is demonstrated by the fact that no uprising of fugitive slaves occurred again; this option was effectively closed.

Within a few weeks the realization spread along the chain of command that it would be beneficial to downplay the significance of fugitive slaves in the affair. The Colonial Office, later followed by Lugard, attempted to shift attention to other factors. While slavery was clearly mentioned as a major cause of the revolt in the reports written at the time and on the spot, the issue was deliberately removed from later reports. This censorship can be directly traced in London even in the case of Lugard's initial cable. That cable stated succinctly that "The rebels are outlaw fugitive slaves."[182] The Colonial Office announcement of the revolt stated something quite different: "The rebels are outlaw fugitives." A marginal note next to Lugard's telegram indicates how the incident was to be handled: "Better say nothing of slaves."[183] By May 9, Lugard had incorporated this cleaned-up interpretation into his official reports.[184] Thus there was a cover-up not only of the severity of the repression, but of the role played by slaves as well. For public consumption, mention of this aspect of the revolt was excised from the record.

Scale of the fugitive exodus

While Satiru was the most dramatic episode in the flight of slaves, many more slaves than the number that gathered at Satiru slipped away from their masters in a manner that is difficult to tabulate. We have suggested a figure in the range of two hundred thousand, but because of the nature of the exodus, it is impossible to estimate the scale with much accuracy. The impression of many colonial officials suggests that the number of escaped slaves was very considerable, however. Agricultural officer Neely appreciated the seriousness of the exodus in his 1904 report on cotton growing in Northern Nigeria: "The Administration does not encourage serfs, who form the farm labourer class, to desert, but it is inevitable that large numbers should have done so."[185] In 1905, Lugard admitted that "the desertion of *bona fide* domestic slaves, who form the labouring classes on the estates of the free-born Mohammedans, was at first keenly felt."[186] Because a "large portion of the population formerly consisted of more or less recently-enslaved persons, who have now left their state of servitude and returned to their homes among the Pagan tribes or taken up land for themselves,"[187] there were "very notable inter-province migrations ... taking place, due to communities returning to their ancient homes, and rejoining their tribes."[188]

As Lugard noted in 1906, the returns of freed slaves accounted for only 3,071 individuals, "only a fraction of the slaves liberated in Northern Nigeria as a consequence of British rule in the past six years." He admitted that the returns

> do not profess to be a complete record [of slaves who had become free], more especially in the earlier years. Large numbers were liberated by various military expeditions, of which no record was kept, and even now the numbers freed by the native courts under the supervision of the Administration are only partially entered. Finally, the vast numbers of newly-enslaved Pagans who have returned to their homes, and of whom the Administration has no knowledge, are of course additional to those shewn on these returns, which only refer to such slaves as have passed through the hands of the political staff.[189]

Later, G. S. Browne noted that "in the early days of the administration," slave owners suffered "great hardship" because of "the assertion of their freedom by large numbers of their slaves." As a result "vast tracts of farm land were left uncultivated for some time, owing to no labour being available for its cultivation."[190]

Orr, who was Resident at Zaria and Sokoto between 1903 and 1908, also admitted that the flight of slaves was of considerable proportions.

> A great number of slaves, many of whom had recently been captured in war, seized the opportunity [of the British occupation] to return to their country, Many deserted their masters and took service under the Government, either as soldiers, police, transport carriers, or labourers in the Public Works Department.[191]

Even by 1908, Girouard thought that as many slaves "sought their freedom by desertion" as through the courts.[192] The problem had been so great that he suspected that fugitives were almost everywhere; they constituted "a certain number of our soldiers, a great proportion of Government carriers, and, I fear also, a large addition to the criminal and depraved classes of the community."[193] In 1910, Governor Hesketh-Bell admitted that the "first inevitable result of the abolition of the legal status of slavery is to prompt a large number of the more recently enslaved population to leave their masters, and establish independent communities."[194]

The scale of the exodus is a subject of speculation. Estimates are few and haphazard. These include Wallace's guess that 30,000 slaves left Bida and crossed the Niger between 1897 and 1901; an estimate of 20,000 slaves who fled Kontagora between 1901 and 1902; tens of thousands of fugitives arriving in Kontagora in the few years after 1902; the reports of whole villages of fugitives in Nassarawa and other places south of Zaria; thousands of escaped slaves at Satiru in 1906; and the notices of fugitive movements other than these. The estimate that large numbers of slaves were liberated during military campaigns, for which no records were kept, also indicates a massive movement of fugitives, while the conviction that desertions greatly exceeded the number of slaves liberated through the courts is another indication that the exodus was very large.

For comparative purposes, there are reasonably accurate estimates of the size of slave desertions in several of the small emirates that were incorporated into French Niger. In 1906, thousands of slaves left Say, Torodi, and Kunari. French officials estimated that the population of these emirates declined by 50 percent in a matter of months. Whereas three-quarters of the population had been slave when the French first arrived, the proportion declined to less than 25 percent as a result of the flight.[195] Although it may be that conditions were different in French territory, we suggest that the events in the western emirates were part of a broader pattern that extended beyond the British sphere and therefore reinforce the impressions gleaned from scattered data.[196] Certainly, the flight of slaves in French territory paralleled the timing and severity of the exodus in the British zone. We further suggest that 1906 was the last year of major desertions that had begun with the European occupation.

While no firm estimate of the scale of the slave exodus can be made, therefore, it is reasonable to suppose that at least 200,000 slaves, and possibly considerably more, fled their masters between 1897 and 1907, and fugitives continued to leave for several more years. This estimate suggests that as much as 10 percent of the total slave population left, although the percentage was certainly much higher in some emirates, particularly Bida and Kontagora. While the number of fugitives appears to have been very large, the exodus was spread out over a decade or more and hence probably had more of an impact on local power arrangements than on factor endowments. Individual masters may have lost many of their slaves and suffered a severe loss of wealth, but other masters probably only lost a slave or two at once, which would have allowed them time to adjust to the loss. On the political level, the exodus was of crisis proportions because the British regime wanted to establish close relations with aristocrats and merchants, who owned most of the slaves.

The evidence is frequently unclear, but it appears that many, if not most, of the slaves who left were recent captives. Many slaves came from areas relatively near to where they were in captivity, and it was not all that difficult for them to return home. Of course, whether or not slaves were welcome depended upon the reasons they had been enslaved. Even those captured in raids or kidnaped could not be sure how they would be received, while those who had been pawned, forwarded as tribute, or convicted of offenses would not have chosen to return. Individual decisions are usually impossible to discern. Furthermore, the evidence on the flight reveals a movement southward into the "Middle Belt," and there was also some movement between Ilorin and Nupe. We have little evidence on the flight of slaves to the east towards Borno, Bagirmi, and Adamawa, from where many slaves came, but it is reasonable to assume, nonetheless, that at least some slaves also attempted to return to their homes there.

Women, including concubines, were numerous among the fugitive population. Webster's reports from Nassarawa establish this fact, and there are sufficient data from other emirates to suggest that women escaped in considerable numbers, perhaps not of the same order as their proportion among the slave population, but still enough to come to the attention of officials. Furthermore, women kept running away even after men no longer did, as a 1907 report from Kontagora suggests. According to Feargus Dwyer, Acting Resident, Kontagora and Borgu, "As a rule men slaves ... never run away; it is the women who do so and always to marry some person in another man's house."[197] The active resistance of women to slavery was a serious concern of the aristocracy and the colonial regime, as we examine below. It is no wonder that the fugitive problem had a major impact on the evolution of colonial policy on slavery.

Gradually, the efforts to prevent the desertion of slaves took hold. As Lugard noted in 1905, "had the Government not taken steps to discourage the too rapid transition from the old to a better labour contract, a complete dislocation of the social conditions of the country might, as I have explained in former reports, have taken place."[198] Reports from the various provinces suggest that fewer slaves were leaving, in some places as early as 1905. In Bauchi, for example, "the masters no longer complain of desertion, and a satisfactory *modus vivendi* appears to have been reached which will, I hope, continue during the transition period till free labour replaces slave labour."[199] In Nupe, for example, almost all the slaves who were going to leave had already done so by 1906.[200] In Ilorin, where "domestic slaves form a great part of the population," they appeared to be "happy and contented, and have no desire to escape from bondage."[201] By 1907, the problem appears to have decreased in Zaria as well; at least it was reported that "complaints about runaway slaves have been fewer than formerly."[202] Even then, however, Governor Girouard still believed that there was a serious problem. He confessed that "continual reports are reaching me as to constant desertions of domestic slaves, who often become banded together as robbers and malefactors when men, or drift into prostitution when women."[203]

By 1912, it was believed that all slaves who were not satisfied with their status had already decamped, but this was not so.[204] The Islamic courts, at least in Kano, were still returning fugitive slaves to their masters as late as 1914. In 1912, for example, forty-six cases of "run-away slaves" were recorded in the Kano courts,[205] and the Judicial Council continued to hear cases concerning fugitives in 1913 and 1914.[206] It is likely that other Islamic courts and Judicial Councils continued to return fugitive slaves to their masters as well. Some slaves left their masters during the famine of 1913–14 as well, and a few continued to leave for years thereafter.[207]

3

The debate on legal-status abolition

Although George Goldie was responsible for the decree that abolished the legal status of slavery in 1897, the real architect of slavery policy in Northern Nigeria was Frederick Lugard, who was first on the scene in the Sokoto Caliphate in the famous march on Borgu in 1894 to forestall French expansion and thereafter was a confidant of Goldie. The choice of Lugard to head the West African Frontier Force in 1897 kept him firmly in the picture, and when he became High Commissioner of the Protectorate of Northern Nigeria in 1900, he was able to implement his ideas.[1] Six years later, when he was transferred away from Northern Nigeria to become Governor of Hong Kong, he could claim to have set in motion an irreversible transition in the slave economy and the condition of slaves in Northern Nigeria.

Lugard had written extensively on legal-status abolition throughout the 1890s. His views, which were widely read, reflected the influence of informed public opinion on this issue, and he owed a special debt to Sir John Kirk, whom Lugard considered to be the "foremost authority on slavery" and who was the official responsible for applying the strategy of abolishing the legal status of slavery to the domains of Zanzibar, also in 1897.[2] Lugard thereby identified with a policy that stretched back over a half-century to India, Burma, Ceylon, and Hong Kong. It is clear that Lugard was selected as High Commissioner not only for his military prowess and organizational skills, but also because he was an authority on the slavery issue.[3] He had acquired his reputation as a result of service in East Africa.

Lugard developed his interest in the topic of slavery well before his first assignment in what was to become Northern Nigeria. In 1888 as an army captain, he joined the Imperial British East Africa Company (IBEAC), under which he served from 1889 to 1892.[4] During those years, when he was still only in his early thirties, Lugard developed a set of several clear ideas as to how a colonial government might cope with an economy based on slaves. In East Africa at that time, as at home in Britain, the desirability of a policy abolishing the legal status of slavery, or "permissive freedom," as such a policy was then often called, was the subject of a keen debate focused on Zanzibar. As a full participant in this debate, Lugard was a firm supporter of legal-status abolition, and consequently rejected the idea of West Indian-style emancipation. As he wrote in 1893,

> Sudden emancipation, enforced alike on owner and slave, causes a complete dislocation of existing social conditions. Unless adequate provision were made for the slaves, it would be regarded by the majority as a misfortune; and though we ourselves may be able to clearly see the justice of such a measure as regards the owners ... they ... would consider compulsory abolition to be an arbitrary and despotic measure, and this would lead to discontent and distrust.[5]

Instead, as he made clear in 1896, he "advocate[d] the less drastic course of abolishing the legal recognition only." In his opinion, "compulsory emancipation would of necessity inflict much suffering and hardship on many of the slaves themselves, especially the aged or infirm; it would cause a dislocation of the whole social fabric, and it would entail an acute financial crisis, and probably lead to outbreaks and disturbances."[6] Nor should owners be compensated with government funds, which, he suggested, had worked poorly in the British West Indies.[7] The language used was, as we shall see, remarkably close to that which he employed in the instructions issued to officials in Northern Nigeria.[8]

When Lugard assumed the administration of Northern Nigeria, it was obvious that his slavery policies were going to be under the close scrutiny of the government, of interested Members of Parliament, and not least of anti-slavery groups in the private sector, including the British and Foreign Anti-Slavery Society.[9] But what would the abolition of the legal status of slavery actually mean in practice? It was soon clear that Lugard had an exceptionally detailed plan of action that involved policies on land, labor, taxation, and the law. As High Commissioner, Lugard was instrumental in modifying the existing institution of slavery, and his decree that pronounced free all children born after March 31, 1901 was a significant mark in the gradual, if bumpy, path down the road to reform.

Nonetheless, Lugard's ideas were only enacted in the midst of a lively and largely secret debate among his political staff and the Colonial Office. Concern over the flight of slaves fueled this debate. In the end British policy remained committed to the abolition of the legal status of slavery, despite the severe criticisms of many of Lugard's subordinates and the reservations of the Colonial Office itself. Only as a result of this debate did it become clear what Lugard intended in his conception of "legal-status abolition."

The crucial dilemma of colonial rule was how to manage the transition from a slave to a non-slave economy. Once slave status was abolished, slaves wanted to desert their places of work, concubines began to move off for other men, the supply of food failed because land fell out of cultivation, the once-powerful and proud became desperate, and ex-slaves began to take the law into their own hands. The proto-colonial state was put into serious jeopardy, since it lacked sufficient soldiers of its own to control the vast spaces, and it was unsure if it had local allies enough to sustain order, let alone trade, food, markets, and prosperity. In short, the old system – slavery by any other name – had to be maintained for the transition. During the initial few years when "slavery" was not maintained very well, there were food shortages, banditry, political instability, and even uprisings, including the one at Satiru.

To the best of our knowledge, every official believed that slavery would continue for some time, but how to avoid drawing attention to the fact was a problem. In establishing the Protectorate of Northern Nigeria, the Colonial Office somehow had to allow local officials to mold slavery to fit the greater aims of the Empire. The CO was less concerned with what happened than with its ability to explain slavery policy if called upon to do so. The lively debate among the officials of Northern Nigeria over slavery policy concerned how best to prevent the flight of slaves, a fact that all of the protagonists realized.

Other scholars have established that the slavery issue was subjected to debate behind closed doors. Polly Hill has pointed to a conspiracy of silence on the part of both the authorities in Northern Nigeria and at the Colonial Office, while Louise Lennihan has claimed that Lugard's policy was shrouded in secrecy.[10] Both Hill and Lennihan focused on Memorandum No. 6, "Slavery Questions," completed in March 1905 and revised slightly in September 1906, which was handsomely printed by Waterlow & Sons in London in 1906, as the key document that Lugard attempted to suppress.[11] Hill and Lennihan are certainly correct in noting that original copies of this memorandum are exceedingly rare; to the best of our knowledge, only the published 1906 revision exists. We have not been able to locate a copy of the March 1905 version, or the many documents that are quoted therein.[12] Yet Lugard's slavery policy was debated at length with the Colonial Office between 1900 and 1904, and by 1904 the CO formally approved Lugard's policy. Secrecy there was, but it was aimed at the British public and Parliament, not the Colonial Office, which was actively engaged in the controversy between Lugard and his subordinates.[13] The CO knew at least as early as November 1901 of the existence of confidential instructions and had the gist of those instructions. Lugard provided full information in the summer of 1903.

These confidential memoranda between 1900 and 1903, if fully known, might well have provoked protests in Britain. It had to be kept carefully under wraps that political officers were attempting to maintain slavery, despite public avowals that the status of slavery was legally abolished and children born after March 31, 1901 were free. There was a conspiracy of silence, therefore, but only for the period before August 1903. Even then a substantial amount of information was available in the *Northern Nigeria Annual Reports.*[14]

Even the attempt to hide the situation from the public was largely abandoned by 1905, and hence the conclusions of Hill and Lennihan that secrecy prevailed through 1906 have to be modified. The disappearance of the 1905 memorandum and the rarity of its revised version in 1906 do not indicate

Colonial Office ignorance of the debate over slavery matters, although the failure of anti-slavery advocates to criticize the accessible 1906 memorandum does reflect the success of the Colonial Office and the Lugard administration in conducting the debate of 1900–1904 behind closed doors.[15] In 1905, Lugard even allowed the publication of a remarkably candid account of how running away was prevented and how a policy of self-ransom was being utilized. Yet more remarkably, he himself was the author, using turns of phrase taken directly from the highly confidential slavery memos themselves.[16] If there was a Lugard-inspired conspiracy of silence after 1903, it was a leaky one.

The secret debate

During 1899, even before he assumed office in Northern Nigeria, Lugard engaged in private correspondence on the slavery issue with the Colonial Secretary, Joseph Chamberlain. Clearly the Royal Niger Company's experiences with slavery had not been satisfactory. The general misunderstanding and confusion among Royal Niger Company personnel had to be checked, and those RNC military officials who were encouraging the flight of slaves and advocating full emancipation had to be corrected.[17] The few missionaries under the protection of the RNC had to be controlled as well. Lugard wanted to make sure that the liberal, indeed humanitarian, view of some military men and missionaries would not resurface among the Protectorate's officials and thereby pose a threat to his policies.

In July of 1899 the Colonial Office took up the question, preparing for Northern Nigeria's protectorate status forthcoming in less than six months' time. *Inter alia* it complained that there had been no correspondence from the RNC on the slavery issue, not even a copy of the decree abolishing its legal status. In response to a minute claiming that the RNC decree actually meant little, Chamberlain counseled caution. "I agree. We must be very careful not to provoke rebellion over this question and we cannot offend unlimited Hausas."[18]

As we have seen, Lugard's first step was to continue the legal abolition strategy of the RNC. The second step was an innovation for Northern Nigeria, more conservative than Goldie's policy had been, and a move that would have to be kept very quiet: slaves were to ransom themselves through money payments to their masters (see Chapter 7). Neither of Lugard's proposals was new for him, each being a direct outgrowth of his East African experience, but the implications for the Sokoto Caliphate with its huge slave population were immense.

On September 12, 1899, Lugard submitted a draft proclamation that extended the Royal Niger Company's decree abolishing the legal status of slavery. His proposal would make slave raiding illegal, control slave dealing, and provide for the freedom of individuals born after a date to be specified later (ultimately March 31, 1901).[19] Slave raiding and slave trading were to be considered criminal offenses to be dealt with in provincial courts, although initially slave trading within emirates would remain legal.[20] Lugard intended to outlaw all trade in slaves only when the conquest was completed, but he did not propose such a measure until January 1902.[21]

Technically, the RNC decree was revoked on January 1, 1900 because it was an "announcement" and not a "regulation." Only RNC regulations became law upon the assumption of the British Protectorate. The attorney-general recommended a new proclamation, but Lugard rejected this suggestion because his own draft was under consideration. Instead, Lugard preferred "to bring into force the Niger Company Decree pro temp," which was enacted as Proclamation No. 11 of 1900 on February 17, 1900.[22] Lugard waited for action on his proposal.

Chamberlain, still cautious, was not certain that Lugard's strategy would work. Commenting on the draft, one Colonial Office official minuted:

> there can be no question of adopting [legal-status abolition] at present in N. Nigeria. Not only is the holding of slaves legal, by religion and long usage, in these territories, but the sudden discontinuance of the system would produce an enormous dislocation of all social conditions; the owner, who is dependent on his slaves for the cultivation of his estates and for every form of his wealth, would be impoverished by their loss; and the slaves themselves, though not immediately, would to a great extent fall into idle habits and bring about a general economical loss ... I do not think Col. Lugard is correct when he says that domestic slavery is not interfered with; it comes to this, that no penalty is attached to the holding of slaves, but otherwise the bottom is taken out of the institution.[23]

There was a suggestion at the Colonial Office that slave dealing be abolished immediately, as had already been done in the Gold Coast and Lagos,[24] but at the time Chamberlain was concerned because WAFF troops had been transferred to Asante. He wanted no action at all until the Asante campaign was finished.[25]

Chamberlain had his own proposal for a proclamation which was based on the Gold Coast Slavery Ordinance No. 1 of 1874 and was designed "with a view to uniformity of legislation in this important matter." He wanted to rationalize slavery policies for all of British West Africa at a time when each territory had a different approach to the slavery issue.[26] He certainly did not want to see an entirely different policy for Northern Nigeria, although in the end that is exactly what emerged. The draft proclamation, dated May 25, 1900, did not provide for the freedom of children born after a specified date. He was more concerned with the termination of slave dealing, although it should be noted that he was in full accord with Lugard in upholding the abolition of the legal status of slavery.[27] Their differences arose from considerations of strategy, not principle.

Lugard made some minor revisions on Chamberlain's draft, which he returned on July 21, 1900.[28] Far from being concerned with uniformity, Lugard observed that the West African colonies and protectorates were very different from each other. Northern Nigeria was "essentially a region of powerful Mohammedan States whose rulers for a long series of years past have exacted tribute from vassal states, paid annually in slaves. Thus a Slavery Decree in any other colony has a different meaning from what it has in Northern Nigeria." Lugard's own proposal had the intention of preventing slave raiding, ending the killing of people associated with raiding, and stopping tribute payments in slaves. He would even "confiscate slaves who have been recently caught and are on their way to Sokoto or elsewhere," which is as far as he would go at this time in outlawing the trade in slaves. If adopted, Lugard's draft would have made the possession and transport of "raw slaves" illegal but otherwise would not interfere with a master traveling with his "domestic slaves." Lugard insisted on a date after which children would be born free, even though this would have had little immediate effect, but "twenty years hence no youth or girl would be legally held slave and after fifty years hence the race of slaves would be practically extinct." Otherwise Lugard's draft did not affect "domestic slavery" any more than Chamberlain's proposal did. The major difference related to the slave trade.

Lugard made it clear that his approach was consistent with the slavery strategy of both Kirk and Goldie.[29] As he noted, he had discussed his draft "clause by clause" with Sir George Goldie, who was responsible for the Royal Niger Company's decree,

> and together we settled its terms ... I afterwards submitted it to Sir John Kirk – an intimate personal friend – who was the Plenipotentiary of Great Britain at the Brussels Slavery Conference, and is, I suppose, admitted to be the greatest living authority on the subject.[30]

Lugard reinforced his position with the opinion of his attorney-general, who agreed that the Gold Coast Ordinance did not go far enough in anticipating a mechanism for implementing the gradual ending of slavery by setting a date after which children of slave parentage would be born free. And there had to be measures to obstruct slave raiding, even if these could not be enforced. In the end, Chamberlain deferred.[31]

The 1901 proclamation included some very important new measures: no claims for government compensation were to be entertained; slave raiding was prohibited; and children born after the date of the proclamation (March 31, 1901) were declared free.[32] The enactment of a date after which all new-born children would be free was particularly important, because it meant that slavery would indeed gradually disappear. Subsequently, there was some misunderstanding, deliberate or not, among the general population as to the date that this provision went into effect. In Hausa, the term 'ya 'yan gwamna applied to children born after the conquest to slaves who were not free.[33] Literally, the term means "children of the [British] governor."

Proclamation No. 2 did not outlaw the trade in slaves, although the movement of slaves over some distance for sale, gift, or transfer was prohibited. Sale within the emirates was not outlawed. Lugard observed that any restrictions on sale "would be practically unenforceable at present."[34] Undoubtedly he was correct in this. He had begun the year 1900 with only five political officers under him, the number reaching nine by March. In 1901, there were still only 104 political officers in every kind of employment.[35] It will be remembered that at this time the British did not control very much of the Caliphate. The Colonial Office kept after him in any case, although for the moment Lugard had his way. According to Lugard, the "time was not ripe" for a slave-dealing clause – an omission that received surprisingly little attention at home in Britain.[36] Lugard was not willing to move against all forms of slave trading until January 7, 1902. Only then did he agree that Chamberlain's 1900 draft, which was based on the Gold Coast Ordinance of 1874, could be "usefully enacted."[37]

Lugard was firmly in control of the situation, or so it must have appeared. Pregnant with future difficulty, however, was section 4 of the new proclamation:

> Any non-native who shall be convicted of being in possession of a slave or of assisting in the surrender of a fugitive slave to his owner, shall be liable to the same penalties as though he were a British subject and all transactions with respect to slaves which are illegal in the case of a British subject shall be equally illegal in the case of any non-native.

Lugard himself asked the CO to set the penalty, which at first was a jail sentence of six months at hard labor.[38] The penalty was later increased to fourteen years.

Lugard initially referred to this clause of the proclamation, when it was still in draft form, in the first of several confidential memoranda on the subject of slavery, issued to Residents in Northern Nigeria soon after the transfer of power from the RNC. The texts of these potentially revealing memos have not come to light, but excerpts and later memoranda allow a partial reconstruction of their contents. Apparently the earliest, dated January 31, 1900, advised Residents that the British intended "to do justice, not merely to the slave but to the master,"[39] although Lugard confused his subordinates when he warned Acting Resident Cochrane in Bida, a year later, that "it is even doubtful whether a British subject (including Residents) rendering up a fugitive slave to his master is not himself guilty of a criminal act."[40] Lugard also issued a Government Notice announcing that "British or Native Officials in the Employment of Government do not capture a run-away slave, nor take him, nor send him to an owner."[41] Implicitly, behind the secret instructions, officials were to find ways that could be interpreted as lawful in apprehending fugitive slaves.

In a strictly legal sense, Lugard clearly forbade his staff from returning slaves to their masters and thereby tolerated a situation in which slaves could run away without legal threat of intervention. In fact, however, Lugard had no intention of encouraging or allowing slaves to desert, as we have seen.

The colonial state could intervene, but only as long as it gave the appearance of observing the fact that slavery had no legal status. In a strictly legal sense, there was no intended contradiction here. Lt.-Gov. G. J. Lethem, who reviewed "early anti-slavery legislation" at Lugard's request in 1931, recognized that early policy was on shaky ground, nonetheless. Before the 1901 proclamation, there was not even a legal enactment concerning slavery. Even so,

> various memoranda had been circulated adumbrating the procedure to be observed in practice in connection with the disallowed Proclamation of 1900 and the Public Notification issued at the instructions of the Secretary of State. Copies of these earliest memoranda have not yet unfortunately been found. But in 1901 Lord Lugard, on his journey to England on leave, prepared a new set of three memoranda (Nos. 3,4,5) superseding the old ones. In these the meaning of the phrase "the abolition of the legal status of slavery" is fully defined, the reasons for non-abolition of domestic slavery are set forth and the procedure to be adopted by officers in administrating the new Proclamation outlined.[42]

These three memoranda, dated November 22, 1901, were probably very similar to the earlier, secret instructions. The new memoranda, which were the first of a series of separate instructions issued between November 22, 1901 and March 15, 1903, elaborated on the Slavery Proclamation of 1901 to such an extent as to nullify much of its apparent meaning. Lugard intended to obscure the slavery issue through legalisms and confusing (to some) instructions. As soon became apparent, Lugard had little tolerance of those who were bewildered and frustrated.

While these memoranda are examined in detail below, it is useful here to summarize their contents as a measure of the issues which Lugard must have addressed in the earlier instructions. Memorandum No. 3, "Slavery," explained how "domestic slavery" was still in force, even though the legal status of slavery was no longer recognized. Memorandum No. 4, "Freed Slaves," outlined the policy that allowed slaves to purchase their own freedom or otherwise have their ransom paid by third parties. Memorandum No. 5, "Slavery: The System of Holding Persons in Pawn," distinguished between the pawning of persons, which was illegal, and the self-purchase or ransom of slaves, which constituted the basis of reformed slavery under British rule. Special Memo No. 10 (Slavery) of January 18, 1902 defined fugitive slaves as vagrants who were to be denied rights to land and otherwise denied freedom of movement. This memo further explained the mechanism whereby slaves were to purchase their freedom. An addendum, dated August 14, 1902, warned against the wholesale desertion of slaves and in that event reaffirmed the policy that denied slaves access to land. The "Master and Servant Proclamation" of September 1902 distinguished between paid servants and domestic slaves. Special Memo No. 32, "Disposal of Liberated Women," dated December 1, 1902, allowed that most matters pertaining to female slaves were to be considered a sub-category of matrimony, which enabled the transfer and redemption of female slaves under the guise of marriage and classified the estrangement of masters and female slaves as divorce, not escape from slavery. This memo also made it clear that most references to "slaves" were aimed at males. The establishment of the first Freed Slaves' Home in early 1902, the subject of another set of memoranda, was intended to provide sanctuary for women and children who could not otherwise be disposed of through marriage or adoption and apprenticeship. Finally, an addendum was enacted in March 1903 that clarified that the enslavement of any person, no matter how achieved, was illegal.

It is our contention that these memoranda were virtually identical to the secret instructions, often verbal, that had been issued earlier, one of the first being to Acting Resident Cochrane in late January 1901. Burdon also received such instructions, and the testimony of Wallace and others suggests that these were widely known in Northern Nigeria.[43] The pattern in Lugard's written communications is revealing. He issued lengthy and frequent directions, but there was extensive repetition from one set of instructions to the next. While Lugard elaborated upon and refined his policies, there is nonetheless remarkable consistency of wording and intent. We would predict that if the despatches to Cochrane, Burdon, and others were to be located, if in fact most existed in other than verbal form, it would be found that they resembled the instructions issued between November 1901 and March 1903. Secret though they may have been, it is highly probable that Lugard's ideas were already shaped when he became High Commissioner in January 1900. He was committed to an ideology based on the abolition of the legal status of slavery while in fact enforcing a gradual transition to a post-slavery society.

The "Movement"

Lugard's warning that colonial officials were subject to criminal prosecution if they returned fugitive slaves to their masters provoked a strong reaction among a group of high officials in Northern Nigeria. In the context of the considerable slave unrest in Nupe, Kontagora, and other parts of conquered territory and the extensive exodus of slaves since 1897, these officials thought that Lugard's public proclamations would further encourage slave desertions. In the opinion of this group, the colonial regime faced serious social and economic dislocation unless British officials were legally empowered to curb the flight of slaves.

His superiors at the Colonial Office and his subordinates in Northern Nigeria misunderstood the genius of Sir Frederick's strategy. The CO, preoccupied with all the other issues of empire, was willing to defer on the matter of slavery, at least at first. Lugard's officers were less tolerant, since they had to deal with the reality of conquest and occupation. Hence the first serious opposition surfaced in Northern Nigeria.

Opposition was led by the two former RNC employees, William Wallace and Alder Burdon, who, as we have seen, had already taken a very conservative position on the slavery issue in the last years of Royal Niger Company rule. As Deputy High Commissioner, Wallace also served as Acting HC during Lugard's frequent absences. Major Burdon was initially Resident at Bida, where the slave exodus had been severe, and later became Resident at Sokoto, where the slave population was particularly numerous. Both men were in positions to effect the implementation of a conservative policy on slavery, whether or not Lugard approved.

Their reaction, which Lugard's erstwhile private secretary Reginald Popham Lobb called a "movement," surfaced in early August 1901. In November Popham Lobb, the new Assistant Resident at Bida under Burdon, wrote to his friend, F. G. A. Butler of the Colonial Office,

> I found myself in the thick of a "movement" ... A fortnight here has opened my eyes in a way that years in an office would never have done ... The general freeing of slaves will lead to such a state of anarchy & robbery that half a dozen Politicals in each province would not be able to cope with it ... If any such idea becomes at all general, the farms will lie waste as they do round Wushishi now ... & the country will be ruined ... It is a most interesting situation ... I'm curious to see what Lugard will do.[44]

Knowingly or not, Lugard's former secretary added fuel to the flames, providing information about a disagreement in Northern Nigeria that may well not have been apparent in London. His letter found its way into the Colonial Office files, to be seen by all the officials dealing with Northern Nigeria.

Wallace, while he was Acting High Commissioner during Lugard's second, lengthy leave of absence, forced a review of slavery policy in a way that can only be interpreted as an attack on Lugard. Thus officials in the Colonial Office must have been already forewarned of the rift among officials in Northern Nigeria. During the summer of 1901, Wallace wrote a series of letters to Chamberlain that dealt with issues of taxation, and hence were not ostensibly concerned with slavery,[45] but in a curious *non sequitur* at the end of one despatch, Wallace raised the issue of slavery in a manner that was bound to produce a strong reaction in the CO. "I am in complete touch and sympathy with the semi-civilized peoples of [the] Hausa States and I can assure you most positively that if a policy of wholesale liberation of domestic slaves is pursued it will mean the ruin of this protectorate at no distant date."[46]

Chamberlain expressed his failure to understand the reference to the "wholesale liberation of domestic slaves." He reminded Wallace that the proclamation of 1901 confirmed the abolition of the legal status of slavery and dealt with issues relating to slave dealing, "but it was not intended to interfere at this stage with domestic relations."[47] Wallace was told to explain himself.

Wallace responded to Chamberlain on November 7. "I regret that in the first instance I did not make my allusion to 'the wholesale liberation of domestic slaves' more clear to you but I should like to explain that I did this advisedly as I hold strong views on this question which I considered it might be out of place for me to express at that time; now however that you call upon me for an explanation of my words, I have no hesitation in writing to you fully on the subject." Wallace charged that Proclamation No. 2 of 1901 "provides for a sweeping abolition of slavery, without distinction."

> There is no doubt that the prevailing opinion amongst Northern Nigerian Officials, and the few Non-Officials, is that the Protectorate law makes it clear that there is no such thing as slavery in any shape or form, and it was the proclaiming of this belief by the Officers and men of the West African Frontier Force ... and the natural belief of the Fulani Chiefs that with the advent of the whiteman, that which had happened before would happen again in the Bida Province, viz: the wholesale liberation of slaves.[48]

Wallace informed Chamberlain that there was a fugitive crisis, which appears to have been the first the CO knew of the extent of the slave exodus. He reported that desertions were so numerous around Wushishi, Bida, and Jebba that the population had been "in a state of semi-starvation for months." This was the first reported "colonial" famine.

Wallace referred back to the 1897 Niger Company Decree and the consequences – large-scale desertion from Ilorin, Bida, and the riverine district between Jebba and Idah (see Chapter 2).

> Before the first month [January 1900] of General Lugard's Administration had expired he had issued a Confidential Memo to Residents on the subject [of mass desertions]. This, although full of very sound and practical advice, was so far as it referred to domestic and farm slavery rendered void by the emasculating sentence "and it is even doubtful whether a British subject (including Residents) rendering up a fugitive slave to his master is not himself guilty of a criminal act."

Wallace clearly identified the existence of the early, secret memoranda, establishing when the first was issued, and he deliberately exposed the contradiction between these memoranda and Proclamation No. 2. As we have seen, Proclamation No. 2 was essentially Chamberlain's draft. Wallace's charges, consciously or not, drove a wedge between Lugard and the CO.

Wallace claimed to have followed Lugard's instructions, rather than to have enforced Proclamation No. 2, when he marched on Yola. He "clearly informed the Emir that we would on no account interfere with the domestic and farm or connubial slaves of himself and his people." He confessed that in taking this action, he was thereby

> laying myself open to censure by His Majesty's Government ... I have so far endeavoured to demonstrate that through injudicious interference with this very grave question of domestic slavery, we have to a great extent, with the exception of at Yola, brought nothing but ruin on the countries, and gained the ill-will of the ruling and influential classes.

The reference to Yola was a dig at Lugard, since Wallace had been in charge of the occupation ("in the absence of the High Commissioner, which is to be regretted"). As we have seen in Chapter 2, however, the fugitive slave crisis was also severe at Yola, despite Wallace's claims to the contrary.

At Bida, where slaves were in open revolt, Burdon had sought to contain the fugitive crisis by returning slaves to their masters. Wallace was in "total agreement" with "Burdon's good work."[49] According to Wallace, Burdon had "repeatedly broken clause 4 of the Slavery Proclamation and thereby rendered himself liable to six months imprisonment with hard labour on different counts."[50] Colonel Morland, who returned a female slave to her master "against her will," was also technically liable, and Wallace admitted that his action at Yola made him subject to criminal prosecution as well. He was not asking that charges be laid but that the proclamation be repealed and a new one introduced. In his opinion, "slaves in the Northern Nigeria Haussa States will be far happier and more prosperous in the future, if ruled by their present native law than by any new code which we could introduce."

Wallace recommended it would be wise to assure the emirs that domestic slavery would be allowed to continue before the British advanced on the central emirates. He claimed that Emir Kwassau of Zaria was requesting clarification of British policy on slavery, and that the Emir would acknowledge the British government if there was no interference with domestic slavery.[51] As we have seen, Kwassau was more disposed towards collaboration than many Caliphate officials, but the slavery issue was a problem that ultimately led to his downfall. Wallace favored an alliance with Kwassau, which was one reason that he intended to "prepare a paper on the subject [of the real status of the domestic slave] ... by the next mail."[52]

As his actions at Bida made clear, Alder Burdon was at least as outspoken as Wallace. He used his post as Resident of one of the most advanced colonial positions to promote the pro-slavery arguments he had first advocated when he was Commandant of the Royal Niger Company Constabulary.[53] Reports from Burdon were included in Wallace's despatch, and they were full of criticism. After pointing out that the slavery problem was the uppermost of his concerns, Burdon stated bluntly that the 1901 Slavery Proclamation could be interpreted to mean that slavery was abolished and all the slaves were free.[54] His reasoning was that since it was criminal for government officials to return runaways, slaves could flee with impunity. Thus slavery was *ipso facto* at an end for any slave who desired to leave.

Burdon believed that Proclamation No. 2 of 1901 was full of contradictions: what could the abolition of the legal status of slavery possibly mean? If it meant that slavery was abolished, Burdon did not "understand why it was not made to say so in plain English." Those born after March 31, 1901 were free; slaves born before that date were not free, but what could that mean if there was no legal status? Certainly this legalism did not conform to Islamic law, which held that concealing an escaped slave was a criminal offense similar to the receipt of stolen property in English law. Furthermore, Burdon did not understand how the status of slavery could be abolished when it was still legal for people to own slaves. His (not so) pretended confusion was clearly intended to expose the contradictions in Lugard's policy.

Burdon proposed an interpretation of Proclamation No. 2 whereby slaves would not become free unless duly and legally freed by a Protectorate court. "The mere fact of flight from a master does not in itself constitute freedom." Otherwise, he contended, the proclamation would result in "the most wholesale and sweeping abolition of slavery."[55] Burdon insisted that he was "governed by the confidential instructions issued by His Excellency Sir Frederick Lugard to Captain Cochrane when he was placed here [in Bida] as Acting Resident. His notes on that document are 'that the Slavery Proclamation is not to be too rapidly or drastically enforced.'" Burdon pursued the point.

> What does this mean? If a master comes to me and reports that half his slaves have run away, by section 4 I must tell him that they cannot be given back, that nothing can be done to the slaves, that he has no redress and can hope for no compensation. The remainder of his slaves hear of this decision and, as they have nothing to fear by running away, promptly do so. The master therefore ... has lost in one overwhelming catastrophe his whole wealth. His farms lie idle ... his house falls down ... his wives or at any rate concubines have gone with ... his children, he is left destitute and as the farm slaves have been careful on going to take all the grain and crops ... he has not even food to support the remnant that stay with him.

The only alternative, Burdon argued, was to return the slaves who attempted to flee: "I must restore or endeavour to restore the original fugitives – then whether I succeed or not the remainder will not run away, knowing that they may be liable to capture or return."[56] In this reading there was no middle ground; the rule had to apply to all fugitives or none.

Burdon asked Lugard for advice in November 1900, because he did not understand a confidential memorandum of January 31, 1900 that the British were "here to do justice, not merely to the slave but to the master."[57] Burdon, to Lugard's frustration, interpreted this to mean that slave escapes were to be prevented. In November 1900, Lugard instructed Burdon not to interfere in cases of slave desertions. The "confused" Resident now considered that he had been instructed neither to uphold Caliphate law that fugitives were to be returned to their masters nor to implement Protectorate laws against returning fugitive slaves. What could Burdon do? He chose to interpret these apparently passive instructions in an active manner. He considered that "to restore all fugitive slaves" was in "the spirit of Sir Frederick's caution against a drastic enforcement."[58] He too inferred that "the Official who drafted the Slavery Proclamation" could not have been Lugard, although it is highly likely that he knew that the Proclamation emanated from the Colonial Office. Whether or not he knew that Chamberlain was the author is uncertain, but he willingly absolved Lugard of blame. The effect was to embarrass both Lugard and Chamberlain, who had approved the revised document and therefore were responsible for it. If a junior official had drafted any part of the Proclamation, it would have been someone with only a marginal role in making policy.

Burdon "urgently" advised total "cancellation" of the proclamation. "Slavery must not be abolished – it must not even be tampered with – until we know something of the laws that govern [the Hausa emirates]." In Burdon's opinion, it would take "generations" to "teach the pagans who form the slave population the meaning of hired labour," and he argued that nothing must be done until that had been achieved. He argued that the revocation of the policy that fugitives were not to be returned to their masters would ease the march on Kano and Sokoto:

> If it is annulled, we can with care enter Kano and even I believe Sokoto in peace ... I consider it most important that all Whitemen should be given to understand that domestic slavery is *not* abolished, that all slaves were not freed, and that no slave is free unless he has been legally freed by his master or in some Protectorate Court.[59]

As Resident in Bida, Burdon was unable to restore order among the slave population, although he certainly tried. "NO – The system of slavery must be legalised. The native laws on it are wonderful in their mildness and liberal spirit and they must be learnt and endorsed by us." There must be penalties for "absconding," because with the abolition of slave trading recaptured fugitives could no longer be sold as a punishment.[60]

Wallace's strategy, as reinforced by Burdon, had the desired effect at the Colonial Office, which now worried "that the operation of Proclamation 2 of 1901 had resulted in several provinces in a wholesale liberation of domestic slaves, and was in danger of producing an entire disorganization of the social and economic system of the country."[61] Antrobus expressed the views of the Colonial Office as follows:

> This is a good despatch, & can only confirm the belief that Mr. Wallace is very wise in his attitude ... The native institution on which ... the whole economic system of the country depends is in danger of being swept away before anything has been devised to replace it ... Mr. Wallace shows quite clearly, I think, that the Proclm. is having precisely the effect which it was intended not to have, and that the political officers in Nor. Nig. are placed in a very awkward position in consequence. There can be no doubt of the right policy in the matter: & there is no divergence between Mr. Wallace and the Colonial Office on this point. The institution of domestic slavery, so far as its practices are not repugnant to civilisation, must be maintained in some form and under some name until another system of labour supply can be substituted for it.[62]

Antrobus seemed to be squarely on the side of the "Movement"; he obviously wanted to maintain slavery in some form. The preferred solution was the adoption of the Southern Nigeria Native House Rule Ordinance of 1901, which in effect legalized the control of the slave population by the heads of houses and effectively continued slavery under another name.[63] Failing that, Antrobus wanted the 1901 proclamation recast, but Chamberlain was reluctant to issue orders to Lugard on the matter, awaiting instead a reply from him upon his arrival back in Northern Nigeria.

Thus Lugard faced a serious crisis within his administration upon his return to Nigeria in November 1901. His two most senior subordinates were in open opposition over the slavery issue, and there is enough information to suggest that they had support among other officials. More than slavery policy was at stake. His very hold on his own colonial staff was in doubt. Lugard considered slavery "the most important question" of his early administration, and Wallace's "condemnation of my action and Policy" required the "use [of] some plain language" in defense.

In his rebuttal to Wallace, Lugard was condescending, implying that Wallace was not capable of understandiung "the meaning of the terms employed" and that the position taken by Wallace, Burdon, Molesworth, and others unnamed was "so very full of illogical deductions and statements that it would have been a waste of time to deal with them in detail."[64] Never one to suffer gladly those he considered fools, Lugard was clearly exasperated with Wallace. Later he was to say to Lady Lugard that "he is a nice old thing of the invertebrate sponge genus (which is usually useful for expunging and effacing everything except itself)."[65] To Lord Scarborough of the Niger Company (Wallace's old employer), he stormed that Wallace "has acted for me in my absence with indifferent loyalty ... Privately & frankly to you, I always thought him *quite useless* & I now begin to think him dangerous to the interests of the country."[66]

Yet on another level Lugard's attitude towards the members of the "Movement" was uncharacteristically placatory. He wrote no answering despatch to the Colonial Office, which had expected him to "take up the cudgels" in defense of his policy, a silence that, years after, some in the Office incorrectly interpreted to mean that the despatch had never been called to his attention.[67]

Lugard contented himself with defending his policy to his subordinates in Northern Nigeria. He turned the criticism around to blame everyone but himself for excesses and the failure to condemn such excesses in the various military campaigns of 1900–1901. Wallace's judgment was repeatedly called into question. The complaints and charges of other officials were dismissed as distortions. Lugard made it clear that he wanted a full investigation and report on all such "domestic matters" within his administration.[68]

Wallace could not have avoided reading these instructions as an order to desist, although Lugard announced that he "would be glad to see the paper" that Wallace had proposed to write. The report never materialized. Finally, Lugard presented himself as a moderate who was an advocate neither of the "infinitely more drastic" measures of the Gold Coast ordinance nor, by implication, the equally severe proposals of the "Movement." He served notice that he would respond verbally to the "illogical deductions and misstatements" that both Wallace and Burdon had made. The coup de grâce was a pointed reminder that British subjects were obliged to uphold British law.[69]

Wallace was humble in his reply. He pretended that he did not have the "faintest idea" that Lugard had written Proclamation No. 2 of 1901. In reiterating his position, he requested that officials be instructed "not to interfere in slavery matters." There was little doubt in Wallace's mind that "the legal reading of it [the Proclamation] is that a slave need only be a slave with his consent." He reminded Lugard that the previous chief justice thought that the proclamation would have to be repealed and a clearer and unequivocal decree enacted. Wallace lamely insisted that he was only following orders in responding to Chamberlain's request for his opinions, although the correspondence makes a persuasive case that Wallace had deliberately provoked Chamberlain, forcing him to ask for Wallace's opinion. Wallace now claimed that his criticism was meant to "strengthen" Lugard's authority by allowing the High Commissioner to "give clear and definite instructions on this most important matter." He believed that his despatch had had a positive impact in securing Chamberlain's statement that "it is not the intention of the Government at present to interfere with Domestic Relations." Wallace noted that Chamberlain "avoided using the word slavery and I think rightly so."[70]

When Lugard issued the slavery memorandum of January 1902, he chose a meeting with Burdon to announce it. As Abadie reported from Wushishi on January 16, 1902,

> I am going down with Lugard to see Burdon who is Resident at Bida; he holds rather different views about slavery and the power given to the Native Chiefs. He is practically in favour of letting them to go on as much as they did before.[71]

Lugard's "Special Memo No. 10 (Slavery)" was dated only two days later, January 18, 1902. In it, he instructed his staff as follows:

> It is important that these farm servants or serfs should not leave their traditional employment in agriculture, and be induced to flock into the big cities as "free" vagrants without means of subsistence. Residents will therefore do their best to discourage wholesale assertion of "freedom" by such persons, explaining to them the difference between their status as serfs, and the status of a real slave.[72]

Here was the distinction between the abolition of the legal status of slavery and the necessity of executive action to prevent the desertion of slaves.

Lugard considered that there were various forms of servility, and thereby played on the ambiguous dividing line between slavery and freedom. As he noted in his Annual Report for 1902, he did not propose

> to interfere with the serfdom of the agricultural peasantry, or the house-born domestics of the cities, in so far as avoidance is compatible with the abolition of the "legal status" which has already been declared. The anomaly under which the law of the Protectorate admits the right of every human creature to assert his freedom, while the executive desires not to interfere with the only existing form of labour contract, or to overturn the social system, is one which, of course, presents constant difficulties. These can only be met in a practical

way by dealing with each case on its merits. The cases which present themselves fall usually into certain classes, and with these I have dealt in a series of instructions to Residents. I regret that space precludes the possibility of a fuller examination here of this very intricate question. I can only say in brief that one class of cases is really rather a question of divorce than of slavery, and can be dealt with as such by Native Courts. Another, that of farm servants, *adscripti glebae*, involves the right of taking up new lands, and, when necessary, can be dealt with on those lines. Others, such as cases of ill-usage, sale of a house-born slave, etc., are already liberally dealt with by the Koranic law, which needs only to be enforced.[73]

According to Lugard's definition, apparently, once the legal status of slavery was abolished, slaves had certain protection under law from ill treatment, and the rights of masters were thereby limited. His distinction between "judicial" principle and "executive" expediency thereby rested on the recognition that there was a middle ground between slavery and freedom. In Lugard's conceptualization of the problem, there were many ways that the "servile" population could be kept in place. It should be noted that the January memorandum and the later addendum were not forwarded to the Colonial Office, but the 1902 Annual Report acknowledges the existence of the confidential instructions and gives a summary of their main points.

Lugard strengthened his fugitive policy further during the summer of 1902 by introducing procedures to deal with fugitives arriving from French and German territory, and from other provinces as well. In an "Addendum to Special Memo No. 10," dated August 14, 1902, Lugard addressed the problem of "fugitive slaves from foreign territory or another Province."

> If an immigration of fugitive slaves from foreign territory is on a large scale the local chief must be told that he is not to encourage immigrants from a foreign country, and must refuse to allow them to settle down ... The foregoing refers to fugitive slaves from French or German territory or other British Protectorates, but it may as a general rule be equally well applied as between Provinces of the Protectorate whose boundaries do not intersect territory under the suzerainty of a single chief.[74]

By now Lugard was willing to admit that the conquest of Kano and Sokoto might well spread the fugitive crisis further, and strong measures, even if they were "temporary" and based on "executive expediency," would have to be adopted. He fell short of actually admitting that Wallace and Burdon might be right.

As this debate makes clear, Lugard understood full well the dangers of a slave exodus, which is why he had issued the confidential instructions to Cochrane, Burdon, and others in 1900 and 1901. Previously in East Africa, Lugard had experienced the problem by runaways (Swahili: *watoro*) who had fled their Muslim masters. In Mombasa as an employee of the Imperial British East Africa Company, he had a part in dealing with the missionaries at up-country Church Missionary Society stations. Some of these missionaries had harbored a large number of runaways, entailing chronic quarrels with the masters. Lugard made it very clear that he did not think highly of fugitive slaves and that slaves should be discouraged from running away. In the earliest of his publications on slavery, published in 1889, he had indicated his hostility to fugitive slaves: the harboring of runaway slaves "would be looked on by the Arabs as theft, pure and simple" and would lead to "disastrous consequences."[75] Whatever the disagreements between Lugard and his critics concerning slavery policy, the High Commissioner was not at odds with his subordinates on the need to curtail the flight of slaves, as we have seen. Lugard did not want his public proclamations on slavery to be enforced too rigorously, but this hypocrisy did not satisfy his critics.

The "Movement" wanted an explicit, public commitment to the maintenance of slavery, and the central issue hinged on the legality of returning fugitives. Nonetheless, Lugard maintained a clear position on this issue from beginning to end. The "Movement" wanted to return fugitives legally; Lugard always opposed any *legal* recognition of slavery and hence had to contrive a policy holding that legal means could not be used to return slaves to their masters. Lugard and his critics wanted to accomplish the same end, that is, ensuring that slaves did not run away. But Lugard's solution meant that political officers had to place themselves in jeopardy. Legal abolition of the status of slavery logically meant that political officers were put in a potentially illegal position if they were to maintain the *status quo*. Lugard's public position held that fugitives could not be returned, but confidential instructions allowed political officers to return them. The "Movement" members were unhappy with the resort to expediency, and it was little solace to them that in fact no official was ever prosecuted for returning fugitives, even though it was common practice.

Lugard's efforts to keep slaves in place

As noted above, Lugard attempted to stop the flight of slaves, and at the same time meet the criticisms of the "Movement," through the memoranda issued between November 22, 1901 and March 15, 1903. A consideration of these instructions provides an outline of slavery policy that was ultimately followed over the next two decades in Northern Nigeria. These memoranda served as the blueprint for Lugard's conception of legal-status abolition.

The first of these memoranda, No. 3, "Slavery," was obviously designed, though without for a moment admitting it, to forge a compromise with the members of the "Movement," in particular addressing fears concerning fugitive slaves. First, No. 3 was straightforward in saying that abolition of the legal status of slavery was not intended to mean abolition of slavery itself. Second, it would not be possible to abolish that institution for some considerable time.

> The wholesale repudiation of their obligation, to labour by the entire slave class would in the case of men, obviously produce in every great town a mass of unemployed vagrants and increase the criminal classes: in the case of women it

would tend to increase prostitution: while both classes would beyond doubt bring upon themselves unforeseen misery by cancelling the obligation under which their masters lie of providing for them in sickness, or caring for their wives and children during their absence from their homes ... The upper classes would be reduced to misery and starvation, and as a consequence to hostility against the Europeans who had brought this chaos about. The result would probably be a rising throughout the Protectorate, with which we have not the Force to deal. Our ill-advised action would therefore possibly result in both ourselves and our supposed philanthropy being swept away.[76]

If a situation arose in which slaves were fleeing their masters in large numbers, then Residents could institute special measures to stop slaves from fleeing in troublesome areas.

Residents could certainly free slaves if masters were cruel, or if slaves were being transported for sale, although simple sale within a province was not outlawed at this time. He realized that some slaves would show "such superior intelligence or such an inherent love of liberty, combined with a definite purpose and intention in life," that it would be advisable to allow them to obtain their freedom.[77] But in cases where freedom was granted, an explanation should be offered that "it is not the Resident's intention to indiscriminately apply it, and giving such arguments as may occur to him why the present case may be considered exceptional." In cases that were *not* exceptional, as when a runaway simply did not want to remain a slave any longer, a Resident "would discourage the assertion of freedom" by withholding assistance and turning the matter over to an Islamic court. Predictably the outcome was expected to be unfavorable to the slave. The use of the Islamic courts as an instrument of colonial slavery policy is considered further in Chapter 4.

Special Memo No. 10 of January 18, 1902 laid the cornerstone of Lugard's strategy to reform slavery under colonialism. On the one hand, Residents were instructed to "do their best to discourage wholesale assertion of 'freedom' by farm slaves." The means of doing so were left unstated, which must have frustrated the "Movement" further. Significantly for future policy, on the other hand, slaves would be allowed to obtain their freedom through self-purchase or ransom by third parties. In his review of early slavery policy in 1931, Lt.-Governor Lethem accurately assessed the importance of Memorandum No. 10, which in his opinion "went so far as to encourage the payment of redemption by the slave to his former master in accordance with native custom." Lethem further noted that "work was provided by Government in such cases in order that a slave who wished to free himself might save the necessary sum." According to Lethem's interpretation, Memo No. 10 was an extension of Memorandum No. 5, which permitted an individual, slave or otherwise, to pledge

his own labour for a limited time in redemption of a debt ... provided that the pawning was entirely spontaneous: but compulsory pawning of a debtor himself was illegal though the amount of time served in such compulsory labour was counted in liquidation of the debt.[78]

The redemption price of a slave was to be considered a debt for which a slave could be held liable. The implications of these provisions in forcing slaves to earn money through the sale of cash crops or the sale of their labor for wages are examined in detail in Chapters 4 and 7.

Memorandum No. 10 left it unclear how Residents were to accomplish the aim of discouraging the desertion of slaves other than by denying them permission to live in government cantonments without Lugard's personal approval.[79] The intent was clear, but the means were not, which was exactly why the "Movement" was so frustrated with the strategy of legal-status abolition. In a supplementary instruction of August 14, 1902, Lugard came close to revealing another of his methods. He ordered Residents to prevent the influx of fugitive slaves across provincial boundaries by refusing permission for the refugees to settle. He instructed the Residents to inform the emirs accordingly.[80] The full implication of this instruction will be considered below in our discussion of land tenure (Chapter 5).

The movements of the slave population were to be monitored as closely as possible. The disposal of freed slaves was the subject of Memo No. 4 of November 1901, but further to override his critics, Memo No. 32 of December 1902 gave more specific instructions:

> The general principle was that all adults should be given an opportunity to return to their own countries and where this was not feasible men were allowed to go where they wished, women to select a husband they desired. The husbands and guardians of freed women or children slaves were subjected to continuous supervision and it was the Resident's duty to see that they fulfilled their obligations.[81]

In many cases slave women and children were placed in the care of guardians, often Europeans but sometimes "respectable Natives." The missionaries willingly looked after some, while a Freed Slaves' Home, the subject of another memorandum, assumed responsibility for others.

Government Freed Slaves' Homes had a very short life under the colonial regime. Initially, a Home was opened at Lokoja to care for the children liberated from slave traders.[82] The Home was relocated to Zungeru in October 1903, and a second Home opened in Borno at the same time. Lugard showed an interest in the wellbeing of these liberated children; indeed he was on the Board of Directors of the Rebecca Hussey Charity, whose funds helped finance the Lokoja, Zungeru, and Borno Homes.[83] The Homes were intended to handle a difficult but minor irritant in the larger scheme to contain the slave population,[84] but the rules for the operation of the Homes make it clear that Lugard's real interest was in preventing the Homes from becoming a sanctuary for escaped slaves. The children were expected to learn useful skills and work hard. The boys were "apprenticed" in the government cart works, and the girls were prepared for "marriage." As Lugard's addenda to his circular memorandum establishing the Homes makes clear, many prominent Muslims considered that "the inmates are still slaves *owned* by Government."[85]

The issue of concubines and slave women was carefully separated from general considerations of slavery, a feature of slavery policy that has been observed elsewhere.[86] As Lethem later noted with respect to "the freedom of a woman slave,"

> the principle concerned was that of divorce and not slavery at all, since the applicants were usually actuated by "a desire to leave one husband or man to whom they were concubines in order to live with another." The right of the Native [Islamic] Court to deal with such cases was therefore recognised and compensation was admitted "not as a debt due to the owner of a slave but on the principle on which damages were awarded in civilized divorce courts."[87]

Memorandum No. 32 was specially directed against abuses associated with the so-called "marrying" of freed women, "which was little better than actual legalized slave dealing." With the establishment of the first Freed Slaves' Home, women and children were to be sent to that institution "except in cases where women obtained satisfactory husbands or could be repatriated without delay."[88] Even then, Lugard's instructions concerning the marriage of liberated slaves in the Freed Slaves' Homes make it clear that the cost of marriage was similar to the cost of redemption. "Every successful suitor will pay £2 at least to his intended bride for her clothes, and £2 (in lieu of the usual present to the parents) to a Fund which will be in charge of the Alkali or a native Chief to be appointed by the High Commissioner. This fund will be devoted to charitable objects approved by the High Commissioner and payments to it will be made direct and not through the Resident or Lady Superintendent."[89]

The "Master and Servant Proclamation" of September 27, 1902, adopted from a Gold Coast model, was enacted as a further effort to control the movement of slaves. The proclamation carefully distinguished between free servants working for wages and fugitive slaves obtaining their subsistence through payment in kind for their labor. Lugard believed that it was essential that servants, particularly those aged ten to thirteen who were apprentices in government departments, receive a wage. Otherwise,

> the people of this country are apt to be unable to discriminate in these niceties. They see the Government seize a slave in transit for whom they have paid hard cash or whom they have received in liquidation of a just debt. If then the Government hands over this freed slave to be the domestic servant of a European or non-Native Clerk without payment of wages they perceive no difference in its new status, and if the slave being a child, is not allowed to run away I confess that the difference, if it exists, is hard to see. I have, in my experience, known Missions to claim a property in their native proteges which accentuated this undesirable position and those who desired to leave were prevented from doing so.[90]

There were good reasons for enacting such a provision. The Sudan Interior Mission, at least, saw children from the Freed Slaves' Homes and fugitive slaves seeking shelter as a source of unpaid labor.[91] The proclamation made it obligatory that servants receive a cash wage, no matter how little.

Lugard did not intend that a situation should arise in which a slave could sue his master for wages; in such an "unlikely contingency" the Slavery Proclamation "would enable a Court to decide against the slave's claim, the more so that the Court is enabled to take into consideration native law and custom, where not repugnant to humanity."[92] The provisions of the proclamation were made stricter with an ordinance to license servants, which commenced March 1, 1905 (and was revised June 23, 1908). Under the terms of the licensing proclamation, domestic servants had to pay an annual fee of 2s. 6d. to obtain a license to work, and there were heavy penalties imposed on any non-native, European or otherwise, who employed a domestic servant without a license.[93] As the missionaries and others discovered, one intent of these measures was to identify fugitive slaves and force their return to their masters.[94]

The Masters and Servants Ordinance became a regular feature of colonial restrictions on the movement of slaves and former slaves, from whom the "servant" class of the colonial state was largely drawn. Freed slaves were expected to take out a license that was comparable to the payments of slaves paying *murgu*, the fee which slaves paid to masters for the right to work on their own account (see Chapter 7). The relationship of the license to slavery is revealed in a chance comment written in 1910, in which it was referred to as the "Freed Slave Boys Servants' License." The Rev. Stirrett had forwarded the money for the servant's license for a boy employed at the SIM mission station at Wushishi. The money was returned. The boy was "now of an age to take out a license ... but as the year is now nearly complete he had better await the 1st Jan when new licenses will be issued. I return you the 2/6."[95] If the boy had still been a slave, he would have had to pay his master the same amount as *murgu*. There was not much, if any, financial advantage for slaves to work as servants.

The colonial vagrancy law

Another of Lugard's strategies to obfuscate the technical problem that fugitive slaves could not legally be returned to their masters was to institute a vagrancy law, a feature of slavery policy that has hitherto been ignored.[96] The imposition of such a law was also closely associated with British perceptions of crime and prostitution, because fugitives were accused of being the core of the criminal element, if males, and the loose women of the cities, if females. In his speech at Kano in 1903, Lugard made it clear to slave owners that the British would not "interfere with the existing domestic slaves" because they "had no desire to convert the existing farm and other labourers into vagrants, idlers, and thieves."[97] As we have seen, Lugard opposed the "Movement" in upholding the illegality of restoring fugitive slaves to their masters, and hence anyone so doing was subject to criminal prosecution. But treating escaped slaves as vagrants provided excellent legal cover for denying these very same slaves their freedom. In combination with restrictions on access to land (see Chapter 5) and the use of the Islamic courts to promote self-redemption and ransom by third parties (see Chapter 4), a measure against vagrancy obstructed the movements of fugitives.

Shortly after the conquest of Kano and Sokoto in 1903, Lugard informed the Colonial Office that "the question of fugitive slaves can be dealt with indirectly but ... effectively by a Vagrancy Law, and by rules as to the taking up of new land."[98] When P. H. Ezechiel reviewed the slavery policy for the Colonial Office in 1904, he too referred to measures against vagrants:

> Sir F. Lugard has instructed his officers to evade the difficulty [involved in returning fugitive slaves to their masters] by a policy of temporary expedients, such as ... dealing with fugitive slaves as vagrants (to be sent back to their masters as paupers were sent back to their parishes in England under the old Poor Law).[99]

Lugard's problem was convincing the "Movement" that a vagrancy law was an adequate substitute for a policy that openly allowed officials to return slaves to their masters. It was only in combination with other policies, especially restrictions on access to land (see Chapter 5), that the vagrancy law would have a significant effect. Lugard's instructions of August 14, 1902, under which fugitive slaves were to be denied the right to settle if they crossed provincial boundaries, become clearer in the light of the vagrancy ordinance.

The vagrancy law became part of the Northern Nigeria Criminal Code as No. 23, Chapter XXIA of September 30, 1904. Its provisions made no specific mention of slaves but nonetheless allowed British officials the powers needed to deal with fugitives:

> Any person who –
> (i.) being a suspected person or reputed thief has no visible means of subsistence and cannot give a good account of himself; or
> (ii.) is found wandering in or upon or near any premises or in any road or highway or any place adjacent thereto at such time and under such circumstances as to lead to the conclusion that such person is there for an illegal or disorderly purpose;
> is guilty of a misdemeanour and is liable to imprisonment for three months for the first offence and for one year for every subsequent offence.[100]

This law was a powerful weapon at the disposal of the colonial state. It allowed British officers to look the other way when emirate officials were apprehending fugitive slaves, and it provided legal cover for Residents when they became involved in such cases. Returning fugitive slaves to their masters was illegal; arresting vagrants and giving them the option of a prison term or a return to their masters was not illegal. When combined with restrictions on access to land, the vagrancy law made it very difficult indeed for slaves on the loose.

On one point, Lugard was unwilling to compromise. The printed instructions continued to make it clear that in any official sense, British authorities were not to participate in the return of runaway slaves: "A British subject assisting in the rendition of a Fugitive Slave commits an illegal act." As he explained to the Colonial Office in August 1903, the laws of Great Britain prevented British officials from returning slaves, a settled point on which the British attorney-general had already ruled with reference to East Africa. These same laws would thus restrict British officials in Northern Nigeria as well. Any law or instruction that contradicted British law on the issue would be "null and ultra vires."[101] Patiently, Lugard continued to tutor the Colonial Office and his subordinates in his theory of legal-status abolition.

Walter Miller, head of the Church Missionary Society in Northern Nigeria at the time, was one of the few foreigners outside the government to comment on the enforcement of the vagrancy ordinance in combination with restrictions on access to land. In 1908 Miller discussed the problems facing a potential deserter:

> He does not want to be a soldier or a labourer; these are the only ones who can obtain their freedom here! He does not want to run away from his wife and to be a fugitive; lastly in no province would anyone give him any land or a farm . . . Moreover in this province [Zaria] as you know, according to the by-law of Captain Orr's [sic] no man is allowed, under heavy penalties, to let runaway slaves [sic] stay in his house, give him food or in any way help him, so that it would be impossible for this man anywhere to get even lodging much less a farm in this province.[102]

Presumably other Residents enacted by-laws for the enforcement of the vagrancy law.[103]

In 1911, Orr explained his actions publicly and candidly. It was necessary to deny a slave "the right to settle on and cultivate land until he had contracted to purchase his freedom from his former master . . . in order to prevent vagabondage and the occupation of land by a horde of masterless runaway slaves, who sought to profit by the Government policy towards slavery by living a life of idleness and lawlessness impossible under native law and custom"; hence

> slaves were plainly informed that Government would not permit them to become vagabonds, but that arrangements would be made whereby they might earn a livelihood and pay from their wages, by a system of installments, the sum of money necessary to purchase their freedom through the native courts.[104]

Orr's reflections on government policy demonstrate that efforts to restrain the slave population preoccupied the early administration. He observed that

> the task of Residents was no easy one, and the difficulty of acting with justice both to owners and slaves was very great. The best course open to them, after full discussion with the Emirs and Alkalis, was to leave the matter as far as possible to the native courts, and to treat each case which could not be so dealt with, on its merits.[105]

The vagrancy law gave emirate officials and the colonial regime alike the power to control the movements of slaves. It was an important component of Lugard's policy to restrain the slave population.

Whether officials relied on the vagrancy law or not, fugitives were frequently returned to their masters. Resident Abadie at Zaria responded quickly to Lugard's secret instructions on fugitives, as he wrote on January 3, 1902, barely a month after Lugard's first memoranda of November 22, 1901:

> During all this time the white man has said "No more slaves" you are all free men and the consequence is that Washishi [sic] has been a haven of refuge ... Now, the white man says, you are not free, you must go back to your masters and we shall help the masters to recover their property. Naturally it is incomprehensible to them.[106]

Similarly, Popham Lobb, who was Assistant Resident at Zaria at the time, also knew what Lugard wanted. In May 1902, six months after Lugard had neutralized the "Movement" with his various memoranda, Popham Lobb explained how British officials dealt with fugitive slaves who had been identified by their masters:

> Of course we give them back, except in cases where ill-treatment is proved, thereby rendering ourselves liable to 15 years. [He was mistaken: the penalty was fourteen years.] It has to be done, however, and it is lucky nothing gets into the papers; you remember the storm over the rendition of slaves on the mainland of Zanzibar? The law of the Protectorate is of course English, and we all have a lengthy series of confidential memos on the slavery question, from the Chief, who is exceedingly wily and up to all sorts of dodges for enthusing a new spirit into and avoiding the letter of the slavery proclamations. If we freed every slave who bolted, the whole country would be a ruin: the masters would be ruined and the slaves would, in numberless cases, as we have found already, roam through the country looting and raiding.[107]

As both Abadie's and Popham Lobb's letters make apparent, Lugard had pre-empted the "Movement," at least to the satisfaction of some of the political officers. Abadie, for one, thought that the High Commissioner's instructions were intended to keep slaves in their place through the return of fugitives, whatever the letter of the law.[108] From Lugard's perspective, Abadie and Popham Lobb, unlike Wallace and Burdon, had the good sense not to discuss matters openly, let alone report to the Colonial Office.

By August 1903, Lugard claimed that he had satisfied the "Movement." On the basis of Memorandum No. 3 of 1901 and the subsequent addenda, Lugard informed the Colonial Office that Deputy High Commissioner Wallace considered the various memoranda "most suitable" and that he and Wallace were "both of one mind on the subject."[109]

The review of slavery policy, 1903–1904

Lugard believed that he had prevailed in the establishment of slavery policy. Accordingly on January 7, 1903, he sent the draft of a new proclamation that combined his various instructions and finally incorporated Chamberlain's draft of 1900 on slave dealing by tacking the existing Southern Nigeria slave-dealing law onto the Northern Nigeria Proclamation of 1901. The penalty for dealing in slaves was to be increased from six months' to seven years' imprisonment, but otherwise the draft merely consolidated existing policies, and depended for its efficacy on the parallel measures – the vagrancy law, restrictions on access to land, the masters and servants ordinance, and the use of the Islamic courts in most matters relating to "domestic" slavery.[110]

The Colonial Office now entered the debate with its own proposal. As is clear, the CO had ideas different from Lugard's. Antrobus, still impressed by the arguments of the "Movement," even after its members out in Nigeria had been pacified, considered the underlying contradiction as strong as ever; there was no intention to interfere with slavery as an institution, but Residents attempting to support it by returning runaways were breaking the law. The earlier objections to the 1901 proclamation "therefore still hold good." Chamberlain agreed: in a message to Lugard he contended that the inability of officials to return slaves

> cuts at the root of the institution on which ... the whole economic system of the country depend. I refrained from answering Mr. Wallace's despatch in the expectation that, on your return to N. Nig. at the end of 1901, his criticisms ... would be brought to your notice, and that you would furnish me with your views upon them. [Your proposals for an attack on slave dealing] do not, it appears to me, in any way remove the objections stated in Mr. Wallace's despatch.[111]

Because Chamberlain wanted uniformity among colonies and protectorates, he let Lugard know that he gave serious consideration to the complaints of the "Movement," although in the end the CO rejected its solutions.

Hence, Chamberlain wanted some assurance that Lugard's proposed proclamation did not "interfere with domestic relations" between slaves and masters; if so, it was time "to substitute for the institution of domestic slavery a legalised form of relationship between employer and labourer," specifically the Native House Rule Ordinance of Southern Nigeria, which gave the heads of houses the legal authority to control their slaves as "members of the house." If that solution was not acceptable because of differences between Northern and Southern Nigeria, then Lugard was to offer his views on whether or not some other "legalised relationship for domestic slavery" should be enacted.

This was indeed a striking proposal. In recommending the adoption of some system akin to the 1901 Native House Rule Ordinance once again, the CO was suggesting that Lugard's strategy of legal-status abolition had serious weaknesses. When the CO first proposed this solution in 1901, the "Movement" had been active, and Lugard had to restrain internal criticisms and override the CO as well.[112] Conditions had indeed changed by 1903. The addition of the central Hausa emirates to the Protectorate increased the danger of slave revolt because of the considerable numbers of slaves in Kano, Sokoto, Gwandu, and Katsina. The CO was deeply concerned; hence the request that Lugard take Wallace's warnings seriously.

Chamberlain's response gave Lugard's Nigerian critics a further opportunity to argue for legalized slavery. This time H. C. Gollan, the Chief Justice of Northern Nigeria, led the attack. Although Gollan opposed the adoption of the Native House Rule Ordinance or any other substitute for domestic slavery, he recommended that slavery be "fully recognized and regulated" through a "slight curtailment of the rights bestowed by the Slavery Proclamation, 1901." Gollan believed that legalization would put the colonial government "in a better position to overlook the upbringing of children born since the 31st March 1901 and prevent them from relapsing into the state of mind which, quite as much as the danger that would be created by a sudden destruction of the basis of native society, makes, in my opinion, the existence of a form of domestic slavery necessary, for the time being in this country, and which would, if not actively combatted, tend to give it continued existence."[113]

Gollan had not been in the vanguard of the "Movement" during the heated debate of late 1901, but it now became clear where his sympathies lay. He had become chief justice in November of that year in the midst of the fight, after serving as a Resident and cantonment magistrate. In these various capacities he had dealt with the full range of slavery cases; as chief justice he only heard charges of enslavement, but as Resident he had handled cases between masters and slaves. On his own admission, he considered himself an expert on the issue of slavery: "during the whole of my service in this country, I have been keenly interested in this question and have taken every opportunity of gathering information on the subject."

Gollan's amending proclamation would have regulated the work of domestic slaves, whereby the obligations of slaves to their masters and the rights of slaves to work on their own behalf were clearly articulated. Masters and slaves alike would have been subject to fines and/or imprisonment for violating the terms and conditions regulating the work regime. Slaves would have been allowed to own property "of every kind and description," and there would have been clear provision for the "release of domestic slaves from customary obligations" through self-purchase, third-party redemption, and concubinage. Severe penalties would have been enforced if slaves attempted to desert their masters, and the Protectorate courts would be able to force slaves to return, pay off their purchase price, or otherwise make arrangements to compensate their masters.[114]

Lugard's marginal notes make it clear that he was not persuaded. Was there danger that slaves would escape as soon as they became aware that their masters had no legal recourse to secure their return, as Gollan claimed? Lugard minuted: "Vide my memos." Was there "an abundance of land available which any man can easily obtain leave to cultivate?" Lugard retorted: "The Government can make it not easy." And as for Gollan's proposal to legalize slavery, Lugard noted curtly: "I do not concur."[115]

Lugard's reply, sent from his home at Abinger Common on August 21, 1903, was even stronger than in 1901. He wanted no part of a "retrograde step" that tolerated "despotic control" in legal form, and he said so explicitly and at length. There was some remonstrance from the Colonial Office that the Southern Nigeria Ordinance did not legalize slavery *de jure*, but this was tantamount to an admission that for all practical purposes it did so.[116] Far better, Lugard argued, "to continue the existing anomaly and in practice to minimise as far as may be the attendant difficulties."[117]

Then he seized the opportunity to review his policy in detail. Though that policy had been in effect at least since November 1901, Lugard had not provided a complete description of it to the Colonial Office, as already noted. Wallace and Burdon had alluded to certain portions with which they disagreed in November 1901, but until Lugard's letter of August 21, 1903 the CO did not have the details. Lugard now included a copy of each of his memoranda from November 22, 1901 to March 15, 1903, in addition to which he presented some aspects of his slavery policy that were not in the various memoranda.

One of these aspects concerned the Islamic courts, a subject to be examined in detail below in Chapter 4. Lugard outlined how these "native" courts would retain an independent jurisdiction "especially . . . in order to deal with such matters as this of domestic slavery." He alluded to the substantial advantage of allowing slavery matters to be dealt with in that venue instead of in the Protectorate courts with the constricting British law. He noted how effectively fugitive slaves could be discouraged by a combination of land regulation and vagrancy law. In his subsequent article in *The Empire and the Century* (1905) he stated that Residents could ensure that village headmen would deny fugitive slaves land on which to settle, or, "if a vagrant in a city would allow the native courts to deal with the matter."[118] These points could have a very practical significance in controlling the slave population if a community of interest were established between the British regime and the slave owners. Only the local authorities could mobilize sufficiently large numbers of police (the emirs' *dogarai*) to deal with such "minor" matters of law enforcement on a wide scale. They could do so because they had legal recourse through the Islamic courts. Once again Lugard was far in advance of his critics. As he complained to Lady Lugard, with obvious reference to Gollan but by inference to those in the CO as well, "almost every week I bowl out the Legal man on some point (or many points) he has missed. Indeed on the *Slavery* cases I have myself taught [them]."[119]

Meanwhile the Colonial Office had delayed its considerations of Lugard's draft proclamation for a considerable period of time; on February 1, 1904, Lugard sent a letter reminding the CO that his draft had been submitted the previous year. He followed that on June 7, 1904 with yet another reminder; in this letter, Lugard proposed that at least some action be taken, perhaps adopting and updating those sections of the proposed revisions that were virtually identical with the 1901 proclamation.[120]

Alfred Lyttleton, who had replaced Chamberlain at the Colonial Office, sought the advice of P. H. Ezechiel, one of the CO secretaries. Ezechiel's summary, submitted on August 6, 1904, accurately described Lugard's policies on slavery but recommended that tougher measures be adopted. Ezechiel noted that slavery

> forms the basis of the whole labour system of the Protectorate. Ultimately it must be replaced ... But it cannot be so replaced at once without turning the country upside down and ruining both the masters and the slaves ... Therefore *domestic slavery must be maintained for the present* [italics in original] – not recognised by law but maintained in practice ... The practical difficulty is that when a slave runs away from his master, a British magistrate is forbidden both by local and by British law to order his return.[121]

Ezechiel recognized that Lugard's vagrancy law could impede the flight of fugitive slaves, but such measures were not enough in his opinion.

Despite Ezechiel's reservations, Lyttleton put his final seal of approval on Lugard's policies two weeks later. On August 19, he wrote to Lugard: "I am willing ... to accept your opinion that the substitution for domestic slavery of a system which would not be slavery and which could therefore be recognized by law, is not at present possible in Northern Nigeria; and I approve the enactment of the draft Proclamation enclosed in your despatch of the 7th June."[122]

Although he deferred to Lugard, Lyttleton tried again to explain the rationale for the CO proposal to adopt some version of the Native House Rule Ordinance. In Southern Nigeria, Lyttleton pointed out,

> domestic slavery has not been legalised *as such* [italics in original], but has been replaced by the house system, so that all former domestic slaves have been made members of a house. It is true that most of the practical features of domestic slavery have been retained; but this was precisely the object of the legislation, while slavery has been abolished not only in name, but also probably in the eye of the strict law, for it is at least very questionable whether a Court in this country would regard the house system as slavery.[123]

Lyttleton continued that there had never been any intention to legalize slavery in Northern Nigeria, thereby making it clear that the CO did not side with the "Movement,"

> but that there should in substitution for it be a system which could be recognised by the law of the Protectorate without coming into conflict with British law. The legislation proposed by Mr. Gollan appears to be inadmissible, because by retaining the name of "domestic slavery" it would immediately challenge criticism in this country, and also because, so far as it purports to authorise a magistrate to make an order for the return of a slave to his master, it is probably ultra vires.[124]

Lugard had finally won the day. Proclamation No. 27 of 1904 was enacted on September 27 of that year.

There were subsequent amendments and modifications of a minor nature, but the basic slavery policy was now firmly in place. On June 12, 1905, an amendment increased the penalty for slave trading to fourteen years' imprisonment, while Memoranda Nos. 3, 4, 5, 10, 12, and 32 of 1901 and 1902 were superseded by Memorandum No. 6 of March 1905, subsequently revised slightly. In September 1906, Lugard published Memorandum No. 22 as an exposition of Islamic law and Caliphate custom with regard to slaves. For purposes of Memorandum No. 22, Lugard drew on the legal opinions of various *alkalai* (judges in Islamic courts), whose expertise was solicited through the Residents in the various emirates.

In November 1906, with regard to a case involving the division of an estate of slaves, the attorney-general issued a ruling on paragraphs 24 and 25 of the Slavery Proclamation of 1904, which held that all slave dealing was illegal, and that a slave could not be handed over to an emir in payment of court fees. The fact that the practice had occurred "shows how long the idea that slaves were realizable assets persisted in the minds of some administrative officers as well as in those of the natives themselves ... It should be noted, however, that the right of a Native Court to deal with cases in which slaves refused to work though they continued to live at their masters' expense was specifically upheld by paragraph 21 of this memorandum."[125] Finally, Slavery Proclamation No. 17 of 1907, enacted December 21, 1907, combined the proclamations of 1904 and 1905 into a single decree.[126]

The four-way debate on the slavery issue thus reached a settlement, as far as the Colonial Office was concerned. The military officers favoring emancipation had lost out early on. The political officers of the "Movement" who had advocated retention of slavery in a legal capacity were bested as well. The Colonial Office officials who wanted to rationalize slavery policy and had therefore proposed that Northern Nigerian law be brought into line with those of the Gold Coast and Southern Nigeria acceded to Lugard's demur. Lugard's own chosen policy of legal subterfuge became the accepted method. Against an impressive array of opponents, Lugard had been able to impose his policy on the military, on his own political family, on the Colonial Office, and by so doing, on the slaves and masters of Northern Nigeria.

Final foray against Lugard's policies

There was one last brief foray against Lugard's slavery policies in 1907 and early 1908, when various officials reported that there were problems with the updated Slavery Proclamation of 1907. The discussion was begun afresh when C. L. Temple wrote to Governor Percy Girouard, Lugard's successor, that

> It is desertions in general, especially to other Provinces, which are the cause of anxiety. At present the Resident finds it hard to deal with these as he is not legally empowered to insist on domestics returning to their homes (although he generally does so and is thereby placed in a very invidious position). I understood that N.N.C.J. [Northern Nigeria Chief Justice] Mendeley had

93

> thought a law on similar lines to the Household Proclamation in S. Nigeria might be required for this Protectorate.[127]

Temple consciously reopened the old debate over Lugard's strategy for dealing with fugitive slaves by once again calling attention to the Native House Rule Ordinance of Southern Nigeria.

C. W. Orr fully identified Temple's intentions in a marginal note a few weeks later:

> This raises the whole question of slavery and whether the present system of dealing with it might not be altered for the better by legislation. H. E. will probably wish to discuss the matter with him and Major Burdon later.[128]

The attorney-general also understood the implications. He (or an assistant) minuted "Yes . . . this is of course illegal but necessary."[129] Should anything be done? The matter was referred to Chief Justice Ernest V. Parodi for consideration.

In January 1908, Parodi proposed that Governor Girouard adopt the Southern Nigeria House Rule Ordinance, as Parodi's predecessor, Mendeley, had also done. The chief justice was concerned with the fact that the proclamation contained "about two pages of printed matter . . . [on] the wholesale assertion of freedom [of slaves]" and twenty-four pages on "methods of dealing with cases of assertion of freedom," which in effect "explained away" a great deal of the proclamation. He claimed that Memorandum No. 22 was intended to achieve virtually the same result as the Southern Nigerian House Rule ordinance; the difference was that the Southern Nigerian solution authorized political officials to enforce compliance, while the Northern Nigerian remedy afforded no legal protection to political officers.[130] If Parodi was aware of the earlier debate, he certainly did not respect the outcome. Girouard appears to have thought the proposal was something new entirely.

After Girouard reflected on the issue, he wrote to the Earl of Crewe at the Colonial Office suggesting either the adoption of the Southern Nigeria model or the granting of full emancipation to all slaves.[131] The Colonial Office responded in disbelief; its curt reply informed Girouard that the issue had been decided in favor of Lugard's strategy of legal-status abolition. There would be no further discussion. Lugard's approach was allowed to stand as it had been reconfirmed in Proclamation No. 17 of 1907, which established "that any Non-Native who assists in the surrender of a fugitive slave to his master or owner shall be liable to be punished."[132] Lugard's policies were finally and firmly entrenched.

In 1910, the Statute Laws Revision Proclamation incorporated the 1907 proclamation *verbatim*, with the exception of redundant sections referring to earlier measures. Chapter 11 of the schedule continued in force until the amalgamation of Northern and Southern Nigeria and its replacement by Ordinances No. 15 and No. 35 of 1916. Ordinance No. 15, later Chapter 21 of the Laws of Nigeria, was enacted on May 16, 1916. Ordinance No. 35, dated August 16, 1916, became Chapter 83 of the Laws of Nigeria. It was identical to earlier legislation, with the exception of superficial revisions.[133]

Fugitive policy in action

At the start of 1906, Lugard could claim that he had successfully adhered to a narrow and even tortuous line between the anti-slavery principles espoused in Britain and the need to maintain political calm and economic stability in Northern Nigeria.[134] Through his response to the "Movement" he had made flight very difficult for the slaves, and so kept many of them at their labor, thereby counteracting the fugitive slave problem to some extent. Yet at the same time he maintained the fiction that the legal status of slavery no longer existed. Later, Margery Perham, Lugard's biographer, would express surprise that his policy did not engender greater overt opposition from the emirs. Apparently, she did not understand that slavery persisted rather than being abolished.[135] Lugard too came to believe that he had abolished slavery, or at least his public image required such an interpretation. His role as an anti-slavery expert in the League of Nations and his request for full documentation on the evolution of his policies in Northern Nigeria attest to this stance. Lethem willingly obliged the father of Indirect Rule in assembling the materials to support this image in his 1931 "Early History of Anti-Slavery Legislation," so that Lugard could maintain his stature as anti-slavery crusader.

The Slavery Proclamation of 1904 was the outcome of long debate. It remained a penal offense for British officials to participate in the return of fugitives, and only in that year did the sale of slaves become illegal.[136] Nonetheless, there was a concerted effort to prevent slaves from escaping. Few wrote quite so openly about the contravention of official policy as did Major H. R. Beddoes in 1904, who stated publicly that the return of fugitives was "continually being done by every official . . . with the connivance of the Government."[137] Restoration was easier when a slave had not crossed a provincial boundary, for then there was no need to involve administrative staff or the system of Islamic courts with attendant paper work and possible disagreements. By and large the Residents said little, either then or later. They quietly went about this particular task, though as Perham noted, some at least must have found their duty a painful one.[138]

There was still only a very small number of British officials in Northern Nigeria: even by 1906, just seventy-five in administrative positions to supervise that vast territory.[139] Their isolation, however, lent them some of the powers of a satrap. Even in Zaria Province, on the main road to Kano and on the line of the railway-to-be, an official could easily find himself seven days away from any superior, no telegraph to bother him, frequent decisions being made on slavery issues, no reports forwarded until long after the event, and strong motives to maintain "face" through mutual support among colonial officers.[140] Under these circumstances a strong position could often be taken towards fugitives, as Popham Lobb and Abadie both admitted.

Even though they rendered themselves liable to prosecution, Residents are known to have instructed or to have authorized Islamic courts "to assist slave owners to recover fugitive slaves."[141] Masters were able to travel to other provinces and to appeal to an Islamic court for the return of a fugitive. In 1907–1908, Residents knew that such actions were occurring and fully collaborated in the return of fugitives. Islamic court records from 1913–14 suggest that Residents still allowed the return of fugitives, despite the colonial law to the contrary.[142]

Thus British officials returned fugitive slaves to their masters. A letter from the Assistant Resident at Sokoto in 1909 is especially revealing. Martin Kisch wrote that

> I engaged a new cook's mate today, a very good looking Fulani called Abdu in place of a runaway slave from Birnin Kebbi, who was reclaimed by his master, and so had to be sent back.[143]

It is striking that even a slave who had succeeded in entering the household of the second-highest British official in the capital of the Caliphate was not safe from the policy of returning fugitive slaves. No matter what the "law" said about the illegality of British participation in their return, the net was tight. In this case, Kisch probably acted under the provision of the Masters and Servants Proclamation, but whatever the technicality of the case, his bold comment reveals what was really happening.

In one of his many frustrated but always secret criticisms of the British regime, the Rev. Miller raised the issue of slavery in a letter to Governor Girouard in 1908. He knew that fugitives were still being returned to their masters on a regular basis, and even more damning, he made it clear that children born after the 1901 slavery proclamation were not being treated as freeborn:

> I have asked at least fifty influential people and malams and I have never yet met one who has heard of any such law [that children born after March 31, 1901 were free], and merely consider it a fancy of my own brain! They are constantly being handed over to their masters, even in the case where one parent is free.[144]

In Kano and Sokoto, it was convenient to believe that the date when children were born free coincided with the conquest in 1903. Whether or not all children born after that date were considered free is open to speculation, moreover.

Although the Rev. Miller was shocked by the continued cooperation of British authorities in maintaining slavery, the SIM missionaries were more accepting. In early 1908, when two slaves sought sanctuary at the Wushishi mission station, claiming that they had fled the Freed Slaves' Home at Zungeru, the Rev. Stirrett sought to learn their true status.[145] They were fugitive slaves, as he dutifully reported to the colonial authorities:

I returned the boy Aku Mugu. He is not a Freed Slaves Home boy at all. On investigation, there turned out to be no particle of truth in his statement of alleged ill treatment, in fact his story was a pack of lies from beginning to end. The other boy Audu expressed his desire to go back to his master, and I have accordingly sent him there.[146]

The colonial regime knew that Stirrett was a willing accomplice in the policy of keeping slaves in line. On another occasion Stirrett was asked to search for a freed slave from the Home, who was a ward of a WAFF soldier. It is not known if the escaped *freed* slave was caught.[147]

The debate over slavery policy may have been decided in Lugard's favor, but it was really only the success of other measures relating to the Islamic courts, land, and taxation that eroded slavery as an institution. These subjects are examined in the chapters that follow. The fugitive question was the focus of debate in the early years, and as we have seen, the colonial state and the Caliphate aristocracy reached an accommodation on the return of slaves, no matter what the stated policy on the question was. Lugard understood the implications of sudden and full emancipation by administrative fiat, a position that some of the early military officers and missionaries had begun to implement, and he demonstrated perspicacity in steering a steady course through the difficult early years of conquest and consolidation. In a sense, therefore, one might easily conclude that Lugard was an intelligent moderate on the slavery issue in a context in which some wanted to retain slavery as a legal institution or under a thinly disguised substitute, while others wanted to abolish it completely.

How correct would such a judgment be? The benefits of the slavery policy were certainly both manifest and large. The colonial government was required to make no cash outlay either for financing emancipation or for the struggles that would have followed any attempt to manumit by force. Northern Nigeria's emirs, nobles, landlords, and proto-capitalists – in short the masters – were also beneficiaries. They were able to salvage far more from the wreck of the Sokoto Caliphate than they could have realistically anticipated. Finally, the Northern Nigerian economy was able to begin its adaptation to these changes with much less wrenching than would have followed an all-at-once abolition of slavery.

These benefits could be obtained, however, only if further huge costs of modified servitude were inflicted on a slave population that had already paid enormously. For most of the slaves, life had been full of uncompensated forced labor, akin to some giant, malevolent tax. Those who had been captured had suffered direct hardships and the rupture of their families. Even before that, the need to defend against slave raids had imposed reduced standards of living and a life of perpetual watching and waiting. For slaves, Lugard's policy changed the way in which they would be exploited, but because they had little political power and influence, their opinions could usually be ignored.

4

Emancipation and the law

Lugard's strategy to reform slavery was off to a hesitant start. While the High Commissioner had prevailed over both the "Movement" and the Colonial Office in the policy debate, slaves had fled in large numbers, with desertions probably numbering in the hundreds of thousands by 1906. Despite the crisis surrounding the slavery issue, however, Lugard maintained a clear vision of the reforms he intended to implement. He still desired that slavery be phased out gradually. By 1903 the supply of new slaves had been reduced to a trickle because slave raiding and the trade in slaves were prohibited and because children born after March 31, 1901 were free. While there was still some kidnapping, and slave raiding continued across the border in German territory, there was no question that the number of slaves entering the market was dwindling rapidly.[1]

The main unfinished issue in Lugard's plan to undermine slavery involved how slaves might obtain their freedom other than through desertion. For that purpose, Lugard looked to Islamic practices that allowed slaves to acquire their freedom through self-purchase or redemption by third parties. British reforms attempted to make these practices obligatory upon demand. This tended to favor male slaves, and hence much of the following discussion is concerned with the fate of male slaves. Female slaves were consigned to a different category that had to do with the male chauvinism of Islamic society and Edwardian England. Women were treated differently on the assumption that their cases were variations on questions of matrimony and their fates tied to that of husbands and masters. Emancipation through self-ransom was not, therefore, intended to apply to women, although to a limited degree it did so.

A major dimension of Lugard's reformist vision was his reliance on the Islamic courts to uphold his policies. Since the legal status of slavery had been abolished, it will seem curious, if not an outright contradiction, that the Islamic legal system would be invoked to regulate reforms of an institution that had no legal recognition under British Protectorate law. To explain how this apparent difficulty could be overcome, Lugard made a careful distinction between the British Provincial courts and the Islamic courts of the

98

emirates that were based on the *shari'a*, but even so, the legalisms of his policies formed a complex web whose legal threads ensnared his critics and somehow enabled him to hold Caliphate society together through the difficult transition under colonial rule.

The use of the Islamic courts to uphold the policy of legal-status abolition was an essential component of Lugard's Indirect Rule. On the one hand, it allowed Lugard to claim that British ideals were being imposed on the conquered peoples of the Sokoto Caliphate, while on the other hand, he could sanction practices and policies that continued the legal tradition of the Caliphate with respect to slavery. In some cases, retreat from British ideals would have attracted far too much attention, and Lugard certainly did not want criticism. Thus slave raiding and slave trading were made illegal in Islamic courts as well as in British courts. Yet for the large slave population of Northern Nigeria, Caliphate law continued to define the terms of slavery and emancipation.

Lugard's views on self-redemption

Lugard was an expert on Islamic law concerning the emancipation of slaves well before he arrived in the Sokoto Caliphate. His experience in East Africa, as employee of the Imperial British East Africa Company, had introduced him to Islamic practices of self-redemption and ransom by third parties, and he had early made it clear that he favored a mechanism whereby slaves could purchase their own freedom. He developed his ideas in 1890 in the context of a crisis over fugitive slaves who had been granted asylum at Rabai, the mission station near Mombasa. G. S. Mackenzie, IBEAC administrator in Mombasa, instituted a program of ransoming escaped slaves with Company funds, much of which was later reimbursed by the missionaries and the government.[2] In all, 1,421 slaves were ransomed with these funds.[3]

Lugard, however, was in profound disagreement with this policy of Company-financed ransom. He foresaw future great expense and difficulty, in particular because there were many runaway slaves in settlements up-country. As Fred Morton has demonstrated, many tens of thousands of slaves had fled into the interior of the Swahili coast by 1890. Fuladoyo and Makongeni, near Rabai, were among numerous fortified settlements ("stockaded villages," wrote Lugard) of these fugitives, all straining relations with Muslim slave owners.[4]

In January 1890, Lugard made his own views clear to Company officials, arguing that Mackenzie's efforts to compensate slave owners should not be extended to the ransoming of the fugitives at Fuladoyo and Makongeni. In criticizing Mackenzie's approach, Lugard argued in favor of a policy wherein "each man shall himself with his own hands and out of his money pay his master, when he has accumulated sufficient."[5] Lugard had found that the Fuladoyo fugitives anticipated that they too would be ransomed by the Company, their expectations heightened by the visit of a "native missionary" who had registered their names in preparation for the payments.[6] The "native missionary" was none other than the Rev. William Jones, a freed slave of Yao origin who had been trained in Bombay and who was responsible for harboring the fugitive slaves at Rabai. Jones had forced the crisis on the IBEAC and was now serving as intermediary in arranging for the legal recognition of freedom for his wards.[7]

Lugard had no intention of letting the Company compensate the former slave owners for the loss of their slaves. He had a very different plan in mind:

> I proposed that those who really valued their freedom should accept work from the Company, & register their names together with a certain monthly deduction from their pay, which when it had reached the sum necessary to purchase their freedom, should be paid by them to their masters ... They eagerly accepted these terms ... We keep before the slave the personal nature of his contract – he earns the money himself, & pays it himself to his master, – & thereby I believe he will value much more the state of liberty he has earned, & appreciate the justice of the transaction ... When I passed through Fuladoyo last month, I was told six villages were ready to accept work, & work off their ransom.[8]

Later in January of 1890, he carried on similar discussions at the near-by slave settlement of Makongeni.[9]

As it happened, the "Fuladoyo experiment" was not a success. Contrary to the "eager acceptance" referred to in the quotation, the fugitive slaves believed that sanctuary at the missionary settlements was sufficient. Lugard was obviously upset. In his diary he wrote that

> it would be an excellent thing to get an Arab to come to Rabai and seize his slave! Extraordinary at this sounds, I believe its effect would be very good. They would learn more than by hours of talking that the missions or Company will not harbour them, and finding they are even safer at Fuladoyo than Rabai, they would all return, and be only too anxious to redeem themselves as I propose.[10]

Wallace, Burdon, and other members of the "Movement" might have been surprised that Lugard had once entertained the idea of letting slave owners seize their escaped slaves – and from missionaries as well! By the time Lugard reached Northern Nigeria, however, he had developed his ideas considerably further and did not need to rely on the expediencies that the "Movement" would have favored.

The Muslim masters of the Swahili coast also exhibited dissatisfaction with Lugard's plan for self-redemption, complaining that the purchase price of MT$15 (Maria Theresa thalers) was low, even lower than the MT$25 paid under the earlier scheme at Fuladoyo. The price was less than £3, compared to prices usually more than double that agreed on by masters and slaves in Northern Nigeria a few years later.[11] Lugard spent considerable time persuading both masters and slaves to accept his mediation, but eventually the slaves agreed to return to their villages and the masters accepted the proffered sum. Lugard wrote that "once more all seemed to augur well for success." The plan for self-emancipation proceeded.[12]

In the event, it was a failure in all but its legacy. Lugard left the coastal district shortly thereafter, leaving the scheme in the hands of William Jones, whose ardent commitment to the abolition of slavery and the emancipation of slaves seemed to have escaped Lugard's full attention. As Lugard wrote in *East African Empire*,

> I regret, however, to say that long afterwards (when in Uganda), I had a desponding letter from Mr. Jones, saying the scheme had fallen through. On my way back, I made inquiries ... at Rabai, and they told me that by the aid of the documents I had left in their hands they had succeeded in arranging for a few men to work out their freedom, but they gave me to understand that the scheme in its entirety, as I had left it, was non-existent.[13]

Instead, the flight of slaves from their masters all along the Swahili coast continued unabated, probably to Jones' satisfaction.

Lugard had learned how difficult it was to stop the flight of slaves once the exodus was underway. On July 4, 1891, Lugard wrote in his diary:

> Anniversary of American slave abolition I believe. This day last year I had the big Fugitive Slave Shauri [meeting] at Rabai, and wrote down all the names of those who wished to redeem themselves (men and women). I took an infinite trouble ... over this matter – all, I fear, to collapse the moment I left the coast.[14]

He would have to wait until he became High Commissioner of Northern Nigeria before he could put into place the policy of self-ransom that he so explicitly advocated in East Africa and continued to champion thereafter.

As he wrote in 1893 after leaving East Africa, it would be better to encourage slaves to purchase their own freedom than to allow missionaries or government to subsidize their redemption.[15] Not only were his ideas clearly developed well before he arrived in the Sokoto Caliphate, but he also decided that missionaries must not be allowed to interfere in slavery matters. Indeed precisely because of his experience at Rabai, he would restrict the movements of missionaries in the Muslim areas of Northern Nigeria. Without missionary interference, he would be prepared to institute his theories on legal-status abolition. He would do so by relying on the Islamic court system and Muslim legal tradition in matters regarding slavery.

Slavery and the courts

Reliance on the Islamic courts was a central component in Lugard's famous theory of Indirect Rule, but it has gone virtually unnoticed that one reason for the importance of the Islamic courts in Lugard's grand scheme was that they dealt with matters relating to slavery. Most scholars have focused on the political and administrative dimensions of Indirect Rule, whereby the British regime governed through the Fulbe aristocracy, retaining most features of the Caliphate state. Colonial reforms centered on the elimination of perceived abuses, but otherwise the existing system was not only allowed to continue but was actually glorified. Such a policy promoted Hausa as the language of administration, relied on Islamic education, and maintained Islamic law.[16] The continuation of slavery as a domestic institution was consistent with Lugard's intentions. The Islamic courts would regulate domestic slavery.

Lugard carefully distinguished between the function of the Provincial courts and the role of the existing Islamic courts. The Provincial courts would uphold British law, whereby the legal status of slavery had been abolished. There was one Provincial court per province, with the Resident or Acting Resident having full jurisdiction. The next senior member of the Provincial Staff could be appointed as commissioner of the court to deal with all but the most serious cases, and all political officers and district superintendents of the Constabulary were ex-officio commissioners of the Provincial courts.[17] Provincial courts dealt primarily with cases of enslavement and slave dealing, both of which were illegal, and heard cases relating to slavery itself only on appeal, such as when ill treatment was a factor. Otherwise slavery cases were left to the Islamic courts and the judicial councils of the emirs, where the *shari'a* was in force in much the same way that it had been under the Caliphate.

The "system of domestic slavery" was not specifically mentioned in section 9 of the Provincial Courts Proclamation, since, under clause 2 of Proclamation 27 of 1904, "the Status of Slavery is in no way recognised by the British Courts." The holding of slaves was "lawful under Native law" and was "not forbidden by the Proclamation." Cases that arose out of "those domestic relations would, therefore, as far as possible, be tried by the Native Courts ... provided that a Criminal case under the Slavery Proclamation was not involved."[18] Criminal cases that properly belonged in the Provincial courts included enslavement and slave trading. As Lugard noted in 1903, "The status of slavery is not recognized by British Courts, and no rights accruing from ownership of slaves can be enforced in them while every person has the right to assert his freedom, and could appeal to the Courts if assaulted or captured in the exercise of that right of assertion."[19] But his intention was that these cases would never reach a British court.

The Islamic courts of the Caliphate were reorganized and "legitimized" as part of the colonial system. Each legally recognized Islamic court was issued a warrant constituting it as a "Native Court," which established its jurisdiction separate from the Provincial courts. As Lugard elaborated in his 1906 *Instructions to Political and Other Officers*:

> Since a Native Court is not precluded (as a British Court is) from taking cognizance of the Status of Slavery, cases relating to the matters [of marriage relations, debt, divorce, inheritance, and petty assaults], and complicated by their relation to the Servile Status, can be dealt with by such Courts to the extent described in Memos. 6 and 22; but, of course, all Criminal cases in

connection with slavery must be dealt with by Provincial Courts, such as enslaving, transactions in slaves, murder or assault upon a slave and even such Civil actions as a complaint against a Slave-owner for forcible detention &c.; for in these cases the Native Code might either fail to recognise that an offence had been committed, or to accord equality before the Law to Master and Slave. A Native Court can, however, usefully decide causes of difference between the Slave and his Master, provided that the right to his freedom is not denied to the Slave by the British Court declining to hear his appeal, and compelling him to go to a Native Court in which that right would not be admitted. Native Courts may, however, deal with cases of persistent refusal to work on the part of a slave who does not assert his freedom, but continues to benefit by the maintenance, &c., as provided by his master, without making an adequate return. (Memo. 6, para. 21)[20]

Lugard clearly did not mean that the abolition of the legal status of slavery deprived the Islamic legal system from handling slavery cases in a legal fashion. Quite the contrary: the existing judicial mechanisms for controlling the slave population were to continue, albeit stripped of any support for enslavement and slave trading.

Initially, the Provincial courts did handle questions of domestic slavery, but gradually fewer of these cases made it to this level. In 1902, for example, the Bauchi Provincial court heard a typical case of ransom by a third party, the decision reading as follows:

> This is to certify that Corporal Ogungwayi has this day paid the sum of Two Pounds and ten shillings to Tambari of Bauchi for the redemption of the Female Domestic Slave Matanyaki and that the latter is therefore free to marry the former if she pleases. Witness my hand and seal of Office, Bauchi Oct 7–02, Ch Temple, Resident.[21]

Very soon, this type of case would fall only within the jurisdiction of the Islamic courts, as had been the case under the Caliphate. It was far too mundane a matter for the Provincial courts.

More typically, the Provincial courts heard serious matters of enslavement, and eventually, slave trading. In 1902, Temple issued a warrant for the arrest of Chief Tsofo of Duguri to stand trial before the Provincial court for murder, enslavement, and other offenses. Tsofo "had refused to deliver" about forty Gwaram slaves:

> about 25 of these I find are domestic slaves bought by Duguri from the ex-emir, so it appears to me reasonable that he should retain them. The remaining 15 who are freeborn and were enslaved I have set free and returned to Guaram. They appear in the Oct. Freed Slave list.[22]

Lugard, demonstrating his infinite capacity to deal in legal distinctions, informed Temple that "it is not illegal to sell a domestic slave (if not deported) at present, but the practice should be checked."[23] In 1902, "deported" meant sale outside of the province. Sale within each emirate was still legal.

Temple, the future Lt.-Governor and great defender of Indirect Rule, had difficulty responding to his chief in his young days, but he tried.

> With regard to Your Excellency's Memo stating that the sale of domestic slaves is not illegal so long as it not effected with the object of deporting the slaves, I think that as regards to this province no domestic slave would be sold except with this object. Certainly in the Case R [Rex] vs Osuman & others (No. 36) recently tried in the Provincial Court I have no doubt that the object was to deport the slave to Kano.

Temple claimed that "little exchange of [slave] property on a large scale takes place between residents of the district of Bauchi itself or of Gombe itself: or Ningi itself: the exchange takes place between Gombe people and Bauchi people, or between Ningi people & Gombe people, or between traders and Bauchi people, so that if a domestic slave entered into the bargaining the slave would almost certainly be deported."[24] Lugard, with patience, minuted, "Yes but this must be *proved* in a legal case. You must always state [the] section" of the legal code.

In 1903 the Provincial courts were still dealing with simple matters of slave emancipation. In Sokoto, Burdon considered it "most important that all Whitemen should be given to understand that domestic slavery is *not* abolished, that all slaves were not freed, and that no slave is free unless he has been legally freed by his master or in some Protectorate Court."[25] Lugard would soon instruct his subordinates to leave such matters to the Islamic courts.

Gollan's draft memorandum on slavery in 1903, which aimed to legalise slavery, would have let all courts, both Provincial and Muslim, deal with issues relating to slavery. On this point, too, Lugard was at odds with the "Movement," because he intended that only Islamic courts would have jurisdiction over such cases. In Gollan's draft, for example, slaves would have had the protection of any court in setting the price of redemption and securing full freedom, once payment had been made. For Lugard, the abolition of the legal status of slavery in the Provincial courts did not preclude the Islamic courts from continuing to recognize that status and thereby uphold slavery as an institution, subject only to the restrictions already noted on "criminal" matters relating to enslavement and trade.[26]

Lugard wanted all slavery cases, other than charges of enslavement and slave trading, shifted to the Islamic courts as quickly as possible. He specifically instructed Residents to

> study the procedure of their own and of other Provinces, and note any point upon which there exists elsewhere an interpretation of the law or a custom more liberal than that which obtains in their Province, and should bring pressure to bear upon the Native Courts and Emirs to adopt it. This is, so to speak, to apply the principle of "the most-favoured-nation clause," and to level up every Province to the most liberal treatment accorded in each particular in any other Province.[27]

In August 1903, Lugard informed the Colonial Office that he was "about to

write one [a memorandum] giving the outline of the Koranic Law as ampli-
fied and interpreted by the Mohamedan Legislators in so far as it defines the
rights of the slave and the liabilities of the master in respect of his slave. The
liberality of some of these rules will I think come as a surprise to many, and
these are inforceable without incurring prejudice and by the Mahomedan
Courts themselves. It is possible gradually to further improve on them."
Lugard began this memorandum in late 1903 or early 1904. It ultimately
became Memorandum No. 22 of 1906 and would constitute instructions to
Residents in upholding the "Native" courts.

Lugard needed to know how the Islamic courts dealt with slavery cases.
Consequently, he asked his subordinates to report on their legal dealings. In
particular, it was necessary to understand the "secular justice" which was an
extension of the *shari'a* but based on local practice and the wisdom of the
emir and his advisors as frequently expressed through the various Judicial
Councils of the emirs. The Judicial Council of each emirate served as the
court of appeal in matters relating to land, violence, theft, and slavery,
among other matters. In disputes relating to land, for example, the courts
followed the principle of *hukm al-basatin lana* (Arabic), "the judgment of
gardens is Ours (the emir's)."[28]

A new principle, *hukm zamanna* (Arabic), "legislation of our time,"
referred to colonial laws and reforms imposed from above, specifically with
respect to slavery.[29] The application of this principle was a slow process that
required frequent consultation with the Residents of each province. As
Christelow has observed with respect to the Judicial Council of Kano:

> Sometimes, particularly in slavery cases, litigants were sent directly to "the
> barracks" [office of the British Resident] for the decision or advice of the
> Resident. Slavery was of direct concern to administrators responsible for
> enforcing the anti-slavery proclamations. Slavery cases sometimes required a
> judgment call, especially about the age of a child, or involved ambiguous
> points of law, such as whether a concubine had the legal status of slave or wife
> ... It is important that these cases seemed to involve no written communication
> to or from the Resident. A representative of the emir would convey the litigants
> to "the barracks," and come back to report orally the Resident's decision.
> Evidently, both the British Resident and the emir saw a need to consult over
> the delicate issue of slavery, but not to record the matter in official communi-
> cations which might be examined by higher authorities.[30]

The Sokoto courts and the Judicial Councils would oversee what was not
recognized as legal in the British courts – the relationship between slave and
master.

Memorandum No. 22, "The Condition of Slaves and the Native Law
Regarding Slavery in Northern Nigeria," consisted of various "rulings by
Alkalis of acknowledged authority, as have reached me from Residents of
different Provinces in reply to circular questions." Its purpose was to
accelerate the shift of slavery cases to the Islamic courts.[31] Residents were
to see that the Islamic courts "acted in accordance with its provisions,

embodying as they would such liberal and humane rules as their own Koranic law prescribed."[32] Lugard wanted "especially retained this independent jurisdiction of Native Courts – with necessary safeguards – in order to deal with such matters as this of domestic slavery."[33]

The *shari'a* court in Bida led the way in dealing with slavery cases. In 1905, this court was praised because it had "eagerly adopted the principle of ransom and self-redemption," with the result that "Complaints of desertion of slaves are decreasing . . . [in part because of] their knowledge that they can redeem themselves for a reasonable sum, while they are allowed more time to work for themselves; and partly [because of] the fact that runaway slaves are not allowed to take up land without permission."[34] In 1905, Orr was encouraging redemption through the Islamic court in Zaria "by every means in my power, thus utilising native customs, native ideas and native machinery in the development of the country along progressive lines, rather than imported ideas and novel machinery which are not understood and are apt to be resented."[35] A similar trend was apparent in Ilorin. By 1906, it was "very rare for slave cases to appear before the [Provincial] court" there.[36]

By 1907, W. F. Gowers reported that the "increase in the number of slavery cases [in the Islamic court in Bauchi] is not due to any increase in crime but to the more effective cooperation of the native administration, by which the large majority of cases tried this year were brought to light."[37] As Howard elaborated,

> the number of cases which were formerly dealt with in the Provincial Court and which are now referred to the Native Court is steadily increasing. I am of opinion that with a Native Court as efficient and trustworthy as that of Bauchi the Provincial Court should only deal with slave dealing cases and with cases in which Government employees are concerned. All cases of importance dealt with by the Alkali are carefully discussed with me; it is the practice at Bauchi for the Alkali and the Liman Ajia to come down every morning to the Resident's Office to discuss cases.[38]

A marginal note on Howard's report stated approval: "very sound so long as the cases are not prejudged." By 1908, "practically all" slaves liberated in the emirates passed through the Islamic courts.[39]

Following Lugard's instructions, the political staff exchanged information on how the Islamic courts dealt with slavery matters. Temple found that the court in Bauchi was much less formal in its proceedings than that in Bida, where Burdon was in charge. In an effort to adhere more closely to the Bida model, Temple instructed the *alkali* to send in written reports on every case. Henceforth, witnesses were expected to be examined more carefully as well.[40] As Tukur has noted, the Islamic court in Yola continued to adjudicate slavery cases in 1904, as it had always done; "Up to this time the [official] position was that only the Provincial Courts could handle such cases." At this time, the Islamic court in Yola, at least, was deciding in favor of slaves trying to establish or obtain their freedom and dealt harshly with masters seeking to prove that plaintiffs were their slaves.[41]

Lugard was not keen on too liberal interpretation of Islamic law with regard to slavery, however. He intended that the Islamic courts would help prevent slaves from deserting by enforcing labor contracts associated with self-redemption. In 1905, he described how the courts would be used to return fugitives to their masters, not because they had run away but because they were not fulfilling their labor obligations:

> whereas the British Courts lend him [the master] no assistance in compelling his slave to do his proper day's work, or in punishing him if he runs away – while the assistance of the Native Courts is but a very precarious one – he can, if he employs free labour, obtain the full assistance of the Administration in enforcing the contract, and punishing its breach, and it should be explained to him how he should enter into a contract enforceable at law. It is not necessary that such contracts (in order to be legally enforceable) should be in writing. A verbal undertaking in the presence of witnesses is sufficient, and it may be enforced either by a Provincial or by a Native Court.[42]

Lugard's highly legalistic approach assured that slavery had no legal status without jeopardizing control of the labor force. As he instructed Residents in 1905, "if the Resident is (according to supposition) convinced that the [fugutive slave] man is unfit to lead an independent life, he may, while admitting the right of the slave to freedom, withhold the special assistance required. He may also utilise the services of the Native Court in the manner described in Memo. 8, para. 10 [which states that the Native Court can make him work, p. 174]."[43]

The Islamic courts could pursue other legal means of dealing with fugitives. In cases where villages were providing sanctuary to escaped slaves, it was possible to summon the villagers to an Islamic court to defend their actions. In 1904, several villages in Nassarawa Province "refused point blank to send any [fugitives] in and have driven out the Emir's messengers with insults or even blows." At least three villages were involved in these episodes. Webster was determined that "these pagan towns should not be allowed to give the runaways asylum, especially in a Province like this where many of the slaves have been caught within the last 20 years from villages one or two days distant."[44] Webster was told to use his own judgment in punishing the villages that refused to cooperate. Webster's solution, which received Lugard's blessing, was to punish these villages for refusing to comply with a court summons, not for harboring fugitives.[45] This is only one instance of the application of collective punishment, a feature of colonial policy that continued an earlier Caliphate principle.[46]

Lugard's instructions in the delicate matter of escaped slaves were to rely on the Islamic courts to enforce the return of fugitives and to punish those who harbored or assisted slaves in running away. In this way, the colonial regime could demonstrate its intention "not to interfere with domestic slavery." As Lugard made clear in 1905,

> If a Native Court summons a runaway slave, with a view to investigating his case – the slave being a *bona fide* domestic slave – and the summons is

107

disobeyed, it may be enforced like any other, in the last resort by the Administration. If, however, the fugitive offers redemption money, it must, in such a case, always be accepted. It must be clearly understood, however, that the summons of the Native Court does not mean that the question of rendition of the runaway is prejudged and will necessarily be ordered, but that the Court will investigate the circumstances and decide equitably whether there is any debt of obligation due from the fugitive. In no case may a Provincial court assist in the capture of a runaway slave, in order that he may be surrendered to his owner in virtue of any claim to his person arising solely from his status as a slave.[47]

Hence the "legal status" was not a factor, but the fact that the slave owed money towards his ransom or was otherwise under "contract" to work in lieu of accommodation, etc. was sufficient to return the slave. In short, the slave was not free to alter the conditions of his relationship with his master.

This important stipulation forced slaves to continue to work for their masters, even though land was available that could have been farmed. British statements about the demise of slavery being bad for the country obviously took the point of view of the masters as uppermost. Presumably, the slaves cared little about what happened to the country and probably would have been at least as well off on their own land as they were on that of their masters. The government did not want roaming bands of ex-slaves interfering with tax collection, commerce, and settled agriculture, which would have entailed a much bigger task of policing the countryside at considerably greater expense.

The Islamic courts and redemption of slaves

Lugard's blueprint for social change in Muslim Northern Nigeria emphasized the redemption of slaves either through lump-sum payments by third parties (*fansa*) or through instalments while slaves worked off their own ransoms (*fansar kai*). The Islamic courts would be the institution that monitored slave emancipation, although in engineering the gradual decline of slavery, Lugard also recognized the importance of pious acts on the part of masters and the eventual emancipation of concubines who bore children. As he observed in Special Memo No. 10 (Slavery), January 18, 1902:

> in some districts the right of a slave to redeem himself is recognised by the owner and ... in such cases a slave is set free on the understanding that for an agreed period he shall pay a proportion of his earnings to his former master. In my view it is desirable to encourage such an arrangement since on the side of the master it enables him to realise money which he in all probability actually paid for the slave under a regime when such an investment was not illegal, and on the side of the slave probably tends to make him value what he has purchased by his own efforts. Residents will therefore promote such arrangements.[48]

Not only was "self-redemption ... recognised by Mohammedan law," but Lugard claimed "that ample opportunity is given, and there is no difficulty in purchasing freedom."[49]

Lugard's opponents, who favored the legal continuation of slavery, shared similar views as to the desirability of promoting self-redemption. Burdon, for example, believed that "slavery will die a natural death within 10 years of our stopping slave-raiding, and by forcing the slaves to ransom themselves we shall give them an incentive to extra work, whereby the prosperity of the country will be increased instead of being killed."[50] It was accepted wisdom that slavery would gradually decline once the source of slaves was eliminated, although the experience of the USA proved that slavery did not necessarily decline under such circumstances.

In 1905 the Islamic court in Sokoto began to enforce the right of slaves to earn their own ransom, no matter whether a master agreed or not. This reform, which Burdon referred to as "compulsory manumission," even meant that the court could set the price of redemption.[51] According to Burdon, Sarkin Musulmi Attahiru II

> directed the native court to adjudicate on all cases in which slaves desire to redeem themselves, fixing an equitable sum, and arranging how it may be earned and paid gradually. A slave thus has an absolute right to redeem himself even against the will of his master, with the result that slaves, instead of running away and becoming vagrants, can now appeal to the native court. Moreover, since they have no longer the fear of being sold or transferred, they are more contented, and less inclined to desert, while the masters, having no longer the power of sale or fear of confiscation or desertion, treat their slaves more as part of the family. In one case, where redemption was refused by a master, the Sultan offered the liberation of the slave without ransom ... This is a remarkable course of action for the highest Mohammedan authorities in the country to take, and illustrates the liberality of the Sultan's views, and his desire to co-operate with the Administration. The gradual extinction of domestic slavery through the initiation of the Head of the Moslem religion, supported by the Moslem jurists on the one hand and by the personal exertions of the slave himself on the other is, in my judgment, a much greater achievement than forcible manumission by the Government, which, while bitterly resented by the masters, is not regarded by them or by the slave himself as really emancipating him from the status of a slave. This movement ... is not confined to Sokoto, though it is here doubly important, first, because Sokoto is the headquarters of the Mohammedan religion, and of the most capable of the Moslem jurists, and secondly, because Sokoto, owing to the former annual slave tribute, possesses a larger slave population than any other province.[52]

Ruxton had to impose a similar measure in Gwandu, where there was resistance to the idea, but he still claimed that "the policy of compulsory manumission on demand to the native courts is working well, as shown by the court returns."[53] Burdon personally intervened in one case in which the master refused to allow the redemption of a slave. As he reported,

> In the case of Aisa (No. 46 Native Court Case 212) the authority of the Native Court had to be supported, and, as a warning to others, by loss to the recusant master of the redemption money. I personally saw the man and warned him of the result of the refusal to accept the Native Court's award. But he persisted. And I therefore gave the money away.[54]

For once, Lugard welcomed Burdon's approach to slavery matters, although he reserved his praise for the aristocracy. He applauded "the liberal and enlightened spirit shewn by such courts as those of the Emirs and Alkalis of Sokoto, Kano, Bida, and Zaria – as evidenced by their initiative in enforcing the prohibition of enslaving and slave-dealing, and even of compelling masters to accept redemption money whenever proferred by a slave."[55] The extent to which the Islamic courts actually enforced "compulsory manumission" is open to question, however, as we will discuss in Chapter 8.

With the supply of new slaves effectively checked, it was possible that the redemption price of slaves might rise above the going price of slaves at the end of the nineteenth century. Indeed an article in the *Société Antiesclavagiste de France* in 1903 claimed that the Caliphate courts were setting the price of manumission so that this would not occur.[56] Travers Buxton at the Colonial Office requested an explanation from Lugard, who responded on December 3, 1903 that "there is no law fixing the sum by which a slave may redeem himself, nor can there be as the legal status is abolished: but I have under consideration to informally assess such a sum."[57] It was a short step from "compulsory manumission" whereby an *alkali* imposed a reasonable ransom price on recalcitrant masters to a situation in which a "fair price" came to be recognized.

For an administration so intent on maintaining its relations with the masters, it might seem curious that the price of redemption was kept down. The *Société Antiesclavagiste de France* seems to have been preoccupied with the mere fact that British courts were upholding the payment of manumission by slaves. The accusation that prices were being set was offered as proof, without comment, on why it might be desirable to fix prices. The far more important point was missed: why would the British not let prices rise to whatever level they might reach? The reason seems to have been related to a recognition that there was a limit to what slaves would be willing to pay – the higher that ransom prices rose, the more likely that slaves would run away. If ransom prices could be fixed at a relatively low market rate, then it would be easier to enforce the various measures to keep slaves in place. It is also clear that restrictions on the sale of slaves and on the ability to punish slaves reduced the value of the slaves to their masters, and thereby reduced the acceptable quit-rent or manumission payment that slaves were willing to make.

In his 1906 *Instructions to Political and Other Officers*, Lugard adopted a policy of court-enforced, low redemption prices, following the lead of the Islamic courts in Sokoto. Masters could legally be "compelled to liberate the slave who desires to redeem himself, and at a fair rate."

This provision should similarly be adopted throughout the country, and the rate should be fixed by the Alkali and not by the master, and should be only the reasonable value of the slave, and not twice the value, and the master should (as is generally the case) maintain the slave while he is working for his ransom. The slave, who is refused the right of redemption, should be encouraged to appeal to the Courts.[58]

110

It was a corollary that "Native Courts should be encouraged to award liberation freely in cases of ill-treatment."[59] But it was also the case that "if a runaway slave is caught and agrees to pay ransom, and is consequently freed, the debt can be enforced in Court, provided that he reiterated the promise of his own free will after liberation."[60]

In practice, fugitives were apprehended and told to pay ransom. The Islamic courts were empowered to uphold these "contractual" payments. Lugard's language was cast in terms of "free will" and "agreement," but in fact these measures were based on coercion. Those slaves who stayed had little choice but to continue to work for their master. In 1908, Alkalin Yabo asked Resident Stanley of Sokoto, "What am I to do when a slave refuses to work for his master?" Stanley told him that

> As a general rule the slave has been granted a farm; if he refuses to work this can be taken from him. Further if a slave refuses to work his master is no longer bound to provide him with food, clothing and a house.[61]

Slaves were not allowed to run away, and they could be denied food and clothing if they failed to work.

The law and slave women

Slave women were a special problem for the colonial regime. Although they probably constituted somewhat more than half of the slave population, British policy was almost entirely preoccupied with male slaves (and their wives and children if the males were married).[62] The large number of female slaves who were concubines or otherwise not married were treated as a separate category that requires some consideration. As far as the colonial state was concerned, their legal status was subsumed under "matrimonial relations" and "prostitution." Unattached women were undesirable from a policy perspective. A woman should either be married or live with relatives. Otherwise she was a prostitute. Since Islamic law dealt with the status of women in great detail, colonial policy generally deferred to the *shari'a*. When it came to women, it was convenient that British law be very simple because Caliphate law was very complex. Much could be disguised in the complexity.

Concubines were a legal category in Islamic law.[63] A man could have four wives and as many concubines as he could afford. The long tradition of concubinage was fully accepted in the Sokoto Caliphate, and this tradition continued under colonial rule. The distinction between free wives and slave women was clear, while the rights of concubines who had borne children by their masters were protected. Similarly, the paternity of a concubine's children could not be questioned; intercourse alone, whether or not the master practiced withdrawal to avoid pregnancy, was sufficient to establish paternity.[64] Not all slave women were concubines, and even if a slave woman was sexually abused, there was no protection for her unless she was a concubine.

In Hausa, concubines were referred to as *sad'aka* (from *sa*, to put, and *d'aka*, room; hence to put in a room), *k'wark'wara* (etymology unclear), *makulliya* (derived from *kulle*, purdah), *wahayiya* (slave woman who has borne a child by her master), or *geru* (etymology unknown).[65] Concubines were invariably slaves, and as has been demonstrated elsewhere, they were often recently captured teenagers.[66] Prenubile girls were also brought into the home, and upon reaching puberty, they too could become concubines. In some cases, girls as young as seven were designated as concubines as a pronouncement of future intentions.[67]

Concubinage was clearly a form of slavery, in case there are any doubts, as a 1905 ruling of the *alkali* of Bida made clear:

> all concubinage proceeds from sale [or the possibility thereof], and ... anyone who procures a concubine and pays a monetary consideration for her, in fact buys her, whether she is a free women, a slave or a *bachucheni* [f. *bacucaniya*, pl. *cucanawa*, children of slaves].[68]

In fact many concubines were newly enslaved and never entered the market. In the nineteenth century, slave girls who had been concubines but who had not given birth by their masters could be sold, and concubines who had children might be sold if they committed adultery or were suspected of theft. Female slaves and concubines who had not borne children could also be given as gifts and thereby become concubines of the receiver, a practice that continued well into the twentieth century.[69] In Kano, officials sometimes gave presents of female slaves to important immigrants as inducements to settle.[70] In most cases such gifts probably resulted in concubinage.

All women were legally minors under Islamic law,[71] but there was a clear distinction between concubines and wives. While concubines by definition were slaves, wives were usually free.[72] The *shari'a* advised that "a freeman should marry a freewoman."[73] As Schacht has observed, "In Muslim law a most rigid distinction is made between marriage and concubinage, so much so that the master cannot enter into marriage with his slave at all. Divergences from this rule are extraordinarily rare."[74] As Baba of Karo noted, "If a man bought a slave woman ... she would be his concubine, never his wife."[75]

A wife had the rights of the freeborn, even though as a woman she had fewer rights than a male. Unlike a slave woman, a free woman could own land, livestock, slaves, and other property. Inheritance practices theoretically followed Maliki norms, in which free women received half the male share of estates. The distinctions between free men and women and their relative wealth and power far exceeded the two-to-one inheritance advantage for men, but marriage contracts and rules of inheritance still allowed a limited degree of autonomy for free women, especially among the aristocrats who owned most of the concubines. There were a variety of marriage contracts between free women and free men, and women who experienced ill treatment could easily get divorced, which probably limited the extent to which men abused their wives. Concubines, by contrast, had little recourse if they were abused, other than running away. Discrimination on the basis of gender aside, there is no doubt that being a wife was preferable to being a concubine.

In the context of Caliphate society and continuing under colonial rule, wives were supposed not only to be free, but also to be Muslims. Families wanted their daughters to marry into respectable families of acceptable origins (*asali*). The aristocracy, the merchant class, the scholar community, craftsmen, prosperous farmers, and Fulbe cattle owners were very careful about whom their daughters married. People tended to marry within their own community or neighbors of an ethnic background with whom "joking relations" (*abokin wasa*) were maintained.

Marriage could not take place unless there was a guardian (*wali*) for the bride, usually the father, but sometimes the father's brother or the bride's older brother. The bride's family provided wedding presents (*gara*), and the groom's family gave a number of presents to the bride and her family as well. The groom also paid *sadaki*, a cash payment that legalized the contract.[76] There also had to be reliable witnesses.[77] Although husbands were allowed a maximum of four wives, they were expected to provide for each on an equal basis. Failure to do so was grounds for divorce.

Both wives and concubines of respectable and sufficiently wealthy men were kept in seclusion. The practice was not wide-spread among the founders of the Caliphate, but Uthman dan Fodio "came to insist on purdah in his own household, [although] it is not clear how widely (or strictly) his example was followed even in his local circle of scholars."[78] By the beginning of the twentieth century, seclusion was common among those who could afford the practice. As M. G. Smith has observed, "like her master's wife or wives, the Hausa concubine was secluded in accordance with the requirement of purdah marriage, and was provided with her requirements of food, clothing, shelter, money, and other goods."[79] Because purdah restrictions applied to both, "free Hausa women and concubines neither farmed nor gathered firewood."[80] As noted above, one of the terms for concubine, *makulliya*, was derived from the word for purdah (*kulle*). When a slave girl became a concubine, the transformation was commonly expressed as "locking her up."[81]

Seclusion for wives and concubines had very different implications. Both were dependent, but the degree of dependency varied considerably. Free women of respectable backgrounds could divorce, if they were mistreated. They had families behind them. Concubines could not leave, except by running away, which was why a common proverb pleaded "Slave girl speak! Say that you will never take manure to the stones bordering the farm [i.e., escape]."[82] Because of their slave status, concubines were relatively powerless to alter their fate. By contrast, wives had distinct advantages. In Sokoto, at least, wives had two rooms, while concubines had only one, which suggestively symbolizes the relative advantage of being free.[83]

The chasm between marriage and concubinage was indeed wide and had to be maintained through strong social pressure, precisely because men could be tempted to bridge the gap. The difficulties of navigating through the turmoil of multiple marriages might well lead the incautious man to favor a concubine. But marrying a slave girl, instead of taking her as a concubine, was unwise and publicly discouraged, for

> He who marries a slave woman, he shall be unhappy.
> He has made war and conquered his own house.[84]

Authorities held that Muslims could marry their slaves, but only if they freed them first.[85] According to the *shari'a*, "a male does not contract marriage with his slave-girl unless he has manumitted her,"[86] but even then such marriages were not encouraged. Since most concubines were of non-Muslim origins and one of the stipulations of marriage was that the woman be a Muslim, a concubine was not usually a desirable candidate for marriage.

In situations in which women competed for the attention of a man, jealousies could become intense. Of course, rivalry could exist among wives, but the most extreme tension prevailed between wives and concubines. Sometimes wives resorted to charms and other supernatural means of keeping concubines in their place or in attempting to dispose of them. There are reports of wives uniting against a concubine, such as in the case of three co-wives who assaulted a teenage concubine in Sokoto in the first decade of colonial rule.[87] Of course, concubines could become embroiled in similar rivalries.

There can be no doubt that one of the reasons for this jealousy is that men wanted concubines for sex. The observation of the learned jurist Imam Imoru represents well male thought on concubines:

> When a man sees a beautiful slave and likes her, he keeps it a secret. He sleeps with her regularly and she becomes his concubine, korkora [*k'wark'wara*].[88]

And the seclusion of concubines was intended to deny these women sexual interaction with anyone other than the master. Homosexual relations among concubines were equally prohibited, as the executions of two concubines who were caught with an artificial penis make clear. Sexual access was the prerogative of the master alone.[89]

Masters were not supposed to sleep with concubines at night; they had to maintain nocturnal commitments to their wives, usually three nights in succession but sometimes four, unless a woman was pregnant, nursing, or ill. Indeed, legally,

> there is no allotting of sleeping-nights to concubines whether they've conceived by him or not ... One goes secretly to sleep with a slave-girl or a concubine who has borne you a child, but a male comes [openly] to his wife's house to sleep with her. Or if he prefers he sends for her to come to him wherever he is.[90]

Failure to discriminate between concubines and wives was worthy of the condemnation of Shehu Uthman dan Fodio himself: "Those who allot days [i.e., nights] to their concubines, treating them as equal like their wives, all of them, the Fire is their portion, be sure of that!"[91]

114

The question of paternity was a central issue in the regulation of concubinage, both in the nineteenth century and under colonial rule. Technically, a concubine's rights were confirmed only when she bore a child by her master. Until then, she could be sold, given away, inherited, or otherwise disposed of. Whether or not *coitus interruptus* was practised, sleeping with a concubine was sufficient to establish paternity. As a consequence, men were careful to seclude their concubines, like their wives, and pregnant concubines usually acquired the full rights accorded under law. Once they were pregnant, it was difficult to deny such rights.

Caliphate law carefully established procedures for determining paternity arising from sexual relations with slave women. Legal advice was clear:

> If you buy a slave-girl and she was before the concubine of her master, do not make her your concubine till she's once menstruated; you can then pay her former master, for otherwise, you don't know whether when he sold her to you she was pregnant by him.[92]

In *Bayan wujub al-hijra 'ala 'l-'abad*, Uthman dan Fodio discussed the "permissibility of taking as concubines the women who have been captured from them [unbelieving belligerents] after waiting for the passing of one menstruation (*istibra'*) even if they have husbands in non-Muslim territory."[93] The Shehu accepted the earlier ruling of Muslim jurists that "captivity nullifies the contract of marriage," whether or not the woman was captured with her husband.[94] The compulsory waiting period of one menstruation was obligatory "whether ownership of her [the slave girl] changes through sale, gift, captivity or other means."[95] The *shari'a* required men "to enquire into the condition of wombs, when ownership changes, with a view to safeguarding questions of parentage."[96]

Once a woman had given birth she could not normally be sold, or otherwise transferred. She was said to have "broken the shackles" (*ta karya mari*), and from then her status was special and she might even be assigned less work than other slave women.[97] It is this feature of concubinage that is so remarkably different from the institution of slavery in general. Concubinage often involved the amelioration of the conditions of slavery, even as the subordination of women continued.

Again the law was clear. Concubines became free on the death of their masters, not before, unless specifically provided for: "He who makes a slave-girl his concubine and she conceives by him, let him not sell her: when he dies, she becomes free so that she may marry the man of her choice."[98] In the first years of colonial rule, British officials found that legal tradition and custom coincided, as the report of Resident Hillary demonstrates: "a slave concubine cannot be sold if she has borne a living child to her master, and becomes free on his death."[99] Only on the death of her master, the father of her children, could she marry or otherwise expect the full rights of a free woman.[100] Before then, a concubine could not inherit, own property, leave the compound, or engage in activities that her master did not sanction.

When she gave birth, the paternity of the father was formally acknowledged, in contrast to the paternity of slave fathers, which was never legally recognized. During the lifetime of her master, who as the father of her child or children had clearly defined responsibilities, her offspring had virtually no danger of suffering the indignities of slavery and were supposed to be treated as equals to the children of free women. The situation provided a strong incentive for concubines to accept their condition. Under such circumstances,

> she is practically free, and if her master were to sell her he would be liable to punishment as for selling a free woman. If he ill-treats her, she has a right to leave him without redeeming herself. Some say that she is freed on the third occasion on which he beats her. If not with child, the Alkali [judge] can marry her to another man, and she is given a paper of freedom. Her children by her master remain with him as his property, and are "bachucheni" [sic]. Others again say that she can leave her master at any time, and he has no redress, but retains the children. If a master dies, his heir cannot sell one who has borne a child.[101]

A concubine could be allowed to go about as she pleased once she was beyond child-bearing age. Her master might even allow her to marry, under certain conditions. Once her master died, as Imam Imoru reported, "she can marry anybody because she is a free woman, just like all freeborn women."[102]

Admittedly, the legal and customary rights gained by concubines were not always perceived as significant or worth while. Power still rested in the hands of the master, as Imam Imoru observed: "when she bears once for him she [will] become a free woman: he doesn't sell her, he doesn't give her away as a gift, nor will he make her pay anything, but he continues to discipline her as he likes."[103] Imoru was a male and jurist, and from such a perspective, the likely reasons for discipline seemed justified. A concubine could be sold if she committed adultery or theft, an ironic commentary on a situation in which men could have many sexual partners and where sexual access was closely regulated through slavery.[104]

The status of slave women who failed to give birth was a difficult problem. Concubines might be freed at the death of a master if there had been a miscarriage and/or they had been in long service. In Daura, children sometimes inherited infertile concubines, presumably to look after them, if they were old and had been concubines for a long time. Otherwise such women were distributed among male slaves, or the inheritors continued to use their services.[105] They were considered step-mothers in the family.[106] Presumably such women, who were fully integrated in the family, whether or not such integration involved respect, faced highly individual futures. Some were probably pushed hard as common slave workers around the compound. Others may have been treated better.

British policy towards slave women

British officials were fully aware of the prevalence of women in the slave population, and the colonial state chose to reinforce the control of masters over their female slaves as a major concession to slave owners. As Lugard noted in his Annual Report for 1902, difficulties relating to female slaves, whether or not they were concubines, was "really rather a question of divorce than of slavery, and can be dealt with as such by Native Courts."[107] By 1906, he claimed that "the majority of the applicants [for freedom] among household slaves are women, who desire to leave a master to whom they are in the relation of wife or concubine, in order to marry another man."[108] Even so, many women were encouraged or coerced into returning to their masters. As Lugard put it, "in many cases where the fugitive is a woman, it will be found to be a domestic quarrel, and the woman may be glad to return and be forgiven."[109] The comment that the *woman* was forgiven obscures the likelihood that many disagreements arose from the condition of servility and that women often had no alternative under the circumstances but to return. This perspective on female slaves was convenient in the context of legal-status abolition. The legal status of the women as slaves could be overlooked. Women were not really considered to be slaves; they were merely women.

In the first instance, the British feared that escaped concubines would become prostitutes and thereby contribute to the criminal class. The Resident of Muri thought "that the immediate result [of the conquest] may be a relaxation of the control over wives and concubines, with a resulting increase in immorality . . . but reforms very commonly result in an initial evil, which rights itself before long."[110] To avoid such an eventuality, Lugard wanted all unattached slave girls and freed slave women to be placed under guardians, "as it minimizes the chances of prostitution."[111] Reports from Sokoto, Bida, Kano, and other places indicate that the incidence of prostitution did increase, and in the context of the times, this increase is an indication that many women could no longer tolerate their masters and saw the opportunity to "break the shackles" in less traditional ways by running away.[112] For this reason, Howard wanted tough measures to discourage "the running away of domestic slaves, mainly young women desirous of living with soldiers and carriers . . . [otherwise] the present social state will be, entirely, disorganised with the result that immorality and disease will increase enormously."[113] Girouard, too, believed that women slaves who had run away tended to "drift into prostitution," a tendency that had to be checked.[114]

Despite these expressions of disapproval, many colonial officials maintained a double standard, since they wanted access to the sexual favors of local women. Many British officials were single men on duty in Northern Nigeria for lengthy periods and fully took advantage of the availability of local women. Even married men dallied, since they were seldom accompanied by their wives, who stayed in Britain. One WAFF officer claimed that the Emir of Katsina offered him a concubine in 1903.[115] SIM missionary Charles Waddell, at Zungeru in December 1905, was "shocked by the evil doings of the Niger Co. white men with Native women [and] even Mr. Davis has fallen & many of the government men also."[116] Not surprisingly, there was a curtain of silence in official reports on relations with women. Understandably, the arrival of the first wives of colonial officials after 1911 required discretion on the part of white males.

While Caliphate officials fully appreciated the desires of European officers, as already observed, slave owners did not like the idea of their slave women running away. Furthermore, slave owners had no intention of supplying or procuring women for the whole colonial establishment, including the average WAFF soldier. Needless to say, British officials were sympathetic to the efforts to control women. Gifts of slave women were acceptable; flight was not. The women who fled to the British fort at Bauchi in 1902, for example, appear to have been concubines. As Temple observed, "far from presenting the aspect of having been ill treated these women generally have a sleek appearance denoting that they have been treated as wives by their owners."[117] Of course Temple returned the women to their masters and instructed the commanding officer not to allow any "persons not connected with the Force" to stay overnight.

When the High Commissioner addressed Waziri Bukhari and other aristocrats after the conquest of Sokoto, March 20, 1903, he gave assurances that their women would not be allowed to leave, except in outstanding instances of brutality that were already covered by Islamic law. After his address, Lugard listened to a number of complaints, one of which was about slaves "especially slave women and concubines, being harboured in [WAFF] camp." Lugard's response was brief: "Reassurance and promise of protection were given." Burdon, who was about to become the first Resident, served as Hausa translator and took notes on the specific complaints.[118] Soon thereafter, Burdon restored the slave women to their masters, but not without protest from his own soldiers:

> Three times in broad daylight, parties of soldiers armed with sticks have attacked my Political Agents when escorting to the Court, Sokoto women who had been claimed by their masters from barracks, who had been handed over by the officers for enquiry. The women were seized and the complainants severely handled.[119]

The soldiers wanted the spoils of war and could not understand why they could not keep women, since they had been allowed to do so in earlier campaigns in Nupe and elsewhere. Burdon and Lugard, of course, understood that they needed the cooperation of the aristocracy now that the conquest was complete, and they could not afford to alienate slave owners over the issue of women. As we have noted, this change in policy was part of the hardening stance of the British regime on the slavery issue.

The way that Webster treated fugitive slave women, who he thought were "mostly concubines," is instructive concerning British policy. Once the fugitives were apprehended, they were brought before the emir, where they were intimidated into returning to their masters. Webster admitted his involvement in many of these cases in 1904:

> I have often been asked to talk to some such recreant wife or slave and "give

her patience," as the term is. In 9 cases out of 10 the original cause of dissension is almost forgotten, some petty fit of jealousy, the refusal of a cloth or a quarrel with the headwife, and the runaway is only too glad to go back on a promise of forgiveness and probably returns next day with a small offering of thanks for having adjusted matters.[120]

In Webster's opinion, these women were "not really slaves" because they were concubines.

Women could still refuse to submit, despite the strong pressure. As Lugard notes, "When a woman, however, declines to return, the Native Court hardly ever, I think insists on her doing so, [and] time is granted for her to collect ransom money."[121] In Nassarawa, if the Emir could not "persuade" fugitive women from leaving, "they are always allowed time to collect ransom or if there is any just cause of complaint to go free."[122] Inevitably the ransom had to be paid by a third party, sometimes a relative but more often some man. In one striking case, a British official discovered a slave woman in irons in the Ilorin jail because she would not "marry" a crippled aristocrat. She was released and "allowed to go where she likes."[123] This extreme case highlights the fact that if a female slave could not obtain the necessary redemption money for her own freedom, she almost certainly had to acquiesce.

By ignoring their slave status and treating slave women as if they were wives, British policy blurred the distinction between concubinage and marriage. As Lugard insisted, slave women were now considered to be free "on marriage,"[124] which sanctified the concubinary rights of masters. As the Resident of Muri stated in 1903, "the emancipation of women at marriage will, moreover, tend to give a woman more choice, and thus to greatly inprove the condition of women in the country."[125] In approving Webster's actions as "marriage counsellor" in Nassarawa, Lugard observed,

> Re runaway slave . . . It is a question of marriage rather than slavery. A woman in England can be forced to return.[126]

The obvious corollary was that women in Northern Nigeria could be too. He was in full agreement with Webster that the "pagan towns [harbouring fugitive slave women] should not be allowed to give the runaways asylum, especially in a Province like this where many of the slaves have been caught within the last 20 years from villages one or two days distant."[127] These were the villages discussed above that were punished, not for actually harboring fugitive slaves but for failure to comply with the order of an Islamic court. Once again legalisms were used to uphold relationships of slavery.

Many women did achieve emancipation from slavery through marriage, but there is considerable difficulty in identifying when women were really married rather than being pressed to concubinage. As has been demonstrated elsewhere, many redemption cases of female slaves were disguised transfers of women for purposes of concubinage.[128] Officially British policy only recognized marriages after the proper payment of redemption money.

> A woman ... who is redeemed by her suitor is married as a free woman, and knows that she has the rights of divorce, etc., which belong to a free woman. Residents should personally investigate any case of which the *bona fides* appear doubtful, and as far as possible keep an eye on ransomed slaves, and see that they are really free – corresponding if need be with other Residents regarding any particular case, when they suspect that the ransomed slave may be sold, transferred or re-enslaved.[129]

Certainly, Makatude, a twenty-year-old Tangale concubine, achieved her emancipation through the Bauchi court in 1906. She had been acquired in 1902 and had subsequently "borne children by her master," who now wanted to marry her. She had to be a free woman to do so, hence the registration in the court.[130] Similarly, in 1906, a Bauchi cleric freed his concubine, twenty-two-year-old Mattan Mallam, because he wanted to marry her. She had also borne children.[131] This must have been the case sometimes in Sokoto, too, where there were "very few emancipations [in 1908] except of women for marriage,"[132] although the evidence here demonstrates the difficulty of distinguishing between actual marriages and disguised transfers for the purpose of concubinage.

When a third party intended to marry a slave woman, he first had to redeem her through an Islamic court. Technically, the ransom money passed from the redeemer to the woman, who gave it to the judge for payment to her master. The woman was then given the certificate of freedom and was released to do as she pleased. The money "given" to the woman was not equivalent to the *sadaki* (marriage payment) that an intending husband gave to his fiancée.

> The important point is that in all cases (except when a slave-girl marries a fellow-slave and both continue in their status of slavery), the woman on marriage must be declared free before the Alkali. The man, in favour of whom the woman has left her master, marries her as a free-woman, and is amenable for slave-dealing if he subsequently treats her as a slave concubine. The same rules apply if the girl is a *bachucheni* [*bacucuniya*] who has now become her master's concubine. The tending husband must pay her the Sadaki, out of which she can make a contribution to her master in return for the maintenance and home she has had at his hands, *since in her case ransom money is not demanded – but his contribution would be optional*, and in any case she is formally declared free.[133]

The implication of this policy was that marriage and emancipation would become indistinguishable and thereby minimize the adjustments to social change under colonialism. The flight into fantasy that is apparent in this policy should be recognized, particularly with respect to Lugard's statement that the "ransom money is not demanded." It is suggested that upon "receiving" the ransom, a woman could make a "contribution" to her master if she wished. Slave women did not have this "option." The ransom went from "husband" to master, no matter how many palms it touched.

Purchase price and the marriage payment were legally to be distinguished, but there were worries about abuses arising from this "reform." Considering the legal opinion of the *alkali* of Bida, a noted jurist, these concerns were justified. The *alkali*, whose ruling has already been cited, argued that concubinage proceeded from sale, that is, slavery, and the fact of purchase or the possibility of sale distinguished concubinage from marriage. In the *alkali*'s opinion, the British reform was incompatible with Islamic law. The money payment in connection with a slave girl was prima facie evidence of a transaction, "and the conditions of such a marriage are virtually concubinage." In effect "the dowry is nothing more nor less than purchase money," and the woman became a concubine.[134] It was for this reason that Lugard insisted that the purchase price be paid to the woman, who in turn gave the money to the court. Thereby, the *alkali*'s ruling could be circumvented.[135]

Temple did not understand the importance of using the courts in 1902 when he registered slave women being freed in order to marry:

> With regard to marriages of soldiers to Freed Slaves I am pursuing the following course. The Soldier first obtains a certificate from the O.C. that he wishes to marry the slave. I then send for the owner & inform him; if he is willing to accept £2 10 or £3 compensation. I put the slave on the Freed Slave List and hand a certificate to the soldier that he has paid compensation. The soldier then shews the certificate to the O.C. and he, I understand, puts the woman on the married register of the Company.[136]

This procedure overstepped Lugard's instructions. His marginal note told Temple: "This must *never* be done. It is a slave transaction." A straight payment between an intending "husband" and a slave owner violated the law abolishing the slave trade.

By contrast, three teenagers who were freed in Kano in 1906 are examples of how the problem of females was supposed to be handled. Aisa, a Bedde girl aged seventeen, Biba, a Fulbe who was also seventeen, and Kolo, a Fulbe aged fourteen were redeemed by their intended husbands, three WAFF soldiers, in the presence of the Resident:

> These three women were married to three soldiers respectively. They were wed with the consent of their owner and in each case, I redeemed them in the presence of the Native Alkali. I warned soldiers that these women were now free, and that they were responsible for their persons and must produce them at any time, unless for good reason shewn.[137]

Lugard was explicit in his instructions on the marriage of slave women to soldiers. These situations were to be governed by the following principles: "If, however, the master (as husband or guardian) will not consent to the marriage (after liberation), she may not be taken by force, but will be sent back to her husband or guardian." Commanding officers were allowed to advance the redemption money, "according to the man's character, precisely as he would if an advance were required for any other purpose, and the full formalities of declaring the person free must be gone through in the Native Court, and a freedom certificate given, and the slave's name changed, before the soldier or constable may marry the ex-slave."[138] Any advance was to be garnished over time.

Thus by 1906, female slaves were frequently being ransomed for purposes of marriage, whether as a disguised form of concubinage or otherwise. In Gombe, for example, the Islamic court issued certificates of freedom so that "those of marriageable age ... [could] be married as free women."[139] As Lugard noted in 1906, "the entry in Native Court returns 'Ransoms and marries her, paid———,' is now a very frequent one, and Residents should be very careful to see that these are genuine cases, and not merely a transaction in slaves disguised in this form."[140] As Orr noted for Zaria, "the majority of slaves freed in the Native Courts have been women whose freedom has been purchased by men in order to marry them."[141]

Marriage and the continuation of concubinage were not the only alternatives for women slaves who did not want to stay with their masters. Under colonialism, it was now possible for relatives to locate lost kin and seek their redemption. Indeed British policy encouraged the restoration of women and children to their families.[142] A typical case involved sixteen-year-old Yaganah, of Kanuri origin. She had been enslaved in Borno in 1903, apparently kidnaped by some "unknown man" and sold in Bauchi. Her brother found her in late 1906 and paid her ransom, whereupon she was "freed to return with her brother to Bornu."[143] Similarly, the girl Mahabauta, aged ten, who had been recently enslaved, was restored to her relatives in 1906.[144]

If relatives were not forthcoming and it was not possible to identify suitable males for slave women on the loose, then female slaves were entrusted to a guardian, placed with a mission, or more rarely, sent to a Freed Slaves' Home (before 1907).

> If the freed slave [who cannot be repatriated] is a woman she will similarly be given a certificate of freedom and registered. She can be employed on suitable tasks for a small wage, preferably in or about the Hospital, where she will be under the eye of a responsible officer, and may be indentured as a nurse, or become a servant of a Nursing Sister, until of her own free will she elects to marry some local Native of good character who is not in Government employ ... Or she may be allowed to engage in some useful occupation, either as servant to a European lady, or in the native reservation so long as she behaves herself and does not lead a notoriously immoral life. Or finally, failing any other method, she may be entrusted to the care of a reliable and trustworthy village Headman ... The Resident will keep a roll of men who have married a freed slave woman who is a Government ward, and satisfy himself from time to time that she is treated as a free woman, and has not been sold or transferred. A freed slave woman cannot be detained by force.[145]

Again the reference to "free will" and "freedom" should be noted. By now the pattern of subtle and not so subtle forms of coercion will be recognized.

In Caliphate society, and continuing under colonial rule, women had to have guardians (Hausa: s. wakali, pl. wakilai; Arabic wakil) who oversaw marriage arrangements and otherwise were responsible for their protection and supervision. As Christelow has demonstrated, the right to *wakili* underlay most relationships involving women. Masters had full authority over their concubines who lacked relatives and therefore needed a male guardian.[146]

Guardians included Europeans and prominent Caliphate officials, as indicated above in Lugard's statement that if all else failed, women were assigned to "reliable and trustworthy village headmen." In Sokoto, for example, slave girls were entrusted to officials, which Hillary found preferable to placing them in the charge of Europeans, and which was certainly better than sending them all the way to the Zungeru Freed Slaves' Home.[147] In any case, unattached female slaves were forced to accept a new dependency that was akin to the old slavery. Many slave women understood that their condition had not really changed. As Larymore reported from Nupe in 1904:

> Freed Slave Women ... have been given to guardians in this place. One or two of them are a source of much trouble to the Resident at present. One (Guardian, Mrs. Williams) refused to do any work, has now commenced to refuse food, speaks no known language, and I am at a loss what to do with her. A police constable has apparently offered her marriage, by some means, and I am told that she is willing to marry the man. Will Your Excellency please sanction? [margin: yes] She will be on the Police books as laid down. I think the woman is most fortunate in having found a suitor. I have seen her. Another is a girl freed slave (guardian, Mrs. Hesse) after having been treated apparently with every consideration, in fact, as Mr. Hesse assures me, "as one of the family" this young woman now refuses to reside with the Hesse household – she wants to marry Sergt. Brown of the Police. I was assured however that she was too young to marry. I therefore offered to send her back to the home in Zungeru. She said, in Hausa, that if she were sent back she would cut her throat. She wants to live with the present Mrs. Brown until old enough to marry Sergt. Brown. Will Your Excellency sanction change of guardianship? [margin: Is a very puzzling case. I see no way of dealing with it except as you suggest.][148]

As this example of unwanted dependency makes clear, freed slave girls as well as female slaves were simply not allowed to be on their own.

The courts intervened to protect the rights of women, albeit within the narrow range of marital relationships that were sanctioned. Masters no longer had full control over their slaves, as a case from Agaye Emirate in Nupe makes clear. On appeal from the Agaye court, the Islamic court in Bida ruled that a girl who had been born into slavery could be allowed to marry a man to whom her parents had given their consent, even though the master refused permission. The conditions of slavery relating to parental control were changing. Whereas formerly, slave parents had no such authority over their children, now the Agaye court was upholding the actions of the slave parents over the wishes of the master. Nonetheless, the court ruled that the suitor first had to ransom the girl. The appeal court in Bida upheld this decision, but the *alkali* observed that because the young wife was a mere slave ("being a bachucheni"), "the suitor should first have asked the owner, and taken action only after his refusal."[149]

The Islamic courts also began to intervene in situations where former masters tried to reclaim female slaves. In one case, the court protected a slave girl who had been freed by Temple: "A slave girl liberated by Mr. Resident Temple was claimed by Mai Yaiki [Yaki] (Ex-Sarkin Ari) who was aware that she had been freed. The Native Court warned me that the girl had been freed by Mr. Temple and fined Mai Yaiki 10/–."[150] Matters of matrimony and slavery could be resolved, but there were serious issues involved because masters still claimed proprietary rights that British rule did not always recognize. The involvement of a Resident suggests ill treatment, but in this case the master rejected the ruling only to discover that the Islamic court upheld it.

Women were taken from their masters when there were criminal charges being investigated. When the Shamaki of Gombe was arrested in 1906, for example, his slaves were freed, which for the women meant free to marry. The Islamic court at Gombe gave each slave a "letter," with "those of marriageable age to be married as free women [and] children to be returned to their homes if possible, if not to be given guardians."[151] As always, women were expected to establish some new dependency on a male, whether a husband or relative.

Men were almost always connected with the court cases involving female slaves. As Feargus Dwyer, Acting Resident, Kontagora and Borgu, noted in 1907, slave women who ran away did so "always to marry some person in another man's house."[152] Similarly, Larymore, reporting from Bida in the same year, observed that when "a woman runs away from her husband or master and the man she goes to can be found, an arrangement of the difficulty is easy enough, by making the latter compensate the original husband or master: the amount varies from £5–£10." If no man could be identified, a woman was put into the custody of the aged mother of the etsu of Bida until a potential husband could be located. The suitor had to pay for the woman's redemption.[153]

Because males dominated the Islamic courts, it is not surprising that slave women were not always protected and their rights were sometimes overlooked. The meanings of "protection" and "rights" were cast in terms in which women had little say. Women could not testify in court, nor could they even be in court. They had to speak through a male intermediary, often standing just outside a window. Consequently, there appears to have been considerable variation in the extent to which these male-dominated institutions served the interests of women. Many transactions involving slave women, in which third parties were paying the ransoms, were thinly disguised transfers for the purpose of concubinage.

In 1908, when Alkalin Yabo of Sokoto asked for clarification of "the Law as regards the redemption of slave-girls who become concubines of the redeemer," Resident Stanley replied:

> Before our advent there was a distinction between the slave bought for labour, and the slave bought in order that the purchaser might make her a "sadakka" or concubine. In the second case the transaction would be called "buying in

order to lock up." When slave-dealing was declared illegal the native ceased "buying in order to lock up" and called it redemption. As in most cases [in which] there was no certificate of freedom this redemption was indistinguishable from purchase. The order at present is that in all cases of redemption the Court gives a properly witnessed certificate of freedom, [and] if this is not done the parties are liable to prosecution for slave-dealing.[154]

In short, masters could "redeem" slave women for purposes of concubinage, and the certificate of freedom actually protected the master, because "if the man married [sic] the slave whom he had redeemed he would have a right to recover the money spent on her redemption in the Native Court," presumably if the woman subsequently left her redeemer for another man.[155] Stanley told the *alkali* that in the case of concubines who did not have certificates of freedom, a master had no recourse: "If the concubine chooses to leave him I can see no legal obstacle and the money is lost."[156]

In the court records from 1905–1906, 39.4 percent of cases involving women slaves led to the "marriage" of the woman to her redeemer, while another 4.6 percent of the women were otherwise married.[157] The other cases involved women being redeemed by relatives, being sent to the Freed Slaves' Home at Zungeru, assigned to missions or other guardians, or otherwise "freed to follow their own inclinations," a vague category that cannot easily be deciphered. How many of the cases were true marriages and how many were disguised transfers for purposes of concubinage is not clear, but it seems likely that many were. As the Resident of Muri noted in 1903, "slave-girls for concubines are plentiful and cheap, while free-born women are costly, scarce, and troublesome."[158] Certainly many women remained in slavery as concubines.

There is no reason to assume, therefore, that the condition of women actually improved in the early years of colonial rule. The response of many concubines that the time had come to terminate their "marriages" through flight indicates that the risks that women were willing to take changed considerably. Certainly British ideas that slave women became emancipated on marriage conflicted with the reality that many women faced, and indeed twisted the meaning of "emancipation" as the term was increasingly being used by women in Britain itself in the struggle for greater rights.

As with male slaves, the colonial approach to female slaves also relied on the Islamic courts, although in the case of women it was convenient to blur the distinction between concubinage and marriage and thereby pretend that matters of slavery were matrimonial in nature. Once again, Lugard could claim that the legal status of slavery was not being recognized. The Islamic courts were allowed to continue to treat women very much as they always had over issues of inheritance, divorce, custody of children, and land ownership, but when it came to slavery, there was a new twist. In some cases, at least, the Islamic courts reenforced concubinage as an institution, and rather than hastening the demise of slavery for women, actually perpetuated it. In the early years, the British regime was more concerned with the potential dangers of the flight of male slaves, and hence the Islamic courts were allowed to impose constraints on male slaves to reduce the attractions of desertion and otherwise keep them with their masters. Self-redemption was encouraged as the mechanism to compensate slave owners for those slaves who could be prevented from running away or who chose to stay. Women mattered primarily because their resistance upset the influential men of Caliphate society, the very people whom the colonial regime needed. By consigning female slavery issues to the Islamic courts as matrimonial disputes, the British deferred to the interests of the aristocracy and merchants. In the short run, this dimension of "legal-status abolition" was expedient, but when young girls who were clearly born after March 31, 1901 became a noticeable portion of the concubine population, a situation that developed by the end of the First World War, British attitudes had to change (see Chapter 8).

5

Upholding proprietary rights to land

The slavery policy instituted by Lugard and maintained by the British administration after his departure in 1906 was heavily dependent for its efficacy on colonial reforms of land tenure. Tenure policies were intended to be, and did in practice serve as, a major element affecting the decisions of both masters and agricultural slaves. Thus even though the institution of slavery was not abolished, economic forces as shaped by the land system worked to keep many slaves, especially males, in place while at the same time diminishing slavery as a viable institution. Policies on land tenure had only a marginal impact on the many women slaves who were not involved in agriculture. Since tenure matters were almost entirely focused on men, even those women slaves who lived in rural areas were only indirectly affected by colonial land policy.

The British regime more or less immediately used land policy to inhibit the wholesale defection of slaves. Even by 1903, it was clear that inability to gain access to land except that available from arrangements with masters was a primary element preventing slaves from deserting. On the one hand fugitive slaves were denied land wherever proprietary rights were clearly established, and that included most of the desirable areas of settlement. On the other hand, those slaves who stayed in place had to rent land or continue to farm their masters' lands in exchange for labor, a share of crops, and other obligations. Freed slaves were only able to acquire proprietary rights to land gradually.

Without access to land, the slaves of Northern Nigeria found it difficult to support themselves if they fled their masters. A primary component in the control of the slave population was therefore the amalgam of Caliphate land law and custom with current British ideas on land tenure that had a significant effect in preventing such access. These measures of control amounted to an informal "Jim Crow" system that ensured that the slaves would for many years remain a class dependent on their masters for access to land.[1] Only rural landholding in the emirates is considered in this chapter, and that only so far as the landholding system affected slaves.[2] Even slaves who attempted to make their way as laborers or artisans in cities and towns were virtually always farmers as well. Most slaves, therefore, were farmers whether they stayed in slavery, were emancipated, or became fugitives. Because they could not easily obtain access to land, the vast majority were forced to remain with their masters, where such access *was* available.

Land tenure under the Caliphate

Before the British conquest, land was held under a variety of tenures. As a result of the *jihad*, the Sokoto and Gwandu areas were declared state lands that could be granted to supporters at the will of the Shehu, and subsequently Caliph Bello and Emir Abdullahi. Previously farmed lands tended to remain state lands, while individuals were given proprietary rights to long-vacant lands. By contrast, the Hausa states of Kano, Zaria, Katsina, and the future emirates elsewhere were declared *waqf*, which in the Maliki school of Islamic law meant that these lands were subject to *kharaj* or land tax (Hausa: *kurdin kasa*).[3] Vacant lands were administered by the various emirates, to be granted to free settlers upon application to local authorities. Some land was recognized as common pasture, and cattle trails were protected from the encroachment of farmers. The emirs also allowed Muslim clerics to work state lands, relying for labor on their students. The land of non-Muslim protected peoples, such as the Maguzawa of Kano and Katsina, involved another category of tenure. As far as Caliphate officials were concerned, these lands were held communally and could not be alienated outside the community. Recognition of these communal rights was dependent upon payment of a special tax (*jizya*). Many of the tributary communities in southern Zaria, Adamawa, Bauchi, and other emirates maintained their lands under similar conditions. For our purposes, a recognition of these land claims is important in understanding why slaves could not easily find vacant land which they could occupy.[4]

Most land, and virtually all of the desirable agricultural land in the emirates, was either state land attached to political office or private land to which individuals had proprietary rights. In both cases, slaves were used extensively to cultivate the land under conditions that resembled slave plantations elsewhere. Many political officials had far more slaves than even the wealthiest commoners, so that there were significant differences in the organization of slave labor depending upon the size of holdings. Some slave-owning officials controlled more slaves than the wealthiest master of the Americas.[5]

The land that was attached to political office, whether the officials were slave or free, changed hands when new officials were appointed. These lands could not be bought or sold. Virtually all political offices had farms and plantations that were worked by slaves, who sometimes passed with the lands as offices changed hands because the officials were slaves themselves and could not inherit. Officials also used their own private slaves to work these lands, and corvée labor was often an obligation of local communities and in effect amounted to an additional tax on the free population. The existence of these official estates has led M. G. Smith to employ terms reminiscent of serfdom in analyzing the Hausa emirates, but we are reluctant to use the same terminology.[6] Most slaves were too recently settled to have acquired the hereditary characteristics of a serf population.

Proprietary rights to land were granted on application and payment of a fee to the emirs. Recipients included aristocrats, scholars, merchants, craftsmen, livestock herders, and other freemen with skills and substantial non-agricultural income. Much of this land was allocated in the early part of the nineteenth century in the central Hausa emirates. These lands could be bought and sold, inherited, and rented. Inheritance and sales had resulted in a bewildering mosaic of land claims, with many individuals owning land in more than one village. Absentee landownership by individual farmers known as *nomijide* was common, especially in Kano Emirate, while some women had acquired land through inheritance. Individuals often had more than one farm, including both irrigated lands (*fadama*) and land where grain and cotton were grown during the rainy season.

As Hill has suggested, smallholders probably constituted a majority of the free agricultural population.[7] Certainly most of the land in the densely populated areas surrounding Kano was divided into small plots, often amounting to only a few acres, and even when allowance is made for dispersed holdings and the *gayauna* gardens of slaves, it seems that the average farmer seldom controlled more than 5–10 acres. Hill has claimed that "a high proportion of farmers owned no slaves," although we believe that many *talakawa* had a slave or two who helped with their farms. She is probably correct, despite our qualifications, in stating that "few private farmers owned more than about ten or twenty [slaves]."[8]

Furthermore, many smallholders worked family farms that were known as *gandu*, which was also a term used to describe plantations. Under colonialism, *gandu* farms increasingly relied on family labor rather than slaves, but this development should not disguise the historical roots of the *gandu*. In the nineteenth century, *gandu* usually meant that a family owned slaves, ranging in numbers from a slave or two to very considerable numbers, in the scores and occasionally in the hundreds. With the demise of slavery, family labor had to substitute for slavery, but many slaves who were working on their own account in return for a fee paid to their masters (*murgu*) augmented family labor for several decades into colonial rule. As slavery declined, hired labor became increasingly common (see Chapter 7).

The plantation sector

There were three categories of large holdings. First, estates attached to political office were worked by slaves who either belonged to the officials or to the office, if the title could only be held by slaves. Known as *gandun sarauta* (*gandu* of office), *rinjin sarauta* (*rinji* of office), or *bado* (gift or grant), the estates could not be sold or otherwise disposed of, since they went with the title. Second, wealthy commoners, especially merchants and members of the aristocracy, including office holders, owned estates that remained in their families and could be sold or rented. These plantations and farms were known simply as *rinji* or *gandu* in Hausa areas and *tunga* in Nupe. Third, the dispersed holdings of many farmers often amounted to considerable estates. Slaves were moved to these scattered farms under the direction of one or more overseers or the master himself. In terms of size and the number of slaves that were employed, the most important holdings were the estates attached to political office. The private estates of the aristocracy were next in importance, followed by the estates of the merchants. Furthermore there were regional variations: there were few large estates owned by commoners near Sokoto, while around Kano there were many such holdings by commoners.

The official estates attached to political office were a feature of Islamic society that would survive into the colonial era as a means of obtaining the support of the aristocracy. They were numerous and extensive. According to Temple,

> the rule that a farm is attached to every office is practically universal ... Certainly every emirship, and headship of a district or village (even the smallest) has a "gandu" attached. To every important court official's office a farm is attached, and very often even the galadimas or village sarkis will be found to have an official farm ... The gandu or state farm goes with the office. The possession passes, when the holder of the office is deposed, to his successor. If he dies, to his official successor, not to his legal heirs. The official may have other farms of which he is the legal occupant by permission of a chief; these he retains when deposed; if he dies they pass to his legal heirs ... There is generally, in the case of important chiefs, a good deal of chattel personal which is attached to their offices (Kayan sarota) [*kayan sarauta*]. This passes to successive holders, just as the "gandu" passes.[9]

Because the aristocracy acquired slaves through annual slave raids and tribute payments, it was possible for most officials to amass considerable holdings in slaves. New captives were distributed as gifts to political subordinates, while the active slave trade from the frontiers made new captives readily available. Slaves were cheap, and for many officials free. Let us consider some of the emirates.

Every official in Sokoto, from the Sarkin Musulmi down to the most insignificant hamlet head, had a *rinji* or *gandu* attached to his office.[10] Many of these officials also had private estates. Based on interviews conducted in the rural areas around Sokoto, Jumare collected information on thirty-seven plantations that were still in operation in 1988. We have already commented on the plantations in the four districts that surrounded Satiru. In 1904 Burdon referred to "chiefs of outlying towns" who "generally owned slaves, who worked their large farms."[11] These estates varied in size from relatively small plantations with a few score slaves, such as the small hamlet of Kaura Alhaji in Silame District, west of Sokoto, which belonged to the Sarkin

Musulmi, to very extensive estates with hundreds of slaves. In 1913, Kaura Alhaji had eight compounds and forty-nine people, but the Caliph had many, many plantations.[12] Other estates, especially in the area of Wurno, to the north of Sokoto, were far more extensive than Kaura Alhaji.

In 1908, Hewby reported from Kano, "nearly every office in the Emirate has a 'Gandu' farm attached to it." Even many of the *jakadu* – tax collectors who were slaves – "had houses of their own in the areas under [their] authority," presumably with land attached.[13] Palmer observed a similar pattern in Katsina, where "every responsible chief has a farm of his own." In Kazaure "one of the chiefs had a very big farm," which is not to suggest that there were no others. Palmer noted that these estates varied in size but were "cultivated by slaves."[14]

The *gandun sarauta* must have numbered well over 10,000 for the Caliphate as a whole. A reasonable estimate for Kano Emirate alone would put the total there at over 4,000.[15] In Sokoto and Gwandu, where there were no land or crop taxes before the British conquest and hence officials did not benefit from land tax (see Chapter 6), state farms and plantations were particularly important to the incomes of officials. Hence the number of *gandun sarauta* in these capital districts was probably at least as great as in Kano. Considering that there were thirty emirates and many large sub-emirates in the Caliphate, the number of official estates may well have been much greater than our intentionally conservative estimate. The variations and exceptions deserve study.

Zaria differed from other emirates, according to Orr, who reported that there was "no evidence" of the existence of official state lands that were designated as *gandun sarauta* "except in cases of village headmen."

> I am assured that there are no official farms attached to the office of Emir or any other office of State, but that every family has its land, which descends in the family from father to son. Thus the family of the late Emir retains its farms, which are situated in a different part of the Province to those belonging to the present Emir. What was attached to the various offices of State was not property in land but property in men to work them, i.e., slaves. They passed with the office.[16]

Zaria was peculiar in having several lineages eligible for the emirship, which passed in rotation. Each lineage had its own lands. Despite this variation, the existence of state slaves who were attached to office allowed officials to deploy state-owned labor on their family lands. And the exception is instructive because members of the aristocracy wanted additional slaves to work the extensive land-holdings under their control, while village headmen did not have access to as much land. They needed official estates as a source of personal revenue.

The private estates of the aristocracy were often substantial. In 1908, Girouard, who would claim before the Northern Nigeria Lands Committee that private rights to land did not exist, even acknowledged these holdings. Girouard recognized that certain areas of cultivated land are held by Emirs or their courts. These in the past have been worked by slaves. Some are probably attached to the office held, though *it would appear that private and individual rights are asserted in others.*[17]

Girouard appears never to have explained his distinction between "private and individual rights" and his testimony before the Lands Committee that no such rights existed.

While only fragmentary evidence on the extent of large holdings has survived, there are enough data to indicate that holdings were often quite large, with some as large as the big plantations of the Americas. One estate in Rafin Yamulu, near Wurno, had 210 acres under cultivation in 1908; it was the remnant of a much more extensive plantation that had been opened in the late 1820s. There were at least two other private estates in the Rafin Yamulu – those of Kasara and Hakimi Atto [Audu?].[18] Information on these plantations was not always easy to obtain, but Stanley, who assessed the area in 1908, identified several.[19]

The estates varied considerably in size. In Dan Isa Sub-District, immediately outside Kano city, bordering the Challawa River, there was a "Gandu village called Rinjin Kashin" which belonged to the Chiroma of Kano, 42 acres in extent. The people of the village were

> slaves of Chiroma's and ... their farms are Gandu farms. Their headman is named Awdu [Audu]; there are 15 men, 20 women and about 25 children in the village ... There are in addition several other smaller Gandu farms in various villages in the Sub-District, some belonging to the mother of the present Emir and others to various Hakimai.[20]

Dan Buram's *rinji* at Wase, also in Kano Emirate, had 255 acres under cultivation at the time of the British conquest.[21]

D. F. H. MacBride's survey of Dawaki ta Kudu District, only six miles from Kano in the bend of the Challawa River, revealed that slave holdings were extensive in this area as well.[22] This densely populated area (299 sq. m.), which had a population of 104,000 in 1937, consisted of about 100 villages in 1900, many of which were inhabited only by slaves. Except for villages that belonged to Muslim clerics, all the land was controlled by officials, mostly free but some slave, and the Emir Aliyu (and subsequently his successors) controlled a considerable number of plantations. Some land, together with the slave population, belonged to descendants of the ousted Hausa dynasty that had been displaced by the *jihad* early in the nineteenth century.

As one of the largest landlords, the Emir of Kano controlled thousands of acres of land that was cultivated by slaves. These included three *rinji* in the Minjibir area: Gasgainu and Yokanna under Jakada Garko and Sawaina under the Shamaki, a slave official who managed other plantations for the Emir as well, including those in the Dawaki ta Kudu area. The Gasgainu plantation had 1,053 acres under cultivation when it was measured in 1912, while the comparable figures for Yokanna and Sawaina were 351 and 264 acres respectively.[23] Further indication of the Emir's holdings can be gleaned from a 1936 report that gives the acreage of seventeen farms and plantations. The list does not include Madarin Taba and other holdings in Dawaki ta Kudu district, which were discovered after the 1936 survey was completed, nor does it include Gasgainu, Yokanna, Sawaina, Gandun Nassarawa, Gogel, and other estates studied by Sa'idu and Yunusa.[24] Nonetheless, the seventeen holdings that were recorded had a combined acreage of 1,235.53 acres under cultivation in 1936. While it is not clear whether all the holdings can be traced to the precolonial period, they probably can.[25] The size of the Emir's holdings was unusual in that there were not many individuals who owned that much land or that many slaves, but the Emirs of Zaria, Adamawa, Katsina, and Gwandu surely did, and the Sarkin Musulmi may well have had holdings that were greater than any of these officials.

The private estates of merchants and other commoners were also extensive around Kano, and again slave holdings were considerable. According to Tahir, "the merchant class owned most of the cultivated land [around Kano]," but emancipation of slaves undermined "much of the capital value of land," while British "inquiries into holdings created apprehension among the class; particularly because of the calculation of tax burdens according to land holdings."[26] Ubah has noted that many slaves were settled on their master's *gandaya*, "for the big agricultural estates of the great men of Kano depended on slave labour."[27] It is difficult to bridge the gap between the reported data on landholdings and the possible size of total acreage belonging to individuals, both because individuals controlled land under a variety of tenures and in different locations and because data are simply hard to come by. Nonetheless, the scattered information that is available suggests lines of inquiry.

In Jaidanawa District, near Kano, "Ex Office holders and other rich men of Kano town have farms of some considerable area there, e.g. the younger sister of the Emir has 89 acres, Ex Dan Buram 59 and so on [and] ... many of the farmers are absentee owners," whose "servants" went out from Kano "to work on the farms." Some of these "absentee owners ... have farms in other districts too."[28] The largest estate had 124 acres under cultivation. "A large number of the villagers are Nomijide [absentee farmers], living in Kano and having farms in the villages."[29] Reports vary on the size of the holdings of Kundilla, reputedly the wealthiest commoner in Kano at the end of the nineteenth century. Accounts credit him with from 600 to well over 1,000 slaves, and most of these worked his lands.[30] There were other wealthy planter-merchants as well.[31] It should be noted that acreage almost always refers to cultivated land, not actual holdings, which included waste land, building sites, rented land, and probably the gardens worked by slaves.

These private estates could be bought and sold, sub-divided, inherited, and rented. In Katsina, as Palmer noted, "farms are sold," a point that Hill has emphasized in her study of Batagarawa, also in Katsina Emirate.[32] Gowers confirmed these observations with respect to Bauchi, where farmers obtained practically a freehold tenure from which they could not be ousted arbitrarily. Further, they could alienate the whole or any portion of their rights in the land either by sale or lease, or in some cases by testamentary disposition.[33]

This was always the case, because slave officials could not pass on state lands, and even some free officials had access to state lands which could not be disposed of.

Gowers summed up the situation by comparing land tenure in Britain and Northern Nigeria:

> as in England so in the Emirates of Northern Nigeria, absolute ownership of land by individuals is unknown, but the fixity of tenure subject to due payment of tribute [tax] and the fact that this tenure can be transferred, practically amounts to ownership (I accordingly use the terms "owner" and "proprietor" in their commonly accepted senses).[34]

We concur and, following Gowers, use these terms in the same way. Furthermore, we avoid the term "private property," because it disguises the fact that there were a variety of tenure arrangements and confuses the issue with respect to slavery. As we will see in Chapter 6, many of the largest slave owners were exempted from the payment of many taxes, other than the tithe, so that even failure to pay the land tax (*kurdin kasa*) frequently could not be used to confiscate land. This was particularly so in the capital districts of Sokoto and Gwandu, for example, because people were not subject to any tax other than the tithe; *kurdin kasa* was not collected before the colonial era.

Territorial administration in the precolonial period

The administration of Caliphate territory followed Islamic principles of government in which officials – elected, appointed, and hereditary – were responsible for specific parts of the emirates. In particularly large emirates, such as Adamawa, there were sub-emirates that were sometimes larger than many of the smaller emirates, but the principles of administration were similar in most, if not all, cases. Officials, both slave and free, maintained the security of their domains, with respect both to police functions and to defense against foreign incursion. They raised military levies, often voluntary when slave raiding was intended but compulsory in the event of invasion. They supervised the assessment and collection of taxes, provided access to the emir, and otherwise attended to the peace, security, and prosperity of the areas of jurisdiction.

This system of government has sometimes been called "feudal" because of the allegiance of the various territorial officials to their emirs. The groupings of towns and villages have been referred to as "fiefs" and the officials as "fiefholders."[35] This analysis, which can be labeled the "serfdom" model of Caliphate society, has been employed by those colonial officials and some scholars to emphasize the importance of political dependency, not only among the freeborn but between slave officials and free aristocrats. The existence of land attached to political office also is a factor in their analysis. According to this interpretation, fief boundaries were often explicitly marked and were often attached to a political office, with the fiefholders responsible to the emir and frequently resident in the emirate capital. Certain anomalies are cited as evidence of this "feudal" arrangement: for example, several Katsina fiefholders owed allegiance direct to Sokoto and not to the Emir of Katsina. In Kano, the fiefholders lived in the city, but in Sokoto, Katsina, and Katagum they resided in the countryside, each in a grand palace at a defensible *ribat*. The establishment of a system of *ribatu* is further evidence that defense was more significant than proprietary rights in land.

Despite the power of this conceptual framework, we contend that the feudal analogy underestimates the importance of slavery, and we agree with Garba that the term "fiefholders" does not accurately define their functions with respect to land. According to Garba,

> the function of these officials was more or less ... administrative control over vacant or waste lands in trust for the community. These territorial chiefs – or even the emirs for that matter – did not claim any "proprietary rights" over the lands under their administrative control; neither did they interfere unduly with local land administration. They were more concerned with the collection of taxes, and left the cultivators undisturbed, provided, that is, they paid their taxes. Even in the case of vacant or waste lands, the villages and hamlets were allowed, under their local heads, to exercise their customary rights of disposal.[36]

These officials controlled taxation over certain categories of citizens, specifically those who owned land in the villages under their jurisdiction. Tax "farming" was a major source of revenue for Caliphate officials, whether these officials were slave or free. Their relationship to the land derived from this function and from the need to raise military levies. They also supervised famine relief and other measures of social security.

Their principal agents were slave subordinates (Hausa: *jakadu*) who administered the collection of taxes, and because of their interest in revenue, were also strongly interested in matters of land tenure. Village heads (Hausa: *mai unguwa, dagatai*) were the local representatives with whom the *jakadu* dealt. They set the rate of taxation, and from the point of view of the land-tenure system, they allocated land for settlement. The personal contacts between the village heads and the *jakadu* were frequent. The village heads, usually Fulani and often respected farmers themselves, were appointed by the territorial officials and usually invested by the emir. They exercised many local administrative functions.[37] No one could occupy or farm land within the jurisdiction of the village head without the consent of that official. The village head also determined the rate of taxation, and this considerable power, added to his jurisdiction over the right to settle, meant that access to land was firmly in the hands of these administrators.[38] Ironically, many of these officials were slaves, which is why their land and slave holdings were attached to the office and not actually "owned."

In Kano, by a tradition given universal accord, a village head and even a hamlet head could "on his own authority forbid transfer" of land "to a man of known bad character."[39] One of the village head's tasks was to report the arrival of strangers to the territorial official. Almost all authorities agree that this system of close control over land was a distinguishing feature of the tenure system. For example, Bello states that in precolonial Kano, the Emir appointed the village heads and that "rights to use the land by peasant households were usually acquired from the officials and particularly the village heads."[40] Mahadi states that in nineteenth-century Kano, the village heads allocated land.[41] Tibenderana shows that village heads in Sokoto and Gwandu had the same power.[42] Oyeyipo reports that in Ilorin, the heads of villages retained this authority under the British "without major changes."[43] Lands were administered by village officials in Nupe also, and these officials and the village heads always judged applications by strangers to take up land.[44]

In many cases the power to allocate land was delegated to hamlet heads, who reported to the village officials. The status of these hamlet heads was encouraged by the British; in the precolonial period they did not exist as a separate office, and village heads major and minor assigned land.[45] During the colonial era, these hamlet heads were often Hausa rather than Fulani, and as such were clients of the village head. They were frequently the officials in the far-flung "bush hamlets" that were in charge of allocating "bush land" (Hausa: *gonar daji*), that is, virgin land or long-unused fallow on the extensive margin of cultivation.[46] When settlement was extended and new villages were established, hamlets were grouped with a parent community as a single unit or placed under a newly appointed village head subject to the territorial official. While no doubt there were instances when this bureaucracy failed to do its duty, the arrangements facilitated the surveillance of slave movements and indeed the settlement of anyone else. It certainly made it possible to supervise access to land for slaves fairly closely.

The options facing slaves after the colonial conquest

With the conquest, slaves faced a decision, whether to remain with their masters as slaves, perhaps making some arrangement to purchase their freedom, or whether to become fugitives. We have already seen that many slaves elected to flee, but the choice to do so was not obvious. Contemporary land tenure and the system of land allocation did much to bias the decision against desertion. Colonial policy to uphold proprietary rights to land added to the problem of slaves who were thinking about leaving. Slaves could choose to return to their places of origin. Many did so, as already discussed in Chapter 2, especially in the first years of British rule. Yet this option was a limited one, because those who had been born into slavery had no personal

136

memory of a former homeland,[47] and no home to go to, and those who *did* have a personal memory of a former home may have found the memory an unpleasant one. Perhaps they had been sold into slavery by their family or their neighbors, or perhaps their enslavement had been a judicial punishment inflicted by the community. There was always a possibility that relatives at home would not welcome the arrival of long-absent slave kin, and would not share their land with the returnee. What if siblings, spouses, or other relatives had established new bonds that excluded the slave? In that case, the returning slave might have great difficulty in obtaining subsistence. An ancestral homeland might be quite far removed – many slaves at Kano, for example, came from southern Adamawa in what is now Cameroun or from lands beyond Borno. Slave raiders were still active, especially in the Adamawa region.[48] The sentiment that slaves should not leave their masters was shared by both the masters and the British; they might be taken on the roads and returned. If a slave had a spouse and children, then the obstacles would be even greater – more mouths to feed on the journey, higher visibility and thus more vulnerability to recapture, more responsibility if a place on a farm was not available in the homeland. If, however, the spouse and the children were left behind, that would obviously be a drastic and often painful sacrifice.[49]

Slaves had options. They sometimes changed masters while remaining in slavery, which involved leaving one master without his permission, and attaching themselves to another or otherwise making a transfer possible. Oral data are particularly rich on this phenomenon, sometimes slaves being credited with "taking themselves to market" for the purpose of sale to new owners. Slaves are even attributed with the right to determine who the new master would be.[50] Such exchanges were intrinsically difficult because legal problems were likely to arise, and because a move might challenge public opinion. There are indications, discussed by Christelow, that slaves nonetheless did sometimes exchange masters during the period up to the First World War, coming to arrangements with prominent slave owners including village heads and others in positions of authority.[51] Such masters could hope to avoid or ignore the ire of the former owner. The frequency of such occurrences is uncertain, but if aggrieved masters thought that slaves might avail themselves of this option, they probably would have been more willing to accommodate the slaves to some extent.

If a male slave decided neither to attempt a return to a homeland nor to exchange masters, then he might consider becoming a fugitive aiming to take up land for farming at some distance removed from his present abode. If the area selected was a settled one, the slave would have to approach the village head where he wished to acquire land, or the hamlet head if that post existed, and announce his intention. Such a meeting would usually be difficult to arrange before the final act of departure from the old home. Visiting a place beforehand involved a conspicuous absence from the master's farm; and even if the slave could arrange this on one pretext or another (say, sale of goods in a market town), the trip itself would be burdensome. Furthermore, it would be dangerous. There are reports of "bounty hunters" in the early colonial period. In 1907, Temple reported that Sarkin Tambawal Shehu "had held runaway slaves to ransom."[52]

Thus fugitive slaves would most likely have to make the approach at the end of the very trip in which they became fugitives. Assuming that a new arrival was judged to be a desirable resident, land could be allocated to him from the unused acreage in the area, but usually this also involved a payment or "gift." Certainly unused land was often available – either land that had been farmed, the last occupant having died, long moved, or decided not to continue farming it or bush land previously not farmed or long in fallow.[53] As M. G. Smith notes,

> Land rights are thus contingent on community membership expressed as allegiance to the community chief, whose office includes trusteeship for the community over its unoccupied land.[54]

Alternatively, with enough ready money, a slave could purchase land from an existing owner, but that had to be registered, too. Lack of ready cash on the part of slaves would have made this procedure rare, to say the least.

In a major respect, the land-allocation mechanism served to put unused land into cultivation, and so improved a fugitive's chances of obtaining a plot of his own. The village heads and *jakadu* were not responsible to the local community of farmers, but instead to the territorial officials (the later district heads). Thus land was probably easier to acquire than otherwise, because putting it into use provided another tax payer to the benefit of the official, and perhaps some regular gifts for the village head. If the local farmers had their way, they might have preferred keeping the land for themselves.[55] As we shall see below, however, the British and indigenous authorities utilized this mechanism to ensure that fugitive slaves would *not* obtain land.

Another possibility was that a fugitive might farm unclaimed "bush" at some distance from where he had worked as a slave. In Islamic legal tradition, "dead" bush land *could* be utilized for farming without permission of the ruler.[56] Thus if a slave found a bush tract so far removed from any hamlet or village that no question of authority arose, he might be able to avoid the surveillance mechanism. This was undoubtedly most feasible in areas of low population density, such as the border lands between the emirates and the low-density areas inhabited by the Maguzawa. Where population was denser, it would have been virtually impossible. But there was little if any such land. Permission to settle was virtually always necessary, even in remote areas.

Girouard wrote in 1908 that "there would appear to be practically no land not subject to village or tribal claim."[57] When Goldsmith was asked "if anyone settled in this presumably waste land could they say whose land it was?", his answer was, "Probably not; but nobody would settle without asking the local chief or the emir."[58] Temple insisted that there is not an inch of land which is not claimed by one tribe or another. To draw any distinction between waste and cultivated land, as regards proprietorship, would be going against native law and custom, and in practice very difficult.[59]

He had already written from Sokoto that "it would be impossible to differentiate in any province between occupied and waste land, I think."[60] Palmer, in a statement about Katsina, noted that "one could not differentiate between occupied and waste land."[61] In Nupe, there was "no waste land, i.e. implying lands absolutely unclaimed." Fremantle noted that village heads "are very tenacious of their rights as regards strangers."[62]

To a significant degree, these British authorities were misstating the facts. There is far too much circumstantial evidence that uninhabited bush lands *were* being taken up at the very time fugitive slaves were leaving their masters in large numbers. On the basis of her work in rural Kano, Hill has asserted that the controls over land allocation did not prevent slaves from clearing bush land immediately after leaving their masters.[63] Tukur Bello Ingawa notes that in most cases of land regulation in Katsina, "the rural administrator ultimately performed the role of the comptroller of land," but even so people did on occasion "carve out" bush land, clearing it for a farm, without permission from any village or hamlet head.[64] Christelow states that "unimproved bush land ... could be appropriated by an individual clearing the land." He cites only one case concerning such land in his study of the Kano judicial records of 1913–14, but that case is instructive:

> When a headman apparently sought to control his subjects' access to bush land, Emir Abbas bluntly told him that "farmland is more valuable to us than bush [Case 98B]." Provided an individual had reliable witnesses to his clearing and farming a piece of land, he could maintain "a secure claim to it.[65]

Christelow does not explain what a "reliable witness" was, but presumably witnesses testified to the character of the settlers, including whether or not they were slaves, but the desire to bring more land under cultivation must have militated against close scrutiny in all cases. M. G. Smith indicates that in Zaria also, many slaves did indeed disperse to bush lands in time, and some of these could have been fugitives.[66]

Slaves fleeing their masters must have been part of the population movements reported by British officials in the years immediately after the uprising at Satiru. Migration appears to have been especially frequent into the uncultivated border lands between Sokoto and Argungu, parts of Gwandu, and into similar derelict land on the Kano–Katsina border, in southern Kano, and in parts of Zaria.[67] Burdon reported from Sokoto in 1905 that there had been a "repopulation" of some deserted areas, and the repatriation of freed slaves "under conditions of self-redemption."[68] Benton, who supervised the assessment of 105 villages in Gwandu in 1906, observed with satisfaction that 74 of these were

> newly re-occupied since the fall of Sokoto in 1903, and the progress of returning to former sites is continuing. There is also a large influx of refugees

> from Tambawel and other districts now that the peace is assured ... Rather more than $\frac{1}{3}$rd of the total population [of 28,449] is in these new villages.[69]

Empty land between Katsina and Zamfara was also taken up, settlement was pushed southeastward towards Ningi, and new farms were opened up in Katagum.[70] All these areas had been subject to precolonial raiding but were now safe for farming.[71] While in some cases, people reasserted their access to land based on existing rights, it is hard to believe that all cases involved farmers returning to land that they already owned.

Major A. H. Festing, the Resident at Kano in 1907, wrote of the "most evident" tendency

> throughout the Province for the peasant class to leave the towns and take up land for cultivation ... But unfortunately it also means that this class are becoming less under control of the Chiefs.[72]

The term "peasant class" when used by British officials in Northern Nigeria was often meant to include slaves, as indeed it appears to do in this quotation. D. F. H. MacBride later described the process in some detail for an area close to Kano city, where some nucleated settlements were being transformed into hamlets. The area, Dawaki ta Kudu District, was characterized by a large slave population. It is not always clear whether people actually obtained permission to settle or not, but in the case of Dawaki ta Kudu, slaves were moving to their farms because of the security of the colonial era and because the relationship to their masters was changing.[73] Wherever there was movement back to previously inhabited villages, as around Gwandu and in Bauchi near Ningi, existing titles were honored, though there were many instances of unclaimed land.[74]

Yet taking up bush land as an individual posed serious difficulties to anyone without resources, which included most fugitive slaves. Because people lived in hamlets and villages, the lone farmer on the land was subject to suspicion, even if he had managed to obtain seed, clear a field, and bring in a harvest. People had to eat during the hungry months before the harvest, and the search for food forced isolated individuals to seek casual employment. These difficulties would have been so severe that they suggest flight by former slaves to individual farms was *not* the common practice. The taking up of land in the bush would very likely have attracted the attention of those who had an interest in keeping the slaves in place. Furthermore, living alone in the bush would have been at all times contrary to the practice in rural Hausaland then and now, where farmers almost always live in villages rather than on scattered farmsteads.

Some slaves had the added handicap of facial and body markings that carried the permanent identification of slave status of a *bacucane* (child of slaves) or a captive.[75] For these fugitive slaves, usufructary rights were insecure no matter what the law said. Even in the case cited by Christelow where Emir Abbas of Kano upheld the rights of a man who cleared and occupied bush land against the claim of a village head in 1913, there was

140

ambiguity. Though the case seems to imply that distant, uncleared bush land was free for the taking, the community still retained rights to the land because "an outsider would need permission from the headman, and the consent of the community to enjoy *secure* [our italics] rights to the land which he had cleared."[76] Slaves could take up distant bush land, farm it, and perhaps not be bothered by the authorities, but the security of tenure that a freeman could count on would not be theirs.

Furthermore, farmers living alone were more or less cut off from the network of larger family support and client relationships that came with village life. Compare the life of a single fugitive to life with a master. Obviously the fugitive would lose his place in the master's *gandu*. Membership in a *gandu* brought protection – it was an individual's insurance policy – and involved some economies of scale. There was access to economically important trees and free use of the tools provided by the master. Finally, slaves-in-*gandu* had their own *gayauna* gardens that could be worked after labor was ended on the *gandu* farm (from the time of afternoon prayer) or on the day or two (usually Friday but occasionally Thursday and Sunday) when the *gandu* field was not worked. Protection provided by the master, economies of scale, access to trees and tools, and use of a private plot of land would all be left behind by the fugitive. While the number of *rinji*, except those on state lands, tended to decline under colonial rule, the institution of *gandu* did not. Instead *gandu* evolved into what Hill and others have described as a mechanism for working farms on the basis of kinship, usually involving fathers and sons but sometimes brothers.[77]

Even if slaves managed to take up bush land, they would have to clear it and put in a crop as soon as possible; otherwise, how would they feed themselves? As slaves in *gandu* or on a *rinji*, they had access to their own production and the communal granaries (Hausa: *rumbu*), but not in some distant location.[78] Slaves would have to suffer from reduced yields for a year or more, because it takes that long to break in the fallow soils of the savanna. Seed would have to come from somewhere, and an individual had to carry that with him or barter some possession for it, for otherwise who would give or lend him seed or the money to buy it? In a year of reduced rainfall and food shortages or famine, which was common between 1901 and 1908, such problems were serious, especially because these conditions meant that slaves on the run would have to seek work for wages.[79] A slave would have to build a hut, and until that was accomplished, he would have to sleep in the open. What if he fell ill? None of the necessary tasks could easily be accomplished in secrecy, and it was likely that the nearest village or hamlet head would be aware of a new arrival within a matter of days.[80]

The many disadvantages militated against individual action by fugitives. The strong implication is that when slaves left their masters to establish bush farms, it was, more commonly than appears in some of the surviving reports, a group decision. Many of the risks entailed in acting as an individual were reduced if the movement occurred in a group. Safety in numbers, enhanced ability to carry tools and seed, inclusion of women, division of labor in ploughing, planting, cooking, and providing shelter all made group action more understandable than individual flight. It is noteworthy that in the *rinji* owned by Baba of Karo's father and that of Hanwa, both near Zaria, many of the slaves fled in groups after the arrival of the British.[81] In the case of Hanwa, the slaves even armed themselves with bows and arrows, so an increased ability to defend themselves to some extent offset their greater visibility on the roads. By the time the authorities had mobilized a force large enough to seize them, with luck they would already be out of reach.

The advantages of group movement and the readiness to band together once on the road explain the existence of independent communities of ex-slaves referred to on occasion. As Lugard observed in 1906, though without details, there was a "strong inducement to farm slaves to leave their masters, and form new communities," particularly by "migrating to distant places," where they owed "allegiance to no chief or clan."[82] The explicit lack of allegiance to village heads in the neighborhood must imply the taking up of bush land; otherwise violence between the former slaves and the existing communities in the area would surely have been the result. We have already noted friction between communities that were harboring fugitives and local Muslim authorities, particularly in Nassarawa, Nupe, and Muri and in the outstanding case of Satiru (see Chapter 2). We suggest that these examples are indicative of a wider pattern.

Many refugee communities were apparently not unlike Satiru, except that they were smaller and without the exuberant Mahdism. Satiru was also founded a decade before the British conquest of Sokoto, and hence was an established sanctuary that was willing to accept individuals. To some degree, once new communities were established they facilitated the flight of slaves, who would presumably receive some welcome rather than having to fend for themselves. The mechanism by which knowledge concerning farm settlements of ex-slaves filtered back to those still enslaved is unknown, although we assume that the trips of slaves to carry their masters' produce to village and town markets were the major factors in assisting the spread of such knowledge.

We speculate that the number of slaves fleeing to such communities of ex-slaves must have been in the low tens of thousands, which is not large considering the total slave population; but the number still represents a major phenomenon.[83] The number was kept low because of the obvious disadvantages of making the move in the first place. An optimistic fugitive might conclude that the disadvantages of fleeing alone to a solitary bush plot could be avoided by deserting with or joining an existing large group of like-minded slaves, assuming he could find such a group. Yet a slave would still have to consider that if he remained with his master, he would have a patron and defender; his access to land, a house, tools, and seed would continue; his food supply would be more assured; he ran no risk of capture on the roads or later, with possibly a worse fate thereafter; marriage partners known to him would likely be available among his fellow slaves, if he were not already married; and his master would facilitate his marriage and probably provide the necessary wedding gifts. These considerations would have to be weighed with care before the choice was made to leave.

We recognize that individuals do not always act rationally but are forced by temperament, passion, or circumstance to act otherwise. The condition of slavery was such that individual slaves ran away regardless. Certainly there was a flood of refugees back to their places of origin or wherever in the early years of colonial rule. After that, however, the evidence – fragmentary and mostly informative by its absence – indicates that the majority of slaves, having duly pondered, decided to remain in captivity or to acquiesce in some form of modified servility rather than to become fugitives. Slaves must often have preferred to stay with their masters.

The effect of land policy on slave decision-making

Thus a slave had to weigh the costs of fleeing his master, with the benefits of freedom, against the benefits of remaining despite the costs of continued enslavement. Lugard saw it as his duty to ease the decision and direct slaves along a path that was more predictable by means of government land policy. Though his 1901 memos to Residents contain no mention of land as a means to keep slaves with their masters, already in 1900 (Land Proclamation No. 8) Lugard implemented a policy that essentially left existing tenure arrangements as they were but made certain that European interests would be prevented from owning land.[84] By 1903 Lugard's thinking on the matter was quite clear. In his reply to the attacks on the "Movement," he noted that the rules against slaves taking up land were a settled part of his policy. As we have already observed, when Chief Justice Gollan warned that slaves would find it easy to settle on vacant land, Lugard scribbled trenchantly in the margin that "the Government can make it not easy."[85]

By 1906 these ideas had been thoroughly worked out. Lugard's own language on the subject, expressed to Residents in his Memo No. 6 of 1905 on "Slavery Questions," is both precise and forceful. He noted that while in the past, the settling of waste land and establishment of new villages could not have been achieved without the permission of local officials, now the situation was different. Given the possibility that slaves would desert and form new villages,

> I foresee that the cultivation of the estates of the upper classes cannot last long. It is not the policy of Government to hasten, but rather to retard, this inevitable outcome, in order to prevent the estates of the upper classes from going out of cultivation (with a consequent dislocation of the social fabric).[86]

Through new methods of subordination, slaves were to be kept on their masters' lands wherever possible.

Land policy proffered a solution, moreover, because "the most effective way of preventing a too sudden and premature tendency to desertion is ... by enforcing proprietary rights in land." Lugard had no intention of "permitting fugitive farm slaves to occupy land to which they have no title, nor to build new villages at will," but instead British policy would transform master/slave relations by "upholding the landlord's right to charge rents to his tenants."

> Government thus does not interfere with the legal right of the serf [sic] to assert his freedom, but, before granting him permission to acquire land, it may, if the occasion demands it, insist on his showing good cause for his desertion of his former work, and if he fails to do so, it may decline to grant him the new land, the ultimate title to which is now, for the most part, vested in Government.[87]

By "ultimate title" for the "most part," Lugard seems to have been alluding to vacant or "waste land," not land already under cultivation. As previously noted, the reference to "serfs" clearly meant agricultural slaves who were now to experience new forms of exploitation.

To inhibit the movement of fugitives and to prevent their occupation of land, Lugard instructed his Residents to

> inform each other of slaves fugitive from their own, or arriving from a neighbouring, Province; and if ... it transpires that there was no sufficient cause for their running away, and that they have not redeemed themselves, the Resident of the Province in which they desire to take up land may decline to grant permission. It will, moreover, be made known that everyone who takes up new land, without having obtained the consent of the Resident, will be liable to ejection, and that Chiefs giving land to fugitive slaves will lay themselves open to censure. The latter should, therefore, report all cases of arrival of fugitive slaves to the Resident. Many slaves or serfs will, unknown to Residents, attach themselves to existing villages, but such cases will be dealt with in the same way as new communities, and Chiefs will be forbidden to accept these immigrants, and to grant them land to farm, without the assent of the Resident.[88]

The determination of "sufficient cause" allowed Residents some leeway in dealing with extreme cases of physical abuse, but otherwise allowed them to send slaves back to their masters. In the years after Lugard's departure from Northern Nigeria in 1906, Residents continued to handle cases of fugitive slaves. Occasionally there was concern, as in 1908, about the legality of returning slaves across provincial boundaries; the Caliphate authorities had no compunction about their actions in doing so, and they had the force of Islamic law and their own interests behind them. Lugard was explicit that the colonial government would do its part as well: fugitive slaves were to be rigorously excluded from government cantonments, denied government employment, and refused permission to join government caravans.[89] Without specific instructions, these avenues could have provided access to freedom.

The Land and Native Rights Proclamation, 1910

In 1907 Governor Girouard circulated a memorandum, "Land Tenure in Northern Nigeria," that marked an ideological divide in the evolution of British policy on land, although the actual impact beyond a change in rhetoric was not very significant. Girouard favored a policy that in effect "nationalized" land and thereby allowed the collection of "land rent" in the form of taxation. His 1907 memorandum to his Residents solicited information on land tenure that was subsequently provided as testimony to the Northern Nigeria Lands Committee of 1908 and laid the foundation for the enactment of the Land and Native Rights Proclamation of 1910. Girouard and a carefully selected group of Residents appeared before the Northern Nigeria Lands Committee in London between June 1 and July 17, 1908. Among those testifying were Temple, Orr, Palmer, and Goldsmith – whose comments on aspects of land tenure have already been cited. Gowers, Stanley, and Arnett were absent, but their views were not dissimilar.

Girouard's inquiries, the Lands Committee hearings, and the 1910 proclamation were part of a carefully staged attempt to impose a theory of colonialism on Northern Nigeria that derived from the writings of the American economist Henry George. George's idea of a "single tax" on land as a means of generating revenue was currently fashionable in Britain, although Girouard's application of this theory diverged significantly from George's model. While George argued that a land tax would garner the economic surplus that was present in land rents, Girouard's land tax was the equivalent of a hut tax. Girouard argued that rents were already being paid for land use, which only needed to be regularized.

The single-tax lobby was strong among these colonialists who were identified as the "Third Party" – Mary Kingsley, John Holt, and E. D. Morel being most prominent. As Anne Phillips has suggested, their vision was "essentially that of mercantile capital," that is, the interests of the large trading firms.[90] Holt was a leading merchant whose firm arrived in Northern Nigeria in 1902. The support of the British Cotton Growing Association for these views should also be noted because the BCGA was particularly interested in Northern Nigeria, where it hoped to develop cotton exports.[91] In the first decade of the twentieth century, under the guidance of Morel, the "Third Party" obtained an important ally in Josiah Wedgwood, MP, who was to sit on the Northern Nigeria Lands Committee. Wedgwood was a radical Liberal who would later join the Labour Party.

Phillips notes that this group did not want to intervene in land matters to "promote individual property rights" but to

> halt further erosion of the principal of public ownership. More concretely, their proposal was that all British colonies in West Africa should adopt the principle already embodied in the Land Proclamation (1902) of Northern Nigeria, which gave the Governor [sic] the right to proclaim areas as public lands.[92]

145

The 1902 proclamation demonstrates that Lugard, too, was strongly influenced by George's ideas, although he is not usually considered a member of the "Third Party." Nonetheless, Lugard also shared their aim of thwarting the penetration of European trading firms in order to develop agriculture through the encouragement of African commodity production.[93] As Phillips has observed, "peasants and plantations began to appear as alternatives, rather than as complementary paths," and by "plantations" Phillips, following Morel's clear meaning, meant "European plantations."[94] Morel and most subsequent commentators, including Phillips, have failed to recognize or have ignored the large holdings that existed in Northern Nigeria at the time. Lugard differed from these observers in this regard. He understood full well that there were large estates in Northern Nigeria.

Girouard was a firm proponent of the Morel/Wedgwood party, and by drawing attention to the land-tenure problem, he intended "to resolve the matter prior to the advent of Europeans in any considerable numbers." In his opinion, "the construction of railways will very probably result in a large access to the white population, and a probable demand for land for plantation purposes," with "regrettable results" if there were to be a delay in devising a clear policy with respect to land tenure.[95] To this end, Girouard distinguished between his advocacy of single-tax ideas and Lugard's recognition of property rights in land, which did not conform to George's theory and which allowed for the possibility of the alienation of land to European interests. We would contend, however, that Girouard's ideas, which sounded so different from those of Lugard, could not be implemented, and that the polemics of the single-taxers did little to alter Lugard's vision. In keeping with George's theory, the tax on land (*kurdin kasa*), the "economic rent" that Girouard wanted to garnish in George's name, was henceforth referred to simply as "rent." For farmers, however, it was still "tax."

While Girouard noted that "in most of the provinces there would appear to be practically no land which was not subject to ... a claim,"[96] he believed that it would not be in the interests of the population of Northern Nigeria "to create a landlord class where apparently they have been non-existent." With considerably more clarity he wanted to prevent the creation of a "white" landlord class. He was suggesting that the Caliphate landlord class did not exist.[97] There was such a class, and Girouard himself recognized its large holdings, as we have seen. Ignoring the reality, Girouard insisted that "the definition and recognition of the native rights in land ... has after the abolition of slavery, and in the interests of development, become a pressing necessity."[98] Land should be nationalized to prevent European settlement. Presumably, Girouard was not concerned about the Caliphate landlord class. Northern Nigeria was

> cut off from development, and largely relied for labour upon the institution of slavery, and their rulers, for their incomes upon extortionate taxation or slave

raiding. The abolition of slave raiding and the manumission of the slaves, placed the ruling class in a very difficult position and threatened their incomes.[99]

Palmer also wanted to "protect the natives against Europeans coming into the country," although he definitely recognized the extent to which there were already large estates.[100] Temple and Orr concurred in compartmentalizing the land issue. In their support of the single-tax idea, they too focused on the exclusion of European settlers and European firms and ignored the existing landlord class. It should be noted that a policy that excluded European settlement was in sharp contrast to British policy in eastern and southern Africa. The government and the British merchant community were at odds, which reveals that profit did not always determine policy. The reason for this division arose from the distrust of capitalism by some British Liberals and leftists.

The Land and Native Rights Proclamation of 1910 ensured that the government's tenure policy would continue to support Lugard's slave policy, despite the ideological overtones that sounded so different from the Lugardian language.[101] For our purposes, the long and complex discussions leading to the enactment of the proclamation can be distilled to several key consequences for slavery policy: First, almost all lands would henceforth be classified as "native lands" where the occupation of the land would continue to give what amounted to title to its current user, whether interpreted as "customary" or "usufructuary." The proprietary rights of the aristocracy, scholars, and merchants to their estates were thereby guaranteed, and slaves would have to obtain permission to use the land. Conforming to earlier regulations, it was made extremely difficult for non-natives to acquire land from indigenous landholders, which meant in addition that slaves moving between provinces would also have difficulty obtaining land.[102] Second, an individual could be dispossessed of land if the holder was unacceptable to the community, which was partly directed at fugitive slaves, but sounded as if it upheld the rights of government as landlord.[103] Third, land law would continue to be administered locally, with little British participation or supervision, which in fact meant that existing tenure arrangements would continue. No full land survey would be attempted, but any transfer of land to a "native of the district" had to have the approval of the local authorities, while transfer "to a strange native" had to have "the consent of the head chief and the approval of the British Resident."[104]

In short, simple sale, rentals, and inheritance for the free residents of the emirates were allowed to continue, as long as transfers were registered with local officials. These practices were already widespread. Sales to other "natives" were still possible, as in the case of Arabs and immigrants from other emirates, but these transfers required the approval of a British Resident, as well as emirate officials. Finally, individual Europeans, expatriate companies, missionaries, and "natives" from outside Northern Nigeria would still not be allowed to obtain land, except on short-term leases from the colonial government. In this context, "natives" meant non-Muslim Africans.

The end result, if it had been realized in practice, was that this British legislation would have upheld the rights of masters to their land while at the same time confirming the existence of state lands attached to political office. Access to land by "non-natives" and Europeans was severely restricted, and therefore no large landholdings would materialize among these interests. The proclamation undoubtedly tried to limit the ability of slaves to leave their masters. Though settlement of unclaimed "bush lands" might provide a way around these barriers for some slaves, the testimony before the Lands Committee makes it clear that the British believed their net would be hard to slip through.[105]

In a statement put before the Lands Committee, W. F. Gowers, then Resident of Bauchi, had this firmly in mind when he wrote that "I think it would be only fair to recognise the rights of the master in the land as compensation for the loss of his rights in the men."[106] Thus did Girouard attempt to implement a system that, under different circumstances and thousands of miles away, would come to be called "exclusionary zoning," or earlier and more pithily, "Jim Crow Laws." Land policy would continue to be a pillar of the British campaign to keep slaves in place.[107]

The disadvantages in running away were so great under the Girouard measures that slaves might reasonably decide to remain with their masters. Masters, too, had a significant incentive to keep slaves in place. Large landholdings could not be worked without labor, the market for hired labor was uncertain, and the size of the master's family was unlikely to be sufficient to offset the loss of slave labor. Selling off plots, while possible, was discouraged because land prices were kept artificially low by the ordinances that followed the Lands Committee's report and the Land and Native Rights Proclamation. The market was depressed because sale to "non-natives" was entirely prohibited and sale to "natives" required official permission yet did not confer full title in the sense that owners could sell to anyone they wished. Land law thus made it difficult to convert property into cash through sale. To that degree, Girouard's efforts had an impact. Restrictions on the sale of land were a factor in the deflationary trend of the early colonial economy (see Chapter 7).

Proprietary rights to land and colonial policy

Girouard's approach to land matters was not a radical departure from Lugard's policies, and the change mattered little to slaves one way or the other. Both Girouard and Lugard had a similar goal with respect to slaves. They differed in how the control of the slave population could be best achieved, whether through the recognition of proprietary rights in land, as Lugard favored, or the nationalization of land and the imposition of a tax to collect the economic rent on land, as Girouard advocated. There were strong similarities in the debate over the Girouard–Lugard models of land tenure and the argument between Lugard and the "Movement" over legal-status abolition. In both cases, the differences of opinion are subtle to the non-specialist. There was a consensus with respect to the desired results; the debate was how best to achieve those results and how to justify the means ideologically.

Girouard chose to overlook the importance of large land-holdings that depended on slave labor. He was preoccupied with individual farms that could be charged an economic rent. As we have demonstrated, Girouard was fully aware of the large holdings, since his regime settled the issue of official estates by allowing one per office. Furthermore, he knew that the emirs and the Sarkin Musulmi controlled much more extensive holdings than this allowance. We would suggest that Girouard used the theory of a single tax which Henry George envisioned would expropriate surplus from the idle rich to cover a different tax, also on land but not on the surplus earned by land. It was another way to make it difficult for slaves to take up new land, which would be subject to Girouard's economic rent.

The fate of the large estates and the substantial dispersed holdings of the aristocracy and wealthy commoners is a matter of considerable importance. In terms of policy, Girouard largely ignored their existence, while Lugard intended that such holdings would play a prominent role in the transitional period from an economy based on slavery to an economy based on small-holder production and wage labor. Girouard's model minimized the import-ance of slavery, while Lugard's analysis always kept the difficult slavery issue in perspective. As was the case with Lugard's earlier dispute with the "Movement," moreover, Lugard prevailed. Girouard had very little impact on slavery policy or land policy, though it has appeared to some scholars and administrators of the time that Girouard imposed his ideological commit-ment to a policy of economic rent on land.

Many officials during Girouard's regime (1907–1909) and the scholars who have been strongly influenced by the arguments of these officials have claimed that land under the Caliphate belonged to the state.[108] There was no private property. We would contend that the issue of "private property" obscures the complex range of proprietary rights to land, including farms that were rented, the private estates of commoners, aristocrats, and royal slaves, and the official estates on state lands, which in combination con-tained a huge slave population. Despite the evidence, Girouard's carefully selected experts insisted that there was no private property and, moreover, few large holdings of land, which justified "nationalization" and the collec-tion of "rent" on the land. According to this argument, farmers obtained only usufructuary rights to land, and their taxes were the "economic rent" that George wrote about. For Girouard and other true believers in George's "socialist" theories, the colonial state could charge a single tax on all adult males that amounted to a collection of rent by the state.

But the important point, and one which Lugard fully subscribed to, was the provision that land could not be alienated without the approval of the colonial officials, and therefore foreigners, especially whites, could not acquire land. As a result no *white* landlord class could evolve. It was not the single tax that kept foreign merchants and white settlers from owning land, but the outright prohibition on their ownership, which was not part of George's theories at all but was definitely compatible with Lugard's anti-business views. Girouard was not instituting a radical shift in policy that protected the peasant class of Northern Nigeria from the consolidation of landholdings by a capitalist class, as Robert Shenton, for example, has argued.[109] Lugard had already made sure that land would not be alienated to foreigners, capitalist or not.

Lugard himself offered a rebuttal to the single-taxers with respect to his intentions on land tenure. Two years after the proclamation was issued, he took the occasion to respond to an article by Wedgwood in the *African Times and Orient Review* (October 1912), now that he was back in Nigeria as Governor of both North and South. Wedgwood, in praising the results of the Lands Committee, attributed the peaceful resolution of the "intimate connection between slavery and the native land question" to Sir Percy Girouard, not Lugard, which must have made Lord Lugard a bit hot under the collar. According to Wedgwood, Girouard had made sure that there would be no "possibility of a landlord class, black or white, ever arising in Northern Nigeria." Wedgwood contended that Lugard had tried to create "a labouring class to till the lands of the ruling classes" by "the enforcement of proprietary rights in land," which anticipates the interpretation of Watts, Shenton, and Lennihan. He commended Girouard for blocking Lugard's "innovation" in trying to establish a landlord class. Wedgwood, committed to theory no matter what the facts were, suggested that the difficulty of obtaining labor "after the abolition of slavery" would be overcome "as long as the natives could work for themselves on free lands." Lugard was mistaken, in other words, in believing that "by depriving natives of free land" he could solve the "difficulty of obtaining labour … [after] the abolition of slavery" even when "labour was scarce and costly."[110]

Lugard wrote to Wedgwood in order to correct the "cynical" interpretation put on his own land policy. He reminded Wedgwood that he had shown the MP a draft of his 1906 memoranda, and at the time had explained that

> I was writing on Slavery, and pointing out to my Residents that an empty title to freedom in the eye of the law would never raise the ex-slave to a sense of his individual responsibility as a free man. I said that only a sense of the possession of land and its produce as his own would create this sense of responsible manhood, and my ideal was that he should become a small landowner, rather than a serf on the lands of a "Master." The Memo – please remember – was written many years ago, long before the land tenure question had arisen as a problem to be solved.

He was at a loss to understand how Wedgwood could ascribe to him the motives described in the article, although he was less than honest in assessing his own intentions, which were to keep slaves on their masters' lands as slaves paying rent, not as freeholding peasants. "So far from desiring to obtain labour by depriving the natives of free land, the exact opposite was the object I had in view."[111] Lugard was stretching a point in feigning such a strong interest in creating a free peasant class of cultivators. He did not state, as he had many times earlier, that he had tried to block slaves from deserting their masters and taking up land.

Nonetheless, Wedgwood had mentioned the omitted word from the whole controversy over land policy – "white." Lugard always assumed that immigration and investment of Europeans would be tightly restricted. He wanted to keep European settlers out of Northern Nigeria and he had no intention of letting European firms acquire land, except under short lease. Even the tin-mining companies only obtained rights to excavate, not title to land. He had no sympathy with missionaries, commercial firms with an interest in large holdings of property, or "non-natives" of any kind taking up more than usufructuary rights in the Protectorate of Northern Nigeria. The review of land tenure between 1908–1910 may appear to have been objective, but Girouard's intention was to introduce radical changes that would have resulted in the confiscation of Caliphate land if fully implemented. Such a course would have obstructed Lugard's vision of how slavery was to be transformed, because it might well have alienated the existing landlord class.[112]

Lugard wanted to prevent the creation of a landed class that was foreign, especially European, but he never pretended that he was blocking the establishment of a propertied class. He knew full well that such a class already existed and wanted its support in the implementation of British rule. He knew that the Caliphate aristocracy and, to a lesser extent, the merchant class controlled considerable land, which was tilled by slaves. Lugard only wanted to assure that land was not alienated to non-natives. It must have seemed to him that Girouard, Temple, Palmer, and the supporters of the "Third Party" were flirting with disaster by pretending that the way to Indirect Rule had been lost over the issue of land tenure. However much Lugard and the others disagreed on land issues, there was full agreement that landholding by foreigners should be prevented.

With Lugard apparently safely exiled to Hong Kong, the supporters of Henry George thought they could attack Lugard's structure of Indirect Rule, not realizing that Lugard would be back to protect his edifice in 1912, first as Governor of Northern Nigeria, Southern Nigeria, and the Colony of Lagos (1912–14) and then as Governor-General of a United Nigeria (1914–18). Lugard's correspondence with Wedgwood, whose seat in Parliament meant that he could not be ignored, attempted to minimize the differences between his own policies and those of the single-taxers. The parallel between Lugard's controversy with the "Movement" over legal-status abolition and the rhetorical debate between Lugard and the single-taxers is strong. The amount of verbiage in both debates was greatly in excess of the differences of opinion, and in both cases actual policy conformed more closely to Lugard's model than to that of his opponents.

After returning to Nigeria, Lugard initiated a review of land policy. In 1913 he despatched a circular inquiring "as to recognition of inheritance of rights of occupancy in land, and in fixtures and improvements on land." Gowers, Palmer, and Arnett, among others, responded at length and once again confirmed that land was inherited, bought, sold, and rented, with disputes settled in the Islamic courts.[113] As Christelow's examination of the Kano judicial records demonstrates, there were particularly serious land claims that reached the Kano courts in 1914 because of the willingness of Emir Abbas to appease litigants who had lost land twenty years earlier during the Kano Civil War (*basasa*). The Judicial Council restored private property to the families of those who had been dispossessed during the civil war. A major settlement involved land that was returned to Alhasan Dantata, a wealthy kola nut trader who had been in exile and would now become one of the largest groundnut buyers.[114] It was hardly necessary for Lugard to reverse Girouard's efforts to implement the theories of Henry George.

In his revised *Political Memoranda* of 1918, he reviewed his differences with Girouard after a lengthy discussion of the theory of economic rent on land, English land tenure, the Indian and Burma colonial systems, and land tenure elsewhere in Britain and French West Africa.[115] In his opinion, the 1908 Lands Committee had used the term "ownership" in a manner incompatible with usage in Northern Nigeria, thus creating considerable confusion.

> Ownership even in English law, as applied to land, is relative, and is qualified by the right of Parliament to expropriate the owner if his land is essential for railway construction, etc. In Africa it is still more qualified, and the owner of land possesses it subject to certain well understood limitations and obligations towards the Community to which he belongs.[116]

Lugard did not reduce the issue to the simple question as to whether private property in land existed. Proprietary rights were complex and varied. As he summarized early colonial land policy,

> The fundamental principle ... which guided the Government, prior to 1910, was the recognition of the advantage of individual occupation rights, combined with the right of Government ... to dispose of lands not in actual occupation, and to control all lands leased to aliens ... It was at that time premature to deal with land questions, for we were engaged in grappling with the slavery question, and endeavouring to find some means of supporting the Rulers, impoverished by the desertion of their slaves.[117]

In other words, the land issue was intimately connected with slavery and of secondary importance to it.

Lugard interpreted the Lands Committee testimony quite differently than Girouard had. Among Lugard's major observations were the following:

First, "individual rights in land" had long been recognized, whereby "payments of small sums (but not periodic rents) were made to Rulers for the right to occupy"; second, individuals "paid for the hire of land to each other (*Suferi*)," and the "sale or hire of use among the peasantry of Kano was subject to the implied or actual consent of the Emir"; third, "the 'occupier' or owner of land would not be evicted except for good cause"; fourth, land was held "subject to payment of taxes, which were based on the profits of the holder's farm and not as a land rent"; and finally, "transfers and inheritance were recognized."[118]

The Land and Native Rights Proclamation of 1910 "introduced fundamental changes" in theory, but Lugard had an explanation as to why the proclamation had virtually no impact:

> That so great a change could be effected without difficulty, in spite of the growing recognition of private rights in land to which many witnesses bore testimony, may be ascribed to two principal causes. In the first place, the local population were entirely ignorant of the fact ... [and] no attempt of any kind was made to issue titles, or to interfere with the existing regime. In the second place, much of the land in Northern Nigeria, except in the vicinity of the great cities, was unpopulated jungle [*sic*], due to the long years of anarchy and slave raiding which had preceded British rule, and ample land was always available. The right to occupy any particular piece of land – except near the big cities – was therefore lightly regarded by the peasantry, while the Chiefs were much more concerned in the fear of losing their slaves.[119]

In the end the Lands Committee could not even impose an economic rent on land, because the theory could not work until the land had greater value. Even Girouard's "nationalization" of land was inoperative because it could not be implemented. We are not sure where Lugard thought the "unpopulated jungle" was located, there being none. It was perhaps Lugard's way of referring to "bush" land, which he had designated "Public Lands" in 1902.

> The wholesale slave raids which had depopulated vast areas, had removed the owners of these lands. Large tracts are to-day called "Jajin [*Dajin*] Allah" ("God's bush"), being ownerless. With the advent of the British, runaway slaves in many cases took up such waste lands without any opposing claims. It was to such lands in particular that I referred, when I claimed that the title to waste land would hereafter vest in the Governor.[120]

He had done so, as we have seen, to prevent fugitive slaves from settling on these lands.

Lugard also disputed the conclusion of the Lands Committee that "there was no landlord class in Northern Nigeria."

> In the strict English sense the assertion was probably true, because the term "landlord" could not be applied correctly to the "owners" of towns and lands. The holders of official farms attached to every office ... were, however, in a sense "landlords" ... [because] much of the land was held by slave-owners, whose slaves tilled the soil.[121]

To the extent that it was possible, Lugard had always wanted "to emancipate the peasant class from the servile attitude of mind which long generations of slavery had induced in them ... [and] promote a sense of individual responsibility," and in his opinion "nothing would so effectively" do so than for farmers to "become proprietors of their own fields; in other words that the slaves ... should be replaced by the individual occupier." But the promotion of smallholdings had to proceed slowly. According to reports that Lugard received after he returned to Nigeria in 1912, this process of "peasantization" had "already happened." Residents reported that "the country is covered with small holders. There are no estates now."[122]

Hence when Lugard revised his instructions to political officers in 1916, there was no reason to change the direction of land policy, other than to restate his earlier pronouncements. The 1910 proclamation of the single-taxers had been a dead letter from its inception. The Land and Native Rights Ordinance, February 25, 1916, reaffirmed Lugard's policies, under which the state claimed "no rights to lands in actual occupation." He repeated what he had said in 1906 that the colonial state "in no way interferes with private titles, transfers or sales between individuals."[123] Lugard specifically rejected Girouard's intention of calculating economic rent on land; by contrast, the taxation in Lugard's Revenue Ordinance of 1916 was "an income tax" pure and simple. Girouard's intention "that the cultivator of the soil is liable to an economic rent ... for the land he occupies over and above the general income tax, has no legal sanction."[124] As far as Lugard was concerned,

> So long as the peasant is allowed to occupy his holding in perpetuity, with absolute ownership of his improvements, and cannot be evicted without full compensation except for good cause, and if expropriated by the State is given equivalent land elsewhere; so long as he can sell or bequeath his rights, subject to Native custom, and is free from rents while he pays the tax recognised by his own customary law ... it matters not in practice whether the State claims a "theoretical ownership."[125]

Furthermore, there were still large landholdings. As he candidly admitted, "though consistently desirous of transforming the 'praedial slave' into a free land-holder, I recognise that it was not without advantage to the country that the Chiefs and leading men of the Community should hold lands, from which they would derive an income to supplement their salaries (see old Memo. 5, #22, and 16 #15)."[126] In Sokoto "most of the Chiefs hold large farms worked by hired labour,"[127] which Jumare's research has confirmed.[128] Lugard must also have been aware of similar holdings elsewhere. C. O. Migeod found that large estates still characterized the area around Yola in 1922.[129] Based on returns supplied by slave owners, Migeod estimated that approximately 10 percent of the population of Yola Emirate were slaves employed on these estates under conditions of *murgu* (see Chapter 7). As noted above, the official estates of the emir of Kano also demonstrate the extent to which large-scale agricultural production continued.

Nonetheless, Lugard had once predicted that the large estates of the slave

154

owners would gradually collapse, and to some extent he claimed that this was happening by 1918: "The farms lapsed to the peasant cultivators, not by confiscation or appropriation of land rights by the State, but because their 'owners' had no slaves wherewith to cultivate them." The break-up of estates because of inheritance was also taking its toll. As Arnett observed in Sokoto in 1925:

> In Sokoto, the division of farm lands on inheritance was strictly carried out unless the coheirs agreed to waive it. When the coheirs lived in different towns or districts, a family of domestic slaves were liable to be separated and divided between them, unless a monetary equivalent were arranged for them.[130]

On the basis of the available information, therefore, Lugard's claim that "the country is a mass of peasant occupiers, who, however, cannot alienate their holdings" requires some revision.[131] Many slaves could not sell their land because they were still working the lands of their masters. Other ex-slaves had become free peasants; indeed by 1924, "many slaves who had gained their freedom have taken up new land on their own account and villages of ex-slaves been formed."[132]

The next opportunity to revise land policy confirms this interpretation that Lugard's understanding of land tenure was the accepted policy, not the Georgian view. In the late 1920s, there was another review, but it had no impact on slavery or land tenancy. The Amendment of the Land and Native Rights Ordinance dealt with land control in the enclaves of the colonial cantonments, the *sabon gari* (new towns that were non-Muslim suburbs), and the commercial districts.[133] It was recognized that conditions were now "different" from the time when the original Land and Native Rights Proclamation was adopted in 1910 and when the Ordinance of 1916 was framed.

> It was then perhaps anticipated that all or the great majority of persons who were not subject to the control of Native Authorities would be resident in Townships, and all others excluded from Townships. That anticipation has not eventualised in fact and partly owing to this and in order to maintain effectively the authority of Native Administrations, His Excellency the Governor has approved legislation to widen the scope of the Native Authority Ordinance and the Native Courts Ordinance.[134]

The purpose of the new legislation was to extend the authority of the emirates into the townships. The question of "native rights to land" as already in existence was not a subject of the revisions. Proprietary rights to land, with the restriction that land could not be alienated to foreigners, were maintained. Neither in 1916 nor in 1930 was there any concern over "native" rights to alienate land to other "natives" or with the continued rights to state lands attached to political office. Consequently, slaves continued to have access to land only on the permission of land owners, often their masters.

Colonial control of land in Northern Nigeria

The layer of administration that prevented the alienation of land to foreigners was the colonial regime itself, and from its inception, that regime prevented the sale of land to "non-natives." Lugard's earliest proclamation on land titles stipulated that land was available to missionaries, European firms, and anyone else who was not a citizen of the Caliphate only on a rental basis for short terms. Furthermore European settlement was confined to specific areas, well segregated from existing towns. Unlike in South Africa and Kenya, non-natives were consigned to "Reserves" – townships and *sabon gari* that were removed from "native" settlements. Subsequent regulations confirmed this policy, well before the Land and Native Rights Ordinance of 1910. It was always stipulated that approval of the British Resident was needed in matters of land unless land transfers were among "natives" of the district.[135] Under the resulting system, even strangers who had *not* been slaves faced substantial difficulties in acquiring land.[136] Because of these restrictions, the British regime did indeed curtail full freehold rights to land. Whereas under the Caliphate, foreigners, as long as they were Muslims, could acquire proprietary rights to land from government officials or through purchase, no foreigner, Muslim or otherwise, could do so under the colonial regime. Despite this considerable limitation on the alienation of land to foreigners, white or black, landowners still retained proprietary rights. Land was bought and sold, inherited, rented, and loaned, which was fully recognized in Islamic law. Such transfers required government registration because of the change in liability for taxation.

The difficulty of selling land because it could not be alienated to Europeans or non-natives made it important for the masters to persuade slaves to stay on the land by coming to some arrangement with them. Masters were aware that unless their relationship with their slaves changed in some degree, slaves were more likely to run away than before the British conquest. If slaves left, masters would have difficulty finding other farm workers, and hence some kind of accommodation was necessary to provide an incentive for slaves to stay. The scarcity of labor could not easily be overcome.

There were strong motives for owners to allow their slaves to continue working their "private plots" that they had farmed as slaves, in a new relationship of dependence and tenancy, without title to the land.[137] Part of the masters' fields never before farmed individually by slaves could also now be worked by them as part of an evolving master/dependant relationship. Indeed, the master class actually did not need as much food output as before. As slaves became tenants paying ransom and rent in money or in kind, the masters no longer faced the necessity of supplying food. In addition, producing food for the emirate armies was, with the disappearance of these armies, no longer required. The necessity for plantation production of food was in decline. If the slaves could be allowed to support themselves, the masters could beneficially sacrifice the use of their land in return for payments of ransom and rent. Giving up the use of land did not, however, amount to sacrificing ownership. When Palmer, after viewing tax records in 1907, commented that there were far more *gayauna* plots paying taxes than there were *gandu* farms, he was undoubtedly commenting on a reality of land tenure that suggested slavery could evolve into a system of tenancy.[138]

Slaves having entered into *murgu* arrangements involving periodic payments that might even include self-ransom could leave the farms of their masters if they found employment elsewhere. Unlike fugitives, slaves on their own might have enhanced opportunities to join other farming communities either nearby or at a greater distance. The question arises, how much easier was it for such slaves to acquire land than it was for fugitives?

Lugard's language in Memo No. 16 of 1906, "Titles to Land," makes it quite clear that even a slave paying ransom or a slave who had already purchased his freedom might be denied permission to settle:

> This right of disposing over waste land is one which in practice the Government only rarely exercises, as in the case of denying permission to settle to freed slaves.[139]

Note that Lugard does not refer to "fugitive slaves": he deliberately addresses the question of "freed slaves," because he expected that freed slaves would acquire land in many cases. For all that, not being a fugitive must have meant that slaves found it at least somewhat easier to pass the barriers erected by the British and local authorities against the acquisition of land. Probably the ability to do so was greatest when slaves paying *murgu*, whether or not they were also acquiring their freedom, stayed in the general locale of their masters. They would then be known to the local authorities, and also they might still be able to depend upon former masters to speak on their behalf or carry out other acts of patronage in case of need. Masters and former masters were certainly among the "respectable" witnesses who were required for the acquisition of vacant lands. Yet, as we have postulated, many slaves who entered the low-density border lands of Kano, Katsina, and Zaria in the early years of colonial rule must also have been from among this group of slaves who were forging a new existence.

The British administration, in alliance with local authorities, made it very difficult for fugitive slaves to acquire suitable land, or indeed any land at all, for farming. Slaves engaged in self-ransom might have an easier time in migrating, but we believe that many slaves found it much safer and more convenient simply to continue farming their masters' lands, at least during the farming season. Much the more practicable course was to stay in place, which brought advantages both to the erstwhile slave and to the former master. The land-tenure system thus imposed serious restraints on running away, but did encourage slaves to reach some local accommodation with their owners and former owners.

In a sense, the land defaulted to the slaves, at the price of continuing provision of labor to the masters. With labor scarce relative to land there was really no good alternative for masters, no other way for them to make the land productive. For the master as for the slave, welfare could plausibly be enhanced by compromise. The usufruct of land fell easily and naturally to the former slaves, but former slaves and their descendants acquired actual ownership of their farms only gradually, and then seldom before the First World War.

6

The role of taxation in the reform of slavery

As we have seen, the decision to enforce proprietary rights in land limited the mobility of male slaves. Before the colonial conquest, slaves could not easily find land because of the danger of slave raiding and kidnaping. Under colonial rule, male slaves continued to find it difficult to gain access to land, and therefore were kept close to their masters. The lack of access to land affected females as well because the Islamic legal system and conservative attitudes about marriage and concubinage meant that women could not easily relocate except in the company of males. Women were forced to remain in their masters' households unless a male or a relative, usually male, was willing to provide for their redemption and assure their subsistence thereafter.

Within a few years after the imposition of colonial rule, the various policies instituted to contain the flight of slaves and make them pay for their own redemption combined with colonial tax reforms in a manner that led masters and slaves into new economic relationships. These tax reforms are examined in this chapter. On the side of the masters, tax policy assisted in persuading them to establish financial arrangements resulting in the emancipation of their slaves. On the side of the slaves, taxes propelled them into cash-crop production, helped push others onto the labor market as wage earners, and sharply increased the numbers of traders in the dry season. The colonial tax reforms had a more direct effect on men than on women, just as did the land policies. With women attached to men for legal and social reasons, however, the indirect impact on female slaves was just as great.

Under the Caliphate, slaves had not been liable to conventional taxation, though slavery itself can obviously be considered an oppressive levy by the masters.[1] After a few years of colonial tax reform, all adult males, slave or free, were supposed to pay taxes directly to the state. The colonial taxes were nominally derived from the old taxes of the Caliphate, but in spite of almost continuous tinkering with the tax system, they basically amounted to a poll-type tax that affected equally almost the entire adult male population. The most important exception, as we shall see, involved slaves who stayed on the official estates attached to political office. These estates were exempted from the colonial tax levy for a considerable time. Though there were rough edges to the tax reforms, and though efforts at tax evasion were partly successful for at least a decade, the colonial officials did not waver in their aim of bringing about universal taxation of males, including slaves. Progress towards this goal increased rapidly after about the year 1910, with direct and powerful consequences for the future of the slave system.

Tax policy had a profound effect on the decision-making of the masters. Masters faced the problem of retaining labor for their farms at a time when a combination of government regulation and depressed market conditions prevented them from selling their land. By law they could not sell their slaves. The dilemma faced by masters was that unless the master/slave relationship could be altered in some degree, the probability was too great that slaves would choose to become fugitives. The masters needed labor, would be worse off than before if they lost it, and therefore had an incentive to persuade slaves to stay by coming to some arrangement with them. It was also the case that many masters needed political support from beneath, and slaves who stayed could provide this support as clients in a new political order. We are less concerned with this evolving political and social dependency than with the economics of the transformation, but it was certainly a factor in the process – and one worthy of considerable further study.

Taxes entered the calculations of masters because of the colonial tax reforms. Masters rapidly lost the many tax exemptions that they had benefitted from, and became liable for what amounted to poll tax on the individuals in their establishments. The liability included adult male slaves, unless – the point is central – the masters could somehow shift the tax burden to the slaves themselves. There was a clear incentive for them to make that shift when they could, diminishing the dependence of their slaves to the degree that they would be responsible for their own tax payments, but with the ties still sufficiently binding that the slaves remained to work the masters' lands.

Masters thus saw the advantages in allowing slaves to work on their own account in return for paying a regular fee, known as *murgu*, and they negotiated suitable self-ransom and rental agreements with the slaves. Masters' income in these forms was either not taxed, or was taxed only lightly. Such agreements would allow masters to escape liability for the slaves' taxes, while receiving income that would not raise their own tax bills. They would also give the slaves sufficient independence, including more mobility or perhaps the greater mobility of freedom itself, to raise the cash to pay the *murgu* fees, ransoms, rents, and taxes. In effect, for many masters the new tax structure encouraged the breakup of large estates and the establishment of financial accommodations with slaves that evolved into landlord–tenant relations.

Crucial to this change was the institution of *murgu*, which was a feature of slavery under the Caliphate.[2] In many cases, masters allowed their slaves to work on their own account in return for weekly, bi-weekly, monthly, or

160

annual payments that were not instalments on the purchase price of the slave and hence did not necessarily lead to redemption. Under the reformed slavery of colonialism, the "right" to have the redemption price set was tied to *murgu* arrangements ("But above all the system of 'Murgu' should be encouraged"). In effect *murgu* was the contract that was recognizable in the Islamic Courts, and it had

> an educational value in the transitional stage from slave to free labour, more especially that form of the system which allows a slave complete freedom, provided he pays a weekly sum to his master. The step from this system to one of a recognised freeman paying a small rental for his holding is but a small one.[3]

Historically, masters had full authority to make slaves work under *murgu* arrangements, if they so decided, and they could deny the requests of slaves who wanted to work accordingly. When it was profitable to do so, masters let their slaves work on their own account, or if masters found that they could not feed their slaves, they made them find work, in return for the fee.

Now, *murgu* would be upheld as a mechanism whereby masters received an additional payment, beyond the ransom price, during the transitional period from slavery to freedom. Because it was a "contract" that could be enforced in the Islamic courts, it was precisely the kind of mechanism that Lugard appreciated as a valuable means of controlling social change. Masters had to adjust to the change; they lost their *right* to determine whether or not a slave could enter into a *murgu* arrangement, just as they lost the right to say whether or not a slave would be freed through the payment of ransom by a relative or would be allowed to pay off his or her own ransom. Nonetheless, slave owners gained the assurance that slaves had to pay *murgu* in order to earn money to pay their taxes, and the *murgu* fee did not contribute towards self-purchase. Indeed, slaves could only earn money towards their ransom if they also paid *murgu*, as we will see in Chapter 7.

The degree to which taxes in any form can be shifted from one group of payers to another is, of course, a staple of economic analysis. In this case of Northern Nigeria's masters, it might be argued that they *could not* effectively shift the new burden of taxation to their slaves because economic adjustments would follow on the attempt. For example, if the masters forced *murgu* and ransom agreements that rid themselves of tax, then the slaves now liable for the tax bills would have fewer resources to make these payments. The amount paid periodically in *murgu*, and the price of ransom, would have to fall.

We contend that this was *not* the result, however, for three reasons. First, the *murgu* and ransom prices were to a large degree set institutionally, rather than in a free market. *Murgu* appears to have stayed constant for many years, while ransom declined very slowly. The new tax on slaves did not appear to affect the size of *murgu* and ransom payments for a long time; their burden was on the slaves. Second, the slaves clearly preferred greater freedom, whether in the half-loaf form of *murgu* or the full loaf of ransom, to slavery under the old conditions. Slaves' new mobility in the dry season, even when still farming for the masters in the wet season, was worth paying for. From all appearances many slaves assumed the tax while keeping up the necessary payments. The mirror image is that the masters ran a greater risk that their slaves would desert if they did not make new arrangements. Paying tax on a suddenly more risky investment was not good business. Finally, slaves in *murgu* could potentially earn larger incomes than before because of their dry-season mobility and greater freedom from menial rainy-season tasks for the masters' good. They were thus *better able* to finance the tax bills, while at the same time paying their masters, in effect allowing some or all of the new taxes to be shifted.

The pressures devolving from the tax system were not equally felt by all masters, as already noted. For a long period the colonial tax policies had much less effect on slave-owning public officials than on the general run of slave owners who held no public office. The protection of the property (including the slave property) of these officials from the new taxes is a noteworthy feature of the British policy, demonstrating vividly the concern of the colonial government to cement relations with the ruling aristocracy. By involving the financial self-interest of that aristocracy, indirect rule received direct encouragement. One result of this obliging British policy, though hardly noticed at home, was that the end of slavery in this sector of the economy was delayed for decades.

With masters establishing relationships with their slaves that allowed them to avoid responsibility for the slaves' tax liabilities, the slaves were now assessed directly by the colonial state. The necessity for slaves to earn income to pay their tax bills would have been revolutionary in any case, but the colonial government's requirement that the payments be made in British currency was even more so. Cash-crop exporting soon became the convenient way for most slaves to earn the needed "hard" currency. The slaves required to pay tax for the first time soon had to face the additional fact that the general level of taxation was rising, which it continued to do during the first three decades of colonial rule despite the fact that this was generally a deflationary period. Rising tax bills combined with the requirement that payment be in sterling multiplied the economic consequences for masters and slaves.

Tax reform, along with land policy, can thus be seen as another prerequisite of Lugard's scheme to modify and eventually to eliminate slavery. These two economic weapons ensured that slaves who had once worked their masters' plantations and farms gradually, over about the first thirty years of colonial rule, were transformed into a dependent population of peasant producers (and tax payers) farming small plots throughout Northern Nigeria.

Taxation under the Caliphate

To understand colonial slavery policy, it is necessary to inquire closely into the colonial tax reforms. The precolonial system's treatment of slaves had been exceedingly generous to the masters; the ending of the exemption for slaves and the requirement that they pay tax themselves were important developments. The evolving structure of taxation wherein *murgu* fees, ransom, and rental payments were lightly taxed or not taxed at all was equally important. Comprehending the economic effects of the colonial reforms requires considerable familiarity with the precolonial tax system of the Sokoto Caliphate, which is considered in this section.

Precolonial taxes were a complicated series of levies that were ultimately based on Islamic precedents and traditions as interpreted by Uthman dan Fodio, Muhammad Bello, and their successors. In 1821 Muhammad Bello wrote a treatise specifically on taxation which outlined official Caliphate policy.[4] Despite Bello's guide, complex differences in types of taxes and their incidence existed from emirate to emirate and between the capital districts of Sokoto and Gwandu and the rest of the Caliphate.[5] Even the method of assessment of these taxes varied among the emirates. The system was certainly not a unified one, which is not surprising considering the size of the Caliphate. The complexity of the tax system, which is often described as confusing or "arabesque," as Watts says with tongue no doubt slightly in cheek, has to this day impeded understanding of how colonialism worked to alter slavery.[6]

The salient detail is that Caliphate taxation bore lightly on slave establishments. The farming population of the capital districts of Sokoto and Gwandu were exempt from the payment of all land and crop taxes other than the religious tithe. This exemption applied whether or not farmers were smallholders or large slave owners. For slave holders elsewhere, especially in populous Kano Emirate, widespread exemptions existed to two major taxes, the land tax and the special crop taxes. While the other major precolonial tax levy – the grain tithe – was not subject to exemptions, farmers who faced famine could escape partial or whole payment. Such conditions may have affected those who owned many slaves if production was not sufficient to feed these dependants. As Garba has observed, "the basic weakness of the [Caliphate] taxation system was that the poorer people, that is to say, the general farmers, paid [relatively] more, while those who were comparatively rich were undertaxed."[7] Because slaves were not subject to taxation, the system had an even more regressive impact on the free poor than Garba has suggested.

The *zakka* tithe on grain

One tax only applied to the whole of the population, no matter how indirect. It was the *zakka* (also spelled *zakah*, *zakat*), a tithe on grain only, which was directly rooted in Quranic principles of taxation and was probably a very old tax in Hausaland.[8] Collected on the harvested amount of guinea corn (sorghum) and millet, it was usually paid in kind.[9] Because of its religious nature, there were no exemptions, not even in Sokoto and Gwandu, unless

163

people simply could not pay because their harvests failed or they claimed that they were threatened by hunger. Because *zakka* was often collected in instalments, the cost of storage was passed onto farmers. Even so, tax payers most often did not pay a full tenth of their grain production. Farmers usually made their own declarations of what had been produced, and it was common, indeed acceptable, practice to misrepresent output. Furthermore, bundles of grain for purposes of assessing *zakka* were often smaller than the normal bundle.

In Cargill's assessment of precolonial Kano, the *zakka* was little more than the private store of the Emir and other officials. In his opinion, "the ruling class and more especially the Emir and his huge following practically subsisted on the Zakka, the whole Emirate forming a sort of granary from which they drew supplies as they wanted."[10] In his survey of Dan Makoyo district, N. M. Gepp found it difficult to guess at the amount of *zakka* that was assessed, let along actually collected; he was convinced that nothing approaching a tenth of the crop had ever been taken:

> Apparently the Maigona [farmer] himself decides how much he will pay. The fact is recognised that some Zakka must be paid, but so long as some, however little is paid, the farmers' conscience appears to be satisifed.[11]

If Gepp understood that the *zakka* was a religious tax, then he certainly placed little store in the convictions of the rural population. We suggest that most farmers willingly and fully paid an amount that was socially acceptable when they could, but that the religious nature of the tax as a method of supporting the needy allowed for the reduction of this tax when circumstances warranted. Because the *zakka* was taken in instalments and was not always collected in full, Festing believed that it was "the biggest channel for extortion and robbery of the whole taxation system."[12] Admittedly, the *jakadu* who collected the tax would have investigated any efforts at circumvention, and they were in a position to confiscate grain, no matter how much had already been paid. Nonetheless, it was the one tax, despite Festing's belief to the contrary, that had a clear social impact through its support of indigents and as a protection against famine. Whatever the tension between farmers and *jakadu*, the moral economy of the Caliphate must have limited excesses on both sides.

In Kano and probably elsewhere, officials attempted to assess this tax as a percentage of production, and it was common to find that the bill was haggled among *jakadu*, village heads, and household heads. In most areas, however, it came to be levied as a fixed sum per village.[13] In 1909, the *zakka* amounted in value to one-quarter of all the taxes collected on the land, or about 200,000 bundles (3,000 tons approximately) of threshed grain, worth £9,000. For poor peasants, the *zakka* represented half of their tax.[14]

According to Lugard, Kano slaves using their "free time" to grow grain for their own personal use were responsible for the *zakka* payment on this grain.[15] In Yola, slaves paid this tax to their masters, who supposedly turned it over to the Emirate.[16] It is not clear from the data if this practice was a colonial innovation or reflected the situation under the Caliphate. If slaves did pay *zakka* under some circumstances in the nineteenth century, it is the only agricultural tax for which they were responsible. Before the British advent masters would have made the payments on the entire grain output of their estates, whoever produced it.

The land tax (*kurdin kasa*)

The basic tax outside of Sokoto and Gwandu was the land tax or *kurdin kasa*. Although it varied from emirate to emirate, and indeed within emirates, basically it was a tax on land farmed during the rainy season but not in the dry season. In Zaria, however, the land tax was based on the "hoe," that is, each adult agricultural laborer.[17] *Kurdin kasa* applied largely to plots that grew millet and guinea corn, with rates usually higher on land closer to cities.[18] It was collected whether or not the land lay fallow. *Kurdin kasa*'s basic principle differed from *zakka* in that it was not tied to production. It was usually paid in money, that is, cowries.

Lugard believed that *kurdin kasa* was a levy on the assessed value of arable land, generally from the cowrie equivalent of 6*d.* to 1*s.* per acre.[19] Hill has noted how misleading this statement is, since there was little indigenous attempt to measure areas accurately, and application of this tax varied substantially.[20] "The usual practice," according to Fika, was for the *kurdin kasa* "to be levied as a poll tax on household heads, probably to avoid a tedious enumeration of all farmsteads."[21] Tax assessment may have been rough and ready, as Hill and Fika contend, but Resident Cargill, a first-hand observer, thought that considerable care was taken. As he noted, "the native assessment itself is detailed and largely concerned with land rights."[22]

In 1909, Festing estimated that *kurdin kasa* represented about half of the land revenue. He reported that the rate was fixed on holders of farms growing grain, whether or not land was fallow. The tax ranged from 2,000 to 10,000 cowries, generally higher near towns. Depending on the locality, the average size of farms varied from 1 to 3 acres, which must indicate that slave plots were included in his estimates (otherwise the large estates would have pulled up the average size); the most usual rate in 1909 was a uniform 4,000 cowries.[23] Data on seven farmers in Gora District, south of Kano, include information on the dimensions of farms and the amount of *kurdin kasa* in cowries (Table 6.1).[24] The largest farm had 62 acres under cultivation; the average tax was 4*d.* per acre. For the district as a whole, *kurdin kasa* varied considerably (Table 6.2).

According to Gepp, who assessed Dan Makoyo Sub-District in 1909, Emir Muhammad Bello (1882–93) set the *kurdin kasa* at a uniform rate of 4,000 cowries per farm, regardless of size. The total amount collected from each village had remained fixed since that time,

The role of taxation in the reform of slavery

Table 6.1. *Rate of kurdin kasa in Gora, Kano Emirate, 1909*

Name	Place	Area (sq.yd.)	Area (acres)	Tax (cowries)	Rate/acre
Chiwake	Konkoso	21,000	$4\frac{3}{4}$	2,000	2d
Idi	Kubarache	72,000	$15\frac{7}{8}$	5,000	$2\frac{1}{2}$d
Jide	Konkoso	61,000	$14\frac{2}{3}$	4,000	3d
Moma	Maria	39,000	$8\frac{3}{8}$	4,000	$3\frac{3}{4}$d
Gaddo	Rikadawa	300,000	62	40,000	5d
Audu	Galinja	8,000	$1\frac{7}{8}$	2,000	$8\frac{3}{4}$d
Baba	Rikadawa	8,000	$1\frac{2}{3}$	2,000	9d

Source: Frewan, Gora District Assessment, 1909, SNP 7/10 3555/1909.

Table 6.2. *Kurdin kasa payments, Gora District, 1909*

Town	Highest tax on a farm (cowries)	Lowest tax on a farm (cowries)
Rikadawa	40,000	1,000
Madobi	30,000	1,600
Konkoso	19,000	300
Chinkoso	15,000	2,000
Hausawa	13,000	1,000
Iakum	10,000	3,000
Rigokwiam	10,000	1,500
Buriji	10,000	1,000
Galinja	9,000	1,500
Gurmina	7,000	1,500
Keffi	7,000	1,000
Kubarache	7,000	300
Shiam	6,000	4,300
Sabon Garu	6,000	3,000
Daburau	6,000	1,500
Dan Auta	5,000	1,000
Gora	5,000	1,000
Kauran Mata	5,000	1,000
Tudun Kwoia	4,000	3,000
Maria	4,000	2,000
Kangwa	4,000	2,000
Dan Mariama	4,000	1,000
Maria Karama	3,000	2,000
Lola	3,000	1,500

Source: Frewan, Gora District Assessment, 1909, SNP 7/10 3555/1909.

although in the meantime the population and number of farms has more than doubled, [and] in fact the village and not the farm is treated as the unit for the purpose of payment of Kurdin Kassa. When enquiries were made as to the amount of Kurdin Kassa fixed by Bello the same reply was received in every one of the 32 villages – that the amount of the Kurdin Kassa paid now is exactly the same as the amount paid 20 years ago. I think there can be small doubt that this is correct.[25]

The original assessment appears to have been based on total acreage. Gepp made allowance for neither the division of farms nor possible exemptions. In some districts, at least, there was also a tax on farmers who possessed a compound in a village but did not farm there (*kurdin daki*). In southeast Kano,

> There exists in two of the Sub-Districts, FAGAM and GWARAM – a Kurdin Daki levied at the same rate as the K. Kassa on Masu Giddaje [household heads] who do not hold farms on the lands of the particular town in which they reside, and therefore identical with the new Compound Tax. The receipts from the K. Daki are said to be paid in as K. Kassa.[26]

Significantly for the slavery issue, territorial officials and members of the aristocracy who did not have official positions and even many local officials were generally exempt from paying *kurdin kasa*,[27] and their slave estates were for the most part untouched by this levy. Numerous commoners who owned plantations also held their estates under a system of tenure that exempted them from paying the *kurdin kasa*, and many merchants were subject only to partial payment. The *gayauna* (farm plots) of the slaves were not subject to this tax either.[28] As already noted, *kurdin kasa* was not even collected in Sokoto and Gwandu. These emirates were not considered to be conquered land (*waqf*); they relied on the *zakka* and tribute payments before the arrival of the British. It was only with colonial rule that the land tax was extended to Sokoto and Gwandu, including much of the land of "fiefholders," other titled officials, and prosperous commoners that had previously been exempted, and most noticeably to the *gayauna* of the slaves.[29] We emphasize that slaves were not subject to the land tax in the precolonial era.[30] These questions of tax exemption receive a detailed treatment later in the chapter.

The special crop taxes

The last of the main taxes to affect rural slavery were the special crop taxes, *kurdin shuka* (from *shuke*, sowing) and *kurdin rafi* (from *rafi*, stream; hence irrigation tax), which was sometimes called *kurdin karofi*, literally the tax on dye pits but more generally meaning an "industrial" tax.[31] Both stemmed from the concept of the tithe, but were applied to crops more easily assessed in the field than after harvest.[32] *Kurdin rafi* was the name applied to the tax on crops grown in the dry season on irrigated (*fadama*) plots. This tax varied with the crop and the district. It was usually based either on the size of the irrigated area, or the length of the furrows. The name *kurdin shuka* was used when the crops were not irrigated. This tax was on special crops planted late in the rainy season and harvested well into the dry season. Again it varied with the crop and the district. Some crops were exempt, cotton in most areas and indigo in some.

The rates for *kurdin shuka* in Kano were 1,000–1,500 cowries per plot. Crops included potatoes, groundnuts, rice, beans, peppers, cocoyams, sugar cane (*takanda*), yams, and cassava. The rates varied with the crop and district, sometimes the rate being fixed, irrespective of size of plot. Potatoes were sometimes assessed at 200 cowries per furrow instead of the patch. Cassava attracted higher rates. Around Kura the tax on cassava ranged as high as 15,000–20,000 cowries. In districts where these crops were not important, they were not taxed. Festing noted that *kurdin rafi* (which he referred to as *kurdin karofi*) was collected on wheat, onions, sugar cane (*rake*), tobacco, henna, dye pits, and productive date trees. Wheat and onion patches attracted full or half rates when fallow in some places. Rates varied from 2,000 to 5,000 cowries; they were fixed in some districts and varied in others. In many parts of Kano neither *kurdin shuka* nor *kurdin rafi* was assessed on cotton, beans (*wake*), or indigo, and minor crops – okra, pumpkins, calabashes, and tomatoes – were generally tax-free. Farms at Kunci were an exception, where there was a high tax on indigo that was imposed forty years earlier because farmers had abandoned other crops to grow indigo. The rate was 40,000 cowries per farm.[33] Both cotton and indigo were taxed in the vicinity of Kura, which was a major center of textile production, apparently to stimulate the planting of other crops.[34] Exemptions on cotton and indigo elsewhere were intended to promote the textile industry, as Dupigny observed in his assessment of Sarkin Dawaki Tsakkar Gidda District.

> I was struck at the large quantity of cotton planted in all parts due no doubt to the fact that it is free from tax . . . Some 30 odd years ago, on representation to the then Emir (Abdulahi – Majin Karofi) [Abdullahi b. Ibrahim, 1855–82, whose nickname was Maje Karofi] that there was a great scarcity of cloth and that in consequence many dye-pits had fallen into disuse the tax on cotton was abolished and has never been reimposed. Indigo is grown plentifully and like Beans (wake) and Lelle [henna] not taxed.[35]

Dupigny also mentioned that "Exemption from payment on these is usually made in favour of Village Heads and others as in the case of Kurdin Kassa."[36] Again it should be noted that these exceptions applied to the largest slave owners.

Tax exemptions (including *hurumi* and *caffa*) for slave owners

Many slave owners, especially those with the largest holdings, were wholly or partially exempt from agricultural taxes, other than the religious tithe. As far as we are aware, no member of the aristocracy or the slaves who held official positions paid *kurdin kasa, kurdin shuka,* or *kurdin rafi.* Plantations and farms on state lands that were attached to political office, as well as the private estates of the aristocracy, were exempt. In addition many commoners, especially merchants, craftsmen, and livestock herders with holdings in land were wholly or partially exempt as well. According to Cargill, exemptions also applied to "sons living and working with their fathers, [and] mallams holding special dispensation."[37] As already noted, the land taxes were not levied at all in Sokoto and Gwandu. The tax exemptions were of importance to the health of the slave economy in the precolonial period, and their withdrawal under colonial rule was rather slow. As long as they were maintained, to that degree slavery was promoted. Eventually all *were* withdrawn, marking the end of the last major government policy that encouraged the retention of slaves.

The two most important exemptions were known as *hurumi (hurmi)* and *caffa (chaffa, chappa).*[38] *Hurumi* exemptions arose from the fact that land was acquired from a political official who was responsible for the administration of waste or abandoned land that technically belonged to the state.[39] Abdullahi dan Fodio discussed the concept in his treatise on Caliphate land law, drawing on Maliki legal precedents.[40] The right to land could be either communal, as in grazing lands, cemeteries, forest reserves for fuel, and other common lands, or it could be individual, as in the case of farms that were allowed tax exemptions. Official farms attached to political office were also declared *hurumi,* but unlike private farms, could not be alienated. According to Cargill, "'Hurumi' farms were the perquisites of jakadas and local 'Sarikis'; they paid no taxes, but subsisted the people, to whom they were reserved as sort of official estates."[41]

According to Bargery, *caffa* involved "attaching oneself to a person of influence for the advantage of his protection, and in return being to a certain extent at his call; volunteering one's allegiance" to that person.[42] By pledging *caffa,* therefore, an individual was subject to "the appropriation, by a privilaged [sic] class usually resident in principal towns, of the taxes of certain talakawa whose allegiance they claim," that is, officials who had granted land concessions to wealthy commoners for an annual rent.[43] Cargill defined *caffa* as being "under the special protection of some powerful man in Kano, who uses his influence to procure his exemption from taxation in return for an annual present."[44]

In both cases these exemptions were associated with absentee farmers, *nomijide,* and dispersed holdings.[45] Often the land appears to have been rented from aristocrats, which is probably the reason why the lands were wholly or partially exempted from taxation. According to Festing, *hurumi* and *caffa* were "the system under which villages, hamlets, farms, or individuals pay a little or a large, sum to some influential 'protector' in Kano (and nothing to the official Revenue) in return for various exemptions."[46]

Table 6.3. *Caffa compounds in Sarkin Dawaki Tsakkar Gidda District, 1909*

Town	Total compounds	Caffa compounds	Caffa (%)
Sindininia	151	122	80.8
Dumus	41	28	68.3
Kangari	84	55	65.5
Kwatai	83	54	65.1
Kawo	34	19	55.9
Maichedia	140	74	52.9
Total	533	352	66.0

Source: Dupigny, Assessment Report, Sarkin Dawaki Tsakkar Gidda District, SNP 7/10 5570/1909.

Hurumi and *caffa* exemptions were numerous and extensive. In Dan Isa Sub-District, immediately outside Kano city, bordering the Challawa River:

> A good many of the farms in the villages belong to farmers living in neighbouring villages ... There are 11 villages, all near Kano, the inhabitants of which formerly paid hurmi to various of the Emir's Hakimai ... In addition to the above there were formerly a good many individual cases of Nomijide, living in Kano and having farms in the villages. All the villages are near Kano and for most intents and purposes can be treated as part of Kano itself.[47]

These absentee farmers, who were "generally more prosperous" than local residents, farmed 1,968 acres. Similarly, in Mundubawa District, several officials and a relative of the Emir of Kano had estates that were not subject to taxation.[48] The town of Kafin Madaki, on the border between Katagum and Kano, had 214 compound holders, 56 of whom farmed on lands across the emirate border in Katagum. The *sarki* of Madaki had no "authority over these nomijide."[49]

In southeastern Kano Emirate, many farmers had acquired land under *caffa* arrangements from a large landholder who was a member of the aristocracy. Dupigny, who assessed the area in 1909, was under the impression that the system had been in effect for over eighty years. Rents were modest, ranging from 1,000 to 2,000 cowries per farm, and including a reduction on *kurdin kasa* as a means of attracting tenants. According to Dupigny,

> In order to attract cultivators, and for other reasons, it has been customary to make rebates in the K. Kassa – thus non-residents (nomijide) are usually charged 500 c (3¾d) per farm; new-comers, semi-nomadic Filani and Mallamai [clerics] pay from 500 to 1000 c per farm.

There was also a "class" of cultivators, *alkalai* (judges), "fadawa" (those associated with the palace), and *jakadu* (slave officials, tax collectors), who paid no tax and presumably no rent. In the six towns that Dupigny assessed,

Table 6.4. *Agricultural taxation and residence, Kura District, 1909*

Town	Tax payers	Total compounds
Kadawa	377	316
Mallam	408	676
Chiromawa	343	543
Dan Hassan	535	349
Tariwa	375	450
Garun Baba	209	205
Kerifi	504	534
Gondusi	357	387
Kampawa	62	32
Kuran	27	87
Ringimawa	143	19
Jebawa	370	266

Source: Frewan, Kura District Assessment Report, 1909, SNP 7/8 2407/1909.

he found that 66 percent of the compounds were governed by *caffa* arrangements (Table 6.3). Though such a high figure may have been atypical, it does focus attention on how important tax exemptions could be in certain areas.

There were further differences in assessment according to whether farmers were immigrants, semi-nomadic Fulani, or Muslim clerics.

> As an illustration, in Fagam, a town of 133 compounds and 993 inhabitants, the total K. Kassa accounted for is 10/–; the reason given for such an insignificant amount being that the town is composed almost entirely of FADAWA who have never paid taxes of any kind except perhaps ZAKKA. In the town of Gwaram there are 5 rates of K. Kassa levied, roughly, according to the ward in which the individual resides and so practically constituting a tribal distinction. Mai Ungwa [*mai unguwa*] Anyokawa collects 1000 and 2000 cowries per farm; Mai Ungwa Warjawa 1500 c, Mai Ungwa Beri Beri [Bare-bari] 1200 c, Mai Ungwa Filani 1000 c. Assuming that this is, as I believe it to be, the correct order of the tribes as agriculturalists, the inference is that, here at any rate, the original idea was to make the rent as far as possible propor-tionate to the size of farm or to the individual's labour.[50]

As already noted, *fadawa* were those associated with the emir's palace, including relatives of the royal family, and hence exempt from taxation. The Warjawa and Anyokawa were non-Muslims living in southeastern Kano and the Ningi hills, and because of their origins they were expected to pay higher tax. Barebari were free immigrants from Borno who were given a special rate to attract them to the district, while the Fulani were often given privileges, including lower taxes, to encourage their settlement.

Finally, the absence of residence requirements for purposes of tax payment meant that equals might not be taxed equally. In Kura District, for example, there were a "large number of owners of compounds who do not

171

acknowledge the Headman of the town where they reside, but pay their taxes to the head of a neighbouring, or at times, distant village where their farms are located." Frewan found the incidence of absentee farming very extensive indeed (Table 6.4).[51]

The discrepancy between the number of local tax payers and the total number of compounds in the towns reflects at least two phenomena. In many cases, farmers lived in one place but farmed in an adjacent community, and they paid their taxes where their farms were located. Hence tax returns might uncover absentee farmers who owned or leased land in the village but who lived elsewhere. It might appear that there were more tax payers than residents. Many farmers had dispersed holdings, and where they paid tax might not relate to their place of residence at all.[52] In most cases, the acquisition of additional farms is indicative of slave ownership, because slaves were needed to work the combined holdings. Hence, in some cases, farmers paid taxes through a village/town head but did not live there. In other cases, they lived in one town where they paid taxes but had farms in other villages, where they did not pay tax. In all these cases of dispersed and absentee farming, the network of tax exemptions for politically influential slaveholders probably applied to some considerable extent.

The widespread nature of the tax exemptions meant that members of the ruling class, their chosen clients, and most other large slave owners were fully or partially exempt from Caliphate land taxes. Thus the full burden of normal state taxation did not attach even indirectly to much of the slave population.[53] Owners of large numbers of slaves were, it is true, visible targets for irregular exactions related to defense, famine relief, other emergencies of state, and the annual *gaisuwa* payments to political superiors that amounted to a type of income tax. *Gaisuwa* involved obeisance or protection money which was perceived as "greetings" or presentations to a superior. The weight of this burden is unknown, although common sense suggests that the amounts involved were relatively modest in relation to income because the highest authorities needed loyal support from the nobles, officials, and merchants making the payments.[54]

British tax reforms and slavery in Northern Nigeria

Colonial tax policy had other important aims in addition to dealing with the slavery issue – most especially the need to raise revenue. At first, Lugard found it advantageous to retain the precolonial taxes as part of his general theory of indirect rule. For the most part the later British attempts to reform the precolonial taxes can be seen as an effort to obtain more favorable results and garner greater tax revenues without a general break with the past. The consequence was that Northern Nigeria's complex and layered precolonial system of taxation continued relatively unchanged for far longer than might have been expected. Even the tax system that emerged after the First World War had distinct links to the earlier mechanism, though the multiplicity of earlier taxes was simplified. Policy gradually did focus on two targets: eliminating exemptions, and finding ways by which the various taxes could be combined and rationalized into a "lump-sum" payment that often amounted to a poll tax. Both these reforms served to alter the incentives to hold slaves.

Lugard quite early came to perceive taxation as a means whereby the government could control the slaves and cause eventual change in the slave system, in conjunction with measures on land tenure and the reliance on the Islamic courts to mediate slavery disputes. He noted that

> Direct taxation ... as being the State recognition of the rights and responsibilities of the individual, is the moral charter of independence of a people. Communities, however, who have only recently emerged from such a state of servitude, are not, at first, wholly fit to appreciate those rights and to assume those duties, and they take some time to acquire the sense of responsibility and its obligations.[55]

Lugard was referring to the plantations or "slave villages" that had previously escaped state taxation but were now expected to pay double – their traditional obligations to their masters and the tax to the colonial state. For public consumption at home in Britain he noted that

> the introduction of a direct and *individual* taxation teaches the peasant his responsibility to the State, and his personal interest in and obligation to it. The law holds him personally responsible for his acts, and the executive holds him personally responsible for his contribution to the revenue.[56]

Again, there can be no doubt that Lugard included the slave population when he used the word "peasant."

That Lugard understood clearly the potential effects of tax reform is shown in his statement that "direct taxation is unsuitable to a people who are held in a state of slavery or serfdom, for the responsibility of the individual is then assumed by the slave-owner."[57] If slaves who stayed on their masters' lands had to meet their own tax bills, a new view of their position vis-à-vis their masters would be encouraged.

We recall that under the Caliphate, no kind of per capita tax was levied on slave ownership.[58] Further, as already noted, the slaves themselves were exempt from the direct payment of most taxes, although occasionally it is noted that slaves paid the tithe (*zakka*) to their masters, who in turn were supposed to forward this religious tax for redistribution to the needy. In general, to the extent that the slaves engaged in activities that attracted a tax bill, the masters were responsible for making the payment.

When Lugard moved to tax the slave population, he did more than provide a "moral charter of independence." He was at one stroke increasing the tax base for the colonial state and implicitly encouraging masters to renegotiate the terms of dependency with their slaves. During the first ten years of colonial rule, income acquired as cash payments from slaves for *murgu* fees, ransom, and rent was rarely subject to tax. After that, the tax burden on such payments was relatively light even when the payments *were* figured in the assessment of tax payers. Any owner, other than officials with access to state exemptions, who maintained a large, rural slave establishment of the precolonial pattern therefore faced a much steeper tax bill than did those who began to emancipate their slaves or allowed them to work on their own account.

The British reforms had to proceed slowly because the common farmers, who had borne the brunt of Caliphate land taxation, initially tried to take advantage of the colonial conquest to escape the discriminatory taxes of the past. There was tax unrest, especially in Kano Emirate. As Lugard reported in 1903,

> At first there was considerable lawlessness in the country districts [of Kano]; the Fulani faction were driven out, and the people refused to pay any taxes ... the peasantry showed a desire to throw off the yoke, and attacked the tax-collectors, and even attacked Captain Phillips when he went to arrest perpetrators of one of these outrages ... [which was] caused by a few malcontents who proposed to obey neither the Fulani nor the British, and whose cry was "no more taxes, no more slaves, no laws and each to do as he pleases."[59]

In 1904, Cargill reported that the "peasantry, however, did not desire the return of the Fulani headmen [after the conquest of Kano], and in some cases refused them admittance to the towns, and ousted the tax-collectors."[60] In 1905, a slave of a tax collector was killed, allegedly for catching a man stealing: "the villagers, who in this Emirate are very ready to take the law into their own hands and resort to blows on little provocation, were collectively guilty of the disturbance, and were punished by a fine."[61] As a result of this resistance, very little tax was forthcoming in the first few years of colonial rule.

Eventually, however, reform did proceed, and as already noted, the most important changes in the tax system for the slavery issue were twofold. The first reform was the elimination of the exemptions on the property of the masters, including land and slaves. Male slaves, never having paid tax to the Caliphate, were now expected to pay taxes to the state. The identification of *murgu* as a form of taxation in Hausa epistemology and the recognition that all forms of slavery constitute a type of taxation that is realized by masters should not disguise the significance of the imposition of the colonial reform. The previously exempt private plots of the slaves offered great potential in terms of the amount of new taxes that could be raised.[62] As Palmer observed,

> Farms are divided into 1. Gandu – big farms. 2. gayemna [*gayauna*] – farms on which the slaves are allowed to work for their own profit generally two days a week, Friday and Sunday ... As may readily be seen, when it comes to paying taxes, there are a good many more "gayemna" than "gandu."[63]

The early assessment reports show low average acreage for farms because colonial tax assessors wanted to capture the potential revenue of these plots, as well as the exemptions related to dispersed holdings.

The second important reform involved the evolution of the multiplicity of Caliphate taxes into a "general tax" resembling a poll tax that all adult males including slaves had to pay. A master keeping slaves would be responsible for the bill, but if *murgu* arrangements that allowed for ransom and rental payments by slaves to masters were struck, the tax would touch this income only lightly if at all.

We are not the first writers to have perceived that colonial tax policy, by giving masters the opportunity to shift part of their tax burden to the slaves, undermined the large slave estates. Adamu Fika saw the importance of this development:

> the British hoped that the system of assessing individuals rather than household-heads would lead to a break-up of the slave or serf farm-estates. In the pre-existing system these farm-estates did not pay [tax on land] since their products belonged to the estate owner or titled official. Neither category of men paid the tax but instead gave presents to the ruler. A sizeable proportion of the emirate's production thus went untaxed. By holding the individual cultivator liable to pay tax on the land he tilled ... the British were deliberately destroying the right of the rich estate-owner or noble to the profits from the labour of his serfs. In effect the colonial regime was saying that ownership of land was valid only if the claimant personally tilled the land or paid for the labour. These developments were of general application throughout the Protectorate.[64]

Fika's observations accurately identify the fact that the British now taxed slaves or "serfs" directly. Jumare similarly saw the connection between slavery and taxation:

> When taxation was introduced by the colonial government in Sokoto, many masters were compelled to enter into *murgu* arrangement[s] with their slaves so that both could pay their taxes, since if slaves were not allowed to pursue some trade or craft, it would be their master who would bear the burden of their taxes.[65]

William Starns perceived this impact as well. He states that the tax burden on large landowners who were expected to pay the bill for all members of this group was a contributing factor to the breakup of many large estates and the negotiation of new tenancy relationships with slaves.[66] Hence the early colonial move to place the tax burden on individuals and separate farm holdings was a significant factor in altering the terms of servility and ultimately in turning slaves into peasants.

These changes were, understandably, not always smooth. In addition to whatever other obligations slaves had to their masters, the colonial state expected that slaves would now contribute a portion of their earnings as a direct tax. Traditional obligations and the new tax had to mesh; the question of who paid taxes had to be resolved. There was thus a struggle between masters and slaves. Some slaves, dunned for tax payments, shrugged their shoulders and pointed to their masters, a strategy that seemed to work for a while. Larymore complained from Nupe in 1907 of the "Slave Farms difficulty." He could not decide how to compel slaves still residing on their masters' lands to pay tax. He believed that

> The assessment problem will however still remain, – the owner declaring that he is unable to pay for all his slaves at the usual rate charged to free men, the slaves folding their hands and saying "Do not ask me, there is my master!"

A marginal note cautioned patience: "Much better leave this question [of] slavery alone."[67] Larymore may have stumbled upon official estates that were still exempt from the land tax, or he may have uncovered a real attempt at tax evasion. In either case, slaves resisted the payment of tax. Similarly, in 1908 Gowers revealed that many slaves were avoiding tax in Bauchi. He testified before the Lands Committee that "the individual who used the hoe did not necessarily pay at all [because] he was usually a slave."[68] As late as 1922, masters were paying taxes on behalf of their slaves in Yola Emirate.[69] Hence there is some evidence that slaves may have resisted the desire of masters to transfer the tax burden to them. That situation did not last for long in most emirates, with the apparent exception of Yola, as is explored in the next section. The incentive for masters to relieve themselves of financial responsibility for their slaves was too strong to be resisted.

The elimination of tax exemptions

The elimination of tax exemptions in addition to augmenting the colonial state's revenue considerably increased the pressures on the slave system. Because the elimination of most exemptions took almost thirty years to implement, the impact on slavery was gradual. The role of tax policy in bringing about a "natural death" for slavery was, deliberately, a measured one. Meanwhile, slaves were caught in the masters' struggle to maintain tax havens and to minimize the effects of the elimination of tax exemptions. Changes in taxation exposed slaves to new forms of compulsion that superseded the old methods of exploitation but left them no less exposed. In the end, the need to acquire cash for their taxes, which was of much less concern to slaves under the Caliphate, pushed them into the world of agricultural production for export and dry-season employment.

As Festing observed in 1908, tax reforms would have a dramatic impact because of

> inclusion under regular taxation of an enormous amount of hitherto untaxed hamlets and estates ... These previous exemptions ... used to absorb something like half the entire [potential] Revenue.[70]

The basic principle of the reform was simple. Each farm would be taxed separately, "whereas by ancient custom in many cases, for intricate reasons, in various manners, a farmer paid his KURDIN KASSA, or farming License, to cover more than one farm."[71] The multiplicity of exemptions that we have already examined was to be ended. It should be noted that the many scholars who have accused the colonial rule of introducing "onerous" taxes and thereby "exploiting" a conquered people have missed this impact of early colonial taxation.[72]

The implementation of full adult male assessment occurred in four stages, three that took place before the First World War and the fourth that occurred much later. While many slaves escaped the stage-by-stage escalation of pressures for a brief period, and some did for as much as thirty years or even longer, in the end all the slaves were expected to pay the same taxes as everyone else. The stages were chronological with overlaps. We summarize them here, and then explore them more fully in the sections that follow.

First, the private lands in Sokoto and Gwandu became subject to *kurdin kasa*, sometimes called *kurdin gona* (farm tax), and masters there needed to shift as much as possible of this burden onto their slaves. Land taxation was applied to Sokoto and Gwandu almost immediately after the conquest in 1903 and was largely in effect by 1905. Many slaves were brought into the assessment pool as soon as their *gayauna* plots came to the attention of British officials, a process that began shortly after the conquest and accelerated over the next seven years. By 1910, most of these plots were being taxed. Masters had an immediate motive to shift as much as possible of this new burden onto their slaves.

Second, *caffa*, and *hurumi* exemptions, particularly numerous in Kano, were largely eliminated in the years 1907–13. The development was related to the consolidation of territorial responsibilities into homologous districts. Slaves working these lands came into view of the taxman as district assessments were completed and then revised, a process that began in 1907 and lasted into the early 1920s. Masters had to decide whether or not to pay the taxes of their slaves or to give them time so that they paid their own taxes. It is clear that in many cases masters thought it was to their advantage to shift the tax burden to the slaves themselves, although many slave owners strenuously objected to these changes because there was considerable guesswork involved, and the possibility for corruption was great.

Third, private estates, often located on state lands and disguised as official holdings, were exposed. These private estates, including their slaves, were placed on the tax rolls whenever they were discovered, usually in the reassessment of districts after 1911. As this was accomplished, yet more masters found that they could reduce their tax bills by methods that made the slaves pay taxes at the same time that the slaves rented land or made cash payments under *murgu* arrangements, whether or not the slaves were also paying off their ransoms.

Fourth and finally, the state lands attached to political office, where a great many slaves resided, were identified and delimited. Initially, officials had to declare which of their holdings should remain exempt from taxation, agreeing to pay tax on the rest, and on those lands slaves became a tax burden. Much of this shift occurred before the First World War. The official farms and plantations that retained their exempt status were the last lands to be taxed, many of them losing their tax exemptions only in the 1930s and some lasting into the 1940s. Only then, after delays ranging up to five decades, did tax reform finally affect slavery on these official lands. Below we present a detailed view of these tax developments.

Extension of land tax to Sokoto and Gwandu

Sokoto and Gwandu, which had only been subject to the religious tithe, now had to pay the land taxes (in practice collected as a poll tax), half the revenues from which were retained by the Caliphate government and half of which were transferred to the colonial state. Thus, a new and large source of tax revenue was suddenly available. From the perspective of the aristocracy in Sokoto and Gwandu, the imposition of this uncanonical tax was essential because tribute from the emirates in the form of a share of booty, accession taxes, inheritance taxes, and other levies were no longer forthcoming. From the perspective of the tax payer, there was a sudden and dramatic increase in the level of taxation. The people in the capital districts had paid very little tax indeed, considering the range of taxes that were collected elsewhere, and they did not welcome the change. Burdon reported that there was considerable dissatisfaction among the *talakawa* in 1904–1905, but he did not recognize its seriousness before the Satiru uprising. Masters especially resented having to pay the new taxes on behalf of their slaves. The "sullen" looks of the peasantry reported by Burdon reflected this discontent in Sokoto and Gwandu.[73]

The principle of a tax on rural areas was firmly established by 1905. This "capitation tax," the term used by Burdon to describe the levy,

> from which no adult male is exempt, except the Sarikin Muslimin [Sarkin Musulmi] himself – is itself a form of graduation. For as every man in a household, slave or free, has either to pay or be paid for, and as it is certain that all sons and domestic slaves will either look to their "pater familias" to pay for them or will demand from him the money, the tax practically comes to a tax on householders, graduated according to the size of the households. And I believe that under present conditions no better or more equitable scheme could be devised. And certainly no other such could be carried out.[74]

Lugard wanted to impose a rate of 3s. per man and 2s. per woman "as a fair start," but Burdon imposed a rate of 6d., and then only on males, on the grounds that "the *bulk* of the people *have* no money, they live from hand to mouth."[75] What he did not say was that even the relatively low rate of 6d. per man was an entirely additional burden over existing levels, and he made no reference to the fact that the "bulk" of the affected population were slaves.

Burdon intended that "every man, slave or free, rich and poor, or beggar (these latter have almost invariably a protection [*sic*] or 'big man' responsible for them) pays, even to the Waziri himself." Initially, there were problems, of course. Indeed there were "a large number of 'masterless men' ... escaping this year [1905]," but he believed rightly that "the amount [of tax] will probably increase automatically as the net is drawn tighter in future."[76] As late as 1908 officials were still discovering many examples of tax evasion, especially on the plantations of the aristocracy. Stanley found that many of the "private estates" around Wurno were not paying. The Habibi plantation in the Rafin Yamulu, for example, had so far escaped: "Habibi and his family pay no land tax; and, until I visited Wurno, Habibi himself paid no tax at all."[77] By that time, however, many farmers had already been snared. Local officials collected the land tax, known as *kurdin gona* (farm tax), keeping a portion for themselves. If the farmer cultivated land in a different village, he paid there as well. The use of the term *kurdin gona* was a thinly disguised effort to make the tax more palatable to farmers who had previously been exempt from paying *kurdin kasa*.

Elimination of *caffa* and *hurumi* exemptions

Early on, the British began to suspect that exemptions from tax were widespread in other emirates as well. Goldsmith stumbled across some in Nupe in 1905, when he undertook tax assessment in the rural areas. He discovered that existing tax assessments were "erroneous, a great number of villages and farms had not been reported, and the population and taxes had been considerably underestimated."[78] While he did not clearly identify these "fraudulent" returns as exemptions, it seems more than likely that they were. The level of assessment was swiftly revised.

The elimination of *caffa* and *hurumi* exemptions was clearly going to be more difficult to implement than was the extension of the land tax to Sokoto and Gwandu. Whereas the addition of a tax on the adult male population in these emirates was simple in principle and hard for individuals to avoid, *caffa* and *hurumi* exemptions turned out to be numerous and complicated, especially in Kano Emirate. The colonial regime first had to determine what they were and where they applied, and since it was not in the interests of those who had these exemptions to provide information, only full assessments, district by district, could uncover them. The problem was complicated further because landholdings were widely scattered. If farmers with holdings in more than one village were paying lower rates to some distant authority, they had no reason to enlighten the tax man. The jumbled territorial organization, especially in Kano Emirate, disguised the location and extent of the farms paying these varying rates.

In Kano, territorial officials were responsible for tax collection and administration in various parts of the Emirate, and as a result they managed these variegated interests from their palaces in Kano city. Their slave retainers, *jakadu* and *masu jimila*, actually dealt with the rural areas.[79] Because of the size of Kano Emirate, rural assessment had to proceed district by district, and that only began after the reorganization of districts into homologous units in 1905. Elsewhere, the need to reorganize territory was not pressing, but the problems of identifying *caffa* and *hurumi* exemptions still obtained.

The immigrant craftsmen and merchants who had acquired land under conditions that came with partial or full exemption from taxation lost their exemptions, both in Kano and in other emirates. Since these free commoners owned many slaves, they faced a crisis in how to pay greatly increased taxes, continue to pay rent in the many cases where they had access to land under *caffa* arrangements, and otherwise weather the famine years of deflation, bad crops, and slaves-on-the-loose. Their exemptions obliged them to demonstrate their loyalty to the officials who had provided them with land through their annual presentations of *gaisuwa*, which supplemented the modest rent that they paid.

In 1910, the *hurumi* farms outside of Kano city that had previously not paid *kurdin kasa* were measured and assessed at 1s. 8d. per acre. There were twenty-two hamlets "known as Hurmi and were in the past regarded as a part of Kano city."[80] In 1911, farmers in Dan Isa's Sub-District, also located just beyond the city walls, were suddenly faced with a compound tax of 1s. 6d. and a farm tax of 1s. per acre. Previously exempt *hurumi* villages were put "on the same footing as the other villages."[81] Many farms in the remaining villages belonged to farmers living in neighboring villages, but in addition "a good many individual cases of hurmi and chappa ... [have] now all been abolished and they (the masu chappa and masu hurmi) now pay their taxes to their own Dagatai, as the other villagers do."[82]

Caffa and *hurumi* exemptions were still being eliminated around Kano in 1912–13. In Jaidanawa District, Foulkes measured 121 farms, only 51 of which were being taxed. The increase in assessment was 27 percent. Foulkes rather generously excused the assessors because the farms that had not been taxed previously "were mostly the larger farms over which the Taki Mallams [tax assistants who measured farms; see below] might excusably make errors at present; (e.g. three farms were respectively 124, 89, 59 acres)"; they belonged to former officials and "other rich men of Kano town."[83] A sister of the emir owned the 89-acre farm. Similarly, several estates in the Mundubawa District of the Chiroma did not pay tax before 1912. These estates belonged to officials, including the Waziri, the Barde, and "a relative of the emir."[84] According to Garba, the districts that had been surveyed by 1913 included Kumbotso, Ungogo, Gezawa, Kunya, Kuru, Minjibir, Dawakin Yamma, and Kura, and in these, presumably, most of the exemptions were exposed.[85]

Hence between 1908 and 1913 in Kano many of the exemptions previously available to the large landowners had been canceled.[86] A similar process of elimination occurred in other emirates at the same time. Backwell, who assessed Moriki District in Sokoto Province in 1913, discovered that 149 leading men in the district did not pay tax.[87] According to Oyeyipo, wealthy landowners in Ilorin only started paying normal taxes in 1913.[88] Emirate officials elsewhere found their tax exemptions steadily whittled away, particularly the many aristocrats who had numerous estates before the tax reforms. Many of the lesser nobility and most of the merchants also discovered that their exemptions were eliminated.

Resistance to reform

There was considerable resistance to these tax reforms, particularly in Kano during 1907–1908.[89] Cargill planned to revise taxes in the Ma'aji's district in 1907 because it surrounded Kano city, where "many of the titular heads held private property ... and their claims could be investigated, settled and placed on record." Until reforms could be introduced, existing taxes were to be paid. The assessment would be based on representative farms in each "village." Cargill was soon to learn why "the native assessment itself is detailed and largely concerned with land rights." The reason related to the existence of the exemptions. The Resident intended to combine the *kurdin kasa*, *shuka*, and *zakka* and require payment in coin, although some grain would be acceptable as payment to "soothe Mohamadan susceptibilities" about the old tithe.

> Each headman would be given a numbered list of his farms, their owners, and their rentals and the number corresponding to the farms would be given to the proprietor.[90]

The *kurdin karofi*, and *jangali* were to be kept separate. There was soon "unrest in Kano," which was "attributed to changes in assessment." The "disturbances" that resulted from the "rejection by the peasantry" arose because of "habitual concealment of the true amount of their harvests."[91] Cargill blamed "the peasantry of the district, always a truculent ignorant lot" for the unrest, not the fact that taxation had suddenly increased by as much as a punishing 300 percent. The assessment "was in excess not only of what had ever been returned in taxation, but of what had been paid altogether in taxation, robbery, and extortion, to and by the Jekada [*jakadu*] fraternity."[92] Unwisely, the *talakawa* received "summary treatment" from a military patrol and many protestors were arrested.

Cargill was sent home, Hewby replaced him, and on February 28, 1908, Cargill's assessment had to be canceled and the old tax rates reintroduced. Girouard's summary trenchantly demonstrates the seriousness of the protest:

> The new assessment was highly unpopular, necessitated the intervention of troops, and eventually, a return to the Native System. It was moreover found that the new assessment of general tax instead of equalling the old native taxes was two or three times as much.[93]

The reason for the unpopularity and the great increase are both clear; Cargill's assessment had eliminated the exemptions. Girouard issued instructions "to enquire into the sentences imposed upon people connected purely with agitation against the new assessment; we are, if anything, responsible for their unfortunate position." As a result, twenty prisoners were immediately released as medically unfit, probably resulting from injuries incurred, and "the sentences were reduced to six months imprisonment for the remainder, who are due for discharge from prison towards the end of

November [1908]."[94] Since the protestors were associated with the propertied class of Kano, these discharges must have been a welcome reprieve for an administration wanting to appease merchants and aristocrats. The old taxes only were paid, and then very late. The *jakadu* collected the *zakka* as before, although not without accusations of corruption: "a large amount of it was taken and consumed by the Jekada gang." The attempt to eliminate exemptions in Kano had to begin afresh, but in the second effort there was no immediate plan to combine the *zakka* with the land tax. Religious sensibilities and favoritism had to be respected for the time being.

Palmer was assigned the difficult task of supervising the next effort to reform the Kano tax system. He began with the districts under the Madaki, Turakin Manya and Dan Iya, even though Emir Abbas was strongly opposed. Perhaps as a result of the emir's objections, resistance continued through 1910, by which time the colonial state was holding local officials responsible for non-compliance. Palmer reported that officials who failed to submit taxes in full were deposed from office:

> it may be safely counted on that the lesson so given during the past year will have most beneficial results in expediting the collection of taxes now proceeding. Although repeatedly warned many of the headmen apparently still believed that Zakka at any rate would not be strictly exacted. The worst failure among the districts was that of Sarikin Dawaki Maituta. In spite of the cleaning sweep given to the district last year little or no improvement took place. The Sub Districts of Kabbo and Godia had large deficits in Kurdin Gidda, Kurdin Kassa, and Zakka. They were proved to have collected these taxes and were convicted under the Revenue Proclamation. Yelwa did rather better but failed to pay up his Zakka.

Palmer submitted a list of those headmen who were deposed, and the tax reforms continued.[95]

Exemption of official estates

There was one major exception to the elimination of tax exemptions. It involved the many estates attached to political offices, including the *gayauna* of the slaves on those estates. This exception was a large one to be sure, since village heads, sub-district and district heads, and palace titleholders all appear to have been allowed one tax-exempt "farm" each. The emirs and Sarkin Musulmi were given even greater privileges. All their estates remained tax-free. This considerable tax exemption was based on the distinction between state lands and private lands. As we have seen, state land that was let to private individuals under *hurumi* and *caffa* arrangements was taxable, but the official estates retained their special status for at least two, sometimes three and even five decades into the colonial era.

The colonial regime justified this major concession to Caliphate tradition as a supplement to the incomes of officials. Once again Lugard had realized the issues involved. He assumed that some lands belonging to officials would remain exempt, although his subordinates and successors only discovered these estates in 1907. Girouard then confirmed the decision to exempt these state lands, which were still worked by slaves and increasingly by corvée labor as well. This benefit of office continued even after formal salaries for officials were introduced in 1909. What better proof that the British were very careful of their relations with the ruling elite, even if that meant scaling back the tax incentive for these particular slave owners to come to new arrangements with their slaves?

Officials debated the wisdom of taxing these lands, and if they were to be exempted, how extensive the allowances should be. Palmer, for one, wanted to "make all farms, including the 'gandu' of Serikis, pay *rent* (kurdin kassa) to Government." His idea was purely symbolic, however, for he too thought that there should be official privileges. He proposed that "the 'gandu' might be put on a nominal rent of 1s. a year." To that end he let one district official in Katsina pay a nominal 4,000 cowries, on condition that he require "all his heads of towns to do likewise with their 'gandus.'"[96] The proposal was not based on acreage, unlike the reform of the *kurdin kasa* with respect to the elimination of *caffa* and *hurumi* exemptions. Cargill had no strong opinions on the matter of official exemptions: "it is immaterial whether the official farms (gandus) are taxed or untaxed. I would regard them as mere perquisites of office. The farms are public property."[97]

Temple's recommendation that "a suitable farm be attached to every office" became colonial policy, however.[98] He believed that state farms were a desirable feature of the colonial political economy:

> This system, if cleared of abuses which have sprung up round it, appears to me a thoroughly sound one, and one to be supported. There must be native officials; the best possible way to remunerate them is to ensure them the opportunity of obtaining a living by either working a farm themselves (as is the case with some) or by overlooking the working of a farm by certain villagers (as is the case with others).[99]

Temple distinguished between personal management of plantations and the assignment of management to slave officials and even slave subordinates under those officials. The abuses that Temple was thinking of included the confusion in some minds between public and private land, and most especially, the number of official estates that were to be allowed per office. It should be noted as well that "working a farm themselves" meant sending slaves out to the fields, while the "certain villagers" were slaves who lived on a *rinji*. Unfortunately, there is little in the archival materials that we have examined to indicate the size of most of these holdings, other than that they were much larger than the average farm.

Despite the great number of exemptions that were continued in Kano alone, the total number of untaxed farms and plantations on state land was considerably reduced. Beyond the single exemption per office, other estates, whether on state lands or not, were assessed whenever and wherever

The role of taxation in the reform of slavery

discovered and no matter who owned them. As Hewby reported from Kano in 1908, some of the *hurumi* estates

> have been taxed, and some have not. Though it is contrary to Memo 5, and probably subversive of a proper system of Land revenue assessment – when the time for that arises, I believe it is a good thing, under the present conditions, of being almost entirely in the hands of the Native Administration, to recognise that every office in our books from village Head to District Hakimi, District Alkali and office holder in Kano, has a tax-free farm, of moderate and limited size; and this has been freely announced.[100]

Neither Hewby nor any other colonial officer indicated what he meant by "moderate and limited size." Palmer, who, as we have seen, was not sympathetic even to this exemption, ferreted out many. In 1911 he taxed the Kashin *rinji* of the Chiroma of Kano, despite the inhabitants' "pleas that they are slaves of Chiroma's and that their farms are Gandu farms." Palmer showed no mercy to the "15 men and 20 women and about 25 children in the village." He was even more demanding when he assessed a neighboring plantation that belonged to the mother of the emir.[101] Other officials lost many of their exemptions as well.

Eventually, the exempted estates were made subject to tax, many losing their special status in the 1920s and 1930s and apparently all of them by the 1940s.[102] In the meantime, the Sarkin Musulmi and the emirs continued to receive special treatment. While all other officials lost their perquisites, the emirs and Sultan avoided the tax, at least on some of their holdings. As Garba has noted with respect to the Emir of Kano,

> By about 1932 the district heads and the *Alkalai* (Muslim judges) were said to be paying taxes on their estates. Only the Emir was exempt. As regards the emir's "slaves" and dependants in revenue-survey districts, they were not taxed if farming in the emir's estates, but in non-revenue survey districts they reportedly paid income tax.[103]

If assessed, the Emir's estates would have fetched about £100. On the basis of the average tax assessment per adult male at the time, it is likely that there were approximately 400 males on the Emir's lands, which on reasonable demographic assumptions suggests a total servile population of perhaps 1,300.

Among the estates of the Emir of Kano was Gandun Nassarawa, the large plantation that gradually became the European quarter outside the walls of Kano city. According to oral tradition, the slaves on Gandun Nassarawa did not pay tax before the coming of the British and only began paying under colonialism very late: "It was only in the time of Emir Abdullahi Bayero that farm tax, 'kudin gona' was introduced."[104] As Rowling's study of land tenure in Kano Emirate in 1946 demonstrates, the Emir's estates were still exempt from taxation that late.[105] The situation in Kano was probably typical of most estates belonging to the emirs and the Sultan. If this is correct, then there were two decades when some 10,000 or more estates

184

continued to be exempted from taxation, and another two decades when the very large holdings of the emirs and Sultan still did not pay tax. As a result, the incentive to encourage slaves to obtain their freedom through self-purchase did *not* apply to these lands.

While there are no figures or estimates on the number of slaves on the 10,000 or more official holdings of the Sultan, emirs and lesser office holders, a very low estimate of ten slaves per estate suggests a minimum figure of 100,000 slaves. An average slave population on these estates of fifty, which is surely a more reasonable figure, suggests a figure of 500,000 slaves. Obviously the protection of official estates was a significant exception to the general pressure to push slaves away from estate agriculture. For two or three decades, and the further years of exemption for estates of the emirs and the Sultan, there were few incentives encouraging slaves to obtain their freedom through self-purchase.

These slaves could still attempt to buy their freedom, and no doubt many did so. Yet several factors discouraged such action among this sub-set of Northern Nigeria's slaves. Some of them continued to receive facial and body markings that clearly identified their status, a practice well documented for the slaves of the Emir of Kano. The application of slave marks lasted into the 1950s, if not later.[106] If the slave stayed in place, such markings would not be a disadvantage, but easy recognition was a problem of slaves who left. Many of these slaves had reasons for remaining, however. They had access to good land, they did not have to pay taxes, and bad treatment would presumably be unlikely in an establishment as visible as the emir's.

Evolution of the poll tax

The relatively early removal of many tax exemptions, and the eventual taxation even of the official estates had a major impact on the economics of slavery. Further consequences flowed from alterations in the specific types of taxation employed, as this section explores. The many British efforts at rationalization and reform are fully as bewildering as the complexities of the precolonial tax system. The end result, however, was relatively simple. Colonial reforms sought to eliminate complexity by combining all taxes into a single tax (that in effect was little more than a poll tax), and making every male pay excepting those on official estates. Although the colonial government vacillated between espousing a graduated income tax and the "single tax" idea of Henry George, in practice a single, general tax did emerge. Villages were told what their bill was. How this bill was apportioned among individuals was of little concern to the colonial state, as long as the total amount was forthcoming. For those who paid the land tax under the Caliphate, the difference may not have seemed significant, but many people had not paid under the Caliphate. For them, the innovation was startling.

From the beginning, the British wanted to introduce a "lump-sum tax," and the first effort to do so was in 1904.[107] According to Garba, efforts to revise the method of assessment varied, but basically

> the unit of assessment was the village, and the aim of assessment was not necessarily to increase taxation, but to see that it was fair and just. The general wealth of the village was assessed and a "lump-sum" amount fixed for it. It was the duty of the village head and the village elders to apportion the rate payable to each taxpayer.[108]

In fact, the applicable rate was often uniform among farmers. The early tax policy, according to Girouard, "practically resulted in the imposition of a poll tax."[109] In 1905, Burdon called the tax in Sokoto "this capitation tax,"[110] while Stanley referred to the tax collected in Wurno as a "poll-tax."[111] In Zaria the tax continued to be based on the "hoe," that is, each adult agricultural laborer, "in other words a poll tax."[112] Temple stated his preference clearly: he favored "the imposition of a poll tax pure and simple."[113]

Lugard's initial thoughts on taxation were not as crude as a simple poll tax, however. The Land Revenue Proclamation of 1904 and the Native Revenue Proclamation of 1906 attempted to institute a "lump-sum" system that would be a general tax of 10 percent of the annual value of production, derived or derivable, according to the average standard of land used in a neighborhood.[114] The aim was to establish a potential level of farm income; tax could be levied on that income. Under the traditional *kurdin kasa*, the *jakadu* had assessed the actual rather than potential level of income from the land.[115] Under the 1904 plan, any ransoms and rentals received from slaves were not taxable. Under a 1906 amendment, however, the tax base was widened to include non-farm revenues, also to be taxed at 10 percent. The provincial Residents were to do the assessing on a village basis, with village heads responsible for apportioning the exact amount of tax among the local residents on the basis of ability to pay. It should be noted that in theory, at least, the figure of 10 percent was a secular tithe, not unlike the basis for *zakka*, *kurdin shuka*, and *kurdin rafi*. As such its imposition, if fully realized, would have been a significant reform in terms of the level of taxation being paid by the average farmer. It would have reduced the amount due from many commoners, who were paying the religious tithe as well as *kurdin kasa*. Furthermore, it would have imposed only the equivalent of the religious tithe on those men who were benefitting from Caliphate exemptions, while not increasing their tax burden beyond the level that they were supposed to be paying according to Islamic tradition. The considerable objection to this attempt at reform is evidence that people had not been paying the full tithe.

Lugard's 1906 reform, if it had been fully adopted, did have the potential to capture a portion of cash income and would have meant taxation of *murgu*, self-ransom, and rental payments received by masters. That would have reduced to some extent the effectiveness of tax policy as a tool for emancipation. Manpower was so limited, however, that assessment of this rough form of income tax virtually failed in Kano and Zaria.[116] As we have seen, the failed attempt to implement this reform in Kano caused Resident Cargill to lose his job; it came close to costing him his sanity as well.[117]

The difficulty with the lump-sum tax was not one of theory – amalgamation of the multitude of precolonial taxes was a sensible idea, and as a concept lump-sum tax based on derived or derivable income receives plaudits to this day from tax economists. The problem was instead implementation, which was mishandled.[118] First, Cargill did not have even the tacit cooperation of Emir Abbas. Second, titled officials were forced to go to their districts in the tax year 1906–1907 to oversee tax collection, while in October 1907, these "district heads" were rusticated from Kano to live in their districts. Their resentment was palpable. Third, Cargill calculated the exchange rate between cowries and sterling at an overvalued rate that caused him to peg tax payments too high by a considerable margin. Fourth, these lump-sum taxes at least potentially hit cash income, including *murgu*, ransom, and rental payments from slaves, whereas the old taxes and even the original 1904 lump-sum tax did not. This innovation was presumably highly unwelcome, and it would clearly have been better to implement the new system over a period of years, not all at once as Cargill tried to do. Finally, the lump-sum tax required a difficult survey and assessment of all land, which included questions such as how to value land of different quality and land under shifting cultivation, as well as requiring an assessment of wealth in other forms.

Hill calls attention to Palmer's "somewhat embarrassed evidence" to the Lands Committee in 1908 that the consolidation of taxes ordered by Lugard in the Native Revenue Proclamation of 1906 had not been achieved, and all the old taxes were still in effect. Garba states that up to 1908, the "taxation system in the emirates remained virtually unchanged," despite the fact that the *gayauna* plots of slaves were supposedly being taxed because all adult males were subject to the agricultural taxes.[119] Even by 1910–11, "native assessment" under the old land tax, often recast in terms of the changing terminology of the colonial vocabulary, was still the rule.[120] Eventually, Mary Bull notes, "the whole concept dropped into obscurity."[121] It was, however, destined to resurface again in modified form, as we shall see below.

Since this first lump-sum tax was largely unsuccessful, slave owners could continue to calculate that income from slaves in the form of *murgu* payments, ransoms, and rentals would not be taxed, whereas taxes *would* be applied to land and the output from land held by a master and worked by his slaves. Lugard himself fully appreciated that the tax system actually in effect would reduce the profitability of slaveholding, although we have seen no indication that he understood that his 1906 reform if fully implemented would have canceled part of the incentive to emancipate.[122]

Girouard's attempt to change the system to an explicit land tax equivalent to the economic rent under the single-tax theories of Henry George was no more successful than Lugard's approach had been. His reform proved very difficult to implement, just as his predecessor's was, because limited manpower made it impossible to survey and map the taxable lands and assess them adequately.[123] In Kano, Festing observed "the futility of attempting, as was practically done in this district, a scientific assessment, much on a Burma system, with a staff insufficient even for its present duties, as well as the suitability of the land in the Kano Province for scientific revenue treatment in 2 or 3 years time."[124] The American invasion of Northern Nigeria through the ideas of Henry George was thus thwarted by the realities of Caliphate political economy and the stinginess of British colonial rule.

If the single land tax had been fully implemented, the effect on slavery would have been similar to that of Lugard's earlier (1904) tax policies. Since a land tax could not capture cash income any more than *zakka* or *kurdin kasa* could, this colonial reform promised to continue the policy of hitting large estates but not cash payments for *murgu*, self-ransom, or rental. This was stated vividly in Temple's testimony before the Northern Nigeria Lands Committee in June 1908. Wedgwood inquired about the new land tax proposal: "On that point, would it not rather tend to be the collection of rent under the name of a tax, and be simply no income tax whatever ...?" Answer: "– Yes."[125]

The most difficult problem in reaching a single tax was the merger of *zakka* with other taxes on agricultural production. People did not like losing their exemptions, but they found good religious reasons to object to the absorption of *zakka* into the single tax. British officials were sensitive to the issue, but they were determined. Until 1910 or so, the colonial regime was attempting to collect the existing taxes, minus exemptions. Thereafter, they concentrated on combining their assessment of the land tax in all its forms with a general merger and simplification of taxation. The *zakka* had to be eliminated. To use the language of Henry George, these taxes could be merged as a "land rent." As Garba has realized, "The implication of the proposed changes was that the institution of colonial taxation – properly so-called – took effect from 1910. The principle of land 'rent' was utterly foreign to the area."[126] Until then the British only tinkered with Caliphate taxes.

The widespread merger of *zakka* with a general tax in 1910 was the initial policy change of consequence, despite the sporadic earlier efforts at reform.[127] The first attempts to merge *zakka* with the land tax occurred in Kano, but as we have seen, the initial attempt failed. Palmer introduced a similar scheme in Katsina in 1908, and some parts of Kano started up a similar plan in 1909. Within two years most of Kano and Zaria had followed suit.[128]

In many places, a separate religious tithe was still collected even after the taxes were merged, whether because tax collectors could get away with double taxation or because farmers refused to recognize that the religious tithe was part of the land tax. In Katagum, for example,

> a general rent was fixed for each village community, and the people were told over and over again that "zakka was included." In spite of this the full

"zakka" was collected in all Emirates but Messau without any complaint reaching the Resident – over and above the general taxes or rent.[129]

There were also charges that officials began to collect the full *zakka*, the difference between the official figure that was usually low and the full tithe being pocketed by the *dagatai* and *jakadu*. One such scheme originated with Maji Dalla, "who was dealt with at Kano." In 1909, Dupigny estimated that at least three-fifths of the *zakka* had been embezzled.[130]

A *kurdin gida*, or compound tax, was an intermediate stage in tax consolidation. It was introduced in 1909 as a measure to capture tax from farmers who had dispersed holdings, which was a feature of the *caffa* system. As applied in Kano, *kurdin gida* was meant to consolidate and replace *kurdin rafi, kurdin shuka*, and *kurdin karofi* and deal with the problem that the more prosperous farmers, who invariably owned slaves, had farms in more than one village and often several districts, under conditions of *caffa*.[131] The intention was to establish the authority of the village heads, making them responsible for tax collection, and thereby reducing the possibility of embezzlement by *dagatai*.[132] Compounds were assessed at £2 per acre; this was raised to £4 per acre in 1914. In some places, compounds were not measured: the tax was a fixed rate per compound, a fixed rate per room, or a fixed rate per married man. The original aim was a fixed rate of 1s. 6d. per compound. In Dutse, Birnin Kudu, and Gwaram, the tax began as a levy on every compound and then became a levy on every married man. *Kurdin gida* had to be paid in coin, not cowries.[133]

Taki assessment

For the most part, the effort to introduce a single land tax had to be scaled back to a simpler attempt to measure roughly the size of individual farms and plots by pacing off the area of cultivated land. This method, called the revenue survey, or more pithily *taki* assessment after the Hausa word for pacing, was introduced from 1909 in parts of Kano and Katsina, where the lowest rate was 6d. per acre, and from 1913 near Sokoto city and around Birnin Kebbi in Gwandu Emirate. By early 1919, a flat rate of 1s. was levied on *taki*-assessed farms, raised to 1s. 6d. in that year. Major increases occurred in 1921, by which time the minimum rate was 1s. 6d. beyond fifteen miles from Kano and a range of 2s. to 4s. within that radius.[134] Note that this tax bore more heavily on farmers with large holdings of less fertile land – different fertilities were not taken into account – which must have had an effect in breaking up these holdings. It probably also reduced the incentives to plant high-risk crops.[135]

Assessments of districts near Kano under the *taki* system raised taxes by huge amounts – Dan Buram increased 134 percent; Ja'idanawa, 195 percent; Chiroma, 137 percent; Madaki, 54 percent; and Shantali, 89 percent. Dan Isa and Dan Mokoyo sub-districts rose by 63 percent and 300 percent

189

respectively. At first Kunci village's increase was 289 percent. Neither Garba nor Ubah make the point, but we would suggest that these increases are so large because they included the revenue now obtained from the elimination of the tax exemptions in these areas.[136]

The spread of *taki* assessment was not without opposition. A major disturbance occurred in 1911 in Dan Isa Sub-District, where there were many *hurumi* and *caffa* farms. Palmer reported that "the taki tax at 1/– an acre caused a certain amount of temporary discontent in some of the villages." Farmers in Limawa and fourteen neighboring villages complained, which resulted in arrests.

> The headman of Limawa was unable to get his people to pay their tax, and on bringing the matter before Dan Isa, he, Dan Isa, together with a few of his followers and the Dagache went to the village, where they were driven out by some of the villagers. The disturbance was probably caused to some extent by want of tact on the part of Dan Isa. At the same time 14 other villages near Limawa came in a body and complained about the new tax. The leaders of the disturbance at Limawa were at once arrested by the Emir and punished. This had an immediate effect, the men of the 14 villages who had complained returned to their villages and no further difficulty has since been experienced in regard to the tax.[137]

These continuing protests over taxation indicate that the imposition of British reforms was a long and painful process.

There were other problems. Corruption in the *taki* assessment was one, as farmers followed *taki malamai* around the fields offering bribes or otherwise being expected to do so. According to oral data collected by Ubah, "It is known that a large number of the more unfortunate mallams were imprisoned by the emir for seeking financial gratification in the field."[138] There were many complaints. As Fika notes,

> Due to the progressive extension in Kano emirate of the taki measurements by which tax was assessed according to farm acreages, there was a corresponding increase in the lodgement of appeals against such assessments. By early 1913, such appeals were causing an excessive back-log in tax collections all over the emirate. Even such legal expedients alarmed the political officers as they feared they could lead to a breakdown of authority. Under the familiar customary taxes, the taxpayer had been able to estimate for himself what was due from him. It seems that the talakawa lodged appeals against taki measurements because they felt the latter was increasing their tax liabilities.[139]

According to Ubah, "it was not unusual for a man to abandon his farm and seek protection in flight if, for whatever reason, he felt that he could not meet the assessment. Hundreds of farms are said to have been abandoned each year in every district."[140]

Where *taki* assessment and the new land tax were adopted, they were intended to replace all former taxes. In those areas *zakka* and *kurdin kasa* were scrapped. *Taki* assessment continued the colonial tradition of providing an incentive to earn income in non-taxed forms, and thus further undermined

190

the large landholdings which were central to the slave economy.[141] It also had the incidental effect of institutionalizing a flat-rate system, so that increments to farm production accrued to farmers and not to the tax collectors. From the standpoint of slaves, any increases in income utilized for self-ransom payments would go untaxed; there was no disincentive to earn more as the colonial economy developed. On both counts, production must have been stimulated.

It was hoped that the *taki* assessment could be transferred rapidly to all other emirates, but that process proved to be slow and difficult.[142] Training sufficient *taki malamai* was always a problem, and so was the fact that this reform generally raised the level of taxes.[143] Implementing it was always likely to cause rural discontent. Thus its spread was limited and uneven. It never covered more than about one-tenth of Kano Emirate, mostly north and northeast of Kano city, and the scheme was abandoned in Sokoto and Gwandu.[144] The colonial state was forced to rely on the assessments of emirate officials, who were rightly suspected of retaining many of the Caliphate exemptions. Still, C. W. Rowling concluded that this method of assessment had been a factor in breaking up the large estates in the areas where it was applied.[145] This claim led Hill to object that since this tax was basically a flat-rate one of 10 percent, its lack of progressivity would have kept it from breaking up landholdings.[146] Though her point is correct as far as it goes, it should be kept in mind that as a tax on *land* and not on income in the form of cash, it did provide a motive to the masters to decrease the size of their estates and to strike arrangements with their slaves. By doing so, they could reduce their tax liabilities considerably.

The result of British fiscal policy after a decade of colonial rule was a patchwork quilt of different taxes. A visitor to Northern Nigeria in 1910 would have found the following: (1) some use of consolidated taxation involving lump-sum assessment, particularly in Sokoto, with individual tax payments left to the village head and his council to divide among each man according to his wealth in land; (2) some *taki* assessment based on land area; and (3) some considerable survival of the old traditional taxes.[147] In general, however, the incidence of all these taxes was heavy on land, with many members of the elite and the *gayauna* of many slaves now included in the net; while tax incidence was virtually nil on rural income not associated with production. From the point of view of the masters, holding slaves meant paying tax on the land they farmed, either for the master directly or for the slaves' *gayauna*.

A major underlying result of tax policy before the outbreak of world war in 1914 was, therefore, that slavery was steadily undermined, except on official estates. The ability of tax policy to achieve this corrosive consequence was deliberate, and the effect was certainly foreseen by some government officials. The statements by these officials that their tax reforms would serve to break up the slave estates were, in the long run, substantially correct.

The "general tax"

Change in the tax mechanism was slow in spite of the huge amounts of time spent by the British in their discussions of tax reform. Yet from about 1910, some greater conformity did begin to emerge.[148] In rural areas where *taki* assessment had not been adopted, at least in principle the British began to standardize on the idea of a single tax assessed on the basis of the community's wealth. This "general tax" bore considerable comparison to Lugard's abortive lump-sum tax, as amended in 1906 to include assessment of wealth held in forms other than land. The major difference between the general tax and the Lugard precursor was that insistence on universal assessment by British officials was dropped, and no land survey was involved.

The general tax was intended as a consolidation of the old taxes. Theoretically it involved an assessment of every adult male by local government officials, and that concept was embodied in the Native Revenue Ordinance of 1916. The incidence of this standardized general tax was designed to be varied according to local estimates of wealth, whether (as was usual) the estimation was carried out by the "native authorities," or by the Resident and his staff. By 1911, *zakka* had been fully merged with the general tax in Kano, Katsina, Sokoto, and Zaria.[149] In Zaria, by 1912, the general tax had completely replaced *all* the old taxes except for the *jangali* cattle tax, while in Kano it (along with *taki* assessment) had superseded the old taxes by 1918.[150] Remnants of the old taxes were still widely found in Northern Nigeria even after the First World War, and in some areas general assessment remained an ideal for some time yet.[151] By the third decade of colonial rule, however, it was the paramount form of taxation.

In theory, under the general tax the village heads would assess the wealth of households, with the household head then responsible for the internal division of the tax burden among family members, dependants, and slaves. The method differed from the assessments carried out under the precolonial *kurdin kasa*, where only land was taxed (after adjustments for exemptions) and where the assessing officials were the *jakadu* of the territorial officials.[152] The theoretical construct of the general tax might have posed much the same problem of removing some incentive to emancipate that arose with Lugard's unsuccessful lump-sum tax of 1906. When slaves paid *murgu*, ransom, and rentals to their masters, that income would add to the wealth of the master. In principle, the lump-sum assessment system would have reflected this greater wealth, and there would have been no special incentive to free the slaves. Tax would be paid either way.

Fortunately for those who supported the use of taxation to degrade the slave system, the assessment of wealth was done haphazardly for a very long time, and even when it was carried out, incomes not associated with land or output were often touched rather lightly. As Garba makes clear, although the wealthy sometimes paid a higher total tax bill than did the small farmers, that bill was usually lower as a percentage of income and hence regressive.[153] Thus even when former masters were assessed on their wealth in all its forms, taking payments from the slaves was for these masters preferable to paying the slaves' share of tax directly.

Furthermore, the British gave only very limited supervision to the mechanism by which the tax was divided within communities. Their goal of raising revenue was satisfied just so long as a village's total assessment was suitably high and the expected payments were forthcoming. In practice at the level of the village, the general tax could in very many cases be nothing more than a poll tax, with each member of the community paying an equal amount toward the village's assessed total sum. Burdon, writing from Sokoto, illustrated how this could happen when he wrote in 1909 that village heads

> disregard[ed] the order to apportion taxes among tax-payers on the basis of each tax-payer's wealth, and ... instead they imposed a uniform tax rate per household thereby eviscerating the terms of the Native Revenue Proclamation.[154]

Garba notes the impossibility of accurately identifying the incidence of the general tax. The assessment was by village heads, and accordingly no written records were kept. He notes that even where wealthier tax payers paid more than the basic rate, the higher rate was still sometimes a flat charge, not further graduated.[155]

The conclusion is that the consolidated tax reinforced the British practice of making the maintenance of a slave establishment more expensive than before.[156] At the very least, even when assessment was tantamount only to a poll tax, masters seeking to preserve slave enterprises would be responsible for paying tax on their slaves, which is what happened in Yola Emirate until 1922.[157] Beyond that, the value of the slaves would theoretically be included in the assessment of the family's wealth, so that the poll-tax rate paid by masters might be higher than the average of poll tax in the locality. Either way, tax could be avoided by the slave owners who took the decision to emancipate their slaves by one means or another.[158] It is true that ransom or rental payments from the former slaves might at times figure in the assessment of a former master's wealth, which could offset some of the original economic motive to emancipate. With the assessment on cash income typically rather small even where it was attempted, however, the inclusion of these payments would not be a major concern for most masters. Taxes thus continued to provide an incentive to alter the master–slave relationship.

The economics of the general tax also altered the motivation of the slaves, but in a quite different way. Slaves entering into some arrangement with their masters were now liable to pay a flat-rate tax bill, a rate that was the higher because in many communities differentials based on income and wealth did not exist. Thus for the slaves a stimulus towards earning a cash income – beyond the cash needed for *murgu*, self-ransom, or rental – was introduced. Economic theory is clear, and was understood at the time, that a

193

head tax increases the incentive to labor.[159] Unlike other forms of taxation, such as a progressive income tax, which alters the trade-off between leisure and labor, a poll tax allows all increment to income to be kept by the tax payer. The single incentive present is to earn enough to pay the tax.

Garba is certainly correct in concluding that colonial tax policy was "generally regressive, in so far as those with higher incomes tended to escape paying it at a rate commensurate with their income ... In general, the tax was not very elastic and was still more in the nature of capitation tax – especially in rural areas – rather than an income tax."[160] The impact of a regressive tax on the slave population had a desirable effect from the colonial perspective. Slaves had to make money for taxes, in addition to paying a share of their crops for rent and raising cash for *murgu* and redemption. As Fremantle assessed the situation in 1918,

> Taxation of the individual, slave or free, has popularized paid labour and done much to determine the status of the slaves. It has been a great help to the [slavery] policy.[161]

Slaves had little alternative other than growing crops that could be sold and seeking employment for wages. Since in general commodity prices were undergoing some decline in these years, in real terms the rate of taxation was actually increasing, adding to the incentives.

The incidence of colonial taxation

It is difficult to assess the degree to which the tax incidence changed in the early colonial period. One problem is that concepts of low taxes or high taxes do not take into account the unknown degree of corruption and extortionate *ad hoc* collections by the officials in charge of the tax system.[162] Another difficulty, a very serious one, is that estimates of tax incidence should, but usually do not, take into account that a slave system is tantamount to a confiscatory tax imposed by the owners on the slaves.[163] Even for free peasants, no one studying Northern Nigeria has ever to our knowledge attempted to quantify the tax burden of conscripted labor for wall and house building and repair, road work, and so forth, before the British, or how that burden changed under colonialism.[164] Finally, the precolonial tax system contained a built-in financial offset for the nobility. That group shared in the distribution of captured slaves following their original acquisition, in what amounted to a subsidy to be netted against the tax bill.

Despite these problems of assessment, it is certain that the amount of tax revenue rose steadily over the first two decades of colonial rule. After an initial drop in revenue resulting from the conquest, precolonial levels were regained within a few years. Thereafter rates rose rapidly, probably surpassing Caliphate levies on agriculture by 1910, at the latest. The revenue must have been considerably above precolonial levels by 1913.

Nonetheless, in the first year or two, the British realized very little revenue

Table 6.5. *Tax revenue, Northern Nigeria, 1905/1906–13*[a]

Year	Total (£)	Increase (%)
1905/1906	53,814	—
1906/1907	102,718	90.0
1907/1908	156,456	52.3
1908/1909	223,376	42.8
1909/1910	256,462	14.8
1910/1911	310,785	21.2
1911/1912	361,649	16.4
1912 (9 mo.)	252,746	—
1913	528,492	46.1

Note: [a] For 1910/1911 and 1911/1912, see *Northern Nigeria Annual Reports, 1911*, 754; for all other years, see *Northern Nigeria Annual Report, 1913*, 31–32. There are two discrepancies in the figures reported in 1913; the figures from p. 31 are preferred to those on p. 32. For the years 1905/1906–1909/1910, the figure for total revenue is calculated on the basis that government revenue was 50 percent of total revenue. Figures for Borno and Bassa Provinces have been subtracted from the totals found in these reports.

from taxation; the land tax only amounted to £21,259 for the whole of Northern Nigeria in 1903–1904.[165] In 1904, when Cargill undertook the first tax assessment in Kano at Gaya, he estimated that Kano could produce an annual tax of £12,000 for the government and £5,000 for the Emir "after payment of the district headmen and the fief-holders... without any increase in old taxes."[166] By 1913, revenue for Kano Emirate had risen to £172,054, a figure that also included the *jangali* cattle tax. In 1905–1906, the Sokoto general tax was only £4,459, but by 1908–1909, it had risen to £31,747, and by 1913, the amount had reached £100,191. While these figures also include *jangali*, most of the increase reflected the collection of land tax where none had previously existed.[167]

For those parts of Northern Nigeria that had been the Sokoto Caliphate (excluding Borno and Bassa Provinces), total tax revenue, including *jangali*, rose steadily from £102,718 in 1906/1907 to £528,492 in 1913, an increase of 414.5 percent in six years (Table 6.5). This was the period when many tax exemptions were being eliminated, and probably the increase was largely due to the greater numbers of tax payers. These figures demonstrate that there was steady pressure on slave owners to shift the tax burden to their slaves, and it shows that slaves who had previously not paid taxes to the state were gradually brought into the revenue stream.

The incidence of taxation varied greatly across Northern Nigeria, with rates rising very generally and sometimes sharply. Sixpence per adult male was a common initial figure.[168] In 1906, Lugard estimated that on average "per adult" the burden of taxation ranged from 2*d.* in Sokoto to 5*d.* in Kano, 11*d.* in Zaria, 1*s* 2*d.* in Bauchi, and 3*s* 2*d.* in Yola.[169] He based his estimate

195

The role of taxation in the reform of slavery

Table 6.6. *Incidence of taxation per adult male, 1913*

Province	Rate of taxation
Muri	2s. 5d.
Bauchi	2s. 7d.
Kano	2s. 10d.
Yola	2s. 11d.
Kontagora	3s. 3d.
Nassarawa	3s. 6d.
Sokoto	3s. 7d.
Zaria	5s. 2d.
Ilorin	5s. 6d.
Kabba	5s. 8d.
Niger	6s. 3d.

Source: Northern Nigeria Annual Report, 1913, 31.

on an average tax per farm at existing rates of 3s. 4d. By 1907 rates were as high as 3s. in some emirates, a sixfold increase.[170] By 1913, the incidence per adult male continued to vary widely (Table 6.6), from lows of 2s. 5d. in Muri, 2s. 7d. in Bauchi, 2s. 10d. in Kano, and 2s. 11d. in Yola to highs of 5s. 2d. in Zaria, 5s. 6d. in Ilorin, 5s. 8d. in Kabba, and 6s. 3d. in Niger. Kontagora, Nassarawa, and Sokoto were in the middle with incidences at 3s. 3d., 3s. 6d., and 3s. 7d. respectively.

The rate on farms in Kano city and its environs had been raised to 4s. per acre by 1914. By 1921, there were four different rates in Kano Emirate: 4s. in Kano city and within a radius of five miles; 3s. per acre for farms within a 5–10-mile radius; 2s. for those within a 10–15-mile radius; and 1s. 6d. beyond the 15-mile limit.[171]

It is illustrative to compare these figures to contemporary estimates of the cost of living. H. R. Palmer made a careful survey of living costs in Katsina Emirate in 1909. He estimated these costs at £1 2s. 9d. per person per year for food, and 12s. 6d. for clothing, or £1 15s. 3d. in all.[172] If we take 1s. per person per year as the average tax rate in 1905, then taxes amounted to 3 percent of subsistence income in the early years, although the allowance for error makes it difficult to assume that this was a low rate for those who actually paid tax at the time. By 1913, when most exemptions other than the tax on official estates had been eliminated, it is possible to make a more accurate assessment of the ratio of tax to subsistence costs. At the rates prevalent in 1913, the tax ranged from a low of 6.7 percent to a high of 17.7 percent of subsistence income. The figure for Kano can be estimated at 8 percent, Sokoto 10.1 percent, and Zaria 14.6 percent. In Katsina, according to Watts, *kurdin kasa* was higher; it "frequently amounted to 20% or more of net returns."[173]

Tax incidence was calculated on the basis of the total revenue and the estimate of population in each province. Since tax assessment and population enumeration were related, it is not particularly significant if the population estimate was low. What does matter is that the population figures would have included slaves on untaxed state farms, so that the actual incidence for the tax-paying population would have been slightly higher. Furthermore, the impact on slaves was even more significant than these relatively modest percentages indicate. Slaves now had to pay tax in addition to *murgu*, and often they paid rent and were trying to ransom themselves or loved ones. It should be noted that the aim of the single tax was an incidence of 10 percent.

A further impact of the new tax system occurred because the British eventually demanded that their share of tax be paid not in cowries and in kind, but in colonial silver coin. The authorities very early (from about 1905) applied pressure to this end, and by 1907 substantial amounts of tax were actually being collected in coin.[174] A major reason underlying the pressure was that the need to acquire coins would eventually lead farmers to produce cash crops for export.[175] Of course, from the British point of view it was also much more convenient to receive the tax revenue directly in the form of coin. The insistence on payment in coin added to the burden of tax payers, and slaves yet again would have felt the burden more than most.

A requirement to the effect that taxes be paid in sterling was instituted in Kano in late 1910.[176] It was meant to coincide with the opening of the railway, though in the event the opening did not occur until more than a year later, in 1912. Yet by the end of 1911, actually much sooner than the authorities expected, the colonial government's share of all taxes in Kano was indeed being paid in colonial silver coin.[177] Before the railway's arrival allowed export crops to be shipped, the coins came to Northern Nigeria through long-distance trade from more southerly areas and through the government payroll. For those who had only grain or cowries to pay their taxes, these items had to be exchanged for coins at village and town markets, with their rows of currency sellers.

The shift to sterling occurred under circumstances that were highly deflationary. Several factors combined to give a deflationary impetus to prices. First, the supply of sterling was tightly controlled by the colonial government, a policy that prevented inflation from the monetary side. Second, in-kind payments for *zakka* were eliminated with the inclusion of the tithe in the general tax. This caused tax payers to use currency that would otherwise have been spent on goods and services for tax payments, which thereby put additional pressure on the money supply. Third, cowries were on the way to demonetization, which took more money out of circulation. Once more, slaves were in the worst position to adjust for these deflationary influences.

The deflationary impact was about to ease, however. Now Northern Nigeria was on the brink of a commercial revolution as the new railway from Lagos approached the population centers of Zaria and Kano, and (via a spur line) the tin mines on the Jos Plateau. When these railways arrived, cash-crop production for export and tin production would boom. Cash incomes associated with the new exports were about to rise accordingly, along with employment in the mines, in the government, and in the establishments of merchants. Lugard accurately anticipated the economics of the future: how the railways would allow exports to expand, while at the same time bringing in cheaper imported goods; how the new imports along with the required tax payments would serve as an incentive for work; how the silver coin earned from the sale of cash crops and employment in the mines would fuel the tax payments and hence allow higher government expenditures, while at the same time eliminating the problem of converting grain and cowries to British money; and how as a result standards of living could rise along with the tax revenue.[178] Events transpired much as Lugard predicted, with further effects on slavery and the remaining slaves. The subject is explored in the next chapter.

Land tenure and taxation were pivotal elements in the British attempt to transform slavery while preventing a breakdown of the rural economy. Land law was rushed into the breach to keep the slaves from deserting. But the law also facilitated the emergence of new relationships between the slaves who stayed on the land, and the masters whose land would have lost value without labor to work it. Tax policy encouraged masters to emancipate slaves, who when free would be responsible for payment of their own tax whether based on output or on the per capita principle. Tax considerations also propelled the slaves into activities that generated cash revenues. Thus did Lugard and his successors enlist the invisible hand of the market in their effort to degrade the slave system while preserving the vitality of the rural economy – an effort that they could claim was ultimately a successful one.

7

The colonial economy and the slaves

Lugard and many other colonial officials fervently believed that colonialism would introduce a period of unprecedented economic expansion for the emirates of Northern Nigeria, which among its other benefits would ease the transition from slavery to freedom. Slaves would be introduced into a variety of economic relationships that would so modify the institution of slavery as to promote its "natural" termination. But the ability to increase economic performance was largely dependent on the provision of better transportation, and that only came about in the second decade of colonial rule. Until the opening of the railway to Kano, the economy performed rather poorly, and the slave population suffered accordingly. Even when economic expansion was firmly underway, moreover, slaves had considerable difficulty in meeting the financial burdens imposed by colonialism, let alone in acquiring their freedom.

As we have seen, British land policies and the legal system limited the movement of slaves unless their redemption had been paid or they had obtained the permission of their masters to work on their own account. Slaves had to meet heavy financial obligations under colonialism, including the payment of taxes to the state for the first time. In addition, they were subject to fees (*murgu*) for the right to work independently of a master, which was often necessary to earn cash for their taxes, and if they wanted their freedom they also had to acquire the money for their ransom, either from relatives, or otherwise from their own resources. If men wanted their wives freed, they needed additional resources. The ability to make these payments, which were often made in cash rather than kind, was enhanced because of the boom in the export economy that began after 1912, but it was nonetheless difficult. The capacity of slaves to earn cash incomes is the subject of this chapter.

The colonial economy developed rapidly after the opening of a railway to Kano in 1912, with a spur to the tin fields of the Jos Plateau.[1] In great anticipation, British commercial interests prepared to tap the vast markets of the emirates once the railway was completed. In particular, the Lancashire textile industry waited for a flood of cotton exports to feed its mills. It was

199

expected that the indigenous textile industry would collapse in the face of cheap imports of cloth, and that farmers would redirect their production of cotton for export to Britain. Tin production would clearly provide an additional stimulus to the colonial economy.

As has been previously demonstrated, British expectations were not exactly realized in detail, although the railway was as important as anticipated. The railway did provide a "vent for surplus" and trade expanded rapidly, but groundnuts (peanuts), not cotton, emerged as the cash crop that transformed the economy.[2] Farmers responded to the relatively high price for groundnuts, which were used in Britain as a source of vegetable oil, an ingredient in soap, and a raw material for margarine. Cotton prices, by contrast, remained too low to spur the export market, and besides, the local textile industry actually flourished in response to the prosperity of the groundnut boom. Eventually, cotton exports also rose, but cotton always lagged far behind groundnuts. Tin performed as it was supposed to. Tin exports developed nicely as the second most important commodity, with cotton taking up a distant third.

Groundnuts were an ideal crop for an economy and society experiencing the transition from slavery to freedom. Groundnuts could be grown on virtually any size plot, including the *gayauna* of slaves purchasing their freedom. They were also ideal for intercropping with millet and sorghum, although intercropping often reduced yields of grain when compared to single stands.[3] As a legume, groundnuts had the added advantage of introducing nitrogen into the soil. Under conditions of intensive labor input into agriculture, groundnuts fitted into the strategies of masters and slaves alike. Masters gained because they too could grow groundnuts, relying on the input of those slaves they still controlled but increasingly turning to paid labor, often slaves as well. Masters also rented land, and received cash payments from slaves who were working for themselves and perhaps paying off their purchase price. For slaves, groundnuts were a source of cash income that enabled them to meet their many financial obligations, but indirectly, the groundnut boom also meant that there were other opportunities to earn money.

The seasonal cycle of the savanna revolved around a rainy season, when farmers worked the land, and a long dry season, when people were underemployed and therefore migrated in search of opportunity. Slaves and other farmers engaged in a variety of strategies that took into account this seasonal dichotomy, including growing groundnuts for sale to European firms during the rainy season and seeking other sources of income during the dry season. Indeed, many people, particularly slaves, were compelled to seek work in the dry season; such migration was known as *cin rani*, literally "eating [or taking advantage of] the dry season." Slaves often had to acquire cash for their taxes, pay their *murgu* obligations, and earn their purchase price, which could only be done out of the supplementary income derived from the sale of crops and the wages obtained from dry-season employment. Migrants found employment as porters, in house, railway, and road construction, as workers in the tin mines, and as laborers in craft production. There were other dry-season occupations as well, including irrigated agriculture, the collection of firewood, and herding animals. As Swindell has demonstrated, people, including slaves, who were involved in dry-season migration often invested their wages in trade goods which were subsequently sold to supplement their non-agricultural incomes.[4] The relative importance of these various types of employment for the slave population and how these changed over the first thirty years of colonial rule are examined below in the context of the economic developments of the colonial era.

Transition from slavery to wage labor

The need to earn cash income to meet new financial obligations was felt by most slaves in the colonial period. The sums necessary to meet tax payments were significant, and the general move to taxes paid by individuals eventually included most slaves in the tax man's net, as discussed in the last chapter. The necessity of paying tax pressured many in the servile population to enter into *murgu* arrangements before they could begin to raise the even larger sums for self-redemption. These additional payments, intended to be made on a regular basis, whether monthly, annually, or on some other schedule, were perceived as a means by which slaves were to be transformed into wage earners.

From the beginning of his mandate, Lugard conceived of the problem of converting slaves into workers who were paid wages as the fundamental labor question of colonialism. He had no doubt that wage labor was "a better system" than slavery.[5] The task facing the British administration was

how free labour can best be provided in a country in which industry has hitherto been largely conducted by slave labour, and where most of the necessities and many of the incentives to work for wages which exist in civilised countries are lacking.[6]

He viewed the transition from bondage to wage labor as requiring the utilization of existing mechanisms for self-redemption and ransom by third parties, modified so that slaves would have to earn money on an expanding labor market and thereby at the same time acquire the discipline of a modern wage labor force. In order to achieve this, in Lugard's vision, slaves would have to earn their freedom by selling their labor on the open market, using the cash so acquired to compensate their masters. Given the rural nature of the economy, the largest market for labor was expected to be provided by these masters acting in the role of employers. The experience of working for wages, Lugard argued, would assist in bringing the slaves into the cash economy, and the opportunity to earn cash by providing an incentive for them to work would boost the productivity of the economy as well.[7]

While Lugard understood that a transition from slavery to wage labor could only come about gradually, he made it clear that his slavery policies were intended directly to further just such a transition. For example, in his Vernacular Proclamation posted at Kano, Sokoto, and Katsina in 1903, he warned slaves that if they left their masters they had to be "willing to work for wages," as we have already observed.[8] He expected that there would be a transitional period in which it would be necessary "to educate both the upper and the servile classes to the idea of a free-labour contract between master and servant."[9] As Abadie predicted in 1902, slavery "[would] die out and paid labour take the place of slave labour," but only "by degrees."[10] Gowers did not doubt that wage labor should be substituted for slavery, but he did worry about the ease of the transition. Writing from Yola in 1905: "It will, I fear, take a long time to educate the Fulani to the employment of paid labour, and indeed the problem of the payment of labour by men whose chief wealth is in slaves is not easy of solution."[11] In 1905, Barclay believed that "the process of evolution . . . is proving a trying and costly experience for the Fulani," but he also supposed that "the advantages of free labor will in time be forced upon the recognition of the Fulanis."[12]

Lugard was optimistic, nonetheless. As he wrote in 1906, "the Mohamme-dan Chiefs . . . are already familiar with the idea of a contract, and merchants already engage free labour by contract for the transport of their goods." He believed that government had an important role to play in employing slaves for wages under "a free contract system." Indeed, government officials and other Europeans engaged "free domestic servants" for wages. The combined impact was that wage employment had become familiar "to many thousands of the labouring class throughout the country." Lugard predicted that the "substitution . . . of this system for domestic slavery should not be a difficult one."[13] He expected that the chief problem would arise from the problem of providing

> the employers of labour with sufficient cash to pay their employés a weekly or monthly wage; for, if payment be in kind only, the servant [sic] is unable to save his wages to purchase when and what he likes, and is dependent on instalments as they become available at arbitrary valuations. In fact, the conditions approximate to the slavery system. Here again, I see reasons for thinking that the difficulty is one which is rapidly decreasing. The existing cowrie currency and the rapid spread of coinage, the fixing of rents and taxes payable in currency, and the increase in wealth due to development and progress under British rule, will, I trust, enable the master to meet his obligations to his servants in the same way that he sees the British Officials doing.[14]

In 1906, therefore, Lugard had a vision of the transition to wage labor that depended only upon economic development and the spread of silver coin.

Lugard's ideas for the conversion of slavery to wage labor were sensible ones, no doubt, but by and large they underestimated the advantages to the slaves of the cash-crop expansion that was to come and oversimplified the process of change. Most slaves found it more advantageous to join in the production of cash crops for their own benefit than to seek work for wages in the wet season. While many could indeed be forced or attracted onto the labor market in the dry season, only a few became full-time wage laborers (those without access to land, or whose alternatives were better in wage labor than in farming). The slaves did learn about wage labor, and for them the motive to learn was often more intense because of their increased need for cash. Sometimes unusual conditions arose that placed slaves in a position in which working for payment was even more necessary. The famine of 1905 was one such incentive, as Barclay reported from Yola. Famine conditions forced slaves "to go and work on Fulani farms for which they receive food and shelter as payment."[15] But slaves did not necessarily work for wages, as this case makes clear.

As we shall explore, for the large part of the slave population that continued to farm in the wet season, entry to the labor market could only be part-time, taking place in the dry season. Thus what actually occurred, as distinct from what had been predicted by Lugard, was that slaves became small farmers, often involved in sharecrop tenancy arrangements with their old masters, rather than a fully developed wage labor force. Their entry into labor markets was basically seasonal, a search for supplements to their income through dry-season migration that might involve trading, working for wages, or indeed any other activity that would raise earnings. Besides paying their *murgu* fees, many of these slaves were also making instalments for their self-redemption.

Economic pressures on the slave population: *murgu*

The new financial obligations put a severe strain on the ability of slaves to become free peasants in the colonial economy. Now that male slaves had to pay taxes for the first time, they had to raise outside income, whether by growing crops for sale on *gayauna* farms or by working on their own account, away from their masters. If they chose the latter course, they had to pay their masters *murgu*, that is, the fee for the right to work alone. When slaves were involved in *murgu* arrangements, they were expected to provide their own subsistence, which was yet a further burden. In this section, we attempt an assessment of the costs of this financial obligation. In the next section, we examine the additional cost of self-redemption.

It should be understood that payment of *murgu* did not mean that a slave would become free. *Murgu* only allowed a slave to work on his own account, during which time he had to fend for himself, whether or not he attempted to earn the cash for his self-redemption payments. In many cases, no price for emancipation *was* ever set; *murgu* was expected by both master and slave simply to continue. There is very little information on female slaves who were paying *murgu*; hence our discussion focuses on men, unless otherwise noted. Gender differences in *murgu* arrangements deserve closer attention.

Numerous authors, including colonial officials and later historians, have frequently compounded *murgu* with self-redemption, considering them as one. The confusion is understandable because a slave attempting to earn cash for redemption by any means had to buy the right to do so; the self-redemption payments and the *murgu* payments would presumably often have been combined and even a knowledgeable observer could easily make the error of believing them to be the same thing.[16] Nonetheless, the distinction between ransom and *murgu* lasted well into the colonial period. When Arnett enquired into the continuation of *murgu* in Sokoto in 1916, he learned from the Sultan and the chief *alkali* that

> Murgu is an arrangement made by mutual agreement between slave and master by which the slave makes a regular money payment in lieu of working for his master.[17]

It was made clear to him that *murgu* was a common mechanism in controlling rural labor. Two years later, he observed further that "the payments of 'murgu' do not affect redemption. They are small payments of cash in lieu of service and continue indefinitely."[18]

The annual *murgu* payment was often 5s.,[19] but the amount varied. Often, however, it was more than was required for tax. In 1906, *murgu* payments in Bauchi ranged from 4d. to 2d. per week, or 5s. per year.[20] At Kudan, in Zaria Emirate, people remember the level of *murgu* at 100 cowries every two weeks or 200 cowries every month, or 2,400 cowries per year, which also suggests a level of a few shillings per year.[21] As early as 1904, Webster reported that

> The masters [in Keffi] complain that they have no power over them [slaves] at all, if a slave is told to do any work that is at all distasteful he refuses and threatens to go away and leave his master, and the latter is so afraid of losing his services altogether that he gives in and hires someone to do the work, and even then frequently has to give his slave a present to pacify him. In short labour has got the whip hand of capital, demands more pay for less work, and is daily becoming harder to get ... Many are craftsmen, and in this case they pay a fixed sum per week from 6d.–1/–., to their master, and all profit over this is their own, and they are liable for no other work. The master also houses them, feeds them, and finds all tools. If a household slave marries and his wife does no work about the house, she also is expected to pay a small weekly sum to the house owner; if she does any work, however slight, she pays nothing.[22]

Webster's report suggests a very high level of payment and probably includes the price of redemption as well. Nonetheless, Webster identified a key change in the relationships of dependence that were emerging out of slavery. Slaves could now insist on the right to work on their own account.

In 1915, H. F. Backwell reported that *murgu* payments had once differed for males and females in Argungu, but the rate had become uniform. After discussing the subject of *murgu* with the *alkali*, he reported that the Islamic court records showed that *murgu* had been 10,000 cowries for a man and 5,000 cowries for a woman, but in 1913 or so, Brackenbury ordered the *alkali* to fix the rate at 10,000 cowries or 5s. for both males and females.[23] He noted that even "quite young slaves are in the habit of paying murgu." This revelation indicates that masters required slaves to pay *murgu*, even though they must have been very young at the time of the conquest. Obligations were being imposed to the bitter end, as far as those who were born just before 1901 were concerned.

In 1918 in Yola, slaves who were still on their masters' lands, and at the time the number was at least 20,000, paid "Murgu averaging in this province about 5 baskets per woman and 10 per man worth in Yola a shilling each and about 4d. to 6d. in the districts," that is, 5s. for women and 10s. for men at Yola prices.[24] In this case masters paid the tax for their male slaves, which explains why the fee was higher for men.

Masters accepted these payments in lieu of service, but their attitude was that *murgu* was "merely an encouragement of laziness among slaves, who are too lazy to work for their masters, or to earn enough to ransom themselves."[25] In 1915, three slaves complained to L. Blake in Gwandu that their masters demanded 10s. apiece in *murgu*, and consequently, they were having trouble paying their taxes. Blake agreed that the amount was too high and negotiated a reduction (to 5s. 5d., so it appears).[26] At Argungu, the amount of *murgu* had fallen to 2s. 6d. per year by the 1930s.[27] By 1936, the *murgu* payments were 12s. 6d. for males and 6s. for females in Gombe Emirate.[28]

Jumare has argued that *murgu* arrangements extended the longevity of slavery because of financial advantages to the masters:

> this long period of [*murgu*] payment would only increase the period of ... bondage to the master, and to the society, whereas ransom (*fansa*) was significant in closing the marginality of slaves because it was done once-and-for-all and the slave became free for ever. In the *murgu* system, even an enterprising skilled slave could be kept for a longer period in view of the benefits which his master reaped from the process.[29]

As Jumare notes, the introduction of taxation in Sokoto compelled many masters "to enter into *murgu* arrangement[s] with their slaves so that both could pay their taxes, since if slaves were not allowed to pursue some trade or craft, it would be their master who would bear the burden of their taxes."[30] It could be more accurate to say that the relationship of servility underwent a commutation. The form of the obligations of the slaves had altered.

While not actually opposing the continuation of *murgu*, some colonial officials were critical of the prevalence of this practice. Arnett believed (rightly) that *murgu* was less beneficial to a slave than was self-redemption, and favored a policy that discouraged the continuation of the *murgu* system:

> I would like to suggest that while not prohibiting the native custom of Murgu, which in certain cases is a very equitable and convenient arrangement for both slaves and masters, it is open to the Administration whenever the arrangements between masters and slaves come before a Political Officer or a Native Court to encourage ransom rather than Murgu.[31]

Backwell believed that "murgu on old slaves, who are past work is liable to be a burden and that in any case their masters would not be able to get any work from them." In 1915, he tried to convince the *alkali* of Argungu that such a burden should be eliminated.[32]

Despite these reservations, the colonial regime accepted the fact that *murgu* was a form of compensation to slave owners that eased *their* transition to a world beyond slavery. Consequently, the incidence of *murgu*, often unattached to self-purchase, increased under colonialism, although estimates of the number of slaves paying *murgu* are rare. Brackenbury reported from Argungu in 1913 that

> freedom by purchase (fansa) is common and the incomplete form of freedom for a small payment (murgu) is still more so ... Many slaves try to continue this system of [paying *murgu* at] 5/– per year indefinitely without attempting "fansa" [and] the owners naturally strongly object.[33]

The *alkali* of Argungu confirmed this impression in 1915. He claimed that "in former times no able bodied man or woman was allowed to adopt this method of escaping work for their masters. It was only allowed in the case of men and women who were past work," that is, capable of undertaking the heavy work that characterized slavery.[34] The question arises whether or not it was more advantageous for slaves to pay *murgu* without attempting self-purchase. While some slaves may have calculated the relative advantages of different strategies, many slaves simply could not afford to make both payments.

The most detailed account of *murgu* comes from Yola in 1922. C. O. Migeod asked the Yola Native Authority to report on the extent to which *murgu* was practiced. He was provided with a return showing that "a remarkable number of slaves – over 10% of the population of the Emirate" were paying *murgu*. At the time, the population of Yola Emirate was estimated at slightly over 195,000.[35] If 20,000 or so adults were paying *murgu*, then a very sizeable proportion of the Yola population was still slave, since the age at which children had been born free now stood at twenty-one.

It would be rash to suggest that the figure of "over 10%" paying *murgu* was typical of the rest of Northern Nigeria. Such knowledge is simply not available. For the sake of argument, however, if the figure of 10 percent is used as a benchmark for 1922, then several hundred thousand slaves may have been paying *murgu* in Northern Nigeria at that late date. Of course, the eligible slave population which could have been paying *murgu* was steadily decreasing to the extent that children born after 1901 were free. Furthermore, the number of slaves who redeemed themselves affects any assessment of the impact. And some slaves died without successfully purchasing their freedom. The estimate for Yola indicates that *murgu* continued to be an ongoing source of income for many slave owners as late as 1922 nonetheless.

Ransom (*fansa*) payments

In addition to their *murgu* fees, ransom payments had to be made by slaves who were attempting to purchase their freedom. Not uncommonly, the annual ransom payments were made over ten to twenty years and amounted to 5–10 percent of the total ransom. Usually the annual ransom payments were somewhat in excess of the annual *murgu* fees. As Gowers reported from Kano in 1912,

> It is the universal practice by Native Courts to allow ransom as a matter of course, and a slave who wishes to ransom himself is always given reasonable facilities to earn the money.[36]

Sometimes the first self-redemption payment was higher than the subsequent ones, which made it difficult for slaves to start paying the ransom price. As Resident Arnett put it, "redemption money is frequently paid in installments but the initial payment at any rate is generally a substantial one as evidence of the payer's bona fides."[37]

Redemption prices seem to have declined gradually in the first two decades of the colonial period. To some extent this should be expected, since the slave population involved in self-ransom was aging. Initially, ransoms were paid in cowries, and prices were often quoted in cowries well into the second decade of colonial rule. In 1905–1906, average prices were 275,000 cowries, with no significant difference between males and females.[38] Prices appear to have stabilized at the price of a prime female slave in c. 1900. The most common redemption price was 300,000 cowries, again irrespective of gender. The average was lower because a significant number of cases involved children, which more than offset the fact that some high-priced females and other exceptions could command prices in excess of 300,000 cowries.[39] Sometimes early prices are quoted in terms of sterling, in the range of £5–10, but the prevalent exchange rate between sterling and cowries suggests a sterling amount that is higher. At the time, 1,200 cowries was equal to a shilling, so that 300,000 cowries, or fifteen bags of 20,000 cowries, was worth £12 10s. The average price (275,000 cowries) was worth £11 9s.

By 1907, the Zaria courts were fixing the price of manumission for both men and women at thirteen bags of cowries valued at £8 2s. 6d.,[40] while in Sokoto, slaves could "buy their freedom if they like for £5" by 1909.[41] Soldiers recruited into the WAFF who were discovered to be fugitive slaves had to buy their redemption for £5.[42] In 1913, the amount of *fansa* at Argungu was £5 5s.,[43] which had become the standard price throughout Sokoto Province by 1916[44] and continued to be the "flat rate for men and women" for the next twenty years.[45]

As the price of cowries declined, the advantage of self-purchase shifted from masters to slaves, although this deflationary trend was somewhat countered by rising taxes and the natural tendency for prices to decline as the population became older. By 1910, a bag of cowries was worth 10s., so that redemption prices of £5 were equivalent to 200,000 cowries; £7 was equivalent to 280,000 cowries. The amount needed for ransom after 1915 (£5 5s.) would have commanded a mere 126,000 cowries at the early colonial rates. By 1918, *fansa* was even fixed at a rate just above £3 in rural Kano. According to Brooke, who investigated procedures in the Wudil court in

Kano Emirate, "the amount fixed is well known throughout the district, a slave coming from the extreme south of the district to ransom himself before the Court, on the day on which I visited it, produced £3:1:6 before stating that he wished to ransom himself."[46] In Gombe, *fansa* had fallen by £1 10*s.* to £3 by 1936,[47] while in Yola ransoms ranged from £3 for aging females and £5 for males and young females at the same time.[48] Those masters who realized a return on their slaves early in the colonial period did not necessarily benefit relatively, because the longer it took for slaves to earn their redemption, the more they paid in *murgu* fees. Without better data, it is difficult to say if there was an incentive for masters to keep slaves in *murgu* or encourage them to purchase their freedom quickly.

There was an added cost to slaves who redeemed themselves through the courts in the form of court fees, which ranged from 1*s.* to 10*s.* These fees were understood to be the legitimate tenth of the costs that courts could charge under Islamic law, but the actual amount of such fees varied among the courts. Usually slaves paid all or a significant portion of the fee. In Katsina, slaves paid 1*s.* to the court scribe who wrote out the certificate of freedom, while in Sokoto the rate varied from 2*s.* to 3*s.* 6*d.*, paid by the slave. The amount that slaves paid in Ilorin ranged between 5*s.* and 14*s.*, while the fee of 6*s.* in Zaria was shared equally by slave and master.[49] In Gwandu 10*s.* 6*d.* was deducted from the amount of the ransom itself, but was not considered a fee for the certificate of freedom.[50]

The length of time it took slaves to pay off their redemption price, given that they also had to pay taxes, *murgu*, and court fees for the certificates of freedom, was seldom less than ten years, and often more. It is clear, moreover, that many slaves who attempted to purchase their freedom never succeeded in doing so. In 1906, the Nassarawa court included *murgu* "for food and lodging" in the amount that a slave who was redeeming himself was expected to pay each week at 4½*d.*, or the equivalent of 19*s.* 6*d.* per year on a ransom price of £7.[51] At this rate, it would have taken the slave seven years to secure his or her freedom. Alisu and Hawa, who were freed in the Bauchi court in May 1906 for sixteen bags of cowries, were allowed to make instalments that amounted to an initial six bags of cowries (120,000 cowries) down, with ten bags to be paid over two years.[52] Informants in Zaria remember that payments were £2 per year until the slave paid off the price,[53] while in Gwandu, the term of payment lasted from two to ten years.[54]

Lugard's stated view on how much time an individual would need to achieve self-redemption appears over-optimistic in the extreme. He stated in 1918, in a passage that distinguishes accurately between *murgu* and self-redemption, that:

> If the slave remains with his master, he must have a fair opportunity of earning the money required for self-redemption within a reasonable time (not more than a year), by working in his own time for wages. This was recognised by the system of *Murgu* under which a slave either paid a certain fee as earnest of his intentions, and was then free for a year (retaining his house and land) to work

off his ransom money, or he paid for his board and lodging and could pay off the ransom by installments in his own time ... That the masters are willing to maintain their slaves, and discharge all their obligations to him [*sic*], while he is earning the money for his ransom, is a proof of the liberal treatment accorded to slaves by their masters in Nigeria. This system of redemption is equitable to the master, since it enables him to realise a part at least of the money, which in all probability he or his father actually paid for the slave under the regime which formerly existed, when property in slaves was as real as any other kind of property, and the investment was sanctioned alike by the law and religion of the country. On the part of the slave ... it is in many cases a reasonable return for benefits received, and the payment tends to make him value what he has won by his own efforts, and to realise his freedom. Self-redemption and ransom are of course only applicable to slaves born or long held in servitude, and not to newly captured slaves or to others held illegally.[55]

Much of this quotation reads intelligently, but the idea that slaves could earn their freedom in a "reasonable time" of a year or less was, if not impossible, undoubtedly a rarity. It is quite true that if a slave could earn 6*d.* per day for a year of 365 days, that would yield him £9 2*s.* 6*d.*, enough to pay a £5–6 ransom and leave enough left over for subsistence during the year. But jobs paying this sum were usually part-time, and even the slave able to earn this amount would be devoting well over half his cash income to the redemption payment. Lugard seems to have been saying that it was at least possible. Possible or not, self-redemption could easily take as long as a decade or more, given the sums involved and the limited potential for earning income.

The exaggeration involved in Lugard's view can be seen with simple arithmetic. To make annual self-redemption payments totaling £6 over ten years, a slave would have to earn an extra 12*s.* per year – a considerable sum when the annual income of poor people could be only £3 or £4 – in addition to the customary 5*s.* for *murgu* and the 5–10*s.* or so for tax payment before any other expense was met (see below). With good fortune, no doubt self-redemption could be accomplished rapidly. But for the average slave, it was reasonable to expect freedom no sooner than ten years or more after payments began. Slaves under these circumstances would have had to work just as hard as slaves always had.

The average age of male slaves who were listed as redeeming themselves in 1916–17 confirms this impression of lengthy indebtedness. In a sample of 161 male slaves from 1916–17, 30.4 percent were age 26–30, 19.3 percent were 31–35, 31.7 percent were 36–40, and 11.2 percent were 41–45 (Table 7.1). That is, 92.6 percent of those who redeemed themselves were 26 or older. While it was possible for males to earn enough to redeem themselves before they were age 30, it was often the case that it took longer.

In many circumstances, ransom and self-redemption were registered with the courts. Jumare's description of the process in Sokoto serves to illustrate the basic process:

In Sokoto City, cases of ransom and manumission were supported by letters signed by the parties concerned in the presence of witnesses and endorsed by an

209

The colonial economy and the slaves

Table 7.1. *Ages of slaves who redeemed themselves, 1916–17*

Age	Male	% Male	Female	% Female	Total	%
16–20	—	—	11	6	11	3
21–25	5	3	31	16	36	10
26–30	49	30	74	39	123	35
31–35	31	19	23	12	54	15
36–40	51	32	34	18	85	24
41–45	18	11	3	2	21	6
46–50	6	4	9	5	15	4
50+	1	1	4	2	5	1
Total	161	100	189	100	350	100

Notes: Male: 46 percent.
Female: 54 percent.
Source: SNP 10/5 435p/1917.

Alkali. It would also be recorded in the court's register and a letter of freedom called *ataqa* or *laya* would be issued to the freed slave. He would be keeping that letter to avoid any attempt to claim him back or his children by his ex-master or his family. Thus the impact of his freedom would be more meaningful to his children as his own average lifespan might be closing by the time he achieved his freedom.[56]

Unfortunately, this registration was frequently not undertaken, because of the fee charged by the courts for the service, because either masters or slaves did not want to get involved with the courts, or because local officials confiscated the fees without notifying the courts.

The records of the Islamic and Provincial courts indicate that approximately 70,000 slaves received certificates of freedom through 1919; while 103,000 did so through 1929 (Table A.2, Appendix). About 36,000 of these were males (Table D.1). Rather scanty data based on returns from 1916 indicate that the proportion of males redeeming themselves (rather than being redeemed by relatives or friends) must have been at least 32 percent of this number (about 11,500), could easily have been 60 percent (21,600), and may have been as high as 78 percent (28,000) (Table D.6). It must be reemphasized that the number of slaves pursuing self-redemption was greater, and probably much greater, than these figures indicate.

The proportions of court cases that involved self-redemption increased steadily during the period of court-monitored redemptions. Self-redemption involved 33.9 percent of the males and 8.3 percent of the females in the 1905–1906 sample of slaves (18.2 percent of the total number of cases), although the category did not exist in the *Northern Nigeria Annual Report* for 1905–1906 (Table D.1). It appears that self-redemptions and cases in which slaves "following their own inclinations" were combined in the *Annual Report*. Those freed on their own devices between 1901 and 1905 were 26.6

210

percent of the freed slaves; the percentage rose to 50.6 percent in 1906, or 30.8 percent for 1901–1906 as a whole (Table A.3). The more detailed sample of court records from 1905–1906 reveals a much lower figure – 12.3 percent (11.2 percent male, 13.1 percent female) (Table D.1).

By 1908, when 1,392 slaves were issued certificates in the courts, the majority of cases involved slaves purchasing their own freedom through the Islamic courts.[57] By 1916, self-redemption accounted for 25.2 percent of all cases; 32.6 percent of males and 21.6 percent of females (Table D.6). The females who were listed as redeeming themselves may well have had their ransoms paid by third-party males (see below, Chapter 8). However, the males almost certainly paid their own ransoms, and when the number of males who were freed to "follow their own inclinations" is taken into consideration, it appears that the incidence of self-ransom had been increasing; at least 65.6 percent of males were so classified.

The slaves who were identified as being freed by their masters/mistresses or freed simply to follow their own inclinations probably redeemed themselves or had been under *murgu* arrangements of long duration. In these cases, masters had already realized a significant return on their investment in their slaves and probably granted them their freedom on the understanding that the relationship had evolved into one of clientship. In 1905–1906, only 2.6 percent of slaves were identified as being freed by masters, and only 12.3 percent were "freed to follow their own inclinations" (Table D.1). By 1916, slaves who were "freed to follow their own inclinations" accounted for at least 21.8 percent (33.0 percent of the males and 16.4 percent of the females; Table D.6). Acts of generosity by masters, death-bed grants of emancipation, and similar pious acts usually affected slaves who had more than paid their way. Besides the financial benefits these slaves provided to their masters, the method of liberation as an Islamic expression of piety also indicates that slaves paid their masters considerable deference and respect.

Rental of farm land

Self-redemption and *murgu* payments usually involved slaves who wished to break their ties with their old masters. However, many farmers rented land, and in the case of slaves and former slaves, they turned to their masters-cum-patrons for access to land. According to Swindell, "many former slaves stayed on as clients or 'tenant' farmers to their former owners; no longer working for them but paying a tenth of their produce as rents."[58] Already in 1909, farms were being leased in the area between Kano and Zaria. J. W. Gill, writing of Faki, on the border between Kano and Zaria, stated that:

> some owners of large farms are said to have let a portion of their farms to others for a yearly fee – a portion of the crops and some money.[59]

Clear proof that slaves and ex-slaves were actually renting such land in 1909 is lacking, but as Gowers observed in 1913, very many household and farm "slaves" ... prefer to remain with their old masters and among their old associates rather than to enter the ranks of casual labour or to set up as independent agriculturalists or traders.[60]

Slaves staying on their masters' land might not be required to embark on redemption payments, or *murgu* either, but in many cases obligations still existed. The slaves farming the land of the masters were widely called upon to pay rent in kind (or sometimes partly in cash).

In Dan Buram District in Kano Emirate, poor farmers who probably numbered slaves among their ranks were already renting land by 1912. According to Foulkes, who assessed the district, these tenant farmers,

> instead of migrating or opening up fresh land, can sometimes get a vacant farm, but when they cannot they rent (awon gona) [*aron gona*] a plot from the larger owners making a small present of 500 c to 2000 c. This is the usual present when approaching another man for a favour; it is not in any sense a rent. They take all the produce and pay the zakka on it to the owner the first year, and to the dagache in succeeding years. The owner pays the whole of the k. kassa [*kurdin kasa*].[61]

As is clear from this report, it was possible for slaves who were paying *murgu* to obtain the land that they needed to farm. They were expected to pay rent; even though Foulkes insisted that *aron gona* was something else.

Land arrangements between masters and former slaves often evolved into sharecropping tenancy, although when sharecropping became common is not certain. Sciortino, writing from Nassarawa in 1914, stated that

> There are a large number of grown-up "slaves" who are perfectly content with their state ... in fact to all intents and purposes they are in full possession of their liberty, but have to assist with farming operations and to supply a certain amount of foodstuffs etc. per annum.[62]

The appearance of sharecropping rent was apparently rapid on the farms where fields once worked by groups of slaves now came to be worked by individual slave families.

Later reports confirm that sharecropping was an important outgrowth of slavery. Rowlings' study of Rano District south of Kano demonstrates that former slaves were paying a portion of their crops to their former masters in the late 1930s and early 1940s.[63] C. K. Meek reported the same pattern:

> On many of the estates the ex-slaves remained as tenants on a métayage [sharecropping] basis, paying to the chief or other landlord a portion of their crops.[64]

In many cases, excepting the individuals who took to their heels or made other arrangements, entire villages of slaves simply stayed in place. Rental payment in kind "bought" them permission from their master, now a landlord absentee or otherwise, to remain on the land. The rent took the place of the labor that had once been required on the *gandu* of the master.

Sharecrop land rentals (Hausa: *galla*) can easily be distinguished from *murgu* and self-redemption payments because the rentals were commonly paid in kind rather than in cash.[65] It should be noted that the payment of rent as a share of the harvest to the master did not provide an incentive for slaves to take paid work or engage in cash cropping as was true of taxes, redemption payments, and *murgu*. All of these were basically fixed sums that had to be paid in cash. With sharecrop rentals, former slaves were required to part with a portion of what they had grown, and did not need to choose the highest-paying alternatives. Of course, other incentives to earn higher incomes existed for the slaves in any case, if only to pay taxes and buy consumer goods. Furthermore, as the prospects for cash-crop agriculture improved, there must have been thousands of cases of masters advising, persuading, or possibly forcing slaves to plant lucrative cash crops if they were not otherwise inclined to do so. Yet it remains true that the system of sharecrop rentals that evolved provided less incentive to slaves to increase their cash earnings than did the other forms of payment discussed above. For these slaves, taxes and the desire to increase the quantity and quality of their consumption were the chief motives for earning more.

The cost of living

Before examining in detail the sources of cash income, it is necessary to establish some estimate of the average cost of living in contemporary Northern Nigeria. Only after slaves had provided subsistence for themselves and their families would their additional earnings be available for financing their tax payments, *murgu*, and self-redemption. Our necessarily cursory examination of the economy in the first three decades of colonial rule indicates that food prices remained relatively stable. There were important seasonal fluctuations, and food prices rose sharply during times of famine, but the long-term trend was relatively flat.[66] Two other features of the colonial economy reinforced this deflationary situation. First, the money supply was carefully controlled, and the removal of cowries from circulation further restricted the quantity of money.[67] Second, as we will see, wages remained relatively stable, varying from 3*d.* to 9*d.* per day, depending upon task and whether or not food was provided.

Most authorities in the early colonial period were in general agreement that sufficient food for subsistence could be purchased for 1*d.* or less per day, that is, about £1 10*s.* per year. According to Grier, writing from Kachia in 1906:

> A native can live on rather less than 1d. [per day]. In some parts of the country, food is much cheaper & a native lives on 100 cowries a day – 400 cowries = 3d.[68]

In Kano in 1909, according to Temple, "a working man and his wife feed themselves well on 200K p.d.," or about £1 3*s.* per adult per year.[69] Palmer's assessment of the cost of living at Shinkafi village in Katsina Emirate in 1909

Table 7.2. *Annual subsistence cost for a family of five, Katsina Emirate, 1909, £.s.d.*

Comfortably off	Food	10.13.0
	Clothing	2.12.0
	Sundries	0.6.6
	Total	**13.11.6**
Moderately off	Food	9.2.0
	Clothing	2.10.0
	Sundries	0.5.6
	Total	**11.17.6**
Sufficiency	Food	7.12.0
	Clothing	2.10.0
	Sundries	0.5.0
	Total	**10.7.6**

Source: Palmer, *Report for 1909, Katsina Division of Kano Province,* Katprof 1/1836; cited in Garba (unpublished, 1986), 372.

confirmed these levels. A family of five at the level of "sufficiency" could eat for £7 12s. per year; total subsistence costs were £10 7s. 6d. (Table 7.2). A family which was "comfortably off" spent £10 13s. on food, with total subsistence costs estimated at £13 11s. 6d.[70] In 1913, it was estimated that the subsistence costs of a family of three in Raba district in Sokoto Province were £2 14s. 1d.[71] This estimate probably referred to food purchases alone.

Palmer's data suggest that a daily ration of food could be obtained for about 1d. per person, while clothing and sundries could be obtained for less than $\frac{4}{10}d$. per day. Housing costs are not apparently included, but the mud brick and grass used universally for building materials could be made at home out of materials almost freely available, and the basic cost unlikely exceeded an amortized value of £1 per year, or 3d. per day. These data make it apparent that subsistence costs must have averaged less than 2d. per person per day, and they were perhaps considerably less than that.[72] If we take the average rate of tax on adults to be 10s. 7d., the figure cited by Swindell for 1906, then taxes added another $\frac{4}{10}d$. per person per day.[73] In Raba District, taxes ranged from 3s. to 6s. per adult male, or about 5–10 percent of the amount spent by a family of three on food.[74]

For the many slaves whose primary occupation was farming, it is unlikely that growing food crops offered any appreciable number a practicable way to pay for self-redemption before the First World War, and even with the groundnut boom it was difficult thereafter. In the early colonial years, as Watts has observed, most farmers, and particularly the poorer ones, including slaves, almost always had to buy grain to feed themselves.[75] Grier noted in 1910 that in poor areas such as Kachia, a "good farmer can not grow more

214

than £5 worth of foodstuffs in a season."[76] Assuming subsistence costs for adults were approximately £1 per year and half that for children, two adults and two children would have had little if anything left after subtracting the income needed for subsistence to pay tax, *murgu*, or rent in kind as applicable. Admittedly the calculations are rough and ready, but they would have to be gravely erroneous to counter the case that farmers after providing for subsistence had little left over to finance self-emancipation. For these farmers, even a relatively lucrative cash crop, if one should present itself, would not necessarily mean that they could make ends meet.

For those slaves able to acquire jobs that paid the government's going rate of 6*d.* per day, the situation was only marginally better. For them, cash income would total nearly £4, if 150 days were worked, but labor contractors usually took a portion of this income, so that the net return was perhaps only £3. Even if they could grow most of their own food during the rainy season, there was only a small margin over subsistence costs that would be devoted to *murgu*, let alone self-redemption payments. The difficulty for slaves meeting all their obligations should not be underestimated. Slaves attempting to free themselves were heavily in debt to their masters, and it was difficult to avoid some kind of ongoing dependency that had financial as well as social implications.

The expansion of the colonial economy

The expansion of the colonial economy followed a decade of hesitant development that was marked by famines, the flight of slaves, and rural unrest over taxes. Even when the railway was ready for use and the boom seemed well underway in 1912, the terrible drought of 1913–14 interrupted economic expansion. Then the First World War retarded development further. Despite these setbacks, the trend over the first three decades of colonial rule was clear. The economy expanded at an accelerating rate under conditions of virtually no inflation. We identify three periods in these developments. The first period lasted from 1900 to 1908 and was marked by military conquest, the consolidation of colonial rule, and intermittent famine conditions. The second period lasted from 1909 to 1916, when the railway was built but the economy was shaken by the drought of 1913–14 and the First World War. The third period, from 1917 to 1930, witnessed the full realization of the export trade; as already noted, groundnuts were most important, followed by tin and cotton. The growth in exports was interrupted only once, during the drought conditions of 1926.

As Swindell has emphasized, "dry season labour migration assumed a heightened significance with the decline of slavery."[77] Early in the colonial period, slaves felt the pressure of the tax and currency policies, the need to provision themselves in the dry season, and their obligations to their masters. According to Swindell, these *cin rani* movements were of "casual"

215

unskilled workers, reflecting the imperfect specialization of labor and the low level of economic development. As he describes it,

> there was a rapid increase in the volume of migration to meet new levels of taxation, and demands for labour in the towns and commercial-crop zones. Notwithstanding these important changes, there was another dimension to the development of labour migration, in that a large sector of the population was able to enter the wage-labour market because of the decay of domestic slavery. Hitherto, slave labour was largely immobilized, but this situation was radically changed by moves towards abolition, a process which sapped the foundations of the pre-colonial economy, in which control and access to labour were vital. The adjustments to abolition were patchy and spread over several decades, but they included the reorganization of agricultural labour and land at the local and regional levels as well as a great increase in personal mobility.[78]

Although it has previously been recognized that *cin rani* migration was common in the 1930s, and has continued to be ever since, Swindell demonstrates that this pattern of labor movement began within a few years of the colonial conquest and helps to explain how slaves were able to meet the severe financial obligations imposed upon them. Without the cash from dry-season employment, slaves could not have fed themselves, let alone paid their taxes or achieved emancipation.[79] And there were other expenses as well, particularly those associated with marriage, naming ceremonies, and funerals.[80] Masters still extracted surplus from slaves. In the absence of dry-season employment, presumably, that surplus would have been lower.

Economic dislocation, 1900–1908

The colonial economy in its earliest period up to about 1908 was marked by government consolidation, the provision of law and order, regularization of taxes, and economic adjustment. But it was also a time of economic dislocation. Many slaves fled, and the time-honored mechanism of grain storage on the estates broke down as exactions for military campaigns and the loss of slave labor took their toll. As a result of the economic shock arising from the conquest and the flight of slaves, famine conditions prevailed for a year or two at different times in various parts of Northern Nigeria during this period. The economic situation improved after 1908, with no famines reported for five more years, but economic growth was still very slow.

The economic dislocation from 1900 to 1908 was significant, particularly as reflected in the famines from 1902 to 1908. Inadequate rainfall in some areas cut food supplies to some extent, thereby exacerbating the problem, but the shortages were local ones. There were stores of grain from previous years, but grain was not moved in sufficient quantities from areas of surplus to areas in need, as it had been before the conquest. Among the areas that were affected were Kontagora and Nupe in 1902; Yola, Bauchi, Muri, Katagum, and Nupe in 1903; and the Gongola River basin in 1905–1906. Katsina was short of grain in 1905, and Kano had bad harvests in 1906. Again it is important to recognize that these famines were localized, unlike

216

the severe drought and famine of 1913–14 that affected all parts of Northern Nigeria, and indeed much of West Africa (see below).[81]

Watts has argued that these famines were a product of capitalist penetration, the cluster in 1902–1908 being the first of this kind.[82] That argument needs to be refined and qualified. The famines of 1902–1908 were related to the process of social and economic change introduced by the colonial conquest, a process that interfered with distribution and left some people with insufficient income to purchase food when they needed to because of deficiencies in their subsistence production. As A. K. Sen has argued, "entitlements" to food are usually more important than the total amount of food produced.[83] Insufficient food in itself was as far as we can determine not the cause of the famines. Sen's argument holds that famine usually involves an interruption in the income of the poor together with some malfunctioning of the supply mechanism, as when merchants bid up food prices, when governments introduce controls with detrimental effects, and so forth. People suffer from hunger because they lose the ability to purchase sufficient food. In the period 1902–1908, from what can be ascertained, there was overall enough food for subsistence, but prices were high, distribution was disturbed, and many people had insufficient income with which to buy grain. Cropping conditions in a given year were sometimes acceptable, and yet the labor to harvest and transport that crop was inadequate, fueling a price rise. Furthermore, many poor people, especially the fugitive slaves, could not afford to buy food.

Despite the unsettled conditions and the frequent famines, there were opportunities for slaves to earn money in the dry season, much as they had been able to do before the conquest. Webster commented on the widespread nature of craft activities among the slave population as early as 1904: "Many are craftsmen, and in this case they pay a fixed sum per week ... to their master, and all profit over this is their own, and they are liable for no other work."[84] The collection of firewood, house repair, and irrigated farming were other activities that slaves could undertake during the dry season, just as they had done previously. Many such tasks could be done without slaves traveling very far from home.

Some features of the new economy, including *cin rani* migration, were already apparent before 1908 and involved greater opportunity to earn cash income. Some slaves were able to find work with commercial firms and the tin-mining companies on the Jos Plateau. Many of these openings for paid labor were limited to the dry season only. As early as 1903, H. W. Laws employed slaves to work his tin mine, but at that time, the slaves came from nearby. According to Freund,

> Laws, in his operations at Tilde, was able to secure labour by hiring out slaves from local masters in the dry season who would often be able to pay for their own manumission with the proceeds.[85]

By 1906–1907 the need for mine workers intensified: "labour began to appear on the Plateau from the central Hausa-speaking areas of Northern Nigeria:

Kano, Zaria, Bauchi, followed by Kanuri from Borno."[86] The pattern of long-distance labor migration had begun. Common *cin rani* occupations in this early period also included droving and construction work, with some slaves already traveling to other emirates in search of work.[87] Many found employment on the construction of government buildings, both for the British and the "Native Authorities."

As noted above, some fugitive slaves joined the WAFF, while many others constituted "a great proportion of Government carriers."[88] Slaves able to enter the West African Frontier Force were paid 1s. per day, a relatively high figure made necessary because the same sum was paid to soldiers in other British territories. At the time of the WAFF advance on Kano, slightly more than one carrier had to be employed for every soldier on the expedition. Some were impressed into this service, but most were paid at half the rate for soldiers, 6d. per day.[89] There were always many more carriers than soldiers. In other areas of government employment, the wage scale was a flat 6d. per day, the same rate paid to workers hired in the private sector in Kano and Zaria.[90] According to Swindell, the average wage for Sokoto migrants in this early period was 6d. per day, or 4d. to 5d. if the employer provided food, for a work day that lasted from 7 a.m. to 3 p.m.[91] Migrant workers from Sokoto could clear £1 net of food and lodging during a four-month period.

As economic stability was restored by 1907 in some places and by 1908 virtually everywhere, the vast majority of slaves who had continued in place with their masters were in the process of forging new arrangements involving sharecrop tenancy. In effect this majority were negotiating new terms of accommodation and dependency that preserved some of the old relationships while obtaining access to land and allowing movement during the dry season in search of extra earnings. For many years these slaves simply continued working the land of their masters, often enlarging their *gayauna* plots.

Whatever form the adjustment took, it involved maintaining a sufficient level of income so that slaves could pay their relatively high taxes, provide their in-kind rental payments if they stayed on the masters' farms, or make their *murgu* and self-redemption payments in cash if that was the arrangement. These requirements were, of course, additional to the need for the slaves to sustain themselves and their families now that their dry-season access to the granaries of the master's *gandu* was lost. The heavy financial commitments ensured that slaves as a group would always be disadvantaged by slow economic growth, and would be particularly vulnerable to economic depression. This explains why so many slaves came to be deeply in debt, ending up as clients (*yara*), retainers, and dependants. Finally, the need for cash income reveals why slaves were so often driven in the farming season, not with whips but by economic circumstances, to shift their cropping patterns towards more remunerative crops, and in the dry season to find employment that would yield additional income. Such involvement of slaves in the market economy included working for wages, engaging in petty trade over long distances, selling local products like firewood, and selling their labor for services such as house repair.

Resettlement and adjustment, 1909–16

The second period of economic development, which lasted from 1909 through 1916, was marked by positive growth as reflected in the construction of the railway to Kano and the spur line to the Jos Plateau, but was interrupted by the disastrous drought of 1913–14 and the first two years of the First World War. It was a period of new opportunities and severe hardship for masters and slaves alike. The principal occupations open to slaves and other seasonal laborers continued to be in construction (the railway, roads, and government buildings, as well as house repair), porterage and droving, and tin mining.

The government demand for carriers was still large. The pay for carriers on the Zaria road for several years before 1912 was 6d. per day. Porters received 6s. for an eight days journey plus 3d. per day for the return journey, making 8s. in all, or 6d. per day for the entire trip.[92] The figure was low compared to what a soldier could earn but high for the economy as a whole, and it was in sterling, thus furnishing a means to obtain the cash that many in the slave population had to have. Temple's observation in 1909 that the "supply of carriers [in Kano] is very large" reflected how avidly the slaves pursued dry-season employment to obtain this cash.[93] In 1911, Temple estimated that a few thousand carriers were employed annually by the government, some tens of thousands by foreign trading and mining firms, and hundreds of thousands by local merchants and other local employers.[94]

Other employment opportunities for laborers existed on the roads and railways, but this was usually very short-term and hence did not provide great opportunity to earn cash income. Much of the labor employed on road construction was "political," that is, impressed, but it was still paid, at the rate of 6d. per day. "Volunteer" labor received half that figure again, 9d. per day.[95] As the building of the rail line to Kano got underway, opportunities for labor also arose in railway construction. In January 1908, the size of the work force on the new Baro-Kano railway was 2,426, rising to 5,466 in October of that year. This work force was seasonal; work was suspended during the period July to September. In 1909, with work progressing northward, 3,191–4,100 workers found dry-season employment near Zaria. By 1910–1911 the pace had picked up: the "Bauchi Light," a narrow-gauge branch from Zaria to the tin fields, had 5,000 men at work on construction, while the Kano line was providing jobs for 8,000. In this period, the total work force may have reached 15,000. As with the roads, however, much of this labor was "political," impressed for the purpose.[96]

The workers were organized in teams under "team leaders," often the eldest sons of village heads in the vicinity of the line. Colonial officials took the lead; the emirs gave the orders to obtain workers; district and village

219

heads assigned labor quotas; family heads decided who would go. Slaves and former slaves undoubtedly made up a substantial portion of the work force; although precise details are lacking, they would have been an obvious choice in the frequent cases where railway work was less preferred to staying at home. The team leaders stayed on as permanent foremen, while the impressed workers were rotated after a work period of three to four weeks. Tasks were set on a daily basis. After these tasks were accomplished, the workers could use the rest of the day for their own purposes.[97] Some income was derived by large numbers of slaves and ex-slaves from this work (assuming that masters did not appropriate it). In Niger Province alone over a five-year period from late 1907, 251,443 laborers had seen service on building the line.[98] In spite of the large numbers, however, there was little chance for slaves to obtain permanent jobs as railway hands, and their earnings from railway work were perforce limited.[99]

By 1909, the emirates were also employing paid labor in construction, as Temple noted in Kano:

> There are more than 1,000 men employed at present [in such construction]. I would draw particular attention to this as I think it is the first time that labour which is *strictly* and *literally* free has been employed on any large scale by the Emir in this Protectorate ... Regular contracts are signed, some with Arabs, the contractor looks to make a profit, and he engages free labour and pays it daily exactly as he would in Europe. If a man does not work properly, he is dismissed. No "moral suasion" or compulsion of any kind is used ... Wages run from 6d per day for skilled labour to 500 Kawries, with food, for unskilled labour.[100]

By "free," Temple meant that no *political* force was used, but rather that wages alone were sufficient to attract workers. It is impossible to determine how many of these laborers were slaves, but it is likely that many were.

A continuing supply of workers for the mines was obtained from the "slave population" as well.[101] Employment in the mines was rising: by 1912, the average monthly size of the labor force in the mines was just over 12,000.[102] By 1909, the mines were also employing thousands of carriers; two years later the number of porters employed by the Niger Company alone was estimated at about 12,000.[103] Demand was so strong that the old wage of 6d. per day for carriers was starting to become obsolete in the tin areas. In Bauchi, demand had pushed up the figure to 9d. and even in some cases to 1s. per day.[104] By 1909, the Niger Company's workers were also being paid 9d. per day. Wages for mine workers were 1d. per hour, up to a maximum of 9d. per day, though by 1910 some miners were being paid 1s. per day. Several efforts were made by the mining firms in the period before 1914 to depress wages on the tin fields, but they failed.[105] The Company's efforts to reduce wages to 6d. led to the first strike in its history.[106] It should be noted that employment in tin remained largely a dry-season occupation through the 1940s.[107]

More traditional opportunities for slaves to find employment presented

220

themselves in a wide variety of craft industries, where they could both produce and market the product as traders. Many slaves had been engaged in craft activities long before the British conquest, and with the slaves' increasing need for cash the incentives to follow a craft were higher than before. No doubt work in craft production and trading had particular appeal to slaves who had inadequate access to land.

Investigations of the composition of the labor force in craft activities during the early colonial period are scarce, but the limited number of studies that do exist often call attention to the role of former slaves. For example, Ifeanyi Anagbogu in his examination of the leather industry points out that

> Our informants are ... in agreement that a number of slaves remained with their masters ... though their conditions of work began to change. In the tanning industry those slaves who had worked for the merchant and received rewards in the form of maintenance – feeding, clothing and housing – began to receive payments. With the money saved from this, as well as perhaps some tanning material, they are said to have produced some tanned skins for themselves which were sold privately. In this way, according to the evidence, many of them were able to establish on their own after resigning from the service of their masters. Those who were unable to save enough migrated or worked for other established tanners within the cities. Some, too, are said to have turned to farm labouring.[108]

Anagbogu's interviews suggest that many migrant professionals in the leather business during the early colonial period were "probably ex-slaves."[109] The supply of these aspiring leather-workers became so abundant that former slaves who learned to work leather flowed to Zinder, Abeche, Fort Lamy, Ilorin, Oyo, Ibadan, Lagos, and Onitsha.

There are also references to ex-slaves finding employment as dyers in the textile industry, an industry to which many slaves had been assigned before the conquest.[110] The sheer size of this industry, together with its growth when the economy expanded following the arrival of the railway, suggests that the employment of ex-slaves in textile production and finishing may have been large. In addition, masters who were involved in the textile industry sent their slaves out to earn wages, subject to the payment of *murgu*.[111] As discussed in the last chapter, craft workers were not allowed to escape a tax obligation of the same sort paid by former slaves in rural areas. In effect by 1912 there was a laborer's tax on non-farm work, collected at a flat rate of 3–4s. per year. The principle that head taxation encourages work effort, discussed in the last chapter, also applied to this laborer's tax.[112]

Migration in search of work was closely associated with petty trading, since many dry-season employees invested their modest incomes in trade goods whose sale could be turned to profit.[113] Migrant workers could double or triple their earnings by successfully buying and selling trade goods (which might include sheep or goats along with a wide variety of consumer goods).[114] Migrants invested part of their earnings in goods for resale in order to increase their profits.[115] By 1906, some slaves in Sokoto were allowed "to leave their masters and tour around the country with their one sheep or one piece of cloth and live on the few cowries profit that they make on the transaction."[116] While some men traveled as far as Ilorin and Lagos and even Accra on their *cin rani* expeditions, the majority went to Kano, Zaria, and Katsina, with Kano being the most important destination. Time spent was usually in the order of three to four months between November and March, during which period a village might lose over half its male population.[117]

Before 1907, trade was not as important as a source of income for slaves and other dry-season workers as it would be thereafter. Initially, Lugard had imposed a caravan toll, payable from early 1903 but repealed in February 1907, which was basically a continuation of the precolonial *fito* and other caravan taxes.[118] It was the only early colonial tax to apply to traders, who otherwise paid nothing for the measures such as policing the routes that made long-distance commerce more secure for them. For a time (1903–1904) the caravan tax accounted for about one-third of all colonial government revenue.[119] It may be that many people, particularly those engaged in the petty trade characteristic of slaves involved in *cin rani* migration, managed to avoid paying the colonial caravan tax. Nonetheless, the tax retarded trade, so that its repeal in early 1907 made it easier for slaves wanting to earn money in the dry season to do so.

With hindsight, it was rather an extreme form of economic liberalism to have abandoned this tax in February 1907, as a hindrance to trade. Because of its abolition, it was many years before traders and merchants were subject to any tax at all except for import duties, the head tax, and the levies on the farms they owned. While no doubt of greatest significance to the larger merchants, the reform also improved the economic environment for slaves attempting to meet their new financial obligations through trading. Removing a tax on trade increased the incentive to invest in goods, no matter how small the quantity, and travel great distances to realize a profit. Particularly as the cash economy expanded, abolition of the toll opened a wider avenue to trade generally, and in particular for slaves to earn the money necessary for their emancipation. By 1911, it was reported in Sokoto Province that the "majority [of men] go off trading in a body" during the dry season.[120] Gowers' comment on Sokoto could apply to the whole of Northern Nigeria: he called attention to "the readiness of the Sokoto peasantry to make the most of their spare time between one harvest and the next sowing."[121] The adoption of internal free trade from 1907 therefore brought improvement in the ability of the slaves to finance their freedom.

During the years from 1909 to 1912, economic conditions clearly improved compared to the years immediately following the conquest. Trade and production were now expanding, albeit slowly; considerable numbers of slaves were able to find paid employment (though the proportion of the whole finding full or lengthy employment must have been quite small); there were no serious famines; taxes were becoming consolidated and more predictable; resettlement of outlying and deserted areas was occurring; and accommodation between masters and the many slaves who remained was taking place. Even so, major new financial obligations had been placed on the slaves. At best these must have imposed a significant burden, while at worst they must have made it impossible for slaves to take any independent action at all, with things remaining in many ways much as they had been before the British arrived. For the slave population as a whole, the outlook would have been more of the same – until, in 1912, Northern Nigeria found itself facing a sudden expansion in the production of crops for export.

Impact of the railway

The impact of the railway was not what the British had expected. The line had been built at the insistence of the cotton interests in the English Midlands, which through the British Cotton Growing Association had persuaded the Imperial government to finance the rail line as a public works project. Northern Nigeria was supposed to supply the looms of Britain. In the event, the farmers along the route found that it was more profitable for them to sell groundnuts than it was to sell cotton, which fizzled as an export crop for some years to come. Groundnuts suddenly became the leading export from Northern Nigeria.

The first full growing season after the railway was opened to Kano on April 1, 1912 resulted in a minimum of £70,000 earned by the local population in the sale of over 10,000 tons of groundnuts. As Fika states, "it is likely that [slaves] played a large role in the expansion of groundnut cultivation, especially in view of the high prices it could fetch and the British insistence that all taxes should be paid in the colonial currency."[122] All of this new revenue was in the form of silver coin. Middlemen in the employ of the European trading companies pioneered new techniques for the region, such as advancing cloth and imported salt to farmers as an inducement to deliver nuts later in the season – for it must not be forgotten that the earnings from groundnut sales were welcome to farmers only in smaller part because of the slavery issue, but in larger measure because of the new goods that could be obtained with the revenue.

Tin production provided another stimulus to the region's cash economy, particularly after the Bauchi Light Railway was opened from Zaria to the Plateau in March 1912.[123] Thereafter, wage employment grew significantly. From about 12,000 in 1912, employment reached nearly 18,000 in 1914 and nearly 22,000 in 1917.[124] A large Hausa community sprang up in the environs of the mines.[125] Freund notes that the many slaves were using their wages to purchase their manumission.[126] Wages were not high, and even the greatly increased demand for labor only raised the going rate to 1s.; the weekly wage in 1926 was 5s. 6d.[127] Though Freund argues that by 1914 there was "collusion to keep labour cheap, both from the point of view of world competition in tin production and the establishment of a low common wage rate in the protectorate of Northern Nigeria," his position seems unnecessarily to rely on an employers' conspiracy.[128] For the period as a whole, wages ranged from 3d. to 1s. per day.[129] If wages elsewhere in the indigenous economy had been higher, then the tin companies and the government would both have had to pay more. The large supply and limited demand for labor in Northern Nigeria were the basic causes of the low wages, not some cabal among employers who, all would surely admit, employed only a small fraction of those who worked for wages anyway.

Farmers, craftsmen, and merchants of all sorts benefitted from the multiplier effects as new spending of export revenues raised the demand for various types of food and locally produced consumer goods. The growing demand for cotton to feed local looms has already been noted. In the production of some other particularly remunerative crops, employment of wage labor arose. We hear that in 1913, rice growing in Silame District west of Sokoto had become

> so lucrative that a regular system of hired labour has sprung up. Men from as far afield as Wurno, and Godabawa, come in to work at the digging. This is really arduous work, for the fadama becomes caked and hard, and the depth to be turned over is much greater than for gero, etc. A man will not do an acre in less than six weeks. These hired labourers, known as "Yanga aiki," or "Yanga lada," work from six a.m. till two p.m. and receive as remuneration 3d. per day ... as much "fura" as they call for to drink, and their evening meal of "tuo" [*tuwo*]. The food and drink from several separate enquiries, works out in cash value from 3.1d. to 3.6d. so that the total cost of hire is about 6½d. per day [based on market value].[130]

Though it was to be a considerable time yet before hired wage labor in agriculture became very significant, for a few slaves it represented another way to earn cash income if they could not grow the crops themselves, and the masters benefitted as well. There is the case of a master in Silame District in 1913 who received *fansa* payments from "two domestics" of 210,000 cowries each. He could afford the loss of this labor because he was a prosperous rice farmer who hired laborers to work his fields.[131]

Another multiplier effect, though a little-noticed one, accompanied the shift away from slave estates to smallholder agriculture. With the decline of many estates, the acquisition of tools became the responsibility of slaves rather than of their masters. Even if the old masters originally allowed the slaves to take some tools with them, hoes in Hausaland wore out quickly, after about two years of use. Then new hoes and other tools often had to be purchased from the artisans able to fabricate them.[132] These artisans benefitted both from the rise in the marketing of tools, and from the multiplier effects caused by the increased cash earnings on the part of farmers. Further "backward linkage," that is, cash earnings by tool producers promoting spending among suppliers to those producers, gave additional multiplier effects that extended to iron makers, to the providers of fuel, and to the wood cutters and handle makers that shaped the implements. No particular barriers existed, as far as we can ascertain, against slaves entering these jobs as well.

The new purchasing power stimulated the growth of dry-season trading and wage labor that had already arisen before the economic boom.[133] Even with increased earnings, the seasonal cycle of the savanna still revolved around a relatively immobile rainy season when farmers worked the land followed by a long dry season when people were underemployed and could therefore migrate in search of opportunity. Many people, particularly slaves trying to earn their *murgu* and redemption price, continued to find it necessary or advantageous to seek work in the dry season. Sometimes the journeys involved were very long: the 1915 *Annual Report* from Gwandu noted "a large number of men ... travelled to the Gold Coast."[134] People so engaged sold their services, worked for wages, accepted commissions, and otherwise received a return in money or in kind.

Famine and war, 1913–16

Shortly after the railway was completed, the growth of the cash economy made possible by the improvement in transport was suddenly stalled by a serious famine on a scale not to be repeated in Northern Nigeria until the early 1970s. A severe drought caused both the cash crops for export and the food crops to fail across a wide swath of savanna countryside. Rainfall at Kano dropped from an average of 25.9 inches to 13.48 inches during the growing season (July, August, and September) of 1913, which, when compared to the next worse subsequent year (16.34 inches in 1949) before the dry cycle that began in the 1970s, demonstrates the severity of the situation.[135] When rainfall drops below about 22 inches in the growing season, yields are substantially reduced. The rainfall total was sufficiently low, especially to the north of Kano, that the guinea corn and millet crops were badly harmed. Output fell by a quarter at best, and in some areas these crops were completely ruined.[136] In May 1914, stocks of staple foodstuffs began to give out, with the September harvest still four months away. Food prices rose tenfold in some areas.[137] Mortality was very high, and in Kano Province alone (then including Katsina) 30,000 people were believed to have perished.[138] Fatalities were especially frequent in the latitudes north of Kano city. The railway facilitated the movement of food to the north, 15,000 tons of it during 1913, and for seventy-four days the government conducted an emergency food distribution.

The famine of 1913–14 had a very different cause from the lesser ones that occurred just after the arrival of the British. The major reason for these earlier famines was economic dislocation, including the departure of so many slaves. The 1913–14 famine, however, took place in conditions of drought so severe that it offset the increasing ability to purchase food as export cropping expanded, and the better transport provided by the new railway. Understanding that the causes of famine differed is essential in determining the impact of colonial rule. For slaves, the famine of 1913–14 had additional significance. No doubt some owners who were still providing

225

some of their slaves' food took steps to cut the old ties, thus ending any further drain on their resources. Even the earlier and less serious period of famine in 1902–1908 is said to have made it more difficult for masters to supply victuals to their slaves, with a resulting incentive to cut some of them loose.

Although agricultural conditions were nearly back to normal in the growing season of 1914, the difficult period arising from the drought lasted another year. Just when more government assistance would have been most welcome for famine relief, the beginning of the First World War in August retarded the recovery. Rice ordered from Britain was delayed, and military movements towards the border of German Kamerun contributed to traffic difficulties on the railway, impeding the relief effort which was in any case inadequate. Furthermore, the shipments of exports overseas were affected, and the military campaign into Kamerun strained resources. For slaves, the war slowed the recovery upon which their hopes for cash income depended. The negative effects of the First World War on transportation and on the market for cash crops only lasted until 1916, however, when the shipping lanes were again relatively safe.

The expansion of the colonial economy, 1916–30

The completion of the railway bridge across the Niger at Jebba in 1916, replacing a slow train ferry, removed the last impediment in the railway system between Northern Nigeria and the coast. The expansion in the earnings of cash incomes soon resumed, and from the point of view of the slaves their ability to earn higher cash incomes either from producing crops for export or from the resulting multiplier effects again began to increase. In 1916 groundnut exports reached 50,000 tons, which remained approximately the average yearly amount exported (49,000 tons) until 1922. Prices temporarily collapsed in 1920 after reaching unprecedented levels, but soon regained their former heights.[139] Tonnage grew as the road system improved, with exports averaging 80,000 tons between 1922 and 1927, thirty-two times the export figure for 1912, the year in which the railway opened. Again there was a temporary setback in 1926–27 because the rains failed, but the drought and associated famine were not as severe as the one in 1913–14.[140] The rapid spread of transport by motor lorry, the building of the new railway line northwest of Kano to Kaura Namoda in 1929, and a further line northeast to Nguru in 1930 all served further to increase shipments. Exports averaged 160,000 tons between 1927 and 1934, sixty-four times the 1912 figure (Table 7.3).[141]

Eventually in the 1920s exports of cotton, too, reached reasonably respectable levels (Table 7.4). It was a good cash crop for smallholders on soils where the groundnut did not thrive. Especially in Zaria and southern Katsina, and later in Sokoto as transport improved, former slaves with access to land could increase their earnings by raising and selling cotton for export. It must be remembered that there was a thriving market for sales of

Table 7.3. *Exports of groundnuts from Nigeria, 1910–30[a]*

Year	Quantity (tons)	Index (1912 = 100)	Year	Quantity (tons)	Index (1912 = 100)
1910	995	40	1921	50,979	2,025
1911	1,179	47	1922	23,890	949
1912	2,518	100	1923	22,887	909
1913	19,288	766	1924	78,266	3,108
1914	16,997	675	1925	127,228	5,053
1915	8,910	354	1926	123,799	4,917
1916	50,368	2,000	1927	90,773	3,605
1917	50,334	1,999	1928	103,000	4,091
1918	57,554	2,286	1929	147,000	5,838
1919	39,334	1,562	1930	146,000	5,798
1920	45,409	1,803			

Note: [a]DeGregori (1969), 340. A quantity rather than a value measure is presented here because, under the conditions prevailing in groundnut purchasing, accurate data are unavailable for the actual price received by farmers. The firms' buying prices in 1914 and 1915 were well below the 1913 price. High prices ensued until the end of the First World War, broke, recovered again to a high point in 1925, and broke again and more sharply in the Great Depression. The correlation between high quantities and high prices is pronounced; the amount received by farmers fluctuated accordingly.

cotton to indigenous manufacturers as well. Time series data are unavailable for this part of the market, which, however, remained strong for many years after the opening of the railway. Yet the maximum expansion in cotton exports during the period (fourteenfold between 1912 and 1926) was far below the thirty- to sixty fold expansion in groundnut exports, and cotton's performance remained a disappointment to the British mercantile community.

By 1918, many workers received daily wages from "native" employers of 9*d.* without food or 6*d.* with food, which was higher than a decade earlier.[142] Wages for carriers had risen as well, to 2*s.* per day in 1920.[143] Work on the railways continued in the 1920s, albeit at a slower pace and at a wage of 9*d.* per day, the same as before the First World War.[144] We recall that with taxes swinging towards a per capita system of assessment just before the opening of the railway, workers had to obtain the cash to pay their tax bills, but were not penalized for earnings at the margin – they could keep whatever they earned once their flat-rate tax had been paid. It followed that the search for means to earn income intensified.

Cash income for long-range human porterage did decline after the opening of the railway and the ending of the First World War. An early visitor, A. F. Mockler-Ferryman, had predicted that improved transport would mean a lessened need for human transport on the part of the indigenous merchant community.[145] He was right. The government and European

Table 7.4. *Exports of cotton from Northern Nigeria, 1911–30*[a]

Year	Quantity (bales of 400 lb.)	Index (1912 = 100)	Year	Quantity (bales of 400 lb.)	Index (1912 = 100)
1911	600	23	1921	12,000	462
1912	2,600	100	1922	10,794	415
1913	2,000	77	1923	12,506	481
1914	2,391	92	1924	18,419	708
1915	1,258	48	1925	27,088	1,042
1916	12,380	476	1926	37,079	1,426
1917	5,190	200	1927	15,379	592
1918	2,871	110	1928	20,238	778
1919	8,000	308	1929	23,458	902
1920	5,500	212	1930	29,208	1,123

Note: [a]Export figures from Northern Nigeria differ slightly depending on the source. For 1911–24, see Lamb (1925), 185. For 1925–30 see Cowley (1966), 169–96. Cowley's figures are for Allen (American) cotton and omit a small quantity of exported "native cotton." Also see Watts (1983), 174 for a different set of figures based on crop year.

employers did indeed require far fewer carriers after the First World War, thus cutting out that source of cash income with which slaves might have met their financial obligations.[146] Yet there was another and more positive side to the issue. The coming of the railway, plus the later expansion of the line and the growing network of motorable roads in the 1920s, meant that the thousands of slaves who had undertaken dry-season porterage could now be dispensed with. Slave carriers offered reduced advantages of ownership to masters who could use, or had to face the competition from, major cost-reducing improvements in transportation. It can therefore be argued that the slaves' loss of ability to earn cash as carriers for the government or private merchants was counterbalanced by the decline in the need for masters to maintain a stable of slave carriers for their own use. Even this *decline* of slaves' ability to earn income from porterage can then be viewed as promoting the prospect of their emancipation.

The new economic vitality was unmistakable. The expansion of exports seen in Tables 7.3 and 7.4 was not seriously reversed until Northern Nigeria felt the world-wide effects of the Great Depression. On average, people had much greater access to cash incomes in 1920 than they had had in 1900. Though they were always on the low end of the income distribution, slaves, too, shared in these opportunities, with the caveat that their potential to achieve higher material levels of living was reduced by the payments that had to be made to masters.

In discussing these developments, Lugard argued in 1918 that the adoption of a "liberal policy" on slavery "has been justified by the results."[147] According to him,

Railways have created a demand for exportable produce hitherto undreamt of, and the Native agriculturalist finds himself able to purchase imported goods which till now were beyond his ken ... [T]he ex-slave, now a peasant proprietor, finds new wants, and a new standard of comfort: the direct tax, which must be paid in cash, adds its incentive – and he is willing to work for wages when sowing time or harvest does not require all his energies, while the large floating class who are not disposed to settle down to agriculture, or who are unable to obtain land in their own particular district, and are too conservative to go far afield, are ready to offer themselves for wages, to procure the articles they covet.[148]

This analysis certainly conflicted with the European perception of the "lazy African."

As was his wont, however, Lugard tended to overemphasize the growth of a wage labor force as opposed to the much more dramatic and pertinent rise in revenues from the sale of export crops. In his 1918 *Political Memoranda*, he noted that "the realisation of the free labour market which it [government] desired to create" was clearly evident.

[W]e find that not only is Government able to count on a fairly adequate labour supply, both for current needs and for great construction works such as railways, but there is a large surplus, working on the minefields and elsewhere, and even willing to accept low wages from Native land owners. The cause, I think, is to be found in the quick appreciation by the African of the amenities of life which he can procure for cash, and his natural aptitude for work.[149]

Lugard's recognition of low wages highlights that feature of the transition from slavery to freedom which pushed slaves and former slaves to grow crops. They might be able to benefit from high prices for groundnuts and cotton, despite the risks in cutting back on grain production, but most farmers, including slaves and former slaves, needed dry-season employment to make ends meet. Wages remained low, despite moderate increases, even though the growth of the export economy introduced a considerable amount of cash into the economy. The supply of potential wage earners was so large that wage rates did not rise significantly.

Impact of the colonial economy on slavery after 1916

Even given Lugard's overemphasis on the importance of wage labor, reports from the field after the end of the First World War confirm that wage labor was indeed springing up widely among the (former) slaves. From Muri, Fremantle reported in 1918 that

It is of much interest to follow the fortunes of masters and their former slaves. The change has no doubt led to the development of the system of wages, and to the voluntary attachment of ex-slaves to Natives in a higher social position than themselves, not necessarily to their former masters.[150]

Labor recruiters, who found workers for employers under contracts that paid a specific amount per recruit, were instrumental in managing this work force, because many wage earners were slaves, even though the "recruiting of slaves qua slaves cannot of course be tolerated."[151] In almost all cases recruiters were officials, which the colonial regime thought was an undesirable but necessary feature of labor recruitment. Officials were the very ones who still controlled large numbers of slaves and had always been the masters with the biggest holdings. Little is known about their recruitment practices, but they probably drew on their own slaves, thereby making it easy to collect *murgu*. Recruitment bordered on "political" or quasi-forced labor, with recruiters receiving a fee for each worker. In those situations in which the slaves actually belonged to the recruiter, the fee was an additional levy on the slave population by the very masters of the slaves! Needless to say, the real level of income that wage earners received was lower than the stated daily rate.

In 1918, Webster identified "two classes of slaves" in the rural areas of Yola. First, many farm slaves had become "hired labourers." These workers included "nearly all the slaves of the small man and those living on the home farm of the big holder." Webster described their working conditions as follows:

> They usually work 5 days a week for their master from 9 a.m. to 3 p.m. The rest of the time is their own. The master feeds them and pays their taxes.[152]

Webster does not state how much these slave workers were paid, but it is clear that the cash amount was only part of the payment, the rest being in the form of food and the money for taxes.

A second type of arrangement involved farm slaves who were paying *murgu* and had become "tenants" on their masters' lands; that is, they became sharecroppers. *Murgu* appears to have been paid in kind, with women paying five baskets of grain and men ten baskets, valued at 4*d.*–6*d.* each in the countryside and 1*s.* each in Yola. According to Webster,

> If they do any work for the master in the dry season he invariably pays their tax and in many cases does so in any case. He also supports them in time of stress. The nett result is that the owner gets little or no profit [*sic*] from his slaves during their life time. That the owner still values his slaves is due partly to sentiment partly to the hope of a good return at their death when according to custom he takes the whole of the deceased's property. This it seems to me cannot continue now that the slaves' children are free.[153]

His comment that owners made "no profit" is difficult to assess, since it was in the interest of masters to avoid paying higher taxes. Nonetheless, Webster establishes that slaves tended to become involved in wage labor on farms or in sharecropping arrangements. Slavery had indeed been modified, which is why he believed that "slavery appears to me dead in all but name."

Large slave owners in Sokoto, including the Majidadin Sokoto, the Galadima, the Magajin Rafi, and the Ubandoma, were hiring workers by 1918. According to Arnett, "it was cheaper to hire labour at a daily wage than to feed and clothe slaves eating their heads off during a large portion of the year."[154] Consequently,

A large number of slaves at Sokoto have acquired a practical freedom because their masters have encouraged them to earn their own living and become independent. The slave has his own house and family, and occupation, & is entirely free, except for occasional calls for such work as repairing the master's house; occasional presents of 6d. or 1/- etc., more as a mark of good will than in quittance of a real obligation.[155]

In short, the payment of *murgu* and the rendering of labor had become the norm for the slave population, and when slaves were not employed on the land they rented from their masters, they were involved in *cin rani* migration in search of work. As Arnett observed, "taxation of the individual, slave or free, has popularized paid labour and done much to determine the status of the slaves. It has been a great help to the [slavery] policy."[156]

In 1924, Browne reflected on the changes that had occurred in two decades. In the early years, he noted, the desertion of slaves had caused considerable dislocation because

vast tracts of farm land were left uncultivated for some time, owing to no labour being available for cultivation. Time has however, brought relief with the result that in the place of slave labour the owner of the land and his family themselves work in the fields, or paid labour is available for the well-to-do farmer where the labour of his own household is insufficient.[157]

In many cases, the farm laborers were former slaves or slaves still working under *murgu*. According to Hill, hired labor had begun to replace slave labor in rural Katsina by this time as well.[158]

Slaves and former slaves continued to enter government employment in lieu of their obligations to their masters. In 1918, Arnett discovered that "a number of the Native Administration Dogarai and also ... the labourers employed by Government as mail carriers are slaves of chiefs and talakawa in Sokoto."[159] Of thirty *dogarai* and fifteen mail carriers, one third were slaves of the Sultan, seven belonged to the Galadima, and the rest were slaves of other officials and a few private persons. After Arnett interviewed these slaves, he concluded that

in every instance the slave had practically achieved his independence before he entered his present duties. He was either rendering no private services at all to his master or else such slight and occasional services as to be practically negligible. This was especially the case with the dogarai. It seems to me necessary to distinguish between the dogarai whose work is purely official and the mail carriers who are merely wage earners of a commercial character. [In many cases the masters had] made no claim on their slaves for many years ... but I did not wish to press this point since the masters might have replied that they had surrendered the services of their slaves at the call of the administration ... With regard to mail carriers I see no occasion to release them from any duties they are now performing for their masters, and they have been told to carry on as before, but that if any master feels that he is or has been deprived of his fair benefits he may appeal to the Native Court. I was first inclined to urge that the mail carriers should pay a ransom out of the good wages they earn, but it was pointed out by the Majidadi that the services they are accustomed to give

231

their masters are of a very slight and occasional nature, and that if the masters had been deprived of any considerable benefit such as would entitle them to a ransom they would have raised the claim some years ago.[160]

Arnett's "discovery" demonstrates that slaves dominated the lower levels of the administration of both the colonial regime and the emirate governments, just as they always had, only now they were being paid wages.

Whatever Lugard's satisfaction that wage labor was becoming widespread, the sharecrop rental and tenancy relations discussed earlier in the chapter became the more common lot of the former slaves. In this situation, the slaves had to depend on the good-will of their landlords. For a very long time their "right of occupancy" of the land was dependent on the willingness of the landlords to let them stay on. It was a mutuality of economic interest and some degree of paternalism, rather than land law or traditional land practice, that provided the ex-slaves with any security of land access that they possessed. As this form of tenancy evolved, the ex-slaves found themselves in a position of dependency not much unlike the landless serfs and peasants of other times on other continents.

An evolving landlord–tenant relation that embodied sharecrop rental payments was especially likely for the slaves on what had been the slave estates. On large estates much of the land would have had to go unused if the slaves departed. There the former masters were usually pleased to retain their services if at all possible, and the slaves in turn appreciated the relatively greater influence of their patrons with their superior wealth and power compared to individual smallholders.

For the one, two, or three slaves of smallholders, the situation was somewhat different. Though many slaves of such owners might be likely to stay on as dependent *gandu* members, some masters were reluctant to reduce the size of a landholding that was small in the first place. Thus access to land was not as certain as for a slave on a *rinji*. If a slave departed, so be it – a brother or even a wife could take up some of the slack.[161] Furthermore, the slaves of smallholders knew that these patrons were relatively weak both politically and economically, with little wealth or power compared to estate owners. That knowledge reduced their motive to stay behind. Thus the slaves of private farmers probably left their masters in greater proportion than did *rinji* slaves on larger estates.[162]

Even for the slaves who found a place in a familial *gandu*, the arrangement seldom survived from one generation to the next. M. G. Smith's observations, based on field work in the late 1940s, are applicable.

> Rarely do brothers continue to operate a gandu for very long after their father's death, and only exceptionally do we find the children of two brothers as the senior members of a common gandu.[163]

Yet on the whole many slaves of private farmers apparently did remain. Staying on where the slave already "belonged" was the more attractive because attaching oneself to another *gandu* at a distance was highly problematical, and only a minority had the skills and initiative to move rapidly into craft activities or wage labor. Hill's conclusion is that the slaves of small-holders were normally allowed to keep possession of their *gayauna* plots, and that eventually they were accepted into the village as full members, often intermarrying with the free population.[164] In time, the descendants of slaves could expect to inherit land from their parents just as if the latter had been free.[165]

The pursuit of accommodation between the slaves and the masters, however forged, continued for years after Lugard had left office. The descendants of many slaves still lacked proprietary rights to land and had to rely on landlords who were often former masters or their descendants.[166] In Zaria until 1936, land cases were dealt with by executive decision on the part of the *imam* and the local headmen. After that date, land cases were brought to the Islamic courts. Elsewhere, the Islamic courts were also involved in decisions pertaining to land. Thus land decisions remained in conservative hands, with such courts unlikely to interpret the law in favor of former slaves.[167] The development was not unlike what happened in the courts of the southern United States after the period of Reconstruction.

The increased opportunities for the slaves to earn cash income that were available from 1912 were instrumental in easing the transition from slavery to freedom. Browne reached the conclusion in 1924 that "the gradual emancipation of slaves by self redemption and by virtue of the [Slavery] Ordinance has set free large numbers of persons who thus have become available for labour in the Government Services, in the Mines and with the Commercial firms, and thus the country has been able to develop to the mutual benefit of its people and the outer world."[168] The new incomes earned from cash-crop exporting or from the multiplier effects of such activity financed *murgu* and self-redemption payments for many slaves. For those slaves who remained on what had been the farms of their former masters, the increased earnings provided the masters with sharecrop rental income larger by far than it could have been in the absence of such opportunities. For virtually all of the male slaves, the new revenue provided the wherewithal for the compulsory tax payments to government. Lugard was right to emphasize the potential of higher cash income to alter the lot of the slaves. True, most did not escape poverty, and many of their descendants are poor today. But in large measure they did become free.

8

The persistence of concubinage

Most of the colonial measures that were designed to reform slavery and to promote its eventual demise were directed at men, as we have seen in the preceding chapters. Yet more than half of the slave population in the early colonial era appear to have been women. As we demonstrated in Chapter 4, issues relating to female slaves were considered to be variations on marital relationships. Women were either married, under the guardianship of relatives or other custodians, or an undesirable element in society that was associated with prostitution and crime. In this chapter, we explore the fate of female slaves after 1910, and more specifically how the institution of concubinage flourished in this period. It is our contention that concubinage presented one of the most persistent difficulties for British colonial policy towards slavery. Theoretically, concubinage resulted in the elimination of slave status for women, since concubines eventually became free. The free status of their children was legally protected even without the declaration that children born after March 31, 1901 were free. In fact, however, the demand for concubines continued, which meant that there had to be young women of servile status who could supply this demand. There were three sources of supply. Initially, females who had been born into slavery before 1901 were available; later girls who were legally free but of servile origin were pressed into concubinage; and finally the clandestine trade in children produced a steady stream of young girls.

Court records provide a window into the workings of British reforms as they affected women (see Appendix). A majority of slavery cases that came before the courts involved women, and a very large proportion of these cases resulted in the transfer of women for purposes of concubinage. Hence we begin this chapter with an assessment of the female population that received certificates of freedom through the courts, and then we examine the difficulties of British policy with respect to female slaves. The issue of concubinage and how men acquired slave women after the slave trade was prohibited tested British reforms. For a decade or more, the Islamic courts were the medium through which concubinage was regulated, but by the early 1920s, the actions of the Islamic courts came under review amid strong criticism.

Thereafter, concubinage continued, but the courts were less involved in the recruitment of concubines.

Throughout the first three decades of colonial rule, and indeed continuing through the 1930s, there was a clandestine trade in slave children, many of whom were girls who eventually became concubines. This illegal source of concubines supplemented the methods of transfer that were sanctioned by the Islamic courts. We attempt an assessment of the scale of this trade and the difficulties in its suppression in Chapter 9.

Women and the courts

A large proportion of the approximately 103,000 slaves who were issued certificates of freedom in the Islamic courts between 1900 and 1929 were women, and many of these women were in fact being transferred for purposes of concubinage. The court records provide data on gender, age, destination, and other information and thereby offer an important insight into the process of change, especially before 1920. These data include slaves who were redeemed by relatives, those who paid off their own ransoms, and women who were freed to marry or who were transferred for purposes of concubinage. Many women who became concubines were recorded under the classification of self-redemption or were simply listed as "freed to follow their own inclinations." Other women, whose families wanted to protect their freeborn status and thereby prevent their reduction to a state of concubinage, arranged to obtain certificates of freedom in the Islamic courts as well.

Far more females than males passed through the courts between 1900 and 1922 (Tables B.1–B.4). The ratio of females to males was 178:100 (64.0 female and 36.0 percent male) in 1905–1906. The lowest ratio (152:100) was recorded in Kano for 1916–1921 (Sample: 11,125 slaves, 60.4 percent female, 39.6 percent male), and the highest ratio (248:100) was recorded for Yola, based on a sample of 1,941 slaves between 1902 and 1922 (71.3 percent female, 28.7 percent male). Of 8,921 slaves receiving certificates before 1918, 64.2 percent were female and 35.8 percent were male (179:100). A slight decline in the gender ratio appears to have occurred between 1917 and 1921. Returns for 4,032 slaves in 1917 indicate a peak of 184:100 (64.8 percent female, 35.2 percent male). Comparable returns of 1,714 slaves in 1918 show a decline to 160:100 (61.1 percent female, 38.4 percent male); while in 1919, the ratio was 152:100 (60.4 percent female, 39.6 percent male, based on a sample of 1,995 slaves).

A common destination for women who received certificates of freedom through the courts was marriage and concubinage, which are often difficult to distinguish in the returns. The percentage of women who were clearly destined for marriage or concubinage was 28 percent in 1905–1906, representing at least 52 percent of the cases involving women. By 1916, the percentage had risen to 35 percent of easily identified cases, or 53 percent of

Table 8.1. *Women freed for marriage and concubinage, 1901–1921*

Year	% of all slaves	Females	Total slaves	% of females	Total females
1901–1905	5	134	2,767		
1906	21	121	581		
1905–1906	28	162	584	45	360
1907	27	43	159		
1916	35	251[a]	706	52	476
1917	24	1,724	7,137	37	4,624[b]
1918	18	1,335	7,540	29	4,644[b]
1919	13	574	4,292	22	2,592[b]
1920–1921	17	359	2,157	28	1,302[b]

Notes: [a] Figure adjusted to include twenty-nine cases where women were ransomed by unrelated males "to follow their own inclinations."
[b] Figures calculated on basis of gender data; see Tables A.5, A.6, A.7 and D.9.
Sources: Northern Nigeria Annual Report, 1905–06, 481; SNP 15/1 Acc 90; SNP 15/1 Acc 121; *Northern Nigeria Annual Report, 1907–08*, 614; SNP 10/5 435p/1917; SNP 10/4 236p/1916; SNP 10/7 331p/1919; SNP 10/8 263p/1920; SNP 10/9 120p/1921.

Table 8.2. *Age of females redeemed for marriage and concubinage, 1905–1906, 1916*

Age	1905–1906	%	1916	%
7–15	39	32	—	—
16–20	43	36	48	24
21–25	16	13	72	36
26–30	13	11	56	28
31–35	3	3	18	9
36+	7	6	4	2
Total	121	101	198	100

Sources: SNP 15/1 Acc 90; SNP 15/1 Acc 121; SNP 10/5 435p/1917.

all cases involving women. Thereafter, the percentage declined from 24 percent in 1917, to 18 percent in 1918, 13 percent in 1919, and 17 percent in 1920–1921. The decline occurred primarily because the Islamic courts began to disguise such transfers (see below).

The age profile of women who were redeemed for purposes of marriage or concubinage reflected the fact that girls born after March 31, 1901 were free. Thus the females in the returns for 1905–1906 tended to be much younger than those a decade later (Table 8.2). In 1905–1906, two-thirds of those destined for marriage or concubinage were aged twenty or younger, in contrast to the percentage in 1916, when only 24 percent were. Girls who

Table 8.3. *Female slaves freed to "marry" in 1916*

Emirate	16–20	21–25	26–30	31–35	36+	Total
Katsina	25	52	41	13	1	132
Daura	—	1	—	1	2	4
Kazaure	2	1	—	—	—	3
Kano	20	13	12	4	1	50
Nassarawa	1	3	2	—	—	6
Niger	—	2	1	—	—	3
Total	48	72	56	18	4	198
Percentage	24	36	28	9	2	100

Notes: 62.5% aged 25 and under.
89.4% aged 30 and under.
Source: SNP 10/5 435p/1917.

were younger than fifteen simply did not show up in the returns for 1916 (Table 8.3).

The 1913 records for Sokoto are perhaps the clearest indication of the relative importance of ransom by third parties for marriage or concubinage. Of the 3,038 cases reported, 40.5 percent (1,229) involved third-party ransoms.[1] The figures for 1917–19 (Tables A.5–A.7) show a decline in the number of cases of "marriage," which probably reflects the change in policy in identifying such cases in the courts (see Chapter 4). In 1916, 46.6 percent of women were freed to "marry," and other women were clearly freed by third-party males to whom they were probably "engaged." The adjusted figure indicates that at least 52.7 percent of women were destined for concubinage or marriage. Another 0.8 percent were freed by their husbands, so that the percentage of women given certificates in association with marriage or concubinage was at least 53.5 percent. The percentage was probably higher still, since the women who were "freed to follow their own inclinations," who technically ransomed themselves, or whom their masters freed, could well have entered concubinage or marriage. The vague category, "freed to follow her own inclinations," disguised at least twenty-nine cases involving a third-party male, for example. A master might well provide freedom papers to a concubine who had borne children, since these women would become free on his death anyway. And self-redemption very often covered cases of transfer for purposes of concubinage. Eventually, all cases of transfer had to be disguised under this category, as we shall see. The 1916 records for Katsina show that 59.5 percent of women issued certificates in the courts were destined to "marry," while in Kano Emirate, at least 52.7 percent of women were given certificates for the same reason. By 1920–1921, the percentage of women in Kano Province who were "freed to marry" had declined to 16.6 percent, while the proportion of women who were recognized as redeeming themselves had risen to 62.0 percent, which indicates the extent to which the courts were responding to the necessity of disguising the acquisition of concubines through the courts. Within a few years, the courts would no longer be used for this purpose at all.

Concubinage and the status of servile women

As we discussed in Chapter 4, the colonial government deferred to the sensibilities of male-dominated Muslim society on the issue of slave women. Concubinage was allowed to continue; indeed concubinage was considered a form of marriage, and consequently the Islamic courts were allowed to sanction the transfer of women for purposes of concubinage under the guise of emancipation. Colonial officials accepted the fact that concubines who gave birth would become free on the death of their masters, and their children would have been free even without the proclamation that declared all children born after March 31, 1901 to be free. Indeed, as far as many officials were concerned, concubines were "practically free" upon "marriage," and there was no reason to interfere with this method of gradual emancipation. Because concubinage automatically led to emancipation, its continuation was consistent with a policy that waited for the "natural death" that was expected of slavery.

Many officials even excused the practice, which in fact was convenient in maintaining the loyalty of the aristocracy. Jumare is certainly correct in noting that the colonial regime was "reluctant" to eliminate concubinage "because it was mainly the members of the ruling class who were involved in keeping concubines."[2] Arnett, who had experience as Resident of Zaria, Kano, and Sokoto and became Acting Lt.-Governor twice between 1921 and 1923, believed that "the status of concubinage is of long standing and a comparatively honourable one, and the Moslem law does not permit a man to enter into concubinage with a free woman."

> The reason for the status of concubinage is rather the social one in the narrower sense, that the woman is of lower social standing than the man. The Fillani especially desires women of Hausa or pagan tribes to be the mothers of his children because the women of his own race and standing are so frequently sterile or mothers of weakly children.[3]

In 1918, he predicted that "within a few years marriage will be the only possible form of union except for those who are content to live in conditions which their religion condemns as sinful (zinna)."[4] Lt.-Governor Goldsmith, who had earlier served in Bida and Sokoto, agreed; in a marginal note he made it clear that the review of slavery policy in 1918 "did not intend ... to touch in any way on the advantages or otherwise of concubinage but solely to deal with [the] Slavery aspect."[5] G. S. Browne, who served in a variety of important secretariat positions between 1906 and 1930, even thought that "concubines in the majority of cases improve their condition by entering the ransomer's house and are no more slaves than is a mistress of a man living in a European community."[6]

There were problems of regulation, however. The difficulty with concubinage was that the women *were* slaves and did not enter into arrangements of concubinage of their own accord. Women who were already concubines at the time of the conquest continued in slavery as all other slaves did. They were already "protected" by Islamic legal tradition and customary practice, and they had recourse to the Islamic courts if abused. Masters who owned female slaves born before March 31, 1901 had access to a reservoir of women that could be drawn on for their own sexual desires. Masters could not sell these women to other men any more than they could have sold any other slave. The methods of transferring women through the courts by-passed this problem of slave dealing. As we have demonstrated, women could be redeemed through the Islamic courts by men who intended to "marry" them. The courts were careful to distinguish between women who were already slaves, who could be transferred if a third party agreed to redeem them, and new captives whose sale was illegal. The Provincial courts assumed responsibility for guaranteeing that the slave trade remained abolished, although as we will examine below, there was a clandestine trade in children that was difficult to suppress. As each year passed, the number of eligible females who could be pressed into concubinage should have decreased. By 1914, there were no longer any slave girls under age thirteen, and by 1920, all teenagers had been born after March 31, 1901. The source of concubines should have dried up, but it did not.

As we have shown, the Islamic courts monitored the transfer of many women for purposes of concubinage. We have observed that 64 percent of the slavery cases before the courts in the first two decades of colonial rule involved women. A high proportion, from 25 to 50 percent of these women, were destined for marriage or concubinage. For a variety of reasons, the methods of classifying the redemption of females disguised the extent of concubinage and the ways in which the courts were used to maintain the supply of desirable females. We suspect that the majority of slave women not freed by relatives were destined for concubinage. The evidence, examined below, seems overwhelming, but we are still left with the classification system of the colonial regime, which has to be deciphered.

We know that 44,800 females were issued certificates of freedom from 1901 to 1919. The number who were destined for marriage or concubinage is not clear. At the low end, there were at least 11,200, but it is likely that the number was at least as high as 22,400. Because unrelated males provided the money to redeem many women who were recorded as having "redeemed themselves," the number may have been as high as 70–75 percent of the total number of cases involving women, that is, 30,000 women or more. Certainly the number of women "freed to marry" was always higher than the returns suggest. The courts were an instrument for the transfer of women among the males who could afford to maintain concubines as long as there was access to eligible females. In fact the returns are a conservative estimate of the extent to which concubinage continued, because there were other sources of females.

The Islamic courts sanctioned the transfer of women by issuing certificates of freedom that clearly allowed for concubinage. As Gowers reported from Kano in 1912, "the great majority" of female slaves were ransomed by their "prospective husbands."[7] This revelation led to an investigation of court ransoms, the results of which were reported the following year. Withers Gill was assigned the investigation, and he discovered that there were

> attempts at an ingenious evasion of the slavery law in the Courts of some of the District Alkalis ... to some extent the paper of ransom – "pansa" [fansa] – for freedom, which the fundamental law alone countenances, has been replaced by the paper of ransom for concubinage, which is legal under the Muslim code. By means of this an illegal transfer of slaves becomes possible and manumission is discouraged.[8]

In Yola, as well, the Islamic courts substituted "for the proper freedom paper (pansa) a paper of 'ransom for concubinage,' thereby perpetuating the state of slavery of the woman, and assisting in the purchase of a slave."[9]

Other officials observed the problem as well. In 1914, J. M. Fremantle suspected that "the line between redemption especially for marriage, and purchase may be very thin."[10] In 1920, Palmer was more certain: "99% of 'slave' cases in which either technically or essentially the action of Alkalai is open to question, are cases where a woman or girl of marriageable age ... is involved."[11] There were problems whenever "the immediate and patent motive of the 'ransoming' [of women] was for purposes of sexual cohabitation."

There were two kinds of ransom for women, one for concubinage and one for marriage. The two methods were not distinguished in the court returns.[12] As Arnett noted in 1918,

> By what amounts to a legal fiction the practice of the Native Courts has permitted women to be ransomed and freed and yet to enter the household of the ransomer in the position of concubines.[13]

Arnett later admitted to M. Delafosse, France's representative to the Temporary Commission on Slavery at the League of Nations, that this "legal fiction" enabled the Islamic courts to register the "ransoms of slave girls with a view to concubinage, as if these ransoms conferred full instead of partial emancipation."[14] Palmer interpreted this "partial emancipation" as "concubinage with deferred freedom, i.e. freedom on the death of the master (husband)."[15]

Whatever their reasons, British officials accepted the legality of concubinage. It is perhaps more surprising that they allowed court-supervised transfers of women for that purposes, but as Palmer observed,

Political Officers were from the earliest days faced with the difficulty of what to do with young female slaves of marriageable age. They took in most Provinces what seemed to them the best course – they handed such girls over to the Alkalai or other persons as wards for *"marriage"* and insisted on their being ostensibly "freed" by the Alkalai.[16]

In most cases, however, the *alkalai* and other guardians of slave girls did not seek out husbands but instead facilitated their entry into harems. Because of the slave status of these girls, "a native of the upper classes would be willing to receive them as concubines but not as legal wives." Palmer fully understood that "concubinage in this sense means 'slavery' (slave status) in Moslem Law ... for no Moslem can legally cohabit with any woman except (a) His legal wife or (b) His slave in the full and proper sense of the term."

The Islamic courts therefore issued certificates of freedom "in contemplation of concubinage, in which case the certificate of freedom was an obvious lie or fiction from the point of view of Moslem Law." According to Arnett in 1918,

> Whether a woman is ransomed for marriage or for concubinage the procedure before the Court is the same in that the money is paid to the master and the woman is handed her certificate of freedom. The difference lies in the declaration of the ransomer. In the one case he says "Na pansa bauya, ta zama diya" (I ransom the slave woman, she becomes free). In that case marriage will follow. In the other case he says, "Na pansa bauya, na sa ta daka" (I ransom the slave woman, I set her in my house). By a legal fiction although she has been certified as free, the effect of the emancipation is held in suspense as long as she remains a member of that man's household.[17]

Hence the actual position with regard to women slaves with a view to marriage was not quite what the official policy stated, although Palmer expressed his opinion that "the spirit of His Excellency's policy has been fully carried out."[18] Technically, according to Arnett, no man should be permitted to ransom a girl unless he "is willing to declare her his wife" in order to prevent a girl from being forced into "unwilling concubinage with a man she may fear and loathe."[19]

Even when certificates of freedom were provided to women so that they could marry their redeemers, there was no mechanism to determine whether or not the women actually did marry. As Palmer noted, "The suitor might of course change his mind – in which case the so called 'enslaving' was not the act of the Alkali,"[20] Hence the Islamic courts might allow the transfer of slave women as concubines, but it was beyond their jurisdiction to monitor such transfers. They could choose to accept testimony that women were actually being freed so that they could marry because it was not the court's responsibility to determine whether or not marriage actually took place. As Palmer admitted, "we have knowingly allowed the Alkalai to pursue these two courses to settle our difficulties for many years."

The Islamic courts also allowed men to reclaim the purchase price should a woman leave her "redeemer." As Arnett noted in 1913, "the tendency of

The persistence of concubinage

Native Courts to permit a transfer on *repayment* of the ransom has been well known for a long time and certainly existed – and perhaps still exists in Sokoto."[21] As A. Holdsworth Groom observed in 1917, "A has a female slave, B ransoms her for £3 and C is made to pay and so ad infinitum, the woman meanwhile being treated as a concubine and not allowed the full privileges of a wife."[22] After studying the legality of these transfers, Palmer concluded that customary law allowed the recovery of costs associated with both marriage and concubinage. Men who acquired rights over women as concubines expected to be compensated if they lost control of their women, just as they recovered the marriage payment should their wives divorce them.

> When one man takes over a woman for another he repays the first husband what the latter has spent in acquiring her. This has nothing to do with Moslem Law – it is a survival of Hausa custom, and a system of marriage by bride price ("mahr") paid to the relatives, as opposed to Sadaki (dowry to the woman herself). In theory of course the Muhammadan Law substituted "sadaki" for "mahr," but in practice "mahr" is still paid in the great bulk of cases, and Alkalai are bound to deal with it on customary lines. It is however the "decay" of the payment of a *substantial* "mahr" consequent on the frequent impossibility of recovering the sum paid, if the woman leaves her husband, which is responsible for the growing tendency to weaken the marriage tie in certain provinces.[23]

Men were willing to pay for the sexual rights in women, but they wanted a refund if they lost control. Palmer thought that this "most pertinacious and universal custom" should be allowed to continue. Fremantle was not so sure; he thought the identification of *fansa* with *sadaki* (marriage payment) "a rather transparent subterfuge."[24]

For the first decade or more of colonial rule, however, the British regime did little to prevent men from claiming compensation for lost women. No one seemed to have realized that there was an issue. Lugard thought that the money given to women for their redemption constituted the marriage payment (see Chapter 4), and apparently he did not envision situations in which women might leave their redeemers. By 1913, however, colonial officials began to realize that the repayment of the ransom money constituted a financial transaction that came very close to being slave trading. Lugard, back in Nigeria as Governor, agreed that the issue had to be clarified.[25] Once women became more active in changing partners, men turned to the courts to redress their financial claims. As a result, the issue of compensation for concubines who absconded assumed more immediacy.

The problem centered on whether or not both the ransom price (*fansa*) and marriage payment (*sadaki*) could be reclaimed if a woman who had been freed for marriage or transferred for purposes of concubinage subsequently left her redeemer. In Kano, the Islamic courts required that a man pay compensation for a slave woman who had been freed by another man because it was considered "inequitable" that the redeemer "should have no redress." The courts refused to allow a man to retain the woman unless he is prepared to repay the £5 which [the redeemer] paid her in the expectation that she would remain with him. The transaction then acquires the aspect of a transfer of the woman for value. It is wrong in strict Moslem law but it does appear to be equitable, though it cannot be sanctioned in view of our law.[26]

According to Arnett, "The Native Courts have, however, always been inclined to strain the letter of the law," even though the further transfer of a woman was not "oppressive" because she was "a free agent."[27] Nonetheless, it was "necessary frequently to impress on Alkalai that the ransom paid for a female slave, whom the ransomer frees with a view to her becoming his wife or concubine is strictly speaking paid for no legal consideration at all."[28]

In September 1914, Lt.-Governor Temple, in response to the confusion over whether or not *fansa* and *sadaki* were distinct, issued instructions that ransom (*fansa*) could not be used to pay the marriage payment (*sadaki*) of a woman being emancipated for marriage, and therefore could not be recovered if a concubine or a wife who had been issued a certificate of freedom subsequently left her redeemer. Temple ruled that

> Ransom paid for a female slave whom the ransomer frees with a view to her becoming his wife or concubine ... is not "Sadaki" (dowry) paid in consideration of marriage because it is paid to enable the woman to be freed. Sadaki can be reclaimed from a man for whom a wife leaves her husband but money paid for ransom cannot be so recovered. If A pays say £5 to a woman B to ransom herself from her master C and she marries A and subsequently deserts him to live with D, A will receive no refund, other than "sadaki," and any man may marry her.[29]

Relatively speaking, the amount of ransom, usually £5–8, was considerably more than the *sadaki*, which was often only a few shillings. This ruling confirmed what men feared: the acquisition of a concubine or wife through the courts involved considerable financial risk.

As Sciortino reported from Nassarawa, the "Moslem courts were notified as to His Excellency's ruling re the distinction to be observed between 'Pansa' [*fansa*] (Ransom) and 'Sadaka' [*sadaki*] (Dowry) when dealing with matrimonial cases where women desire divorce from husbands who have purchased or given them their freedom."[30] Kontagora quickly fell in line as well. The question of redemption for purposes of "marriage" had cropped up on several occasions, and Resident Hamilton Moore dutifully ruled that "'Pansa' [*fansa*] under these conditions, is not recoverable in the event of the wife leaving her husband, and that it must not be regarded as forming any position of 'Sadaki,'"[31] Fremantle still worried "that unless close supervision be exercised, or the abuse stamped out at once if so possible, there exists a tendency to combine or confound ransom-money with the marriage portion."[32] Nonetheless, by 1918, the Sokoto courts were "emphatic" in maintaining that the redeemer could not recover ransom money from a woman whom he had freed or from a future husband of the woman and "that any claim to treat this ransom money as sadaki is illegal."[33] Customary compensation for expenses incurred in marrying a woman no longer extended to the recovery of the redemption price.[34]

Ransoming of women classified as self-redemption

One method of making sure that the ransom money was not confused with *sadaki* was to record all cases in which women were being redeemed as cases of self-redemption. According to this approach, it was no concern of the Islamic court, or indeed the colonial state, how a woman obtained the money for her redemption or what happened to the woman after she was issued a certificate of freedom. She was a free woman, and the responsibility of the courts ended with her emancipation. Two provinces, Muri and Yola, stand out in particular because of the efforts of colonial officials there to implement this approach.

In the Muri courts, at least, the men who were paying the ransom were not allowed in court, which emphasized the fact that women were securing their own redemption, no matter what the source of the ransom.[35] Fremantle argued that redemption and marriage should "be kept rigidly separate."

> The Alkali need have no cognisance of how the woman has obtained her ransom money which should be paid by her to him and handed by him in Court to her master. If her intending husband has paid the money he should not be present in Court. The Alkali must give the woman a certificate of freedom and, if she has a slave name, should re-name her in Court. If after marriage the woman deserts or wishes to leave her husband the latter can claim the sadaiki [*sadaki*] but not a penny of the ransom money. To preserve effective control I think it is necessary to be very strict on these points.[36]

This approach had the advantage of disguising the source of ransom and the destination of the women receiving the certificates of freedom, but it did not change the practice of third-party ransoming for purposes of concubinage. Nonetheless, this procedure explains why the court records do not always show returns for "ransomed to marry" and "ransomed by intending husband" and have higher totals for "self-redemption" and "ransomed to follow her own inclinations" when in fact men were paying the ransoms.

Fremantle and his assistant, Groom, began to enforce their restrictions on court redemptions in Muri Province in 1915 after they uncovered "all sorts of ingenious devices, sometimes by open, sometimes by secret means, to circumvent the Slavery Law," including the "confusion, accidental or deliberate, between dowry-money (sadaiki) [*sadaki*] and ransom (pansa) [*fansa*]."[37] The *alkali* of Wukari, along with his scribe, was removed from office, and their court abolished. In Muri Emirate the Islamic courts in the districts were no longer allowed "to touch any cases dealing with the ransom of slaves." All cases involving slavery had to be heard in a new Islamic court in Muri itself, where the colonial office could monitor them.[38] After reviewing the evidence, Temple informed Fremantle that he had been "well advised to do this."[39]

244

The returns for Muri, where "the great majority of slaves ransomed are women," show the results of these tighter restrictions.[40] There were sixty-nine cases in 1917; twenty-four were classified as self-redemption, while fifteen were "freed by order of the Native Court." In 1918, twenty-eight of thirty-four cases were "self-redemption," the others by order of the Islamic court, while in 1919, twenty-two of thirty-four were cases of "self-redemption." Other cases were heard in the Provincial court and involved the freeing of children seized from slave traders.[41] As these returns demonstrate, Fremantle's action to control "the abuse of redemption in the Native Courts has resulted in a great reduction of the number of slaves so freed"; indeed the "Alkali has refrained from dealing with cases of redemption for marriage without specific instructions."[42] In 1917, however, Fremantle and Groom were out of line with existing policy, which would not change for several more years. Fremantle was warned that "control has been carried too far."[43] In any event official intervention stopped the Muri courts from active involvement in the transfer of women, and the number of slavery cases in Muri continued to decline.

The Yola courts also stopped recognizing third-party redemptions by males. Instead women were listed as having redeemed themselves. When Webster submitted the slave returns for 1916, he noted that most slave cases in the Islamic court related to "marriage."

> The women are always clearly given to understand that they are free and that they can at any time claim a divorce. They take the redemption money to the court themselves and should they repudiate the marriage contract whether before or after consummation no claim for return of the money for redemption is entertained. This is treated as a free gift to the woman by the prospective bridegroom. The woman receives a certificate of freedom and is entered on both Native Court and Provincial Registers.[44]

Thereafter the Yola courts were no longer registering ransoms by "intending husbands," although one case slipped through in 1917.

As in Muri, the Resident of Yola was directly involved in these cases. According to Webster, the woman appeared before the court with the money which she handed to her master.

> The late slave then receives her certificate of freedom and is sent up to the Resident for his counter signature, and there the responsibility of the court ends, unless there should be any question as to her freedom. No claim for money thus advanced by the intending husband is entertained should the woman divorce him. The Emir and the Alkali were both of opinion that unless this line was taken it would be impossible to check slave dealing under guise of marriage. The women would consider themselves sold.[45]

In short, Webster had to approve every case of redemption. In 1917, there were eighty-one self-redemption cases (out of a total of ninety-five cases), of which at least fifty-six appear to have been women being transferred for purposes of concubinage or otherwise being married. In 1918 and 1919 there was a similar pattern, and we assume that most cases of self-redemption were in fact situations in which unrelated males were paying the ransom. Returns for 1918 show forty-three of fifty-two slaves listed as redeeming themselves; in 1919 seventy-five out of ninety-eight slaves were similarly listed. Approximately 70 per cent of these cases involved women.[46]

The Islamic courts in Sokoto, Kano, Bauchi, Nassarawa, and Kontagora still recognized the category "ransomed by intending husband" in 1917, and in 1918 the Zaria returns did so as well. In 1919, the returns for Nupe also show this category, so that only Yola, Muri, and Ilorin did not recognize such cases in these years, and it seems that Nupe and Zaria sometimes did and sometimes did not. Even where this category remained, the trend was towards listing women being "freed" by unrelated males for purposes of concubinage and marriage as cases of self-redemption; Yola and Muri set the trend. And as we note in the Appendix, slavery cases were kept away from the courts in Ilorin, and hence there was no need to redefine categories there.

The distinction between *fansa* and *sadaki* may have lowered the price of redemption for women destined for concubinage, but it probably did not lower the total costs involved. In most cases, ransom prices hovered between £5 and £7, but in Kano the price had fallen to just over £3 by 1918. According to Brooke, who investigated procedures in the Wudil court in Kano Emirate,

> The procedure regarding the ransoming of slaves is clearly understood [in the Wudil Islamic Court]; the ransom however has become a fixed sum of £3:1:6, due to the fact, I believe, that the Emir fixed the maximum for the ransom of female slaves at this sum.[47]

In short, if the distinction between *fansa* and *sadaki* had to be maintained and males could not recover their financial commitment towards the acquisition of women, then the amount of non-recoverable *fansa* could be lowered and the amount of recoverable *sadaki* greatly increased.

According to Mahmudu K'ok'i, if a "man had the money, and saw a young slave girl, he would offer to buy her, maybe [for] twenty pounds," after which the two would "marry before an alkali" at the going rate of £8. After the *alkali* noted the payment, the "marriage" would be duly recognized. As Mahmudu blithely observed, "A lot of women became concubines in this way."[48] The contradiction between Mahmudu's testimony and Brooke's account demonstrates that the amount of the marriage payment and the ransom were being manipulated. Arnett claimed that the *sadaki* had always been a small amount, "by custom only a few shillings," and hence it was highly likely that a slave woman could use the *sadaki* for her self-redemption; the *sadaki* "would go a very little way towards ransom."[49] Arnett apparently did not realize that the ransom had been lowered and the *sadaki* increased in many transactions.

Resistance to the perpetuation of the servile status of women

The unfortunate women who were caught in the struggle between the Muslim establishment and the colonial regime over their fate had few options at their disposal. Women could acquiesce and accept concubinage, which perpetuated their slave status. Many clearly did, whether or not there was temporary resistance. After all, as Arnett claimed, women "frequently prefer to be concubines in rich men's harems rather than wives of poor freemen." Arnett's comment overlooks the coercion underlining slavery, and indeed the extent to which wives were subject to coercion from their husbands. Nonetheless, there certainly were slave women who cherished material possessions and wanted their children to have opportunities.[50] We cannot fault the decision, however unconscious, of these women, but it is important to point out that their response was not unusual for oppressed persons, and the extent to which women acquiesced did depend upon coercion and the implementation and/or threat of physical punishment.

Slave women faced sale, referred to euphemistically as "transfer," if their masters did not want them or if money was a problem. Some were turned out of their homes because they miscarried or otherwise did not please their masters. and if they left their "redeemers" for another man, as we have already examined, they had to be paid for again. Slave owners pushed girls into relationships that not only perpetuated subordination to males but maintained slavery as an institution. Slave parents had little influence on the fate of their daughters because they did not possess the right of guardianship; indeed from a parental perspective, it might even have seemed better to put a daughter into the harem of an official than to let her marry a local boy, also of slave descent. Whether or not parents thought concubinage was desirable, they were often under pressure to provide their daughters to their masters. As slaves themselves, they had no customary rights over their children anyway. Legal-status abolition aside, women continued to experience slavery, not as a legacy but as a reality.

Despite their handicaps as slaves and as females, women resisted in a variety of ways. Concubines continued to run away, as they had during the early years of colonial rule. In 1913–14, the Kano Judicial Council heard a number of cases involving fugitive women, who in most cases were returned to their masters.[51] Hamman Yaji, the Emir of Madagali, recorded six instances in which his own or one of his son's concubines escaped between 1921 and 1927.[52] The Emir's anger was stirred on one occasion because one slave "refused to cook me my food, and gave as her excuse that she had no water." On another occasion he reported that three of his concubines, Ni'ma, Dadiya, and Koita, "came shrieking out against me saying that they did not get enough to eat and that they could not give birth to any children."[53] Khalid, a concubine in Kano Emirate, refused to stay with her master because "she did not like him." Her master complained to the Emir's Judicial Council, which referred the case to the Resident.[54]

Some instances of friction between slave women and their masters are not explained in the court records, but nonetheless it is clear that there were problems. One Kano concubine was forced to leave the house of her master, and when he refused to let her marry another man, the Emir freed her.[55] Finally, one master let his slave woman marry and live with her husband, but when she refused to work for her master, the Emir rebuked the husband. Emir Abbas told the master that if the husband prevented the woman from working, he should go to the Islamic court and have the couple divorced, whereupon the woman would have to return to the master's house so that he could "make her work."[56]

As Arnett reported from Sokoto in 1918, "it frequently occurs that a man who ransoms a slave girl with a view to marriage or concubinage, treats her harshly or as a slave and the girl then complains or returns to her home."[57] Finding another man was one technique that was common enough to become a legal problem for the colonial regime, as we have observed. Men wanted recourse to the courts, if necessary, in recovering their women or their money. As we have noted, Palmer tried to explain the tradition behind this resort to the legal system, but in fact his explanation was not historical. There was no tradition whereby someone who redeemed a woman who subsequently left could expect compensation for his loss. Under the Caliphate, custom dictated that concubines who ran away were sold, if they were caught. If a man received a fugitive concubine, he had to be willing to pay the price. This was not a question of a marriage payment, as Palmer argued; it was a question of slavery. Under colonialism, Palmer, at least, was convinced that custom now covered the difficulties associated with women who failed to honor the obligations that men expected in financing their redemption. But this had not been "customary" before the British occupation.

Because a male perspective dominates the available data, it is difficult to assess what women tried to do and how successful they were in achieving their aims. Nonetheless, there are occasional glimpses into the resistance of some women to the changing nature of concubinage and slavery. For example, sometime before 1913, the Emir of Zaria informed Arnett that there were "a number of women in the town who had debts on their heads" because they had left the men who had redeemed them, and as a result "no man would marry them." Inquiries revealed that "in every case the woman's reply had been that although nominally freed by [a man] he had treated her as a slave and she had therefore left him." It must have been difficult for the women, since other men refused to marry them because of the necessity of refunding the ransom. Nonetheless, there may have been some solace in embarrassing a redeemer who everyone knew had not been "careful to treat the woman well so that she would not leave him."[58] The nature and the amount of the "debts" these estranged women "owed" is not explained, but it seems reasonable to assume that it included both ransom and *sadaki*.

Some slave women were accused of taking advantage of the demand for concubines. Arnett even suggested that concubines in Sokoto were actually "freer" than wives.

> The most curious result ... is that the woman so ransomed for concubinage is actually freer than the woman ransomed and married as a wife. The matrimonial

248

law undoubtedly gives the wife great freedom and facility for divorce, but nevertheless if a woman desires a divorce she must either show good cause or else repay the dowry into Court. But in the case of the concubine there is no tie of any sort. She leaves the man at her will as a free woman and she may at once marry whom she likes. Cases have occurred of *girls* inducing rich men to ransom them as concubines in order that they may immediately leave them and go and marry some one else. The man who has paid the ransom money has no redress and the Court contents itself with reprimanding the *girl's* dishonesty. It is obvious that under such circumstances the ransom for concubinage will not take place unless the woman really desires it or has led the man to suppose that she will be a contented inmate of his household. It is also certain that the man will treat the woman fairly or else very quickly lose her and his money.[59]

Arnett's reference to "girls" in 1918 stretches the credibility of his report, since anyone seventeen or younger was born free. It is difficult to tell if Arnett's male bias is attributing motives to girls who may have been leaving men because they did not want to be their concubines and knew that legally they could not be stopped. Whether or not they also collected some money in the process is hard to tell. Hidden behind Arnett's comments is circumstantial evidence that concubines did not always accept their status.[60]

Once the date of birth began to affect the supply of slave women who could become concubines, females and their parents turned to the Islamic courts to protect the rights of the freeborn. By 1913, when all girls under age twelve were technically free, there were already numerous disputes over age that came before the Kano Judicial Council. In one case, a man from Gwaram paid the redemption price of six cows and 140,000 cowries to the master of a girl in order to "marry" her, but the mother of the girl protested that her daughter was born in *zaman turawa*, the time of the Europeans, and hence could not be redeemed. The Council canceled the "redemption," and the daughter remained with her mother, who of course returned to her master's house.[61] In 1918, by which time girls under seventeen had been born free, Webster observed that

> the question of concubinage is ... becoming a pressing one. A Moslem cannot hold a free woman in concubinage. The supply of concubines thus ceased 18 [*sic*] years ago. This will cause great heart burnings and takes away the last benefit the Fulani has from his slaves.[62]

Webster was off by one year in his calculation, but his observation was still valid. There were fewer and fewer females who had been born into slavery.

In the intervening years, attempts to impress under-age girls into concubinage or otherwise make them work as slaves continued. Masters tried to pass off girls as older than they were. In Kano and Sokoto, there were even attempts to substitute the date of the British conquest (1903) for the March 31, 1901 date after which children were born free, even though it was clearly known that the correct date in the Muslim calendar was Zulhija 10, 1318.[63] Sometimes the Kano Judicial Council found in favor of masters, but when witnesses supported the contentions of the parents, children were declared free and given certificates as insurance.[64] As Webster noted in 1917, the lack of female slaves available for concubinage "is being got round by a certain amount of convenient mistakes in age or status on both sides, as the women are often anxious to get into the harem, but it will increase in importance year by year."[65] It should be noted that Webster emphasized the willingness to err on the part of girls eager to become concubines, because the freeborn daughters of slaves became the major source of concubines by 1920, as we shall see. Webster's report is more revealing for what it does not say: the only cases of error concerning the ages of girls that would have come to his attention were ones in which girls and their parents objected to concubinage. Otherwise there was no reason for Webster to be involved. Here as elsewhere, Webster's bias against females and slaves is evident.

The response of parents and teenagers themselves was to request certificates of freedom from the Islamic courts that verified their birth as free persons. As G. S. Browne noted in 1920,

> It is quite common for persons to ask to have the declaratory certificate when they realize they are free born and feel they are in danger of being treated as slaves. As Your Honour knows they are never satisfied with the certificate from a Political Officer, but do not really feel free until they have been before an Alkali.[66]

Palmer "frequently directed Alkalai to issue Certificates declaratory of the status of a person free under our Law owing to being born since 1901."[67]

In 1920, Webster reported a case from Sokoto that demonstrates the difficulties that parents faced in trying to protect their daughters from the pressure to force them into concubinage.

> A puzzled father came to me to ask what he could do. Two men wanted his daughter, one as a concubine and one as a wife. He took her to the Alkali to free her and the Alkali said he could not as she was born in our time. Obviously their master would not part with the girl for nothing. She was condemned to perpetual virginity or a life of vice? Enquiries showed this is a common state of affairs.[68]

As Christelow has demonstrated, the phrase "born in our time" (*zaman turawa*) refers to the Muslim legal rubric, legislation of our time (*hukm zamanna*), which referred to colonial legislation.[69] Once again parents wanted certificates of freedom in order to confirm the free status of their children. Palmer, at least, only issued certificates to persons born after 1901 "on the application of either the person to be 'free' or his or her parents, guardians or some other person in a fiduciary capacity."[70]

By 1921, other officials believed that the courts should no longer issue certificates of freedom to those born after 1901, and Attorney-General Donald Kingdom even claimed that "executive instructions have been issued to Native Tribunals to the effect that such certificates cannot be granted to persons born in or brought within the Northern Provinces after March 31 1901, but must be confined to the cases of persons who were slaves in the

Northern Provinces prior to that date."[71] Palmer, however, had "never heard of these instructions."[72] The importance of such certificates rapidly receded after 1921 anyway, because there was little room for mistaking the ages of females.

The provision of certificates of freedom to females as proof that they were born after 1901 appears to be reflected in the returns of the Islamic courts under the category "ransomed by relatives." Of 21,832 slaves freed through the courts between 1916 and 1921 whose destination is known, 12.2 percent (2,658) were freed by relatives. In 1916, 11.5 percent of court cases involved slaves redeemed by relatives; while in 1917, the percentage was 12.9 percent, in 1918, 11.5 per cent, 1919, 9.8 percent, and in 1920–21, 12.4 percent. While there is no direct evidence that the certificates of freedom given under this category were to protect females born after 1901, it seems certain that many, if not most, were. Only in 1916 is there a breakdown by gender, and in that year females constituted 53.1 percent of those ransomed by relatives. Hence by no means all slaves who were given certificates as a result of the intervention of relatives were females, but at least half seem to have been. There were also strong desires to protect male children from the payment of unnecessary ransom and *murgu* as well.

Concubinage and the free children of slaves

As the availability of slave women declined, men sought other sources of females for concubinage. By 1915 or so, masters were pressing the free daughters of their slaves into concubinage. The servile status of the parents was considered inheritable as far as the eligibility of girls for concubinage was concerned, even though the girls were technically born free. The acceptance of these girls as a proper source of concubines involved a legal innovation, since only slaves could become concubines under Islamic law. The Islamic courts now recognized that slave status for purposes of concubinage could be inherited, although the "condition" of slavery ceased to exist.

Many females thereby became concubines without the medium of the courts because their parents had not or could not easily protect their status. In popular opinion, according to information collected by Ibrahim Jumare, the offspring of slave parents continued to be considered servile: "their master can choose his concubine or *sadaka* from among their children."[73] The most vulnerable were girls on the estates of those officeholders and other slave owners who maintained rural slave establishments.[74]

In 1920, Webster thought that "the attitude of all classes towards slavery questions is most correct," except with respect to concubinage. Those men who could afford it still wanted concubines, only by 1920 "the pinch is ... being felt owing to the lack of fresh concubines."

> The temptation to parents to accept money for their daughters is very great and once in a big harem, though nominally able to get out at will, in practice they would never do so or only when discarded. I have also just received evidence

251

that children of slave parents are being treated as slaves by the masters of the latter.[75]

Hence it would be necessary to maintain "a close watch ... for the next few years." Webster was off in his assessment of how long concubinage would last, but his observations help establish when it became acceptable to recruit concubines from the freeborn girls of slave parents.

Some of these girls were being transferred through the courts under the guise of ransom as late as 1921, even though they were born free. While most political officers were opposed to the continuation of these transfers, they did not object to concubinage. As Browne admitted,

> there are undoubtedly hard cases, e.g. where a young girl born after 1901 is fraudulently ransomed to be put into the harem of an old leper *against her will*. She should receive the protection by other sections of the criminal code, and this would be a sufficient safeguard.[76]

Otherwise Browne did not think that there was very much wrong with the persistence of concubinage, "as long as the girl *wishes* to be a concubine or wife of the ransomer." As far as he was concerned, such cases did not involve "'enslaving' unless ... she is regarded merely as a manual labourer without marital rights." Even then, there was little that could be done to prevent the exploitation of a woman as a slave after she had been ransomed through the courts, because "it is hard to see how her subsequent treatment can be foretold."[77] By the end of 1922, Webster believed that the children of slave parents "must all know they were free," and consequently there was no longer any reason for colonial officials to be involved, "unless appealed to."[78] The usefulness of the Islamic courts as a mechanism for the transfer of females for purposes of concubinage was drawing to an end.

Nonetheless, "girls of slave parentage born since 1901" were still being pressed into concubinage, although the Sultan of Sokoto insisted that girls appear "before a court or someone of standing and ... a report [be] made." For the first time, the transaction leading to concubinage could be monitored by "someone of standing" outside the courts. In the words of the Sultan, this measure was adopted in order "to be sure that they are not lost in some big house against their will, to the detriment of their liberty and infraction of the Koranic law."[79] Soon, such cases would not be referred to the courts.

An important dimension of the concubinage issue related to the right of guardianship (*wali*) over female slaves and the female offspring of slaves. It is clear that masters continued to claim this right, even over the daughters of their slaves who were born after 1901. When girls stayed with their parents, it was relatively easy for masters to maintain the right of *wali*. The problem, to which the Sultan of Sokoto appears to have addressed himself, was how to supervise other females. As Palmer reported in 1921,

> The proper person to be Wali (guardian) of all and sundry women or girls of servile origin who float about the country looking for husbands, is not an Alkali, but either an Emir, District Head or other tribal Head or Chief. These

252

are the men who should give in marriage where no parents are available, and on whose shoulders should fall the punishment if marriage or other sexual relations by purchase or compensation, an idea which runs all through Native Law and Custom and is too deeply rooted to eradicate, is used as a cloak to slave-trading transactions.[80]

As Christelow has demonstrated in his examination of the Kano Judiciary Council records, the right of *wali* over slave girls was a long-standing issue in Kano.[81] In one case, the Judicial Council made it clear that the man who redeemed a slave woman retained guardianship should she marry someone else.[82] In another case, the principle was upheld that masters even retained guardianship over freeborn children; a master had the rights to "service" as long as he was recognized as the guardian of the child's father "and others of your slaves."[83]

By 1924, the practice of pressing freeborn girls into concubinage was well established, so much so that Arnett was candid in response to an inquiry from the League of Nations. He informed the League's Temporary Committee on Slavery, that many women "prefer to continue in the category of slaves rather than of free persons," particularly "the daughters of domestic and other slaves [who] frequently prefer to be concubines." Arnett admitted that "many thousands of girls have been ... ransomed who were in fact born free under the Nigerian Ordinance," which he blamed on "the connivance of their parents."[84] Concubinage was still widely practiced over two decades after the imposition of colonial rule, although Arnett predicted its demise. He anticipated that concubinage would continue to "operate for a certain limited number of years."[85]

The ending of court involvement in concubinage

The colonial regime had no intention of allowing the Islamic courts to continue to oversee the transfer of concubines once the legal source of girls no longer existed. Each year, there were fewer female *slaves* available for concubinage, since girls born after 1901 were supposed to be free. It was one matter to allow slave girls to be transferred through the courts under the fiction that they were being emancipated; it was quite another matter to allow the courts to transfer girls who did not need certificates of freedom. The crisis in policy hit in 1920–21, when the youngest slaves were already nineteen to twenty. Considering Muslim sexual practices, most females had married or become concubines by the age of fourteen to fifteen, and there were few females who had not given birth by the age of nineteen, let alone maintained their virginity. The crisis in policy, therefore, was not the result of unclear thinking but because those who were born free or otherwise were technically free were still being treated as slaves in 1920–21.

One of the reasons why Palmer wanted a tighter policy on the issuance of certificates of freedom was that it would make sure that there was a "voluntary" dimension to freeborn girls becoming concubines. By 1921, in his opinion, the Islamic courts should no longer be involved in cases of concubinage anyway. He thought that "the parents of all girls of the servile class of marriageable age [should] be in a position to make their own terms with suitors." There was no reason for an *alkali* to "be responsible for the nature of the sexual relation entered into."

> If the "parents" like to take "bride price" (mahr) from the suitor and to call the relation "concubinage" or "amre" in its loose sense, as was done in a recent case at Sokoto, I do not see that Government is called on to interfere, or that we are bound to vindicate the letter of the Moslem Law.[86]

Concubinage involving girls of servile origin could continue, as far as Palmer was concerned, but any payments thereby made would no longer be considered ransom but "brideprice."

As already noted, the instructions of the Sultan of Sokoto that girls being pressed into concubinage could appear before an official to ensure that they were not becoming concubines "against their will" was an attempt to shift the responsibility for monitoring concubinage away from the courts. When a girl was the child of slaves of the man who wanted her, these appearances before officials, if and when they actually occurred, were perfunctory, but when a man wanted a girl whose parents belonged to someone else, it was difficult to detect when a financial transaction amounting to purchase actually took place. It is not clear if the Sultan intended to prevent cash transfers, except under the guise of "brideprice," or to provide a screen behind which the sale of concubines could continue. Some officials certainly considered that the transfer of concubines outside of the Islamic courts was now legitimate.

Colonial officials attempted to intercept this trade in concubines. In 1920, for example, the Sarkin Kabi of Jega was fined £10 "for attempting to ransom a free girl to make her his concubine." The girl was only fourteen, and besides the fine, the two men who had "removed her from the custody of her parents for that purpose were sentenced to six months each by the Alkalin Sokoto." The case was not isolated, for the *sarki* of Illo "also issued ransom papers for two virgin girls to be used as concubines."[87] The designation of these girls as "virgins" suggests that they were in their early teens and almost certainly indicates that they were younger than nineteen. Whatever the Sultan's intentions, the Sokoto courts had to punish these officials.

There was an increase in transactions outside of the courts in Kano as well. Mahmudu K'ok'i personally remembered that "trading in slaves, in concubines, went on in secret" as late as 1919 because his family was awarded custody of some girls who were freed by British officials. According to Mahmudu, "it was done under the pretence of free marriage."[88] Whereas previously girls were transferred through the courts, now they had to be bought from traders.[89]

In 1920, Emir Usuman of Kano proposed that matters relating to concubinage should remain out of the view of the Provincial courts. His approach differed from the way the Sultan handled matters, in that no official sanction would be required when girls of servile origin became concubines. Slave girls and female offspring of slave parents would be available for concubinage, whether or not they consented. The Emir drafted an ordinance that would have transferred the responsibility for preventing the slave trade from the Provincial courts to the Islamic courts, therby reinforcing the role of the Islamic courts in matters relating to concubinage. His draft rule No. IV stated that

1. Any Native born since the advent of the British Administration is born free.
2. Any Native who buys or sells a slave during the British Administration is guilty of an offence.
3. Any Native who ransoms any Native born since the British Administration or enslaves such Native is guilty of an offence. Any Native who commits any of the above offences is liable on conviction to imprisonment for a period not exceeding 5 years.
4. Any Native who ransoms a slave except before an Alkali is guilty of an offence. Any Native who commits this last offence is liable on conviction to imprisonment for 2 years.[90]

If the Emir's ordinance had been accepted, the payment of a high price for *sadaki* in order to obtain a girl for concubinage would have been legal, and any dispute as to whether the *sadaki* was ransom would have been decided in the Islamic courts, without reference to British officials.

At first, Lt.-Governor Goldsmith favored the Emir's initiative, although he would have substituted "person" for "Native" throughout.[91] But other officials were quick to point out that "slave dealing cases ought not to be tried before Native Courts."[92] The Provincial courts (i.e., the Residents) should retain the control over slavery matters. The Emir's proposal was dropped, and as G. F. L. Tomlinson pointed out, the more serious "question of preventing abuse of 'ransoming' is under consideration."[93]

The issue to which Tomlinson referred arose from the dismissal of the Alkalin Kano, Mohammadu Aminu, on charges of slave dealing in 1921. The charges against the chief *alkali* arose directly from a case involving the transfer of two women for purposes of concubinage. The case was complicated by the fact that one woman had been brought from the Cameroons, and hence was technically free on entering British Northern Nigeria. For the *alkali* and other officials as well, there was room for confusion, since the British had occupied German territory in 1916 and subsequently acquired control under a mandate from the League of Nations. The area in question had been part of the Sokoto Caliphate, furthermore, and it was logical enough for the *alkali* to ignore the relevance of the Cameroons origin of the woman. British officials thought otherwise, Mohammadu Aminu was dismissed, and criminal charges were laid against him. Two other cases, one involving the district *alkali* of Gwarzo, and the other the *galadima* of Zaria, came under consideration at the same time. When these cases are considered alongside the prosecution of officials in Sokoto, as noted above, it is apparent that the colonial regime had moved forward in redefining the full extent of legal-status abolition. The resolution of these cases, particularly that of the Alkalin Kano, put the Islamic courts out of commission with respect to concubinage.

British officials were concerned about the transfer of female slaves from the Cameroons as early as 1918. The Islamic court in Muri heard the case of a slave girl who wished to ransom herself in 1918. Her master had come from the Cameroons, but apparently as a result of Fremantle's orders,

> The Alkali refused to free her on the grounds that she was free already. But in her own eyes and in those of her friends she was not. In such a case I think the Alkali is not only right but wise. If ransom was once accepted it would be a dangerous precedent. It is a case where public opinion needs forming.[94]

The Alkalin Kano seems to have been unaware that this case had occurred, but he certainly must have known that British officials were arresting Kano slave traders dealing in slave women from the Cameroons. The activities of J. H. Carrow, Assistant District Officer after 1919, are credited in particular with ferreting out slave dealers.

According to Mahmudu K'ok'i, Karaye was a major center for the importation of females from the Cameroons, and it was not until Carrow's arrival in Kano in 1919 that the trade came to an end.

> Mr. Carrow would go right into the huts in their compounds where they were concealing slaves and fetch them out. And then the slave dealers were collected and told that they were to stop it. After that, the girls were divided among different households. We were given some. My father was allotted two and they became like members of our family.[95]

According to the records of Carrow's investigation in 1920, many slaves, particularly females, were being imported from the Cameroons.[96] Carrow provides data on forty slaves (twenty-three females and seventeen males), all brought from the Cameroons, who were liberated in Karaye town, Godiya, Igi, Bebeji, Gezo, Dal, Kaura, and Kofa. Most, if not all, of the females were destined to become concubines. Carrow's data raise other issues relating to the continuation of the slave trade, which we examine in the next section, but our concern here is with the change in policy with regard to the involvement of the Islamic courts in slavery cases.

Alkalin Mohamadu Aminu of Kano was removed from office on February 19, 1921 and was tried in the Provincial court on a charge of "aiding and abetting slave dealing" in issuing certificates of freedom to two slave women. In both cases the Mudi of Kano paid ransom "ostensibly" with the intention of marriage. One girl, Mairo, had been brought from Ngaundere in the Cameroons by Nana five years earlier and was "freed" for £8.[97] The other, Ilori, had been born in Garko, in Kano Emirate, and was freed for £13.[98] There had been other problems in the Kano court, but the "matter of real importance" involved the two women.

The Alkali himself gave the freedom papers, mentioning in the first case that the girl Mairo was born in Cameroons. Apart from other factors in the two cases, i.e. age of the girls, doubts as to the right of Nana and Haruna to dispose of them; the one glaring point stands out that the girl Mairo was brought into Nigerian territory 5 years ago, and ransomed as a slave. The law is thereby contravened.[99]

As a result, Mohammadu Aminu was sentenced to three years' imprisonment.

It was subsequently determined that the second slave, Ilori, had been born in Garko about 1899, and hence her ransom was legal. Her fate upon "emancipation" was unclear, but it is instructive that Hastings attempted to convict the *alkali* on the grounds of slave dealing in this case, too. He thought she was born after 1901 and wanted to make the point that such persons could not be transferred through the courts for purposes of concubinage.[100] In the parallel case of the Alkalin Gwarzo Mustapha, the conviction was based on exactly this point; the Alkalin Gwarzo was sentenced to three years "for permitting children born free, to be ransomed before him." Resident Hastings deplored the "culpability of Alkalai in their dealing with these ransom cases."[101] As far as Hastings was concerned,

> The trials of the Alkalis of Kano and Gworzo ... tend to show, how criminally careless to say the least of it, are many of the native judges, in failing to ascertain in cases of ransoming either that the persons concerned are lawfully free born, or brought from without the boundaries of Nigerian territory. Further it seems certain that the less reputable permit the traffic of others, under the guise of ransom for marriage or other purposes. It is hoped that the convictions of these two Alkalis, will have an effect upon others worthy of suspicion, and in addition, it will be made certain that all have knowledge, beyond any doubt, of the facts which constitute the offence.[102]

The judges were certainly careless, as Hastings charged, but higher officials thought it was excessive for the colonial state to allow the dismissal of the chief *alkali* of Kano merely because two concubines were transferred.

The matter became the subject of lengthy review of slavery policy. Palmer submitted a detailed defense of existing practice whereby the Islamic courts were allowed to transfer slaves for purposes of concubinage,[103] and while Tomlinson and other officials would not go as far as Palmer in upholding court-sponsored transfers, they were reluctant to see the two *alkalai* convicted for slave dealing.[104] In the end, Donald Kingdom, the attorney-general, overturned the conviction of the Alkalin Kano because the "granting of a certificate of freedom is the act of a Court – not the act of an individual person," and hence the *alkali* could not be punished. The Alkalin Gwarzo was granted a free pardon.[105]

On a technicality, therefore, both judges were set free, but they were not returned to their courts. Colonial policy had adjusted to the fact that there were no more female slaves who could be transferred through the courts for purposes of concubinage or "marriage." After 1921, some slaves still received certificates of freedom in the courts, but third-party ransoms for the purpose of concubinage were no longer valid. Since concubinage had been a major reason for court-sanctioned redemptions, it is not surprising that the number of "redemptions" declined drastically. For almost two decades, the Islamic courts had been a primary vehicle for the transfer of female slaves into concubinage, but after 1921, men had to find other ways of obtaining concubines.

"Fictitious Ransom," as Brown's circular of November 10, 1922 labeled the transfer of women through the Islamic courts, was illegal. Henceforth, the certificate of freedom was "merely a declaration of the status of the person in question and ... not an instrument which confers status either present or future." *Alkalai* could no longer be guardians to persons of servile status, nor could they be responsible for the marriages of such persons. In cases of individuals born before 1901, certificates could only be issued "on the application of either the person to be 'free' or his or her parents, guardians, or some other person in a fiduciary capacity." The court could require "a receipt from the master or mistress for 'pansa' [*fansa*] and proof of its authenticity" as evidence that the person being given a certificate was no longer a slave. Certificates could only be given to persons born after 1901 "if so directed by a Political Officer, when the question whether the man or woman concerned was or was not born after April 1901 has been in dispute, and has been investigated and determined by him."[106]

The persistence of concubinage, 1926–36

By the second half of the 1920s, most concubines were recruited from the children of servile families. Certainly, P. C. Butcher was correct when he pithily observed in 1931 that "there is not a virgin slave of age to be taken as a concubine in the country."[107] Instead a socially inferior class of former slaves and their descendants (the "children of the governor," *'ya 'yan gwamna*) emerged as the reservoir from which concubines could be drawn. As Webster observed from Adamawa in 1929,

> The old practice of concubinage dies hard, and men, women and children who owing to their age could by no possibility be treated as slaves are still brought up to consider themselves as such.[108]

Seven years later, the situation had not changed. According to G. Miles Clifford, "girls born of slave parents in the larger households have grown up with concubines as their almost certain destiny."[109] Clifford suspected that concubinage continued in all the emirates, although the recruitment of freeborn girls was "more likely in Provinces such as Adamawa where the female slaves were more usually of pagan origin who after years of severance from their own kith and kin would become virtually detribalised."[110] In 1936, Clifford believed that legislation would not eliminate concubinage, especially the recruitment of freeborn girls of servile origin. In his opinion, "the remedy would appear to lie rather in the building up of public opinion."

Some female slaves, although probably a decreasing number, were still available through the clandestine slave trade well into the 1930s. In 1926, Haman Joda was sentenced to two years' imprisonment in Muri in connection with the transfer of four slave girls who were thirteen to eighteen years old.[111] By 1929, Webster reported a few cases of trans-frontier enslaving in the Mubi area but claimed that "these are very few compared with the number that used to occur."[112] Pawning continued as well, and may have revived during the Depression of the 1930s (see Chapter 9). In Adamawa "certain rich men in the larger villages encourage pagans to deposit their children with them with the intention of later on making them their concubines." By 1929, however, these cases were treated as enslaving and severe punishments inflicted.

Futhermore, the Islamic courts in Yola, at least, no longer accepted cases involving the ransoming of slaves by 1929 because

> It merely led to enticing away of slaves from one master to another or to the practical enslavement through concubinage of a girl already free by law. The ransom was never paid by the person nominally applying for freedom but by the would-be acquirer of his or her services.[113]

This prohibition, which went beyond the instructions of 1921–22 to limit the transfer of women through the Islamic courts, was attributed to a decision of the Emir.

In 1931, an Advisory Council on Concubinage and Dowry was established to investigate the continuation of concubinage and the extent to which *sadaki* was being used to purchase girls of servile origin for purposes of concubinage.[114] The colonial government wanted to know "the trend of public opinion brought about by the changes introduced into the social system by the slavery policy introduced with our administration of the country."[115] Because children born after March 31, 1901 were free, technically there were no female slaves available for concubinage. As Butcher observed in his instructions to Residents,

> By the letter of the Moslem law, as interpreted in Nigeria as in other countries, a man can have only four legal wives but an unlimited number of slave concubines, though it may be held by authorities that only four wives or concubines may be maintained on legal status. It is perhaps possible that the custom of concubinage is dying out, but if not, it is difficult to see in what way the new social order will evolve.[116]

From a purely legal standpoint, a man who took a freeborn girl of servile origin as his concubine was living in "an extra-legal relationship," unless some "legal fiction" or "adjustment of the law" occurred. Butcher asked the Residents, "How then is the Moslem conscience moulding public opinion on this question?" Despite the inquiry of the Advisory Council on Concubinage and Dowry, concubinage did continue, indeed well into the 1980s, as Jumare has demonstrated.[117]

Conclusion

By the 1920s, slavery was not dead, despite repeated predictions of its early demise. The supposedly free daughters of slaves were becoming concubines, which meant that their status as the freeborn children of slaves was conveniently blurred. For all intents and purposes, they remained slaves, although it was increasingly difficult to transfer them from one owner to another. Furthermore, there was no reason to suppose that either the trade in children (see Chapter 9) or the impressment of free girls of servile origin into concubinage was about to end. The colonial regime was sporadic in its success in preventing enslavement and intercepting slave traders because pawning and kidnaping were difficult to eliminate. While the Islamic courts were no longer accessible to men wanting to transfer women for concubinage, there were sufficient numbers of girls of servile origin in the countryside and among young girls imported from non-Muslim areas to maintain the supply. It would take another ten years of continued pressure on the slave supply mechanism to reduce the flow of slaves to a trickle, and not until 1936 would the final measure in the abolition of the legal status of slavery be enacted. These last developments from the mid 1920s to 1936 are the subject of the volume's final chapter.

9

Legal-status abolition: the final phase

Many officials predicted that slavery would die a "natural death" as a result of the abolition of the legal status of slavery and the provision that children born after March 31, 1901 were free. There were repeated pronouncements that slavery was "virtually dead" or "no longer existed" beginning in the first decade of colonial rule and continuing almost annually for the next two decades. In 1924, G. S. Browne could claim that there had been "no disruption" caused by the Slavery Ordinance, and those slaves who had not taken "even more advantage . . . of the liberal terms of the Ordinance" had failed to do so

> not because the people of the Northern Provinces are not aware that they can ransom themselves at any time they so desire, but because in many cases, and especially in the cases of the elder people, they are unwilling to leave those families to which they are connected by long ties of mutual cooperation and trust.[1]

Browne insisted that slavery "is gradually dying out."

Yet a state akin to slavery persisted, as we have seen. Slaves remained on their masters' lands, sometimes tilling the soil under sharecropping arrangements and other times paying rent and *murgu*. Women remained in the harems of the wealthy, and the free daughters of slaves were pressed into concubinage. Even the slave trade persisted, with children filtering through the net of the anti-slavery patrols. The "natural death" that was frequently announced by the architects of legal-status abolition was slow and tortuous.

The final decade of legal-status abolition ended in 1936 with the enactment of Ordinance No. 19, which eliminated the clause that maintained the status of slavery for those individuals born before April 1, 1901. With Ordinance No. 19, "all persons born in or brought into Northern Nigeria" were free. It was no longer necessary for individuals to pay their ransoms or acquire certificates of freedom in the Islamic courts. Ordinance No. 19 was the last piece of legislation in the long history of legal-status abolition in Northern Nigeria.

This chapter examines the pressures brought to bear on Northern Nigeria by the League of Nations that resulted in tighter restrictions on slave trading and slavery in the late 1920s and ultimately led to the enactment of Ordinance No. 19 in 1936. Few scholars have noticed this law, but we would suggest that it was a significant watershed in the history of slavery. Thereafter, slavery truly had no legal status, and all slaves at least in theory were thereby emancipated without further compensation to their masters.

As in most societies in which slavery has been important, the legacy of slavery continued well after its final abolition, in this case 1936. Indeed illegal enslavement lasted through the 1980s, and people of slave origin continued to admit publicly to a slave status well into the 1970s. Nonetheless, we have chosen 1936 as the year to end our study, knowing that the legacy of slavery, and indeed the illegal continuation of slavery, are topics that require further study.

The clandestine slave trade

As Ubah has demonstrated, the clandestine slave trade through the emirates of Northern Nigeria was difficult to stop.[2] The trade continued for at least four decades, despite steady pressure from the colonial regime to end it. Ubah has divided the trade into three periods, the first from 1900 to 1908, the second lasting from 1909 to 1919, and the third covering the 1920s and 1930s. During the first phase, the colonial regime concentrated on closing the slave markets and overcoming resistance to its policies on slavery. As a result, the slave trade was driven underground, although its scale was considerably reduced from its precolonial level. In the second period, the area from which new slaves came was gradually restricted to Borno and the eastern emirates, particularly Yola, Muri, and Gombe. The effort to confine the trade was temporarily undermined during the First World War, when the volume of the trade appears to have increased. Most new slaves came from the former German territory of Kamerun. In the third period, efforts at suppression concentrated on the Mandated Territory of Cameroon, but despite greater cooperation from emirate officials and more police patrols, the trade continued for another two decades.

The clandestine trade was an understandable if unfortunate by-product of the policy to abolish the legal status of slavery. As we have seen, slavery continued to be a viable institution, despite colonial reforms that allowed many slaves to secure their freedom. In a situation in which large numbers of slaves still worked for their masters, it is not surprising that slaves were in demand, even though outright sale was now illegal. Because it was possible to disguise the transfer of slaves, most notably in the case of females for purposes of concubinage, there continued to be some movement of slaves through supposedly "legal" means. These transfers satisfied some of the demand for slaves, but by no means all. Furthermore, these transfers establish clearly that demand was sufficient to induce some merchants to risk trading in "raw slaves," to use the common expression of colonial officers.

Demand for new slaves was strong for three purposes. First and foremost, men wanted concubines in greater numbers than could be supplied by the transfer of women through the courts and by the recruitment of the free daughters of slave parents. Concubines were easy to hide because they were secluded and because there were "legitimate" sources of females for this purpose. Second, there was a steady demand for household servants of both sexes, and in the case of female servants there was the possibility of eventually pressing them into concubinage as well. As with concubines, domestic servants who were in fact slaves could be hidden from the colonial authorities with relative ease as long as the general attitude of the population tolerated their presence. Third, Fulani herdsmen wanted boys to tend their cattle and goats.[3] Once more, it was relatively easy to keep slave boys out of view, since herds wandered through the bush away from settled areas.

After the colonial conquest, "raw slaves" were primarily children who came from the non-Muslim populations that bordered the various emirates, especially Zaria, Bauchi, Gombe, Adamawa, and its many sub-emirates in German Kamerun and subsequently in the Mandated Territories shared between British Northern Nigeria and Afrique Equatoriale Française. "Child smuggling," as Lethem called it in 1911, was particularly prevalent along the Benue River.[4] Not only was the trade almost entirely in "small children," as Groom noted in 1917, but "the smaller the better, provided they have been weaned."[5] Children were easier to move, especially after some preliminary acculturation. The children were often held for a period of a year or more, during which time they were taught Hausa and otherwise acquired the appearance of Muslim children who would escape detection.

> They are made to look as much like Hausas as possible by dressing them in the Hausa fashion and even cutting Hausa marks on their faces. They are taught to speak Hausa, often with the aid of the whip, and have it carefully instilled into them by threats of dire punishment that they are to swear that their owners are their parents if questioned by anyone. It is surprising the control these Hausa Slave Traders have over the children. The natives say they give them medicine – I myself have seen a little pagan girl with a pierced upper lip and tattooed stomach and other pagan characteristics stoutly declare that an old Hausa man of about 60 years of age was her father.[6]

Sometimes children were fully acculturated and even resisted being returned to their parents. Vereker, at least, claimed as much in several cases that he investigated in the mountainous area of Northern Cameroon in 1927:

> Pagan parents appear and claim the return of a child stolen from them in infancy many years ago, before the British Administration appeared. These children are now growing up, they often do not recognise their parents, nor do they speak the Pagan dialect, and are quite happy with the Fulani people with whom they have lived happily for most of their lives. They stoutly refuse to return to their parents and prefer to proclaim their status as free persons and to remain with their so-called "masters" – who are often more like "foster-parents."[7]

Haughton noted that "kidnapped children are said to be given a drug which makes them forget their homes and relations," which probably refers to some kind of amulet or local medication with a stronger psychological than medicinal impact.[8]

Children tended to be of both sexes, although there was a preference among slave traders for females. Of the sixty slave children whom Laing freed at Zang in 1916, for example, the proportion of little girls to boys was four to one.[9] The boys were being trained to become "servants," while the girls were being prepared for "marriage" when old enough. Dupigny, reporting on four slave-dealing cases in Niger Province in 1917, noted that the "offenders had either sold or bought young pagan girls belonging to Bauchi Province."[10] A woman slave dealer apprehended in Nupe in 1919 had purchased six female children and one boy during a period of eighteen years.[11] Other data, however, demonstrate that boys were often as numerous as girls.[12]

Methods of enslavement

Children became slaves as a result of pawnship, kidnaping, and slave raiding – the very methods of enslavement that had operated before the imposition of colonial rule. Under colonialism, many children were enslaved through pawnship, perhaps even more so than previously. Pawnship showed no signs of disappearing well into the 1930s. Kidnaping only gradually subsided because it was difficult to prevent until local people themselves, with or without the assistance of local officials, refused to tolerate the seizure of children and women. Nonetheless, kidnaping was still common in the 1920s and occurred sporadically in the 1930s. Remarkable as it may seem, slave raiding continued in some areas of Adamawa under colonialism (see below). Organized slave raiding *should* have ended soon after the colonial conquest, but large-scale slave raiding was still being conducted as late as 1920; we have no evidence of raiding after that date. Because enslavement was illegal, it is impossible to assess the relative importance of these methods of enslavement, other than to note when raiding ended and kidnaping declined.

Children became slaves as a result of the debts of their parents or other kin, often during famines. Parents, and occasionally other kin when children were orphans, used the children as pawns to secure food or the money to buy food. The famines of 1903–1904, 1907–1908, and 1913–14 are particularly noteworthy, and there was a resurgence of pawning during the Depression of the 1930s.[13] As Webster noted in 1916, the "recrudescence of slave dealing amongst the Mumuye ... may be attributed to the famine in 1914 which aggravated the natural tendency of these tribes to sell their children, whom they look on as their natural currency."[14] As another official noted, "the Pagans' readiness to pawn their children and their apathy as regards their neighbours' losses of children have contributed to the success of this abominable traffic."[15] In 1916, Webster described the activities of "Hausa traders who spend some years among raw pagans, either in the South West of [Yola] Province or in the Cameroons, and 'adopt' children."

In other words in a time of stress they promise to maintain the parents if they will let them "adopt" a child or two to train as servants. After the child has learnt Hausa they remove to some other part of the country and the child becomes in practice a slave. A number of these Hausa returning from Cameroons, when liberated by our columns, endeavoured to smuggle such children through. The children were freed. A small colony of Hausas in Mumye [Mumuye] country was also broken up and for the time this industry is crushed. So long as Hausa colonies exist in Pagan areas it will inevitably rise again.[16]

Conditions among the Mumuye had been bad for at least several years. When Laing freed the 60 children at Zang in 1916, he observed that all had "been pawned or pledged by their relatives for a trifle of food or a pittance of money in times when food was scarce." Another forty children were missing and had presumably been sold away.[17] Traders made an initial payment, often 5s., to the parents, whereafter the debtors had difficulty collecting more. In 1921, the trade was also observed in the unsettled Kaleri district in the extreme southwest of Bauchi: "It can best be described as adoption on payment . . . carried on between the parents (usually of the Kaleri tribe) and the neighbouring Fulani."[18]

Fremantle thought child pawning would only end with "the gradual sophistication of the primitive pagans" who supplied the trade. He echoed a theme that was to characterize colonial attitudes towards the hill people of Northern Nigeria for decades to come: "through their transference to the plains from the rocky hills whose poor soil renders them liable to famine" the "pagans" would come to know peace, prosperity, and security.[19] In the meantime, according to Groom, "the Hausa trader living, often for long periods amongst the pagans for the ostensible purpose of trading in groundnuts or some such article of commerce, takes advantage of a famine or an intercommunal feud or the death of both parents to obtain the children he needs."[20] Despite the bias in these reports, the legacy of Caliphate slave raiding that first drove people into the hills and then kept them there unless they surrendered as conquered peoples was being painfully realized. The hill peoples did not trust the colonial administration that was reinforcing Muslim rule on the plains, and they chose to stay in the famine-sensitive hills even though it meant selling their children. In the end, they would move to the plains.

Kidnaping, particularly of "tiny Pagan children with intent to enslave or sell as slaves," was also common.[21] The Mumuye, for example, not only pawned their children but could not protect them from kidnapers either. As Groom reported in 1916, "Complaints have constantly been brought in from the Mumuye pagans that their children have been stolen and no trace of them can be found."[22] Sciortino reported a similar problem near Jema'a in 1917; there had been "a certain amount of kidnapping of Mada children and subsequent marking them with Hausa tribal marks."[23] Other reports demonstrate that kidnaping continued as late as 1923 along the frontier in the

Table 9.1. *Madagali slave raids, 1912–20^a*

Year	No. of raids	Slaves	Cattle	Goats/sheep	Horses
1912	6	1	3	14	—
1913	15	198	88	30	1
1914	2	0	70	—	—
1915	4	52	176	—	—
1916	14	169	303	—	10
1917	22	291	157	102	—
1918	17	271	421	350	—
1919	15	416	319	744	—
1920	24	627	371	522	2
Total	119	2,025	1,908	1,762	13

Note: [a] Vaughan and Kirk-Greene (forthcoming). It should be noted that there were at least two raids in which slaves were captured, but the number is not stated. Not all livestock was reported in the diary.

Cameroons, where the traders were usually Muslim, while kidnapers were more often "pagans," a neat division of labor in the clandestine slave trade.[24] In 1924, Yola officials claimed that there was a decline in the slave trade from the Mandated Territory, "though until the border pagan villages are completely under control, it will be impossible to stamp out kidnapping of young women and children as these villages act as depots."[25]

In some areas there was still organized slave raiding during the second decade of colonial rule. In 1916, Webster reported that "slaves are openly sold now in Madagalli and Mubi, and the chiefs are indulging in an orgy of oppression and confiscation."[26] Madagali, a sub-emirate in northeastern Adamawa on the border with Borno, was especially notorious as a slave-raiding center. As Captain Wilkinson reported in 1927,

> Before British occupation [1920] the armed bands of the District Head [Hamman Yaji] openly moved among the pagans plundering, slaughtering and capturing ... On a visit to Sina Galli last March the pagans showed me the ruins of their village and a rock on which many had perished when the village was plundered and burnt by Hamman Yaji's armed bands just prior to British occupation. The charred guinea corn is still preserved and the village head has been sworn never to enter the town of Madagali. The spoil and captives obtained in these raids were brought to Madagali sold and distributed. Young children were separated from their mothers. Madagali was famous as a slave market.[27]

There was also slave raiding along the frontier between French and British territory in 1918, particularly in Mandara,[28] and we suspect that other Adamawa sub-emirates also indulged in raiding.

The most detailed account of slave raiding is contained in the diary of Hamman Yaji, Emir of Madagali. Between September 22, 1912 and

December 23, 1920, Hamman Yaji recorded 119 raids on the non-Muslim populations in the hills around Madagali. In eight years, his forces enslaved over 2,025 people[29] and killed another 225 people who resisted enslavement (Table 9.1). In addition, at least 1,908 cattle, 1,762 goats and sheep, 13 horses, and 2 donkeys were seized, and some cloth was taken as well. Apparently the records for smaller livestock are incomplete before 1917. In eight years, eleven of Hamman Yaji's troops died in these raids, and several raids failed. In general, there is little information contained in the diary on the gender or age of those who were enslaved. While the diary begins in late 1912, only one slave is recorded for that year, and Hamman Yaji does not mention slaves being taken in 1914, a period of quiescence that may have resulted from the 1913–14 drought or the advent of the First World War. Whether or not these were complete returns is unclear. Under pressure from the British, Hamman Yaji had to stop raiding in 1920.[30] Even then, he "resorted to more subtle means of obtaining slaves i.e. through the medium of witchcraft or holding persons to ransom."[31]

If Madagali is representative of the Adamawa frontier, then many thousands of slaves were seized in organized raids before 1920. Thousands more must have been kidnaped, and unknown numbers pawned. The scale of enslavement, as suggested by the figures for Madagali, was shocking given the sanctimoniousness of the colonial regime on the question of ending slave raiding, and was certainly much greater than suggested by the registers of slaves freed in the Provincial courts, where slave-trading cases were heard. There is every reason to believe that the court returns were indeed only a small portion of the total trade, as some British officials suspected.

Sources of slaves

Adamawa had been a major source of slaves in the nineteenth century, not only for the Sokoto Caliphate but also for Borno and adjacent areas to the south and southwest. This vast region continued in this traditional role under colonialism, and since Germany occupied much of the slaving grounds of Adamawa before 1914, it is not surprising that German Kamerun was a notorious source of slaves in the first decade of colonial rule. As Groom reported during the War, "the native chiefs in the Cameroons while under German rule ... settle[d] their accounts with ... traders for gowns, swords, etc ... by a payment of slaves."[32] The border area produced even more slaves during the First World War. The "disturbed state of the Cameroons" made it "the happy hunting ground of the Hausa trader who does not care where he goes and what he deals in, provided he gets a large profit."[33] As a result of the War, Hausa traders flocked to the Cameroons in search of slave children.

> Many of these men have slaves with them usually small girls and in a few cases boys, which have as a rule all been purchased or stolen within the last five years. These slave children ... fetch as much as £15 a head in Kano and Lokoja.[34]

Slaves were traded openly in Madagali, Mubi, and Rei Buba, among other places. The British were able to close the market at Rei Buba, but to little effect. As Webster reported in 1916, "a certain number of slaves are imported by every immigrant, but as there is no proof of intention to sell there is no ground for prosecution."[35]

British administration of the Mandated Territories had little immediate impact on the slave trade to Kano, despite considerable efforts to stamp it out. The scandal surrounding the Alkalin Kano and the Alkalin Gwarzo in 1921 revealed the extent of the Cameroons slave trade. Hastings proceeded to prosecute twenty-one cases of slave dealing in the fifteen months after January 1921, which he concluded were "only a small percentage of the actual transactions." Clearly

> there has been a recrudescence of these offences, owing to the large number of persons brought into Nigeria for this purpose from the Cameroons since the termination of the war, and the lack of adequate supervision in the Emirate, in the last few years, has tended to encourage the activities of the offenders.[36]

Carrow's efforts to apprehend slave traders have been noted, particularly in relation to the market at Karaye. Even so the trade continued, and in 1922, Emir Usuman, "on his own initiative," raided Karaye. One of the principal merchants was captured, the buildings used to house slaves were destroyed, and "all the slaves found were given freedom certificates." None of the slaves were children or recent imports, however; at least none were reported to Resident Arnett.[37]

Even after the First World War, Northern Cameroon was still "chaotic and lawless," and slave dealing continued apace.[38] Indeed Palmer claimed that "there was more kidnapping in 1919 than in 1913."[39] In 1922, the Resident observed that

> a considerable traffic still exists in slaves throughout this region. Not only are children kidnapped, or bought from Pagans but also grown persons are often seized and sold to slave dealing agents on both sides of the Anglo-French Frontier ... [A]s the sympathies of all the Chiefs and the well-to-do persons in these Districts are distinctly with the slave traders, it is little use, at present, attempting to rely upon very much help from them in detecting or catching slave dealers ... Pagans themselves take a part in the slave traffic, for various reasons, and constantly seize persons from one side or the other of the Frontier, and sell them on the other side. I have found Pagans, Bororo Fulani, Town Fulani, Beri-Beri [Kanuri], and Hausa traders all equally prone to deal in slaves in these areas, when they see the opportunity to do so.[40]

Among the cases that preoccupied the Resident were two men trying to sell several Fulani women in February; a "pagan" man selling children in April; and a Fulani man caught selling slaves, also in April.

In 1923 the slave traffic was "considerably more active in the Northern Division [of the Cameroons] than in the Southern Division," although now the District Heads were "beginning to co-operate in suppressing this traffic," because they "realize that times have changed and it cannot be indulged in any longer with impunity."[41] Even so, there continued to be reports of kidnaping along the Cameroons frontier.[42] By the mid 1920s, local officials were more cooperative in suppressing the trade, even though children were still smuggled through for another decade at least.[43]

Slaves also came from the Jos Plateau and other hilly territory near the Benue River in British Northern Nigeria.[44] As Sciortino reported from Nassarawa in 1914, there was

> a certain amount of quiet slave-dealing going on. This is mostly done by the purchase of young children from among some of the lower pagan tribes where children are oftener than not merely looked on as realisable assets. As children thus purchased are kept hidden until they can speak the language of the purchaser (generally Hausa and sometimes Yoruba) by which time they come to look on their owners as their parents, it is next to impossible to detect such cases, or to prove them.[45]

Mada children were being purchased in southern Zaria, on the borders of Jos Plateau, in 1917.[46] In 1922, Fulani were buying children on the Plateau itself. The boys were trained to tend cattle, while the girls were kept until they were old enough to become concubines. When a teenager or adult was captured by mistake, "he (or she) is either held to be ransomed for a suitably youthful child or failing that is kept carefully guarded as a slave by the Pagan captors or purchasers."[47] Undoubtedly, new slaves came from elsewhere as well, but the available documentation suggests that the Jos Plateau, the hill communities of the Benue Valley, and the uplands of Adamawa were the primary source of new slaves throughout the whole period from c. 1903 to 1936.

The slave trade radiated outward from the hills of Adamawa and the Benue Valley in at least four directions. Many slaves went north through Dikwa and Borno to the Lake Chad basin and the Sahara Desert.[48] These slaves are beyond our view and are not considered further. Second, pilgrims leaving Northern Nigeria for Mecca sometimes took slave children with them for sale in the Sudan and the Hijaz, a phenomenon that came to the attention of British officials in the 1920s.[49]

Third, many other slaves traveled down the Benue River to Southern Nigeria, and these slaves, when intercepted, show up in the Provincial court returns for Muri Province in particular. This trade was "exceedingly difficult to prevent on a waterway like the Benue."[50] As Groom noted in 1917, children were taken at night to

> certain well known encampments on the banks of the river Benue and sold to Nupes, Kakandas, Igarras and Igbirras who come up in large numbers and are ostensibly engaged in the fish trade, or the salt trade with Garua. These children are taken down river to Lokoja, Etobe, Shintako, Ida, Onitsha and, I am told, even to the Niger Delta. I have heard though this is probably an exaggerated native rumour that there is living today in Onitsha a well known wealthy woman-trader who possesses 200 slaves obtained during the course of the last 10 years or so.[51]

269

Presumably children who were destined for southern markets were taken overland as well, but they are not visible in our sources.[52]

The fourth destination for slaves from Adamawa was Kano and the central Hausa emirates. Sometimes slaves followed the Benue for part of the way, and other times they were taken via one of several overland routes that passed through or near Bauchi. Butchers were the middlemen in the trade through Fika: "they have a regular code of language for discussing it in public, ostensibly referring to cattle." By 1922, the routes via Fika and Jellum were no longer important; instead slaves were taken through Bauchi Province via Nafada. According to Harris, the trade from Kano was conducted as follows:

> "A" residing in Kano Town sends one of his "yara" to Adamawa or else goes there himself leaving one of his "yara" in Kano or the villages outside. At Adamawa he buys perhaps 2 or 3 slaves (mainly young girls) and stays there for a year or so teaching the children Hausa so that they forget their mother tongue and drop into the way of speaking good Kananchi [Kano dialect of Hausa]. Then he either sends them with his women to Kano to his agent or returns with them himself; a ready market being found for them as concubines to the rich men of Kano.[53]

Harris thought that the trade was on a small scale because of the length of time needed to teach the children.

Thus, the clandestine slave trade persisted well into the 1920s and indeed longer because of the difficulty of ending enslavement and the high demand for children, especially girls. The trade remained largely invisible to the outside world, and colonial officials themselves were often reluctant to intervene dramatically to stop it. Suddenly, however, the slave trade came to the attention of the League of Nations, and the activities in Northern Nigeria could no longer be conveniently overlooked. Public opinion in Britain and elsewhere now became concerned about the persistence of slavery, even if that concern was only marginal to many other world issues.

The League of Nations and the slavery question in Northern Nigeria

In the mid 1920s, the League of Nations undertook to investigate the prevalence of slavery and the policies of various governments in its suppression. As Suzanne Miers and Dogbo Daniel Atchebro have both demonstrated, the League's involvement in the suppression of slavery had rather dubious origins, and in the fifteen years during which the League was concerned with the slavery issue, more was done to protect the interests of colonial governments than to eradicate slavery.[54] Nonetheless, the inquiries of the League impinged on developments in Northern Nigeria and indirectly moved British policy towards a tougher stance on the slavery issue. For public consumption, at least, the colonial regime had to appear to have the slavery situation under control.

When the League of Nations initiated an investigation into the persistence of slavery in Ethiopia in 1922, Sir Frederick Lugard once more resurfaced in the slavery debate. At the time, Lugard was Britain's appointee to the League of Nations' Permanent Mandates Commission.[55] He was also Vice President of the Abyssinian Corporation, which promoted British commercial interests in Ethiopia.[56] On November 10, 1922, Lord Balfour transmitted a memorandum to the League through Lugard recommending an investigation of slavery in Ethiopia. Lugard assumed an appearance that he was not directly interested in the Ethiopian question, despite his connection with the Abyssinian Corporation, but as William Rappard, Director of the Mandates Section of the League, noted at the time, "the British Government or certain colonial circles were considering the possibility of using the League and Sir Frederick Lugard as a means of intervention in Abyssinia."[57] Conflict of interest aside, the Anti-Slavery and Aborigines Protection Society, especially through the tireless activities of J. S. Harris, quickly entered the debate over slavery in Ethiopia.[58]

The slavery inquiry expanded into an investigation of former German colonies that had been mandated to other colonial powers. As Britain's representative on the Mandates Commission, Lugard was well placed to play a role here, too. The Mandates Commission issued reports to the League in 1922, 1923, and 1924, which were subsequently forwarded to the International Labour Office.[59] Slavery was visible to anyone who wanted to notice.

In December 1923, the Fourth Assembly of the Council of the League adopted a resolution to continue the inquiry into the question of slavery. A Temporary Commission on Slavery was established, with Lugard as Britain's representative. The Commission was instructed to gather information on what legislative and other means were being taken to secure the suppression of slavery. Further, it was to report on the results of the efforts at suppression and whether slavery was completely suppressed or was still dying out. Finally, the Commission was to examine the economic and social impact of anti-slavery measures on former masters, slaves, governments, and the development of territories where slavery was or had been important. The Council wanted replies from the different governments by June 1, 1924.[60]

Lugard drafted the questionnaire to be addressed to governments throughout the world. As might be expected considering his experience in East Africa, Nigeria, and Hong Kong, the questionnaire was written in terms that were compatible with his commitment to the abolition of the legal status of slavery. The questions addressed slave raiding, slave dealing, domestic or praedial slavery, concubinage and payment for females disguised as dowry, adoption of children through slavery, pawnage, and compulsory labor. Lugard convinced the Commission to take a broad perspective – "to enquire into the question of slavery from every point of view." Whether or not particular governments wanted to minimize the extent of slavery in their domains or anti-slavery groups tried to exaggerate the extent of slavery in particular countries, the volume of data that came before the Temporary Commission simply could not be ignored. So much material was submitted that the French delegate, Maurice Delafosse, former official of Afrique Occidentale Française, agreed to summarize the documentation for purposes of discussion.[61]

Colonial response in Nigeria

In preparation for the League's inquiry, the colonial government in Nigeria reviewed existing legislation, only to discover that the Mandated Territories were not fully covered. G. S. Browne had issued a circular on November 10, 1922, which extended Northern Nigerian laws to Northern Cameroon, but this circular had questionable legality.[62] Particularly difficult to explain was the practice whereby Islamic courts issued certificates of freedom in situations where individuals had been born free, which was innocently admitted in the report to the Mandates Commission in 1923. In order to repair the damage, the legal status of slavery was formally abolished in the Mandated Territories on February 28, 1924. Confusion continued, nonetheless. As the Resident of Cameroons Province tried to explain in October 1924,

> although the status of slavery was not statutorily declared by us to be abolished till 28 February 1924, we never have from the date of our political occupation on April 1st 1916 recognised the status of slavery. If a former slave left his master, as some have done, nothing was done by the Administration to prevent him doing so. At the same time native public opinion has continued to assign the status of slavery to the old slaves and their children, unless they are duly ransomed. The social status of slavery is clearly distinguished in the right of the master to the estate of the slave, to dispose of his women in marriage, and to share in the dowries paid on the slave's daughters. Their work is usually the more menial task[s] ... Many of the slaves have been so long in the state that they do not know their homes and are not sure of a welcome there if they do. They are therefore inclined to remain with their masters, especially if they have been humanely treated. But a slave who wishes to leave his master will probably desire a freedom certificate as a protection against molestation by his former owners, and sometimes will insist on paying a ransom if he intends to stop in the neighbourhood, because until he has properly discharged his liability to his master, he will still remain in public opinion a slave.[63]

In short, the situation in the Cameroons was similar to that in Northern Nigeria, but it was embarrassing to admit as much. Furthermore, the Ordinance of 1924 compounded the problem because it applied the laws of *Southern* Nigeria to the Mandated Territories. Unlike the laws of Northern Nigeria, there was no role for the Islamic courts, and there was no reference to the freeing of slaves after March 31, 1901. The Mandates Commission wanted an explanation.

Ordinance No. 3, the Slavery Abolition Ordinance of Nigeria, did not actually resolve the sensitive questions being asked at the League of Nations, therefore. The Ordinance confirmed the abolition of the legal status of

272

slavery in the Mandated Territories and stated that "all persons heretofore or hereafter born in or brought within the area were free." This provision made it clear that all children were born free, although it was noted that "non-recognition by the Administration of the legal status does not imply equal non-recognition in native public opinion."[64] In the 1924 report to the League, it was now possible to "explain ... away the unfortunate sentence, which had been introduced into the 1923 report, regarding the jurisdiction of Native Courts in Slavery Cases."[65]

The public image may have improved, but officials in Northern Nigeria were quick to point out that Ordinance No. 3 created problems over the status of persons born in Northern Cameroon before 1901. The dilemma in taking over the Cameroons was that "it was impossible to proclaim a general emancipation, for that would have caused social chaos; and on the other hand, if we made no such proclamation and yet forbade the courts to issue certificates of freedom, we might not improbably have hampered the gradual elimination of slavery."[66] Officials thought that it was impossible to amend the law and were concerned about what the League of Nations would think.

A second attempt to clarify the situation in the Mandated Territories was made in early 1925. Ordinance No. 1 of 1925 confirmed that all persons born in or brought into the Mandated Territories were free; there was no reference to March 31, 1901 or any other date. Whether or not the Islamic courts could grant certificates of freedom was left unresolved, even though in Governor Clifford's opinion, Ordinance No. 1 placed "the inhabitants of the Cameroons at a disadvantage in comparison with their neighbours in Nigeria."[67] Initially, Clifford wanted Northern Cameroon to be on the same footing as Northern Nigeria:

> it is evident that in the Northern Cameroons it is essential to provide persons of servile birth with the means of ridding themselves of the stigma of their origin. To deny them such opportunities might have the effect of perpetuating slavery rather than of promoting its elimination.[68]

In the end, it was decided to let the Islamic courts continue to issue certificates of freedom; "although the issue of certificates is not strictly in accordance with the law, it is not forbidden by the law and therefore not an offence." It would be undesirable "to legalize the practice of the [Cameroons] Native Courts by a Nigerian Ordinance." Instead, Thompson recommended that whereas

> we do not by British law take cognisance of slavery in the Cameroons ... we allow the Native Courts to provide machinery to enable persons, who of their own free-will wish to do so, to receive a "hall-mark" of freedom in a form which satisfies native public opinion.[69]

Ordinance No. 1 was justified because of the difficulty of explaining to the League of Nations why the laws of Northern Nigeria should be applied to the Mandated Territories. The Ordinance seemed to be the logical extension of the 1924 Ordinance and hence easier to explain. Lt.-Governor Gowers agreed to the modifications introduced in the 1925 Ordinance, but he may not have realized the consequences. There was now a significant difference between the Northern Mandated Territory and Northern Nigeria that would remain unresolved until 1936, when all reference to March 31, 1901 would be deleted from Nigerian law.[70] Until then, persons born into slavery before 1901 were still slaves in Northern Nigeria but not in the Mandated Territories.

In the short run, the colonial government in Nigeria was able to maintain a low profile on the slavery issue. The League continued to focus on Ethiopia and other parts of Africa, particularly Liberia and Bechuanaland [Botswana]. Lugard even introduced a lengthy report on forced labor in July 1925 that led to considerable discussion and deflected attention from Nigeria.[71] Delafosse summarized the many reports that had been submitted in his own interpretation of slavery, and this report in turn led to lengthy review.[72] In 1925, Lugard asked Arnett for comments on Delafosse's memorandum, which allowed officials to stay abreast of League discussions without drawing attention to Northern Nigeria.[73] Lugard made it clear that he disagreed with Delafosse on the approach that should be adopted in dealing with "slavery in all its forms."[74]

The result of the activities of the Temporary Commission on Slavery was the Slavery Convention, adopted by the League on September 25, 1926, which included twelve articles outlawing slavery and slave trading.[75] As Perham has noted, the Convention was largely based on Lugard's draft.[76] The Slavery Convention recommended the abolition of the legal status of slavery along "the Indian model." According to Miers, slavery that no longer had legal status "was now euphemistically called 'permissive' or 'voluntary' slavery since slaves might remain in servitude if they wished."[77] The similarity to Lugard's policy in Northern Nigeria is obvious. The Temporary Commission was thereby terminated, its assignment complete. Thereafter, the League contented itself merely with receiving reports from various governments and made no effort to enforce or otherwise expose slavery practices.[78]

The campaign against the slave trade, 1927–38

Under pressure because of the possibility of adverse publicity that might arise from the League's investigations, the colonial regime in Northern Nigeria renewed its commitment to the complete suppression of the slave trade. Its new-found determination was not easily realized, however. The trade persisted through the second half of the 1920s and into the 1930s, and Northern Cameroon continued to be the origin of many newly enslaved children.[79] Local authorities became more active in cooperating with the colonial regime, even though their interest in recruiting children, especially females, was at odds with their official duties. The French and British worked more closely together to monitor the movement of kidnapers and

274

traders across the border, and the two colonial regimes found that stopping trans-frontier slaving was possible in many cases. By this time, at least, individuals were intercepting kidnapers and liberating children without resort to official channels.

The export of slave children to Mecca was checked through the requirement that pilgrims obtain passports, but children were still smuggled out of Northern Nigeria to the east. Steps were taken to prevent the export of slaves by pilgrims as early as 1926, after Lethem returned from an intelligence mission to the Sudan and the Hijaz. The colonial regime was concerned about Mahdist propaganda and the possibilities of another uprising, but in the course of Lethem's investigation, it was discovered that there were many destitute pilgrims who needed repatriation, and even more disturbing, that pilgrims often financed their journeys through the sale of children. Upon Lethem's recommendation, pilgrims now had to apply for passports so that their movements could be monitored. The intention was to check Mahdism, reduce the number of destitute individuals, and curtail the export of children. The implementation of the passport policy clearly undermined the slave trade to the east. Several men applying for passports to Mecca in 1926 were turned down because, as H. H. Middleton reported from Yola, they had a suspicious number of children (between four and eight each) with them. It was clear that the children were to be sold "once they had left our territory."[80]

In a particularly dramatic move in 1927, the British even ousted Hamman Yaji as Emir of Madagali; his diary was used as evidence against him. As Captain Wilkinson observed,

> the terrible sufferings of the people will be seen from the callous remarks in Hamman Yaji's diary regarding these raids. The bitterness of the pagans towards this man is inconceivable to one who has not seen it.[81]

After his arrest, one hundred slaves were freed through the Islamic court and an even greater number of slaves obtained their liberation without resort to the court. As Wilkinson reported,

> There are many more names to record and cases keep coming up daily. In addition, large numbers who have asserted their right to freedom have not come before the Native Court. Cases only come to light through the claims of parents, complaints of ill treatment or in some such way. Prior to the removal of Hamman Yaji it would have been quite impossible for these unfortunate people to either complain or assert their right to freedom.[82]

Many of the slaves were children under age ten. Parents came in from the hills to find their children, but in some cases the children did not recognize them, or so it was claimed. It is difficult to disentangle situations in which adults falsely tried to claim children as their own and situations when children tragically had been separated too long.[83] The removal of Hamman Yaji closed "a great slave centre," and "as the people themselves say, the doors of their prison have been opened."[84] Because of the closure of such

275

Table 9.2. *Ransoms through the Islamic courts, Kano Province, 1926–35*

Year	Kano	Kazaure	Hadejia	Gumel	Total
1926	362	—	25	—	387
1927	39	—	19	2	60
1928	18	5	15	2	40
1929	22	—	9	—	31
1930	9	—	4	—	13
1931	4	—	—	—	4
1932	2	—	9	—	11
1933	—	—	—	1	1
1934	—	—	—	1	1
1935	—	—	—	—	—
Total	456	5	81	6	548

Source: Resident Kano, October 27, 1936, SNP 17 No. 20216.

markets as the one at Madagali, parents of kidnaped children felt freer to approach British authorities in their attempts to locate their children.[85]

By 1930, people began to take action against slave raiders and merchants without resort to official approval.[86] When a party of men from French territory entered Kilba District and kidnaped a number of children while their parents were in the fields, nomad Fulani intercepted the kidnapers and freed all but one of the children. As Webster reported,

> There have been one or two other cases of outrages of a similar nature on a smaller scale, all attributed to this gang. The victims have all found their way back except one. The French authorities have the matter in hand.[87]

Many communities that had suffered from enslavement and slave trading for three decades under colonial rule were no longer willing to tolerate this oppression.

By the 1930s, local officials had accepted the inevitable and enforced the anti-slavery laws of the colonial state. Kidnapers were intercepted, children were returned to their parents, and slave traders were prosecuted. Even the boundary with French territory no longer offered an opportunity to avoid detection.[88] The six convictions of slave dealing in the northern districts of Adamawa in 1932 were brought about by emirate officials, which led the Acting District Officer at Yola to praise "the energetic action which has been taken throughout the year by local native authorities, in particular the District Head of Madagali [who had replaced Hamman Yaji], to stamp out this trade."[89] Throughout the first half of the 1930s, the principal slaving ground was Wandala (Mandara) in French Cameroon, especially the area inhabited by the Wula, but by then the trade went mainly north and east and not towards the central Hausa emirates. Once again children were the victims, their parents "willingly" selling them, "the chief contributing cause for their action being shortage of food in their own country."[90] The trade limped along through the 1930s but apparently at a reduced scale over previous decades. The total number of slaves freed in the Northern Provinces for 1933 was 129, in 1934, 84, and in 1935, 71, apparently all as a result of the interception of slave traders.[91] The declining importance of slavery was also reflected in the Islamic courts, where fewer and fewer cases were heard. In Kano Province, for example, the number of slavery cases had declined to only 387 by 1926, and the numbers dropped off precipitously thereafter (Table 9.2). Between 1926 and 1934 there were only 548 cases, and there were none in 1935.

Renewed pressure from the League of Nations, 1932–36

The League of Nations, dormant in its campaign to undermine slavery for five years after 1926, once again directed its attention to the slavery issue in 1931. A new Committee of Experts on Slavery was instructed to examine the material that had been submitted by various governments since 1926 and to report on the extent to which slavery was being suppressed throughout the world. Lugard was not only Britain's representative again, but he also served as the Vice Chairman of the Committee.[92] In its report of September 1932, the Committee recommended that a bureau be established to process documentary material and that a permanent commission be appointed "because the mere existence of such a Commission could enlighten world public opinion in regard to slavery in the world." The pressure on officials in Northern Nigeria, as elsewhere, was renewed.

By this time, Lugard's credentials as an authority on slavery were unsurpassed. He had even written the entry on Islamic slavery for the 14th edition of the *Encyclopaedia Britannica* in 1928.[93] In preparation for his continued duties, he wrote to Lt.-Governor Lethem in Northern Nigeria asking for detailed information on his own contribution to the evolution of slavery policy in Northern Nigeria, since he intended to demonstrate that legal-status abolition had worked.[94] It must have come as quite a surprise, therefore, when he was inexplicably not appointed as the British representative to the Advisory Committee of Experts on Slavery, which met from 1934 to 1939.[95] He had to content himself with writing letters to the British newspapers.[96]

The Committee of Experts was "circumscribed" in its duties because it could only collect information from governments and not from individuals and private organizations. As a result, the Colonial Office apparently wanted someone who had not been connected with the slavery issue, and Lugard's history in Nigeria did not allow him to fill that role.[97] Britain's new champion in the fight against slavery was George Maxwell, who had formerly served in Malaya.[98] Perhaps to everyone's surprise, as Miers has observed, Maxwell turned out to be "the only truly independent member of the committee."[99] He raised issues such as why ex-slaves did not leave their masters, and he put a large amount of pressure on the British in particular.

The renewed interest of the League of Nations was anticipated with caution in Northern Nigeria. In response to Lugard's request for information, Lethem reviewed slavery policy in preparing his "Early History of Anti-Slavery Legislation" (1931), and, as noted above, the Northern Provinces Advisory Council was already investigating the continuation of concubinage. Subsequently, there were lengthy files collected, as colonial officials gathered material required for its reports to the League.[100] The establishment of the Permanent Commission of Experts, with Maxwell as the British representative, was not welcomed in Northern Nigeria.

In the summer of 1935, Maxwell warned Nigerian officials that the League inquiry into the suppression of slavery was serious. The Slavery Committee would give "special attention" to the whole issue of "voluntary slavery" in British and other colonies and in the Mandated Territories. Furthermore, the Committee would "raise the question of the approximate numbers of persons involved," and hence he requested a census of "ex-slaves."

> The Slavery Committee, in its next report, aims to show, not merely that slavery is said to be dying out, but to indicate the manner in which the ex-slaves are being, or have been, absorbed into the normal life of the free population ... Bald statements such as "Slavery has been abolished" or "Slavery is unlawful" carry little weight (and less perhaps today than ever) unless they are supported by circumstantial evidence.[101]

A census was duly manufactured and forwarded to Maxwell after some last-minute alterations. The census revealed a population of slaves and ex-slaves and the children of slaves who were still "living in their previous mode" at 121,005, and these were only the slaves, former slaves, and slave descendants that authorities in Northern Nigeria were willing to confirm (Table 9.3). Problems with the methods of estimating the number of slaves and unaccountable variations between provinces raise serious questions as to the accuracy of the census, but it is amazing in itself that the government of Northern Nigeria was willing to admit publicly to a slave population of this scale.[102]

The 1935–36 census deserves closer analysis. If the figures for Borno are excluded, then the reports suggest a population of 116,000 slaves, former slaves, and children of slaves who were still identified as living in conditions approximating slavery. All the figures are highly suspect. The figures for Sokoto (40,000) are rounded off to the nearest ten thousand, which confirms that no census was attempted. Officials merely guessed at what they thought would be an acceptable figure for the large slave population that still existed. The figure for Adamawa (11,900) conforms reasonably well with Migeod's estimate of fourteen years earlier, when he thought that the number of slaves in *murgu* was 10 percent of the total population of Yola, or about 20,000 people.[103] By 1936, presumably, many of these people had either died or achieved self-redemption. The Bauchi figure (14,245) is of the same order and may have been a reasonable estimate. Similarly the figures for Katsina (8,430), while low, suggest the existence of a visible slave population, but its

Table 9.3. *Slaves reported to the League of Nations, 1936*

Province	A	B	C	D	Total
Adamawa	5,000	1,500	3,500	1,900	11,900
Bauchi	13,643	602	—	—	14,245
Benue	50	30	70		150
Bornu	3,000	—	1,000	1,000	5,000
Ilorin	350	40	700	—	1,090
Kabba	600	850	3,400	—	4,850
Kano	500	250	200	—	950
Katsina	2,800	2,030	3,600	—	8,430
Niger	24,380	420	8,850	—	33,650
Plateau	60	—	30	—	90
Sokoto	20,000	10,000	10,000	—	40,000
Zaria	500	50	100	—	650
Total	70,883	15,772	31,450	2,900	121,005
Revised	71,880	15,570	30,490	1,090	119,030

Notes: A Slaves who did not take advantage of the law to ransom themselves prior to Ordinance No. 19 of 1936.
B Slaves who took advantage of the law to ransom themselves (or had been ransomed), but continued "in their previous mode of living."
C Children of slaves, who though born after 1901 and therefore free, continued to live with their parents' masters, as the latter's "dependants."
D Ex-slaves in the Cameroons (who became free on the enactment of Ordinance No. 1 of 1925) who continued "in their previous mode of living."
Sources: E. S. Pembleton, December 5, 1936, CSO 26/11799 Vol. IV; revised totals, League of Nations, Slavery, Report of the Advisory Committee of Experts, Fourth Session of the Committee, April 5–10, 1937, C.188.M.173. 1937. VI, p. 44.

size must have been at least as large as that for Bauchi or Yola. The estimates for Kano (950) and Zaria (650) are so low as to be ridiculous, however. The Emir of Kano alone had many more slaves than were being reported. Still, this "census," despite its clear under-representation and outright fabrication, is an interesting commentary on colonial perceptions of what must have been considered "acceptable" levels. The League inquiry made colonial officials nervous, but they had to admit to the presence of slavery on an enormous scale nonetheless.

When some of the unaccountable differences between provinces and categories are eliminated, the report to the League suggests that at least 400,000 people fell into the categories defined by the League. British officials estimated that 70,883 slaves had not taken advantage of the opportunity to ransom themselves before Ordinance No. 19 was enacted in 1936.[104] All these slaves had to be over thirty-five, since anyone younger was born free. While the figures for Kano and Zaria are suspiciously low and should be dismissed, the estimates for Bauchi, Adamawa, Niger, Sokoto, and Katsina

279

should be taken more seriously. In all cases, however, there was good reason to underestimate the slave population. We assume that the figures for the latter set of provinces are conservative but nonetheless useful for purposes of analysis. If adjustments are made to allow for the relative proportions of slaves that were reported in 1916–19, when 85 percent of court cases were in the central Hausa emirates, then the total number of slaves over thirty-five who had not purchased their freedom may well have been as high as 220,000, not 70,883.[105] Similar distortion can be detected in the estimates for the number of slaves who had been ransomed but continued "in their previous mode of living" and the children of slaves who continued under conditions approximating slavery. Once again the Kano and Zaria figures are suspiciously low, but if they are adjusted proportionately, then the League figures should be adjusted upwards by another 47,000, so that the revised total for individuals "in their previous mode of living" would be in the order of 170,000. It seems likely, therefore, that a reasonable guess based on the report to the League would suggest something approaching 390,000 or 400,000 slaves, former slaves, and the descendants of slaves, rather than the 116,000 who were reported.

Even the more modest estimate of the number of individuals who were still slaves or who were living under modified conditions of slavery was an embarrassment to the British government in London and officials in Nigeria. The examination undertaken by the League was more detailed than any previous inquiry. Documentation that was provided to the League revealed that the Yoruba system of pawnship (*iwofa*) had been abolished, that the Native House Rule Ordinance of Southern Nigeria, which had allowed slavery to continue, had been repealed, and that slavery was abolished in the Mandated Territories. The question was raised: Why was there still a law in Northern Nigeria that only allowed for the freedom of persons born after March 31, 1901?

The Slavery Ordinance of 1936

In 1936, the Advisory Committee of Experts, with Maxwell now chair, made it clear that "voluntary slavery" would not be tolerated as "a cover for the fact that individuals fear persecution or oppression if they avail themselves of the law."[106] Governments were instructed to investigate whether or not slaves could gain access to land and "thereby earn their own living." The Committee also wanted to know if there were any signs of "the mental helplessness of a depressed class," especially in Muslim countries, where every attempt should be made to emphasize "the liberal attitude of the Koran and tradition (Sunnah) to slavery."[107]

Maxwell warned Ormsby Gore, the Under-Secretary of State for the Colonies, of the seriousness of the League's intent, specifically with respect to Nigeria. If there were slaves in any British territory, he considered that "either the slavery abolition law of the country is more or less inoperative, or else the circumstances of the country are so extraordinary that the life of a 'slave' is preferable to that of a free man." In either case, the Committee expected an explanation:

> the Government of Nigeria should prepare a detailed report upon the situation in the Southern Provinces, where apparently there are still some "voluntary" slaves, and the Northern Provinces, where only slaves born after the 31st March, 1901 are "free." The Slavery Committee understands the official reports to mean that slaves born before the 31st March, 1901, are expected by local custom as administered by the Native Courts, to purchase their freedom by a system of ransom.

Maxwell did not accept the official interpretation that because Northern Nigeria was Muslim "this is some reason for non-interference with slavery." Quite the contrary: he made it clear that "the whole subject of the continuance of slavery in the Northern Provinces of Nigeria requires the most earnest attention from every point of view, and that the solution can best be found by asking the Potentates and Chiefs for their advice as to the methods to be employed, and by securing their cooperation in carrying out these methods."[108] Maxwell's letter was forwarded to officials in Nigeria.

The Colonial Office instructed Governor Bernard Bourdillon that slavery policy in Nigeria had to change. It was no longer acceptable to abstain from interference "with the relation of master and slave so long as the relation is voluntarily maintained by both parties in districts which recognise Moslem law and are under the jurisdiction of Moslem Courts." Whatever justification there had been for non-interference in the past, the colonial government of Nigeria should "carefully consider whether the time has not now arrived for the legislation relating to slavery in Nigeria to be amended so as to include in the declaration of freedom contained in Section 3 of Chapter 83 *all* persons in the Northern Provinces and not only those 'born in or brought within' those provinces after 31 March, 1901."[109]

Some officials expressed concern over the proprietary rights of masters, particularly with respect to the right to *murgu* and ransom payments. The Emirs of Bauchi and Gombe opposed the proposition

> as an interference with a master's rights of receiving pansa [fansa] and murgu. The latter in Gombe runs to 12/6 and 6/– per annum for male and female "slaves" respectively.[110]

Although redemption prices for slaves had fallen to £1.10s. to £3 by 1936 because eligible slaves were "quite old," the potential income for some masters still had to be taken into consideration.[111] As the Emir of Argungu complained, "a slave who did not live with his master, but worked his own farm, used to pay his master 2/6 every year that he should secure his freedom ... [as] 'murgu,'" in addition to the ransom set in court.[112] In Yola, ransoms were still being collected in 1936, "the actual ransom which was paid to the former owner varied from £3 in the case of an aging female to £5 for a male or young female, from which sum the 'ushira' [court fee] prescribed by law was deducted."[113] It is not explained how there could be a "young female" slave as late as 1936. Presumably *murgu* was also being collected.

There was also concern that slaves would be dispossessed of land and other property. Izard worried that

> some persons who have been regarded as slaves have been allowed by their masters to enjoy the possession of and inherit farms etc. in the same way as ordinary persons and if they are now declared to be free their former "masters" may wish to resume possession of their property.[114]

MacMichael reported from Argungu that there are "many ex-slaves who still live under the tutelage of their former masters ... [and] work their own farms." When they performed tasks for their former masters, they were paid for their services.[115] MacMichael did not explain the terms of tenancy of these former slaves, but they did not appear to be at risk as a result of any change in the slavery law. Similarly, Sharwood Smith stated that there was "no restraint on the movements or activities of ex-slaves in the matter of land tenure or private occupation" in Zaria.[116]

As far as Izard was concerned, "the question is whether consideration for these people can be allowed to outweigh the desirability of removing once and for all any grounds for suspicion that people can still be held as slaves in Nigeria."[117] Indeed the collection of *murgu* and ransom were greatly exaggerated, according to some Residents. The Resident of Kano even claimed that there were only 500 slaves left in 1936 who had not already ransomed themselves.[118] In Zaria, Sharwood Smith asserted that

> ransom has been unknown for the past fifteen years in that the technical condition of slavery has involved no form of obligation and a change of status entailing no material gain has been considered too dearly bought at the statutory price of £5–5–0d.[119]

The fear that some Residents expressed that former slaves would be dispossessed of land was also dismissed, although it was expected that the Islamic courts might be faced with complaints.[120] Izard concluded that "the continued existence of such consequences of the slave status as inability to hold property and the practice of 'murgu' appears somewhat anachronistic and is not easy to defend."[121]

Objections aside, there would be change, and "approval" if the total abolition of the legal status of slavery was pushed through. Izard summarized the various responses in a detailed report completed in record time on 25 June, only six weeks after the Colonial Office called for a report:

> Residents and Native Authorities in general see no great objection to the proposed amendment of the law and think that it would have little effect in the territories with which they are concerned.[122]

The way was clear for a new law. The Nigerian government took "appropriate action" to appease Maxwell and the League of Nations with the enactment of the Slavery (Amendment) Ordinance No. 19 of September 24, 1936.

282

As Pembleton noted, Ordinance No. 19 provided that "all persons in the Northern Provinces have now been declared free" by deleting reference to March 31, 1901.[123] Section 3 of chapter 83 of the Laws of Nigeria, 1923 now read that "all persons heretofore or heretoafter born in or brought within the southern provinces, and all persons heretofore or hereafter born in or brought within the northern provinces are hereby declared to be free persons."[124] The tortuous path of legislation surrounding the abolition of the legal status of slavery had reached its end. There was a final report in December 1936 that was forwarded to Maxwell's committee to demonstrate that Ordinance No. 19 had been well received. Officially, at least, there was no further social disruption, and few individuals were affected by the new decree. Indeed one official even reached the startling conclusion that "the explanation lies in the fact that slavery did not really exist." Since so-called slaves "owned or cultivated their own farms or traded on their own account there was nothing to differentiate their position from that of their 'free' neighbours except a certain social stigma which in a few places was attached to slave origin."[125]

In fact, however, the slaves who remained behind with their masters had to assume a sharecrop rental obligation for the lands that they farmed, including their old *gayauna* plots. Careful work by M. G. Smith in Zaria Province in the late 1940s uncovered the relationships that had developed between slaves and their masters. As he discovered, large slave holders continued to assert their rights to the land that had constituted their *rumada*. Ex-slaves worked this land

> under the authority of its owner, and were indebted to him for rent which they paid in kind [*galla*]. In other words persons were thereafter controlled indirectly through property in land. This system of control still persists in Zaria, but its bases and objectives are of necessity hidden from the British, who consequently find the logic behind the system of land tenure in Zaria somewhat obscure and puzzling.[126]

Part of the payment by former slaves to their old masters was expected to be in the form of gifts given at the time of the Islamic festivals, and part by sending a portion of the *zakka* grain tithe to the former master. The custom continued, with the children of ex-slaves paying the old masters' descendants with grain as *gallan gona* (also known as *aron gona*), rent for the loan of farms and compound sites. The payments "are commonly increased by addition of the Koranic tithe known as *zakka*."[127] Several phrases reported by M. G. Smith from his field work convey the flavor of the relationship that developed: "Kowanne gari yana da iyayen gijinsa, ko ba shi da sarauta" ("Every settlement has its owner, even if the latter has no title"); and in describing how long the relationship would last, "Har gobe, za a yi" ("Until tomorrow, i.e., for ever, this will remain").[128] In the late 1940s, it was still general practice for land to be occupied by descendants of slaves "at the pleasure of their *ubangiji* [landlord, descendant of former master] in return for specified rents."[129]

283

In Kano, the case that masters became sharecrop rentiers has been debated with some vigor. Hill contends that the evolution of sharecrop rents did not occur in the vicinity of the city, even though she agrees that permanent rent did arise in northern Zaria.[130] The slaves in this reading obtained control of their *gayauna* plots in an evolutionary process during which rent did not spring up. C. W. Rowling, however, notes that in parts of Kano rents paid by (former) slaves *did* arise, with the rent often in the form of sharecropping involving one-quarter to one-third of the crop.[131] Fika comments that this existence of sharecropping in Kano Province may demonstrate a connection between present-day domestic clientage and a former relationship of slave to master.[132] We conclude that, on the basis of the differing results of field studies, local conditions varied sufficiently to account for the differences. No doubt this is not surprising in a territory as large as Northern Nigeria. One factor contributing to Hill's findings may be proximity to a large urban center. Kano, for example, may have exerted such a pull on slaves in its immediate vicinity that masters hoping to retain slaves on the land found it more difficult to impose rental arrangements on the slaves. Further local field studies may well shed additional light on this debate.

By 1936, legal-status abolition had completed its final phase. Slowly over the previous thirty-six years, the colonial regime had eroded the foundations of the slave system that the British had inherited with the conquest of the Sokoto Caliphate. The prevention of enslavement and slave trading had proven to be difficult and had been pursued with vigor for three decades. International attention revealed that colonial practices could not easily suppress either enslavement or trade. Even in 1936, there was some trading in children, and concubinage was far from over. These dimensions of slavery would continue into the future, but after 1936 there was no legal foundation under Islamic law as practiced in Nigeria that could be used to rationalize existing demand. To the extent that concubinage depended upon slavery, the recruitment of women as concubines was no longer legal.

An assessment of legal-status abolition

Lugard and other supporters of legal-status abolition had wanted to avoid a sudden and turbulent ending of slavery in the Protectorate of Northern Nigeria. To some extent they were successful in this attempt, although there *was* considerable unrest and dislocation, much more than officials usually admitted. The desertion of perhaps 10 percent of the slave population and the uprising at Satiru seriously disturbed the tranquillity of the colonial regime and its Caliphate allies. Even so, officials predicted, repeatedly, that slavery would die a "natural death," and in the not too distant future. That these predictions were made for over twenty years suggests that they were misconceived. Despite claims that slavery *had* died or was *almost* dead, the institution persisted in modified form into the 1930s. Slavery proved to be far more resilient than Lugard and other officials believed.

Because of the size and complexity of the slave population of the Sokoto Caliphate, the transition from slavery to freedom could hardly have been easy in any case. There is ample evidence that many slaves already resented their bondage under the Caliphate, and certainly resistance to slave raiding by Caliphate forces demonstrates that the larger issue of slavery as a functioning system was far from being peacefully resolved at the time of the British conquest. That slave raiding and kidnaping continued is sad proof that it was not so easy to dismantle this slave regime. Many people in the Protectorate of Northern Nigeria opposed Caliphate slavery, but they were mostly the slaves themselves and the non-Muslim populations that provided new slaves. The British administration was not especially interested in these people, because they lacked political power. In the long run, colonial policies stopped slave raiding, almost eliminated kidnaping, and reduced slave trading to a trickle, but it took more than three decades to achieve these results.

British policy was essentially gradualist, and its implementation depended upon a consensus among colonial officials that Lugard's reforms would be allowed to take hold. Lugard had a very clear vision of how he wanted to handle the slavery issue, but he had difficulty convincing his immediate subordinates and his superiors at the Colonial Office that his plan would work. Subsequent officials were not certain that the Lugardian vision was all that clear after he left the scene in 1906, and there were attempts to refine the rough edges over the next several years as taxation and land policies were implemented. Lugard was able to retain a relatively firm grip on the course of change, however, once he returned to amalgamate Northern and Southern Nigeria in 1912. The Lugardian scheme remained largely in place thereafter.

That scheme tried to keep slaves in place while they paid compensation to their masters in a variety of forms. Male slaves usually had to continue to serve their masters unless they entered into *murgu* arrangements, and slaves seldom achieved their freedom unless they or someone else purchased it. Concubines retained their status until their masters died; their sexual and domestic obligations continued as before. Furthermore, many slave parents had to endure the recruitment of their daughters into concubinage. Slaves and their descendants, even if born free, paid rent for access to farmland, and in some cases paid *murgu* as well. Because the process leading to emancipation was uneven and often lengthy, slave owners received compensation to an extent that is difficult to evaluate. Nonetheless, the colonial administration made sure that slaves were heavily taxed, both directly by the state and by their masters.

The indebtedness of the peasantry of Northern Nigeria can be traced in large measure to the method by which slavery was eroded. For several decades, slaves paid for the right to work on their own account, and they had to pay taxes and other levies whether they wanted to or not. The expansion of the export sector allowed these slaves the opportunity to earn the necessary income to meet these financial obligations, but with considerable difficulty. Northern Nigeria did indeed become a mass of peasant cultivators under colonialism. That process of "peasantization" was closely associated with the transition from slavery to freedom. Furthermore, the peasant sector expanded haphazardly. Many slaves and their descendants became share-croppers or tenant farmers and were forced to find dry-season employment, often migrating great distances in search of temporary work. Finally, slaves on the official estates of the aristocracy continued to work under conditions that were more akin to the plantation agriculture of the late nineteenth century than to the peasant farms of the colonial period. Many of these estates were still in operation in the late 1930s.

Frederick Lugard was indeed a foremost authority on slavery. As the architect of change in one of the largest slave societies in modern history, he had the opportunity to observe slavery in operation and to implement reforms designed to bring about its gradual demise. His role in the League of Nations was perhaps clear recognition of his importance in the recent history of slavery. His activities there were to convince other countries that the abolition of the legal status of slavery was an effective method for ending slavery and, in the process, thereby protect his own record on the slavery issue. Lugard was also one of the most conservative abolitionists in the long fight against slavery. He did participate in the decline of slavery in Northern Nigeria. No doubt even those who continued as slaves had gained to a degree, but at a tremendous personal cost by comparison to the free land-holding peasantry.

Appendix   Court records of slaves issued certificates of freedom

The number of court cases involving slaves rose slowly in the early years of colonial rule (Table A.1). A total of 2,767 had passed through the courts by 1905; the number was only 7,199 by 1909. Thereafter there was a dramatic increase. In 1914, the total reached 35,814, of whom 28,615 (79.9 percent) appeared in court after 1909. By 1919, at least 69,785 slaves had been issued certificates of freedom, and by the end of 1929, the number was approximately 102,750 (Table A.2). By then the number of cases fell off considerably and by the early 1930s there were almost no cases.

The detailed returns for 1905–1906 (Table D.1) and the more general figures for 1901–1906 that appeared in the *Annual Report* for 1905–1906 (Table A.3) can be taken as a base from which to measure subsequent change. There are important differences between these sets of data. The sample of 584 cases reported for 1905 and 1906 (and a few cases dating back to 1904) have the disadvantage of under-representing Kano, Katsina, Sokoto, Gwandu, and several smaller emirates near these major centers. Undoubtedly, the great majority of slaves were held in these emirates. Zaria, Bauchi, and Yola, which were also important emirates, are well represented, however. There is no reason to suppose that these emirates differed significantly from the central emirates in terms of the profile of the slave population.

Despite these variations, a comparison of the figures for 1901–1906 with data from 1914 (Table A.4), the more detailed information from 1916–1919 (Tables A.5–A.7) and the scattered returns thereafter are instructive of the impact of Lugard's reforms. An analysis of the returns suggests that the fate of most slaves was not directly tied to the courts. Only 102,750 of the estimated slave population of 2.5 million or so made it to the courts. Far more slaves deserted their masters during the conquest or died in slavery without achieving their freedom. Many women, probably more than the number of slaves who appeared in court, became free because they had borne children by their masters. Slaves who had official positions, no matter how low or high, do not figure in the court records either.

In the early years, the British were not informed of most cases before the

Islamic courts, and hence the returns are incomplete. In Kano, for example, Cargill noted that fifteen slaves were set free in the Provincial court in 1905, but there were "many more [freed] by self-redemption or manumission [by third parties] through the Native Courts."[1] The Resident of Yola noted that the returns of slaves freed by the courts in 1905 "do not profess to be a complete record, more especially in the earlier years ... [and] even now the numbers freed by the native courts under the supervision of the administration are only partially entered."[2] In Ilorin, it was "very rare for slave cases to appear before the court."[3] The Church Missionary Society was freeing slaves "by perfectly legitimate means" in 1909, but without reporting the cases to the authorities.[4] By 1909, when 7,199 slaves had been manumitted through the courts, it was admitted that "there were, doubtless, many more of whose manumission a record has not been obtainable."[5] Even as late as 1910, the Resident of Bida noted that "the absence of any return of freed slaves is no evidence to the number of slaves who become free. The vast majority purchase their freedom by private arrangement with the owner."[6] In 1914, Lugard also observed that the official returns were, "of course, very far from including *all* who had been liberated, since large numbers were, no doubt, omitted from the records of the Native Courts, especially in the earlier years."[7] Furthermore, certificates continued to be issued outside the courts at least as late as 1913. In that year, Arnett reported that village headmen near Sokoto "had made a practice for many years past of arranging for freedoms and ransoms to be made before them on payment of a fee instead of sending them before the Native Courts."[8] It is uncertain how widespread this practice was.

Cases that were heard in Provincial courts are prominent in the early years. These courts dealt almost entirely with slave trading, enslavement, and ill treatment. Gradually, however, the number of cases before the Provincial courts dropped off to insignificance. Slavery convictions declined from 194 in 1908 to 137 in 1909, 134 in 1910, 66 in 1911, and 64 in 1912. Of the 35,814 slaves who were freed through all the courts between 1900 and 1914, only 6.5 percent were freed through the Provincial courts.[9] Since many of the cases before these courts dated from the early years of colonial rule, the shift to the Islamic courts was even more pronounced.

As we demonstrate in Chapter 5, many of the slavery cases that came before the Islamic courts after 1906 would never have appeared in court before colonial rule because British policy looked to the "Native Courts" to ease the transition from slavery to freedom. Consequently, the Islamic courts and the Judicial Councils assumed two new functions which account for most of the slave returns. First, the Islamic judicial system had always allowed ransoming, either by third parties or through self-redemption, if masters agreed. The British encouraged these courts to uphold the right of slaves to redemption, either through self-ransom or by relatives. In general, the courts complied and thereby regulated what had once been largely a private matter settled outside the courts. Second, the courts allowed the transfer of women for purposes of concubinage. Under the Caliphate, when the slave trade had been legal, the purchase of females for concubinage had been conducted openly. Whereas the Islamic courts had previously supervised the emancipation of slave women so that they could marry as free persons, now that the trade in slaves was illegal, all cases involving concubinage and marriage had to be controlled. Because concubines eventually received their emancipation after they had given birth and their masters died, these transfers for purposes of concubinage were tolerated for almost two decades and account for a large percentage of court cases.

The Islamic courts became active in promoting these reforms at different times in the first decade of colonial rule. The Zaria courts led the way. In the first quarter of 1906, there were already 40 cases of redemption before its Islamic courts; the returns for the year for both Islamic and Provincial courts were 145.[10] In 1907, the number of cases of self-redemption and manumission had risen to 513, and by 1914, over 6,500 slaves had been issued certificates of freedom in Zaria.[11] Sokoto, with its much larger slave population, quickly followed suit. In 1906, 106 slaves were "freed" through the Islamic courts; the number rose to 250 in 1907,[12] and by 1913 the figure reached 3,038. Between 1903 and 1914, 14,678 slaves received certificates in the Sokoto courts.[13] Kano followed the lead of Zaria and Sokoto. There were only 22 slaves listed in 1907, but by 1910 the number had increased enormously to 1,295, and in 1912, the total reached 2,764.[14] By 1914, the Kano courts had accounted for 8,000 slaves.[15] Thereafter the Kano courts issued more certificates than those at Sokoto.

The emirates that comprised the two provinces of Kano and Sokoto, which had the majority of slaves in the Sokoto Caliphate in the nineteenth century, accounted for 63.4 percent of all slavery cases between 1900 and 1914; 80.4 percent of all cases in 1917 and 77.3 percent of those in 1918 (Table A.4).[16] For the whole period through 1919, Kano and Sokoto accounted for 69.9 percent of the court returns (Tables A.5, A.6, and A.7). If Zaria is included in these figures, then the proportion of slavery cases in the central Hausa emirates amounted to 81.7 percent through 1914, 88.1 percent in 1917, 86.9 percent in 1918, and 83.4 percent for the whole period through 1919.[17] These proportions are in accordance with what is known about the concentration of slaves in the central Hausa emirates under the Caliphate.

Nonetheless, there are some anomalies in the court records that reflect gaps in the early years, as noted above. The figures for Ilorin are suspicious. It is possible that relatively high court fees kept people away. Certainly, the low numbers suggest that the Islamic courts there never fulfilled the functions of their counterparts in other emirates. Only 0.3 percent (101) of the total slavery cases between 1900 and 1914 were in Ilorin, which probably represents the returns for the Provincial courts there and not the Islamic courts. The number through 1919 (277, or 0.4 percent) suggests that there was no improvement in the intervention of the courts in Ilorin. It seems that court-induced reforms did not apply to the Emirate of Ilorin. Low figures for

Kabba, Kontagora, and Nassarawa reflect the relative smallness of the emirates in these provinces, which had large non-Muslim populations. Kontagora had also experienced extensive slave desertions. Court-induced reforms understandably had little impact in these provinces. The various Nupe emirates also appear to be under-represented in the official figures. There are no figures before 1905, although the Islamic court at Bida was involved in slavery reform at an early date. As late as 1910, the Islamic court returns for Nupe were still patchy at best.

The figures for Bauchi and Yola appear to be reasonable considering the relative size of the emirates in these provinces. Bauchi accounted for 7 percent of total slavery cases through 1914 and 7.2 percent of total cases through 1919. Yola, which had been stripped of its large sub-emirates by the German conquest of Adamawa, accounted for 3.1 percent of slavery cases through 1914 and 2.2 percent through 1919. The figures for Muri are relatively large (4.8 percent through 1914; 3.0 percent through 1919), considering that the only emirate in the province was a small one. The reason for this anomaly arises from the fact that the clandestine trade in slave children along the Benue operated through Muri Province, and therefore many slave children were freed as a result of the arrest of slave traders. Of the 1,720 slaves freed in Muri by 1914, 1,106 (64.3 percent) had passed through the Provincial courts, where slave-dealing cases were heard.[18] To a lesser extent the figures for Yola and Bauchi also included a disproportionate number of slave-dealing cases, because most new slaves came from Adamawa and passed through Yola and Bauchi.[19]

Far more females than males received certificates of freedom in the courts (Tables B.1–B.4). Of 630 slaves from the court records of 1905–1906 whose gender is known, 64.0 percent (403) were female and 36.0 percent (227) male, a ratio of 178:100. Of 8,921 slaves receiving certificates before 1918 whose gender is known, 64.2 percent were female and 35.8 percent were male (179:100). A slight decline in the gender ratio appears to have occurred between 1917 and 1921. Returns for 4,032 slaves in 1917 indicate a peak of 184:100 (64.8 percent female, 35.2 percent male). Comparable returns for 1,714 slaves in 1918 show a decline to 160:100 (61.1 percent female, 38.4 percent male); while in 1919, the ratio was 152:100 (60.4 percent female, 39.6 percent male, based on a sample of 1,995 slaves). The gender ratio for 11,125 slaves freed in Kano from 1916 to 1921 was also 152:100 (60.4 percent female, 39.6 percent male), which seems to confirm the decline.[20] The reasons for the decreasing proportion of females was related to the change in British policy that prevented the courts from allowing the transfer of female slaves as concubines, a development that is examined in Chapter 8.

Gender ratios varied considerably, despite the trend. Scattered returns from Yola between 1902 and 1922, based on a sample of 1,941 slaves, suggest a high ratio of 248:100 (71.3 percent female; 28.7 percent male), while a small sample of sixty-nine slaves from Muri in 1917 suggests the lowest ratio of 123:100 (55.1 percent female, 44.9 percent male).[21] Both of these extremes can be explained. On the one hand, relatively few males made their way to court in Yola, where *murgu* arrangements without a quest for self-redemption appear to have prevailed. On the other hand, the Muri slaves were largely children freed as a result of the arrest of slave traders, and the gender ratio of new slaves during the colonial period reflected patterns of pawnship and kidnaping, processes that tended to be gender-neutral (see Chapter 9).

The ages of slaves who received certificates in the courts became greater as each year passed, which reflected the fact that slaves born after March 31, 1901 were free. Occasionally there were slaves under age, which resulted from the liberation of children upon the interception of slave traders, although some children born after 1901 who should have been free were still being given certificates in the courts.

There were slightly more slaves aged twenty and under in 1905–1906 than would have been normal in a stable population, which partially reflected the relative importance of liberating young slaves from slave traders. Of the 525 cases in which age is known for 1905–1906, 40.8 percent were aged fifteen or under, while 50.1 percent were aged six to twenty (Table C.1). The female slaves aged fifteen and under constituted 37.1 percent of the total number of females; for males the comparable proportion was 47.6 percent. For females between ages six and twenty, the proportion was 52.3 percent while for males it was 45.9 percent. The greater proportion of small boys under age six and the greater proportion of girls between sixteen and twenty account for the differences in the ratios. These differences suggest that the sexual demand for young women was high and the market for young children who could be trained in a variety of domestic services that did not preclude the eventual sexual role for females meant that gender was not very significant at an early age.

Returns for 1916, based on a sample of 671 slaves, reveal a predictable shift in the age structure, since all persons aged fifteen and under should have been free by birth and only children rescued from the illegal slave trade should have appeared in the returns (Table C.3). In fact this expectation is realized in the figures. Only 1.0 percent (1.3 percent of the males and 0.8 percent of the females) were under 16. It can be assumed that virtually all of these cases were children liberated from slave traders.

The most striking features of the 1916 returns are that 50.5 percent of all slaves were aged twenty-one to thirty and that many more slaves over thirty (36.3 percent) were obtaining certificates of freedom in the courts in 1916 than had been the case a decade earlier. This upward shift in the age profile reflects not only the free status of children born after 1901 but also the impact of other colonial policies. If the 1905–1906 figures are adjusted to exclude all slaves under age sixteen, 38.9 percent were aged twenty-one to thirty and 31.2 percent were over thirty (Table C.2). That is, 29.9 percent of slaves were aged sixteen to twenty, while 70.1 percent of slaves were older. A decade later, 13.2 percent of slaves were aged sixteen to twenty-one, while 86.8 percent were over twenty-one. This shift towards an older age of emancipation reflects the fact that by 1916 more slaves were redeeming themselves than in 1906, and consequently there was a lower proportion of young women who were being sought for purposes of concubinage and marriage. By 1921, this shift towards older slaves purchasing their own freedom was even more pronounced, and appears to have been reflected in the decline in the ratio of females to males as well as in the upward movement in the average age of slaves acquiring their freedom.

The court returns allow an examination of the destination of slaves who received their certificates of freedom in the years from 1905 to 1921, although the methods of classification have to be interpreted carefully because the language of legal-status abolition kept changing. Slave cases were usually classified according to self-redemption (Table D.2), "freed to follow their own inclinations" (Table D.3), simply freed by masters but otherwise no reason given (Table D.4), ransom by relatives (Table D.5), "ransomed by intending husband," or ransomed by a third party other than a relative, which was another method of expressing third-party ransoms of women by non-relatives who were males. There are a number of difficulties with this classification. There seems no reason to doubt the category of slaves who were freed by relatives, which appears to have been a common occurrence, but the reasons that relatives did so appears to have changed. In the early years, relatives ransomed long-lost kin who had been seized in slave raids. The *pax britannica* allowed relatives to locate their kin and make arrangements for their redemption. By 1916, however, such cases of ransoming appear to have declined. Relatives had either found their kin or stopped looking. Now ransoming by relatives resulted from one of two causes. Either slaves who had paid off their own ransoms were freeing their wives and children, or parents of children born after March 31, 1901 were obtaining certificates of freedom in the courts to protect the freeborn status of their offspring.

Sometimes the reason for emancipation was the result of an "order" by the Provincial or "Native" court, which in the first instance usually meant liberation as a result of the arrest of slave traders, and in the second instance as a result of ill treatment. The number of slaves so designated tended to be relatively small, and the proportion of trade slaves to total slavery cases fell off after 1906. A few other categories occasionally appeared. In the early years, slaves assigned to missions, Freed Slaves' Homes, or other guardians were so indicated. These slaves tended to be children liberated from merchants. Deaths, escapes, apprenticeship, and enlistment in the WAFF were recorded in the early years as well. Ransoming by a spouse or as a result of "long service" was also noted, but only rarely.

Early on there were a considerable number of slaves assigned to guardians of one form or another, including missions, Freed Slaves' Homes, and other custodians. In the 1905–1906 sample, 20.4 percent of the freed slaves were so destined. Other records for the period through 1906 indicate that these categories were even more important (Table D.1). In the period 1901–1905, 48.3 percent of liberated slaves were assigned to the Zungeru Freed Slaves' Home or to guardians, while 0.4 percent were apprenticed and 0.6 percent were enlisted in the WAFF. That is, almost half of the 2,767 slaves freed by the end of 1905 were placed in some kind of dependency other than that arising with a relative, husband, or position in a harem. In 1906, these categories became much less significant; only 13.1 percent of the 581 slaves given certificates that year were assigned to guardians, including the Zungeru Home. A decade later these categories virtually disappeared. In the first instance, the Freed Slaves' Homes were closed in 1909, and thereafter children were assigned to guardians. In some cases missions were awarded custody, but most of the time the children ended up in the homes of "respectable" members of Muslim society.

Cases of self-redemption have to be considered carefully. When men were listed as redeeming themselves, we have no reason to doubt the accuracy of the classification (Table D.2). As we demonstrate in Chapter 7, these records provide some insight into the process of emancipation through *murgu* arrangements for men, whereby male slaves were allowed to earn the money for their own redemption. But when a woman was classified as redeeming herself, we cannot be certain that she was paying off her ransom with her own resources. As we examine in Chapter 8, women who were being liberated in order to marry or were being transferred for purposes of concubinage were often reported as redeeming themselves, when in fact a third-party male actually provided the money. By 1916, females who were listed as redeeming themselves (21.6 percent) may well have had their ransoms paid by third-party males. Furthermore, women who were designated as destined for "marriage" were often intended to become concubines. Hence the recorded explanations for the fate of women have to be treated with particular caution (Tables D.6–D.9).

Similarly, the explanations that slaves were freed by their masters or were freed "to follow their own inclinations" are open to interpretation. In many cases, we suspect that male slaves who are listed under these categories were involved in *murgu* arrangements and probably also purchased their own freedom or otherwise acquired the means to pay their ransom. In cases involving women slaves, however, these designations may well be a further disguise related to transfer for purposes of concubinage.

Table A.1–A.7 Returns of slaves "freed" through the courts

Table A.1. *Court cases involving slaves, 1900–29*

Year	Total to date	%
1905	2,767	2.7
1909	7,199	7.0
1914	35,814	34.9
1919	69,785	67.9
1929	102,750	100.0

Source: Tables A2–A7.

293

Table A.2. *Slaves freed through the courts, 1900–29*

Province	1919[a]	1929[b]
Bauchi	5,044	7,291
Ilorin	277	279
Kano[c]	21,992	32,000
Kontagora[d]	431	450
Muri	2,132	3,073
Nassarawa	613	701
Nupe[e]	1,540	2,363
Sokoto[f]	26,703	34,430
Yola	1,581	2,373
Zaria	9,472	19,796
Total	69,785	102,756

Notes: [a] Unless otherwise noted, the figures for 1919 are from SNP 10/7 331p/1919.
[b] Unless otherwise noted, the figures for 1920 are from SNP 17/2 14432. Not all figures for 1929 are acceptable, but it is reasonable to suggest increases of 45–50 percent over the 1919 total. Figures for Kano, Sokoto, and Zaria are suspect. The figure for Kano, 13,011, is clearly too low, while the figure for Sokoto from 1918 to 1929 of 12,540 seems low as well. The figure for Zaria, 19,796, seems to be too low also, based on earlier figures.
[c] It was thought that an error had been introduced into the total for Kano for the period before 1919, but subsequent correspondence and reports suggest that the figure used here was accurate: see SNP 10/7 331p/1919 and SNP 10/8 263p/1920. The figure given for Kano in 1929 (13,011) is clearly incorrect: see SNP 17/2 14432. The total for Kano through 1921 was 24,149; 2,157 slaves were freed in 1920–21 alone: see SNP 10/9 120p/1921. The figure suggested here, 32,000 is based on a comparison with the figure for Sokoto and the ratio between Sokoto and Kano in earlier years.
[d] There is no figure for Kontagora in 1929. The estimate used here is a projection from the 1919 total.
[e] There are no figures for Nupe prior to 1905; the total for 1905–14 was 894, and 646 for 1915–19, which yields a total of 1,540. See SNP 10/8 263p/1920.
[f] There is no figure for Sokoto in 1919; instead the figure used here is based on a projection from the 1918 total, which is found in SNP 10/7 331p/1919. In 1918, Sokoto had a total of 24,537. In 1917, Sokoto courts freed 2,698 slaves, or 38.6 percent of total returns for the year; in 1928, its courts freed 2,321 slaves, or 35.1 percent of total returns, while in 1920, 2,011 slaves were freed in Sokoto. We have adopted the average for 1918 and 1920, or 2,166, which seems reasonable since the annual total appears to have been declining. For the 1920 figure, see G. W. Webster, Sokoto Province Report No. 58 for the Half-Year ending June 30, 1920, SNP 10/8 256p/1920.

Table A.3. *Returns of freed slaves, 1901–1906*

Destination/Fate	1901–1905	%	1906	%	Total	%
Zungeru FSH	979	35.4	21	3.6	1,000	29.9
Own inclinations	737	26.6	294	50.6	1,031	30.8
Restored to relatives	511	18.5	87	15.0	598	17.9
Died	23	0.8	3	0.5	26	0.8
Married	134	4.8	121	20.8	255	7.6
Allotted to guardians	356	12.9	55	9.5	411	12.3
Enlisted in WAFF	17	0.6	0	0.0	17	0.5
Apprenticed	10	0.4	0	0.0	10	0.3
Total	2,767	100.0	581	100.0	3,348	100.0

Source: *Northern Nigeria Annual Report, 1905–06*, 481.

Table A.4. *Returns of freed slaves, 1900–14*

Province	Ill treatment	Contravention of slavery proclamation	Self-redemption	Redemption by relatives	Manumission by owners	Decease of owner	Various and unknown	Total	%
Bauchi	—	180	1,050	696	538	54	—	2,518	7.0
Ilorin	76	2	20	3	—	—	—	101	0.3
Kabba	—	29	2	—	2	—	68	101	0.3
Kano	—	—	1,554	207	1,736	—	4,540	8,037	22.4
Kontagora	7	9	167	64	11	8	—	266	0.7
Muri	26	1,067	102	—	5	—	520	1,720	4.8
Nassarawa	24	—	22	7	18	3	135	209	0.6
Niger	—	—	80	380	—	—	33	493	1.4
Sokoto	19	36	6,264	8,328	20	20	—	14,687	41.0
Yola	113	482	386	—	—	64	72	1,117	3.1
Zaria	—	—	2,968	1,899	1,664	10	24	6,565	18.3
Total	265	1,805	12,615	11,584	3,994	159	5,392	35,814	100.0
Percentage unknown	0.9	5.9	41.5	38.1	13.1	0.5			

Sources: SNP 17/2 14432.
Figures for Zaria are for 1905–14; see SNP 10/8 263p/1920.

Table A.5. *Returns of freed slaves, 1917*

Province	Order of Provincial court	Self-redemption	Manumission by owner	Ransomed by relatives	Order of Native court	Ransomed by intended husband	Total	%
Bauchi	1	329	18	63	2	54	467	6.5
Ilorin	—	—	—	—	24	—	24	0.3
Kano	—	1,563	204	253	14	951	2,985	41.8
Kontagora	1	20	—	2	—	5	28	0.4
Muri	29	24	1	—	15	—	69	1.0
Nassarawa	7	17	12	14	8	9	67	0.9
Nupe	—	96	—	1	2	—	99	1.4
Sokoto	—	1,585	5	457	1	705	2,753	38.6
Yola	—	81	—	—	14	—	95	1.3
Zaria	—	335	81	133	1	—	550	7.7
Total	38	4,050	321	923	81	1,724	7,137	100.0
Percentage	0.5	56.7	4.5	12.9	1.1	24.2		99.9

Source: SNP 10/4 236p/1916.

Table A.6 *Returns of freed slaves, 1918*

Province	Order of Provincial court	Self-redemption	Manumission by owner	Ransom by relatives	Order of Native court	Ransom by intending husband	Other	Total	%
Bauchi	1	541	10	75	34	44	1	706	9.4
Ilorin	—	—	—	—	40	—	—	40	0.5
Kano	—	2,030	156	384	3	606	—	3,179	42.2
Kontagora	—	26	1	8	—	2	—	37	0.5
Muri	4	28	—	—	2	—	—	34	0.5
Nassarawa	34	17	53	9	3	5	—	121	1.6
Sokoto	—	1,606	18	350	29	644	—	2,647	35.1
Yola	—	43	—	—	9	—	—	52	0.7
Zaria	—	437	214	39	—	34	—	724	9.6
Total	39	4,728	452	865	120	1,335	1	7,540	100.0
Percentage	0.5	62.7	6.0	11.5	1.6	17.7	0.0	100.0	

Sources: SNP 10/7 331p/1919 for all provinces, except Yola. For Yola, see SNP 10/6 489p/1918.

Table A.7. *Returns of freed slaves, 1919*

Province	Order of Provincial court	Self-redemption	Manumission by owner	Ransom by relatives	Order of Native court	Ransom by intending husband	Total
Bauchi	5	539	10	87	60	50	751
Ilorin	—	8	—	—	—	—	8
Kano	—	1,343	205	219	3	429	2,199
Kontagora	—	29	2	13	—	4	48
Muri	10	22	2	—	—	—	34
Nassarawa	3	39	73	7	5	3	130
Nupe	8	160	4	1	1	5	179
Yola	1	75	—	—	22	—	98
Zaria	—	445	222	95	—	83	845
Total	27	2,660	518	422	91	574	4,292
Percentage	0.6	62.0	12.1	9.8	2.1	13.4	100.0

Source: SNP 10/8 263p/1920.

Table B.1–B.4 Gender of slaves "freed" through the courts

Table B.1. *Gender of freed slaves by province, 1900–17*

Province	Male	%	Female	%	Total
Bauchi[a]	182	39.0	285	61.0	467
Ilorin[a]	1	4.2	23	95.8	24
Kano[b]	2,074	37.5	3,450	62.5	5,524
Kontagora	128	38.9	201	61.1	329
Muri[a]	31	44.9	38	55.1	69
Nassarawa[a]	127	34.0	247	66.0	374
Nupe[a]	41	41.4	58	58.6	99
Yola	426	28.7	1,059	71.3	1,485
Zaria[a]	186	33.8	364	66.2	550
Total	3,196	35.8	5,725	64.2	8,921

Notes: [a] 1917 only.
[b] Figures for Kano and Katsina Emirates, 1917 only; Hadeija Emirate, 1915–17; Katagum Emirate for 1917 and earlier.

Source: SNP 10/4 236p/1916.

Appendix

Table B.2. *Gender of freed slaves by province, 1917*

Province	Male	%	Female	%	Total
Bauchi	182	39.0	285	61.0	467
Ilorin	1	4.2	23	95.8	24
Kano	654	38.9	1,028	61.1	1,682
Katsina	197	25.7	570	74.3	767
Muri	31	44.9	38	55.1	69
Nassarawa	127	34.0	247	66.0	374
Nupe	41	41.4	58	58.6	99
Zaria	186	33.8	364	66.2	550
Total	1,419	35.2	2,613	64.8	4,032

Notes: ^a 1917 only.
^b Figures for Kano and Katsina Emirates, 1917 only; Hadeija Emirate, 1915–17; Katagum Emirate for 1917 and earlier.

Source: SNP 10/4 236p/1916.

Table B.3. *Gender of freed slaves, 1918*

Province	Male	%	Female	%	Total
Bauchi	287	40.7	419	59.3	706
Ilorin	—	—	40	100.0	40
Kontagora	19	51.4	18	48.6	37
Muri	18	52.9	16	47.1	34
Nassarawa	47	38.8	74	61.2	121
Yola	10	19.2	42	80.8	52
Zaria	278	38.4	446	61.6	724
Total	659	38.4	1,055	61.6	1,714

Source: SNP 10/7 331p/1919 for all provinces, except Yola. For Yola, see SNP 10/6 489p/1918.

Table B.4. *Gender of freed slaves, 1919*

Province	Male	%	Female	%	Total
Bauchi	281	37.4	470	62.6	751
Ilorin	—	—	8	100.0	8
Kontagora	16	33.3	32	66.7	48
Muri	19	55.9	15	44.1	34
Nassarawa	54	41.5	76	58.5	130
Nupe	82	45.8	97	54.2	179
Zaria	339	40.1	506	59.9	845
Total	791	39.6	1,204	60.4	1,995

Source: SNP 10/8 263p/1920.

300

Table C.1–C.3 Age profile of slaves "freed" through the courts

Table C.1. *Ages of slaves freed through the courts, 1905–1906*

Age	No. Females	% Females	Total	%
0–5	25	7.4	44	8.4
6–10	37	10.9	81	15.4
11–15	64	18.8	89	17.0
16–20	77	22.6	93	17.7
21–25	40	11.7	54	10.3
26–30	44	12.9	67	12.8
31–35	16	4.7	33	6.3
36+	37	10.9	64	12.2
Total	340	100.0	525	100.0

Sources: Register of Freed Slaves, 1905, SNP 15/1 Acc 90; Register of Freed Slaves, 1906, SNP 15/1 Acc 121.

Table C.2. *Ages of slaves over fifteen freed through the courts, 1905–1906*

Age	No. Females	% Females	Total	%
16–20	77	36.0	93	29.9
21–25	40	18.7	54	17.4
26–30	44	20.6	67	21.5
31–35	16	7.5	33	10.6
36+	37	17.3	64	20.6
Total	340	100.0	525	100.0

Sources: Registers of Freed Slaves, 1905, SNP 15/1 Acc 90; Register of Freed Slaves, 1906, SNP 15/1 Acc 121.

Table C.3. *Ages of freed slaves, various emirates, 1916*

Age	Male	%	Female	%	Total	%
6–10	1	0.4	2	0.4	3	0.4
11–15	2	0.9	2	0.4	4	0.6
16–20	12	5.4	69	15.4	81	12.1
21–25	19	8.5	116	26.0	135	20.1
26–30	55	24.6	149	33.3	204	30.4
31–35	37	16.5	41	9.2	78	11.6
36–40	61	27.2	41	9.2	102	15.2
41+	37	16.5	27	6.0	64	9.5
Total	224	100.0	447	100.0	671	100.0

Note: Emirates include Katsina, Daura, Kano, Azare, Hadeija, Niger (Bida), Nassarawa, Muri and Yola.

Source: SNP 10/5 435p/1917.

Appendix

Table D.1. *Destination of freed slaves, 1905–1906*

Destination	Male	%	Female	%	Total	%
Ransom, third party	4	1.8	162	45.0	166	28.4
Self-redemption	76	33.9	30	8.3	106	18.2
Ransom by relatives	41	18.3	57	15.8	98	16.8
To follow own inclinations	25	11.2	47	13.1	72	12.3
Custody of guardians	33	14.7	17	4.7	50	8.6
Missions	20	8.9	15	4.2	35	6.0
Freed slave homes	11	4.9	23	6.4	34	5.8
Freed by owner	10	4.5	5	1.4	15	2.6
Escaped	1	0.4	3	0.8	4	0.7
Long-service	2	0.9	0	0.0	2	0.3
Died	1	0.4	1	0.3	2	0.3
Total	224	100.0	360	100.0	584	100.0

Source: Register of Freed Slaves, 1905, SNP 15/1 Acc 90; Register of Freed Slaves, 1906, SNP 15/1 Acc 121.

Table D.2. *Cases of self-redemption, 1905–21*

Year	%	No.	Sample
1905–1906	18.2	106	584
1916	25.2	178	706
1917	56.7	4,050	7,137
1918	62.7	4,728	7,540
1919	62.0	2,660	4,292
1920–1921	62.0	1,337	2,157

Sources: SNP 15/1 Acc 90; SNP 15/1 Acc 121; SNP 10/5 435p/1917; SNP 10/4 236p/1916; SNP 10/7 331p/1919; SNP 10/8 263p/1920; SNP 10/9 120p/1921.

Table D.3. *Slaves freed to follow their own inclinations, 1901–16*

Year	%	No.	Sample
1901–1905	26.6	737	2,767
1906	50.6	294	581
1905–1906	12.3	72	584
1916	17.7	125	706

Sources: *Northern Nigeria Annual Report, 1905–06*, 481; SNP 15/1 Acc 90; SNP 15/1 Acc 121; SNP 10/5 435p/1917.

Table D.4. *Slaves freed by masters through the courts, 1905–21*

Year	%	No.	Sample
1905–1906	2.6	15	584
1916	9.2	65	706
1917	4.5	321	7,137
1918	6.0	452	7,540
1919	12.1	518	4,292
1920–1921	7.0	152	2,157

Sources: SNP 15/1 Acc 90; SNP 15/1 Acc 121; SNP 10/5 435p/1917; SNP 10/4 236p/1916; SNP 10/7 331p/1919; SNP 10/8 263p/1920; SNP 10/9 120p/1921.

Table D.5. *Slaves redeemed by relatives, 1901–21*

Year	%	No.	Sample
1901–1905	18.5	511	2,767
1906	15.0	87	581
1905–1906	16.8	98	584
1916	11.5	81	706
1917	12.9	923	7,137
1918	11.5	865	7,540
1919	9.8	422	4,292
1920–1921	12.4	267	2,157
1916–1921	12.2	2,658	21,832

Sources: *Northern Nigeria Annual Report, 1905–06*, 481; SNP 15/1 Acc 90; SNP 15/1 Acc 121; SNP 10/5 435p/1917; SNP 10/4 236p/1916; SNP 10/7 331p/1919; SNP 10/8 263p/1920; SNP 10/9 120p/1921.

Table D.6. *Destination of freed slaves, selected emirates, 1916*

Method of liberation	Male	%	Female	%	Total	%
Marriage	—	0.0	222	46.6	222	31.4
Relatives	38	16.5	43	9.0	81	11.5
Own inclinations	76	33.0	78[a]	16.4	154	21.8
Freed by masters	39	17.0	26	5.5	65	9.2
Self-redemption	75	32.6	103	21.6	178	25.2
Other	2	0.9	4[b]	0.8	6	0.8
Total	230	100.0	476	100.0	706	100.0

Notes: [a] Twenty-nine women were freed by third-party males, probably for purposes of concubinage/marriage. If these cases are shifted to the category "marriage," then the adjusted percentages would be 52.7 percent of women liberated for purposes of "marriage" and 10.3 percent liberated to follow their own inclinations.
[b] Three women freed by spouses.
Emirates include Katsina, Daura, Kano, Azare, Hadeija, Niger (Bida), Nassarawa, Muri, and Yola.
Source: SNP 10/5 435p/1917.

Table D.7. *Destination of freed slaves, Kano Emirate, 1916*

Method of liberation	Male	%	Female	%	Total	%
Marriage	—	0.0	50	33.3	50	22.2
Relatives	11	14.7	8	5.3	19	8.4
Own inclinations	18	24.0	29[a]	19.3	47	20.9
Self-redemption	45	60.0	60	40.0	105	46.7
Ransomed by spouse	1	1.3	3	2.0	4	1.8
Total	75	100.0	150	100.0	225	100.0

Note: [a] All were freed by third-party males. Adjusted percentage for women freed for "marriage" is 52.7 percent.

Source: SNP 10/5 435p/1917.

Table D.8. *Destination of freed slaves in Katsina, 1916*

Method of liberation	Male	%	Female	%	Total	%
Marriage	—	—	132	59.5	132	38.4
Ransomed by relatives	27	22.1	26	11.7	53	15.4
To follow own inclinations	56	45.9	38	17.2	94	27.3
Freed by masters	39	32.0	26	11.7	65	18.9
Total	122	100.0	222	100.1	344	100.0

Source: SNP 10/5 435p/1917.

Table D.9. *Destination of freed slaves, Kano, 1920–21*

Method of liberation	No.	%
Order of Provincial court	29	1.3
Self-redemption	1,337	62.0
Manumission by owner	152	7.0
Ransomed by relatives	267	12.4
Order of Native court	13	0.6
Ransomed by intending husband	359	16.6
Total	2,157	100.0

Source: SNP 10/9 120p/1921.

Notes

Preface

1 Hogendorn and Lovejoy (1988), 391–414.
2 Hogendorn and Lovejoy (1989), 1–43.
3 Hogendorn and Lovejoy (1992), 49–75.
4 Lovejoy and Hogendorn (1990), 217–44; Lovejoy (1988), 245–66; and Lovejoy (1990), 159–89.

1 Slavery and the British conquest of Northern Nigeria

1 Estimates for the size of the Caliphate's population, let alone the number of slaves, have to be based on conjecture, in the absence of census data. Polly Hill has hazarded a guess that "the ancient and flourishing slavery systems" of Northern Nigeria "probably involved several million men and women" (1976), 395. Also see Hill (1982), 249. Michael Watts has also estimated the slave population at "several million slaves" (1983), 191, 216. Our own estimate is based on the assumption that slaves constituted between a quarter and a half of the population of the Caliphate, which certainly numbered many millions and perhaps as many as 10 million.
2 Among other sources, see Lovejoy (1981), 201–43; (1978), 341–68; Hogendorn (1980), 477–93; Tambo (1976), 187–217; and Yakubu (unpublished, 1985).
3 The journal *Slavery and Abolition* regularly explores slavery in all its aspects, and Joseph C. Miller's bibliographical updates that are published therein provide a useful introduction to this complex and extensive subject. Also see M. Klein (1993) and Watson (1980).
4 See Toledano (1982).
5 The comparative demography of slavery world-wide is still in its infancy. Figures on the size of the slave populations in the Americas are generally known, but not so for elsewhere. For the US, Brazil, the British Caribbean, and Cuba, see Fogel and Engerman (1974); H. Klein (1986); Slenes (unpublished, 1976); Higman (1985); Scott (1985); and Knight (1970).
6 A preliminary examination of this process was undertaken in Hogendorn and Lovejoy (1988), 391–414.
7 Roberts and Klein (1980), 375–94.
8 Rudin (1938), 393–95.
9 See especially Lovejoy (1983) and Miers and Roberts (1988).
10 Genovese (1979).
11 Conrad (1972).
12 Scott (1985).
13 Hogendorn and Lovejoy (1989), 1–43; Hogendorn and Lovejoy (1992), 49–67; but also see

Temperley (1972), 93–110; Coupland (1933), 220, 243; Coupland (1939), chapter 11; Miers (1975), 157–60; Cooper (1980), 34–55, and especially 295–96, where the Zanzibar decree is reproduced; Morton (1990); Hollingsworth (1953), 141, 158, 217–19; Cave (1909), 20–33. Lugard discussed the policy in his *East African Empire* (1893), I, 182–83, and he reproduced the India Act as appendix Ia, in "Slavery under the British Flag" (1896), 340–41. The India Act is also in Miers (1975), appendix II, 364.

14 Swindell (1984), 3–19; M. G. Smith (1954a), 239–80.
15 See, for example, B. G. Smith and Wojtowicz (1989); Mullin (1972); Price (1979); Brode (1989); and Ross (1983).
16 M. G. Smith (1954a), 116–61.
17 Boahen (1964), 71–74.
18 Temperley (1991).
19 See Miers (1975), 42; and Temperley (1972), 54–61.
20 Report of July 2, 1841, Albert, Sierra Leone, No. 38, CO 2/33.
21 See chapter 4, "Telescopic Philanthropy." The model farm was abandoned in 1842.
22 Crowther to Venn, November 2, 1841, CMS C A1/079, as cited in Mason (unpublished, 1970), 128.
23 See Richardson (1853); Barth (1857–58); Boahen (1964), 186, 203–204; and Miers (1975), 51.
24 Instructions to Baikie, May 1, 1857, FO 2/23.
25 Boahen (1964), 219; Mason (1981), 85.
26 Oroge (1975a), 40–53; Oroge (1975), 61–80; and Agiri (1981), 141–42.
27 Samuel Crowther reported that one of the Caliphate officials at Rabba recognized among the carriers "two of his own soldiers, who were captured during the Umora war about two years ago [i.e., 1856], and sold away"; see extract of letter, August 16, 1858, *Church Missionary Record* (1858), 315.
28 Hastings (1926), 206. Haywood and Clarke (1964), 5, state that Glover had "great faith in the loyalty and courage of these Hausa freed slaves."
29 Pedraza (1960), 59.
30 *Ibid.*, 65.
31 No. 180, FO 97/435/1.
32 *Ibid.*
33 See Parliamentary Papers, 1865, Report of a Select Committee of the House of Commons on West African Settlements, 1865, and Orr (1911), 15.
34 See Dusgate (1985), 21, who cites the relevant Foreign Office documents, and Geary (1927), 167–70.
35 Flint (1960), 44–46.
36 Fürster, Mommsen, and Robinson (1988); and Miers (1975), 173, 181.
37 See Flint (1960), 137.
38 The treaties are summarized in FO 84/2109/2179. For the Muri treaties, see Hamman (unpublished, 1983), 437–46. For the treaty with Bida, see Mason (1981), 124–25.
39 Flint (1960), 86, 333.
40 Geary (1927), 189–90.
41 Flint (1960), 95.
42 Report on the Administration of the Niger Territories, January 9, 1890, FO 84/2109. Also see Dusgate (1985), 33. Anene (1966) also presents details on the activities of the Company.
43 Miers (1975), 315. For a discussion of the Brussels Conference, see 190–235; the Act is reprinted as appendix I, 346–63..
44 Mason (1981), 132.
45 Flint (1960), 234.
46 *Ibid.*, 235.
47 *Ibid.*
48 Geary (1927), 186.

49 See Flint (1960), 175–76; Dusgate (1985), 42–43; and Hamman (unpublished, 1983), 464–504.
50 Tukur (unpublished, 1979), 12–13.
51 Goldie to Scarborough, January 22, 1896, as cited in Flint (1960), 240.
52 Flint (1960), 246–47.
53 Somerset to Oliver, October 22, 1898, CO 446/1, as cited in Dusgate (1985), 261, n74.
54 See Goldie's introduction in Vandeleur (1898), xviii.
55 Dusgate (1985), chapters 5–7.
56 Ibid., 67; Adeleye (1971), 179–84; and Mason (1981), 144–47.
57 Dusgate (1985), 71.
58 Mason (1981), 147–48.
59 Tukur (unpublished, 1979), 121.
60 Mason (1981), 148–9; Tukur (unpublished, 1979), 121.
61 The decree is contained in the Niger Gazette of the Royal Niger Company, No. 55 of March 6, 1897.
62 Mason (1981), 124; Tukur (unpublished, 1979), 28, 36, 71, 125.
63 Ukpabi (1966), 485–501; Ukpabi (1987); Haywood and Clarke (1964). "Royal" was not added until the 1920s. WAFF is pronounced "woff" (p. 31). The official records of the WAFF are in CO 445.
64 Orr (1911), 39.
65 For details see Flint (1960), 307–12; Geary (1927), 205–206, and Orr (1911), 41–42.
66 Geary (1927), 209. The name Nigeria had been coined by Flora Shaw, Lugard's wife-to-be, in a letter to The Times dated January 8, 1897.
67 The proclamation is appendix IV of Adeleye (1971); also see 221–22.
68 Lugard to Chamberlain, August 28, 1900 (African (West) No. 580. Correspondence (1899–1901) Relating to the Administration of Lagos and Nigeria. No. 29, 42, CO 879/58/580.
69 Dusgate (1985), 134; and Lugard to Chamberlain, December 27, 1900, NO. 34, p. 46, paras. 2 and 4. The Bida explanation that the raids were to punish predatory raids on farms and villages by "pagan tribes" was not given credence. W. H. Grey, an agent of the private trading company Lagos Stores, made a journey from Lagos to Kano in 1902. He commented at length on the number and condition of villages and towns in the area that Kontagora was accused of raiding. See Crown Agents to Colonial Office, November 15, 1902, No. 26, p. 55, African (West) No. 695. Lagos: Nigeria. Further Correspondence (November 20, 1901–April 19, 1905) Relating to Railway Construction in Lagos and Nigeria. CO 879/76/695.
70 Mason (1981), 154.
71 Ibid.
72 Adeleye (1971), 226–29; Dusgate (1985), chapter 11; Orr (1911), 88–89, 98. More troops were lent to Southern Nigeria in 1900 for the Aro expedition, and another contingent (600–700 troops) was sent to the Asante War in April 1901, returning in October.
73 See Adeleye (1971), 222–25.
74 Ibid., 229–31; Dusgate (1985), 136; Mason (1981), 156–57; Ubah (1979), 36–45.
75 Mason (1981), 154.
76 Ibid., 155, 157.
77 Adeleye (1971), 259; Dusgate (1985), 137; and Tukur (unpublished, 1979), 72.
78 Argungu was the successor state to Kebbi, which had fallen in the jihad but whose emir retained the title Sarkin Kebbi; he was the senior member of the ruling triumvirate among Dosso, Birnin Konni, and Argungu. For the alliance of Dosso with the French see Rothiot (1988) and Idrissa (unpublished, 1987).
79 W. Wallace to Chamberlain, July 1901, No. 55, pp. 157–58, African (West) No. 580. Correspondence (1899–1901) Relating to the Administration of Lagos and Nigeria, CO 879/58/580.
80 Northern Nigeria Annual Report, 1900–01, and Dusgate (1985), 138.
81 Adeleye (1971), 245. Also see Tukur (unpublished, 1979).
82 Ubah (1979).

83 Lugard to Chamberlain, Jebba, March 15, 1902, No. 15, p. 16, paras. 5–6, African (West) No. 684. Lagos: Nigeria. Further Correspondence (January, 1902, to February, 1905). Relating to the Administration of Lagos and Nigeria. CO 879/72/684. It should be noted that the accusation that the slaves were "recently captured" almost certainly confused recent captives, recaptured fugitive slaves, and slaves being moved to prevent their escape. Of course, some slaves were probably sufficiently intimidated or otherwise loyal to have accompanied the Kontagora forces as well.

84 Tukur (unpublished, 1979), 52.

85 R. Popham Lobb to his mother, Zaria, April 25, 1902. Reginald Popham Lobb, later known as Reginald P. Nicholson, had been private secretary to Lugard during the period 1900–1901; Lugard Papers, Mss. Brit. Emp. s.64 (Vol. 35), Rhodes House.

86 The Waziri of Sokoto, who came to accept the slaves, had a strong escort which enabled the movement of the tribute out of Zaria; see Popham Lobb to his mother, Zaria, May 6, 1902.

87 Popham Lobb to his mother, Zaria, August 24, 1902. In his journal he wrote that "several times I had to send out WAFF patrols to round them up and rescue enslaved people" and that "The Emir's men had caught several Soba villagers, probably to go to Sokoto as part of the slave tribute, & sent them in to Zaria. My agents in the city confirmed this, so I chanced my luck & sent a demand to the Emir for their release & delivery to me. To my surprise, & far more to theirs, he surrendered them, possibly because he heard that on the previous day I had got the O.C. [officer commanding] to send out a patrol of 50 men which split up & covered two roads & many villages, though it left at an hour's notice in the night." See Mss. Afr. r.81, Rhodes House. Reginald Popham Lobb, Northern Nigeria Notes, 1900–1905, handwritten in a journal apparently transcribed in the 1930s from his diaries and road books, pp. 36–37.

88 Diary, August 26, 1902 and September 9, 1902. The former Galadima, Suleiman, was appointed to succeed him. That did not, however, end all attempts to send slaves to Sokoto, as reported by Popham Lobb, diary, December 4, 1902. Lugard described these events as follows: "At the time ... the Resident of Zaria, Captain Abadie (an especially able Officer, who is in close touch with the natives, and has sources of information through spies and traders, &c.), reported to me that the situation at Zaria was becoming exceedingly strained. The King, in defiance of the Resident, was sending out 'gunmen' to catch slaves in every direction, and to enforce extortionate demands upon the people, giving out that it was done by order of the whiteman. Our own men were not safe a few miles from the town, and our patrols came into collision more than once with these Dokari [dogari] (gunmen). The King of Kano is an intimate personal friend of the King of Zaria, and though the latter professed ignorance of these acts, it was clearly demonstrated that they were done by his orders, and though he professed loyalty it was more than probable that he was intriguing with Kano." CO 879/79/713. African (West) No. 713. Northern Nigeria. Correspondence (December 1, 1902, to January 28, 1903.) Relating to the Expedition to Kano, 1903. No. 28. High Comm. Sir F. Lugard to Mr. Chamberlain (rec. Jan. 19, 1903). P. 13, para 2.

89 Adeleye (1971), 253. Lugard stands accused of various exaggerations at this period. He said he had received a letter from the Caliph in May 1902, demonstrating hostile intent on the part of the Caliphate. D. J. M. Muffett, however, casts doubt on Lugard's straight-forwardness in his use of this letter; see (1964), chapter 3. Lugard stated that he received word that in October 1902, Emir Aliyu had actually sortied from Kano to attack Zaria but had turned back on hearing of the death of Caliph Abdurrahaman. The evidence for this appears weak; see Muffett (1964), 71. Orr (1911), 124, says that Emir Aliyu of Kano was busily "intriguing" with the Emir Suleiman of Zaria. Finally, Lugard's claim that the Emir's dogari (police) were running amok at Zaria is stated by Muffett (1964), 74–75, to be a misunderstanding, deliberate or not, of the normal activities of police.

90 Tukur (unpublished, 1979), 1–2. Also see Fika (1978); Adeleye (1971), 279–83; Dusgate (1985), 187–94.

91 Enclosure 3 in No. 35, extract from Lugard's despatch, No. 597, of November 21, 1902, p. 21, African (West) No. 713. Northern Nigeria. Correspondence (December 1, 1902, to January 28, 1903.) Relating to the Expedition to Kano, 1903, CO 879/79/713.

92 Adeleye (1971), 266–68; and Tukur (unpublished, 1979), 52. Keffi was sacked by the WAFF troops, with many casualties.

93 Adeleye (1971), 261–62.

94 This is the letter which has been subjected to close scrutiny by a skeptical Muffett (1964), chapter 3.

95 Dusgate (1985), 173. Part of Lugard's policy was "occupying the territory along whose borders they would pass, and safeguarding it from attack," according to Orr (1911), 125.

96 Earl of Onslow to Lugard, January 28, 1903, No. 35, p. 19, para. 6, African (West) No. 713. Northern Nigeria. Correspondence (December 1, 1902, to January 28, 1903.) Relating to the Expedition to Kano, 1903, CO 879/79/713.

97 Adeleye (1971), 270, and Orr (1911), 125–26.

98 Adeleye (1971), 272–73.

99 Ibid., 275–79; Muffett (1964), chapter 10.

100 Dusgate (1985), 189, whose figures are used, and Adeleye (1971), 283. Also see Tukur (unpublished, 1979), 77.

101 Dusgate (1985), 190; Adeleye (1971), 283.

102 Adeleye (1971), 282–85.

103 Tukur (unpublished, 1979), 52.

104 Adeleye (1971), 308–309; Dusgate (1985), 221, whose numbers are used. Also see Tukur (unpublished, 1979), 145.

105 For British anti-slavery activities in the nineteenth century, see Miers (1975).

106 Cooper (1980), 25–27, has argued as much in the context of his discussion of British policies in East Africa.

107 Lugard to Chamberlain (rec. February 16, 1903), No. 6, p. 5, para. 8, African (West) No. 718. Northern Nigeria. Further Correspondence [February 5, 1903, to October 12, 1903] Relating to the Expedition to Kano, CO 879/80/718.

108 Abadie, April 18, 1902, Zaria, Abadie Papers, Rhodes House.

109 R. Granville, Nassarawa Province Report, June 1903, SNP 10/7.

110 The African Review (January 16, 1904) 89.

111 Walter R. Miller, "Fillani Rulers and their Atrocities, as Narrated by Trustworthy Hausas and some Royal Fillanis," May 20, 1904, Lugard Papers, Mss. Brit. Emp. s.53/6, Rhodes House.

112 Adeleye (1971), 255; Geary (1927), 216; and Dusgate (1985), 166–67. The reinstallation is further proof of the way in which Lugard used the issue of slave raiding to justify the conquest. Ibrahim had been detained in 1901. The British then appointed his successor, and when he failed to prove accommodating, yet a second replacement was installed. Lugard was still not pleased, and in a remarkable turn of events, he reappointed Ibrahim in 1903; also see Duff and Hamilton-Browne (1920), 12.

113 E. S. Pembleton, Secretary Northern Provinces, "Slavery – Report of the Advisory Committee, League of Nations," October 17, 1936, Sokprof 3/1 c.33, Nigerian National Archives, Kaduna; the Nigerian Gazette (December 10, 1936).

114 Ordinance No. 19 of 1936 has hitherto mostly escaped the attention of scholars. Neither M. G. Smith nor Hill has mentioned this ordinance, as far as we are aware. Hill has even claimed that "slave-holding was never legally prohibited ... dying a natural death by about 1930" (1982), 249. Lennihan (1982) ends her study of early slavery policy before the 1930s. Swindell (1984), 15, is the only scholar we know of who has noticed that "abolition in full was not achieved until 1936." We must confess our own ignorance of Ordinance No. 19 until well along in our research. For a full discussion, see Chapter 9.

2 Fugitive slaves and the crisis in slavery policy

1 *Northern Nigeria Annual Report, 1905–06*, 371.
2 Kopytoff (1988), 485–503.
3 *Northern Nigeria Annual Report, 1905–06*, 371.
4 For earlier slave flights in the Caliphate, see Lovejoy (1986b), 256–62 and Lovejoy (1986c), 71–95. For the pattern of flight occurring during military operations, see Mason (1981), chapter 7, and Mason (unpublished, 1970), 394–95.
5 The comments of Captain Richard Somerset in 1898 exemplified the anti-slavery view of many officers. He was not a Company employee, having come as an officer in the new imperial West African Frontier Force. Somerset attacked the RNC's policy on slavery in the following terms: Ilorin had *"never been* subjugated," slavery was everywhere, "and you can see the lines of poor manacled devils working in the fields." He charged that the Company's agent-general deliberately arranged with Emir Suleyman of Ilorin that a visiting bishop of the Church Missionary Society was kept from seeing slaves when he visited Ilorin, and that the Emir treated this as a good joke. Somerset concluded his letter: "I came out here with the greatest possible admiration for the Niger Company but that changed very quickly indeed." See Somerset to Oliver, October 22, 1898, in FO Conf. Print 7653, as cited in Flint (1960), 246–47.
6 See Ayandele (1966a), 503–22; and Ayandele (1968), 397–419.
7 Ukpabi (1987), 100.
8 Vandeleur (1898), 191–92.
9 Goldie to Harford Battersby, May 17, 1897, Upper Niger Précis Books, 1897–1906, Church Missionary Society Papers, University of Birmingham, G3/A3/P4.
10 Burdon to Wallace, November 1, 1901, contained in Wallace to Chamberlain, November 7, 1901.
11 Abadie, June 18, 1902, Wushishi, Abadie Papers, Rhodes House.
12 Mason (1981), chapter 7; Mason (unpublished, 1970), 394–95.
13 *Northern Nigeria Annual Report, 1904*, 271.
14 Mason (1981), 150.
15 Report of Sir George Goldie, encl. in Morley to Salisbury, April 19, 1899, CO 147/124, as quoted in Mason (1973), 464n. The report is credited to Makun Muhammad, who first became *etsu* of Bida in February 1897; see Dusgate (1985), 83.
16 Hazzledine (1904), 75, 81.
17 Vandeleur (1898), 293–94.
18 Dusgate (1985), 92.
19 Extract of letter received February 20, 1897, Emir of Ilorin to Goldie; encl. in Goldie to Earl of Scarborough, March 6, 1897, CO 147/124. We wish to thank Ann O'Hear for this reference.
20 Goldie to Scarborough, March 6, 1897, CO 147/124.
21 Mason (1981), 151.
22 Wallace to Chamberlain, November 7, 1901, CO 446/17.
23 *Northern Nigeria Annual Report, 1904*, 271, 277.
24 SNP 33p/1913, as quoted in Mason (1973), 464 n; and Mason (1969), 561 n.
25 Vandeleur (1898), 294.
26 Ayandele (1966), 124.
27 Willcocks (1904), 225–26; Lugard to Secretary of State, June 13, 1898, CO 446/1.
28 Speech by Goldie, 17th Ordinary General Meeting of the RNC, July 16, 1897, contained in Despatch No. 19829 of July 27, 1899, CO 446/4.
29 Ukpabi (1987), 100–106, 112.
30 Gann and Duignan (1978), 109. They add that "The supply of ex-slaves began to dry up by

the end of the nineteenth century as slave raiding and slave trading were progressively eliminated. Ex-slaves, moreover, were prone to desert when they could."

31 Vandeleur (1898), xxv.

32 Maimaina, who was employed by the British as a secret agent, went to Kano to discover whether slaves had been sent "to Lokoja to join the army there who, after their training, had returned to Kano and were now instructing the Emir's men in the arts of European warfare." See Maimaina's autobiography, published at Zaria in 1958 and translated by Kirk-Greene as "Maimaina's Story," in Kirk-Greene and Newman (1971), 143.

33 Girouard to Crewe, Zungeru, November 16, 1908, "Slavery in Nigeria," No. 46301, CO 446/76.

34 Orr (1911), 39.

35 Recruiting Report of Lt. H. Bryan, September 1898, CO 446/4.

36 Ukpabi (1987), 103.

37 Captain N. M. Lynch, 2nd WAFF, "Reporting on Recruiting in the Benue Country," December 18, 1898, Enclosure in No. 12, Correspondence (1899–1901) Relating to the Administration of Lagos and Nigeria, African (West) No. 580, CO 879/58/580. Also see Ukpabi (1987), 101–103.

38 N. M. Lynch, December 18, 1898, CO 446/4.

39 Willcocks (1904), 225–26.

40 According to Willcocks, "As soon as the women saw the "Union Jack" floating over the town and knowing it to be the same as they had seen at Illorin, they rushed and laid hold of the flag staff and claimed their freedom, as they said they knew slavery was not allowed where that flag floated." See Lugard to Secretary of State, Jebba, June 13, 1898, CO 446/1.

41 *Northern Nigeria Annual Report, 1900–01*, 20.

42 Lugard (1906), 141–42. As he stated in a footnote, "The greater part of this para. is reproduced from an early Memo. I have allowed it to stand, though the contingency it contemplates has long since ceased, I think, to be one which can possibly arise." Lugard explained what he meant by "executive necessity" and "legal theory" in his response to Gollan's proposals for legalization of slavery, even if by some other name; see Lugard to Secretary of State, Surrey, August 21, 1903, CO 446/36.

43 *Northern Nigeria Annual Report, 1900–01.*

44 Wushishi, a sub-emirate under Kontagora, was established as the advance post of the WAFF in early 1900. See Mason (1981), 153.

45 Mason (1981), 155.

46 *Ibid.,* 153.

47 *Northern Nigeria Annual Report, 1900–01*, 11.

48 Abadie, Monthly Report, Zungeru, January 3, 1902, Abadie Papers, Rhodes House.

49 Abadie referred to these fugitives as "all those worthless, lazy slaves who wanted a good time with nothing to do." *Ibid.*

50 Walter Miller to Bayliss, Lokoja, April 1, 1901, Upper Niger Précis Books, 1897–1906, Church Missionary Society Papers, University of Birmingham, G3/A3/P4.

51 *Northern Nigeria Annual Report, 1900–01*, 14.

52 *Northern Nigeria Annual Report, 1904*, 280.

53 Molesworth to Wallace, August 1, 1901, contained in Wallace to Chamberlain, November 1, 1901. Also see Popham Lobb to Butler, November 12, 1901.

54 George Abadie, Wushishi, December 19, 1901, Nigerian Letters, 1897–1904, Mss. Afr. s.1337, Rhodes House.

55 Burdon, Report from the Resident of Nupe Province, August 31, 1901, in Wallace to Chamberlain, November 7, 1901. Also see Mason (unpublished, 1970), 401; Mason (1981), 163 n.

56 Wallace to Chamberlain, November 7, 1901.

57 *Ibid.* Also see Mason (unpublished, 1969), 401; Mason (1981), 163n.
58 Notes on Administrative History, BIDANA 6, B 655, as quoted in Köhnert (1982), 92 n.
59 See Gibson (1903), 51.
60 Burdon, Report from the Resident of the Nupe Province, September 1901, enclosed in Wallace to Chamberlain, November 7, 1901.
61 R. Popham Lobb to Butler, Bida, November 12, 1901, in Despatch 504, CO 446/17. Note that Popham Lobb had been at Bida for only two weeks and hence the earlier report of Burdon concerning trouble at Paieko in September and this report cannot be referring to the same events. In short, there were additional unrest and seizure of property by slaves.
62 Popham Lobb to his mother, May 6, 1902, Lugard Papers, Mss. Brit. Emp. s.62, Rhodes House. Also see Ukpabi (1987), 121.
63 Burdon, Report from the Resident of the Nupe Province, September 1901, enclosed in Wallace to Chamberlain, November 7, 1901.
64 Abadie, Wushishi, December 19, 1901, Nigerian Letters, 1897–1904, Mss. Afr. s. 1337, Rhodes House.
65 Abadie, Monthly Report, Zungeru, January 3, 1902, Abadie Papers, Rhodes House.
66 Mason (1981), 157.
67 *Northern Nigeria Annual Report, 1902,* 1. See also *Northern Nigeria Annual Report, 1904,* 281. According to Lugard, "At the capture of Ibrahim on Kontagora, some thousands of newly enslaved persons were freed;" see *Northern Nigeria Annual Report, 1902,* 133.
68 Abadie, February 21, 1902, Maska, Abadie Papers, Rhodes House: Grier later noted that the Emir of Kontagora and his officials "held vast numbers of slaves who worked on farms. When the Emir was defeated at Kontagora he fled into the north of Zaria Province, and as a natural result the slaves disappeared – many in fact found their way back to their original homes." See S. U. Grier, minute on Browne's report, May 26, 1924, CSO 26/11799, Vol. I.
69 Abadie, February 21, 1902, Maska, Abadie Papers, Rhodes House.
70 *Northern Nigeria Annual Report, 1902,* 1.
71 Lugard to Chamberlain, Jebba, March 15, 1902, CO 879/72/684.
72 Abadie, March 6, 1902, Birnin Gwari, Abadie Papers, Rhodes House.
73 Abadie, April 6, 1902, Zaria.
74 Abadie, April 18, 1902, Zaria.
75 *Ibid.*
76 *Ibid.*
77 Popham Lobb to his mother, May 6, 1902, Lugard Papers, Mss Brit. Emp. s.62, Rhodes House.
78 Mary Smith (1954), 67.
79 Hogendorn (1977b), 372, 382; see also interviews conducted on May 27, 1975 with Malam Najuma and Malam Audu Goma at Biye (Hogendorn/Maccido Collection). Also see interview with Audu Goma, May 20, 1975.
80 Maccido Alhassan, b. 1897, interviewed at Kwarbai, Zaria, June 11, 1975 by Ahmadu Maccido; Ali Barlarabe, Sarkin Farin Kasa, Zaria Emirate, b. 1907, interviewed July 7, 1975 by Ahmadu Maccido; Tukur Yero, b. 1905, Zaria, interviewed September 12, 1975 by Ahmadu Maccido; Boyi Ibrahim, b. 1880, Bani-Wuri ward, Zaria, interviewed September 2, 1975 by Ahmadu Maccido; Ahmadu Ibrahim, b. 1905, Sundu, Zaria Emirate, interviewed July 20, 1975 by Ahmadu Maccido; Aliyu Muhammadu, b. 1895, Dambo, Zaria Emirate, interviewed August 22, 1975 by Ahmadu Maccido; Muhamman Bello, b. 1890, interviewed August 17, 1975 by Ahmadu Maccido.
81 *Northern Nigeria Annual Report, 1905–06,* 386.
82 G. W. Webster, Nassarawa Provincial Report, September 1904, SNP 7/5 285/1904.
83 Wilkin to mother and father, Wilkin Papers, October 28, 1901, Mss. Afr. r.152, Rhodes House.

84 *Northern Nigeria Annual Report, 1905–06,* 390. Many of those enslaved may originally have been pawns.
85 C. L. Temple, Bauchi Report No. 2, March 8, 1902, SNP 15/1 Acc 38.
86 Temple wrote, "Further I am taking steps to cause all owners of serfs to know that every serf has the right to demand to be brought before the Provincial Court to state his grievance if he have one, and that any owner who refused to grant this privilege will on conviction be declared unfit to own serfs and may be further punished as the Court may think fit." As far as Lugard was concerned, Temple was going too far. Lugard wanted to prevent the flight of slaves, but he was not willing to use the threat of emancipation to keep masters from punishing slaves. After underlining the phrase *"all his serfs being,"* Lugard commented in the margin: "Deal with each case on its own merits and free a man if ill usage is found." Threats to liberate more slaves violated the British promise not to interfere in domestic relations. In another marginal note Lugard underlined Temple's phrase *"be declared unfit to own serfs"* and commented "note supra"; that is, Temple was told to follow the exact letter of his instructions not to make any sweeping declarations freeing slaves which might give the impression that slaves were being encouraged to escape. See Bauchi Report No. 2, March 8, 1902, SNP 15/1 Acc 38.
87 Abubakar (1977), 151; and Tukur (unpublished, 1979), 903–12.
88 Notes on Yola Province, c. 1904, Lugard Papers, Mss. Brit. Emp. s.64, Rhodes House. Also see *Northern Nigeria Annual Report, 1904,* p. 261, where Lugard states: "The Resident [of Yola] reports that criminality is rare except among the runaway slave class."
89 Yola Provincial Reports, 1903–1904, Yolaprof A5.
90 Notes on Yola Province, c. 1904 (no author given), Lugard Papers, Mss. Brit. Emp. s.64, Rhodes House.
91 Fika (1978), 198, quoting *Northern Nigeria Annual Report, 1902,* 41–42. Okediji (unpublished, 1972), 54–57, has concluded that

> The unsettled state of affairs during the British occupation caused insecurity among the population. Large numbers of the productive class in the emirates decided to leave their homes and emigrate to the east. A report by a British column on the Kano–Samfara–Sokoto [that is, Kano–Zamfara–Sokoto] route testified that the movements of the inhabitants from the emirates would result in the depopulation of the countryside. The report further mentioned that to allow such a mass migration to continue would bring a reduction in the total output of production in the emirates.

Although Okediji does not attribute this exodus to fugitive slaves, it is clear from other reports that slaves were a principal element in the movement. Okediji cites Report No. 8, file 129/1903, Sokoto Series, paragraphs 72 and 87. Her reference is to Burdon, Sokoto Province, Report No. 8 for July, August and Part of September, 1903, Sokprof 2/1 129/1903.
92 Minute on Browne's report by S.U.G. [Grier ?], May 26, 1924, CSO 26/11799, Vol. I.
93 Enclosure No. 2 in No. 14, Lugard to Chamberlain, received May 2, 1903, CO 879/80/718.
94 *Northern Nigeria Annual Report, 1902,* 250.
95 *Northern Nigeria Annual Report, 1902,* 99–100. Perham's rendition of this story is virtually identical, with one word change: "unhappy" rather than "disagreeable"; see her (1960), 130–31.
96 Burdon to Lugard, March 1, 1903, encl. in Sokoto Province, Report No. 1 by Burdon, March 31, 1903, Sokprof 2/1 7/1903.
97 Cargill, as cited in *Northern Nigeria Annual Report, 1903,* 173.
98 *Ibid.*
99 As quoted *ibid.,* 177.
100 Cargill, as cited *ibid.*
101 *Northern Nigeria Annual Report, 1904,* 24.
102 *Ibid.* Also see Ukpabi (1987), 120–21.

103 Cargill, in *Northern Nigeria Annual Report, 1904*, 290.
104 See his comments *ibid.*
105 F. Cargill, Kano Province Annual Report, 1907, SNP 7/9 1538/1908.
106 *Northern Nigeria Annual Report, 1907–08*, 613.
107 Mai Dawakai Gwadabe Dogari, who was born in 1921, told Yusufu Yunusa (interview, Emir's Palace, Kano, July 11, 1975) that "when the British came, they prevented the slave trade and slavery. Everybody left for where he wanted to go. Those who knew their home towns went there." Also see the account of Idrisu Dan Maisoro, b. 1900, interviewed in Hausawa ward, Kano, August 7, 1975. by Yusufu Yunusa; Abdullahi Adamu Ningi, b. 1932, interviewed in Kano, August 3, 1975 by Yusufu Yunusa; Sa'a Mai Itace, interviewed in Gini ward, Kano, August 8, 1975 by Aliyu Musa; Muhammadu Rabi'u, b. 1916, interviewed in Fanisau, July 13, 1975 by Yusufu Yunusa.
108 Based on family tradition, as reported by Ibrahim Tahir. Tahir notes that "many slaves left as soon as the [British] administration took over," and that such desertions undermined the activities and wealth of many big merchants and craftsmen. See Tahir (unpublished, 1975), 330.
109 Yeye was born at Kabo in 1893, where his family had its plantation. The merchants at Kabo were known as Zumbulawa, but the meaning of this term is not known. Yeye was interviewed in Gini ward, Kano, August 8, 1975 by Aliyu Musa. Also see the account of Mairo Iya Babba, who was born before the British arrived, who remarked that not only plantation slaves ran away: "actually almost everybody was running away, but then the British made it clear that they would have nothing to do with slavery," that is, not interfere with slavery. Mairo Iya Babba is of slave descent and was interviewed in Gini ward, Kano, August 10, 1975 by Aliyu Musa.
110 Hill (1976), 420n.
111 Kanoprof 5/24, No. 764 of 1932, as quoted in Hill (1976), 419n.
112 Sarkin Bagarmi was born in 1907 of slave parents who stayed on the Gogel plantation, which is located about twenty kilometers southeast of Kano in Dawakin Kudu District. Bagarmi was interviewed by Yusufu Yunusa on August 23, 1975.
113 Da'u Bello, interviewed in Gini ward, Kano, August 23, 1975 by Aliyu Musa. Da'u Bello was born in 1895. Amarawa is near Gogel.
114 S. U. Grier, minute of May 26, 1924 on report of G. S. Browne, Slavery in British and Mandated Territories: Information Required by League of Nations Concerning, May 3, 1924, CSO 26/11799, Vol. I.
115 Grier, minute of May 26, 1924 on report of G. S. Browne.
116 Burdon, Sokoto Province, Report No. 2, April 30, 1903, Sokprof 2/1 23/1903.
117 C. W. Orr, Sokoto Province Report for January and February 1904, February 29, 1904, Sokprof 2/2 51/1904.
118 E. J. Arnett, May 27, 1918, in "Revision to Memo on Slavery," SNP Supplementary Acc 612 1598/1918.
119 Stanley, Report No. 36 on Sokoto Province for Half-Year ending June 30, 1908, Sokprof 2/9 985/1908.
120 One observer ("E.W.") noted that already-issued regulations stated that "no 'freed' slave was ever to be given to a soldier or policeman." The observer went on to ask why "the O.C. troops and the Resident" could not "cooperate to prevent slaves running away to barracks. If the native owners come up to the Resident and complain, it would surely be an easy matter to have a search made for the missing slave, and impose a punishment under Sec: 35(9) of the N.N.R. Reg. upon the soldier in whose house he or she is found. It does not seem to me that any further legislation is necessary"; May 22, 1907, "Slavery in Sokoto Province," SNP 6/3 137/1907.
121 E. A. Brackenbury, Assistant Resident, Argungu, in E. J. Arnett, Sokoto Annual Report, 1913, Sokprof 2/12 581/1914.

122 Lugard (1906), 138. Webster, Nassarawa Province Report, September 1904, SNP 7/5 285/1904.
123 *Northern Nigeria Annual Report, 1904*, 269, 290.
124 Webster, Nassarawa Monthly Report, March 1904, SNP 15/1 Acc 59.
125 *Ibid.*
126 Webster, Nassarawa Province Report, December 1904, SNP 7/5 346/1904.
127 Webster, Nassarawa Monthly Report, March 1904, SNP 15/1 Acc 59.
128 Webster, Nassarawa Province Report, September 1904, SNP 7/5 346/1904.
129 Webster, Nassarawa Province, December 1904, SNP 7/5 346/1904.
130 Lugard referred to Memorandum No. 2 of 1901, which is discussed in the next chapter. The quotation is Lugard's marginal note on G. W. Webster, Nassarawa Monthly Report, July 1904, SNP 15/1 Acc 59. On the issue of upholding proprietary rights to land, see chapter 5.
131 Webster, Nassarawa Province Report, September 1904.
132 Lugard (1906), 137.
133 Arthur Festing, Annual Report on Zaria, 1908, Zarprof 7/1 2555; Hill (1976), 411n; and Lugard (1906), 308, citing Orr. Also see E. C. Duff, Annual Report on the Nupe Province for 1906, SNP 7/8 1520/1907.
134 Grier to Dorothy Grier, Zaria, September 30, 1906, Grier Papers, Mss. Afr. r.1379, Rhodes House.
135 Grier to his mother, Zaria, c. Christmas 1907.
136 Grier to his mother, February 24, 1908.
137 Grier to his mother, January 23, 1911.
138 Duff, Nupe Annual Report, 1906.
139 *Northern Nigeria Annual Report, 1905–06*, 399–400.
140 Lugard (1906), 137.
141 *Northern Nigeria Annual Report, 1906–07*, 498.
142 Mason (unpublished, 1970), 383; Banfield (1905), 14.
143 Judd to R. V. Bingham, August 2, 1903, Pategi, Edwin George Judd Book of Letters, Nigeria 1903, DD–2/4, SIM Archives.
144 *Ibid.* A search of the SIM archives reveals remarkably little on the subject of slavery.
145 Obayemi (1978), 81–82, 85; Mason (1969), 551–64; and Mason (1970), 193–208.
146 Annual Report, Kabba Province, 1907, SNP 7/9 1130/1908; *Northern Nigeria Annual Report, 1907–08*, 630.
147 *Northern Nigeria Annual Report, 1905–06*, 407.
148 *Ibid.*, 504.
149 *Northern Nigeria Annual Report, 1906–07*, 508. The Report noted that "The few slaves that remain to the upper classes seem contented as such."
150 *Northern Nigeria Annual Report, 1905–06*, 407.
151 *Northern Nigeria Annual Report, 1904*, 265.
152 *Northern Nigeria Annual Report, 1907–08*, 634.
153 G. N. Barclay, Yola Province Annual Report 1905, SNP 15/1 Acc 116.
154 *Northern Nigeria Annual Report, 1905–6*, 404.
155 *Ibid.*
156 Mahmudu K'ok'i, G. A. Bargery's scholarly associate on the compilation of *A Hausa–English Dictionary and English–Hausa Vocabulary* (1934), recounted this tradition to Yunusa (unpublished, 1976), 65.
157 Hiskett (unpublished, 1969), 462.
158 From a poem of an anonymous Kano poet, shortly after 1903, but note that Hiskett is incorrect in referring to the "abolition" of slavery; he is really describing a situation that resulted from the slave exodus. See Hiskett (unpublished, 1969), 462.
159 Hiskett (unpublished, 1969), 471.
160 As translated by Mohammed (unpublished, 1983), 170.

161 Watts (1983), 78, 172.
162 Lovejoy and Hogendorn (1990), 217–44. Also see Adeleye (1972), 193–214; and Mohammed (unpublished, 1983). Also see Büttner (1973), 1–18; Al-Hajj (unpublished, 1973); Idrissa (1981), 171–75; Tibenderana (unpublished, 1974), 164–72; and Tukur (unpublished, 1969), 283–330.
163 Lovejoy and Hogendorn (1990); Al-Hajj (unpublished, 1973).
164 For a full discussion see Lovejoy and Hogendorn (1990); Idrissa (1981); and Mohammed (unpublished, 1983).
165 The location of Satiru has been the object of some confusion. Various sources have placed the village haphazardly. See, for example, Shenton (1986), 27; Harrison (1988), 45; Idrissa (1981), map; and our own earlier discussion, Lovejoy and Hogendorn (1990).
166 Mohammed (unpublished, 1985); Mohammed (unpublished, 1983), 183–84; Burdon to Lugard, March 21, 1906, Shillingford Papers. The Shillingford Papers, Mss. Afr. s. 547, Rhodes House, include a file on Satiru that contains a large collection of official reports and telegrams on the rebellion, many otherwise unavailable. A. A. Shillingford held an education portfolio, and the presence of the Satiru file in his papers, presumably a transfer at some point from other files at headquarters, is unusual.
167 The coordination with the uprising in French Niger and the debate on this subject is treated in Lovejoy and Hogendorn (1990).
168 We have benefitted from the interpretation of Asmau G. Saeed, who has identified three groups of Mahdists, viz., the devotees of the Mahdi of the Nilotic Sudan, "spontaneous Mahdists" or "those who followed self-styled Mahdists" like the leaders of Satiru, and "revolutionist Mahdists" who awaited the coming of the Mahdi but did not emigrate or emigrated only reluctantly but did not revolt and who generally represented the official view of the aristocracy. See Saeed (unpublished, 1986) and (1982–85), 95–119. The revolutionary possibilities of Mahdism, particularly with reference to Satiru, were accurately identified by Mohammed (unpublished, 1983), 168, 172–173. Adeleye (1972), 194–97, has an excellent discussion of Mahdism.
169 Burdon to Lugard, telegram, February 28, 1906, Shillingford Papers, Mss. Afr. s.547, Rhodes House; Burdon to Lugard, March 15, March 21, 1906 Shillingford Papers, Mss. Afr. s.547, Rhodes House.
170 Burdon to Lugard, telegram, March 11, 1906, Shillingford Papers. Mss. Afr. s.547, Rhodes House. The WAFF casualties numbered thirty dead, including three British officers.
171 See Mohammed (unpublished, 1985). For a discussion of the terminology of Caliphate slave estates, see Lovejoy (1979), 1267–92.
172 Burdon to Lugard, telegram, February 28, 1906, and Lugard to Secretary of State, May 9, 1906, Shillingford Papers, Mss. Afr. s.547, Rhodes House. As one Sokoto cleric wrote at the time, "We have been conquered. We have been asked to pay poll tax and *jangali* [cattle tax]. We have been made to do various things, and now they want us to fight their wars for them. Let them go and fight themselves." Malam Bako to Malam Jafaru of Argungu, February 1906; manuscript in the Nigerian National Archives, Kaduna and quoted here as cited in Al-Hajj (unpublished, 1973), 199. The capital districts of Sokoto and Gwandu had not been subject either to *jizya* (poll tax) or *jangali* before the conquest, and their imposition under colonialism was clearly a major grievance (see Chapter 6).
173 According to Alkali Modi at Bodinga, Alhaji Bello of Danchadi, and Madawaki Shehu at Dange; interviews conducted in 1978–79 and cited in Mohammed (unpublished, 1983), 164.
174 Mohammed (unpublished, 1983), 171, and Mohammed (unpublished, 1985).
175 Cited in Mohammed (unpublished, 1983), 171, and based on an interview by Saleh Abubakar, August 14, 1975.
176 Burdon to Lugard, February 21, 1906, CO 446/53.
177 Conference of February 28, 1906, No. 11115, CO 446/53.

178 Lugard to CO, March 7, 1906, CO 446/53. On the Mahdist connections of Isa's father, see Lovejoy and Hogendorn (1990).
179 C. L. Temple, Extract of Sokoto Provincial Report, March 31, 1907, in "Slavery in Sokoto Province," SNP 6/3 137/1907.
180 Burdon to Lugard, March 15, 1906 CO 446/53.
181 Mohammed (unpublished, 1983), 164.
182 Lugard to CO, telegram, February 14, 1906, CO 446/52.
183 CO 446/52, p. 567.
184 Lugard to Secretary of State, May 9, 1906 .
185 Neely, Memorandum on Cotton, May 25, 1904, encl. in Lugard to Lyttelton, May 16, 1904, CO 819/84.
186 *Northern Nigeria Annual Report, 1905–6,* 409.
187 *Ibid.,* 427.
188 *Ibid.,* 412.
189 *Ibid.,* 408–409. In 1914, Lugard admitted that in the early years of colonial rule "very many (probably many thousands) were ... set free or left their masters without the knowledge of the Government, as the result of the conquest of each Emirate." See *Colonial Reports, Annual, Nigeria, 1914,* 50.
190 G. S. Browne, May 3, 1924, CSO 26/11799, Vol. I.
191 Orr (1911), 203.
192 Girouard to Crewe, Zungeru, November 16, 1908, CO 446/76.
193 *Ibid.*
194 *Northern Nigeria Annual Report, 1910–11,* 804–805. Hesketh Bell appears to have quoted *verbatim* from Lugard, Memorandum on the Taxation of Natives in Northern Nigeria, November 22, 1906, Colonial Reports, Miscellaneous, 1907 [Cd. 3309].
195 H. Lousteau, Rapport annuel 1903 du cercle commencé le 1er mars 1903, terminé le 31 mars 1904, cercle de Say, 16.2.4; Rapports d'ensemble des mois de fév., mai, juin, aôut et déc. 1906, Cercle de Say, 16.5.1; Rapport du Cercle de Say, 30 avril 1906, 16.5.2; Archives Nationales du Niger; and Taillebourg, Histoire du Cercle de Say, c. 1921, IRSH.
196 See Roberts and Klein (1980).
197 Report of Acting Resident Feargus Dwyer, enclosed in C. W. Orr to Elgin, September 9, 1907, Despatch No. 459, CO 446/64.
198 *Northern Nigeria Annual Report, 1905–06,* 409.
199 *Ibid.,* 390.
200 E. C. Duff, Annual Report on the Nupe Province for 1906, SNP 7/8 1520/1907; see also *Northern Nigeria Annual Report, 1906–7,* 509.
201 *Northern Nigeria Annual Report, 1906–07,* 509.
202 *Ibid.,* 508.
203 Girouard to Crewe, Zungeru, November 16, 1908, CO 446/76.
204 *Northern Nigeria Annual Report, 1912,* as cited in Ubah (unpublished, 1973), 373.
205 W. F. Gowers, Annual Report Kano Province, 1912, SNP 10/1 134p/1913.
206 Cases included the following, as cited in Christelow (1993):

1. Case No. 84I: Harun, a slave of Muhammad from Yardakuna who had fled to Kano, was returned to his master.
2. Case No. 2B: Maiduki from Julare had a brother Ciroma, whose slave had ran away. "He did not see him for years." When the slave was identified as being in the possession of D'an 'Iya Majeli, the master filed a complaint with the Emir. The slave was returned to Maiduki.
3. Case No. 14C: Madaki from Kafuw complained that a man named Sarki had encouraged his slave woman not to work. The Emir rebuked Sarki, and returned the woman to her master.

Notes to pages 63–67

Case No. 15A: A slave woman, Amina, was "stolen" from Uthman of Gamuji. Four months later, Uthman saw her in the possession of Shaya in Ganbawa, in the land of Yuanbu. Witnesses confirmed that this was his slave woman and that "she [had] fled from him." The slave woman was taken from Shaya and returned to Uthman.

4. Case No. 25G: The slave woman of Maina of Fagim ran away to the Emir's palace in Kano, where she had a grandmother. Maina learned of this and claimed her. She was returned to Maina.

5. Case No. 28B: Sarkin Raki of Warure ward in Kano city had a slave who ran away to Kumurai. A year later, the Sarkin Raki saw the slave in the possession of the headman of Kumurai. The headman claimed that when the slave came he "never knew where she came from." The slave returned to Sarkin Raki.

207 Hill (1976), 416, 418.

3 The debate on legal-status abolition

1 On the West African Frontier Force, see Haywood and Clarke (1964); Ukpabi (1987); Ukpabi (1966), 485–501.

2 Kirk was former Consul at Zanzibar, Director of the Imperial British East African Company, and prominent in slavery issues. See Coupland (1939).

3 Lugard explored the issue in two early works: (1893), I, especially chapter 7; and (1896), 335–55.

4 Perham (1956), 71, 73. Lugard's experiences with slavery during his East African service are also discussed by Lennihan (1982), 111–39.

5 Lugard (1893), I, 177.

6 Lugard (1896), 344.

7 Lugard (1893), I, 175–76; (1896), 344. For a comprehensive account of the British West Indian policies and their results, see Green (1976).

8 In East Africa he himself had already practiced what he preached when he announced and enforced local legal-status abolition in one area of Uganda. See (1893), I, 186.

9 Contemporary issues of the *Anti-Slavery Reporter* concentrated on Zanzibar, Pemba, and elsewhere in East Africa, but they did have notes, reviews, and articles of interest on Northern Nigeria. After the conquest, a regular section entitled "Northern Nigeria" appeared in most issues, together with occasional other notes of interest.

10 Hill (1977), 200; and Lennihan (1982), 112. Also see Hill (1976), 395–426. Both *West Africa* and the *Morning Post* (February 2, 1902) complained about the lack of news from the Lugard administration and the lateness of what was published.

11 Memorandum No. 6, "Slavery Questions," in Lugard (1906).

12 I. F. Nicolson, in his debunking study (1969), 135, wrote that "Lugard went to some lengths to conceal from the Colonial Office the existence of these memoranda, prohibiting their removal from the territory, and later having them printed in England without the Office's knowledge. When the Colonial Office got wind of them, and insisted upon seeing a copy, Lugard was markedly hesitant about sending one, and finally sent the revised, printed version, not the originals. Nothing obviously wrong was seen in them in the Colonial Office, although Antrobus remarked: 'Sir F. Lugard's jealousy of our seeing these instructions is absurd. They can have no "confidential character" in regard to the S of S'" (Nicolson cites CO 446/44).

13 Hogendorn and Lovejoy (1989), 19.

14 Nonetheless, Nicolson (1969), 153–54, is correct in his charge that the reports were both tardy and sanitized.

15 Hogendorn and Lovejoy (1992), 49–75.

16 Lugard (1905), 849–54. Lady Lugard was less forthcoming in her widely read book, *A Tropical Dependency*; see Shaw (1905), 460–65.

318

17 Willcocks (1904), 225–26; and Vandeleur (1898), 191–92. Also see Hogendorn and Lovejoy (1989), 6–8.
18 Despatch No. 19829 of July 27, 1899, CO 446/4. Lennihan (1982), 115–16, notes that the RNC proclamation meant that Lugard did not have to argue the question of his preferred strategy of legal-status abolition versus general emancipation. True, but given the Colonial Office's attitude, and particularly that of Chamberlain himself, there was no need for argument.
19 September 12, 1899, No. 24433, CO 446/8.
20 A later slavery proclamation, addendum (Special Memo No. 2) of March 1903 clarified the legal intent in upholding the enslavement of any person as an illegal act. Initially the trade in slaves between provinces (i.e., emirates) was banned; then all slave trading was prohibited. For the evolution of British policy towards slave trading, see Ubah (1991), 447–70.
21 Hogendorn and Lovejoy (1991), 62–63; and "Early History of Anti-Slavery Legislation," compiled by G. J. Lethem in 1931, SNP 17/2 15849.
22 Minutes of Lugard, February 15, 17, 1900; attorney-general, February 15, 1900; Lugard to Chamberlain, April 7, 1900, in "Early History of Anti-Slavery Legislation," SNP 17/2 15849.
23 Mercer to Antrobus [Sir Reginald Antrobus, the Assistant Under-Secretary of State in charge of West Africa], Despatch No. 24433, September 12, 1899, CO 446/8.
24 Memo by H. B. Cox, No. 24433, September 12, 1899.
25 Perham (1960), 171–72. It was also a year with heavy demands for officers to serve in the Boer War, as noted in Chapter 1.
26 See Grace (1975); Ohadike (1988), 437–61; McSheffrey (1983), 349–68; Dumett and Johnson (1988), 78–82; and Phillips (1989), 26–34.
27 Chamberlain to Lugard, May 25, 1900, SNP 17/2 15849.
28 Lugard to CO, July 21, 1900, Despatch No. 166, CO 446/10; also quoted in G. J. Lethem, "Slavery Legislation in Northern Nigeria," October 1931, SNP 17/2 15849. Lethem's important document contains a summary of the various ordinances, to which is attached the complete instructions, many relevant despatches, and correspondence.
29 The consultation with Goldie and Kirk is referred to in a minute by Antrobus, in Despatch No. 4, January 7, 1903, CO 446/30.
30 Lugard to CO, July 21, 1900.
31 Between the time Chamberlain sent his despatch of May 25 and Lugard responded on July 21, Proclamation No. 11 of 1900 was disallowed on technical grounds. Chamberlain thought that his own proclamation would be acceptable, but because of Lugard's reservations, a cable was sent to authorize the enactment of Lugard's draft, subject to minor amendments; see Chamberlain to Lugard, June 25, 1900, SNP 17/2 15849. The amended draft was forwarded to Lugard on November 26, 1900, and it was enacted on February 28, 1901 as Proclamation No. 2 of 1901. See Despatch No. 24433 of September 12, 1899 for the original draft, which with only a few changes in due course became Proclamation No. 2 of 1901. For its text, see the *Northern Nigeria Gazette*, Vol. 2, No. 2 (February 28, 1901). There is a supporting statement by Lugard, "Memorandum Re Slavery," in No. 24433. Also see P. H. Ezechiel, a Colonial Office secretary, "Slavery in Northern Nigeria," August 6, 1904, CO 520/95. This very useful document, written as a summary of developments to that time, is misfiled with Southern Nigeria papers.
32 Zulhija 10, 1318 in the Muslim calendar; see the marginal note in Arthur Festing, Zaria Province Annual Report, 1908, February 9, 1909, Zarprof 2555.
33 According to Bargery (1934), p. 1114, 'ya 'yan gwamna is defined as "descendants born after 1903 to slaves who have not claimed their freedom."
34 Lugard to CO, Despatch No. 166, July 21, 1900, CO 446/10.
35 Perham (1960), 35.
36 Ezechiel, "Slavery in Northern Nigeria." A minute by Antrobus notes that Goldie and Kirk

advised the CO to approve the 1901 proclamation even in the absence of a slave-dealing clause; see Despatch No. 4 of January 7, 1903, CO 446/30.

37 Lugard to Chamberlain, January 7, 1902, SNP 17/2 15849.
38 Despatch No. 24433 of September 12, 1899 for the question; and William Wallace's statement as to the penalty in Despatch No. 504 of November 1901, CO 446/17.
39 As quoted in Burdon to Wallace, November 7, 1901, SNP 17/2 15849.
40 As quoted in William Wallace to Chamberlain, November 7, 1901, Despatch No. 504, CO 446/17.
41 Lugard to CO, July 21, 1900, Despatch No. 166, CO 446/10.
42 Lethem, "Slavery Legislation."
43 Hogendorn and Lovejoy (1989), 16–17.
44 Popham Lobb to Butler, November 12, 1901, in Despatch No. 504, November 7, 1901, CO 446/17.
45 Wallace to Chamberlain, May 21, August 2 and August 14, 1901, SNP 17 15849. The letter of August 2 is also in CO 446/16, Despatch No. 368.
46 Wallace to Chamberlain, August 2, 1901, SNP 17/2 15849.
47 Chamberlain to Wallace, September 21, 1901, SNP 17/2 15849.
48 Wallace to Chamberlain, November 7, 1901, SNP 17/2 15849.
49 Ibid. Also see Despatch No. 504, CO 446/17.
50 Wallace to Chamberlain, November 7, 1901. One clear example of Burdon's actions was reported to Wallace on November 1, 1901. In response to a request for details, Burdon reported that he had returned a slave girl to her master against her will; see Burdon to Wallace, November 1, 1901, SNP 17/2 15849; also in Despatch No. 504, CO 446/17.
51 No such letter has been located.
52 Wallace to Chamberlain, November 7, 1901.
53 Burdon was later Resident at Sokoto. Nicknamed *mai farin kai* ("the one with white hair") because of his premature gray, he was the son of a bishop, had enlisted as an army private, was commissioned from the ranks, and ended his career as Governor of British Honduras, 1925–31. See Heussler (1968), xv; and Muffett (1964), 214.
54 Letter from Burdon to Wallace, dated Bida, November 1, 1901, and included by Wallace in Despatch No. 504. Two months before, Burdon had made much the same case in a report of August 31, 1901, also enclosed in Despatch No. 504.
55 Burdon to Wallace, November 1, 1901.
56 Ibid.
57 Ibid.
58 Ibid.
59 Wallace, Report on Nupe Province, August 31, 1901.
60 Burdon to Wallace, November 1, 1901.
61 Ezechiel, "Slavery in Northern Nigeria," August 6, 1904.
62 Despatch No. 504 of November 7, 1901, CO 446/17.
63 See "Domestic Slavery," No. 34322 of 1903, CO 446/36. The Southern Nigeria "House Rule" scheme had been proposed by Sir Ralph Moor, and had resulted in a 1901 law that converted slaves into house members. The chief or head of a house was given legal authority over the members. The Colonial Office waxed enthusiastic over this scheme, which has been the subject of ridicule by Anene (1966), 294, 305–308. Lugard himself presided over the repeal of this Southern Nigeria law when he was Governor-General of united Nigeria in 1914. Repeal took effect on January 1, 1915. Lugard explained that "House rule was not thereby abolished, but the denial of the assistance of British courts in enforcing the will of the head of the House, and of Government police in capturing fugitive members, struck a death blow to the system." In effect Lugard thus abolished the legal status of slavery in Southern Nigeria as well. Among his numerous complaints concerning the system were (1) acceptance of the uncorroborated oath of the head of a house was sufficient to convict a

vagrant; (2) arrest could be without warrant; and (3) the penalty, a year's imprisonment, was severe. See Cmd. 468 of 1919, "Report by Sir F. D. Lugard on the Amalgamation of Northern and Southern Nigeria, and Administration, 1912–1919," 23, p. 14, and Perham (1960), 458. A copy of the Southern Nigeria 1901 House Rule Ordinance can be found in CO 446/76 of 1908, No. 46301 of November 16, 1908. Also see Talbot (1926), chapter 28, "Slavery," 693–707.

64 Lugard to CO, August 21, 1903, Despatch No. 34322, CO 446/36.
65 Lugard to Lady Lugard, December 11, 1905, Mss. Perham 309, file 2, ff 58, Rhodes House.
66 Lugard to Scarborough, February 9, 1907, Royal Niger Company papers, Vol. 18, p. 245, Rhodes House. Wallace's career did not end happily. He left Colonial Office service in 1910 amid charges of favoritism in the granting of prospecting licenses in the tin fields: see Freund (1981), 42.
67 See Ezechiel's memo, August 6, 1904, CO 520/95, but as we have seen, he did see the despatch as soon as he returned to Nigeria in November 1901.
68 Lugard to Wallace, November 23, 1901, SNP 17/2 15849. In "Lugard's Policies Toward Slavery" (Hogendorn and Lovejoy (1989)) we stated that this correspondence had not survived, so far as we knew, but it could be reconstructed from a letter sent by Lugard to the Colonial Office, August 21, 1903, in No. 34322, CO 446/36. The correspondence has now been found in "History of Early Anti-Slavery Legislation," SNP 17/2 15849.
69 Lugard to Wallace, November 23, 1901.
70 Wallace to Lugard, December 29, 1901, SNP 17/2 15849.
71 Abadie, January 16, 1902, Wushishi, Abadie Papers, Rhodes House.
72 "Special Memo No. 10 (Slavery)," January 18, 1902.
73 *Northern Nigeria Annual Report, 1902*, 132.
74 "Addendum to Special Memo No. 10," August 14, 1902, No. 34322, CO 446/36.
75 Lugard (1899), 13–14.
76 Enclosure in Despatch No. 34322, CO 446/36. This gloomy prediction was widely believed. Dr. Walter Miller, the most outspoken of the missionaries, used much the same language in warning against a large population loose on the country, and ensuing social chaos; letter of Miller, cited in Despatch No. 46301 of November 16, 1908, CO 446/76.
77 See Memorandum No. 3 of November 22, 1901 for this and the following. Later Lugard added to this list of deserving cases slaves who had fled and then been recaptured by the Northern Nigeria equivalent of "bounty hunters" – headmen and other local officials who made a practice of capturing fugitives on the road in return for a reward or bribe; see Lugard (1906), 155.
78 "Early History of Anti-Slavery Legislation," SNP 17/2 15849.
79 Special Memo No. 10 in Despatch No. 34322, CO 446/36.
80 Addendum to Special Memo No. 10, August 14, 1902, CO 446/36, No. 34322, and also contained in SNP 17/2 15849.
81 SNP 17 15849.
82 Ubah (1992); and Olusanya (1966), 523–38.
83 Olusanya (1966), 427n. The Rebecca Hussey Charity was established in 1865 for the redemption of slaves.
84 We have not been able to locate Circular Memorandum No. 1 of 1902, which established rules for the Freed Slaves' Home at Lokoja, but we have located the addendum to Circular Memo 1, Rules for Freed Slaves Home, which was enacted on August 4, 1902. See the *Northern Nigeria Gazette* (August 30, 1902), 118.
85 Addendum to Circular Memo 1, Rules for Freed Slaves Home, August 4, 1902; the *Northern Nigeria Gazette* (August 30, 1902), 118.
86 Lovejoy (1988), 245–66.
87 Lethem, "Early History of Anti-Slavery Legislation," SNP 17/2 15849.
88 *Ibid.*

89 Addendum to Circular Memo 1, Rules for Freed Slaves Home, August 4, 1902; the *Northern Nigeria Gazette* (August 30, 1902), 118. Furthermore, "No Native will be allowed to marry a freed slave girl without the sanction in writing of the High Commissioner. When such applications are submitted, adequate guarantees will be given that the suitor intends to make the girl his *bona fide* wife, and if a Christian that he does not already possess a wife and will marry her according to civilised usage, and does not intend to abandon her when he returns to his country on expiry of his contract."

90 Lugard to Chamberlain, September 23, 1902, Zungeru, CSO 1/27/2.

91 "We have four slave children here at the mission now. Three Bro. Taylor brought from Lokoga [Lokoja] and one we are holding for the Government until we can find out what they want us to do with her, she had been a slave in Beda [Bida] but ran away ... She makes a good nurse for the baby and we want her if we can arrange it with the government. We have taken the other children from the slave home to make servants for us and thereby save the expense of paying a native cook and house boy." Judd to R. V. Bingham, August 2, 1903, Pategi, SIM Archives.

92 Lugard to Chamberlain, September 23, 1902, CSO 1/27/2. The Master and Servants Ordinance commenced on September 27, 1902; it was further revised May 26, 1903, September 15, 1904, April 1, 1907, and June 30, 1909. See Speed (1910), xiii–xvii. For the full text of the proclamation, as it was incorporated in *Laws of Northern Nigeria, 1910*, see 561–78.

93 For the full text of the Master and Servant Proclamation, see Speed (1910), xiii–xvii; 561–78; for the Proclamation for Licensing of Servants, see 579–80. Also see White to Stirrett, April 26, 1905, Wushishi–Government Correspondence, 1905–14, CC–2/A, SIM Archives. White observed that all servants of whites and non-Natives had to be registered, according to the Proclamation of March 1, and they had to pay a yearly fee of 2*s*. 6*d*. "Boys who attempt to obtain work with Europeans or non-natives after 1.3.05 and are not registered are liable to a 40/– fine."

94 According to Swindell, the Master and Servant Proclamations, were also intended "to protect the interest of the natives, but were seen as further attempts to raise revenue while at the same time controlling the labour market. The Proclamations of 1902, 1903 and 1904 controlled the engagement of labour within the Protectorate for service outside it, and for what were termed extra-local contracts. Workers recruited for outside service attracted a capitation fee of £1.0.0 rising to £2.12.0 while for extra-local contracts (taking workers more than 100 miles from the place of engagement) it was 5/–. In this way the government tried to inhibit the mobility of wage labour, especially carriers in order to secure the local supply around the major centres where the administration frequently required transport labour." See Swindell (1992).

95 H. C. Wall [?] to Stirrett, 19/11/10, Wushishi–Government Correspondence, 1905–14, CC–2/A.

96 Lennihan (1982), 136n, for example, states that to the best of her knowledge, "Lugard refrained from imposing vagrancy laws in Northern Nigeria."

97 Quoted in Ubah (1985), 217. Also quoted in the *Anti-Slavery Reporter*.

98 Lugard to Secretary of State, August 21, 1903, CO 446/36.

99 P. H. Ezechiel, Slavery in Northern Nigeria, August 6, 1904, CO 520/95.

100 Speed (1910), 259.

101 Lugard to CO, August 21, 1903, Despatch No. 34322, CO 446/36.

102 Miller to the Resident of Zaria, n.d. [1908], SNP 7/9 82/1908, as quoted in Lennihan (1982), 136. This letter has now apparently been misfiled in the Kaduna archives, and hence we have not been able to consult it.

103 As Fremantle reported from Muri in 1918, "the responsibility of chiefs and village heads for law and order carried the right to exclude undesirables. There was also the Vagrants' Proclamation. I regarded both these (as I do many of the Laws) as weapons to be employed

with discretion, ready to hand and extremely useful as a support but seldom required." See J. M. Fremantle, Muri, September 19, 1918, in "Revision of Memo on Slavery," SNP Supplementary Acc 61 1598/1918.

104 Orr (1911), 202–203.

105 Ibid., 202. As Orr indicates, vagrancy cases were probably all heard in the Islamic courts. Since records of these courts have been little investigated, it is not possible to know the frequency of prosecutions or the range of sentences that were pronounced in such cases.

106 Abadie, January 3, 1902, Abadie Papers, Rhodes House. These comments were repeated in the Zaria monthly report to Lugard of January 1902, extracts from which are in the copies of these letters at Rhodes House. In a later letter written April 18, 1902 (vol. 3, p. 58), Abadie expressed his support: "I am so afraid that all slaves will run away. They have been so often misled by whitemen (who ought to know better) saying 'no more slavery, everyone is free, etc. etc.' and what is the result? Slaves run away and the whole country whose constitution is built up on slavery becomes a desert."

107 Popham Lobb to his mother, May 6, 1902, Lugard papers, Mss. Brit. Emp. s.64, vol. 35, Rhodes House. The reference to Zanzibar referred to the outcry concerning government participation in the return of escaped slaves on the Kenya coast in the 1890s.

108 Letter of 18 April, 1902.

109 Lugard to CO, August 21, 1903, in Despatch No. 34322, CO 446/36.

110 "Draft Slavery Proclamation 1903," Despatch No. 4, January 7, 1903, CO 446/30; also see Lugard to Chamberlain, January 7, 1903, enclosing draft proclamation, SNP 17/2 15849, and Lugard to Lyttleton, June 7, 1904, SNP 17/2 15849.

111 Chamberlain to Lugard, April 17, 1903, CO 446/30.

112 Butler suggested this approach in response to Despatch No. 4 of January 7, 1903, CO 446/30; Antrobus minuted his agreement on March 28; Chamberlain asked whether it was not possible to substitute in place of the present anomaly some legalized form of domestic slavery, as had been done in Southern Nigeria.

113 H. C. Gollan to Lugard, June 24, 1903, CSO 8/6/3.

114 "Draft Amending Slavery Proclamation," June 24, 1903, CSO 8/6/3.

115 Minutes on Gollan to Lugard, June 24, 1903.

116 One minute in No. 34322 put it this way: "our suggestion was not to legalise domestic slavery, but to substitute for it a relationship which, while having the same effect in practice as domestic slavery, would not bear the name of slavery & could be recognised by the law of the Prot[ectorate] without appearing to come into direct conflict with recognised law." Also see Lyttleton to Lugard, August 19, 1904, CSO 1/28/34, where Lyttleton defended the Southern Nigeria House Rule system, but accepted that Lugard would have his way on the issue.

117 Lugard to Co, August 21, 1903, Despatch No. 34322, "Domestic Slavery," CO 446/36; Ezechiel, "Slavery in Northern Nigeria," August 6, 1904, CO 520/95.

118 Lugard (1905), 852.

119 Lugard to Lady Lugard, May 1904 [no more exact date given], Mss. Perham 309, file 2, p. 6, Rhodes House.

120 Lugard to Lyttleton, June 7, 1904, SNP 17 15849. At this point, Lugard also proposed that any canoes suspected of being involved in slave trading should be confiscated. This proposal appears to have been dropped shortly thereafter; there is no later mention of it. The letter included a copy of Lugard's earlier despatch of August 21, 1903 and another copy of the draft slavery proclamation.

121 Ezechiel, "Slavery in Northern Nigeria," August 6, 1904.

122 Lyttleton to Lugard, August 19, 1904.

123 Ibid.

124 Ibid.

125 W. W. Fraser, Circular No. 53, November 29, 1906, SNP 17/2 15849.

126 Lethem, "Early History of Anti-Slavery Legislation," SNP 17/2 15849.
127 C. L. Temple, Sokoto Provincial Report No. 33, July 22, 1907, SNP 7/7 137/1907; also included in "Slavery in Sokoto Province," SNP 6/3 137/1907.
128 Marginal note by C. W. Orr, August 7, 1907, in "Slavery in Sokoto Province," SNP 6/3 127/1907.
129 Marginal note, anonymous but probably that of the attorney-general or an assistant, August 7, 1907, in "Slavery in Sokoto Province," SNP 6/3 137/1907.
130 Ernest V. Parodi, attorney-general, to Girouard, January 9, 1908, SNP 17 15849.
131 Girouard to Crewe, November 16, 1908, CO 446/76.
132 Oliver Howard, Resident, Bauchi, to Parodi, February 14, 1908, enclosure in Parodi, Memo on Slavery Laws, enclosed in Girouard to Crewe, November 16, 1908, CO 446/76.
133 Lethem, "Early History of Anti-Slavery Legislation," SNP 17/2 15849.
134 This judgment follows Perham (1960), 171–72.
135 Perham (1960), 171.
136 For the complete text, see "Slavery Proclamation No. 27 of 1904," *Northern Nigeria Gazette*, Vol. 5, No. 12 (September 30, 1904). Under the amended "Slavery Proclamation No. 12 of 1905," the penalty for non-Natives in violation of the slavery laws was a prison sentence of up to fourteen years with or without hard labor, with fines also a possibility; see *Northern Nigeria Proclamations 1905–1913*, CO 587/2.
137 Beddoes (1904), 710. Also see Despatch of March 17, 1905, CO 446/44.
138 For the Residents' presumed discomfort, see Perham (1960), 171–72.
139 Bull (1963), 47.
140 So wrote Selwyn Grier in a letter to his mother dated Rahamma, Zaria Province, April 25, 1907, Grier Papers, Mss. Afr. r.1379, Rhodes House.
141 Howard to Parodi, February 14, 1908.
142 Christelow (1992).
143 Kisch (1910), 164.
144 Miller to Resident, Zaria, no date given other than 1908, SNP 7/9 82/1908, cited by Lennihan (unpublished, 1983), 80.
145 Kirkpatrick to Stirrett, January 16, 1908, Wushishi–Government Correspondence, 1905–14, CC–2/A, SIM Archives.
146 Kirkpatrick to Stirrett, January 19 [1908], Wushishi–Government Correspondence, 1905–14, CC–2/A, SIM Archives.
147 Kirkpatrick to SIM, January 16 [1908], Wushishi–Government Correspondence, 1905–14, CC–2/A, SIM Archives. The letter read: "The bearer of this note, Sgt. Barro, has reported to me, that a ward of his, from the Freed Slaves Home, ran away yesterday, and is reported to be at Oshishie [Wushishi]. Will you kindly give Sgt Barro every facility to make a search for the boy?"

4 Emancipation and the Law

1 Ubah (1991).
2 Lugard (1893), II, 222–24; Perham (1956), 191; Perham and Bull (1959), I, 29; and see the account by C. H. Crauford, who took part in these operations, contained in a personal letter to Mackenzie dated May 12, 1893, and now in the Lugard Papers, Mss. Brit. Emp. s.71, Rhodes House. There is a comprehensive discussion in Morton (1990), 119–44. Also see Herlehy and Morton (1988), 395–426.
3 At a cost of £3,500; see Morton (1990), 118, 139. According to Morton, by 1894 the total number of redemptions under this and other schemes was about 3,200 slaves. Also see the Report of the Court of Directors to the Shareholders dated July 25, 1890 and May 18, 1892, both in Imperial British East Africa Company Miscellaneous Papers 1888–1894 (Rhodes House 740.14.s.25).

4 Morton (1990), 19–51, 77–97; Lugard (1893), I, 222, 224–25.
5 Perham and Bull (1959), I, 87, diary entry for January 22, 1890. See Lugard (1893), I, 224–24, for Lugard's objections to Mackenzie's plans.
6 Lugard to Euan-Smith, June 9, 1890. FO 84/2062. The diary for January 2, 1890, says two missionaries, not one.
7 William Jones remained an unsung hero until Morton's portrayal; (1990), 98–118.
8 Perham and Bull (1959), I, 206–208, especially the entry for April 21, 1890, and Lugard (1893), I, 61–62, 67, 227–28, 231–33. For a full discussion, see Morton (1990), 121–27.
9 Lugard (1893), I, 233, and Perham and Bull (1959), I, 71–72, 105, diary entries for January 16 and February 15 1890.
10 Perham and Bull (1959), I, 206–208, entry for April 21, 1890. Indeed, in 1890 and subsequently there were occasions on which patrols of the IBEAC itself actually attacked fugitive settlements in order to return runaways who were not making payments to their masters. This policy had Lugard's "solid backing." Also see Morton (1990), 126–27.
11 Perham and Bull (1959), I, 216 (May 10, 1890), 233 (August 6, 1890); Lugard (1893), I, 296–97. It will be noted below that the ransom amount per slave in these East African transactions, at MT$15 per slave or the sterling equivalent of less than £3, was only about 40 percent of the usual market price for slaves in this region. True, these East African slaves had already escaped, so perhaps a substantial discount was appropriate. Morton notes that the redemption price for the IBEAC-sponsored redemptions at Fuladoyo had been MT$25; the price under Lugard's redemption scheme was first set at MT$16 and then lowered to MT$15; see Morton (1990), 118, 122.
12 Perham and Bull (1959), I, 245–46, entry for August 18, 1890; Lugard (1893), I, 298–99 (the quotation is from 298). In the Lugard Papers, Mss. Brit. Emp. s.71, f.123, Rhodes House, there is a typewritten copy of a "freedom paper" that was given to a slave who had completed his self-redemption payments. It should be noted that Lugard in East Africa always made a direct connection between his plans for self-redemption and other plans for settlement and employment, an emphasis that was lost in Northern Nigeria, where he thought in terms mainly of long-term evolution to a system of wage labor. Lennihan (1982) also discusses the subject. The work projects are noted by Morton (1990), 122–26, 137–39.
13 Lugard (1893), I, 299.
14 Perham and Bull (1959), II, 228. In the survey of Lugard's slavery activities in Mss. Brit. Emp. s.71, f.119, Rhodes House, the comment is made that the "scheme worked well at first, but he had to leave it in the charge of others when he left East Africa, and it finally faded out." See Morton (1990), 123.
15 Lugard (1893), I, 484.
16 See, for example, Tibenderana (1988); Ubah (1985); and Fika (1978).
17 Lugard (1906), 58.
18 *Ibid.*, 66. Lugard referred to Memoranda 6, 15, 16, and 22 with reference to the power of the Islamic courts in matters relating to slavery.
19 Lugard to Secretary of State, August 21, 1903, CO 466/36.
20 Lugard (1906), 174.
21 C. L. Temple, Bauchi Monthly Report for September 1902, September 18, 1902, SNP 15/1 No. 42.
22 *Ibid.*
23 *Ibid.*
24 *Ibid.*
25 Wallace, Report on Nupe Province, August 31, 1901.
26 Gollan's Draft Amending Slavery Proclamation, 1903, CO 446/36.
27 Lugard (1906), 309.
28 Christelow (1993).
29 *Ibid.*

30 *Ibid.*
31 Lugard (1906), 295. As is the case with the background material for Lugard's Memorandum No. 5 of 1905 (revised 1906), we have not been able to locate the original documentation that is quoted at length in Memorandum No. 22. It is our impression that the extensive quotations in both these memoranda are not drawn from the monthly, quarterly, or annual reports from each province. Each of these regular reports contains a section on slavery, and except for those that are missing in the Kaduna archives and are not found at Rhodes House, we have examined all of these reports. We suspect, therefore, that the documentation for the slavery memoranda was separate, but we have not found the circular requesting such information or any portion of the documentation itself, either in Kaduna or in Lugard's papers at Rhodes House.
32 Lugard to Secretary of State, August 21, 1903, CO 446/36.
33 *Ibid.*
34 *Northern Nigeria Annual Report, 1905–06*, 400.
35 C. W. Orr, Zaria Province Annual Report, 1905, March 23, 1906, Zarprof 2552.
36 *Northern Nigeria Annual Report, 1906–07*, 508–509.
37 W. F. Gowers, Annual Report on the Bauchi Province for the Year 1907, SNP 7/9 889/1908.
38 O. Howard, Quarterly Report, Bauchi Province, March 1907, SNP 7/9 1655/1907.
39 *Northern Nigeria Annual Report, 1908–09*, 679.
40 Temple, Bauchi Monthly Report for September 1902.
41 Tukur (unpublished, 1979), 467, citing G. N. Barclay, Yola Report No. 10 for August 1902, Yolaprof A1; Barclay, Yola Report for October 1904, Yolaprof 2; Barclay, Report No. 45 for September and October 1905, Yolaprof A6 and 7.
42 Lugard (1906), 139–40.
43 *Ibid.*, 142.
44 Webster, Nassarawa Province, December 1904, SNP 7/5 346/1904.
45 *Ibid.*; and minutes by Lugard, SNP 7/5 346/1904.
46 On the application of the principle of collective punishment under British rule, see Christelow (1993).
47 Lugard (1906), 149–50. Tibenderana (unpublished, 1974), 190, had recognized how the Islamic Courts were to deal with fugitives, while Provincial Courts were not:

> Native courts were empowered to summon a runaway slave to show cause why he or she ran away without paying his or her redemption fees and they were also empowered to enforce the authority of the master over his slave who objected to do slave work. In other words, native courts were to continue disposing of cases involving slaves and their masters as they had done prior to the establishment of the British administration. But Provincial courts were barred from assisting in the capture of a runaway slave in order that he may be surrendered to his owner.

48 Lugard, Special Memo No. 10 (Slavery), January 18, 1902, CO 446/36. Virtually the same wording was later incorporated into Lugard (1906), 147–48.
49 Lugard (1906), 147–48.
50 Burdon, Report on Nupe Province, August 31, 1901.
51 Burdon first identified "compulsory manumission" in the summer of 1905:

> A great step towards the gradual abolition of slavery has been taken by the Sarikin Muslimin. He has directed the Native Court to undertake all cases of desire for self redemption, arranging the amount, making provision for its being earned and paid and enforcing the acceptance of the award on the master. The result is that slaves instead of running away can go to the Alkali and obtain immediate conditional release.

See Burdon, Report No. 26 for July and August 1905, Province of Sokoto, SNP 15/1 Acc

109. A few months later, he reported that "I therefore gave my full approval to the Sarkin Musulmin of the course that he proposed to adopt in compulsory manumission"; Report No. 28 on Sokoto Province for Months of November and December 1905, Sokprof 2/4 85/1906.

52 *Northern Nigeria Annual Report, 1905–06*, 362–63.

53 *Ibid.* As Burdon reported, "The policy of compulsory manumission on demand on the Native Court, adopted by the Sarikin Muslimin . . . is working well here, as is shewn by this month's [slave register] returns. The principle is of course followed in the Gando [Gwandu] Courts, but there, in the absence of any enlightened ruler, it is by direct European intervention." See Burdon, Report No. 28, November and December 1905, SNP 15/1 Acc 109.

54 Burdon, Report No. 28, November and December 1905.

55 *Northern Nigeria Annual Report, 1905–06*, 411.

56 September 1903, contained in Lugard to Travers Buxton, December 3, 1903, Despatch No. 427, CO 446/33.

57 Lugard to Travers Buxton, December 3, 1903, Despatch No. 427, CO 446/33.

58 Lugard (1906), 309.

59 *Ibid.*

60 *Ibid.*, 306–307.

61 Stanley, Report No. 36 on Sokoto Province for Half-Year ending June 30, 1908, Sokprof 2/9 985/1908.

62 Lovejoy (1988), 248. Female slaves may even have numbered considerably more than half, yet references to slaves often imply that slaves were men. As we have seen, female slaves were common among fugitives, and cases of enslavement and slave trading more often referred to girls and young women than to males. It is difficult to know if women were as numerous as Martin Klein has reported among the slave populations of the Islamic portions of the western Sudan that were so similar to the Sokoto Caliphate, but there is no reason to assume that the proportion of women was lower in the central Sudan than in the western Sudan. See M. Klein (1983), 68–72.

63 Lovejoy (1990), 167–76. Also see Fisher and Fisher (1970), 97–109; Levy (1957), 77–81; Schacht (1964); Schacht (1934), 1012–15; Cooper (1977), 195–96; Mack (1992a), 109–29; Mack (1992b), 89–110; Christelow (1991), 130–44.

64 Convenient legal citations on concubinage in the Caliphate can be found in "Notes on Muslim Law," in Abraham (1940), 159; Lovejoy (1990), 168–69.

65 Bargery (1934).

66 Lovejoy (1990), 164–66; Lovejoy (1988), 256.

67 Case of Gagi, freed in 1905, SNP 15/1 Acc 90.

68 Cited in Lugard (1906), 144. Technically, of course, free Muslim women could not be bought.

69 See, for example, Vaughan and Kirk-Greene (forthcoming).

70 Mahadi (unpublished, 1982), 466.

71 Schacht (1934), 1014–15.

72 There is some uncertainty over the issue of whether men married slave women in the Sokoto Caliphate and early colonial Northern Nigeria. On the basis of Islamic legal texts, Fisher and Fisher (1970), 100, claim that wives could be slave or free, but concubines always had to be slaves. We have no evidence that free men married slave women in Northern Nigeria, except in cases where the woman was freed first.

73 "Notes on Muslim Law," in Abraham (1940), 209.

74 Schacht (1934), 1015.

75 Mary Smith (1954), 41.

76 Levy (1957), 95, 111. According to Bargery (1934), 879, the smallest payment that was acceptable in the early twentieth century was 1,250 cowries.

77 For a description from 1905, see Tremearne (1913), 85–88; also see Baba's account in Mary Smith (1954), 127–66; and Coles (unpublished, 1983), 187–226.
78 Boyd and Last (1985), 287.
79 M. G. Smith (1954a), 134.
80 M. G. Smith (1954b), 22.
81 Stanley, Report on Sokoto Province for Half-Year ending June 30, 1908, Sokprof 2/9 985/1908; and Bargery (1934), 689, 759.
82 Merrick (1905), 27. That is, slave girls should stay in the compound and not even take household sweepings and nightwash to the fields, which might seem a good excuse to go out.
83 Jumare (unpublished, 1988b).
84 Hiskett (1985), 123.
85 Yunusa (unpublished, 1976), 26. Also see Levy (1957), 79, 111–12; and group interview, Runjin Biyo, Sokoto (Jumare Collection). But see Fisher and Fisher (1970), 100.
86 "Notes on Muslim Law," in Abraham (1940), 209.
87 Jumare (unpublished, 1988b), and group interview, Runjin Biyo.
88 Ferguson (unpublished, 1973), 231.
89 The owner of these concubines was none other than Caliph Abdurrahaman (1891–1902), who had the throats of the two concubines slit, their heads hung on a pole by their plaited hair, and his other concubines and wives forced to examine the spectacle. See Skinner (1977), III, 27.
90 Hiskett (1985), 122, citing Tabbat hakika.
91 Ibid.
92 "Notes on Muslim Law," in Abraham (1940), 159.
93 Uthman dan Fodio (1978), 117. Hiskett (1985), 122, states that the statutory period of abstention from intercourse with female captives was four months.
94 Uthman dan Fodio (1978), 118, citing the Mukhtasar. That the legal stricture was followed has been confirmed by oral tradition; group interview, Runjin Biyo.
95 Uthman dan Fodio (1978), 118, citing the Risala.
96 Ibid., 118.
97 Yunusa (unpublished, 1976), 28; testimonies of Muhammadu Rabi'u, Fanisau, Kano Emirate, July 13, 1975; and Alhaji Wada, Kano, July 18, 1975 (Yunusa Collection).
98 "Notes on Muslim Law," in Abraham (1940), 159.
99 Report of Hillary, in Lugard (1906), 303.
100 Other scholars, including Christelow (1985), 69, and M. G. Smith (1954a), 134, state that a concubine became free upon giving birth to a child, but we do not believe that the evidence lends sufficient support to this interpretation. Similarly, Mary Smith (1954), 41, reports that Baba said that when a concubine had children by her master "she became free, and she could leave his house and marry someone else." We suggest that Baba meant that eventually a concubine could do this.
101 Lugard (1906), 303. It should be noted that the reference to the children of a concubine as the "property" of the father is certainly inaccurate. Furthermore, children of concubines were not known as cucanawa (s. bacucane), which was the term used for children born into slavery. Children of concubines were not slaves.
102 Ferguson (unpublished, 1973), 231; also see Yunusa (unpublished, 1976), 28–29.
103 Ferguson (unpublished, 1973), 231. Ferguson's translation has been modified in two important respects. First, women were free on the death of their master, not upon giving birth, and hence the future tense is appropriate. Second, Ferguson's translation states that concubines were exempt from the payment of "tax," by which he presumably means murgu. For a discussion of murgu, see Chapter 7.
104 Lugard (1906), 303.
105 M. G. Smith (1978), 49. For a comparison with East Africa, see Cooper (1977), 196–97.

328

106 Personal communication from Ibrahim Jumare.
107 *Northern Nigeria Annual Report, 1902*, 132.
108 Lugard (1906), 143.
109 *Ibid.*, 149–50.
110 *Ibid.*, 145.
111 H. R. P. Hillary, Sokoto Monthly Report, January 1905, Sokprof 2/2 401/1905; enclosed letter of July 31, 1905, Hillary to Lugard.
112 Larymore, Report No. 58 on Nupe Privince for Quarter ending 31st March 1907, SNP 7/8 2017/1907; Lugard (1906), 136, 145.
113 Howard, Resident Bauchi to Secretary of Administration, Zungeru, April 29, 1908; CSO 1/127/8.
114 Girouard to Crewe, November 16, 1908, CSO 1/27/8.
115 Crozier (1932), 154. Also see 87, 123, 144, 146–47, 161, 163, 168.
116 Charles Waddell "Travelling in Nupe Country," 1905, DC–2/A, SIM Archives. Waddell's uncle was the famous Hope Waddell of Calabar.
117 C. L. Temple, Bauchi Monthly Report for September 1902, September 18, 1902, SNP 15/1 No. 42.
118 Orr (1911), 295.
119 A. Burdon, Sokoto Province, Report No. 2 April 30, 1903, Sokprof 2/1 23/1903.
120 Webster, Nassarawa Province, December 1904, SNP 7/5 346/1904.
121 Lugard (1906), 149–50.
122 Webster, Nassarawa Province, December 1904.
123 Register of Freed Slaves, Illorin, Year ending 31st December 1906, SNP 15/1 Acc 121.
124 Lugard (1906), 145. Also see Duff's comments on the reforms at Bida, in Lugard (1906), 144: "It follows that practically all women are already emancipated. A slave woman who bears a child to her master is not only free at his death but practically so during his life, and even if she bears no child but if well behaved she is free at her master's death." Of course she was not free to leave.
125 Lugard (1906), 145.
126 Minute by Lugard to Webster, Nassarawa Province, December 1904, SNP 7/5 346/1904.
127 Webster, Nassarawa Province, December 1904.
128 Lovejoy (1988), 264–65.
129 Lugard (1918), 233.
130 Return of Freed Slaves, Bauchi Province for Quarter ending 31st December 1906, SNP 15/1 Acc 121.
131 *Ibid.*
132 Kisch (1910), 155.
133 Lugard (1906), 143–44. Italics added.
134 *Ibid.*, 143. We have been unable to identify the *alkali*.
135 According to Lugard's instructions, "whenever a woman whose status is that of a slave marries a man, and any 'dowry' is demanded by the owner of the woman, it must be regarded as purchase money, and the transaction is consequently illegal. It may, however, be paid as redemption-money, provided that the woman is first freed with all proper formalities by the Native Court." See Lugard (1906), 146.
136 C. L. Temple, Bauchi Monthly Report for September 1902, September 18, 1902, SNP 15/1 No. 42.
137 Register of Freed Slaves, Kano Province, September 1906, SNP 15/1 Acc 121.
138 Lugard (1906), 146.
139 The political assistant, Northern Nigeria, to the Resident, Bauchi Province, June 7, 1906, SNP 15/1 Acc 121. The letter refers to an earlier report dated February 10.
140 Lugard (1906), 143.
141 C. W. Orr, Zaria Province Annual Report, 1905, March 23, 1906, Zarprof 7/1 2/552.

142 See, for example, the certificate of freedom for Dije, in Skinner (1977), 253–54.
143 Return of Freed Slaves, Bauchi Province for quarter December 31, 1906, SNP 15/1 Acc 121.
144 Register of Freed Slaves, Zaria, August 1906, SNP 15/1 Acc 90.
145 Lugard (1918), 237–38.
146 According to Christelow (1993), there was a distinction in Arabic between *wala* and *wilaya*: *Wala* refers to the patron–client relationship between former master and ex-slave and is not the same as *wilaya*, guardianship. The legal import is similar in conferring the right to give the ex-slave in marriage. Legal texts are concerned with who inherits the rights to *wala*. Also Bargery (1934), 1076.
147 H. R. P. Hillary, Sokoto Monthly Report, January 1905, Sokprof 2/2 401/1905; enclosed letter of July 31, 1905, Hillary to Lugard. Also see Ubah (1992).
148 H. D. Larymore, Kabba Province Monthly Reports, March 1904, SNP 15/1 Acc 64.
149 Lugard (1906), 304.
150 O. Howard, Quarterly Report, Bauchi Province, March 1907, SNP 7/9 1655/1907.
151 Political Assistant, Northern Nigeria to Resident, Bauchi, June 7, 1906, SNP 15/1 Acc 121.
152 Report of Acting Resident Feargus Dwyer, enclosed in C. W. Orr to Elgin, September 9, 1907, Despatch No. 459, CO 446/64.
153 Larymore, Report No. 58 on Nupe Province for Quarter ending 31st March 1907, SNP 7/8 2017/1907.
154 Stanley, Report No. 36 on Sokoto Province for Half-Year ending June 30, 1908, Sokprof 2/9 985/1908.
155 *Ibid.*
156 *Ibid.*
157 Register of Freed Slaves, SNP 15/1 Acc 90, SNP 15/1 Acc 121.
158 Lugard (1906), 143.

5 Upholding proprietary rights to land

1 In addition to the specific citations in the chapter, several works that consider the territorial system and the slaves were generally depended upon. M. G. Smith was the first scholar to consider the question in detail. His analysis is scattered through a number of publications, including M. G. Smith (1955); (1960); (1965a); (1965b); (1954a), 239–90; (1952), 333–47. Hill (1972) and (1977) both contain treatments of land-allocation patterns that have informed the discussion here. Starns (1974), working mostly with secondary sources (including Smith and Hill), made a judicious summary in his "Land Tenure among the Rural Hausa." Several academic theses consider the issue, among which those of Bello (unpublished, 1982) and Mahadi (unpublished, 1982) should be noted. Official documents on the subject from the colonial period, though hardly comprehensive, provide more information than has generally been appreciated. These are cited below.
2 Other land-tenure questions, such as ownership by Europeans, town and city plots, common lands including cattle trails, and some religious lands (*waqf*) are not treated here. The term *waqf* usually refers to an endowment of a pious foundation, but in the Maliki school of law, it also refers to state-held land, and in that context *waqf* lands are examined.
3 According to Garba (unpublished, 1986), 165, 169–70, the Hausa states of Kano, Zaria, Katsina and others were declared *waqf* lands for purposes of taxation; that is why they were subject to *kharaj* or *kurdin kasa*.
4 There are indications, nonetheless, that these "tribal" lands could in fact be alienated and that "communal" tenure was more complicated than we are suggesting here. See, for example, Gowers, n.d., but sometime after July 23, 1907, SNP 6/3 162/1907. It does seem, however, that *jizya* lands could not easily be transferred to "outsiders."
5 Lovejoy (1979).
6 For the classic discussion, see M. G. Smith (1960).

7 Hill (1977), 4.
8 *Ibid.*, 208–209.
9 Cited in E. P. C. Girouard, "Land Tenure in Northern Nigeria," November 2, 1907, Northern Nigeria Lands Committee, Minutes of Evidence and Appendices, 1910 [Cd. 5103]. The reference to slaves "passing with the office" includes titles that were reserved for slaves.
10 Jumare (unpublished, 1990).
11 Resident to Lugard, June 14, 1904, Sokprof 151/1904, as cited in Garba (unpublished, 1986), 117.
12 H. B. Foulkes, Silame District Assessment Report, Sokprof 2/11 230/1913.
13 Ubah (1985), 47.
14 Evidence of H. R. Palmer, June 1, 1908, in Northern Nigeria Lands Committee, Minutes of Evidence and Appendices, 1910 [Cd. 5103].
15 At the time, there were fourteen districts, each with its own *hakimi* and *alkali* (judge). Ten of the districts had been sub-divided into a total of forty-five sub-districts, each under a *mai jimila*. The central district around Kano had eleven sub-districts, under the Chiroma. The number of these office holders, therefore, amounted to about 185. Ubah (1985), 117, states that there were some 4,000 village and town heads at this time. The number of office holders in Kano city is unknown, but they included many palace officials, ward heads, *alkalai*, and occupational heads, certainly totaling more than one hundred. Even allowing for the possibility that some officials were not provided with a tax-free farm, the total number of tax-free official farms and estates probably exceeded 4,000, of which at least the 185 belonging to high officials were particularly large. There were other estates as well; the Emir of Kano owned at least two dozen, so that the total might well have approached 5,000. See also C. L. Temple, Annual Report on Kano Province, 1909, SNP 7/10 6415/1909.
16 Orr to Girouard, November 14, 1907, in Northern Nigeria Lands Committee, Minutes of Evidence and Appendices, 1910 [Cd. 5103].
17 Girouard, "Land Tenure in Northern Nigeria," November 2, 1907. Italics have been added because Girouard insisted before the Lands Commission that there were no proprietary rights in land; see below.
18 Stanley, Report No. 36 on Sokoto Province for Half-Year ending June 30, 1908, Sokprof 2/9 985/1908.
19 According to Stanley, Temple had earlier "dealt" with the assessment of the two private estates in the Rafin Yamulu – Kasara and Hakimi Atto – which were transferred from Dinawa to Wurno, but because Hakimi Atto lived in Dinawa and "the bulk of the farmers of the Kasara's estate also live in Dinawa," Temple was not aware of the other private estates. Stanley had "no doubt that investigation will show that there are private estates on the same scale as those in the Rafin Yamulu, all round Kworgaba." Perhaps if Temple had realized the extent to which there were private estates, he would have altered his testimony before the Lands Committee in London in 1908. See Stanley, Report No. 36 on Sokoto Province for Half-Year ending June 30, 1908, Sokprof 2/9 985/1908.
20 Gepp, Assessment Report, Dan Isa's Sub-District, May 5, 1911, SNP 7/12 1035/1911. We do not suggest that these holdings were identical to those of the precolonial period.
21 H. B. Foulkes, Assessment Report, Dan Buram District, Kano Emirate, SNP 7/13 5785/1912. Unless otherwise noted, acreage refers to land under cultivation.
22 D. F. H. MacBride, Dawaki Ta Kudu District, Assessment Report, October 9, 1937, SNP 15/1 Acc 289.
23 Foulkes, Assessment Report, Dan Buram District.
24 Yunusa lists seventeen estates belonging to the Emir, of which Fanisau, Gogel, and Giwaran were the largest; see (unpublished, 1976), 55–63. Gandun Nassarawa was approximately 9 sq. km. in extent; see Sa'idu (unpublished, 1981), 105–40. For information on the extensive holdings of the Emir in Dawaki ta Kudu, see D. F. H. MacBride, Dawaki Ta Kudu District, Assessment Report, October 9, 1937, SNP 15/1 Acc 289.

25 Revenue Survey Assessment, Kanoprof 1708/Vol. 1, 5/6/36, as cited in Garba (unpublished, 1986), 292.
26 Tahir (unpublished, 1975), 332.
27 Ubah (1985), 56.
28 Foulkes, Assessment Report, Jaidanawa District, SNP 7/13 4817/1912.
29 Gepp, Assessment Report, Dan Isa's Sub-District, May 5, 1911, SNP 7/12 1035/1911.
30 Ubah (1985), 57, drawing on oral sources.
31 Lovejoy (1978).
32 H. R. Palmer, "Land Tenure in the Haussa States [Katsina]," May 19, 1907, SNP 15/1 Acc 369; and Hill (1972), 84, 240–41.
33 Gowers, 1907, SNP 6/3 162/1907.
34 Ibid.
35 M. G. Smith (1965a), 233–35; Fika (1978), 171. Territory was not automatically inheritable, although the rumada owned by many officials in their lands were inheritable unless they were attached to an office. See M. G. Smith (1955), 102. Territorial responsibilities were often scattered about the map, as in Kano and Sokoto; a territorial official might have as many as twelve to twenty parcels. Territorial boundaries were more compact in Katsina and also in small emirates like Katagum. The British instituted an early reform that consolidated these dispersed territories into districts, and though this had importance for tax collection, it was of little significance for the land-allocation mechanism considered in this chapter. The former territorial officials usually became the district heads under the new rules. See Lugard, Memo on the Taxation of Natives in Northern Nigeria, 1907 [Cd. 3309], pp. 6, 28, 31–32, 34, 37–38, 40, 43, 46, 51, 53, and 55; Percy Girouard, "Land Tenure and Land Revenue Assessment," Memo No. 25, September 1908, CO African (West) Confidential Print No. 906, ff. 7–8; and Meek (1957), 160. Lugard noted that by the end of 1906 the reform had been fully accomplished in Nupe, was not needed in Kontagora, which had not originally been so divided, was progressing rapidly in Borno, more slowly in Zaria and Bauchi, more slowly yet in Ilorin and Yola (where only three of thirteen districts had been reformed), and not at all in Nassarawa. In Kano, the title holders were required to live in their district capitals from October 1907. See Fika (1978), 171.
36 Garba (unpublished, 1986), 165.
37 On the position of village head, see Mahadi (unpublished, 1982), 288–91. Dupigny, referring to traditional practice, stated that a "Fulah" was invariably the village headman. See Kano Province Assessment, 1909–10, SNP 7/10 5570/1909. Among the Maguzawa the village head might often be the senior male member of the village's founding lineage group.
38 M. G. Smith (1955), 96.
39 Rowling (1949, 6. Although Hill (1977), 35–39, has contended that the position of village head was relatively weaker in the precolonial and early colonial periods, on balance there appears no reason to doubt that the village heads were central to the land-allocation system both before and after the British advent.
40 Bello (unpublished, 1982), 19, 27–28.
41 Mahadi (unpublished, 1982), 450; also 374–75, 460, and 461–62.
42 Tibenderana (1988), 26.
43 Oyeyipo (unpublished, n.d.).
44 See Nadel (1942), 183.
45 Fika (1978), 115–16, notes that the creation of the hamlet layer was carried on in the period 1905–1908. For an early study of the development of local government authorities, called "Native Administrations" – a term that long survived Nigerian independence – see Wraith (1966), 201–202. The Native Authority Proclamation was issued in 1907, while the first Native Treasuries were established in 1911.
46 M. G. Smith (1965b), 137–38; Hill (1972), 265; Starns (1974), 17; Fika (1978), 98.
47 As discussed by M. G. Smith (1960), 254–59. Also see Sa'idu (unpublished, 1981), 146–48.

48 Diary of Hamman Yaji, Emir off Madagali; see Vaughan and Kirk-Greene (forthcoming).
49 Compare Christelow (1993), chapter 8.
50 Testimonies of Alhaji Wada of Kano, July 18, 1975; Malam Zubairu, Gandun Swaina, Kano Emirate, September 11, 1975; and Malam Rabi'u, Fanisau, Kano Emirate, July 13, 1975 (Yunusa Collection).
51 See Christelow (1993), chapter 9.
52 C. L. Temple, Sokoto Provincial Report, No. 33, Quarter ending 31 March 1907, Sokprof 343/1907, as cited in Tukur (unpublished, 1979), 830. Lugard observed: "It has been reported that Chiefs and others in outlying towns or on important roads receive bribes or rewards for capturing fugitive slaves." Residents were advised that either they could punish the seizer for "re-enslaving the person" or they could "abstain from interference"; see Lugard (1906), 155. G. N. Barclay (Annual Report, Yola Province, 1905, Yolaprof A6, A7) also reported that runaway slaves were being recaptured in Yola in 1905.
53 Following the description in M. G. Smith (1965b), 137–38. Also see Hill (1972), 20, 213–15, 264–65; and Meek (1957), 164–65.
54 M. G. Smith (1965b), 137–38.
55 See Starns (1974), 34.
56 Meek (1957), 164–65.
57 Northern Nigeria Lands Committee, Minutes of Evidence [Cd. 5103] of 1910, f. xviii.
58 *Ibid.*, f. 30.
59 *Ibid.*, f. 11.
60 *Ibid.*, f. 31.
61 *Ibid.*, f. 15.
62 *Ibid.*, ff. 96–97.
63 Hill (1977), 211–12. It is clear enough, however, as seen above, that the British based their land policy on a broad assumption that permission *would* be necessary for taking up land.
64 See Ingawa (unpublished, 1984), 141, and also 32, 46–51.
65 Christelow (1993). The case refers to a farm carved out of bush land at Bakarari.
66 M. G. Smith (1955), 104–105.
67 A. H. Festing reported from Kano that people were "leaving the towns and settling in the agricultural districts" (Report on the Kano Province for the Quarter ending 31 December 1906, SNP 7/8 1545/1907). In 1908, he wrote in his report "Conditions on Zaria-Kano Border," SNP 15/1 Acc 394, that three years before, rich uncultivated lands still existed in the border region, but that now heavy migration was taking place, largely from the direction of Kano into Zaria. Cargill in 1908 stated that "During the past year 20,000 people have crossed from the Western part of Kano into [southern Katsina]," where land was being rapidly cleared and put into cultivation (Kano Province Report for the Year ending 31 December 1907, SNP 7/9 1538/1908). A year later, Dupigny reported "an enormous acreage of virgin land . . . is being brought under cultivation" (Kano Province Assessment, 1909–10, SNP 7/10 5570/1909). Most such accounts linked the movements to an increased safety in the border regions. Thus a 1909 document from Kano, SNP 7/10 3555/1909, speaks of a "new sense of security from raid and rising which is rapidly growing up in the country districts, the natural consequence of which is continual exodus from the town onto the land."
68 *Northern Nigeria Annual Report, 1905–06*, 360.
69 Goldsmith, Sokoto Province Quarterly Report No. 31, September 30, 1906, Sokprof 2/2 977/1906. Benton estimated the population at 5,391 free males, 8,786 females, 9,296 children, and 4,976 slaves, for a total population of 28,449. These estimates suggest a slave population of at least 17.5 percent, but it should be noted that many of the women were probably slaves, including concubines, and the status of the children is unclear. Of the adult population (19,153), at least 26 percent were slave, and if allowance is made for the probability that the disproportionate number of females included concubines, then at least 30 percent of the population must have been slave.

70 *Annual Report, Northern Nigeria 1907–08*, 613, 625; and Dupigny, Assessment Report, Sarkin Dawaki Tsakkar Gidda District, SNP 7/10 5570/1909. The area borders Katagum and Ningi. Dupigny noted: "The effect of established order is to be seen today mainly in the enormous acreage of virgin land which is being brought under cultivation, in the depletion of the towns and increase in farm holdings, and in the influx of strangers from outlying populous districts."

71 Wallace, while traveling for the Royal Niger Company in the 1890s, had written of a belt of "robber-haunted" border districts made uninhabitable because of raiding by the troops of the Emir of Katsina. Between Fawa and Guzo, Wallace states that his party went seventy miles without seeing a single person. See Wallace (1896), 215.

72 Festing's report on trade in Kano Province dated May 8, 1907, SNP 7/7 1867/1907.

73 D. F. H. MacBride, Dawaki Ta Kudu District, Assessment Report, October 9, 1937, SNP 15/1 Acc 289.

74 Goldsmith, Sokoto Province Quarterly Report No. 31, September 30, 1906, Sokprof 2/2 977/1906; and Gowers, Report on Land Tenure in Bauchi, 1907, SNP 6/3 162/1907.

75 M. G. Smith (1960), 254. *Dimajai* was another term for the children of slaves; the less familiar term *matankara* means "grandchildren of slaves." Sa'idu, commenting on Gandun Nassarawa, the large plantation just outside the walls of Kano that belonged to the Emir, notes that the Emir's slaves were given their own facial marks; see (unpublished, 1981), 137, 254.

76 Christelow (1993).

77 For discussions of the institution of *gandu*, see Hill (1972), 41–43, 250, 292. Hill notes that "all writers on land tenure have ignored gandu," but see M. G. Smith (1965a), 241–44; and (1965b), 140–41.

78 Hill (1972), 254–55. These private granaries became more important as tax payments moved from kind to cash.

79 Hill (1972), 231; Watts (1983), 99–102, 370; *Northern Nigeria Annual Report, 1907–08*, 613. Ubah (1985), 367, notes that many slaves changed hands at this time, ostensibly because their masters could not take care of them.

80 These difficulties are addressed by M. G. Smith (1960), 257.

81 Mary Smith (1954), 67; Hogendorn (1977b), 372, 382.

82 Lugard (1906), 137; Memorandum on the Taxation of Natives in Northern Nigeria, 1907 [Cd. 3309], 18.

83 The situation should be compared with the East African coast, where fugitive slave settlements appear to have been far more common; see Morton (1990), 11–51.

84 The 1900 proclamation is cited in SNP 17 42367. The Land Registry Proclamation was drafted as Proclamation No. 10, June 15, 1901 and is enclosed in the same file.

85 August 21, 1903, CO 446/36, p. 10; and the enclosure in this file from Chief Justice H. C. Gollan, Zungeru, June 24, 1903.

86 Lugard (1906), 138.

87 *Ibid.*, 142.

88 *Ibid.*, 142–43.

89 *Ibid.*, 140–42.

90 Phillips (1989), 66.

91 *Ibid.*, 74; Hogendorn (1978), 16; Watts (1983), 156, 172–73.

92 Phillips (1989), 67–68. In 1902, Lugard was High Commissioner, not Governor.

93 Phillips (1989), 67–68.

94 *Ibid.*, 73.

95 Girouard, "Land Tenure in Northern Nigeria," November 2, 1907, Northern Nigeria Lands Committee, Minutes of Evidence and Appendixes, 1910 [Cd. 5103]. This memorandum was the outgrowth of "A Memorandum on Land Tenure and Land Revenue in Northern Nigeria," July 5, 1907, SNP 15 Acc 374.

96 Girouard, "Land Tenure in Northern Nigeria," November 2, 1907.

97 *Ibid.*

98 Girouard, "A Memorandum on Land Tenure and Land Revenue in Northern Nigeria," July 5, 1907.

99 Girouard, "A Memorandum on Land Tenure and Land Revenue in Northern Nigeria," July 5, 1907. Also see Girouard, "Land Tenure in Northern Nigeria," November 2, 1907.

100 Cited in Girouard, "Land Tenure in Northern Nigeria," November 2, 1907.

101 See Report of the Northern Nigeria Lands Committee, Cd. 5102 of 1910, and Minutes of Evidence, Cd. 5103 of 1910. In preparation for the meetings of this committee, which convened in June 1908, much evidence was submitted by Girouard, and two of the most knowledgeable British officials, Temple and Orr, testified personally in London. A large amount of material (over one hundred typed pages) not published in the Command Papers is in the "Lands Committee's Report," October 17, 1908, in CO 446/75 of 1908 following Despatch No. 545. Lennihan discusses at length the Lands Committee's membership and its affection for the single tax ideas; see (unpublished, 1983), 86–103. There are useful discussions in Watts (1983), 158–66; Hill (1977), 35–36; and Shenton (1986), 41–45. We would contend that the difference between Lugard and Girouard has been exaggerated, both at the time and in the recent scholarship of Lennihan, Watts, and Shenton. As Lugard commented on the fugitive slave problem in 1906, "the rights of the Fulani in the land have, in theory, been transferred to Government as the suzerain power," an idea that is very similar to Girouard's. See Lugard (1906), 137. Phillips (1989), 67–74, has presented a more balanced view.

102 By the language of Proclamation No. 8 of 1900 and No. 11 of 1906, no non-Native could acquire land from a Native without the prior written consent of the High Commissioner. Before 1900, the Royal Niger Company had acquired small and scattered posts, which appear to have been the only foreign holdings that the colonial regime recognized; see Cd. 5102, pp. vi–vii. In fact, merchants from North Africa and immigrants from Borno, among other places, had regularly acquired property; see Lovejoy (1980), 68–69; and Lovejoy (1986a), 201–209.

103 The Lands Committee's Minutes of Evidence, Cd. 5103, p. 28, noted that a major reason for precolonial eviction from land was failure to perform military service when called upon, failure to pay taxes, or failure to participate in the compulsory building or rebuilding of fortifications. A year before the Lands Committee met, Cargill wrote that

> In Kano in the event of a man applying for a *vacant* plot he does pay a purchase amount to the local headman and the plot then remains his and is heritable so long as he or his heirs pay the land and produce taxes, or their land is not confiscated on account of crime; he may however be dispossessed by the Emir without compensation. Telekawa [*tala-kawa*] are not admitted to have proprietary rights outside the will of the Emir or suzerain. (Cargill Papers, SNP 15/3 Acc 373 A7, dated September 3, 1907)

Also see Gowers' 1907 report on Bauchi, SNP 6/3 162/1907.

104 See Meek (1949), 151.

105 Cd. 5102 of 1910, p. xviii; Cd. 5103 of 1910, p. 11.

106 Cd. 5103 of 1910, p. 39. Lennihan (unpublished, 1983), 86–87, makes the point that the Lands Committee's report ensured that smallholder agriculture would predominate, rather than the estates favored by Lugard where ex-slaves could find work as the hired labor of their former masters. The election of a Liberal government in Britain in 1905 probably furnished a political underpinning to this development, according to Lennihan. Note that Lennihan (1982) uses this phrase, quoted in the text, for the title of her article, "Rights in Men."

107 Woodward (1957).

108 Watts (1983); Shenton (1986); Lennihan (1982).

109 According to this view, the major way in which the area was incorporated into the world economy was through the profits of merchant capital. See, for example, Shenton (1986), 11–20. Also see Watts (1983) and Lennihan (unpublished, 1983).

110 Lennihan (1982) prefers Girouard's interpretation.

111 Lugard to Wedgwood, November 15, 1912, Mss. Brit. Emp. S.76, Lugard Papers, Rhodes House.

112 The ideas of the single-taxers had further opportunity for implementation through the West African Lands Committee of 1916, which was an extension of the Northern Nigeria Lands Committee hearings and which represented a further move towards George's views on land by emphasizing the role of peasant production. Phillips has observed that even after the all-West African hearings, policy was largely one of intent and "barely influenced practice." Policy was "little more than a cloak for inactivity." Phillips' observations apply equally well to Northern Nigeria. For Phillips (1989), 75–79, "inaction" meant that the colonial state "could not impose conditions which would create free labour without destroying communal land tenure, and they could not destroy communal tenure without weakening the chiefs on whom they relied in the interim for forced labour and political order." This valuable insight on areas where communal tenure was common also applies to the Northern Nigerian situation, where proprietary rights to land under a variety of tenures continued to exist, despite the rhetoric.

113 Lugard (1918), 358–59.

114 Christelow (1993); Lovejoy (1980), 90, 94, 129, 145; and Hogendorn (1978), 85–86, 108, 141, 142.

115 Lugard (1918), 340–43.

116 *Ibid.*, 343.

117 *Ibid.*, 350.

118 *Ibid.*, 345.

119 *Ibid.*, 350.

120 *Ibid.*, 346.

121 *Ibid.*, 346–47.

122 *Ibid.*

123 *Ibid.*, 349.

124 *Ibid.*, 168–69.

125 *Ibid.*, 347.

126 *Ibid.*, 356.

127 *Ibid.*

128 Jumare (unpublished, 1988a), 90, 138–65. Jumare's interviews are being prepared for publication.

129 C. O. Migeod, Annual Report, Yola Province, 1922, SNP 9/10 72/1923.

130 Arnett's memorandum for Lugard on slavery, 1925, Arnett Papers, Mss. Afr. s.952/2–3, Rhodes House.

131 Lugard (1918), 356.

132 Memorandum on Slavery in Nigeria, June 5, 1924, CSO 26/11799, Vol. I. This memorandum was an expansion of G. S. Browne's draft and incorporated S. U. Grier's lengthy comments.

133 Memorandum dated April 11, 1930, SNP 18/2 13696/36.

134 *Ibid.*

135 Meek (1957), 151; Lugard (1906), 137–38, 142–43.

136 A point emphasized by Meek (1957), 122.

137 Greenberg (1947), 209.

138 SNP 15/1 Acc 369, 1907. Palmer was also observing the impact of making slaves pay taxes on their plots; see Chapter 6.

139 Lugard (1906), 252.

6 The role of taxation in the reform of slavery

1 Slaves had, of course, been "taxed" under the Caliphate in the sense that slavery was a form of exploitation, but the benefits of this "tax" accrued directly to the master, not the state. Slaves were, however, used for public purposes such as building and repairing city walls and service in the army, especially the transport corps, and as government carriers as well. In this regard, it is instructive that Bargery equates *murgu*, the fee slaves had to pay to their masters for the right to work on their own account, with *galla*, "any kind of tax"; see (1934), 350. Of course *murgu* was a "tax" that was between master and slave, not between the political state and the slave (see below).

2 Lovejoy (1993).

3 Lugard (1906), 309.

4 *Al-Gaith al-Wabl fisirat as Iman al adl*; see the discussion by Lawal (1992).

5 For the best discussion of taxation, see Garba (unpublished, 1986), which to a great extent corrects the observation of Hill (1977), 50, that "much less was known about variations in pre-colonial taxation systems . . . than Lugard supposed." In addition to Garba, see Okediji (unpublished, 1972); Tukur (unpublished, 1979), chapter 8; Fika (1978), chapter 5; Hill (1972), 323–25; Hogendorn (1978), chapter 4; Bello (unpublished, 1982), 32–34; Mahadi (unpublished, 1982), 456–73; Tibenderana (1988), 103–14; and Ubah (1985). Also see Orr (1911), chapter 4, "Taxation Problems in 1903–1904"; and Memorandum on the Taxation of Natives in Northern Nigeria, Cd. 3309 of 1907.

6 Watts (1983), 69.

7 Garba (unpublished, 1986), 193.

8 *Ibid.*, 71. In areas inhabited by non-Muslims, such as the Maguzawa, who had accepted political subordination, *zakka* with its roots in religion was not levied. In its stead a special tax (*jizya*) was collected. *Jizya* was comparable in amount to *zakka*, and was assessed on the community, not on individuals.

9 Garba (unpublished, 1986), 114, 166–67, notes that *zakka* was assessed by the *jakadu* after the harvest had taken place. It was easier to assess grain when stored than when growing in the fields. Also see Hill (1972), 51–52; Mahadi (unpublished, 1982), 320, 418; Watts (1983), 257–58; Fika (1978), 39; and Lugard (1906), 89.

10 F. Cargill, Resident Kano, May 27, 1908, in File 7173, "Kano Province Economic Survey, 1909," as reproduced in Paden (unpublished, 1968), 1302–1304.

11 N. M. Gepp. report on Dan Makoyo Sub-District, 1909, encl. in H. R. Palmer, Kano Annual Report, 1910, SNP 15/1 Acc 167.

12 Festing report, 1907, in W. P. Hewby, Report on Kano emirate, July 10, 1908, SNP 6/4 c.111/1908.

13 Lugard (1906), 90; Girouard, "Land Tenure and Land Revenue Assessment," Memo No. 25, September 1908. These principles were sufficiently unlike the Quranic injunction to pay a tithe that many peasants regarded it not as an Islamic tax, but a tax on grain (*kurdin hatsi*). See Mahadi (unpublished, 1982), 320, 418. For a discussion of the Islamic base of taxation, see Sa'id (1983), 117–25; and Garba (unpublished, 1986), 20.

14 Garba (unpublished, 1986), 111–12. In 1908, W. P. Hewby estimated that *zakka* made up about a quarter of all taxes, SNP 6/4 c.111/1908.

15 Lugard (1906), 300.

16 *Ibid.*, 303.

17 Orr to Girouard, no date, in Northern Nigeria Lands Committee, Minutes of Evidence and Appendices, 1910 [Cd. 5102]. Also see his testimony before the Lands Committee, June 30, 1908.

18 See Watts (1983), 69.

19 Lugard (1906), 90.

20 Hill (1977), 50. Lugard had some excuse for failing to identify *kurdin kasa*'s features with accuracy. It was indeed complex. Sometimes it was paid to an official in the emirate's capital, sometimes to the tax payer's village head. Sometimes payment was made where a person's farm was located even though he did not live there. Many people paid partially because they had bought or inherited a farm that had been sub-divided and assessed as part of the original holding. According to Festing, the amount of *kurdin kasa* could be adjusted when new farms were opened up or when farms were transferred from one owner to another. In some places when a farm was divided, each part had to pay the tax, but in other places several farms could be held under one title and pay only one tax. This was one feature of the tax system that Festing thought was "a matter deserving of regularisation." See Festing report, 1907, in W. P. Hewby, Report on Kano Emirate, July 10, 1908, SNP 6/4 c.111/1908.

21 Fika (1978), 39. Fika states that *kurdin kasa* had become a flat-rate poll tax about the year 1882. Also see Tukur (unpublished, 1979), 552, citing C. L. Temple.

22 Cargill to Festing, April 26, 1907; SNP 15/3 Acc 368.

23 Festing report, 1907, in Hewby, Report on Kano Emirate, July 10, 1908, SNP 6/4 c.111/1908.

24 H. Frewan, Gora District Assessment, 1909, SNP 7/10 3555/1909.

25 The amount of *kurdin kasa* collected in 1909 was £231. 11s. 6d., based on the flat assessment of 4,000 cowries per farm. At the rate of 2,000 cowries per shilling, Gepp estimated that the total number of farms twenty years earlier had been 2,316, although in 1909 the actual number was 4,632, "rather more than double [sic] the number of 20 years ago." Gepp thought that the population must have at least doubled in the same period and hence that "the Kurdin Kassa has remained unaltered and has not increased proportionately with the population and the number of farms. In fact it may be said that, in respect of Kurdin Kassa the individual farmer is now paying rather less than half the rent he paid 20 years ago." N. M. Gepp, report on Dan Makoyo Sub-District, 1909, encl. in H. R. Palmer, Kano Annual Report, 1910, SNP 15/1 Acc 167.

26 E. G. M. Dupigny, Assessment Report, Sarkin Dawaki Tsakkar Gidda District, SNP 7/10 5570/1909.

27 Garba (unpublished, 1986), 368; Tukur (unpublished, 1979), 200; Okediji (unpublished, 1972), 107; Bello (unpublished, 1982), 104n; Mahadi (unpublished, 1982), 315, 433–34, 464, 495.

28 Garba (unpublished, 1986), 368.

29 Tukur (unpublished, 1979), 532–33, 562–639.

30 Yunusa (unpublished, 1976), 63.

31 Okediji (unpublished, 1972), 94; Hill (1977), 50–51; Watts (1983), 258; Lugard (1906), 91. According to Gepp, "The Kurdin Shuke, Kurdin Rafi and Kurdin Karofi [were] the taxes on certain specified forms of cultivation on irrigation crops and on dye pits and certain forms of industry ..."; see Report on Dan Makoyo Sub-District, 1909, encl. in Palmer, Kano Annual Report, 1910, SNP 15/1 Acc 167. Also see Dupigny, Assessment Report, Sarkin Dawaki Tsakkar Gidda District, SNP 7/10 5570/1909.

32 Fika (1978), 39.

33 Festing report, 1907, SNP 6/4 c.111/1908.

34 According to Frewan, the list of crops attracting *kurdin shuka* or *kurdin rafi* in Kura District included rice, groundnuts, pepper, cotton, artichokes, yams, *gujia* groundnuts, indigo, *rama*, tobacco, beniseed, *rizga*, *tumuku*, *yalo*, potatoes, cassava, sugar cane (both *takanda* and *reke*), onions, okra, and *yakuwa*.

> Kurdin shuka and kurdin rafi are fixed according to the crop. Sweet potatoes and others are assessed on the furrow, which varies from 10 to 40 yards and is called kunia. Each of these over 10 yards pays $1\frac{1}{2}$d, the talakawa naturally making them as long as possible. Furrows under 10 yards in length are called yan kunia [*kunya*], and are not considered for taxation purposes unless there appear to be too many of them. (Frewan, Kura District Assessment Report, 1909, SNP 7/8 2407/1909)

338

In Gora District, *kurdin shuka* was collected on groundnuts (2,000–3,000 cowries), potatoes (3,000 cowries), rice (2,000–3,000 cowries), cassava (2,000–5,000 cowries), pepper (1,000 cowries), and *gwaza* (2,000 cowries): see Frewan, Gora District Assessment Report, 1909, SNP 7/10 3555/1909.

35 Dupigny, Assessment Report, Sarkin Dawaki Tsakkar Gidda District.

36 *Ibid.*

37 F. Cargill, Resident Kano, May 27, 1908, in File 7173, "Kano Province Economic Survey, 1909," in Paden (unpublished, 1968), 1302–1304.

38 Garba (unpublished, 1986), 174. *Chappa* or *chaffa* is often seen in the sources, but the Hausa "c" is normally a "ch," and "p" is more often rendered "f."

39 According to Bargery (1934), 470, *hurumi* is defined as: 1. A compound not assessed for tax but which has to pay heavy demands made on it by a district head or other native official. 2. A cemetery. 3. Common land. 4. A forest or other reserve. 5. An official farm which cannot be alienated. 6. Any private property.

40 In *Ta'lim al-radi*, a tract written in c. 1809–10 on land tenure; see Zahradeen (unpublished, 1976), 263–66. also see Lugard (1918), 360.

41 Cargill, May 27, 1908, in Paden (unpublished, 1968), 1302–1304.

42 Bargery (1934), 146.

43 Dupigny, Assessment Report, Sarkin Dawaki Tsakkar Gidda District.

44 Cargill, in Paden, (unpublished, 1968), 1302–1304. For Zaria, see the interview of Malam Ali of Kudan, December 8, 1975, Maccido Collection, Tape No. 3. Kudan was an important cotton-growing district.

45 According to Bargery (1934), 822, a *nomijide, nomijidi,* or *nomijiji* was a person "living in the jurisdiction of one, and farming in the jurisdiction of another." *Nomi-* is derived from *noma,* farming, and hence invariably referred to scattered holdings. Dupigny defined a *nomijide* as an "absentee farmer ... who resides in one town and farms on the lands of another town paying his taxes to the latter and, as a rule, not acknowledging fealty to either town"; Assessment Report, Sarkin Dawaki Tsakkar Gidda District.

46 Festing report, 1907, SNP 6/4 c.111/1908.

47 N. M. Gepp, Assessment Report, Dan Isa's Sub-District, May 5, 1911, SNP 7/12, 1035/1911.

48 H. de C. Matthews, Report on the Sub-District of Mundubawa District of Chiroma, Kano Province, SNP 7/13 157/1912.

49 Dupigny worried about this situation because these farmers could not be conscripted: "if they were asked to assist in clearing the roads they would only do so if they felt disposed to (the inclination was usually unfavorable) but that there could be no compulsion in the matter. Beyond exacting his land rents I doubt if Audubu [of Katagum] could demand any form of homage from these people – they therefore remain without a recognized local chief, a state of affairs eminently adapted to foster lawlessness"; see Assessment Report, Sarkin Dawaki Tsakkar Gidda District, SNP 7/10 5570/1909.

50 Dupigny, Assessment Report, Sarkin Dawaki Tsakkar Gidda District, SNP 7/10 5570/1909.

51 Frewan, Kura District Assessment Report, 1909, SNP 7/8 2407/1909. For further examples of absentee farmers, see Frewan, Gora District Assessment, 1909, SNP 7/10 3555/1909. A conspicuous case was Rikadawa, where there were 186 compounds under Rikadawa, 33 under Bebeji, 15 under Madobi, 9 under Kura, and 15 under Kubarache, for a total of 259 compounds. "In most ... areas ... there are some half dozen houses or so held by members of outside communities."

52 Also see Gepp, Report on Dan Makoyo, Sub-District, 1909, encl. in Palmer, Kano Annual Report, 1910, SNP 15/1 Acc 167.

53 Compare this to the similar situation in the United States before the Civil War, where masters were often able to structure local property taxes (the only direct tax they had to pay) so that slaves were not subject to assessment and charge.

54 For *kurdin gaisuwa*, see Mahadi (unpublished, 1982), 325–26; Garba (unpublished, 1986), 146–47; Lovejoy (1980), 138; Lovejoy (1986a), 219.
55 Lugard (1906), 86.
56 Lugard (1905), 852.
57 *Ibid.*
58 See M. G. Smith (1955), 103.
59 *Northern Nigeria Annual Report, 1903*, 173.
60 *Northern Nigeria Annual Report, 1904*, 240.
61 *Northern Nigeria Annual Report, 1905–06*, 377.
62 A factor that Garba (unpublished, 1986), 368, has clearly recognized.
63 Palmer, "Land Tenure in the Haussa States," May 19, 1907, SNP 15/1 Acc 369.
64 Fika (1978), 200–201.
65 Jumare (unpublished, 1988a), 123–24.
66 Starns (1974), 17.
67 Larymore, Report No. 58 on Nupe Province for Quarter ending 31st March 1907, SNP 7/8 2017/1907.
68 Evidence of W. F. Gowers, June 26, 1908, in Northern Nigeria Lands Committee, Minutes of Evidence and Appendices, 1910 [Cd. 5103].
69 C. O. Migeod, Annual Report, Yola Province, 1922, SNP 9/10 72/1923.
70 Festing report, 1907, SNP 6/4 c.111/1908.
71 *Ibid.*
72 See, for example, Tukur (unpublished, 1979); Shenton (1986), 50–58; Watts (1983).
73 Burdon to Lugard, March 21, 1906, Shillingford Papers, Mss. Afr. s.547, Rhodes House; and H. R. Palmer to Resident Kano, August 20, 1907, in Paden (unpublished, 1968), 1222.
74 Burdon, Sokoto Report No. 28, November and December 1905, Sokprof 2/2 85/1906.
75 "I certainly left out women, for the mere suggestion of women paying offended the Sarikin Muslimin [Sarkin Musulmi] – very naturally in a Mohammedan country" (Burdon, Sokoto Report No. 28, 1905).
76 Burdon, Sokoto Report No. 28, November and December 1905, Sokprof 2/2 85/1906.
77 Stanley, Report No.36 on Sokoto Province for Half-Year ending June 30, 1908, Sokprof 2/9 985/1908.
78 Goldsmith to Girouard, January 2, 1908, in Northern Nigeria Lands Committee, Minutes of Evidence and Appendices, 1910 [Cd. 5103].
79 The Kano hierarchy consisted of twelve senior officials appointed from the royal family, twenty hereditary offices, six non-hereditary offices, and eight slaves of the emir. Below these forty-six were many petty officials; see *Northern Nigeria Annual Report, 1902*, 109. Cargill reorganized the emirate administration in 1905, when thirty-four districts were consolidated. The *hakimai* had to move to their districts in early 1907. There were additional changes in late 1907, when the number of districts was reduced to fourteen. Until 1907, *jakadu* collected tax in all thirty-four districts, at which time Cargill abolished the system. The *hakimai*, who had been sent to their districts, were now supposed to collect the tax. Nonetheless, the *jakadu* continued to operate as tax collectors in their own right at least as late as 1909. In the Madaki's district, the Madaki oversaw tax collection himself, according to Festing, and applied fixed rates per farm. But it is doubtful that this official or any others who were now banished to their country estates did much more than they had previously. British officials objected to the *jakada* system because the *jakadu* were slaves; an "army of unpaid and unknown 'boys,'" according to Festing. Festing's designation of *jakadu* as "boys" is revealing, because once they were officially banned, the new "officials," who were also slaves or of slave descent, were known in Hausa as *yara*, "boys." According to Festing, there were five *masu jimila* (also *jami'i*) in the Madaki's district, and the Madaki had an efficient assistant in his *makada*. See Festing's report, 1907, SNP 6/4 c.111/1908. Also see Ubah (1985), 92, 98, 102–103, 203, 215.

80 Palmer, Kano Annual Report, 1910, SNP 15/1 Acc 167.
81 Palmer, Assessment Report, Dan Isa's Sub-District, May 5, 1911, SNP 7/12 1035/1911.
82 *Ibid.*
83 Foulkes, Assessment Report, Jaidanawa District, SNP 7/13 4817/1912.
84 H. de C. Matthews, Report on the Sub-District of Mundubawa District of Chiroma, Kano Province, SNP 7/13, 157/1912.
85 Garba (unpublished, 1986), 292. C. W. Rowling later observed that these Resident surveys, "aided the break up of large official estates"; see "General Investigation into Northern Provinces Land Problems and Land Tenureship," May 20, 1946, RG/R2.
86 See Bello (unpublished, 1982), 104; and H. Q. Glenny, Assessment Report, Rano District, Kano Emirate, SNP 7/10 3272/1909. Further references to the elimination of exemptions are found in the Annual Reports for Kano Province, 1909 and 1910.
87 See H. F. Backwell, Moriki District Assessment Report, May 23, 1913, Sokprof 3/2 264/1913, as cited in Tibenderana (1988), 107.
88 Oyeyipo (unpublished, n.d.), 8–9. Oyeyipo points out that gifts to the emir from such people were *de rigueur* even when they escaped normal taxation, which was the standard practice elsewhere as well.
89 Hewby, Report on Kano Emirate, 1908, SNP 6/4 c.111/1908.
90 Cargill to Festing, April 26, 1907, SNP 15/3 Acc 368.
91 Festing report, 1907, SNP 6/4 c.111/1908.
92 The protesters even rejected an attempted compromise that reduced the assessed tax from the £33,000 figure to £16,000; see Hewby, Report of Kano Emirate, 1908, SNP 6/4 c.111/1908.
93 Governor to Hewby, July 10, 1908, SNP 6/4 c.111/1908.
94 SNP 6/4 c.111/1908. Also see Ubah (unpublished, 1973), 107–108.
95 Palmer, Kano Annual Report, 1910, SNP 15/1 Acc 167.
96 Palmer to Girouard, November 24, 1907, in Northern Nigeria Lands Committee, Minutes of Evidence and Appendices, 1910 [Cd. 5103].
97 Cargill to Girouard, December 8, 1907, in Northern Nigeria Lands Committee, Minutes of Evidence and Appendices, 1910.
98 Cited in E. P. C. Girouard, "Land Tenure in Northern Nigeria," November 2, 1907, Northern Nigeria Lands Committee, Minutes of Evidence and Appendices, 1910.
99 Cited in Girouard, "Land Tenure in Northern Nigeria."
100 Hewby's report, July 10, 1908, SNP 6/4 c.111/1908.
101 Palmer, Assessment, Dan Isa's Sub-District, SNP 7/12 1035/1911.
102 C. W. Rowling reported that some official exemptions continued in 1946; see "General Investigation into Northern Provinces Land Problems and Land Tenureship," May 20, 1946, RG/R2.
103 Revenue Survey Assessment, Kanoprof 1708/Vol. 1, 5/6/36, as cited in Garba (unpublished, 1986), 292.
104 Interview with Alhaji Ado Ahmed of Gandun Nassarawa, July 12, 1980, in Sa'idu (unpublished, 1981), 151, 219.
105 Rowling, "General Investigation into Northern Provinces Land Problems and Land Tenureship."
106 One of the authors employed a research assistant, a student at Ahmadu Bello University in the early 1970s, who had such markings. He was born in the 1950s.
107 Hill (1972), 323.
108 Garba (unpublished, 1986), 300.
109 Girouard, "A Memorandum of Land Tenure and Land Revenue in Northern Nigeria," July 5, 1907, SNP 15 Acc 374. Girouard described the process of assessing tax as follows: "The usual procedure is to take the 'Native assessment' add to it certain direct taxes on trades and divide the total by the number of adult inhabitants. As the number of

inhabitants is not accurately known it is usually estimated by counting the number of compounds or householders. If a figure of taxation thus obtained does not exceed what is considered to be a reasonable incidence per head it may be adopted or the old 'native assessment' increased to produce a fair figure. Such a procedure appears to me in effect to produce a hut or poll tax."

110 Burdon, Sokoto Report No. 28, November and December 1905, Sokprof 2/2 85/1906.

111 Stanley, Report No. 36 on Sokoto Province for Half-Year ending June 30, 1908, Sokprof 2/9 985/1908.

112 Orr to Girouard, no date, in Northern Nigeria Lands Committee, Minutes of Evidence and Appendices, 1910 [Cd. 5103]. Also see his testimony before the Lands Committee, June 30, 1908.

113 Temple to Girouard, December 9, 1907, in Northern Nigeria Lands Committee, Minutes of Evidence and Appendices, 1910 [Cd. 5103].

114 Lugard (1906), 110–11; Okediji (unpublished, 1972), 96.

115 Garba (unpublished, 1986), 227, 241.

116 With hindsight, limited manpower (as elsewhere) made the idea of Resident assessment rather ridiculous from the outset. Kano had no more than two British officials at times during the first seven years of colonial rule, and the number never exceeded six in the period 1910–26. The income-tax aspect is clearly noticed by Swindell (1984), 13. Also see Hill (1972), 324; Fika (1978), 118; Okediji (unpublished, 1972), 97–100; and Shenton (1986), 51.

117 Cargill was acting strangely in 1907–1908: He was a recluse who would not come out of hiding to meet official visitors, and he was apparently responsible for burning many of the provincial records.

118 Fika (1978), 115–24, covers most of these issues. Cargill himself discussed the tax plan at length in Cargill to Festing, Zungeru, April 26, 1907, SNP 15/3 Acc 368.

119 Garba (unpublished, 1986), 247.

120 Hill (1972), 324; Hill (1977), 49.

121 Bull (1963), 65–66.

122 Swindell (1984); 15; Lugard (1906), 86.

123 Okediji (unpublished, 1972, 104; Shenton (1986), 39–40; Tukur (unpublished, 1979), 663–64.

124 Festing report, 1907, SNP 6/4 c.111/1908.

125 Northern Nigeria Lands Committee, Minutes of Evidence, Cd. 5103, 1910, p. 78.

126 Garba (unpublished, 1986), 245–46.

127 Ibid., 247.

128 Cargill, May 27, 1908, in Paden (1968), 1302–1304; and Garba (unpublished, 1986), 248.

129 Palmer, Kano Annual Report, 1910, SNP 15/1 Acc 167.

130 Dupigny, Assessment Report, Sarkin Dawaki Tsakkar Gidda District, SNP 7/10, 5570/1909.

131 Ubah (1985), 216, 305.

132 Ibid., 304.

133 Ibid., 306–309. It was abolished in 1918.

134 For taki assessment see Garba (unpublished, 1986), chapter 6; and Fika (1978), 182–86. Fika notes that the changes in the basis of assessment and collection of taxation instituted in 1909–10 formed the basis of Kano emirate taxation well into the mid 1920s. He states that in Hausa taki literally means "by the foot." Also see Hill (1977), 49, 53; and Hill (1972), 312–13.

135 Watts (1983), 165, notes the regressivity involved. See also Garba (unpublished, 1986), 245.

136 Garba (unpublished, 1986), 381; and Ubah (1985), 309, 315.

137 Palmer, Assessment, Dan Isa's Sub-District, May 5, 1911, SNP 7/12 1035/1911.

138 According to oral data, Ubah (1985), 317.

139 Fika (1978), 202.

140 Ubah (1985), 318, based on oral data.
141 Okediji (unpublished, 1972), 107.
142 Hill (1977), 53.
143 See Swindell (1984), 14; Tibenderana (unpublished, 1974); and Watts (1983), 260, 279–80.
144 Hill (1972), 313.
145 Rowling (1949), 19.
146 Hill (1972), 313.
147 Garba (unpublished, 1986); Hill (1972), 324–25; Shenton and Freund (1978), 14.
148 Garba (unpublished, 1986), 246.
149 *Ibid.*, 248.
150 M. G. Smith (1960), 211; Hill (1972), 324; Hill (1977), 49, 50, 52. Hill claims that *kurdin kasa* and *zakka* were still being paid in parts of Kano in 1917.
151 Hill (1972), 325.
152 Garba (unpublished, 1986), 353.
153 *Ibid.*, 396.
154 Tibenderana (1988), 107. Burdon had specific knowledge of collection on the basis of a uniform flat rate rather than on the basis of ability to pay.
155 See Garba (unpublished, 1986), 362–63.
156 *Ibid.*, 364–65.
157 C. O. Migeod, Annual Report, Yola Province, 1922, SNP 9/10 72/1923.
158 For the poll tax in later years, see Hill (1972), 265–66, and Hailey (1957), 76–77.
159 Economists such as Francis Edgeworth had already published largely accurate accounts of the principles involved. Technically the income effect of a head tax is paramount. More labor is exerted to pay the bill, and there is no substitution effect.
160 Garba (unpublished, 1986), 400.
161 J. M. Fremantle, Muri, September 19, 1918, in "Revision of Memo on Slavery," SNP Supplementary Acc 61 1598/1918.
162 There had been times in the precolonial period when the degree of oppression and extortion involved in tax collection had reached "crippling levels," according to Garba (unpublished, 1986), 72. The corruption continued into the colonial period, a problem that greatly troubled the British (as, indeed, it must have troubled the tax payers). Illustrative is a letter from Selwyn Grier dated March 10, 1907, Mss. Afr. r.1379, Rhodes House, pointing to many Zaria towns in arrears and about twenty village headmen accused of having embezzled the tax collections. Collections may have been significantly greater than shown in the records, and it would probably have been unwise for a villager to complain. A great many cases of tax revenue embezzlement in Kano are discussed by Fika (1978), 163–67.
163 Girouard recognized this when he wrote that the "original taxes of a primitive nation are those of service and slavery." Girouard, "Land Tenure and Land Revenue Assessment," Memo No. 25, September 1908, CO African (West) Confidential Print No. 906.
164 The colonial government ordered the cessation of corvée labor in Kano in 1912, but it survived anyway, well into the 1920s. See Bello (unpublished, 1982), 133, citing SNP 10/7 316p/1920; and Mason (1978), 56–79.
165 Garba (unpublished, 1986), 218; *Northern Nigeria Annual Report, 1904*, 436.
166 *Northern Nigeria Annual Report, 1904*, 226–27. The British originally took one-quarter of the revenue collected in an emirate as their share; this was raised to one-half in 1905, which remained the proportion from that time on. Garba (unpublished, 1986), 225. Of the tax allotted to the emirate government, 50 percent was paid to Ma'aji, the Native Treasurer in Kano, and the remaining 50 percent was divided locally into fifths, two belonging to the district heads or *hakimai*; one-fifth to sub-district heads or *mai jimila*; and two-fifths to village heads, who handed over half of this to subordinates, *dagatai*. See Festing's report.
167 Burdon, Sokoto Province, Report for Half Year ending 30 June 1909, SNP 7/10 4964/1909.
168 Burson, Sokoto Report No. 28, November and December 1905, Sokprof 2/2 85/1906.

169 Lugard, Memo on the Taxation of Natives in Northern Nigeria Cd. 3309 of 1907, p. 62. The figures did not include *jangali* or death duties, according to Lugard, and they probably did not include *zakka*.
170 Tukur (unpublished, 1979), 569; also see N. M. Gepp, Report on Dan Makoyo's Subdistrict, Kano Province, Enclosure in Palmer, Report for the Kano Province for the Year ending 31 December 1910, SNP 15/1 Acc. 167.
171 Ubah (1985), 315.
172 See Garba (unpublished, 1986), 372, citing Palmer, Katprof 1/1836/1909. Temple thought the food costs were somewhat high, however, which would increase the implicit tax rate.
173 Watts (1983), 261.
174 Lugard discussed the form taken by tax payments to the British authorities at some length in his 1907 Command Paper. In Sokoto and Zaria, the colonial government's share of tax payments was in British silver, the payments having been converted by the indigenous authorities from cowries and commodities; Lugard described the difficulties involved. In Bauchi, payment was optional, taking the form of coin, cowries, or grain, with a "considerable part" paid in coin. Auctions of cowries and grain were managed by the government. In Nupe and Ilorin, all tax was paid in "cash," meaning silver coin. In Muri, two-thirds of the payments were in coin, with the remainder mostly in the local cloth currency. In Nassarawa, payment was apparently mostly in cowries. In Yola, the government share came in coin. In Kontagora, 70 percent was paid in coin and 30 percent in kind, the latter then auctioned by the government. For this information see F. D. Lugard, Memo on the Taxation of Natives in Northern Nigeria, 1907 [Cd. 3309].
175 Watts (1983), 160.
176 The plan to have *kurdin kasa* paid in coin, at a rate of 6*d.* per 1,000 cowries, was implemented in December 1910; only the districts of Barde, Wombai, Dutse, and Sarkin Dawaki Tsakar Gida were exempt. Because of tax collection, the value of cowries dropped from 10*s.* per bag of 20,000 to 8*s.* over the several months before December 1910. Cowries ranged from 2,600 per 1*s.* in Kano to 3,000 per 1*s.* further east. See H. R. Palmer, Kano Annual Report, 1910, SNP 15/1 Acc 167. Also see Ubah (1985), 335.
177 Fika (1978), 189, notes that during 1911, the Kano Baitulmali [Native Treasury] adopted silver currency as its unit of account, and disposed of its large stocks of cowries, which resulted in a loss of more than £2,000 due to the depreciation of the cowrie in part caused by these sales. Fika cites SNP 3546/1911, paras. 45, 47. Also see Bello (unpublished, 1982), 125; Hogendorn (1978), 66; and Hogendorn and Johnson (1986), chapter 10.
178 Lugard, Memo on the Taxation of Natives in Northern Nigeria, 1907 [Cd. 3309], p. 16. Also see Garba (unpublished, 1986), 16.

7 The colonial economy and the slaves

1 See the account in Hogendorn (1978).
2 *Ibid.*; Hogendorn (1976), 15–28. For a critique, see Freund and Shenton (1977), 191–96; and Hogendorn (1977a), 196–99.
3 Watts (1983), 193.
4 Swindell (1984).
5 Lugard (1906), 136.
6 Lugard (1922), 390–91.
7 These questions have been explored at length by Lennihan (unpublished, 1983).
8 Enclosure No. 2 in No. 14, Lugard to Chamberlain, received May 2, 1903, CO 879/80/718.
9 Lugard (1906), 139–40. In his revised version of the *Political Memoranda* (1918), 237, Lugard was still expounding on the shift to wage labor. "Slaves who have been long in slavery and who are liberated by manumission, or by ransom, etc., have usually some

344

definite object in view. Men can find work as free labourers or agriculturists and women usually desire to be married."
10 Abadie, April 18, 1902, Zaria, Abadie Papers, Rhodes House.
11 W. F. Gowers, Yola Province Monthly Reports, April 1905, SNP 15/1 Acc 116.
12 G. N. Barclay, Yola Province Annual Report, 1905, SNP 15/1 Acc 116.
13 Lugard (1906), 139.
14 *Ibid.*, 139–40.
15 Barclay, Yola Province Annual Report, 1905.
16 Lovejoy (1993).
17 E. Arnett, April 12, 1916, SNP 10/3 850p/1915. In this document, Arnett advocated that tax bills be adjusted downward for slaves paying *murgu* and upward for masters receiving it. Lugard minuted his agreement with this opinion (in W. H. Sykes to Arnett, May 26, 1916, SNP 10/3 850p/1915), but as we saw in the last chapter, taxes most often resembled a fixed poll tax, and such adjustments appear to have been infrequent.
18 Arnett, Sokoto, May 23, 1918, in "Revision of Memo on Slavery," SNP Supplementary Acc 61 1598/1918.
19 Jumare (unpublished, 1988a), 123, citing Classification of Native Court Cases, December 1913, in Annual Report, Sokoto, Gandu, Argungu Divisions, 30th March, 1914, Sokprof 2/12 581/1914; and E. A. Brackenbury, Assistant Resident, Argungu, in E. J. Arnett, Annual Report, Sokoto, Gwandu and Argungu, 1913, Sokprof 581/1914.
20 Register of Freed Slaves, Bauchi Province, May 1906, SNP 15/1 Acc 121.
21 Abubakar Cindo (born during reign of Sarkin Zazzau Yaro), Kaura, Zaria city, interviewed September 10, 1975 by Ahmadu Maccido.
22 G. W. Webster, Nassarawa Provincial Report, March 1904, SNP 15/1 Acc 59.
23 H. F. Backwell, April 5, 1916, in "Suggested Abolition of Murgu, Sokoto Province," SNP 10/3 850p/1915.
24 G. W. Webster, Yola, May 15, 1918, in "Revision of Memo on Slavery," SNP 17 Supplementary Acc 61 1598/1918. According to C. O. Migeod, Annual Report, Yola Province, 1922, SNP 9/10 72/1923, there were approximately 20,000 slaves paying *murgu* at that date.
25 Backwell, April 5, 1916, SNP 10/3 850p/1915.
26 L. Blake, November 16, 1915, in "Suggested Abolition of Murgu, Sokoto Province," SNP 10/3 850/1915.
27 MacMichael, DO Argungu, to Resident, Sokoto, October 28, 1936, Sokprof 3/1 c.33.
28 Resident Bauchi, June 24, 1936, SNP 17/2 20216.
29 Jumare (unpublished, 1988a), 123–24.
30 *Ibid.*
31 E. Arnett, April 12, 1916, in "Suggested Abolition of Murgu, Sokoto Province," SNP 10/3 850p/1915.
32 Backwell, April 5, 1916, SNP 10/3 850p/1915.
33 E. A. Brackenbury, Assistant Resident, Argungu, in E. J. Arnett, Annual Report, Sokoto, Gwandu and Argungu, 1913, Sokprof 2/12 581/1914.
34 Backwell, April 5, 1916, SNP 10/3 850p/1915.
35 See Migeod, Annual Report, Yola Province, 1922, SNP 9/10 72/1923. Atypically, *murgu* payments in Yola were in kind (baskets of corn) according to Migeod. Migeod also mentions that the Emir of Yola had taken steps in 1922 to lower the *murgu* slaves paid to masters by the amount of tax that the slaves were required to pay to the government. "The custom obtaining previous to this was for the masters to pay their slaves' tax out of the 'Murgu' they received."
36 W. F. Gowers, Annual Report for Kano Province, 1912, SNP 10/1 134p/1913.
37 Arnett, Sokoto, May 23, 1918. As Grier observed in 1924, gradual emancipation of slaves gave those owners who still retained their slaves (in fact the majority) an opportunity of adapting themselves to changed conditions:

I am doubtful whether *large* numbers of slaves ransomed themselves in the *early* days. They first had to obtain the ransom money ... [Consequently,] the emancipation of slaves by self redemption was gradual.

See minute on Browne's report by S. U. G. [Grier ??], May 26, 1924, CSO 26/11799, Vol. I.
38 The following slave ransoms were recorded in the Register of Freed Slaves, Zaria Province for Quarter ending Sept 1906 (SNP 15/1 Acc 121):

1 Maguashie, aged thirty-five, male, Gwari, "ransomed himself for 15 bags from Ibrahim. To follow his own inclinations."
2 Mero, aged fifteen, female, Jaba, "ransomed by her father from Amina for 15 bags."
3 Hadgiratu, aged thirty-five, female, Arago, "ransomed by Mahomma Sambo for 15 bags and married her."
4 Hamma, aged thirty, female, Yasko, "ransomed by Abdulahi for 15 bags and married her."
5 Arsatu, aged twenty-five, female, Jaba, "ransomed herself for 15 bags."
6 Hadiratu, aged forty, female, Nupe, "ransomed herself for 15 bags from Adamu."
7 Habibatu, aged one, female, Nupe, "ransomed by her mother for C 70,000."

At 1,200 cowries to the shilling, fifteen bags of 20,000 cowries each were equivalent to £12. 5s.
39 The highest redemption prices were for males, two at 400,000 cowries and one at 430,000 cowries. There were several women priced over 300,000 cowries, but there is no clear pattern for such pricing for either males or females. It is possible that high male prices reflected skilled craftsmen, and some of the female prices were probably associated with concubinage, but there are not enough cases and the information is insufficient to substantiate these remarks, however logical they appear to be. When the British came to Zaria, the master of the Hanwa *rinji* called the slaves together, told them that there was no more slavery, that there was no more buying and selling of slaves, and that slaves could get their freedom for £5. Not only did most pay, but they stayed at Hanwa (Malam Bawa, Hanwa, Zaria Emirate, June 16, 1975, Interview No. 21). Oral traditions collected by Yunusa in Kano have it that the value of slaves seeking their freedom was usually estimated at 200,000–300,000 cowries: see Yunusa (unpublished, 1976), 29–30.
40 Grier to Dorothy, January 9, 1907, Grier Papers Mss. Afr. r.1379, Rhodes House. One bag was worth 12s. 6d.
41 Kisch (1910), 155.
42 Lugard (1918), 241. In 1910, Edwardes freed a slave girl in Bida, whose relationship to Edwardes is otherwise unexplained, for the low amount of £1 10s. (Edwardes Diary, March 9, 1910, Mss. Afr. r.106, Rhodes House).
43 E. A. Brackenbury, Assistant Resident, Argungu, in E. J. Arnett, Annual Report, Sokoto, Gwandu and Argungu, 1913, Sokprof 2/12 581/1914.
44 Jumare (unpublished, 1988a), 123, citing Classification of Native Court Cases, December 1913, in Annual Report, Sokoto, Gandu, Argungu Divisions, 30th March, 1914, Sokprof c. 27, 581/1914.
45 G. S. Stewart, DO Gwandu, to Resident, Sokoto, September 28, 1936, Sokprof 3/1 c.33. The Alkali would take 10s. 6d. as "ushurin kurdin da Bawa ya biya ga Ubangiji £5.5/–" (the commission of the money paid the slave to his master, £5.5/–). See "Wannan ita che takardar labarin Bayi Kasar Gwandu, 1901–1936", in Sokprof 3/1 c.33, as translated in Jumare (unpublished, 1988a), 151.
46 Report of Brooke on District Court, Wudil, Kano Emirate, October 2, 1918, Wudil District, Alkali and Prison Report, Kanoprof 5/1 244.
47 Resident Bauchi, June 24, 1936, SNP 17/2 20216.
48 G. Miles Clifford, Yola, November 11, 1936, SNP 17 20216.

49 E. S. Pembleton, Secretary, Northern Provinces, to Chief Secretary, Lagos, December 5, 1936, CSO 26/11799, Vol. IV. At Yelwa, in Sokoto Province, the "fee of one shilling was paid by slave to alkali's assistant who prepared the certificate"; telegram, n.d. (1936) to Resident, Sokoto, Sokprof 3/1 c.33. Also see Jumare (unpublished, 1988a), 152.
50 "Wannan ita che takardar labarin Bayi Kasar Gwandu, 1901–1936", in Sokprof 3/1 c.33, as translated in Jumare (unpublished, 1988a), 151. In 1935, Maybin estimated that "the average figure of the fee [for a certificate of freedom] was 4/–; it was paid sometimes by the master, sometimes by the slave and sometimes shared between them, and it accrued to the Native Treasury. It was not of course in the nature of a ransom, but merely a fee for registration by the Native Court and for the preparation of the certificate of freedom." See J. A. Maybin to W. G. A. Ormsby Gore, December 16, 1936, CSO 26/11799, Vol. IV.
51 G. W. Webster, Report for August 1904, Nassarawa Province, SNP 15/1 Acc. 59.
52 Register of Freed Slaves, Bauchi Province, May 1906, SNP 15/1 Acc 121.
53 Nuhu Salmanu (b. 1898), Zaria city, interviewed by Ahmadu Maccido, June 10, 1975.
54 G. S. Stewart, DO Gwandu, to Resident, Sokoto, September 28, 1936, Sokprof 3/1 c.33.
55 Lugard (1918), 233.
56 Jumare (unpublished, 1988a), 123–24.
57 *Northern Nigeria Annual Report, 1908–09*, 679.
58 The quotation is from Swindell (1984), 16.
59 J. W. Gill, "Notes on Taxation and Industrial Organisation of Hausa Towns of Zaria Emirate, May 1909," SNP 7/4252/1909, cited by Garba (unpublished, 1986), 106.
60 Gowers, Annual Report for Kano Province, 1912, SNP 10/1 134p/1913.
61 H. B. Foulkes, Assessment Report, Dan Buram District, Kano Emirate, SNP 7/13 5785/1912.
62 J. C. Sciortino, Nassarawa Province Annual Report, 1914, SNP 15 146p/1914.
63 C. W. Rowling, "General Investigation into Northern Provinces Land Problems and Land Tenureship," May 20, 1946, RG/R2. Also see Watts (1983), 234–35; Hill (1972), 205; Hill (1977), 131–32.
64 Meek (1949), 149.
65 For a discussion of the evolution towards sharecropping rents paid in kind (or sometimes in cash), see M. G. Smith (1965a), 245; Hill (1972), 178–80; Meek (1957), 161–62; and Starns (1974), 18. M. G. Smith (1965a), 263, first called our attention to one meaning of *galla* in Bargery's dictionary: "payment made by a slave in lieu of work (= murgu)." See Bargery (1934), 350. A definition such as this makes it even more understandable why so many observers have not identified the meaning of *murgu* with complete accuracy.
66 For millet prices, for example, see Watts (1983), 289, 309.
67 Hogendorn and Johnson (1986), 148–51.
68 S. Grier, July 10, 1906, Grier Papers, Mss. Afr. s.1379, Rhodes House. Grier, writing from Zaria in 1910 when 20,000 cowries = 10s., stated that "In this country 100 cowries will buy enough food for a man for a day." Grier to his mother, March 3, 1910, Grier Mss. Papers, Afr. s.1379, Rhodes House. With 1d. = 166 cowries at the time, the cost of food would have been $\frac{6}{10}d.$ per day.
69 C. L. Temple, Annual Report, Kano Province, 1909, SNP 7/10 6415/1909.
70 Palmer, Report for 1909, Katsina Division of Kano Province, Katprof 1/1836; cited in Garba (unpublished, 1986), 372.
71 Watts (1983), 280, citing a Raba District report.
72 According to Swindell (1984), 9, based on oral sources, the cost of food was less than the figures cited by Palmer, $\frac{1}{10}d.$ per person per day in Kano and $\frac{1}{2}d.$ per day in Sokoto.
73 Swindell (1984), 13.
74 Watts (1983), 280.
75 *Ibid.*, 195–99. According to Watts, citing a report on Tudun Wada District in the 1920s, the average farmer who had only 3.5 acres under cultivation would have had to devote his whole

acreage to grain production to meet the needs of a household of one man, a wife, and two children, and in most cases a third of the acreage was devoted to cash crops. According to Forde, as late as 1937, when recorded incomes in rural Kano averaged £18 6s. 3d., households spent an average of £3 18s. on food, or about 21 percent of recorded income; see Forde (1946), I, 125, 153.

76 Grier Papers, Mss. Afr. s.1379, ff. 1–24, Rhodes House, Letter dated Kachia, January 28, 1910.
77 Swindell (1984), 6, 12, 16–17, notes that seasonal migration expanded greatly in the 1930s, but it had become an established practice long before then.
78 Swindell (1984), 14.
79 By 1937, the value of non-agricultural income for adults in Dawaki ta Kudu District near Kano amounted to 40 percent of total income; see Watts (1983), 198–99; and Forde (1946), 149.
80 The cost of marriage rose steadily over the first four decades of colonial rule; see Watts (1983), 219.
81 For a survey, see ibid., 276–78.
82 Watts (1983), 276–78; 285–97, 305–12.
83 Sen (1981). Also see Drèze and Sen (1990); Curtis (1988); Reutlinger and Pellekaan (1986); McAlpin (1983).
84 G. W. Webster, March 1904, SNP 15/1 Acc 59.
85 Freund (1981), 47, citing Laws, 1903.
86 Freund (1981), 50.
87 Swindell (1984), 11, 17.
88 Girouard to Crewe, November 16, 1908, CO 446/76.
89 Swindell (1992). On the employment of slaves in the WAFF, see Crozier (1932), 122.
90 Swindell (1984), 14, citing Kisch.
91 Swindell (1984), 9. The figure for wages of 6d. per day recurs frequently in the contemporary accounts. It seems to have been the standard amount. Lugard believed the figure was overly high by comparison to the situation in other British possessions, but he seems to have forgotten the dictates of demand and supply. Northern Nigeria was not an area of abundant labor like India or Hong Kong. See Freund (1981), 53.
92 E. A. Biggs, "Report on the New Road from the Railway to the Mines," July 12, 1910, Royal Niger Company Papers, Vol. 14, Misc. Papers 1910–13. In the recollection of A. C. G. Hastings (1925), 136, "Carriers are among the best and hardest workers in the country, earning well the money they are paid. They pick up their head load of 50 lb. or more, and march their 17 to 20 miles a day. As a rule they must be left to travel in their own way, resting after two hours or so, and moving at about 3 miles an hour. In cases of necessity they can do wonderful distances, and I have pushed my gang 70 miles in two days, letting them travel when they would." The demand for carriers was raised because the government would "provide carriers for any traveller who gives notice of requiring them." See Tremlett (1915), 73.
93 Temple, Annual Report, Kano Province, 1909, SNP 7/10 6415/1909.
94 Temple to Harcourt, August 18, 1911, Despatch No. 646, CO 446/99. Also see Watts (1983), 222–23.
95 "Plus accessories and [they] are 'allowed women.'" E. A. Biggs, "Report on the New Road from the Railway to the Mines," July 12, 1910, RNC Papers, Vol. 14, Misc. Papers 1910–13. For the wages also see Mason (1978), 63, 65, 78. Sometimes the wage paid to workers on the railway was lower. Mason mentions that about 1908, wages could be as low as 1s. per week, while near the completion of the Lagos extension they could be as high as 8d. per day.
96 "The workers recruited by means of political coercion were not expected to remain on the line of rail for more than a few weeks at most." See Mason (1978), 60, 62, 71. On the Bauchi Light, "The drafts are changed monthly." Edwardes Papers, Mss. Afr. s.769, f. 26, Rhodes House.

97 For the work arrangements see Oyemakinde (1974), 303–24; Oyemakinde (unpublished, 1970); Mason (1978); Tamuno (1965); Morel (1912), 198; and *Northern Nigeria Report, 1910–11*, 40.

98 Mason (1978), 71.

99 Pedraza (1960), 105, thought that "slaves working on the railway in the early days could earn the requisite money to purchase their freedom," but he is probably wrong in this interpretation.

100 Temple, Annual Report, Kano Province, 1909, SNP 7/10 6415/1909.

101 Freund (1981), 51–52. Freund cites Gonyok (unpublished, 1977).

102 Freund (1981), 36, 50–51, 76. Freund notes (p. 51) that much of this was "political labour."

103 Freund (1981), 51.

104 Temple to Harcourt, August 18, 1911, Despatch No. 646, CO 446/99.

105 E. A. Biggs, "Report on the New Road from the Railway to the Mines," July 12, 1910, RNC Papers, Vol. 14, Misc. Papers 1910–13; Mason (1978), 73; Freund (1981), 54.

106 Freund (1981), 54.

107 *Ibid.*, 78. Freund discusses the labor contractors' recruitment of workers for these mines on pp. 89–90. For the corruption sometimes displayed by these labor contractors, see Mason (1978), 64.

108 Anagbogu (unpublished, 1986), 117–18.

109 *Ibid.*, 118. According to Anagbogu, "migration became necessary because the ex-slaves usually could not compete with their former masters or with established artisans who already had long years of association with foreign and indigenous traders in the leather business."

110 For references to slaves as dyers, see interviews by Philip Shea: Ishiaka Abdurahman (b. 1900), Takalmawa ward, Kano, interviewed February 3, 1971; Garba (b. 1903), Limawa, Kumbotso District, Kano Emirate, interviewed October 27, 1971; Uban Gila (b. 1901), Rogo, Karaye District, Kano Emirate, interviewed November [no day given] 1971.

111 According to Baliya (b. 1898), Karofin Sudawa ward, Kano, interviewed May 6, 1971 by Philip Shea.

112 Garba (unpublished, 1986), 322–29.

113 According to Malam Gwadabe, Sabon Sara ward, Kano, "After the Europeans gave the slaves their freedom, not many of them left – but some did go trading because there was not enough land for them." Malam Gwadabe (b. 1904), Sabon Sara ward, Kano, interviewed May 27, 1970 by Philip Shea.

114 Swindell (1984), 9.

115 *Ibid.*, 7.

116 Goldsmith, Sokoto Province, Report for December 1906, SNP 7/8 1643/1907.

117 Swindell (1984), 4.

118 Lengthy discussions of the caravan tolls are contained in CO 446/51 of 1905 under the heading "Lugard." See especially September 12, October 2, November 3, and November 11. See also CO 446/58 of 1906, communications with West African Trade Association, January 4, August 2, and September 6.

119 Garba (unpublished, 1986), 215.

120 The comment was made specifically of the village of Bagayawa. See Swindell (1984), 4, citing 1911 Assessment Report, Sokoto Home Districts.

121 Swindell (1984), 5, citing W. F. Gowers, "Notes on Trade in Sokoto Province, February 1911," Mss. Afr. s.662(2), Rhodes House. In this report Gowers made some calculations on the profitability of dry-season trading. He estimated that the average return on donkey loads of rice and salt, less feed, was $7\frac{1}{2}d.$ per day after a thirty-five-day round trip. Raw cotton was also an important item in *cin rani* trade.

122 Fika (1978), 210.

123 Hogendorn (1978), 23.
124 The average monthly size of the labor force in the tin mines was as follows:

Year	Number	Year	Number	Year	Number
1911	5,832	1915	14,316	1918	21,568
1912	12,037	1916	19,250	1919	22,289
1913	16,883	1917	21,817	1920	22,976
1914	17,883				

See Freund (1981), 76.
125 Freund (1981), 51.
126 *Ibid.*, 52, citing Josprof 1/1 329/1920.
127 Freund (1981), 82. As Freund notes, wages in the tin fields reached 6s. to 7s. in 1927, but after 1928, wages fell. By 1932–35 they had been cut to 2s. 6d. or even less.
128 Freund (1981), 41.
129 Lugard in 1918 noted that "a free labour market has sprung up, with a daily wage, and is freely resorted to by Native land owners, not only in Sokoto, but also in Yola, where ... the recognised wage is from 3d. to 1s. per diem according to quality." See Lugard (1918), 222.
130 H. D. Foulkes, Silame District Assessment Report, Sokprof 2/11 230/1913.
131 Foulkes, Silame District Assessment Report. Also see E. A. Brackenbury, Assistant Resident, Argungu, in E. J. Arnett, Annual Report, Sokoto, Gwandu and Argungu, 1913, Sokprof 2/12 581/1914. Hill discusses farm laboring, or *kwadago*: see (1972), 105–23.
132 For a discussion of tools, see "The Importation of Hoes," Edwardes Papers, Mss. Afr. s.769, ff. 52–53, Rhodes House.
133 See Bello (unpublished, 1982), 123, with further sources cited there; and Watts (1983), 160.
134 As quoted in Swindell (1984), 3.
135 Hogendorn (1978), 118. Also see Watts (1983), 285–97.
136 Kano Province Report for the Quarter ending 30th September 1913, para. 42.
137 Watts (1983), 289.
138 Hogendorn (1978), 118. Also see Shenton (1986), 132.
139 Watts (1983), 275, 300.
140 *Ibid.*, 305–12.
141 Hogendorn (1978), 123, 133, and the sources cited there.
142 Lugard (1918), 241.
143 Shelford (1920), 167.
144 Mason (1978), 74.
145 The argument is traced in Mockler-Ferryman (1900), 371–78.
146 As stated by Palmer (1942), 109: "The sturdy, cheerful Hausa carrier ... all but ceased to exist after the war of 1914–1918."
147 Lugard (1918), 224.
148 *Ibid.*
149 *Ibid.*
150 Fremantle, Muri, May 3, 1918, in "Revision of Memo on Slavery," SNP 17 Supplementary Acc 61 1598/1918.
151 Freemantle, Muri, September 19, 1918.
152 G. W. Webster, Yola, May 15, 1918, in "Revision of Memo on Slavery."
153 Webster, Yola, May 15, 1918.
154 Arnett, Sokoto, May 27, 1918, in "Revision of Memo on Slavery."
155 Arnett, Sokoto, May 27, 1918.
156 Arnett, September 19, 1918, "Revision of Memo on Slavery."

157 G. S. Browne, May 3, 1924, CSO 26/11799, Vol. I.
158 Hill (1972), 105, 193.
159 Arnett, Sokoto, May 27, 1918.
160 *Ibid.*
161 Hill (1972), 43, suggests that the labor shortages resulting when slaves deserted small-holders may have been alleviated by the contributions of labor time by the wives of the *gandu* heads.
162 A point made by Sa'idu (unpublished, 1981), 155.
163 M. G. Smith (1965b), 141.
164 Hill (1972), 42–43; also see Starns (1974), 18, who cites Hill and Meek in making this same judgment.
165 Fika (1978), 209.
166 M. G. Smith (1965a), 261–62. Smith notes that the legal claim of the landlord was usually based on some original grant after the *jihad*, the original clearing of the property, and status as the recognized landlord.
167 M. G. Smith (1965a), 266, which continued the pattern examined by Christelow (1992) for Kano in 1913–14.
168 G. S. Browne, May 3, 1924, CSO 26/11799, Vol. I. Also reprinted in the League of Nations Report, "The Question of Slavery," September 5, 1924: "Letters from the British Government Transmitting Despatches Showing the Situation with Respect to Slavery in the British Colonies and Protectorates and Territories under British Mandate," A.25(a).

8 The persistence of concubinage

1 E. J. Arnett, Annual Report, Sokoto, Gwandu and Argungu, 1913, Sokprof 2/12 581/1914.
2 Jumare (unpublished, 1988a), 106.
3 E. Arnett, Sokoto, May 23, 1918, in "Revision of Memo on Slavery," SNP Supplementary Acc 61 1598/1918.
4 *Ibid.*
5 *Ibid.*
6 Minute of G. S. Browne, July 15, 1921, Alkalin Kano, SNP 8 10/1921.
7 W. F. Gowers, Kano Province Annual Report, 1912, SNP 10/1 134p/1913.
8 W. Gill, quoted in Kano Province Annual Report, 1913, in "Money Paid for Slave (Female) Ransom," SNP 10/2 549p/1914.
9 In 1918, these events were said to have occurred "some years ago"; see Lugard (1918), 233.
10 J. M. Fremantle, Muri Province Annual Report, 1914, SNP 10/2 549p/1914.
11 Minute of H. R. Palmer, July 10, 1921, Alkalin Kano, SNP 8/10/1921.
12 Arnett's Memorandum to M. Delafosse, August 9, 1925, Arnett Papers, Mss. Afr. s.952/2–3, Rhodes House; A. C. G. Hastings, Kano Province Report No. 59 for 15 months ending 31 March 1921, SNP 10/9 120p/1921; Sa'idu (unpublished, 1981), 76; and Skinner's notes on Mahmudu interviews.
13 E. Arnett, Sokoto, May 23, 1918, in "Revision of Memo on Slavery," SNP Supplementary Acc 61 1598/1918. According to Arnett, "The result of these ransoms and the consequent freedom of the women has undoubtedly been some increase of immorality, but at the same time it has prevented the wealthier men from keeping large numbers of women and so depriving poorer men of wives. On the whole I think the result of this practice has been satisfactory and it has undoubtedly softened the social changes that are taking place with the gradual disappearance of slavery."
14 Arnett's Memorandum to M. Delafosse, August 9, 1925, Arnett Papers, Mss. Afr. s.952/2–3, Rhodes House.
15 Minute of Palmer, July 10, 1921, Alkalin Kano, SNP 8 10/1921.
16 *Ibid.*

17 E. Arnett, May 23, 1918, in "Revision of Memo on Slavery," SNP 17 Supplementary Acc 61 1598/1918.
18 Minute of Palmer, July 10, 1922.
19 Arnett, May 23, 1918.
20 Minute of Palmer, July 10, 1921.
21 Arnett, Kano Province Annual Report, 1913, in "Money Paid for Slave (Female) Ransom," SNP 10/2 549p/1914. Italics added.
22 Quoted in J. M. Fremantle, Muri Province Annual Report, 1917, in "Money Paid for Slave (Female) Ransom," SNP 10/2 549p/1914.
23 Minute of Palmer, July 10, 1921.
24 Fremantle, Muri Province Annual Report, 1917.
25 Lugard, Governor, Northern Nigeria, as quoted in G. R. Matthews, September 15, 1914, "Money Paid for Slave (Female) Ransom," SNP 10/2 549p/1914.
26 Kano Province Annual Report, 1913, in "Money Paid for Slave (Female) Ranson," SNP 10/2 549p/1914.
27 *Ibid.*
28 Arnett believed that the ability to recover ransom payments thereby "rather encourages manumission than otherwise, for the would-be ransomer naturally hesitates to pay a sum of money which he can under no circumstances recover." See Kano Province Annual Report, 1913, in "Money Paid for Slave (Female) Ransom," SNP 10/2 549p/1914.
29 Précis of Ruling Referred to by His Excellency in Comment on Paragraph 54, in J. C. Sciortino, Nassarawa Province Annual Report, 1914, SNP 15/2 146p/1914. The circular was issued on September 15, 1914 (No. 4897), according to Fremantle, January, 23 1917, "Money Paid for Slave (Female) Ransom," SNP 10/2 549p/1914. We have not been able to locate the original. The wording of these instructions appears to be drawn *verbatim* from Arnett, Kano Province Annual Report, 1913, in "Money Paid for Slave (Female) Ransom," SNP 10/2 549p/1914.
30 J. C. Sciortino, Nassarawa Province Annual Report, 1914, SNP 15/2 147p/1914. *Sadaki* is more accurately translated as "marriage payment" than "dowry."
31 Moore had already ruled accordingly the previous year, when the *alkali* of Kontagora had requested a ruling on whether the *fansa* of £5 5s. being paid by a man "with the object of freeing and marrying a certain female slave ... could be regarded as Sadaki." The man paid the ransom and "married" the slave anyway, but Moore took the precaution of "personally" explaining the conditions of marriage to the woman. See N. Hamilton Moore, Kontagora, October 3, 1914, "Money Paid for Slave (Female) Ransom," SNP 10/2 549p/1914.
32 Fremantle, Muri Province Annual Report, 1917.
33 Arnett, May 23, 1918, in "Revision of Memo on Slavery," SNP 17 Supplementary Acc 61 1598/1918. According to Arnett, if a concubine who received a certificate of freedom in the court decided to leave her master, she was free to do so. "The moment she leaves him, and she can do so at will, the emancipation takes effect and she is a free woman. Should the man attempt to restrain her, the certificate of freedom or the records of the Court will defeat him."
34 According to Groom, as quoted in Fremantle, Muri Province Annual Report, 1917, "Money Paid for Slave (Female) Ransom," SNP 10/2 549p/1914: "The proper procedure is that if B wishes to ransom and marry the female slave of A, B presents the woman with the necessary ransom say £3 to £5 and she and A appear before the Native Court and a Certificate of freedom is granted. Later, B and the woman are married by a malam in the usual way and the usual marriage portion (sadaki) say 7/6 is paid which in the event of divorce is returnable but *not* the ransom money."
35 In 1918, Fremantle asked Lt.-Governor Goldsmith, "Is it necessary for the ransomer to appear in Court at all? I have found it safest to insist that the woman pays the ransom money herself, the Court having no official knowledge as to who gave it to her." A marginal note

read, "I agree." See Fremantle, Muri, September 19, 1918, in "Revision of Memo on Slavery," SNP 17 Supplementary Acc 61 1598/1918.

36 Fremantle, June 6, 1918, in "Revision of Memo on Slavery," SNP 17 Supplementary Acc 61 1598/1918.

37 *Ibid.*

38 Fremantle, Muri Province Annual Report, 1915, SNP 10/4 365p/1916.

39 Ironically, the name of the official in question was Mr. Groom. See *ibid.*

40 Fremantle, Muri, September 19, 1918, in "Revision of Memo on Slavery," SNP 17 Supplementary Acc 61 1598/1918.

41 *Ibid.*

42 Fremantle, January 1917, "Money Paid for Slave (Female) Ransom," SNP 10/2 549p/1914.

43 Fremantle protested that he had been following the procedures set down in Temple's circular of September 15, 1914. According to Fremantle's interpretation of Temple's circular, "If the suitor pays the ransom money this is no concern of the Court whether the fact is known to the Court or not. The woman pays the money herself to the Alkali who pays it over to the master and gives the woman her certificate of freedom. The suitor does not appear at all; the *wrong* procedure would be for him to pay the money to the master. Technically the latter has nothing to do with the matter. The certificate of freedom must be given to the woman. The money must be recognised as having been paid for redemption and nothing else. If there is any special marriage gift paid by the suitor he can claim it later in the event of the woman deserting him, but he can have no claim whatever to the money paid for redemption." See Fremantle, January 23, 1917, "Money Paid for Slave (Female) Ransom," SNP 10/2 549p/1914. Temple had always taken a hard line on the slavery issue. As discussed above in Chapter 2, Lugard was to caution Temple on handling slavery matters, when Temple was Resident of Bauchi in 1902; see Bauchi Report No. 2, March 8, 1902, and Lugard's minute, SNP 15/1 Acc 38.

44 G. W. Webster, Yola Province, Report No. 95 for Quarter ending 30 June 1916, SNP 10/5 540p/1917.

45 Webster, Yola Province, Annual Report, 1917, SNP 10/6 201p/1918.

46 As Webster wrote in 1918, "With regard to the freeing of women with a view to marriage, the Emir of Yola and the Alkali both agree that the only way in which this can be done so as to avoid a camouflaged sale is for the money to be treated merely as a ransom paid by the woman. Should a divorce take place it cannot be reclaimed. In practice it thus becomes the Rubu and Sadaki is paid separately. This course has been followed for some years here and does not seem to hinder the freeing of women in this way." See Webster, May 15, 1918, in "Revision of Memo on Slavery," SNP 17 Supplementary Acc 61 1598/1918. All but one of the other slaves, most of whom were women, were issued certificates on the order of the Islamic courts without further explanation.

47 Report of Brooke on District Court, Wudil, Kano Emirate, October 2, 1918, Wudil District, Alkali and Prison Report, Kanoprof 5/1 244.

48 Skinner's notes on Mahmudu interviews.

49 He claimed that he had never heard of such a case; see his report from Sokoto, May 23, 1918, in "Revision of Memo on Slavery," SNP 17 Supplementary Acc 61 1598/1918.

50 Arnett's Memorandum to M. Delafosse, August 9, 1925, Arnett Papers, Mss. Afr. s.952/2–3, Rhodes House.

51 See, for example, Case No. 15A, in which a master reported his female slave "stolen" by another man. Witnesses confirmed that the woman had actually "fled from him." She was returned to her master. Also Case No. 25G, in which a slave woman hid with her grandmother in the emir's palace. She was returned to her master as well. For these and other cases, see Christelow (1993).

52 Vaughan and Kirk-Greene (forthcoming).

53 *Ibid.* Also see Case No. 41C, Kano Judicial Records, in which a slave woman complained

that her masters did not "give [her] food and drink." The master was rebuked; see Christelow (1993).

54 Case No. 17B in Christelow (1993). The Resident did not know what to do, so he let her go. Also see Case No. 44D; in this case the concubine and her master were "reconciled," with the assistance of the Resident.

55 Case No. 148G, in Christelow (1993).

56 Case No. 55B, in Christelow (1993). Also see Case No. 14C, in which a woman also refused to work, apparently at the instigation of a man.

57 E. Arnett, Sokoto, May 23, 1918, in "Revision of Memo on Slavery," SNP 17 Supplementary Acc 61 1598/1918.

58 Lugard, Governor, Northern Nigeria, as quoted in G. R. Matthews, September 15, 1914, "Money Paid for Slave (Female) Ransom," SNP 10/2 549p/1914.

59 Arnett, May 23, 1918. Italics added.

60 See Case No. 28C in Christelow (1993), in which a woman had run away from her master eighteen years earlier but was allowed to stay with the man with whom she had been living because "he has never frightened me." Two women also ran away from their Argungu master, returning to the original master of one of the women in Kano. They were allowed to remain, although the possibility that the master in Argungu might file suit was recognized: see Case No. 29G.

61 Case No. 13F, in Christelow (1993).

62 Webster, May 15, 1918, in "Revision of Memo on Slavery," SNP 17/2 1598/1918. For Webster's comments on the situation in Yola, see Annual Report for Yola Province, 1917, SNP 10/6 201p/1918.

63 Marginal note in Arthur Festing, Zaria Province Annual Report, 1908, February 9, 1909, Zarprof 2555.

64 Case No. 33A, in Christelow (1992), in which a slave woman claimed that her daughter was under eleven, but the Judicial Council held that she was fourteen and had to work for the master.

65 Webster, Annual Report for Yola Province, 1917, SNP 10/6 201p/1918.

66 Minute of G. S. Browne, July 15, 1921, Alkalin Kano, SNP 8 10/1921.

67 Palmer refers to a case from Zaria in which a mother was "anxious" to obtain a certificate of freedom from the *alkali* of Makarfi for her daughter who had been born after 1901. Palmer claimed that "the case is entirely typical, and I can recollect many instances of mothers with young children coming to ask for such certificates, in order to give them the 'Hall Mark' which so much affects their status in Native Society." See Minute of Palmer, July 10, 1921, Alkalin Kano, SNP 8 10/1921. Also see minutes of W. F. Gowers, April 1, 1921, and Donald Kingdom, attorney general, May 26, 1921.

68 Webster, Sokoto Province Report No. 58 for Half Year ending 30th June 1920, SNP 10/8 256p/1920.

69 Christelow (1993).

70 Minute of Palmer, July 10, 1921, Alkalin Kano, SNP 8 10/1921. Also see minutes of Gowers, April 1, 1921, and Kingdom, May 26, 1921.

71 Minute of Kingdom, May 26, 1921, Alkalin Kano, SNP 8 10/1921.

72 Minute of Palmer, July 10, 1921.

73 Testimony of Balarabe Junaidu, Sokoto, March 1986, as quoted in Jumare (unpublished, 1988a), 108. Jumare also cites other oral sources.

74 Jumare cites an anonymous source that "concubines are obtained from slave settlements outside the City [of Sokoto] by the families whose forefathers had established such settlements"; see (unpublished, 1988a), 109. For Kano, see Sa'idu (unpublished, 1981), 157.

75 Webster, Sokoto Province Report No. 58 for Half Year ending 30th June 1920, SNP 10/8 256p/1920.

76 Minute of G. S. Browne, July 15, 1921. Alkalin Kano, SNP 8 10/1921.

77 *Ibid.*
78 Webster, December 31, 1922, Annual Report, Sokoto Province, 1922, SNP 9 3013/1923.
79 As quoted in Webster, December 31, 1922, Annual Report, Sokoto Province, 1922, SNP 9 3013/1923. Webster claimed that "this action is entirely unprompted by me."
80 Minute of H. R. Palmer, July 10, 1921, Alkalin Kano, SNP 8 10/1921. Palmer was concerned that *alkalai* were assuming the right of *wali* over girls of servile origin, but in his opinion, "It is the function of an Alkali to dissolve marriages and to adjust the relations of subsisting marriages, but it is not his function to register and make marriages or give certificates of marriage."
81 Christelow (1993). Also see the case of a master in Kano who attempted to claim the daughter of one of his slaves. The slave had apparently run away to Bauchi sometime in the late 1870s, where he married and had a family. He returned to Kano in c. 1912 because his daughter was being married. His master thereupon laid claim to the daughter, and the case duly came before the Judiciary Council and then to the attention of the Resident. Gowers considered that the master had the right to receive ransom for the woman, although in this particular case the matter appears to have been settled out of court. In Gower's opinion, "The Alkali's Court would undoubtedly have held as the Mallamai did that, legally [the man] was a slave until proved otherwise," and therefore the master had the right of *wali* over the daughter, who was also a slave. See W. F. Gowers, Annual Report for Kano Province, 1912, SNP 10/1 134p/1913.
82 Case No. 7E, in Christelow (1993).
83 Case No. 13A, in Christelow (1993). Residence of the slave parents was an important element in determining whether or not a master had guardianship over the free children, as was clear in Case No. 35D. When the master tried to take one of the children of his slave woman who was married to another man by force, the Judicial Council ordered that the boy be returned to his mother.
84 Arnett's Memorandum to M. Delafosse, August 9, 1925, Arnett Papers, Mss. Afr. s.952/2–3, Rhodes House.
85 *Ibid.*
86 Minute of Palmer, July 10, 1921, Alkalin Kano, SNP 8 10/1921.
87 Webster, Sokoto Province Report No. 58 for Half Year ending 30th June 1920, SNP 10/8 256p/1920.
88 Skinner's notes on Mahmudu interviews.
89 A. C. G. Hastings, Kano Province Report No. 59 for 15 months ending 31st March 1921, SNP 10/9 120p/1921. Also see Sa'idu (unpublished, 1981), 76.
90 That is, before March 1903.
91 Rules made by the Emir of Kano under Native Authority Ordinance Prohibiting Slave Dealing, SNP 10/8 415p/1920.
92 Minute by G. J. F. Tomlinson, February 24, 1921, Rules made by the Emir of Kano under Native Authority Ordinance Prohibiting Slave Dealing, SNP 10/8 415p/1920. Gowers agreed with Tomlinson: "The trial of offences connected with slavery [i.e., slave trading and enslavement] should be left to Provincial Courts." Minute by W. F. Gowers, March 1, 1921.
93 Minute of Tomlinson, June 21, 1921.
94 Fremantle, June 6, 1918, in "Revision of Memo on Slavery."
95 Skinner's notes on Mahmudu interviews.
96 Carrow, Karaye District, Kano Province, June 1920, in "Slave Dealing, Nigeria and Cameroons," SNP 17/2 12577.
97 The certificate given by the Alkalin Kano Aminu read as follows: "Know that a man of the people of city of Kano called Mudi has ransomed a female slave born in Adamawa, a girl of 25 years of age or thereabouts called 'Uwaye Tawa' and the reason of the ransoming is that she may be free and in order that he may marry (nikah) her. The ransom paid was eight

pounds. Her master Mama has agreed, and was paid the amount in the presence of the Alkali of Kano, etc. etc." Translated in the minute of Palmer, July 10, 1921, Alkalin Kano, SNP 8 10/1921.

98 H. R. Palmer, July 10, 1921. It should be noted that the ransom prices reported here were much higher than the "fixed sum" of £3 1s. 6d. that was reported by Brooke in 1918 for Wudil District; see Report on District Court, Wudil, Kano Emirate, October 2, 1918, Wudil District, Alkali and Prison Report, Kanoprof 5/1 244.

99 According to Resident Hastings (January 19, 1921, Alkalin Kano, SNP 8 10/1921),

The Emir, Waziri, District Officer Kano and myself met and discussed the matter at length and the Alkali was personally interrogated by the Emir. His sole defence was that he had not been told the girl Mairo came from Cameroons. Confronted by the Emir with this freedom paper given by himself, in which her birth place was mentioned, he had nothing further to say. The Emir Usumanu has written to me officially asking that the Alkali should be removed from office for this grave offence, pointing out that the law upon the subject of "slavery" and all its circumstances is known to all, and that its infringement must be punished – I recommend most strongly that the Emir's request be complied with. A further point arises – Mudi, Nana and Haruna are being tried in the Provincial Court for slave dealing; the two former have been convicted, the case of Haruna is remanded for further evidence.

100 Case No. 1/KD 1/1921, January 12, 1921 before Major T. A. G. Bugden, Kano. Rex v. Nana, aged sixty of Kano; Haruna, aged fifty-two of Garko; and Mudi, aged thirty-five, of Kano. Mairo was eighteen to twenty years old, brought into Nigeria by Mudi five years ago; Mudi had accepted ransom for her in the Alkali's court in Kano about six months ago, "thus treating her as a slave." Haruna had transferred one Ilori, eighteen to twenty years old, to Mudi in the Alkali's court six months earlier. Mudi was charged with paying the ransom for the two girls. Mairo's testimony: "I know accused Nana and Mudi. Nana brought me from Ngaundere some 5 years ago, and I have been living with him until I was ransomed by Mudi in the Court of the Alkali of Kano. Since then I have been living with him as his wife. Mudi has known me since I came from the Cameroons. He knew that Nana brought me from the Cameroons. My father died some 10 years ago long before I left Ngaundere." Testimony of Komai na gari, a native youth of eighteen to twenty years: "I know accused Nana. He brought me from Ngaundere in the Cameroons together with Mairo, some 5 years ago. I have been living with Nana since then." Ilori: "I know Haruna and Mudi. I have lived with Haruna since I was small. My father Isa died when I was about 5 years. He was a slave of Haruna. Assubar was my mother. She died 2 years ago. I have been kept by Haruna as his slave until ransomed some 6 months ago by Mudi. Mudi gave me 8/– sadaki when he married me." Nana's testimony: "Mario's father was my slave in the Cameroons. I heard that my house in Kano was likely to be taken away so I came back to Kano with Mairo and Nana to Kano some 5 years ago. Mudi ransomed her, Mairo, at the court of the Alkali of Kano some 6 months ago. He paid £8. Mudi knew I brought her from the Cameroons. I did not know that persons brought into Nigeria during the past 20 years were free." Mudi states: "I know Nana and Mairo and Ilori. I ransomed them before the Alkali of Kano some 6 months ago and married them. I paid £8 ransome [sic] for Mairo and £13 for Ilori. I did not know that it was illegal to ransome children brought into Nigeria since March 1901. I thought that if the Alkali approved of the transaction it must be legal." Haruna states: "I know Mudi and Ilori. Ilori was my slave. Her father was my slave. He was called Madugu ta Gobara. He died some 20 years ago at Bida. She has been at Gerko [Garko] for 24 years. Her mother Assabat died 15 years ago at Gerko. She was my slave. Ilori was born in my house. The Liman of Gerko knows Ilori's parents." Mallam Dogo of Garko: "I know Ilori, and Haruna. Ilori was born at Gerko, before the advent of the British, about 4 years before Emir Aliu succeeded to his rank. Her mother was Assubar.

Her father was Isa. They were slaves." The court concluded that it was legal to ransom Ilori, and hence Haruna was found not guilty. Testimony before Provincial court, Kano, January 12, 1921 and January 24, 1921, Alkalin Kano, SNP 8 10/1921.

101 Minutes on Annual Report on Kano, 1920, SNP 10/9 120p/1921; A. Hastings, March 2, 1921, Alkalin Kano, SNP 8 10/1921.

102 Hastings, Kano Province Report No. 59 for 15 months ending 31st March 1921, SNP 10/9 120p/1921.

103 Minute of Palmer, July 10, 1921, Alkalin Kano, SNP 8 10/1921.

104 Minute of Tomlinson, April 7, 1921, Alkalin Kano, SNP 8 10/1921. Also see the minute of M. L. Tew, April 7, 1921.

105 Minute of Kingdom, attorney general, May 26, 1921, Alkalin Kano, SNP 8 10/1921. Tomlinson (minute of March 17, 1921) did not think the *alkali* should be tried, but ransoming before the Islamic courts could "be made an instrument of slave dealing and should therefore be carefully watched, but such cases are difficult and need to be reviewed with great care." Gowers (minute of April 1, 1921) did not think that "the 'ransoming' and the giving of a certificate of freedom to a girl who is already free in the eyes of British law constitutes an offence against the sections of the C.C. [Criminal Code] which deal with slave-dealing."

106 G. S. Browne's circular of November 10, 1922, entitled "Fictitious Ransom," CSO 26/11799, Vol. I. The wording was very similar to Palmer's minute of July 1921; see Alkalin Kano, SNP 8 10/1921.

107 P. C. Butcher to Resident, Sokoto, October 17, 1931, Advisory Council on Concubinage and Dowry, Sokprof 3/27 s.1646.

108 Webster, Annual Report on Adamawa Province, 1929, SNP 17/2 12447, Vol. 1. In 1930, Webster reported that "a certain number of girls are still technically enslaved by being taken in concubinage, and that others free by law are treated as slaves, but most, if not all, of these are fully aware that they are really free and only continue in nominal serfdom in order to enjoy certain privileges. Enslaving except in this sense is apparently quite dead." See Webster, Adamawa Annual Report, 1930, SNP 17/2 14985.

109 G. Miles Clifford, Yola, November 11, 1936, SNP 17/2 20216.

110 *Ibid.*

111 H. H. Middleton, March 10, 1926, in "Slave Dealing, Nigeria and Cameroons," SNP 17/2 12577. Hebini returned to her parents near Banyo; Jamveli was placed with Sarkin Gashaka's mother until she was ready to marry; Allaidi, aged eighteen, who had run away from her mistress, had been illegally brought from Banyo and had recently married; while Bormi, a Mambila girl, returned to her mother.

112 Webster, Annual Report on Adamawa Province, 1929, SNP 17/2 12447, Vol. 1.

113 *Ibid.*

114 Jumare (unpublished, 1988a), 105. See also Northern Provinces Advisory Council, 1931; Subject: Concubinage and Dowry, SNP 17/2 14841/24.

115 P. C. Butcher to Resident, Sokoto, October, 17, 1931, Advisory Council on Concubinage and Dowry, Sokprof s.1646.

116 *Ibid.* 3/27.

117 Jumare (unpublished, 1988b). See also Slavery Concubinage, 1922–47, Yolaprof No. 239.

9 Legal-status abolition: the final phase

1 G. S. Browne, May 3, 1924, CSO 26/11799, Vol. I. Browne repeated the earlier claims: he noted that as early as 1918 "slavery in the Kano Province was to a very large extent already dead."

2 Ubah (1991).

3 Testimony of Arande, an "adult Fulani," before H. F. Mathews, ADO Keffi, November 26, 1911, in H. F. Mathews, November 26, 1917, in "Slave Dealing, Nigeria and Cameroons,"

SNP 17/2 12577. Also see J. C. Sciortino, November 30, 1917, in "Slave Dealing, Nigeria and Cameroons," SNP 17/2 12577.

4 Lethem was writing from Ilorin; see the letter to his mother, October 17, 1911, Lethem Papers, Mss. Brit. Emp. s.276, Box 22, Rhodes House.

5 A. Holdsworth Groom, Muri, February 10, 1917, in E. H. B. Laing, Yola Province, Quarterly Report No. 96, 30 September 1916, SNP 10/4 695p/1916. Also in SNP 17/2 12577. Also see Summary of Reports to the League of Nations for 1922, 1923, and 1924, submitted to the International Labour Office, October 14, 1925, CSO 26/11799, Vol. I.

6 J. M. Fremantle, Muri Province Annual Report, 1915, SNP 10/4 365p/1916. For another description of the techniques of disguising these slave children as Hausa, see Groom, Muri, February 10, 1917.

7 S. H. P. Vereker, Yola, July 18, 1927, in "Slave Dealing, Nigeria and Cameroons," SNP 17/2 12577.

8 T. H. Haughton, Yola Province, Annual Report, 1924, SNP 9/12 639/1925.

9 Zang was a slave-smuggling center near Numan, on the border between Yola and Muri Provinces. It was on the road from Yola to Mutum Biu and Lau. See E. H. B. Laing, Yola Province, Quarterly Report No. 96, 30 September 1916, SNP 10/4 695p/1916.

10 E. G. M. Dupigny, Niger Province Report No. 10 for Year ending 31st December 1917, SNP 10/6 199p/1918.

11 E. H. B. Laing, Nupe Annual Report, 1919, SNP 10/8 9p/1920.

12 Register of Freed Slaves, 1905–1906, SNP 15/1 Acc 90; SNP 15/1 Acc 121.

13 Ubah (1991).

14 The Mumuye were located in Yola Province; see G. W. Webster, Yola Province, Report No. 94 for Quarter ending 31 March 1916, SNP 10/3 373p/1916.

15 Mair, in E. H. B. Laing, Yola Province, Quarterly Report No. 96, 30 September 1916, SNP 10/4 695p/1916.

16 G. W. Webster, Annual Report, Yola Province, 1916, SNP 15/5 103p/1917. A marginal note made the point that "As long as political staff are instructed what to look for amongst these Hausa colonies this form of slavery should die a natural death in a very short while." Once more the "natural death" of slavery was being predicted.

17 Mair, in E. H. B. Laing, Yola Province, Quarterly Report No. 96, 30 September 1916, SNP 10/4 695p/1916.

18 Fremantle, December 22, 1921, in "Slave Dealing, Nigeria and Cameroons," SNP 17/2 12577.

19 Fremantle, Muri Province Annual Report, 1916, SNP 10/5 95p/1917.

20 *Ibid.*

21 E. H. B. Laing, Yola Province, Quarterly Report No. 96, 30 September 1916, SNP 10/4 695p/1916. For Pankshin Division, see A. J. Hicks Gower (?), Resident, Jema'a, October 2, 1923, in "Slave Dealing, Nigeria and Cameroons," SNP 17/2 12577.

22 A. Holdsworth Groom, Jalingo, March 2, 1917, in "Slave Dealing, Nigeria and Cameroons," SNP 17/2 12577. Also see the information on kidnaping in German Cameroons in 1916, in Summary of Reports to the League of Nations for 1922, 1923, and 1924, submitted to the International Labour Office, October 14, 1925, CSO 26/11799, Vol. I.

23 J. C. Sciortino, November 30, 1917, in "Slave Dealing, Nigeria and Cameroons," SNP 17/2 12577.

24 Resident Yola, October 2, 1923, in "Slave Dealing, Nigeria and Cameroons," SNP 17/2 12577.

25 According to Rosedale, as quoted in T. H. Haughton, Yola Province, Annual Report, 1924, SNP 9/12 639/1925. Haughton claimed that the "past year has shown a considerable improvement in respect to slavery in the Mandated Areas, and although it cannot be denied that a relatively mild form of trafficking in children as slaves still continues to exist, the traffic is now only a shadow of its former self."

26 Webster, Yola Province, Report No. 94 for Quarter ending 31 March 1916, SNP 10/3 373p/1916.
27 Captain Wilkinson, November 21, 1927, contained in G. S. Browne, February 28, 1928, in "Slave Dealing, Nigeria and Cameroons," SNP 17/2 12577.
28 Lucien Fourneau to Gouverneur Général de la Nigeria, June 5, 1918, SNP 10/6 447p/1918.
29 The diary records one entry in which "Abangu and his people" were enslaved, but the number involved is not stated.
30 Captain Wilkinson, November 21, 1927, contained in G. S. Browne, February 28, 1928, in "Slave Dealing, Nigeria and Cameroons," SNP 17/2 12577. See Vaughan and Kirk-Greene (forthcoming).
31 Captain Wilkinson, November 21, 1927, contained in G. S. Browne, February 28, 1928, in "Slave Dealing, Nigeria and Cameroons," SNP 17/2 12577. In 1926, Backwell reported three cases of slave dealing in Madagali, which continued to be a center of the trade even after Hamman Yaji stopped raiding for slaves in 1920. See H. H. Middleton, September 4, 1926, in "Slave Dealing, Nigeria and Cameroons," SNP 17/2 12577; S. H. P. Vereker, Yola, July 18, 1927, in "Slave Dealing, Nigeria and Cameroons," SNP 17/2 12577.
32 Fremantle, Muri Province Annual Report, 1915, SNP 10/4 365p/1916.
33 Ibid.
34 Ibid. For another description of the techniques of disguising these slave children as Hausa, see Groom, Muri, February 10, 1917, in Laing, Yola Province, Quarterly Report No. 96, 30 September 1916, SNP 10/4 695p/1916. The report is also in SNP 17/2 12577.
35 Webster, Yola Province, Report No. 94 for Quarter Ending 31 March 1916, SNP 10/3 373p/1916.
36 A. C. G. Hastings, Kano Province Report No. 59 for 15 months ending 31st March 1921, SNP 10/9 120p/1921.
37 E. Arnett, Kano, August 8, 1922, in "Slave Dealing, Nigeria and Cameroons," SNP 17/2 12577.
38 C. O. Migeod, Annual Report, Yola Province, 1922, SNP 9/10 72/1923.
39 H. R. Palmer, March 19, 1926, CSO 26/11799, Vol. I.
40 Resident, Northern Cameroons Districts, in despatch from the Resident of Yola, June 14, 1922, in "Slave Dealing, Nigeria and Cameroons," SNP 17/2 12577.
41 Resident Yola, October 2, 1923, in "Slave Dealing, Nigeria and Cameroons," SNP 17/2 12577.
42 Ibid.
43 As T. H. Haughton, Resident Yola, noted in 1925: "In the North [Cameroons] complaints of slave dealing have grown fewer and fewer, no doubt because of the fact that an Officer has been in residence for the greater part of the year, and the border pagan villages, that have been the centres for slave dealing are gradually being brought under effective control ... The Chiefs – formerly themselves slave-dealers – have now begun to help to put a stop to the traffic." See T. H. Haughton, January 16, 1925, in "Slave Dealing, Nigeria and Cameroons," SNP 17/2 12577. Also see Haughton, Yola Province, Annual Report, 1924, SNP 9/12 639/1925.
44 E. G. M. Dupigny, Niger Province Report No. 10 for Year ending 31st December 1917, SNP 10/6 199p/1918. Also see Summary of Reports to the League of Nations for 1922, 1923, and 1924, submitted to the International Labour Office, October 14, 1925, CSO 26/11799, Vol. I.
45 J. C. Sciortino, Nassarawa Province Annual Report, 1914, SNP 15/2 146p/1914.
46 H. F. Mathews, November 26, 1917, in "Slave Dealing, Nigeria and Cameroons," SNP 17/2 12577; J. C. Sciortini, November 30, 1917, in "Slave Dealing, Nigeria and Cameroons," SNP 17 12577.
47 A. J. Hicks Gower, Resident, Jema'a, October 2, 1923, in "Slave Dealing, Nigeria and Cameroons," SNP 17/2 12577.
48 See, for example, G. W. Webster, Yola Province, Report No. 95 for Quarter ending 30 June

1916, SNP 10/5 540p/1917 and H. H. Middleton, March 10, 1925, in "Slave Dealing, Nigeria and Cameroons," SNP 17/2 12577. For slave dealing from Mandara north into French territory around Lake Chad in 1934, see P. Boittoy to Governor-General of Nigeria, January 13, 1934; Donald Cameron to Governor-General, Dakar, February 2, 1934, Zarprof 5/1 C.4089.

49 Lethem to Hugh Clifford, July 24, 1925; R. W. Bullard to Lethem, August 27, 1925; Lethem to Civil Secretary, Sudan, August 28, 1925, Lethem Papers, Mss. Brit. Emp. s.276, Rhodes House; H. H. Middleton, March 10, 1926, in "Slave Dealing, Nigeria and Cameroons," SNP 17/2 12577. Also see Miers (1989), 102–28.

50 Fremantle, Muri Province Annual Report, 1916, SNP 10/5 95p/1917. Also see Webster, Yola Province, Report No. 101, Half Year ending 30th June 1918, SNP 10/6 489p/1918.

51 A. Holdsworth Groom, Muri, February 10, 1917, in E. H. B. Laing, Yola Province, Quarterly Report No. 96, 30 September 1916, SNP 10/4 695p/1916. Also in SNP 17/2 12577. Also see J. M. Fremantle, Muri Province Annual Report, 1915, SNP 10/4 365p/1916.

52 There are numerous files in the Enugu archives that deal with the overland slave trade between the Benue Valley and southeastern Nigeria which we have not been able to examine, including "Hausa Slave Traders from Cameroons via Yola and Muri Province, Annual Report, 1916–17," Calprof Conf. 31/1916, 4/5/46; "Influx of Slaves into the Southern Provinces from the North, 1916," Rivprof C.31/16, 1/2/2; and various files on slave dealing.

53 P. Graham Harris, January 24, 1922, in "Slave Dealing, Nigeria and Cameroons," SNP 17/2 12577.

54 Miers (unpublished, 1986); Miers (1991); and Atchebro (unpublished, 1990), 25–32.

55 Perham (1960), 645–48. He served from 1922 to 1936.

56 Atchebro (unpublished, 1990), 40.

57 As quoted *ibid.*, 54.

58 Atchebro (unpublished, 1990), 25–32, 34.

59 Summary of Reports to the League of Nations for 1922, 1923, and 1924, submitted to the International Labour Office, October 14, 1925, CSO 26/11799, Vol. I.

60 Eric Drummond, Secretary-General, League of Nations, December 23, 1923, "Questions of Slavery in British West Africa," CSO 26/11799, Vol. I.

61 See Temporary Slavery Commission, Report to Council, July 12, 1924; "The Question of Slavery," Memorandum by the Secretary-General, August 4, 1924; and Temporary Slavery Commission, Minutes of the First Session, July 9–12, 1924.

62 G. S. Browne, February 6, 1925, CSO 26/11799, Vol. I.

63 W. Hunt, January 31, 1925, CSO 26/11799, Vol. I.

64 Summary of Reports to the League of Nations for 1922, 1923, and 1924, submitted to the International Labour Office, October 14, 1925, CSO 26/11799, Vol. I.

65 Graeme Thomson to Harding, December 1, 1925, CSO 26/11799, Vol. I. See the two-page report to the League, "The Question of Slavery, 5 September 1924: Letters from the British Government Transmitting Despatches Showing the Situation with Respect to Slavery in the British Colonies and Protectorates and Territories under British Mandate."

66 Graeme Thomson to Harding, December 1, 1925, CSO 26/11799, Vol. I.

67 Clifford, Governor of Nigeria, April 1924, but letter not sent, CSO 26/11799, Vol. I.

68 *Ibid.*

69 Thomson to Harding, December 1, 1925, CSO 26/11799, Vol. I.

70 *Ibid.*

71 Atchebro (unpublished, 1990), 75.

72 Temporary Slavery Commission, Minutes of the Second Session, July 13–25, 1925.

73 Arnett to Strachey, August 10, 1925, Arnett Papers, Mss. Afr. s.952/2–3, Rhodes House.

74 Atchebro (unpublished, 1990), 74. Also see Lugard (1933), 1–14.

75 The Slavery Convention, Report Presented to the Assembly by the Sixth Committee, September 24, 1926, dealt with the legal details.

76 Perham (1960), 656.
77 Miers (unpublished, 1986).
78 Atchebro (unpublished, 1990), 81–82. Annual reports were issued between 1927 and 1933.
79 S. H. P. Vereker, Yola, January 30, 1926, in "Slave Dealing, Nigeria and Cameroons," SNP 17/2 12577. Reports on the slave traffic in the Cameroons were submitted to the League of Nations twice annually from 1924 to 1928 and then annually through 1938; see Minute of April 18, 1939 in "Slave Traffic from Cameroons to Nigeria," CSO 26/50127, Vol. II. There are annual reports on "Slave Traffic in the Cameroons" in "Slave Dealing, Nigeria and Cameroons," SNP 17/2 12577 and in SNP 17/2 20216, Vols. I and II. These files are voluminous and contain extensive information on slave trading and kidnaping in Borno, Dikwa, Northern Cameroon, Mubi, Southern Cameroon, and elsewhere near Yola, Muri and Bauchi.
80 H. H. Middleton, March 10, 1926, in "Slave Dealing, Nigeria and Cameroons," SNP 17/2 12577.
81 Captain Wilkinson, November 21, 1927, contained in G. S. Browne, February 28, 1928, in "Slave Dealing, Nigeria and Cameroons," SNP 17/2 12577. Also see Vaughan and Kirk-Greene (forthcoming).
82 Captain Wilkinson, November 21, 1927, contained in G. S. Browne, February 28, 1928, in "Slave Dealing, Nigeria and Cameroons," SNP 17 12577.
83 *Ibid.* As Wilkinson observed, "On perusal of the attached list [not included] it will be seen that a large number of children have been freed, many of whom are under ten years of age. The gratitude of parents on the restoration of their children is abundant whereas the disappointment when their children fail to recognize them through long separation is distressing."
84 Captain Wilkinson, November 21, 1927, contained in G. S. Browne, February 28, 1928, in "Slave Dealing, Nigeria and Cameroons," SNP 17/2 12577.
85 S. H. P. Vereker, Yola, July 18, 1927, in "Slave Dealing, Nigeria and Cameroons," SNP 17/2 12577.
86 For British efforts at suppression, see Ubah (1991).
87 Webster, Adamawa Annual Report, 1930, SNP 17/2 14985.
88 Webster, February 19, 1931, in "Slave Dealing, Nigeria and Cameroons," SNP 17/2 12577.
89 Acting Resident, Yola, n.d. [1932], and also contained in H. B. James, Annual Report on Slave Traffic in Cameroons, March 18, 1932, in "Slave Dealing, Nigeria and Cameroons," SNP 17/2 12577. Patterson reported child stealing in Idoma country for purposes of sale to Southern Nigeria; some cases of slave dealing in children in Nassarawa Emirate in 1934; and forty-two persons convicted in Benue Province in the previous five years, with nineteen persons freed as a result; sentences ranged from two to fourteen years' imprisonment. There was extensive slave traffic in Pankshin Division, Plateau Province in 1933 – pagan children sold by their parents to Fulani as a result of the economic depression. Fifteen children had been freed. See J. R. Patterson, League of Nations, Report on Slavery, December 28, 1935, SNP 17/2 20216.
90 E. V. Dalwyn, Resident Bornu, "Slave Dealing, 1931–1935," n.d., SNP 17/2 20216.
91 G. W. Izard, June 24, 1936, SNP 17 20216.
92 Slavery, Report of the Committee of Experts on Slavery Provided for by the Assembly Resolution of September 25th, 1931, dated September 1, 1932. The formation of a new commission was recommended in 1929.
93 Lugard, "Mohammedan Slavery" (1928), 784–87. The entry was revised in 1938. See Perham (1960), 656–57.
94 Lethem, "Early History of Anti-Slavery Legislation," SNP 17/2 15849.
95 Miers (unpublished, 1986).
96 "The Abolition of Slavery," letter to *The Times*, December 13, 1932; "Slavery and the League," *Spectator*, July 21, 1933; "Slavery To-day," letter to *The Times*, August 3, 1934.

361

He also published "Slavery in all its Forms" in 1933. These reports had almost nothing to say about Northern Nigeria. His earlier article (1923), 491–97, also had nothing to do with slavery in Northern Nigeria.

97 Miers (unpublished, 1986).
98 Atchebro (unpublished, 1990), 103.
99 Miers (unpublished, 1986).
100 Lethem, "Early History of Anti-Slavery Legislation," SNP 17/2 158489; Northern Provinces Advisory Council, 1931: Subject: Concubinage and Dowry, SNP 17/2 14841/24; Slave Dealing in Nigeria and Cameroons, SNP 17/2 12577, Vols. I and II; Slavery in Nigeria: League of Nations' Report on Slavery, SNP 17/2 20216 Vols. I and II; Slavery: Report of the Advisory Committee, League of Nations, Zarprof 5/1 c.2480; Slave Dealing General: Slaving Grounds in Cameroons, Yolaprof 1563, Vol. II.
101 George Maxwell to Under-Secretary of State for the Colonies, June 15, 1936, Sokprof 3/1 c.33.
102 Pembleton, December 5, 1936, CSO 26/11788, Vol. IV. The revised figure of 119,030 was printed in League of Nations, Slavery, Report of the Advisory Committee of Experts, Fourth Session, April 5–10, 1937, C.188.M.173. 1937, p. 44.
103 C. O. Migeod, Annual Report, Yola Province, 1922, SNP 9/10 72/1923.
104 The figures for Borno (3,000 slaves who had not ransomed themselves before 1936, 1,000 children of slaves, and 1,000 former slaves from Northern Cameroon) should be excluded for comparative purposes with the rest of this study.
105 These calculations are derived as follows: the census reports 23,800 slaves in the central emirates, which was approximately 35 percent of the total (Bornu, Plateau, and Kabba Provinces are not included). In 1916–19, these central emirates had 85 percent of the court cases involving slaves. If it is assumed that the estimates for other provinces are reasonably accurate but should only constitute 15 percent of the total instead of 65 percent, then there must have been 221,000 slaves in total, with 187,850 or 85 percent of the slaves in the central emirates. Another approach would be to assume that the number of slaves in Kano was approximately the same as in Sokoto, and the number in Zaria about the same as in Katsina. This approach would account for another 21,800 slaves, giving a total of 92,000 slaves. However, the methods of estimating the slave population in Sokoto were very rough and appear to have involved considerable underestimation.
106 Atchebro (unpublished, 1990), 106. The context of the 1936 Session should be noted briefly. Italy was partly justifying its invasion of Ethiopia on the basis that slavery was still widespread and that its suppression required formal occupation. For a fuller discussion of the relationship between the Permanent Committee of Experts and the Ethiopian question, see Miers (1991); Miers (unpublished, 1986).
107 Report of the Advisory Committee of Experts, Third (Extraordinary) Session, Geneva, April 15–24, 1936; Sokprof 3/1 c.33.
108 George Maxwell to Under-Secretary of State for the Colonies, June 15, 1936, Sokprof 3/1 c.33.
109 J. H. Thomas at the Colonial Office wrote to Governor Bernard Bourdillon on May 4, 1936. His despatch was forwarded to Northern Nigeria; Minute by K. A. Sinker, May 28, 1936. The Residents were immediately consulted; see G. W. Izard, June 6, 1936, SNP 17/2 20216. This correspondence is contained in "Status of Slavery in Nigeria," Sokprof 3/2 4277. For a summary of the replies of the Residents, see G. W. Izard, June 24, 1936, SNP 17 20216, and G. W. Izard, June 25, 1936, in "Status of Slavery in Nigeria," Sokprof 3/2 4277; also in SNP 17/2 20216.
110 Resident Bauchi, June 24, 1936, SNP 17/2 20216.
111 *Ibid.*
112 According to MacMichael, DO Argungu to Resident, Sokoto, October 28, 1936, Sokprof 3/1 c.33. The ransom could be paid off over three years.

113 G. Miles Clifford, Yola, November 11, 1936, SNP 17/2 20216.

114 G. W. Izard, June 24, 1936, SNP 17/2 20216.

115 MacMichael claimed that these ex-slaves "are in no sense to be regarded as voluntary or domestic slaves. They have entire freedom of action." Indeed, he claimed that "these people are happier living under these conditions, being well cared for, and supplied with food & clothing, and given assistance in their matrimonial affairs." The provision of food, clothing, and assistance in marriage payments suggests that these "ex-slaves" were actually in *murgu* and not free, but it is virtually certain that they were using land that they did not own; see MacMichael, DO Argungu to Resident, Sokoto, October 28, 1936, Sokprof 3/1 c.33.

116 Sharwood Smith, Zaria, October 22, 1922, SNP 17/2 20216.

117 Izard, June 24, 1936, SNP 17/2 20216.

118 Resident Kano, October 27, 1936, SNP 17/2 20216.

119 Sharwood Smith, Zaria, October 22, 1922, SNP 17/2 20216.

120 The Resident Gwandu replied that "the Emir and Council are unanimously of the opinion that the freeing, by administrative decree, of all slaves would meet with no difficulties. Even now it is the rule for the near relations, and not the master, of a slave to inherit a deceased slave's property. The master only inherits when there is no close relative. Any doubtful case would be referred for decision to a competent Court, but it is thought that this would be a rare occurrence and that no special regulations are required on this point." See DO, Gwandu to Resident, Sokoto, June 20, 1936, at Birnin Kebbi, in "Status of Slavery in Nigeria," Sokprof 3/2 4277.

121 Izard, June 24, 1936, SNP 17 20216.

122 *Ibid.*

123 Pembleton, October 16, 1936, in "Questions of Slavery in British West Africa," CSO 26/11799, Vol. IV.

124 League of Nations, Slavery. Report of the Advisory Committee of Experts, Fifth (Extraordinary) Session of the Committee, March 31st to April 5th, 1938, C.112.M.98. 1938. VI, pp. 117–18.

125 W. Pembleton, December 5, 1936, CSO 26/11799, Vol. IV.

126 M. G. Smith (1960), 223. Smith cites Cole (1944), for the point that the British found the system obscure and puzzling.

127 M. G. Smith (1960), 254.

128 *Ibid.*, 258–59.

129 M. G. Smith (1965a), 260.

130 Hill (1977), 212.

131 Rowling (1940), 52. Also see Rowling, "General Investigation into Northern Provinces Land Problems and Land Tenureship," May 20, 1946, RG/R2.

132 Fika (1978), 235.

Appendix Court records of slaves issued certificates of freedom

1 *Northern Nigeria Annual Report, 1905–06*, 38. The Zaria courts did not report such cases until 1905; see C. W. Orr, Zaria Province Annual Report, 1905, March 23, 1906, Zarprof 7/1 2252.

2 *Northern Nigeria Annual Report, 1905–06*, 39–40, 408.

3 *Northern Nigeria Annual Report, 1906–07*, 508–509.

4 Arthur Festing, Zaria Province Annual Report, 1908, February 9, 1909, Zarprof 7/1 2555.

5 *Northern Nigeria Annual Report, 1909*, 706.

6 Resident's report included in C. Temple to Harcourt, July 17, 1911, Despatch No. 539, CO 446/98.

7 *Colonial Reports, Annual, Nigeria*, 1914, 50.

8 E. J. Arnett, Annual Report, Sokoto, Gwandu and Argungu, 1913, Sokprof 2/12 581/1914. Arnett caught two village heads engaged in this practice, and he had "not the least doubt that there are many other instances of this which have not yet come to light." In these cases, "the headmen were punished and made to disgorge the fees taken and the freedom formerly [sic] verified and recorded in the Native Court."

9 Statistics for Borno and Bassa have been excluded from these totals; SNP 10/1, 45p/1914 and SNP 17/2 14432.

10 Northern Nigeria Annual Report, 1905–06, 411; Northern Nigeria Annual Report, 1906–07, 508.

11 Northern Nigeria Annual Report, 1907–08, 623; SNP 17/14432.

12 Northern Nigeria Annual Report, 1906–07, 506–507; Northern Nigeria Annual Report, 1907–08, 610.

13 SNP 17/2 14432.

14 Northern Nigeria Annual Report, 1907–08, 614; Northern Nigeria Annual Report, 1910–11, 739; W. F. Gowers, Kano Province, Annual Report, 1912, SNP 10/1 134p/1913. Also see Ubah (1985), 368–69.

15 SNP 17/2 14432.

16 Ibid.; SNP 10 236p/1916; SNP 10 331p/1919.

17 Ibid.

18 J. M. Fremantle, Muri Province Annual Report, 1916, SNP 10/5 95p/1917. In his Annual Report for 1915 (SNP 10/4 365p/1916), Fremantle accounted for the 1,106 slaves freed through the Provincial court as follows: 1,067 were freed on the conviction of their merchant owners; 26 were freed as a result of ill treatment and 13 were deserted by their owners, which usually meant that the slave trader escaped arrest.

19 In Yola, for example, 22 of 141 (15.6 percent) slaves were freed through the Provincial court in 1916; see G. W. Webster, Yola Province Annual Report, 1916, SNP 15/5 103p/1917.

20 SNP 10/9 120p/1921.

21 C. O. Migeod, Yola Province Annual Report, 1922, SNP 9/10 72/1923.

Glossary

abokin wasa – "joking relations"; denoting acceptable marriage partnerships
afuma – a special levy on grain
alkali (pl. *alkalai*) – Muslim judge
aro – a system of borrowing
aron gona – farm leasing
asali – origins; kinship
attajirai – wealthy merchants

bacucane (pl. *cucanawa*) – second-generation slave
bado – gift or grant
basasa – the Kano civil war, 1893–94
bayi (pl. *bawa*) – slave
benu – the Bida official responsible for Lokoja
birni – walled city

caffa – clientage with associated access to land
cin rani – dry-season labor migration
cowrie shells – Caliphate currency

dagaci (pl. *dagatai*) – village head, subordinate
dimajai – children of slaves; see *bacucane*
dogarai – emirate police

fadama – irrigated lands
fadawa – those associated with the palace
fansa (*pansa*) – slave ransom or redemption price
fansar kai – self-ransom
fito – tax on caravans at river crossings
Fombina – Adamawa
Fulbe – Fulani
Fulfulde – the language of the Fulani

gaisuwa – (a) gift-giving to political officials; (b) greetings

galadima – common title for officials

galla – (a) sharecrop rental for land; (b) a tax

gallar k'asa – farm tax

gandu (pl. *gandaye*) – (a) large agricultural estates; (b) central field farmed by fathers and sons and occasionally by brothers

gandun sarauta – *gandu* estates attached to political office

gara – wedding presents

gayauna – (a) small farms or gardens worked by slaves; (b) small farms worked by individual members of a *gandu* unit

gonar daji – bush land

gujia – groundnuts

hakimi (pl. *hakimai*) – district heads

hurumi – special land grants with tax exemptions associated with privileges of political office

jakada (pl. *jakadu*) – slave officials; tax collectors

jangali – cattle tax

jihad – Muslim holy war, specifically the one founding the Sokoto Caliphate, 1804–1808

jizya – poll tax on non-Muslim populations

Kakanda – Nupe river merchants and fishermen

karofi – dyepit centre

kharaj – land tax, *kurdin kasa*

kitaba (Arabic) – contract

kulle – purdah

kurdin d'aki – tax on compounds

kurdin galma – tax calculated per hoe

kurdin hatsi – tax on grain

kurdin karofi – literally, the tax on dye pits but more generally, an industrial tax

kurdin kasa – land tax

kurdin rafi – tax on special dry-season crops

kurdin shuka – tax on special dry-season crops

madugu – caravan leader

Maguzawa – non-Muslim Hausa

mahdi – Islamic messianic figure, "the rightly guided one"

mai gida (pl. *masu gidaje*) – (a) household head; (b) landowner; (c) slave master

mai jimila – sub-district head

mai unguwa – hamlet head

makulliya – concubine

murgu – practice whereby slaves paid a fee to their masters in order to work on their own account

nomijide – non-residents or absentee farmers

pansa – see fansa

ribat – a fortified settlement
rinji (pl. *rumada*) – plantation; *also see gandu*
rinjin sarauta – estate attached to political office
rumbu – granary

sad'aka – concubine
sadaki – marriage payment
sarki (pl. *sarakuna*) – (a) emir; (b) town head
Sarkin Musulmi – Hausa title for Caliph of Sokoto, later known as Sultan
shaida – witness
shari'a – Islamic law

taki assessment – revenue survey
talakawa – freeborn peasantry
torodbe – Fulbe or Fulani clerical class

WAFF – West African Frontier Force
wahayiya – slave woman who has borne a child by her master
wali – guardian
wakili – a relationship in which the ex-owner of a slave acted as the slave's representative or guardian
waqf – state land, according to the Maliki school of law

yanci – a free person
yara – (a) boy; (b) servant; (c) former slave

zakka/zakat –Islamic tithe on grain
zaman turawa – "time of the European," as pertaining to colonial laws

Bibliography

I Oral data

1 Yusufu Yunusa Collection
Sarkin Bagarmi, Kano, August 23, 1975
Mai Dawakai Gwadabe Dogari, Emir's Palace, Kano, July 11, 1975
Idrisu Dan Maisoro, b. 1900, Hausawa ward, Kano, August 7, 1975
Abdullahi Adamu Ningi, b. 1932, Kano, August 3, 1975
Muhammadu Rabi'u, b. 1916, Fanisau, July 13, 1975
Alhaji Wada, Kano, July 18, 1975
Malam Zubairu, Gandun Swaina, Kano Emirate, September 11, 1975
Malam Rabi'u, Fanisau, Kano Emirate, July 13, 1975
2 Aliyu Musa Collection
Da'u Bello, Gini ward, Kano, August 23, 1975
Yeye, Gini ward, Kano, August 8, 1975
Mairo Iya Babba, Gini ward, Kano, August 10, 1975
Sa'a Mai Itace, Gini ward, Kano, August 8, 1975
3 Ahmadu Maccido Collection
Maccido Alhassan, b. 1897, Kwarbai, Zaria, June 11, 1975
Ali Balarabe, Sarkin Farin Kasa, Zaria Emirate, b. 1907, July 7, 1975
Tukur Yero, b. 1905, Zaria, September 12, 1975
Boyi Ibrahim, b. 1880, Bani-Wuri ward, Zaria, September 2, 1975
Ahmadu Ibrahim, b. 1905, Sundu, Zaria Emirate, July 20, 1975
Aliyu Muhammadu, b. 1895, Dambo, Zaria Emirate, August 22, 1975
Muhamman Bello, b. 1890, August 17, 1975
Abubakar Cindo, b. during reign of Sarkin Zazzau Yaro, 1890–97, September 10, 1975
Malam Ali, Kudan, December 8, 1975
Nuhu Salmanu, b. 1898, Zaria City, June 10, 1975
4 J. S. Hogendorn and Ahmadu Maccido Collection
Malam Najuma and Malam Audu Goma, Biye, May 27, 1975
Audu Goma, May 20, 1975
Malam Bawa, Hanwa, Zaria Emirate, June 16, 1975
5 Ibrahim Jumare Collection
Group interview, Runjin Biyo, Sokoto, July 23, 1989
6 Philip Shea Collection, appendix in Shea (unpublished, 1975)
Malam Gwadabe (b. 1904), Sabon Sara ward, Kano, May 27, 1970
Baliya (b. 1898), Karofin Sudawa ward, Kano, May 6, 1971
Ishiaka Abdurahman (b. 1900), Takalmawa ward, Kano, February 3, 1971

368

Garba (b. 1903), Limawa, Kumbotso District, Kano Emirate, October 27, 1971
Uban Gila (b. 1901), Rogo, Karaye District, Kano Emirate, November [no day given] 1971
7 Neal Skinner, Typescript summary of interviews with Mahmudu K'ok'i

II Archival materials

Nigerian National Archives (Kaduna)
  Secretariat, Northern Provinces (SNP)
    SNP 6/3, 6/4
    SNP 7/5–7/13
    SNP 8
    SNP 9/10
    SNP 10/1–10/9
    SNP 15/1, 15/2, 15/3
    SNP 17/1–17/2
    SNP Supplementary Acc 61 1598/1918
  Sokoto Provincial Files (Sokprof)
    Sokprof 2/1, 2/2, 2/8, 2/9, 2/11, 2/12
    Sokprof 3/1, 3/2, 3/3, 3/27
    Sokprof 230/1913
  Kano Provincial Files (Kanoprof)
    Kanoprof 5/1
    Kanoprof 1708
  Zaria Provincial Files (Zaraprof)
    Zaraprof 5/1
    Zaraprof 7/1
  Katsina Provincial Files (Katprof)
    Katprof 1
  Jos Provincial Files (Josprof)
    Josprof 1/1
  Yola Provincial Files (Yolaprof)
    Yolaprof A1, A5, A6, A7
    Yolaprof 239
    Yolaprof 1563
  Bauchi Provincial Files (Bauchiprof)
    Bauchiprof 390
  C. W. Rowling, "General Investigation into Northern Provinces Land Problems and Land Tenureship," May 20, 1946, RG/R2
Nigerian National Archives (Ibadan)
  Central Secretariat Office (CSO)
    CSO 1/27, 1/28
    CSO 8/6
    CSO 26/11799
Rhodes House (Oxford)
  Frederick Lugard Papers
    Mss. Brit. Emp. s.53
    Mss. Brit. Emp. s.62
    Mss. Brit. Emp. s.64
    Mss. Brit. Emp. s.71
    Mss. Brit. Emp. s.76
    Mss. Perham 309

Bibliography

George Abadie, Nigerian Letters, 1897–1904, Mss. Afr. s.1337
Selwyn Grier Papers, Mss. Afr. r.1379
A. A. Shillingford Papers, Mss. Afr. s.547
Royal Niger Company Papers, Mss. Afr. s.85–101
A. J. H. Lethem Papers, Mss. Brit. Emp. s.276
W. F. Gowers, "Notes on Trade in Sokoto Province, February 1911," Mss. Afr. s.662(2)
H. S. W. Edwardes Papers, Mss. Afr. s.769
H. S. W. Edwardes Diary, Mss. Afr. r.106
W. H. Wilkin Papers, Mss. Afr. r.152
E. J. Arnett Papers, Mss. Afr. s.952
Reginald Popham Lobb, Northern Nigerian Notes, 1900–1905, Mss. Afr. r.81
Imperial British East Africa Company Miscellaneous Papers 1888–1894, 740.14.s.25
Archives Nationales du Niger (Niamey)
H. Lousteau, Rapport annuel 1903 du cercle commencé le 1er mars 1903, terminé le 31 mars
   1904, cercle de Say, 16.2.4
Rapports d'ensemble des mois de fév., mai, juin, aôut et déc. 1906, Cercle de Say, 16.5.1
Rapport du Cercle de Say, 30 avril 1906, 16.5.2
Centre Nigérien de Recherches en Sciences Humaines, Niamey
Taillebourg, Histoire du Cercle de Say, c. 1921
Public Record Office (Kew)
   Colonial Office
      CO 147/124. Despatches Relating to the Royal Niger Company
      CO 445. West African Frontier Force Despatches
      CO 446 1–99. Despatches of the British Administration of Northern Nigeria
      CO 520/95. Southern Nigeria, 1910
      CO 579/58/580. Correspondence (1899–1901) Relating to the Administration of Lagos and
         Nigeria
      CO 587/2
      CO 819/84
      CO 879/58. Administration of Nigeria
      CO 879/72/684. Lagos: Nigeria. Further Correspondence (January, 1902, to February,
         1905) Relating to the Administration of Lagos and Nigeria
      CO 879/76/695. Lagos: Nigeria. Further Correspondence (November 20, 1901–April 19,
         1905) Relating to Railway Construction in Lagos and Nigeria
      CO 879/79/713. Northern Nigeria. Correspondence (December 1, 1902, to January 28,
         1903) Relating to the Expedition to Kano, 1903
      CO 879/80/718. Northern Nigeria. Further Correspondence [February 5, 1903, to October
         12, 1903] Relating to the Expedition to Kano
   Foreign Office
      FO 84/2062. Documents Relating to the Royal Niger Company Activities
      FO 84/2109. Further Documents Relating to the RNC
      FO 97/435
Parliamentary Papers, 1865, Report of a Select Committee of the House of Commons on West
   African Settlements, 1865
E. P. C. Girouard, "Land Tenure in Northern Nigeria," November 2, 1907, Northern Nigeria
   Lands Committee, Minutes of Evidence and Appendices, 1910 [Cd.5103]
Report of the Northern Nigeria Lands Committee, 1910 [Cd. 5102]
F. D. Lugard, Memo on the Taxation of Natives in Northern Nigeria, 1907 [Cd. 3309]
E. P. C. Girouard, "Land Tenure and Land Revenue Assessment," Memo No. 25, September
   1908, CO African (West) Confidential Print No. 906

Sudan Interior Mission (Toronto)
Wushishi–Government Correspondence, 1905–14, CC–2/A
Edwin George Judd Book of Letters, Nigeria 1903, DD–2/4
Charles Waddell, "Travelling in Nupe Country," 1905, DC–2/A
Church Missionary Society (University of Birmingham)
Upper Niger Précis Books, 1897–1906, G3/A3/P4

III Periodicals

Church Missionary Record
Anti-Slavery Reporter
West Africa
Morning Post (London)
Times (London)
Spectator

IV Official publications

Northern Nigeria Annual Reports, 1900–12
Gazette, Royal Niger Company, 1897
Northern Nigerian Gazette, 1901–1904
Nigerian Gazette, 1936
Colonial Reports, Annual, Nigeria, 1914

V League of Nations reports

Temporary Slavery Commission, Minutes of the First Session, July 9–12, 1924. A.17
"The Question of Slavery," Memorandum by the Secretary-General, August 4, 1924. A.25
"The Question of Slavery, 5 September 1924: Letters from the British Government Transmitting Despatches Showing the Situation with Respect to Slavery in the British Colonies and Protectorates and Territories under British Mandate." A.25(a)
Temporary Slavery Commission, Minutes of the Second Session, July 13–25, 1925. C.426.M.157
The Slavery Convention, Report Presented to the Assembly by the Sixth Committee, September 24, 1926. A.104
Slavery, Report of the Committee of Experts on Slavery Provided for by the Assembly Resolution of September 25th, 1931, September 1, 1932. C.618
Report of the Advisory Committee of Experts, Third (Extraordinary) Session, Geneva, April 15–24, 1936.C.180(1).M.145
Slavery, Report of the Advisory Committee of Experts, Fourth Session, April 5–10, 1937, C.188.M.173.1937
Slavery. Report of the Advisory Committee of Experts, Fifth (Extraordinary) Session of the Committee, March 31st to April 5th, 1938, C.112.M.98. 1938. VI

VI Unpublished theses and scholarly papers

Al-Hajj, Muhammad, 1973. "The Mahdist Tradition in Northern Nigeria," Ph.D. thesis, Ahmadu Bello University
Anagbogu, Ifeanyi, 1986. "The History of the Indigenous Leather Industry in Sokoto and Kano, Northern Nigeria," Ph.D. thesis, University of Birmingham
Atchebro, Dogbo Daniel, 1990. "La Société des Nations et la lutte contre l'esclavage, 1922–1938," Mémoire du diplôme, Institut Universitaire des Hautes Etudes Internationales

371

Bibliography

Bello, Sule, 1982. "State and Economy in Kano, 1894–1960," Ph.D. thesis, Ahmadu Bello University

Coles, Catherine Mary, 1983. "Muslim Women in Town: Social Change among the Hausa of Northern Nigeria," Ph.D. thesis, University of Wisconsin

Ferguson, Douglas E., 1973. "Nineteenth Century Hausaland, being a Description by Imam Imoru of the Land, Economy and Society of his People," Ph.D. thesis, University of California, Los Angeles

Garba, Tijani, 1986. "Taxation in Some Hausa Emirates, c. 1860–1939," Ph.D. thesis, University of Birmingham

Gonyok, C. K., 1977. "Creation of Labour for the Tin Mining Industry in the Plateau 1909–14 (or Proletarianisation?)," Seminar Paper, Department of History, Ahmadu Bello University

Hamman, Mahoud, 1983. "The Rise and Fall of the Emirate of Muri," Ph.D. thesis, Ahmadu Bello University

Hiskett, M., 1969. "Hausa Islamic Verse: Its Sources and Development Prior to 1920," Ph.D. thesis, University of London

Idrissa, Kimba, 1987. "La Formation de la Colonie du Niger, 1880–1922. Des mythes à la politique du 'mal nécessaire,'" Thèse pour le doctorat d'état ès lettres et sciences humaines, Université de Paris VII, 6 vols.

Ingawa, Tukur Bello, 1984. "A Study of the Rural Economic History of the Major Cotton Producing Districts of Katsina Emirate during the Colonial Period c. 1900–1939," Ph.D. thesis, University of London

Jumare, Ibrahim, 1988a. "Slavery in Sokoto City, c. 1804–1936," MA thesis, Ahmadu Bello University

1988b. "Kwarkwara (Concubinage): A Persistent Phenomenon of Slavery in the Centre of the 'Sokoto Caliphate,'" Seminar paper, Department of History, Usumanu Danfodiyo University

1990. "Slave Agricultural Estates in the Sokoto Sultanate," paper presented at the World Conference on Slavery and Society in History, Kaduna

Lennihan, Louise, 1983. "Origins and Development of Agricultural Wage Labor in Northern Nigeria: 1886–1980," Ph.D. thesis, Columbia University

Mahadi, Abdullahi, 1982. "The State and Economy: The Sarauta System and its Role in Shaping the Society and Economy of Kano with Particular Reference to the Eighteenth and Nineteenth Centuries," Ph.D. thesis, Admadu Bello University

Mason, Michael, 1970. "The Nupe Kingdom in the Nineteenth Century: A Political History," Ph.D. thesis, University of Birmingham

Miers, Suzanne, 1986. "Britain, the League of Nations and the Suppression of Slavery," paper presented at the Ninth International Economic History Congress, Bern

Mohammed, Abubakar Sokoto, 1983. "A Social Interpretation of the Satiru Revolt of c. 1894–1906," M.Sc. thesis, Ahmadu Bello University

1985. "The Songs and Poems of the Satiru Revolt, c. 1894–1906," seminar paper, Department of Sociology, Ahmadu Bello University

Okediji, Francis, 1972. "An Economic History of Hausa-Fulani Emirates of Northern Nigeria, 1900–1939," Ph.D. thesis, Indiana University

Oyemakinde, Wale, 1970. "A History of Indigenous Labour on the Nigerian Railway, 1895–1945," Ph.D. thesis, University of Ibadan

Oyeyipo, I. N. R., n.d. "'Tax Agitation' in Ilorin Province 1900–1935: An Attempt at a Reconstruction of the British Styled 'South Inspired Tax Revolts,'" paper presented at the Ahmadu Bello University Niger-Benue Seminar

Paden, John N., 1968. "The Influence of Religious Elites on the Community, Culture and Political Integration of Kano, Nigeria," Ph.D. thesis, Harvard University

Saaed, Asmau G., 1986. "British Fears over Mahdism in Northern Nigeria: A Look at Bormi

1903, Satiru 1906 and Dubulwa 1923," paper presented at the School of Oriental and African Studies, London

Sa'idu, Abdulrazak Giginyu, 1981. "History of a Slave Village in Kano: Gandun Nassarawa," B.A. thesis, Bayero University, Kano

Slenes, Robert W., 1976. "The Demography and Economics of Brazilian Slavery: 1850–1888," Ph.D. thesis, Stanford University

Tahir, Ibrahim, 1975. "Sufis, Saints and Capitalists in Kano, 1904–1974: Pattern of a Bourgeois Revolution in an Islamic Society," Ph.D. thesis, Cambridge University

Tibenderana, Peter Kazenga, 1974. "The Administration of Sokoto, Gwandu, and Argungu Emirates under British Rule, 1900–1946," Ph.D. thesis, University of Ibadan

Tukur, Modibbo, 1979. "The Imposition of British Colonial Domination on the Sokoto Caliphate, Borno and Neighbouring States, 1897–1914," Ph.D. thesis, Ahmadu Bello University

Ubah, Chinendu Nwafor, 1973. "Administration of Kano Emirate under the British, 1900–1930," Ph.D. thesis, University of Ibadan

Yakubu, Mahmood, 1985. "A Century of Warfare and Slavery in Bauchi, c. 1805–1900," B.A. thesis, University of Sokoto [Usumanu Danfodiyo University]

Yunusa, Yusufu, 1976. "Slavery in 19th Century Kano," B.A. thesis, Ahmadu Bello University

Zahradeen, Muhammad Sani, 1976. "'Abd Allah ibn Fodio's Contributions to the Fulani Jihad in Nineteenth Century Hausaland," Ph.D. thesis, McGill University

VII Published works

Abraham, R. C., 1940. *An Introduction to Spoken Hausa and Hausa Reader for European Students*, London

Abubakar, Sa'id, 1977. *The Lamibe of Fombina. A Political History of Adamawa, 1809–1901*, Zaria

Adeleye, R. A., 1971. *Power and Diplomacy in Northern Nigeria, 1804–1906: The Sokoto Caliphate and its Enemies*, New York

1972. "Mahdist Triumph and British Revenge in Northern Nigeria: Satiru 1906," *Journal of the Historical Society of Nigeria*, 6, 2: 193–214

Agiri, Babatunde, 1981. "Slavery in Yoruba Society in the 19th Century," in Paul E. Lovejoy, *The Ideology of Slavery in Africa*, Beverly Hills, 123–48

Anene, J. C., 1966. *Southern Nigeria in Transition 1885–1906*, Cambridge

Ayandele, E. A., 1966a. *The Missionary Impact on Modern Nigeria, 1842–1914: A Political and Social Analysis*, Harlow, Essex

1966b. "The Missionary Factor in Northern Nigeria, 1870–1918," *Journal of the Historical Society of Nigeria*, 3, 3: 503–22

1968. "The Relations between the Church Missionary Society and the Royal Niger Company," *Journal of the Historical Society of Nigeria*, 4, 3: 397–419

Banfield, A. W., 1905. *Life among the Nupe Tribe in West Africa*, Berlin (Kitchener), Ont.

Bargery, G. P., 1934. *A Hausa–English Dictionary and English–Hausa Vocabulary*, London

Barth, Heinrich, 1857–58. *Travels and Discoveries in North and Central Africa*, 3 vols., London

Beddoes, H. R., 1904. "The British Empire in West Africa," *National and English Review*, 44, 262: 701–17

Boahen, A. Adu, 1964. *Britain, the Sahara, and the Western Sudan 1788–1861*, London

Boyd, Jean and Murray Last, 1985. "The Role of Women as 'Agents Religieux' in Sokoto," *Canadian Journal of African Studies*, 19, 2: 285–300

Brode, Patrick, 1989. *The Odyssey of John Anderson*, Toronto

Bull, Mary, 1963. "Indirect Rule in Northern Nigeria 1906–1911," in Kenneth Robinson and Frederick Madden, eds., *Essays in Imperial Government*, Oxford, 47–87

Bibliography

Büttner, T., 1973., "Social Aims and Earlier Anti-Colonial Struggles: The Satiru Rising of 1906," in T. Büttner and G. Brehme, eds., *African Studies*, Berlin, 1–18

Cave, Basil S., 1909. "The End of Slavery in Zanzibar and British East Africa," *Journal of the African Society*, 9, 33: 20–33

Christelow, Allan, 1985. "Slavery in Kano, 1913–14: Evidence from the Judicial Records," *African Economic History*, 14: 57–74

———— 1991. "Women and the Law in Early Twentieth Century Kano," in Catherine Coles and Beverley Mack, eds., *Hausa Women in the Twentieth Century*, Madison, 130–44

———— 1993. *Thus Ruled Emir Abbas: Selected Cases from the Records of the Emir of Kano's Judicial Council*, East Lansing, Mich.

Cole, C. W., 1944. *Report on Land Tenure, Zaria Province*, Kaduna

Conrad, Robert, 1972. *The Destruction of Brazilian Slavery, 1850–1888*, Berkeley

Cooper, Frederick, 1977. *Plantation Slavery on the East Coast of Africa*, New Haven

———— 1980. *From Slaves to Squatters: Plantation Labor and Agriculture in Zanzibar and Coastal Kenya, 1890–1925*, New Haven

Coupland, Reginald, 1933. *The British Anti-Slavery Movement*, 2nd ed., London, 1964

———— 1939. *The Exploitation of East Africa 1856–1890: The Slave Trade and the Scramble*, London

Cowley, E. J., 1966. "Development of the Cotton Growing Industry in Nigeria," *Empire Cotton Growing Review*, 43, 3: 169–96

Crozier, F. P., 1932. *Five Years Hard*, London

Curtis, Donald, 1988. *Preventing Famine*, Boston

DeGregori, Thomas R., 1969. *Technology and the Economic Development of the Tropical African Frontier*, Cleveland

Drèze, Jean and Amartya K. Sen, 1990. *Hunger and Public Action*, Oxford

Duff, E. C. and W. Hamilton-Brown, 1920. *Gazetteer of Kontagora Province*, London

Dumett, Raymond and Marion Johnson, 1988. "Britain and the Suppression of Slavery in the Gold Coast Colony, Ashanti, and the Northern Territories," in Suzanne Miers and Richard Roberts, eds., *The End of Slavery in Africa*, Madison, 71–116

Dusgate, Richard H., 1985. *The Conquest of Northern Nigeria*, London

Edgar, Frank, ed., 1911–13. *Litafi na Tatsuniyoyi na Hausa*, 3 vols., Belfast

Fika, Adamu M., 1978. *The Kano Civil War and British Over-rule*, Ibadan

Fisher, Allan G. B. and Humphrey J. Fisher, 1970. *Slavery and Muslim Society in Africa. The Institution in Saharan and Sudanic Africa and the Trans-Saharan Trade*, London

Flint, John, 1960. *Sir George Goldie and the Making of Nigeria*, London

Fogel, Robert W. and Stanley Engerman, 1970. *Time on the Cross: The Economics of American Negro Slavery*, 2 vols., Boston, Mass.

Forde, Daryll, 1946. "The North: The Hausa," in Margery Perham, ed., *The Native Economies of Nigeria*, London, I, 119–79

Freund, Bill, 1981. *Capital and Labour in the Nigerian Tin Mines*, Harlow

Freund, W. H. and R. W. Shenton, 1977. "'Vent-for Surplus' Theory and the Economic History of West Africa," *Savanna*, 6, 2: 191–96

Fürster, Stig, Wolfgang J. Mommsen, and Ronald Robinson, eds., 1988. *Bismarck, Europe, and Africa: The Berlin Africa Conference 1884–1885 and the Onset of Partition*, London

Gann, L. H. and Peter Duignan, 1978. *The Rulers of British Africa, 1870–1914*, London

Geary, William N. M., 1927. *Nigeria under British Rule*, London

Genovese, Eugene, 1979. *From Rebellion to Revolution: Afro-American Slave Revolts in the Making of the Modern World*, Baton Rouge

Gibson, A. E. M., 1903. "Slavery in West Africa," *Journal of The African Society*, 3, 10: 17–54

Grace, John, 1975. *Domestic Slavery in West Africa, with Particular Reference to the Sierra Leone Protectorate, 1896–1927*, New York

Green, William A., 1976. *British Slave Emancipation: The Sugar Colonies and the Great Experiment 1830–1865*, Oxford.

374

Bibliography

Greenberg, Joseph, 1947. "Islam and Clan Organization Among the Hausa," *Southwestern Journal of Anthropology* 3: 193–210

Hailey, Lord, 1957. *An African Survey*, rev. ed., London

Hall, Herbert C. (Johnny), 1923. *Barrack and Bush in Northern Nigeria*, London

Harrison, Christopher, 1988. *France and Islam in West Africa, 1860–1960*, Cambridge

Hastings, A. C. G., 1925. *Nigeria Days*, London

1926. *The Voyage of the Dayspring*, London

Haywood, A. and F. A. S. Clarke, 1964. *The History of the Royal West African Frontier Force*, Aldershot

Hazzledine, George Douglas, 1904. *The White Man in Nigeria*, London

Herlehy, Thomas J. and Rodger F. Morton, 1988. "An Ex-Slave Community in the Regional and Colonial Economy of Kenya: The Wamisheni of Rabai, 1880–1963," in Suzanne Miers and Richard Roberts, ed., *The End of Slavery in Africa*, Madison, 254–81

Heussler, Robert, 1968. *The British in Northern Nigeria*, London

Higman, B. W., 1984. *Slave Populations of the British Caribbean, 1807–1834*, Baltimore

Hill, Polly, 1972. *Rural Hausa: A Village and a Setting*, Cambridge

1976. "From Slavery to Freedom: The Case of Farm-Slavery in Nigerian Hausaland," *Comparative Studies in Society and History*, 18, 3: 395–426

1977. *Population, Prosperity and Poverty: Rural Kano 1900 and 1970*, Cambridge

1982. *Dry Grain Farming Families. Hausaland (Nigeria) and Karnataka (India) Compared*, Cambridge

Hiskett, M., 1985. "The Image of Slaves in Hausa Literature," in John Ralph Willis, ed., *Slaves and Slavery in Muslim Africa*, London, I. 106–24

Hogendorn, J. S., 1976. "The Vent for Surplus Model and African Cash Agriculture to 1914," *Savanna*, 5, 1: 15–28

1977a. "Vent-for-Surplus: A Reply," *Savanna*, 6, 2: 196–99

1977b. "The Economics of Slave Use on Two 'Plantations' in the Zaria Emirate of the Sokoto Caliphate," *International Journal of African Historical Studies*, 10: 369–83

1978. *Nigerian Groundnut Exports: Origins and Early Development*, Zaria and Ibadan

1980. "Slave Acquisition and Delivery in Precolonial Hausaland," in B. K. Swartz, Jr., and Raymond A. Dumett, eds., *West African Culture Dynamics*, The Hague, 477–93

Hogendorn, Jan S. and Marion Johnson, 1986. *The Shell Money of the Slave Trade*, Cambridge

Hogendorn, J. S. and Paul E. Lovejoy, 1988. "The Reform of Slavery in Early Colonial Northern Nigeria," in Suzanne Miers and Richard Roberts, eds., *The End of Slavery in Africa*, Madison, 391–414

1989. "The Development and Execution of Frederick Lugard's Politics Toward Slavery in Northern Nigeria," *Slavery and Abolition*, 10, 1: 1–43

1992. "Keeping Slaves in Place: The Secret Debate on the Slavery Question in Northern Nigeria, 1900–1904," in Stanley Engerman and Joseph Inikori, eds., *The Atlantic Slave Trade: Effects on Economies, Societies and Peoples of Africa, the Americas and Europe*, Durham, NC., 49–75

Hollingsworth, L. W., 1953. *Zanzibar under the Foreign Office 1890–1913*, London

Idrissa, Kimba, 1981. *Guerres et sociétés. Les Populations du "Niger" occidental au XIXe siècle et leurs reactions face à la colonisation (1896–1906)*, Niamey

Kirk-Greene, A. H. M. and Paul Newman, eds., 1971. *West African Travels and Adventures: Two Autobiographical Narratives from Northern Nigeria*, New Haven

Kisch, Martin S., 1910. *Letters and Sketches from Northern Nigeria*, London

Klein, Herbert, 1986. *African Slavery in Latin America and the Caribbean*, New York

Klein, Martin, 1983. "Women in Slavery in the Western Sudan," in Claire Robertson and Martin Klein, eds., *Women and Slavery in Africa*, Madison, 67–92

ed., 1993. *Breaking the Chains: Slavery, Bondage and Emancipation in Africa and Asia*, Madison

Bibliography

Knight, Franklin W., 1970. *Slave Society in Cuba during the Nineteenth Century*, Madison

Köhnert, Dirk, 1982. *Klassenbildung im ländlichen Nigeria: Das Beispiel der Savannenbauern in Nupeland*, Hamburg

Kopytoff, Igor, 1988. "The Cultural Context of African Abolition," in Suzanne Miers and Richard Roberts, eds., *The End of Slavery in Africa*, Madison, 485–503

Lamb, P. H., 1925. "The Past, Present, and Future of Cotton Growing in Nigeria," *Empire Cotton Growing Review*, 2, 3: 184–97

Lawal, S. U., 1992. "The Fiscal Policies of Amir al-Muminin Muhammadu Bello: Al-Gaith al-Wabl fisirat al-Iman al-adl," *African Economic History*, 20

Lennihan, Louise, 1982. "Rights in Men and Rights in Land: Slavery, Wage Labor, and Smallholder Agriculture in Northern Nigeria," *Slavery and Abolition*, 3, 2: 111–39

Levy, Reuben, 1957. *The Social Structure of Islam*, London

Lovejoy, Paul E., 1978. "Plantations in the Economy of the Sokoto Caliphate," *Journal of African History*, 19, 3: 341–68

1979. "The Characteristics of Plantations in the Nineteenth-Century Sokoto Caliphate (Islamic West Africa)," *American Historical Review*, 84: 1267–92

1980. *Caravans of Kola. A History of the Hausa Kola Trade (1700–1900)*, Zaria and Ibadan

1981. "Slavery in the Sokoto Caliphate," in Lovejoy, *The Ideology of Slavery in Africa*, Beverly Hills, 201–43

1983. *Transformations in Slavery. A History of Slavery in Africa*, Cambridge

1986a. *Salt of the Desert Sun. A History of Salt Production and Trade in the Central Sudan*, Cambridge

1986b. "Problems of Slave Control in the Sokoto Caliphate," in Lovejoy, ed., *Africans in Bondage. Studies in Slavery and the Slave Trade*, Madison, 235–72

1986c. "Fugitive Slaves: Resistance to Slavery in the Sokoto Caliphate," in Gary Okihiro, ed., *In Resistance: Studies in African, Caribbean, and Afro-American History*, Amherst, 71–95

1988. "Concubinage and the Status of Women Slaves in Early Colonial Northern Nigeria," *Journal of African History*, 29, 2: 245–66

1990. "Concubinage in the Sokoto Caliphate (1804–1903)," *Slavery and Abolition*, 11, 2: 159–89

1993. "Murgu: The 'Wages' of Slavery in the Sokoto Caliphate," *Slavery and Abolition* 14.

Lovejoy, Paul E., and J. S. Hogendorn, 1990. "Revolutionary Mahdism and Resistance to Colonial Rule in the Sokoto Caliphate, 1905–6," *Journal of African History* 31: 217–44

Lugard, F. D., 1889. *Coercive Measures for Suppression of the Slave-Trade*, London

1893. *The Rise of Our East African Empire*, 2 vols., Edinburgh

1896. "Slavery under the British Flag," *The Nineteenth Century*, 39: 335–55

1905. "West Africa," in Charles Sydney Goldman, ed., *The Empire and the Century*, London, 849–55

1906. *Instructions to Political and Other Officers, on Subjects Chiefly Political and Administrative*, London

1918 (1970). *Political Memoranda: Revisions of Instructions to Political Officers on Subjects Chiefly Political and Administrative*, ed., A. H. M. Kirk-Greene, 3rd. ed., London

1922 (1965). *The Dual Mandate in British Tropical Africa*, London

1923. "The Passing of Slavery in Africa," in *The Story of the Cape to Cairo Railway and River Route* from 1887 to 1922, London, I, 491–97

1928. "Mohammedan Slavery," *Encyclopaedia Britannica, 14th*. ed., London, XX, 784–87

1933. "Slavery in all its Forms," *Africa*, 6, 1: 1–14

Lugard, Flora Shaw. *See* Shaw, Flora

McAlpin, Michelle, 1983. *Subject to Famine*, Princeton, N.J.

McSheffrey, G. M., 1983. "Slavery, Indentured Servitude, Legitimate Trade and the Impact of Abolition in the Gold Coast, 1874–1901, "*Journal of African History*, 24, 3: 349–68

376

Mack, Beverly B., 1992a. "Royal Wives in Kano," in Catherine Coles and Beverly B. Mack, eds., *Hausa Women in the Twentieth Century*, Madison, 109–29

1992b. "Women and Slavery in Nineteenth-Century Hausaland," in Elizabeth Savage, ed., *The Human Commodity: Perspectives on the Trans-Saharan Slave Trade*, London, 89–110.

Mason, Michael, 1969. "Population Density and 'Slave Raiding' – The Case of the Middle Belt of Nigeria," *Journal of African History*, 10, 4: 551–64

1970. "The *Jihad* in the South: An Outline of the Nineteenth Century Nupe Hegemony in North Eastern Yorubaland and Afenmai," *Journal of the Historical Society of Nigeria*, 5, 2: 193–208

1973. "Captive and Client Labour and the Economy of Bida Emirate, 1857–1901," *Journal of African History*, 14, 4: 453–71

1978. "Working on the Railway: Forced Labor in Northern Nigeria," in Peter C. W. Gutkind, Robin Cohen, and Jean Copans, eds., *African Labor History*, Beverly Hills, 56–79

1981. *The Foundations of the Bida Kingdom*, Zaria

Meek, Charles K., 1949. *Land Law and Custom in the Colonies*. London

1957. *Land Tenure and Land Administration in Nigeria and the Cameroons*, London

Merrick, G. 1905. *Hausa Proverbs*, London

Miers, Suzanne C., 1975. *Britain and the Ending of the Slave Trade*, London

1989. "Diplomacy versus Humanitarianism: Britain and Consular Manumission in Hijaz, 1921–1936," *Slavery and Abolition*, 10, 3: 102–28

1991. "Britain and the Suppression of Slavery in Ethiopia," *Proceedings of the Eighth International Conference of Ethiopian Studies*

Miers, Suzanne and Richard Roberts, eds., 1988. *The End of Slavery in Africa*, Madison

Mockler-Ferryman, A. F., 1900. *British West Africa: Its Rise and Progress*, London

Morel, E. D., 1912. *Nigeria: Its Peoples and Problems*, 2nd ed., London

Morton, Fred, 1990. *Children of Ham: Freed Slaves and Fugitive Slaves on the Kenya Coast, 1873 to 1907*, Boulder

Muffett, D. J. M., 1964. *Concerning Brave Captains*, London

Mullin, Gerald W., 1972. *Flight and Rebellion: Slave Resistance in Eighteenth-Century Virginia*, New York

Nadel, S. F., 1942. *Black Byzantium*, London

Nicolson, I. F., 1969. *The Administration of Nigeria 1900–1960*, Oxford

Obayemi, Ade, 1978. "The Sokoto Jihad and the 'O-Kun' Yoruba: A Review," *Journal of the Historical Society of Nigeria*, 9, 2: 61–87

Ohadike, Don, 1988. "The Decline of Slavery among the Igbo People," in Suzanne Miers and Richard Roberts, eds., *The End of Slavery in Africa*, Madison, 437–61

Olusanya, G. O., 1966. "The Freed Slaves' Homes – An Unknown Aspect of Northern Nigerian Social History," *Journal of the Historical Society of Nigeria*, 3, 3: 523–38

Oroge, E. A., 1975a. "The Fugitive Slave Crisis of 1859: A Factor in the Growth of Anti-British Feelings among the Yoruba," *Odu*, 12, 40–53

1975b. "The Fugitive Slave Question in Anglo-Egba Relations, 1861–1886," *Journal of the Historical Society of Nigeria*, 8, 1, 61–80

Orr, Charles, 1911. *The Making of Northern Nigeria*, London

Oyemakinde, Wale, 1974. "Railway Construction and Operation in Nigeria, 1895–1911: Labour Problems and Socio-Economic Impact," *Journal of the Historical Society of Nigeria*, 7, 2: 303–24

Palmer, H. Richmond, 1942. "Arriving in Northern Nigeria (About 35 Years Ago)," *Journal of the African Society*, 41: 158

Pedraza, Howard J., 1960. *Borrioboola-Gha: The Story of Lokoja*, London

Perham, Margery, 1956. *Lugard. The Years of Adventure 1858–1898*, London

1960. *Lugard: The Years of Authority 1898–1945*, London

Perham, Margery, and Mary Bull, 1959. *Diaries of Frederick Lugard*, 4 vols.

Bibliography

Phillips, Anne, 1989. *The Enigma of Colonialism: British Policy in West Africa*, London

Price, Richard, ed., 1979. *Maroon Societies: Rebel Slave Communities in the Americas*, 2nd. ed., Baltimore

Reutlinger, Shlomo and Jack van Holst Pellekaan, 1986. *Ensuring Food Security in the Developing World: Issues and Options*, Washington

Richardson, James, *Narrative of a Mission to Central Africa in 1850–1*, London, 1853

Roberts, Richard and Martin Klein, 1980. "The Banamba Slave Exodus of 1905 and the Decline of Slavery in the Western Sudan," *Journal of African History*, 21, 3: 375–94

Ross, Robert, 1983. *Cape of Torments. Slavery and Resistance in South Africa*, London

Rothiot, Jean-Paul, 1988. *L'Ascension d'un chef Africain au début de la colonisation: Aouta le conquérant (Dosso-Niger)*, Paris

Rowling, C. W., 1949. *Report on Land Tenure, Kano Province*, Kaduna

Rudin, Harry R. 1938. *Germans in the Cameroons, 1884–1914. A Case Study in Modern Imperialism*, London

Saaed, Asmau G., 1982–85. "The British Policy towards the Mahdiyya in Northern Nigeria: A Study of the Arrest, Detention and Deportation of Shaykh Said b. Hayat, 1923–1959," *Kano Studies* 11, 3: 95–119

Sa'id, H. I., 1983. "Notes on Taxation as a Political Issue in Nineteenth Century Kano," in B. M. Barkindo, ed., *Studies in the History of Kano*, Ibadan, 117–26

Schacht, Joseph, 1934. "Umm al-Walad," *Encyclopedia of Islam*, London, 1012–15

1964. *An Introduction to Islamic Law*, Oxford

Scott, Rebecca J., 1985. *Slave Emancipation in Cuba. The Transformation to Free Labor, 1860–1899*, Princeton

Sen, Amartya K., 1981. *Poverty and Famines: An Essay on Entitlement and Deprivation*, Oxford

Shaw, Flora, 1904. "Nigeria," *Journal of the Society of Arts* (March 18), 376

1905. *A Tropical Dependency*, London

Shelford, F., 1920. "Transport in Africa by Road, Rail, Air and Water," *Journal of the African Society*, 19, 75: 165–75

Shenton, Robert, 1986. *The Development of Capitalism in Northern Nigeria*, London and Toronto

Shenton, Bob and Bill Freund, 1978. "The Incorporation of Northern Nigeria into the World Capitalist Economy," *Review of African Political Economy* 13, 8–20

Skinner, Neil, ed. and trans., 1977a. *Alhaji Mahmudu K'ok'i: Hausa Malam*, Zaria.

1977b. *Hausa Tales and Traditions*, Madison, III

Smith, Billy G. and Richard Wojtowicz, 1989. *Blacks who Stole Themselves: Advertisements for Runaways in the Pennyslvania Gazette, 1728–1790*, Philadelphia

Smith, M. G., 1952. "A Study of Hausa Domestic Economy in Northern Zaria," *Africa* 22: 333–47

1954a. "Slavery and Emancipation in Two Societies," *Social and Economic Studies*, 3, 3–4: 239–90

1954b. Introduction to *Baba of Karo: A Woman of the Moslem Hausa*, ed. Mary Smith, London.

1955. *The Economy of Hausa Communities of Zaria*, London

1960. *Government in Zazzau, 1800–1950*, London

1965a. "Hausa Inheritance and Succession," in J. D. M. Derrett, ed., *Studies in the Laws of Succession in Nigeria*, London, 230–81

1965b. "The Hausa of Northern Nigeria," in James L. Gibs, ed., *Peoples of Africa*, New York, 119–25

1978. *The Affairs of Daura*, Berkeley

Smith, Mary, ed., 1954. *Baba of Karo: A Woman of the Moslem Hausa*, London

Speed, Edwin Arney, 1910. *Laws of the Protectorate of Northern Nigeria, being the Schedule to the Statute Laws Revision Proclamation, 1910*, London

Starns, William W., 1974. *Land Tenure among the Rural Hausa*, Land Tenure Center Paper No. 104, Madison

Swindell, Kenneth, 1984. "Farmers, Traders, and Labourers: Dry Season Migration from North-West Nigeria, 1900–33," *Africa*, 54, 1: 3–19

1992. "The Struggle for Transport Labour in Northern Nigeria, 1900–1912: A Conflict of Interests," *African Economic History*, 20

Talbot, P. Amaury, 1926. *The Peoples of Southern Nigeria*, 3 vols., London

Tambo, David Carl, 1976. "The Sokoto Caliphate Slave Trade in the Nineteenth Century," *International Journal of African Historical Studies*, 9, 2: 187–217

Tamuno, T. N., 1965. "The Genesis of the Nigerian Railway, II," *Nigeria Magazine*, 84 (March)

Temperley, Howard, 1972. *British Antislavery, 1833–1870*, Columbia, S.C.

1991. *White Dreams, Black Africa. The Antislavery Expedition to the Niger 1841–1842*, New Haven

Tibenderana, Peter Kazenga, 1988. *Sokoto Province under British Rule, 1903–1939*, Zaria

Toledano, Ehud R., 1982. *The Ottoman Slave Trade and its Suppression*, Princeton

Tremearne, A. J. N., 1913. *Hausa Superstitions and Customs. An Introduction to the Folk-lore and the Folk*, London

Tremlett, Mrs. Horace, 1915. *With the Tin Gods*, London

Ubah, C. N., 1979. "Etsu Nupe Muhammadu and the British, 1900–1916," *Ikenga*, 4, 1: 36–45

1985. *Government and Administration of Kano Emirate, 1900–1930*, Nsukka

1991. "Suppression of the Slave Trade in the Nigerian Emirates," *Journal of African History*, 32, 4: 447–70

1992. "Disposal of Freed Slave Children in Northern Nigeria," *Journal of African History*, 33: 1992

Ukpabi, Sam C., 1966. "The Origins of the West African Frontier Force," *Journal of the Historical Society of Nigeria*, 3, 3: 485–501

1986. *Strands in Nigerian Military History*, Zaria

1987. *The Origins of the Nigerian Army (A History of the West African Frontier Force, 1897–1914)*, Zaria

Uthman dan Fodio, 1978. *Bayan wujub al-hijra 'ala 'l'abad*, ed. and trans. F. H. El-Masri, Khartoum

Vandeleur, Seymour, 1898. *Campaigning on the Upper Nile and Niger*, London

Vaughan, James and A. H. M. Kirk-Greene, eds., forthcoming. *Hamman Yaji's Diary*

Wallace, William, 1896. "Notes on a Journey through the Sokoto Empire and Borgu in 1894." *Geographical Journal*, 8 (September), 211–21

Watson, James L., ed., 1980. *Asian and African Systems of Slavery*, Oxford

Watts, Michael, 1983. *Silent Violence: Food, Famine and Peasantry in Northern Nigeria*, Berkeley

Willcocks, James, 1904. *From Kabul to Kumasi: Twenty-four Years of Soldiering and Sport*, London

Woodward, C. Vann, 1957. *The Strange Career of Jim Crow*, New York

Wraith, R. E., 1966. "Local Government," in J. P. Mackintosh, ed., *Nigerian Government and Politics*, London

Index

Index

Godiya, 182, 256
Gogel, 47, 133, 314, 331
Gold Coast, 68–70, 78, 84, 93, 225
Goldie, Sir George, 13–18, 31–36, 64, 67, 69, 307, 310, 319
Goldsmith, H. S., 145, 179, 238, 255, 333–34, 340, 349, 352
Gollan, Chief Justice H. C., 90–92, 104, 143, 311, 323, 325, 334
Gombe, 23, 27, 37, 104, 122, 124, 205, 208, 262–63, 281
Gongola River, 216
Gonyok, C. K., 349
Gora, 37, 165–66, 339
Gordon, General Charles "Chinese," 55
government, 6–9, 11–12, 14, 16, 19–20, 22, 25, 28, 31–32, 34, 36, 40, 45–46, 53–56, 59–62, 64–65, 69–70, 74–75, 79, 82–84, 87, 90, 95, 97–98, 101, 106, 108–109, 117, 122, 134, 143–44, 147, 152, 156–57, 160, 162, 169, 173, 175, 178, 183, 185, 191–92, 195, 197–98, 202, 215–19, 222, 224–29, 231–33, 238, 254, 259, 270–72, 274, 277–78, 280–82
Gower, A. J. Hicks, 358–59
Gowers, William F., 106, 133–34, 145, 148, 152, 176, 202, 207, 211, 222, 240, 273, 317, 326, 330, 332, 334–35, 340, 345, 347, 349, 351, 354–55, 357, 364
Grace, John, 319
grain, 76, 129, 163–65, 181, 197–98, 200, 215–17, 229–230, 283
Granville, R., 309
Green, William A., 318
Greenberg, Joseph, 336
Grey, W. H., 307
Grier, Dorothy, 315, 346
Grier, Selwyn U., 45, 47–48, 50–51, 213–14, 312–15, 324, 336, 343, 345, 347–48
Groom, A. Holdsworth, 242, 244–45, 265, 267, 269, 352–53, 359–60
groundnuts, 168, 200, 215, 223, 227, 229
guardianship, 83, 113, 117, 121–24, 234, 241, 247, 250, 252–53, 258
Gumel, 276
Guzo, 334
Gwadabe, Malam, 349
Gwandu, 14, 19, 22, 24–26, 48–49, 56, 90, 109, 128, 131, 133–34, 136, 139–40, 163, 165, 167, 169, 177–78, 189, 191, 205, 208, 225, 287, 316, 327, 327, 363
Gwaram, 167, 171, 189, 249
Gwarjiko, 39
Gwarzo, 255

Habibi, Malam, 179
Hadejia, 24, 26, 276
Hailey, Lord, 343

Hall, Herbert C. (Johnny), 42
Hamilton-Browne, W., 309
Hamman, Mahmoud, 306–307
Hanwa, vii, 142, 346
Harcourt, Lord, 348–49, 363
Harding, Alfred, 360
Harris, J. S., 271
Harris, P. Graham, 270, 360
Harrison, Christopher, 316
Hastings, A. C. G., 257, 268, 306, 348, 351, 355–57, 359
Haughton, T. H., 263, 358–59
Hausawan Maiwa, 57
Haywood, A., 306–307, 318
Hazzledine, George Douglas, 34, 310
Herlehy, Thomas J., 324
Hesse, Mr. and Mrs., 123
Heussler, Robert, 320
Hewby, W. P., 131, 181, 184, 337–38, 341
Higman, B. W., 305
Hijaz, 269, 275
Hill, Polly, 47, 66, 129, 139, 165, 187, 191, 233, 284, 305, 309, 314, 318, 330–35, 337–38, 341–43, 347, 350–51, 363
Hillary, H. R. P., 115, 123, 328–30
Hiskett, Melvyn, 53–54, 315, 328
Hogendorn, Jan S., xiii, 305, 312, 315, 317–21, 334, 336–37, 344, 347, 350
Hollingsworth, L. W., 306
Holt, John, 145
Hong Kong, 6, 64, 151, 271, 348
Howard, Oliver, 106, 117, 324, 326, 329–30
Hunt, W., 360
hurumi, 168–70, 177, 179–80, 182–84, 190
Hussey, Rebecca, 321

Ibadan, 221
Ibi, 53
Ibrahim, Sarkin Sudan, of Kontogora, 20–23, 29, 40, 42–43, 309, 312
Idah, 35, 74, 269
ideology, 10, 17, 27, 32–33, 56, 59, 72
Idrissa, Kimba, 307, 316
Idrisu Dan Maisoro, 314
Igi, 256
Illo, 19, 22, 37, 254
Ilorin, 11, 16–19, 21, 23, 27, 33–37, 41, 51–52, 62, 74, 106, 136, 180, 196, 208, 221–22, 246, 279, 288–89, 310, 332, 344
Imoru, Imam, 54, 114, 116
India, 1, 64, 152, 348
Ingawa, Tukur Bello, 139, 333
inheritance, 102, 112, 125, 129, 147, 152–53, 155, 178
irrigation, 129, 167, 201, 217, 224
Isa, 56, 58, 317
Izard, G. W., 282, 361–63

Index

Other books in the series